THE MILITARY BALANCE 1989-1990

Published by **Brassey's** for

THE INTERNATIONAL
INSTITUTE FOR
STRATEGIC STUDIES
23 Tavistock Street London WC2E 7NQ

THE MILITARY BALANCE 1989–1990

Published by
The International Institute for Strategic Studies
23 Tavistock Street, London WC2E 7NQ

Director
François Heisbourg

Assistant Director
for Information
Col. Andrew Duncan

This publication has been prepared by the Director of the Institute and his Staff, who accept full responsibility for its contents. These do not, and indeed cannot, represent a consensus of views among the world-wide membership of the Institute as a whole.

First published Autumn 1989

ISBN 0 08 037569 3 (Flexi)

ISSN 0459-7222

Printed in Great Britain by Nuffield Press, Hollow Way, Cowley, Oxford OX4 2PH

CONTENTS

THE MILITARY BALANCE
FORMAT, LAYOUT AND PRINCIPLES OF COMPILATION

The Military Balance is updated each year to provide a timely, quantitative assessment of the military forces and defence expenditures of over 140 countries. This volume contains such data as at 1 June 1989. This introduction explains how *The Military Balance* is laid out and the general principles followed. There are no changes from the format used in 1988/89.

GENERAL ARRANGEMENT

There are two main sections in *The Military Balance*. The first comprises national entries grouped by regions; the Index on p. 10 gives the page references of individual national entries. Each group is preceded by a short introduction describing significant changes in the defence postures and economic positions of the countries concerned and in their international treaties, agreements and military aid arrangements. Inclusion of a particular entity or military organization connected to it in no way implies legal recognition for or IISS approval of it.

The second section contains analytical essays which cover Developments in Strategic Arms Control and the Conventional Forces of NATO and the Warsaw Pact, in the light of published data and arms-control proposals (both accompanied by tables showing the relative strengths of the Alliances), the implications of demographic change for NATO and the Warsaw Pact, and the utility of reserve forces. Other tables provide information on nuclear delivery means, the capabilities of artillery, multiple rocket launchers and mortars, the vital statistics of the major navies of the world, and comparisons of defence expenditure and military manpower.

Finally, there is a list showing the type, name/designation, maker and country of origin of all aircraft listed in *The Military Balance*.

A map of the Middle East showing the deployment of key land/air equipment and the areas covered by significant SSM is provided as a loose insert.

ABBREVIATIONS AND DEFINITIONS

Limitations of space force us to use abbreviations. A list is at the fold-out sheet on pp. 250–51. Punctuation is not used, and the abbreviation may have both singular or plural meanings, e.g., 'elm' = 'element' or 'elements'. The qualification 'some' means 'up to' whilst 'about' means 'the total could be higher than given'. In financial data, the $ sign refers to US dollars unless otherwise stated; the term billion (bn) equals 1,000 million (m).

NATIONAL ENTRIES

Information on each country is given in a format as standard as the available information permits: economic and demographic data, and military data including manpower, terms of service, outline organization, number of formations and units, the inventory of major equipments of each service, followed where applicable by a description of their deployment.

GENERAL MILITARY DATA
Manpower

The 'Active' total comprises all servicemen and women on full-time duty, including conscripts and long-term assignments from the Reserves. Unless otherwise indicated, the 'Reserves' entry includes all reservists committed to rejoin the armed forces in emergency. Where national reserve service obligations last almost a lifetime our strength estimates of military effective reservists are based on the numbers available within five years of completing full-time service, unless there is good evidence that obligations are enforced for longer. Some countries have different categories of Reserves, often kept at differing degrees of readiness; where possible we denote these differences using the national descriptive title, but always under the heading of Reserves, so as to differentiate them from full-time active forces.

Reserves

In *The Military Balance* the term 'Reserve' is used to describe formations and units not fully manned or operational in peacetime but which can be mobilized by recalling reservists in emergency, except for Warsaw Pact countries where we use the categorization described on pp. 33–4. Reserve stocks of equipment are listed as 'in store'.

Other Forces

Many countries maintain para-military forces whose training, organization, equipment and control suggests they may be usable in support, or in lieu, of regular military forces. We list all such known para-military forces, describing their role, after the military forces of each country, but do not normally include their numbers in the Armed Forces totals at the start of each entry. We count Home Guard units as para-military. Where para-military groups are not on full-time active duty we have added the suffix (R) after the title to indicate that they are of reserve status. When internal opposition forces are armed and appear to pose a significant threat to the internal security of a state, their details are shown separately after national para-military forces. In each country we also show any stationed foreign forces, whether allied or peace-keeping.

Equipment

Numbers are shown by function and type and represent total holdings including active and reserve operational and training units and 'in store' stocks. Inventory totals for missile systems (e.g. SSM, SAM, ATGW, etc.) relate to launchers and not to missiles.

GROUND FORCES

We normally use the national designation for army formations. The term 'regiment' can be misleading. In some cases it is to all intents and purposes a brigade of all arms; in others a grouping of battalions of a single arm; and lastly (the UK and French usage) a battalion-sized unit. We indicate which sense is meant. Where there is no standard organization we show the intermediate levels of command as HQ, and then list the total numbers of units which could be allocated between them. Where a unit's title overstates its real capability we put the title in inverted commas and our estimate of the comparable NATO unit size in parentheses: e.g., 'bde' (coy).

Military Formation Strengths

The table below gives the approximate manpower and major equipment strengths of the main military formations of selected countries.

	Armoured/Tank Division						Mechanized/Motor Rifle/Infantry Division[a]					
	Men[b]	MBT	AIFV	APC[c]	Arty/Mor[d]	ATGW[e]	Men[b]	MBT	AIFV	APC[c]	Arty/Mor[d]	ATGW[e]
US	16,800	348	216[f]	–	117	168	17,100	290	270[f]	–	113	204
USSR	11,000	328[h]	273	–	174	9	13,300	271[g][h]	245[i]	290	216	117
China	9,900	323	–	–	32	52	13,400	80[g]	–	–	60	54
UK	14,900	285	225[f]	–	72	120	14,000	–	–	129	54	126
FRG	21,750	308	164	–	124	141	22,000	252	190	–	130	171
France	9,000	190	114	–	68	60	7,200	–	–	400	42	96

[a] Type of Division: US Mechanized; Soviet Motor Rifle; China, UK, France Infantry; FRG Armoured Infantry.
[b] Manpower is for war establishment
[c] Only basic inf APC and not specialist versions incl.
[d] Incl MRL, SP and towed arty and mor of 100mm calibre or over.
[e] Figures comprise only dismounted ATGW and those mounted on vehicles with a *primary* ATK role.

[f] When *Bradley/Warrior* issues complete.
[g] Tank strengths are for divisions in Eastern Europe, other Soviet MRD have 220 tanks.
[h] Tank strength, after unilateral reductions and restructuring have been effected will be 234 for TD and 177 for MRD.
[i] Number of AIFV depends on number of BMP regts. This example assumes one BMP regt and an appropriate ATGW count.

Equipment

We do not list weapons with calibres of less than 14.5mm or, for major armies; hand-held ATK weapons or mortars of under 100mm calibre. By AIFV we mean all light armoured wheeled or tracked infantry fighting vehicles with a cannon of not less than 20mm; it is not necessary for an ATGW to be mounted. APC roled as ATGW or other weapons platforms are shown under the relevant weapon heading and not as APC.

NAVAL FORCES

Categorization is based partly on operational role, partly on weapon fit and partly on displacement. Ship classes are identified by the name of the first ship of that class. Where the class is based on a foreign design we add the original class name in parentheses.

Each class of vessel is given an acronym designator based on the NATO system. All designators are included in the abbreviations list on pp. 250–51.

The term 'ship' is used to refer to vessels of over both 1,000 tonnes full-load displacement and 60 metres overall length; vessels of lesser displacement but of 16 metres or more overall length are termed 'craft'. Vessels of less than 16 metres length overall have not been included.

Classifications and Definitions

Naval entries have been sub-divided into the following categories:

Submarines   Submarines with SLBM are listed separately under 'Strategic Nuclear Forces'.

Principal Surface Combatants   All surface ships with both 1,000 tonnes full-load displacement and a weapons system other than for self-protection. They comprise aircraft carriers (with a flight deck extending beyond two-thirds of the vessel's length), battleships (armour-protected, over 30,000 tonnes, and with armour-protected guns of at least 10in./250mm bore); cruisers (over 8,000 tonnes) and destroyers (less than 8,000 tonnes), both of which normally have an anti-air warfare role and may also have an anti-submarine capability; and frigates (less than 8,000 tonnes), which normally have an anti-submarine role.

Patrol and Coastal Combatants   All ships and craft whose primary role relates to the protection of the sea approaches and coastline of a state. Included are: corvettes (600–1,000 tonnes and carrying weapons systems other than for self-protection); missile craft (with permanently fitted missile launcher ramps and control equipment); torpedo craft (with an anti-surface-ship capability). Ships and craft which fall outside these definitions are classified 'patrol'.

Mine Warfare   This category covers surface vessels configured primarily for minelaying or mine countermeasures, which can be minehunters, minesweepers or dual-capable vessels.

A further classification divides both coastal and patrol combatants and mine warfare vessels into: offshore (over 600 tonnes), coastal (300–600 tonnes) and inshore (less than 300 tonnes).

Amphibious   Only ships specifically procured and employed to disembark troops and their equipment over unprepared beachheads have been listed. Vessels with an amphibious capability but which are known not to be assigned to amphibious duties are not included. Amphibious craft are listed at the end of each entry.

Support and Miscellaneous   This category of essentially non-military vessels provides some indication of the operational sustainability and outreach of the Navy concerned.

Weapons Systems   We list weapons in the order in which they contribute to the ship's primary operational role. After the word 'plus' we add significant weapons relating to the ship's secondary role. Self-defence weapons are not listed. To merit inclusion, a SAM system must have an anti-missile range of 10 km or more, and guns must be of 100mm bore or greater.

Organizations   Naval groupings such as fleets and squadrons are often temporary and changeable; we show organization only where it is meaningful.

AIR FORCES

The following remarks refer to aviation units forming an integral part of Ground Forces, Naval Forces and (where applicable) Marines, as well as to separate Air Forces.

The term 'combat aircraft' comprises aircraft normally equipped to deliver ordnance in air-to-air or air-to-ground combat. Combat helicopters are divided into armed helicopters (equipped to deliver ordnance over the battlefield or beachhead) and ASW helicopters, which have a purely maritime role. The 'combat' totals include aircraft in operational conversion units (OCU) whose main role is weapons training and those training aircraft of the same type as those in front-line squadrons and assumed to be available for operations at short notice.

Air Force operational groupings are shown where known. Squadron aircraft strengths vary; attempts have been made to separate total holdings from reported establishment strength.

We try to keep the number of categories of aircraft listed to a minimum. 'Fighter' is used to denote aircraft with the capability (weapons, avionics, performance) for aerial combat. An aircraft shown purely as a fighter can do little but attack other aircraft; dual-capable aircraft are shown as FGA, etc. Often different countries use the same basic aircraft in different roles; the key to determining the roles lies mainly in aircrew training. For bombers, long-range means having an unrefuelled *radius of action* of over 5,000 km, medium-range 1,000–5,000 km and short-range less than 1,000 km; light bombers are those with a payload of under 10,000 kg (which is no greater than the payload of many FGA).

ECONOMIC AND DEMOGRAPHIC DATA

Economic Data

We provide GDP figures but use GNP and NMP when necessary (GNP equals GDP plus net income from abroad; NMP equals GNP minus non-earning state services). GDP figures are quoted at current market prices (at factor cost for East European and some other countries). Where available, published sources are used, but we estimate figures when data is incomplete. GDP/GNP growth rates cited are real growth in real terms. Inflation rates are based on available consumer price indices and refer to annual averages. By 'Debt' we mean foreign debt and include all long-, medium- and short-term debt, both publicly and privately owed; no account is taken of similar debt owed to the country in question by others.

Wherever possible the UN System of National Accounts, based on the latest available International Monetary Fund (IMF) *International Financial Statistics* (IFS), has been used. For Eastern Europe, data from *Economic Survey of Europe in 1987–1988* and *1988–1989* (New York: UN, 1988, 1989) and *World Economic Outlook* (Washington DC: IMF, 1988) is used. Estimates for the USSR's GNP, and those of other Warsaw Pact countries, are based on commercial banking estimates; for Hungary, Poland and Romania GDP is taken from IFS; other East European GDP/GNP figures at factor cost are derived from GNP. China's GDP/GNP is as given by the IMF.

Defence Expenditure

We quote the latest defence expenditure or budget data available as at 1 June 1989. Some countries include internal and border security force expenditures in their defence budgets, where separate budgets exist they are indicated in footnotes. Figures may vary from previous years, often because of updates made by the governments themselves.

NATO countries use a 'standard definition' of defence expenditure which includes all spending on regular military forces, military aid (including equipment and training) to other nations, military pensions, host government expenses for NATO tenant forces, NATO infrastructure and civilian staff costs; but excludes spending on para-military forces.

We are including Foreign Military Assistance (FMA) figures with other economic data in country entries (except for non-Soviet WP countries). The total of FMA received is shown, together with the providing countries. FMA includes both cash grants and credits; it may also include the cost of military training.

Currency Conversion Rates

National currency figures have been converted into US dollars to permit comparisons. The rate is averaged for the national financial year (for 1989–90 figures, the mid-1989 rate is used). Wherever possible, exchange rates are taken from IFS, though they may not be applicable to commercial transactions. For the USSR no adequate conversion ratio of roubles to dollars is available. For those East European countries which are not members of the IMF, and Hungary and Romania (which are), the adjusted conversion rates used are calculated by the method described in T.P. Alton, 'Economic Growth and Resource Allocation in Eastern Europe', *Reorientation and Commercial Relations of the Economies of Eastern Europe*, Joint Economic Committee, 93rd Congress, 2nd Session (Washington DC: USGPO, 1974).

Population

All population data are taken from the latest census data available in *World Population Projections 1984* (Washington DC: World Bank, 1984) and *1986 Demographic Yearbook* (New York: UN, 1988), latest national statistics where available, as well as calculated trends and projections.

WARNING

The Military Balance is a quantitative assessment of the personnel strengths and equipment holdings of the world's armed forces. It is in no way an assessment of their capabilities. It does not evaluate the quality of units or equipment, nor the impact of geography, doctrine, military technology, deployment, training, logistic support, morale, leadership, tactical or strategic initiative, terrain, weather, political will or support from alliance partners.

Nor is the Institute in any position to evaluate and compare directly the performance of items of equipment. Those who wish to do so can use the data provided to construct their own force comparisons. As essays in many editions of *The Military Balance* have made clear, however, such comparisons are replete with difficulties, and their validity and utility cannot but be suspect.

The Military Balance provides the actual numbers of nuclear and conventional forces and weapons as we know or can reasonably confidently estimate them – not the number that would be assumed for verification purposes in arms-control agreements (except in the sole case of the Soviet–American nuclear strategic balance table on p. 212).

This means that great care must be taken in assembling the data presented here for specific purposes. We provide an up-to-date and detailed catalogue of military forces in as many dimensions as possible and in a way which we hope will be generally useful. We make no judgments on quality, effectiveness or the political purposes underlying the aggregation of power.

The data presented each year in *The Military Balance* reflect judgments based on information available to the Director and staff of the Institute at the time the book is compiled. Information in subsequent volumes may differ from previous editions for a variety of reasons, generally as a result of substantive changes in national forces but in some cases as a result of our reassessment of the evidence supporting past entries. Inevitably, over the course of time we come to believe that some information presented in earlier versions was erroneous, or insufficiently supported by reliable evidence. Hence, it is not always possible to construct valid time series comparisons from information given in successive editions.

CONCLUSION

The Institute owes no allegiance whatever to any government, group of governments, or any political or other organization. Our assessments are our own, based on the material available to us from a wide variety of sources. The co-operation of all governments has been sought and, in many cases, received. Not all countries have been equally co-operative, and some of the figures have necessarily been estimated. We take pains to ensure that these estimates are as professional and free from bias as possible. The Institute owes a considerable debt to a number of its own members and consultants who have helped in compiling and checking material. The Director and the staff of the Institute assume full responsibility for the facts and judgments contained in this study. We welcome comments and suggestions on the data presented, since we seek to make it as accurate and comprehensive as possible.

Readers may use items of information from *The Military Balance* as required, without reference to the Institute, on condition that the Institute and *The Military Balance* are cited as the source in any published work. However, reproduction of all major portions of the work must be approved in writing by the Institute prior to publication.

1

COUNTRIES AND
PRINCIPAL PACTS

INDEX

The United States

United States defence planning for FY 1990 and beyond has been delayed first by the Presidential election process and the subsequent change of Administration, and secondly by the lengthy Senate confirmation hearings which led to the rejection of Senator John Tower as Secretary of Defense. Since the appointment of Congressman Richard Cheney has been confirmed, some of the findings of the policy review ordered by President Bush have been released and are reflected in the revised defence budget requests for FY 1990 and 1991 and in the five-year spending plan for FY 1990–94 which have been submitted to Congress. The budget request for FY 1990 is $299.3 billion which, if it were to survive Congressional scrutiny unscathed, would maintain 1989 funding levels in real terms. Current plans envisage modest increases in defence spending thereafter of approximately 2% growth per year, but there can be little confidence that this will be achievable. Some of the effects of this static defence budget picture may, however, be alleviated by savings and value-for-money measures such as base closures and a tightening of the Department of Defense procurement system.

Strategic Defense Initiative

President Bush has confirmed his resolve to continue with research and development for SDI. The original budget request for SDI in FY 1990 was set at $5.6 bn but this has been reduced by $1 bn by Secretary Cheney and it is expected that Congress will reduce this further to about $4 bn. The main focus is now on the *Brilliant Pebbles* concept; this envisages placing in orbit several thousand small rockets equipped with their own sensors which would each track and destroy an incoming ICBM during its boost and post-boost phase, before its MIRVed warheads were released. The defence provided, though only partial, is said by its proponents to cost significantly less than the SDI Office's current Phase I SDI concept which has been put at $69 bn. The US hopes to carry out tests related to *Brilliant Pebbles* within two years which would be carefully constrained so as not to breach the narrow interpretation of the 1972 ABM Treaty. SDI research has continued throughout the year, and in March 1989 a test in which a Mid Infra-Red Advanced Chemical Laser successfully intercepted an AGM-129A cruise missile flying at supersonic speed was carried out.

Nuclear Forces

Strategic Systems

The full 50 MX *Peacemaker* ICBM have now been deployed in *Minuteman* silos, the last eleven having displaced *Minuteman* III missiles during the past year. After further reviews of the land-based element of the strategic nuclear triad the new Administration has announced plans to mount the 50 *Peacemakers*, currently sited in silos, in pairs on railway trains. Once this 'rail-garrison' re-deployment is well advanced, production and deployment of the small ICBM *Midgetman* will commence. No figure for the final number of *Midgetman* to be produced has yet been given but estimates range from 250 to 500. The first *Midgetman* test firing took place on 11 May but a fault in the second stage caused the missile to be destroyed 70 seconds after launch. The Administration's ICBM deployment plan met with numerous reservations in the US Congress.

Although the first *Ohio*-class SSBN to be armed with *Trident* D-5 SLBM has been accepted for service, the D-5 SLBM are not yet ready for deployment and the first submerged test firing on 21 March 1989 was unsuccessful. Two *Lafayette*-class SSBN each with 16 *Poseidon* C-3 SLBM have been decommissioned. A further *Lafayette* will be decommissioned when USS *Tennessee*'s *Trident* D-5 SLBM becomes operational, probably in early 1990.

The B-2 bomber, incorporating low-observable ('stealth') technology has been unveiled but has not yet been flown. No performance details are available. For budgetary reasons the planned introduction of the B-2 has been both delayed (by at least a year) and extended in time; the production goal of 132 aircraft by mid-1996 is likely to be reduced and/or delayed. The organization of the B-1 bomber force has altered, there are now six operational squadrons with 90 aircraft, leaving seven in store. The programme of modification to equip B-52H aircraft to carry AGM-86B ALCM has been completed with 84 aircraft in squadron service and 12 in store.

Sub-Strategic Nuclear Forces
The Navy has added further platforms capable of launching SLCM: one improved and two modified *Los Angeles* SSGN, a fourth *Iowa*-class battleship, three *Ticonderoga*-class cruisers, and six destroyers.

Withdrawal and elimination of both *Pershing* II SSM and GLCM under the terms of the INF Treaty have proceeded. To date 34 *Pershing* II missiles and 28 (out of 165) launchers, and 130 GLCM and 25 (out of 123) launchers have been eliminated. We are unable to give accurate figures for INF weapons still operationally deployed.

Short-Range Nuclear Systems
While the replacement of nuclear artillery ammunition and limited initial development of a Tactical Air-to-Surface Missile is taking place with little publicity or fuss, much political attention has been given to NATO's plans with regard to a follow-on weapon to replace *Lance* SSM. The decision reached at the NATO summit on 29 and 30 May was that: 'The allies concerned recognize the value of the continued funding by the United States of research and development of a follow-on for the existing *Lance* short range missile', but 'The question concerning the introduction and deployment of a follow-on system for the *Lance* will be dealt with in 1992 in the light of overall security developments'.

Against this background, US development efforts are increasingly focusing on a surface-to-surface missile which will be fired from the MLRS launcher vehicle but with an increased range and with a different and easily recognizable configuration from the conventional army tactical missile system (ATACMS) which is also to be fired from MLRS, so as to ease the problems of verification.

The Navy has announced its intention of withdrawing from service the nuclear element of three weapons systems: the *ASROC* submarine-launched and *SUBROC* surface-launched ASW (introduced in 1961 and 1965 respectively) will be withdrawn from all ships by the end of 1989 and 1991 respectively. The 1956 vintage air-defence weapon *Terrier* (previously thought to have been withdrawn in 1988) is also to be taken out of service. This development will leave the Navy with only *Tomahawk* SLCM (land attack) and free-fall bombs and depth charges in its nuclear armoury.

Conventional Forces

Ground Forces
Some minor reorganization of the main ground forces structure has taken place. The 9th Motorized Infantry Division deployed in Washington State is being converted to a mechanized division and two Army National Guard (ARNG) armoured cavalry regiments have been reformed as armoured brigades. The number of CONUS-based active divisions whose third brigade is now provided by the National Guard or Army Reserve has risen from five to six. Fresh information has allowed us to revise our holdings of aviation units; there are now six corps aviation brigades, of which two are in West Germany. Each brigade consists of three active attack helicopter battalions, each with 18 AH-64 *Apache* and 13 OH-58 *Kiowa* scout helicopters (and with a further three reserve battalions on mobilization), two assault-transport battalions each with 45 UH-60 *Black Hawk*, and a medium transport battalion with 64 CH-47 *Chinook*, as well as command and medical evacuation helicopter assets. All divisions (including ARNG) other than light divisions have aviation brigades which are planned to consist of a cavalry battalion with eight AH-1S *Cobra* and 12 OH-58 *Kiowa*, an anti-tank battalion (two for divisions in West Germany) with 18 AH-64 *Apache* and 12 OH-58, and an assault-transport battalion with 15 UH-60 *Black Hawk*. Some 70 AH-64A

Apache helicopters have been procured during the year, allowing a total of 15 battalions to be equipped with the *Apache*.

The programme for prepositioning equipment (POMCUS) in Europe is now virtually complete for six divisions, an armoured cavalry regiment, and appropriate corps combat support and service support units. While a proportion is physically stored in Belgium and the Netherlands, all is intended for formations destined for deployment in West Germany.

The main re-equipment programmes have continued, and holdings of *Abrams* M-1 tanks have increased by some 700 and of *Bradley* M-2/M-3 fighting vehicles by nearly 900; both these are being placed in POMCUS wherever the CONUS-based unit is equipped with them. M-1 production is to continue for five years at a rate of 516 tanks a year. A further 110 MLRS have entered service. Three further *Patriot* SAM battalions have been formed to make a total of nine, of which eight now comprise three batteries (towards the final planned organization of six) each with eight launchers. Six further batteries will be activated in FY 1990, all for deployment in Europe. Last year we overestimated the number of *Patriot* launchers deployed; there are now 204 launchers in service.

The Army has suffered less than the other three services from cuts made to previous spending requests presented by the Reagan Administration – $1.7 bn in FY 1990 and $2.2 bn in FY 1991. Only two weapons programmes have had to be cancelled: the Army Helicopter Improvement Program (for the OH-58) which has already upgraded two thirds of the 375 helicopters originally budgeted for; and the production of AH-64 *Apache* after 1991. Production of UH-60 *Black Hawk* has been reduced by eleven helicopters a year. However, funding has been provided for development of the next-generation Light Helicopter Experimental (LHX).

Naval Forces

One 'improved' (SSN-751) and two modified (SSN-719) *Los Angeles*-class SSGN have been commissioned. A further two 'improved' *Los Angeles* SSN-751 have been launched and three more ordered. A total of six submarines have been retired: three *Permit* SSN-594, one *Skipjack* and one *Skate* SSN and one non-nuclear *Barbel*.

The fourth *Iowa*-class battleship, *USS Wisconsin*, was re-commissioned in October 1988. An accident on *USS Iowa* destroyed a 406mm gun turret but the ship continues in operational service for the present without this being repaired. Three *Ticonderoga*-class guided-missile cruisers all equipped with *Aegis* command-and-control system and *Tomahawk* SLCM have been commissioned. Six *Spruance*-class destroyers have been upgraded by the addition of the Vertical Launch System which has the capability to launch any combination of missile (but for the *Spruance* is restricted to *Tomahawk* only since that class has no air defence radar). The early retirement of 14 frigates (eight *Garcia*-class and 6 *Brooke*-class) has taken place, but the last of 51 *Oliver Hazard Perry*-class frigates has been commissioned. Finally, the first of a new class of amphibious assault ship, *USS Wasp* with the capacity to lift 1,900 troops and 60 tanks and to operate six AV-8B *Harrier* II, 24 helicopters and either 12 LCM or 3 LCAC (which can carry a tank ashore), has been commissioned.

The Navy's budget requests for FY 1990 and 1991 have been cut by $5.8 bn; to achieve these savings a number of new procurement programmes will be cancelled or extended in time and some early retirements made. Planned cancellations include the V-22 *Osprey* tilt rotor plane for the Marine Corps, the F-14D new production and two coastal mine-hunters. In a reversal of a previous policy, one of the two *Los Angeles* SSN-688, previously cut from the procurement budget, has been reinstated. This effectively delays change-over to *Sea Wolf* SSN-21; the first SSN-21 was ordered in January 1989 but will not enter service before 1995, with two further planned for FY 1991. Other budgetary cuts include early retirement of the *USS Coral Sea* once the fifth *Nimitz*-class carrier joins the fleet (implying the dropping of the 15 carrier battle-group target) together with seven destroyers, while ten frigates will be transferred to the Naval Reserve Surface Forces; these moves will save 5,600 posts.

The Secretary of Defense has testified that, in view of the cuts proposed, the Navy could not reach the Reagan 1980 target of a '600-ship' fleet in the near future.

Air Forces

In addition to unveiling the B-2 bomber the US Air Force has also revealed details of the F-117 aircraft which also incorporates low-observable technology, after several years speculation on its introduction into service. A tactical group of 52 F-117 aircraft exists and is based in Nevada. No performance details have been released nor has the plane's role been defined, but it could be well employed in attacking early warning and fire control radars and possibly in carrying out strategic reconnaissance. It has been reported that the dimensions of the F-117 permit it to be carried by a C-5 transport. This would make possible clandestine deployment of F-117 in limited numbers for special missions. New evidence on the primary tasking and pilot training of multirole tactical aircraft squadrons has led us to some re-attribution between the fighter and FGA roles. We now list 71 fighter squadrons and 66 FGA as compared with 53 fighter squadrons and 82 FGA last year (these totals include Air National Guard (ANG) and Air Force Reserve (AFR) units). Aircraft holdings show an increase of some 70 F-15 and 160 F-16.

The Air Force has managed to absorb its budget cuts of $2.76 bn in FY 1990 and $3.6 bn in FY 1991 by extending programmes rather than cancelling them, but the production of F-15E fighters will be terminated after 1991 and some 78 aircraft will not be built. There is no reduction in funding for the Advanced Tactical Fighter programme nor for the C-17 strategic transport.

Special Operations Command

Special Operations Command has further enhanced its independence from the four primary services by being granted, after a long bureaucratic struggle, its own budget. This will come into effect in FY 1992 but until then Special Operations Command will have responsibility for the execution of relevant Major Force programmes. Therefore, this year we have, listed all Special Operations Units together, separately from their parent services. Special Operations equipment is, however, still listed with those of the appropriate service. Two additional Air Force Squadrons with HC-130 aircraft and one with MH-53 helicopters have been formed.

Defence Spending

Fiscal constraints during 1988–9 continued to erode the Reagan Administration's defence budget plans for a real increase of 2% over the next two years. After the inauguration of the new President, the defence budget request was twice revised and reduced from an original $305.6 bn to $299.3 bn. Congress will impose further cuts before the FY 1990 defence budget is approved. The scope for further reductions in expenditure without major adjustments to force size, structure, readiness and sustainability appears very limited because, as several observers have noted, when military personnel costs are added to the cost of authorized programmes (Congress has already authorized $266 bn for weapon programmes and services for the period FY 1990–94) only 15% of the defence budget is left in the hands of the Secretary of Defense.

These fiscal and political constraints, coupled with the far less threatening image of the Soviet Union, have placed the Administration in an uncomfortable position. (The President's offer to reduce by 20% US combat troops in Europe to about 275,000 in return for a similar Soviet limit in effect is not only an answer to President Gorbachev's initiatives, but also is to assuage his Congressional critics, and to reduce the financial burden of the US contribution to the Alliance.) The public debate over the level of defence outlays has become increasingly complicated, and is no longer just linked to the issues of the fiscal deficit, the need to increase spending on social programmes while avoiding tax increases, and equitable burden-sharing within the Alliance, but also to the nature of the US response to President Gorbachev's force reductions, future investment in strategic forces, and to modernization programmes.

Explanatory Note:
Each year the US government presents its Defense Budget to Congress for the next two fiscal years, together with a long-term spending plan covering a further three years. Until approved by Congress the Budget is referred to as the Budget Request, after approval it becomes the Budget Authority (BA). The term 'outlay' refers to moneys expended; each year the government estimates what the outlay will be, the difference between this and the BA providing for contingencies. However, moneys authorized, particularly in the procurement and construction areas are rarely all spent in the year of authorization though contracts are signed which commit the government to payment in future years. On average, carried forward authorities constitute some 40% of each year's outlay, while similarly some 40% of each year's BA will be carried forward to future years.

Table I: Selected Budgets 1979–90 ($ bn)[a]

FY 1 Oct– 30 Sept	National Defense Function[b] (BA)	(outlay)	Department of Defense (BA)	(outlay)	Atomic Energy Defence Activities (outlay)	Inter- national Security Assistance (outlay)	Veterans Admin- istration (outlay)	Total Govt Exp (outlay)	Total Govt Budget Deficit (outlay)
1979	126.467	116.342	123.595	113.605	2.541	3.655	19.931	503.464	40.162
1980	143.859	133.995	140.651	130.12	2.878	4.763	21.185	590.920	73.808
1981	180.001	157.513	176.110	153.868	3.398	5.095	22.991	678.209	78.936
1982	216.547	185.309	211.513	180.741	4.309	5.416	23.958	745.706	127.940
1983	245.043	209.903	238.900	204.410	5.171	6.613	24.846	808.327	202.784
1984	265.16	227.413	258.176	220.928	6.120	7.924	25.614	851.781	185.324
1985	294.656	252.748	286.27	245.154	7.098	9.391	26.292	946.316	212.260
1986	289.146	273.375	281.436	265.480	7.445	10.499	26.356	990.258	221.167
1987	287.427	281.999	279.469	273.966	7.451	7.106	26.782	1,003.830	149.687
1988 (est)	292.008	290.361	283.755	281.935	7.913	4.500	29.428	1,064.044	155.090
1989 (est)	298.805	298.255	290.186	289.800	7.945	2.823	29.218	1,137.030	161.496
(Administration request)									
1990	315.193	302.991	305.645	293.820	8.647	8.428	29.872	1,151.848	92.509

[a] Data is from *Historical Tables, Budget of the United States Government Fiscal Year 1990* (Washington DC: USGPO, 1989), *Budget of the United States Government Fiscal Year 1989* (Washington DC: USGPO, 1989). All categories include off-budget items.
[b] The National Defense budget function includes DoD Military Activities, Department of Energy Atomic Energy Defense Activities, and smaller support agencies such as the Federal Management Agency, the Selective Service System and the General Services Administration Stockpile of Strategic Materials, National Defense Function. International Security Assistance and Veterans Administration is not included nor is spending by NASA and the Coast Guard.

Table II: Defense Budget Authorities

	FY 1979	1985	1986	1987	1988	1989	1990[c] requested
	Billion current $ (*Billion constant 1985 $*)						
Personnel	37.6 *(55.7)*	67.8 *(67.8)*	67.8 *(66.6)*	74.0 *(70)*	76.6 *(69.7)*	78.6	79.8
Operations & Maintenance	38 *(56.3)*	77.8 *(77.7)*	74.9 *(73.4)*	79.6 *(75.3)*	81.6 *(74.2)*	85.9	91.7
Procurement	31.4 *(46.5)*	96.8 *(96.8)*	92.5 *(90.7)*	80.2 *(75.9)*	80.1 *(72.8)*	79.2	84.1
RD&TE	12.4 *(18.4)*	31.3 *(31.3)*	33.6 *(32.9)*	35.6 *(37.7)*	36.5 *(33.2)*	37.5	41.0
Military construction	2.3 *(3.4)*	5.5 *(5.5)*	5.3 *(5.2)*	5.1 *(4.8)*	5.3 *(4.8)*	5.7	5.3
Other	1.8 *(2.7)*	7.5 *(7.5)*	7.3 *(7.2)*	4.9 *(4.6)*	3.6 *(3.3)*	3.2	3.3
Total DoD spending (incl Family Housing)	123.6 *(183.0)*	286.8 *(286.8)*	281.4 *(275.8)*	279.5 *(264.4)*	283.8 *(258.2)*	290.2	299.3
Atomic energy	2.7 *(4.0)*	7.3 *(7.3)*	7.3 *(7.2)*	7.5 *(7.1)*	7.7	8.1	9.0
Other	0.1 *(0.1)*	0.5 *(0.5)*	0.5 *(0.5)*	0.5 *(0.5)*	0.5	0.5	0.5
TOTAL NATIONAL DEFENSE	126.5 *(187.1)*	294.6 *(294.5)*	289.1 *(283.5)*	287.4 *(271.9)*	292.0 *(265.7)*	298.8	315.2

[c] Reagan Administration Request.

THE UNITED STATES

GDP 1987: $4,484.3 bn
1988: $4,839.2 bn
Growth 1987: 2.9% 1988: 3.9%
Inflation 1987: 3.6% 1988: 4.0%
Debt 1987: $287.3 bn 1988: $349.3 bn
Def bdgt* 1988: BA $288.6 bn, outlay
$274 bn
NATO defn: $286.04 bn
1989: BA $290.3 bn, outlay
$289.8 bn
Request 1990: BA $299.3 bn, outlay
$291.2 bn

Population: 248,917,000

	13–17	18–22	23–32
Men	8,487,000	9,483,000	21,257,000
Women	8,076,000	9,128,000	21,170,000

TOTAL ARMED FORCES:
ACTIVE: 2,124,900 (211,200 women) (excludes
Coast Guard).
Terms of Service: voluntary.
RESERVES:
READY RESERVE: 1,655,900. Selected Reserve
and Individual Ready Reserve: to augment active
units and provide reserve formations and units:
NATIONAL GUARD: 587,000. Army (ARNG)
472,000; Air (ANG) 115,000.
RESERVE: 1,068,900. Army 610,800; Navy
242,600; Marines 86,800; Air Force 128,700.
STANDBY RESERVE: 37,500. Trained
individuals for mobilization: Army 400; Navy
11,200; Marines 1,400; Air Force 24,500.
RETIRED RESERVE: 175,500. Trained
individuals to augment support and training
facilities: Army 87,300; Navy 28,800; Marines
5,200; Air Force 54,200.

STRATEGIC NUCLEAR FORCES:†

NAVY: 608 SLBM in 35 SSBN.
SSBN (incl 6 in refit):
9 *Ohio* (SSBN-726)
1 to get 24 UGM-133A *Trident* D-5 (0 msls)
USS Tennessee, currently testing *Trident D-5,*
is now expected to be operational in early
1990, when a further *Lafayette* will be
decommissioned to remain within SALT limits.
8 with 24 UGM-93A *Trident* C-4 (192 msls)
12 *Franklin* (SSBN-640):
6 with 16 *Trident* C-4 (96 msl)
6 with 16 UGM-73A *Poseidon* C-3 (96 msl)
8 *Madison* (SSBN-627):
6 with 16 *Trident* C-4 (96 msl)
2 with 16 *Poseidon* C-3 (32 msl)
6 *Lafayette* (SSBN-616) with
16 *Poseidon* C-3 (96 msl)

STRATEGIC AIR COMMAND (SAC):
2 Air Forces. 8 div (1 trg/spt).
ICBM: 1,000. 6 strategic msl wings (20 sqn, each
with 5 launch control centres):
3 wings (9 sqn) with 450 *Minuteman* II (LGM-30F).
3 wings (10 sqn) with 500 *Minuteman* III
(LGM-30G).
1 sqn with 50 *Peacekeeper* (MX; LGM-118A); in
mod *Minuteman* silos.
AIRCRAFT: 372 cbt ac; plus 50 in store;
21 bbr wings (14 B-52, 4 B-1B, 2 FB-111, 1 trg).
BOMBERS: 372; plus 50 in store.
LONG-RANGE: 324; plus 36 in store.
4 wings (6 sqn) with 90 B-1B; plus 7 in store.
4 wings (6 sqn) with 84 B-52H (with AGM-86B
ALCM); plus 12 in store.
10 wings (10 sqn) with 150 B-52G; plus 17 in store:
6 sqn (89 ac) with ALCM/SRAM; plus 9 in store.
4 sqn (61 ac) with *Harpoon* or bombs
(conventional role only); plus 8 in store.
MEDIUM-RANGE: 48; plus 14 in store.
2 wings: 5 sqn with FB-111A (to be modified to
111G and to transfer to TAC in the 1990s).
RECCE: 60; plus 5 trg, 12 in store.
3 wings: 6 sqn:
1 with 6 SR-71A, 1 SR-71B (trg); 12 in store,
11 T-38A (trg). Withdrawn by 10/89.
1 with 11 U-2R, 2 U-CT (trg).
2 with 23 TR-1A, 2 TR-1B (trg).
2 with 20 RC-135.
COMMAND: 44:
6 sqn:
1 with 4 E-4A/B.
5 with 40 EC-135.
TANKER: 706: (plus 48 in store):
6 wings: 54 sqn (51 with ac, incl 1 trg):
31 USAF with 512 KC-135.
4 USAF with 60 KC-10A tkr/tpt.
13 ANG with 110 KC-135.
3 AFR with 24 KC-135.
3 KC-10 AFR Associate sqn (no ac).

STRATEGIC RECCE/INTELLIGENCE COLLECTION (SATELLITES)
IMAGERY: KH-8: 80–220-mile orbit, photographic
film return. KH-11: 160–400-mile polar orbit,
digital imagery. KH-12 (*Ikon*).
OCEAN SURVEILLANCE (OSUS): 4 satellites to detect
ships by infra-red and radar.

NAVIGATIONAL SATELLITE TIMING AND RANGING
(NAVSTAR): 7 satellites, components of global
positioning system (21 by 1992).

ELINT/COMINT: *Chalet, Magnum, Aquacade*; 'Ferrets'
(radar-monitoring satellites).

NUCLEAR DETONATION DETECTION SYSTEM (NDS):
Detects and evaluates nuclear detonations. Sensors
to be deployed in NAVSTAR satellites 1989–92.

STRATEGIC DEFENCES:

US Air Force Space Command: (HQ: Peterson
AFB, Colorado).
North American Aerospace Defense Command
(NORAD), a combined US-Cdn org (HQ: Peterson
AFB, Colorado).

EARLY WARNING:

SATELLITE EARLY WARNING SYSTEM (SEWS): 1 each
over Indian, Atlantic and Pacific Oceans;
infra-red surveillance and warning system.
Control and tracking stations at Guam and Pine
Gap, Nurrungar (Australia).

BALLISTIC MISSILE EARLY WARNING SYSTEM
(BMEWS): 3 stations: Clear (Alaska); Thule
(Greenland) Fylingdales Moor (UK). Radars detect
and track satellites, ICBM and IRBM, 4,800-km
range. Thule has been updated with phased-array
radar, Fylingdales is in process of update.

SPACETRACK: USAF radars Pirinclik (Turkey),
Shemya (Aleutians), Clear, Thule and
Fylingdales; optical tracking systems in New
Mexico, at St Margarets (NB), Choejong-San (S.
Korea), San Vito (Italy), Maui (Hawaii), Diego
Garcia (Indian Ocean).

PACIFIC RADAR BARRIER (PACBAR): detection and
tracking radars: at San Miguel, Philippines,
Kwajalein Atoll, North Mariannas.

USN SPACE SURVEILLANCE SYSTEM (NAVSPASUR): 3
transmitting, 6 receiving sites field stations in
south-east US.

**PERIMETER ACQUISITION RADAR ATTACK
CHARACTERIZATION SYSTEM** (PARCS): 1
north-facing phased-array system at Grand Forks
ND; 2,800-km range.

PAVE PAWS: phased-array radars in Massachusetts,
Georgia, Texas, California; 5,500-km range.

MISCELLANEOUS RADARS: US Army: Kwajalein
Atoll (Pacific). USAF: Ascension Island
(Atlantic), Antigua (Caribbean), Kaena Point
(Hawaii); MIT Lincoln Laboratory, Westford, MA.

UNDER DEVELOPMENT: Ground-based Electro-
Optical Deep Space Surveillance system
(GEODSS): White Sands NM, Taegu (S. Korea)
and Maui (Hawaii), Diego Garcia (Indian
Ocean); 1 more planned for Portugal.

AIR DEFENCE:

RADARS:

OVER-THE-HORIZON-BACKSCATTER RADAR (OTH-B): 4
systems planned: 1 in Maine, 1 in Oregon/N
California, 1 in south central US, 1 in Alaska.
east coast system operational; construction of the
west coast system has started; construction to
start in Alaska in FY 89. Range 900 (minimum)
to 3,300 km.

NORTH WARNING SYSTEM: to replace DEW line
(q.v.). 15 automated long-range radar stations
now operational. 39 short-range (110–150 km)
stations due in service by 1992.

DEW LINE: 31 radars in Alaska (7), Canada (20), and
Greenland (4) roughly along the 70°N parallel
from Point Lay, Alaska to Greenland.

AIRCRAFT:

REGULAR: 84: 1 Air Force, 5 air div:
2 with 36 F-15A (CONUS).
2 with 30 F-15C (Alaska).
1 with 18 F-15C (Iceland).

ANG: 216: 12 sqn:
7 with 126 F-4C/D.
1 with 18 F-15A (Hawaii).
4 with 72 F-16A/B.

TAC augmentation: ac on call from Navy, Marine
Corps and Air Force.

AAM: *Sidewinder, Sparrow.*

ARMY: 766,500 (82,700 women).

7 Army HQ, 6 Corps HQ (1 AB).
4 armd div (3 bde HQ, 6 tk, 4 mech inf, 3 SP
  arty, 1 MLRS/SP arty, 1 AD bn; 1 avn bde)
  (incl 1 ARNG bde in 1 div).
7 mech div (3 bde HQ, 5 tk, 5 mech inf, 3 SP
  arty, 1 MLRS/SP arty, 1 AD bn; 1 avn bde)
  (incl 1 ARNG/AR bde in 3 div).
1 inf div (3 bde HQ, 8 inf, 1 mech inf, 1 tk, 3
  arty, 1 AD bn; 1 avn bde).
4 lt inf div (3 bde HQ, 9 inf, 3 arty, 1 AD bn)
  (incl 1 ARNG/AR bde in 2 div).
1 air aslt div: (3 bde HQ, 9 air aslt, 3 arty bn, avn
  bde (8 bn: 4 attack, 2 aslt, 1 comd, 1 tpt)).
1 AB div (3 bde HQ, 9 para, 3 arty, 1 AD bn, 1
  ATK coy, 1 air recce sqn; 1 avn bde).
2 indep armd bde (2 tk, 1 mech inf, 1 SP arty bn).
1 indep mech bde (1 tk, 2 mech inf, 1 SP arty bn).
2 inf (theatre def) bde (3 inf, 1 lt arty bn, 1 tk coy+).
6 corps avn bde (2 attack, 1 avn bn).
2 avn trg bde.
3 armd cav regt.
9 arty bde.
5 AA arty bde.
4 *Pershing* II SSM bn (plus 1 school bty) (being
  disbanded).
8 *Lance* SSM bn (each 6 launchers).
9 *Patriot* SAM bn: 8 with 3 bty (all to form 6 bty
  as eqpt becomes available).
8 *HAWK* SAM bn.

READY RESERVE:
ARMY NATIONAL GUARD (ARNG): capable after mob of manning 10 div (2 armd, 2 mech, 5 inf, 1 lt inf); 20 indep bde (5 armd, 6 mech, 9 inf (3 lt) (incl 5 'Roundout' (1 armd, 3 mech, 1 lt inf) for Regular Army div)); 2 armd cav regt; 1 inf gp (Arctic recce: 5 scout bn); 20 fd arty bde HQ. Indep bn: 5 tk, 3 mech, 1 mtn inf, 50 arty, 4 ATK (*TOW*), 13 AD (1 *HAWK*, 7 *Chaparral*, 1 M-42 40mm, 4 *Vulcan/Stinger* SP AA arty), 62 engr.

ARMY RESERVE (AR): 12 trg div, 3 trg bde (no cbt role). 3 indep bde: 1 mech, 1 inf (theatre def), 1 lt inf ('Roundout'); 3 arty bde HQ, 72 indep bn (1 tk, 2 inf, 16 arty, 53 engr).

EQUIPMENT:
MBT: some 15,992: 1,111 M-48A5, 3,487 M-60/M-60A1, 5,400 M-60A3, 5,994 M-1/M-1A1 *Abrams*.
AIFV: some 4,883 M-2/-3 *Bradley*.
APC: some 26,480, incl 4,500 M-577, 18,080 M-113.
TOWED ARTY: 1,945:
   105mm: 300 M-101, 800 M-102, 35 M-119;
   155mm: 220 M-114, 590 M-198.
SP ARTY: 3,452:
   155mm: 2,423 M-109A1/A2;
   203mm: 1,029 M-110A1/A2.
MRL: 227mm: some 416 MLRS.
MORTARS: 81mm; 107mm: 2,670 (incl 920 M-106); 120mm: some.
SSM: 109 *Pershing* II launchers (to be destroyed); 65 *Lance* launchers.
ATGW: 7,400 *TOW*, 3,900 M-901 with *TOW*, 7,700 *Dragon* launchers.
RCL: 3,560 90mm and 106mm.
AD GUNS: 20mm: 220 M-167 *Vulcan* towed, 380 M-163 SP; 40mm: 500 M-42 SP.
SAM: *Redeye*, FIM-92A *Stinger*, 39 *Avenger* (vehicle mounted *Stinger*), 618 M-54 and M-48 SP *Chaparral*, 400 *Improved HAWK*, 204 *Patriot* launchers, 8 *Rapier*, 4 ADATS.
AMPHIBIOUS: 15 ships:
   4 *Frank Besson* LST: capacity 32 tk.
   1 *John Page* LST: capacity 16 tk.
   10 *Runnymede* LSM: capacity 7 tk.
   Plus craft: some 180 LCM, 30 ACV.
AVIATION:
   AIRCRAFT: some 520, incl 111 OV-1C/D, 26 RV-1D, 28 RU-21, 2 RG-8A, 6 Short-330, 19 C-7, 134 C-12 (113 C-12D, 21 RC-12D/G/H), 49 U-8, 6 UV-18A, 115 U-21, 24 T-42.
   HELICOPTERS: some 8,376 (2,250 armed hel) incl hel in store; 1,074 AH-1S, 454 AH-64A, 18 AH-6/MH-6, 3,085 UH-1 (being replaced), 15 EH-1H ECM, 985 UH/MH-60A (40 to be EH-60A, ECM on conversion), 197 CH-47A/B/C, 271 -D, 71 CH-54, 335 OH-6A, 1,871 OH-58A/C/D.

NAVY: 583,900 (55,000 women): 4 Fleets; 2nd (Atlantic), 3rd (Pacific), 6th (Mediterranean), 7th (W. Pacific).
SUBMARINES: 133:
STRATEGIC SUBMARINES: 35: (see p. 16).
TACTICAL SUBMARINES: 96: (incl 31 in refit).
   SSGN: 10:
      2 improved *Los Angeles* (SSN-751) with 12 × *Tomahawk* SLCM (VLS), 533mm TT (Mk 48 HWT, *Harpoon*, *Tomahawk*).
      8 mod *Los Angeles* (SSN-719) with 12 × *Tomahawk* SLCM (VLS); plus 533mm TT (Mk 48 HWT, *Harpoon*, *Tomahawk*).
   SSN: 83:
      31 *Los Angeles* (SSN-688) with Mk 48 HWT, plus *Harpoon*; 22 with *Tomahawk* SLCM.
      37 *Sturgeon* (SSN-637) with Mk 48 HWT; 5 with *SUBROC*, plus *Harpoon*; 13 with *Tomahawk* SLCM.
      10 *Permit* (SSN-594) with Mk 48 HWT, *SUBROC*; plus *Harpoon*.
      1 *Lipscomb* (SSN-685) with Mk 48 HWT, *SUBROC*.
      1 *Narwhal* (SSN-671) with Mk 48 HWT; plus *Harpoon*.
      3 *Skipjack* (SSN-585) with Mk 48 HWT.
   SS: 3:
      2 *Barbel* (SS-580) with Mk 48 HWT.
      1 *Darter* (SS-576) with Mk 48 HWT.
SUBMARINES, OTHER ROLES: 2:
   2 *Houston* (SSN-609) (special ops).
PRINCIPAL SURFACE COMBATANTS: 229:
AIRCRAFT CARRIERS: 14 (incl 2 in refit, excl 1 in SLEP).
   CVN: 5:
      4 *Nimitz* (CVN-68) (92,900t).
      1 *Enterprise* (CVN-65) (91,500t).
   CV: 9 (plus 1 *Kitty Hawk* in SLEP):
      2 *Kitty Hawk* (CV-63) (81/83,000t).
      1 *Kennedy* (CV-67) (82,500t).
      4 *Forrestal* (CV-59) (80,500/82,400t).
      2 *Midway* (CV-41) (65/66,300t).
   AIR WING 13 (average 86 ac, dependent on ship):
      2 ftr sqn with 24 F-14A; or (*Midway*-class) F/A-18A.
      3 FGA/attack sqn:
         2 lt with 24 F/A-18A or A-7E.
         1 med with 10 A-6E.
      2 ASW sqn:
         1 with 10 S-3A ac; 1 with SH-3H hel.
      1 ECM sqn with 4 EA-6B.
      1 AEW sqn with 4 E-2C; 4 KA-6D tkr.
BATTLESHIPS: 4 *Iowa* (BB-61) with 3 × 3 406mm guns, 8 × 4 *Tomahawk* SLCM, plus 4 × 4 *Harpoon* SSM.
CRUISERS: 41 (incl 6 in refit):
   CGN: 9:
      4 *Virginia* (CGN-38) with 2 × 2 SM-2 MR SAM/*ASROC* SUGW; plus 2 × 4 *Tomahawk*

SLCM, 2 × 4 *Harpoon*, SH-2F hel (Mk 46 LWT), 2 × 3 ASTT, 2 × 127mm guns.

2 *California* (CGN-36) with 2 × SM-2 MR; plus 2 × 4 *Harpoon*, 1 × 8 *ASROC*, 2 × 3 ASTT, 2 × 127mm guns.

1 *Truxtun* (CGN-35) with 1 × 2 SM-2 ER SAM/*ASROC*; plus 2 × 3 ASTT, 1 × SH-2F hel, 1 × 127mm guns.

1 *Long Beach* (CGN-9) with 2 × 2 SM-2 ER; plus 2 × 4 *Tomahawk*, 2 × 4 *Harpoon*, 1 × 8 *ASROC*, 2 × 3 ASTT, 2 × 127mm guns.

1 *Bainbridge* (CGN-25) with 2 × 2 SM-2 ER plus 2 × 4 *Harpoon*, 1 × 8 *ASROC*, 2 × 3 ASTT.

CG: 32:

14 *Ticonderoga* (CG-47 *Aegis*):
5 Baseline 1 with 2 × 2 SM-2 MR/*ASROC*; plus 2 × 4 *Harpoon*, 2 × 1 127mm guns, 2 × 3 ASTT, 2 × SH-2F or SH-60B hel.
9 Baseline 2/3, with 2 × VLS Mk 41 (61 tubes each) for combination of SM-2 ER, and *Tomahawk*. Other weapons as Baseline 1.

9 *Belknap* (CG-26) with 1 × 2 SM-2 ER/*ASROC*; plus 2 × 3 ASTT, 2 × 4 *Harpoon*, 1 × 127mm gun, 1 × SH-2F hel.

9 *Leahy* (CG-16) with 2 × 2 SM-2 ER/*ASROC*; plus 2 × 3 ASTT, 2 × 4 *Harpoon*.

DESTROYERS: 68: (incl some 6 in refit).

DDG: 37:

4 *Kidd* (DDG-993) with 2 × 2 SM-2 MR/*ASROC*; plus 2 × 3 ASTT, 2 × SH-2F hel, 2 × 4 *Harpoon*, 2 × 127mm guns.

10 *Coontz* (DDG-37) with 1 × 2 SM-2 ER; plus 1 × 8 *ASROC*, 2 × 3 ASTT, 1 × 127mm gun. 8 with 2 × 4 *Harpoon*.

23 *Adams* (DDG-2) 13 with 1 × 2 SM-1 MR; 10 with 1 × SM-1; plus 1 × 8 *ASROC*, 2 × 3 ASTT, 2 × 127mm gun; 18 with *Harpoon*.

DD: 31:

31 *Spruance* (DD-963) (ASW):
21 Baseline 1, with 1 × 8 *ASROC*, 2 × 3 ASTT, 1 × SH-2F hel; plus 2 × 4 *Harpoon*, 2 × 127mm gun; 7 with 2 × 4 *Tomahawk*.
10 Baseline 2, with 1 × VLS Mk 41 (*Tomahawk*), 2 × 3 ASTT, 1 × SH-60B hel; plus 2 × 127mm guns, 2 × 4 *Harpoon*.

FRIGATES: 102: (incl some 12 in refit).

FFG: 51:

51 *Oliver Hazard Perry* (FFG-7) (15 in NRF), all with 2 × 3 ASTT; 24 with 2 × SH-60B hel; 27 with 2 × SH-2F hel; all plus 1 × SM-1 MR/*Harpoon*.

FF: 51:

46 *Knox* (FF-1052) (7 in NRF) with 1 × 8 *ASROC*, 1 × SH-2F hel, 4 × ASTT; plus *Harpoon* (from *ASROC* launcher), 1 × 127mm gun.

2 *Garcia* (FF-1040) with 1 × 8 *ASROC*, 2 × 3 ASTT; plus 2 × 127mm guns. Note: To decommission 8/89 and 9/89.

1 *Glover* (FF-1098) with 1 × 8 *ASROC*, 2 × 3 ASTT; plus 1 × 127mm gun.

2 *Bronstein* (FF-1037) with 1 × 8 *ASROC*, 2 × 3 ASTT.

PATROL AND COASTAL COMBATANTS: 30:

Note: Mainly responsibility of Coast Guard.

MISSILE CRAFT: 6 *Pegasus* PHM with 2 × 4 *Harpoon*.

PATROL, INSHORE: 24⟨.

MINE WARFARE: 29:

MINELAYERS: None dedicated, but mines can be laid from SS classes and also by B-52 bbr.

MINE COUNTERMEASURES: 29:

1 *Avenger* (MCM-1) MCO.

21 *Aggressive* (MSO-422)/*Acme* (MSO-509) MCO (18 with NRF).

7 MSB-15 MSI⟨.

AMPHIBIOUS: 66:

COMMAND: 2 *Blue Ridge*: capacity 700 tps.

LHA: 6:

1 *Wasp*: capacity 1,900 tps, 60 tk; with 6 AV-8B ac, 12 CH-46, 4 CH-53, 4 UH-1N, 4 AH-1T hel; plus 12 LCM-6 or 3 LCAC.

5 *Tarawa*: capacity 1,700 tps, 100 tk, 4 LCU, 6 AV-8B ac, 12 CH-46, 4 CH-53, 4 UH-1N, 4 AH-1T hel.

LPH: 7 *Iwo Jima*: capacity 1,750 tps, 4 AV-8B ac, 2 CH-46, 10 CH-53, 1 UH-1N hel.

LPD: 13: 11 *Austin*, 2 *Raleigh*: capacity 930 tps, 4 tk.

LSD: 13:

5 *Whidbey Island* with 4 LCAC or 21 LSM: capacity 450 tps, 40 tk.

5 *Anchorage*, 3 *Thomaston*: capacity 350 tps, 38 tk.

LST: 20 *Newport* (2 NRF): capacity 400 tps, 10 tk.

LKA (amph cargo ships): 5 *Charleston*: capacity 360 tps, 10,000 tonnes stores.

CRAFT: some 75:

14 LCAC: capacity 1 MBT.

53 LCU-1610: capacity 3 MBT.

Numerous LCVP, LCU, LCM.

SUPPORT AND MISCELLANEOUS: 152:

(Total includes 66 USN ships, 78 ships of the Military Sealift Command Fleet Auxiliary Force, and 8 AGOR owned by the US Navy, but operated by civil research institutes.)

UNDERWAY SUPPORT: 59:

AO: 31: 5 *Cimarron*, 7 *Wichita*, 6 *Henry Kaiser*, 6 *Neosho*, 5 *Mispillion*, 2 *Caloosahatchee*.

AOE: 4 *Sacramento*.

AE: 13: 8 *Kilauea*, 2 *Suribachi*, 3 *Nitro*.

AF: 11: 7 *Mars*, 1 *Rigel*, 3 *Sirius*.

MAINTENANCE AND LOGISTICS: 50:

9 AD, 12 AS, 3 AR, 7 AT, 14 AOT, 3 AK, 2 AH.

SPECIAL PURPOSES: 22:

2 comd, 14 AGOS (towed array), 5 technical spt, 1 avn trg.

SURVEY AND RESEARCH: 21:

12 AGOR, 9 AGHS.

NAVAL AVIATION: incl 13 attack carrier air wings.

AIRCRAFT:

FIGHTER: 26 sqn with F-14A.

FGA/ATTACK: 42 sqn:
16 med with A-6E, KA-6D (tanker).
12 lt with A-7E.
14 with F/A-18A.

ELINT: 2 sqn with EA-3, EP-3.

EW: 11 sqn with EA-6B.

MR: 24 land-based sqn with P-3B, P-3C, P-3CIII.

ASW: 12 sqn with S-3A.

AEW: 15 sqn with E-2C.

COMD: 2 sqn with EC-130Q (TACAMO) (E-6A to replace).

OTHER: 14 spt sqn with C-130F, LC-130F/R, EC-130G/Q, C-2A, CT-39, C-131, UC-12B ac; and hel (see below).

OCU: 17:
4 ftr/strike (2 with F-14, 2 with F-18).
4 attack with TA-7C, A-7E, A-6.
3 EW with EA-6B, EA-3.
2 MR with P-3B/C.
2 AEW with E-2B/C.
2 ASW with S-3A.

TRAINING:
5 'Aggressor' sqn with F-5E/F, T-38, A-4, F-16N.
18 trg sqn: 2 with F/A-18B, 16 with T-2B/C, T-34C, T-39, T-44 ac; and hel (see below).

HELICOPTERS:

ASW: 25 sqn:
5 with SH-60B (LAMPS Mk III).
6 with SH-2F (LAMPS Mk I).
14 with SH-3H (SH-60F to replace).

MCM: 2 sqn with RH-53D, MH-53E.

MISC: 6 spt sqn with SH-3, 4 with CH-46, 1 with CH-53E.

OCU: 9 with SH-2/-3/-60B, UH-1, CH-46, CH-53.

TRG: 2 sqn with TH-57A/B/C.

EQUIPMENT:
1,579 (incl 247 NR) cbt ac; plus 568 in store; some 376 (incl 46 NR) armed hel.

AIRCRAFT:

F-14: 398. **-A:** 372 (312 ftr, 60 OCU); **-A plus:** 26 (ftr); plus 210 in store.

F/A-18: 246. **-A:** 213 (168 FGA, 45 OCU); **-B:** 33 (trg); plus 118 in store.

F-5E/F/T-38: 21.

F-16: 26. **-N:** 22 (trg); **TF-16N:** 4 (trg).

A-4: 426 (trg). **-F:** 177 (trg); **TA-4J:** 249 (trg).

A-6: 340. **-E:** 212 (160 FGA, 52 OCU); **-F:** 12 (trials); **EA-6B:** 64 (EW); **KA-6D:** 52 (tkr); plus 125 in store.

A-7E: 210 (FGA); **TA-7C** (OCU).

E-2C: 86. 72 (AEW, incl 12 NR): **-B/C:** 14 (OCU).

A-3: 18. **EA-3:** 14 (ELINT); **KA-3:** 4 (tkr).

P-3: 385: **-A/-B/-C/-CIII:** 333 (MR, incl 117 NR); 40 (OCU); **EP-3:** 12 (ELINT); plus 115 in store.

S-3A: 140 (110 ASW, 30 OCU).

C-130: 28. **-Q:** 15 (comd); **-F/LC-130F/R:** 13 (misc).

CT-39: 9 (misc). **C-117** (C-47): 4 (misc). **C-9B:** 27 (tpt). **UC-12A:** 38 (misc).

T-2B/C: 178 (trg). **US-3:** 6 (tpt). **T-34C:** 334 (trg). **T-44:** 46 (trg).

HELICOPTERS:

RH-53D: 31 (MCM); **MH-53E:** 16 (MCM).

SH-60B: 97 (ASW); **-F:** 12 (ASW). **HH-60:** 16 (cbt spt, NR).

SH-2F: 147 (ASW, OCU; to be mod to -2G).

SH-3D/H: 104 (ASW, OCU; remaining 26 -D being converted to -H standard).

CH-46: 88 (tpt, OCU) being updated.

MISSILES:

AAM: AIM-120 AMRAAM being delivered. AIM-7 *Sparrow*, AIM-54A/C *Phoenix*, AIM-9 *Sidewinder*.

ASM: AGM-78D *Standard* ARM, AGM-45 *Shrike*, AGM-88A *HARM* (anti-radiation); AGM-84 *Harpoon*.

RESERVES:

NAVAL RESERVE SURFACE FORCES (NRF): 45 ships: 15 FFG, 7 FF, 18 MCMV, 2 amph and 3 spt/misc vessels. Incl in main Navy entry. Crewed by about 70% active USN and 30% NR.

AVIATION: 247 cbt ac; 46 armed hel.
2 attack carrier wings: 16 sqn:
6 attack (4 with 48 A-7E; 2 with 24 F/A-18).
1 med attack with 10 A-6E.
4 ftr with 48 F-14.
2 AEW with 12 E-2C.
2 ECM with EA-6A/B.
1 tkr with KA-3B.
2 MR wings: 13 sqn with 117 P-3A/B/C.
1 tac spt wing: 13 sqn:
2 composite with TA-4J.
11 spt with C-9B.
1 hel wing: 11 sqn:
4 ASW (1 with 6 SH-3D, 3 with 24 SH-2F).
2 lt attack with 16 AH-1J.
2 MCM with 24 RH-53D.
1 SAR with HH-3.
2 cbt spt special sqn with 16 HH-60.
(To form: aircrew associate units).

COMBAT SUPPORT FORCES (provision of units for MCM, underwater ops, ashore contruction, cargo handling).

AUGMENT FORCES (provision of additional manpower to regular org).

MARINE CORPS: 195,300 (10,500 women).
3 div (2 bde HQ, 3 inf (with 9 inf, 1 armd inf with LAV-25 bn), 1 arty regt, 1 recce, 1 tk, 1 cbt engr, 1 aslt amph, 1 AD bn).
2 bn Marine Corps Cbt Security Force (deployed 1 each in Atlantic and Pacific).

RESERVES (MCR):

1 div: (3 inf, 1 arty regt; 2 tk, 1 armd inf (with LAV-25), 1 aslt amph, 1 recce, 1 cbt engr bn). 1 SAM bn with *HAWK*

EQUIPMENT:

MBT: 716 M-60A1.
AIFV: 422 LAV-25 (25mm gun)
APC: 805 AAV-7A1/LVT-7A1 (all roles) incl 50 LAV-M (mor), 94 LAV-L (logistic)
SP ARTILLERY: 155mm: 143 M-109A3; 203mm: 108 M-110A2.
TOWED ARTILLERY: 105mm: 282 M-101A1; 155mm: 422 M-198, 90 M-114
MORTAR: 81mm: ε400.
ATGW: 1,117 *TOW*, 1,054 *Dragon*, 96 LAV-AT (*TOW*).
RCL: 83mm: ε700.
SAM: *Redeye, Stinger.*

AVIATION: 3 active air wings.

AIR WING: (no standard org but an optimal option is shown below): 174 fixed-wing aircraft, 156 hel: 48 F/A-18, 48 P/A-18, 20 A-6, 60 AU-8B, 9 T/O A-4, 20 A-6, 60 AV-8B, 9 T/OA-4, 7 RF-4B, 6 EA-6B, 12 OV-10, 12 KC-130, 60 CH-46, 48 CH-53, 24 AH-1, 24 UH-1.

AIRCRAFT:

FIGHTER: 12 sqn with F/A-18.
FGA: 13 sqn:
  8 lt: 6 with AV-8B, 2 with A-4M.
  5 med with A-6E.
RECCE: 1 sqn with 21 RF-4B.
EW: 1 sqn with 18 EA-6B.
FAC: 2 sqn with OV-10.
COMD: 5 sqn with OA-4/TA-4.
TANKER: 3 sqn with KC-130.
TRAINING: 7 sqn.

HELICOPTERS: 30 sqn:

ARMED: 6 lt attack/utility sqn with AH-1/UH-1N.
TRANSPORT: 15 med with CH-46E, 9 hy with CH-53 (5 with -A/-D, 4 with -E).

SAM:

3 bn with *Improved HAWK*.
3 bn with *Stinger* (forming).

RESERVES (MCR):

AVIATION: 1 air wing: 96 cbt ac, 8 armed hel.
AIRCRAFT:
FIGHTER: 2 sqn with 24 F-4S; 1 with 12 F/A-18A.
FGA: 5 sqn with 60 A-4M.
EW: 1 sqn with 4 EA-6A.
FAC: 1 sqn with 18 OV-10A.
TANKER: 2 tkr/tpt sqn with 18 KC-130F/T.
HELICOPTERS:
ARMED: 1 sqn with 8 AH-1J.
TRANSPORT: 3 sqn (2 med with 24 CH-46E, 1 hy with 18 CH-53A).

UTILITY: 2 sqn with 24 UH-1N.

EQUIPMENT: 488 cbt ac (incl 96 MCR); plus 5 in store; 84 armed hel (incl 8 MCR).
AIRCRAFT:
F/A-18: 186. **-A:** 120 (ftr; 12 MCR); **-B:** 20 (trg); **-C:** 36 (FGA); **-D:** 10 (trg).
AV-8B: 141. 134 (FGA); **TAV-8B:** 7 (trg); plus 5 in store.
RF-4B: 21 (recce).
A-4: 122. **-M:** 98 (60 MCR); **OA-4M:** 15 (comd); **TA-4F:** 9 (trg).
A-6: 76. **-E:** 54 (attack); **EA-6A:** 4 (ECM, MCR); **-B:** 18 (ECM).
OV-10A/D: 36 (FAC).
F-21: 13 (trg).
KC-130F/T: 42: 36 (tkr), 6 (trg).
HELICOPTERS:
AH-1J/T/W1: 84: 72 (armed), 12 (trg).
UH-1N: 80: 72 (tpt), 8 (trg).
CH-46E: 206 (186 aslt, 20 trg).
CH-53: 170: **-A/D:** 94 (84 aslt, 10 trg); **-E:** 76 (66 aslt, 10 trg).
VH-60A: 9 (VIP tpt).
VH-3D: 11 (VIP tpt).
MISSILES:
SAM: *Improved HAWK, Stinger.*
AAM: *Sparrow, Sidewinder.*
ASM: *Maverick.*

COAST GUARD (By law a branch of the Armed Forces; in peacetime operate under and are funded by the Department of Transportation. Budgets are not incl in the figures at p. 15):

Budget 1987: BA $2.595 bn, outlay $2.581 bn.
  1988: BA $2.534 bn, outlay $2.785 bn.
Strength: 38,100 (2,700 women).

PATROL AND SURFACE COMBATANTS: 158:

PATROL, OFFSHORE: 49:
  12 *Hamilton* high endurance with hel deck, 2 × 3 ASTT, 1 × 127mm gun (5 in refit).
  11 *Bear* med endurance with HH-52A hel.
  16 *Reliance* med endurance with hel deck.
  10 other med endurance cutters.
PATROL, INSHORE: 99:
  30 *Farallon* PCI, 13 *Cape Higgon*, 3 *Sea Hawk* SES, 53 *Point Hope*⟨.
SUPPORT AND OTHER: 13:
  3 icebreakers, 9 icebreaking tugs, 1 trg.
AVIATION: 74 ac, 125 hel.
FIXED WING: 2 E-2C, 41 HU-25A, 29 HC-130H, 1 VC-4A, 1 VC-11A.
HELICOPTERS: 58 HH-65A, 36 HH-3F, 2 CH-3E, 29 HH-52A.

COAST GUARD RESERVE: 18,350. Selected: 12,100; Ready 5,700; Standby 550.

STRATEGIC SEALIFT:

Military Sealift Command, in addition to the Fleet Auxiliary Force, operates and administers strategic sealift resources.

TOTAL SEALIFT SHIPS: 311:

ACTIVE: 69:

STRATEGIC MOBILITY: 44:

2 ro-ro veh ships, 4 ro-ro container, 5 AK, 1 AK (container), 22 tankers, 8 fast veh/cargo, 2 hospital.

AFLOAT PREPOSITIONING: 25:

7 AK, 4 barge lift, 13 Maritime Prepositioning (to support MEB), 1 semi-submersible heavy lift ship.

RESERVE: 242: (in preservation in CONUS ports).

READY RESERVE FORCE (RRF): 93 (5 to 20 days reactivation notice):

48 AK (incl 18 veh carriers), 9 gasoline tkr, 1 pax, 8 crane ships, 20 ro-ro, 7 barge lift.

NATIONAL DEFENCE RESERVE FLEET (NDRF): 149 (60 to 90 days reactivation notice, but many ships very old and of doubtful serviceability): 45 dry cargo, 27 tkr, 77 'Victory' WW II cargo.

AUXILIARY STRATEGIC SEALIFT. A further 318 US-flag and effectively US-controlled ships potentially available to augment these holdings.

AIR FORCE: 579,200 (69,000 women); 3,577
cbt ac (incl ANG, AFR); plus 1,000+ in store.

STRATEGIC: (organization: see p. 16).

TACTICAL: 25 active cbt wings, comprising 82 sqn (sqn may be 18 or 24 ac). 2 active wings to be disbanded by 1991.

FIGHTER: 45 sqn (also have FGA commitment):
18 with F-15.
27 with F-16.

FGA: 37 sqn, 1 gp:
7 with F-4.
10 with F-111.
14 with A-10.
6 *Wild Weasel* (1 trg) with F-4.
1 tac gp with F-117.

SUPPORT:

RECCE: 6 sqn (1 trg) with RF-4C.

AEW: 1 Airborne Warning and Control wing; 4 sqn (incl 1 trg) with E-3.

EW: 4 sqn with EC-130, EC-135, EF-111.

FAC: 7 tac air control sqn:
6 with OA-10/OV-10/OA-37.
1 with CH-3 hel.

SPECIAL OPERATIONS (4,100): 3 wing, 10 sqn: (see p. 23)

OCU: 14: 2 with F-111; 3 with F-16; 2 with F-4; 1 with F-5; 2 with F-15; 3 with A-10; 1 with RF-4.

TRAINING:
2 'Aggressor' sqn with F-16.
30 trg sqn with F-16, T-37, T-38, T-39, T-41, T-43, UV-18, Schweizer 2-37, C-5, C-12, C-130, C-141 ac and UH-60, HH-3, HH-53, U/TH-1 hel.

TRANSPORT: 32 sqn:
19 strategic: 4 with C-5; 15 with C-141.
13 tac airlift with C-130.
Units with KC-10, C-135, C-137, C-140, C-9, C-12, C-20, C-21, C-23, CT-39.

SAR: 6 sqn (incl SAC msl spt) with HC-130 ac, HH-3, UH-1, UH-60 hel.

MEDICAL: 3 medical evacuation sqn with C-9.

WEATHER RECCE: 2 sqn with WC-130, WC-135. WC-130 to be withdrawn.

TRIALS/weapons trg units with F-4, F-5, F-15, F-16, T-38, C-141 ac, UH-1 hel.

GLCM:
3 wings with BGM-109G (being disbanded).

EQUIPMENT:

STRATEGIC: 372 cbt ac (plus 50 in store).

B-52: 234: **-G:** 150, plus 17 in store (98 with ALCM, 69 with *Harpoon*); **-H:** 84 strike (with ALCM) plus 12 in store.

B-1B: 90 (strike trg); plus 7 in store.

FB-111A: 48 (strike, trg); plus 14 in store.

SR-71: 7: **-A:** 6 (recce; 12 in store); **-B:** 1 (trg). Are being withdrawn.

U-2CT/R: 13 (11 recce, 2 trg).

TR-1: 25: **-A:** 23 (recce); **-B:** 2 (trg).

E-4: 4 (comd/control): **-A:** 1; **-B:** 3.

C-135: 706: **RC-135:** 20 (surveillance, comd/control); **EC-135:** 40 (comd/control); **KC-135:** 646 (tankers; 512 USAF, 110 ANG, 24 AFR).

KC-10A: 60 tkr/tpt.

TACTICAL: 3,205 cbt ac; (incl 818 ANG, 241 AFR); plus 1,150+ in store, no armed hel.

F-4: 677. 348 (FGA; incl 188 ANG, 60 AFR); 77 (OCU); **-G:** 72 (*Wild Weasel*); **RF-4C:** 180; plus 350+ in store.

F-15: 642 (incl 450 ftr, 120 OCU, 54 ANG; **-E:** 18 (FGA); plus ε250 in store.

F-16: 1,083. 822 (ftr; incl 168 ANG, 84 AFR); 196 (OCU); 65 (trials); plus some 367 in store.

F-111: 219. **-D/E/F:** 140 (FGA); **-A:** 43 (OCU); **EF-111A:** 36 (ECM).

F-117: 52 (FGA).

A-7: 270 (ANG); plus 96 in store.

A-10A: 538. 447 (FGA; incl 72 ANG, 87 AFR); 91 (OCU); plus some 100 in store.

E-3: 34 (AEW).

EC-135K: 2 (AEW).

EC-18B: 4 (Advanced Range Instrumentation).

E-8A: 2 (J-STARS ac).

WC-135B: 5 (weather recce).

AC-130: -A: 10 (special ops, AFR); **-H:** 10 (special ops, USAF); **EC-130/E/H:** 15 (ECM); **HC-130H/N/P:** 53 (31 spec ops; 22 SAR with AFR); **MC-130E/H:** 14 (special); **WC-130E/H:** 10 (weather recce: 6 USAF, 4 AFR).

OA-37B: 36 (FAC).

OA-10: 48 (FAC).

OV-10: 53 (FAC).

TRANSPORT:
  C-5: 97. **-A:** 70 (strategic tpt; 36 with Reserves);
    -B: 27 (incl 6 trg).
  C-141B: 249 (217 strategic tpt, 16 trg, 8 ANG, 8 AFR).
  C-130: 534 (incl 296 ANG/AFR). 490 (tac tpt, incl
    279 ANG/AFR); 44 (OCU, incl 17 ANG/AFR).
  C-135: 7.
  C-137: 7: **-B:** 3 (VIP tpt); **-C:** 4 (VIP tpt).
  C-9A/C: 20. **-A:** 17 (medical); **-C:** 3 (VIP).
  C-12: 86 (liaison). **C-20A/B/C:** 13 (tpt). **C-21A:** 82.
    C-22A/B: 5 (tpt). **C-23A:** 16 (tpt). **CT-39:** 2 (tpt).
    C-140B: 4.

TRAINING:
  MiG-21: 24. **MiG-23:** 4. **T-37B:** 608. **T-38:** 812. **T-39:**
    4. **T-41A/C:** 100. **T-43A:** 19. **UV-18A:** 2. **Schweizer
    2-37:** 8.

HELICOPTERS:
  CH/HH-3: 58 (SAR, trg).
  MH-53-J: 24 *Pave Low* (special ops).
  UH-1H/N: 68.
  MH-60G: 10 (special ops).

MISSILES:
  AAM: *Sidewinder, Sparrow.*
  ASM: 1,100 AGM-69A SRAM, 1,500 AGM-86B
    ALCM; 15,000 *Maverick;* 5,000 *Shrike;* 5,000
    HARM.
  GLCM: 98 BGM-109G launchers (to be destroyed).

RESERVES:

AIR NATIONAL GUARD (ANG):
  24 wings, 96 sqn; 818 cbt ac.
FIGHTER 26 sqn; 476 ac.
  12 AD sqn (see p. 12),
  4 sqn with 72 F-16A/B,
  10 sqn with 188 F-4C/D/E.
FGA: 17 sqn; 342 ac.
  13 with 270 A-7D/K; 4 with 72 A-10. 96 more
    A-7 in store.
RECCE: 5 sqn (TAC) with 90 RF-4C.
ECM: 1 sqn (MAC) with 6 EC-130.
FAC: 3 sqn (TAC): 2 with 36 OA-37B, 1 with 18 OA-10.
TRANSPORT: 21 sqn (MAC):
  19 tactical with 168 C-130A/B/E/H.
  2 strategic: 1 with 11 C-5; 1 with 8 C-141B.
TANKER: 13 sqn (SAC) with 110 KC-135E.
SAR: 2 sqn (MAC) with 8 HC-130 ac, 9 HH-3E, 1
  CH-3 hel.
TRAINING: 7 sqn with 142 ac, incl 40 T-33, 4 T-43A.

AIR FORCE RESERVE (AFR):
  20 wings, 58 sqn (37 with ac); 241 cbt ac.
FGA: 12 sqn (TAC):
  4 with 84 F-16; 3 with 60 F-4D/E; 5 (incl 1 trg)
    with 87 A-10.
TRANSPORT: 17 sqn (MAC):
  14 tactical with 124 C-130B/E/H (incl 1 with
    C-130/WC-130).

3 strategic: 2 with 25 C-5A, 1 with 8 C-141B.
TANKER: 3 sqn (SAC) with 24 KC-135E.
SPECIAL OPERATIONS: 2 sqn (MAC):
  1 with 10 AC-130A.
  1 with 5 H/CH-3 hel.
SAR: 3 sqn (MAC) with 13 HC-130H ac, 11
  H/CH-3, 5 HH-1H hel.
ASSOCIATE: 21 sqn (personnel only):
  MAC: 4 sqn for C-5, 13 for C-141, 1 aero-
    medical for C-9.
  SAC: 3 sqn for KC-10.

CIVIL RESERVE AIR FLEET (CRAF): 367
  commercial ac (numbers fluctuate):
LONG-RANGE: 320
  246 passenger (Boeing 747, L-1011, DC-8/-10),
    74 cargo (Boeing 707, 747, DC-8/-10).
SHORT-RANGE: 47 (Boeing 727, DC-9).

===

SPECIAL OPERATIONS FORCES:
Units only listed – manpower and eqpt shown in
  relevant single service section.

ARMY: (3,000):
  4 SF gp (each 3 bn).
  1 Ranger inf regt (3 bn).
  1 avn gp.
  1 Psychological Operations gp (4 bn).
  1 Civil Affairs bn.

RESERVES:
  2 ARNG SF gp (6 bn).
  2 AR SF gp (6 bn).

NAVY: (3,360):
  2 Navy Special Warfare Gps.
    3 Naval Special Warfare units.
    6 Sea-Air-Land (SEAL) teams.
    2 SEAL delivery veh teams.
    3 Special Boat units.
    2 amph tpt submarines (2 SSN-608).
    3 Drydeck shelters (DDS).
RESERVES: (1,400):
  5 Naval Special Warfare gp det.
  3 Naval Special Warfare unit det.
  3 SEAL team det.
  2 Special Boat sqn.
  4 Special Boat unit.
  1 engr spt unit.
  2 cbt spt special hel sqn.

AIR FORCE: (4,100)
  3 wings, 10 sqn:
    3 with MC-130.
    1 with AC-130.
    3 with HC-130.
    2 with MH-53 hel.
    1 with MH-60 hel.

RESERVES:
  2 sqn (MAC):

1 with 11 AC-130A ac,
1 with 4 HH-3, 1 CH-3 hel.

DEPLOYMENT:

Commander's NATO appointments also shown.
(e.g. COMEUCOM is also SACEUR)

EUROPEAN COMMAND (EUCOM): 326,400:

HQ Stuttgart-Vaihingen (Commander is SACEUR).
ARMY: HQ US Army Europe (USAREUR),
Heidelberg (Commander is COMCENTAG).
NAVY: HQ US Navy Europe (USNAVEUR),
London (Commander is also CINCAFSOUTH).
AIR FORCE: HQ US Air Force Europe (USAFE),
Ramstein (Commander is COMAAFCE).

FRG:
   ARMY: 202,500 (assigned to CENTAG unless
   shown otherwise).
   V Corps with 1 armd, 1 mech inf div, 1 armd
      cav regt, 2 arty (incl 3 bn *Lance*), 1 engr, 1
      corps avn bde.
   VII Corps with 1 armd, 1 mech inf div, 1 mech
      inf bde (elm of CONUS div), 1 armd cav
      regt, 3 arty (incl 3 bn *Lance*), 1 engr, 1 corps
      avn bde.
   1 armd bde (elm of CONUS div) (assigned to
      NORTHAG).
   1 inf bde: (Berlin).
   1 arty bde with 3 bn *Pershing* II (being withdrawn).
   Army AD Comd with 5 bn (30 bty) *HAWK*, 7
      bn *Patriot*.
   1 engr bde.
   Prepositioned equipment (POMCUS) for 2
      armd, 3 mech, 1 lt inf div, 1 armd cav regt.
      Approx 70% stored in FRG.
   EQUIPMENT (incl POMCUS in FRG, Be and Nl):
   Some 5,000 MBT, 940 AIFV, 1,600
      arty/MRL/mor, up to 120 SSM.
   AIR FORCE: 40,300, 264 cbt ac (assigned to 4 ATAF).
   1 air force HQ: 2 air div.
   4 tac ftr wings: 11 sqn (5 with 156 F-16C/D, 3
      with 36 F-4G, 3 with 72 F-15C/D).
   1 tac recce wing, 1 sqn with 18 RF-4C.
   1 tac msl wing; GLCM being withdrawn.
   1 electronic cbt, 2 cbt spt, 1 tac air control
      wings and 1 gp of 3 sqn (2 with 42 OV-10A
      ac, 1 with 7 CH-53C hel).
   1 tpt wing (MAC): 4 sqn (incl 18 C-23A *Sherpa*,
      16 C-130E).
   1 special ops sqn (MAC) with 4 MC-130E, 2 air
      base gp.
BELGIUM:
   ARMY: 1,500. Approx 15% of POMCUS stored in Be.
   AIR FORCE: 1,600.
GREECE:
   ARMY: 500.

NAVY: 500. Base facilities Suda Bay (Crete).
AIR FORCE: 2,300, 2 air base gp. Facilities at
   Hellenikon (Athens) and Iraklion (Crete).
ITALY:
   ARMY: 3,900. 1 AB bn gp.
   NAVY: 4,900. HQ Gaeta, bases at Naples, La
      Maddalena, 1 MR sqn with 9 P-3C Sigonella.
   MARINES: 300.
   AIR FORCE: 5,800: 1 tac, 1 air base gp, 1 tac msl
      wing; GLCM being withdrawn.
MEDITERRANEAN:
   NAVY: 20,100.
   Sixth Fleet: typically 4 SSN, 1 CVBG (1 CV,
      6–8 surface combatants, 2 fast support ships),
      1 URG (4–6 support ships, 2 or 3 escorts), 1
      amph ready gp (3–5 amph ships with 1 MEU§
      embarked), 1 MPS, 4 depot ships.
NETHERLANDS:
   ARMY: 800. Approx 15% of total POMCUS is
      stored in Nl.
   AIR FORCE: 2,000: 24 cbt ac.
   1 tac ftr sqn with 24 F-15C/D.
NORWAY: Prepositioning for 1 MEB§ to be
   complete late 1989.
PORTUGAL: (for Azores, see Atlantic Command).
   NAVY: 400.
   AIR FORCE: 1,200.
SPAIN:
   NAVY: 3,700, base at Rota.
   1 MR sqn with 9 P-3C.
   AIR FORCE: 4,900: 1 air force HQ, 72 cbt ac.
   1 tac ftr wing of 3 sqn with 72 F-16A/B
      (planned redeployment to Italy).
   1 ftr trg wing (no ac assigned).
   1 air base gp.
   1 SAR det (MAC) with 3 UH-1N hel.
TURKEY:
   ARMY: 1,300.
   NAVY: spt facilities at Iskenderun and Yumurtalik
   AIR FORCE: 3,600, facilities at Incirlik.
   Installations for SIGINT, space tracking and
      seismic monitoring.
UNITED KINGDOM:
   NAVY: 2,500. HQ London, SSBN base Holy Loch.
      1 AS, 1 floating dock. To spt about 8 SSBN.
      Comms facilities, Thurso.
   AIR FORCE: 25,400: 279 cbt ac.
   1 air force HQ: 5 tac ftr wings: 16 sqn (7 with
      140 F-111E/F, 1 with 12 EF-111, 6 with 108
      A-10, 1 with 19 F-16, 1 with 13 TR-1A).
   1 special ops sqn with 5 MH-53 J.
   1 tac tpt wing with 16 C-130 (MAC): 4
      EC-135H (SAC).
   1 SAR sqn with 5 HC-130, 5 HH-53.
   1 tac msl wing, GLCM being withdrawn.
   2 air base gp.
NATO REINFORCEMENTS: Committed US–NATO
   goal to provide from CONUS further 6 div, 37 tac
   ac sqn, 1 MEB (Norway)§ within 10 days of mob.

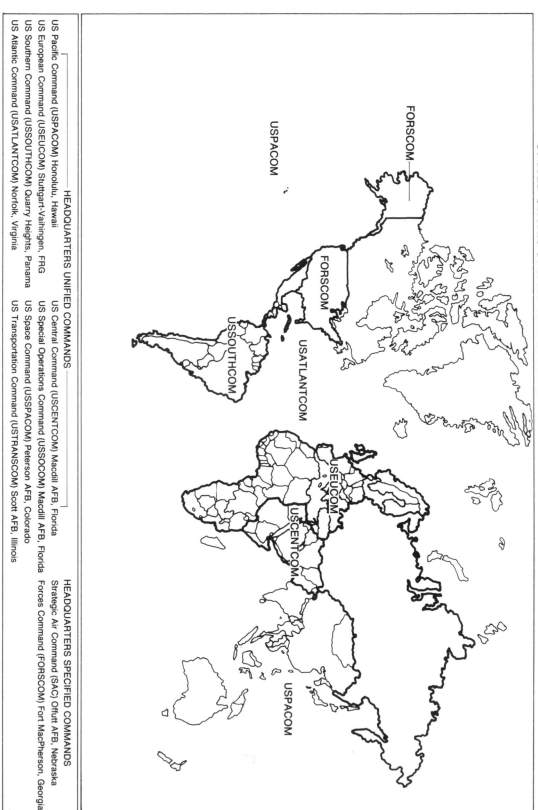

UNITED STATES UNIFIED AND SPECIFIED COMMANDS' AREAS OF RESPONSIBILITY

HEADQUARTERS UNIFIED COMMANDS

US Pacific Command (USPACOM) Honolulu, Hawaii
US European Command (USEUCOM) Stuttgart-Vaihingen, FRG
US Southern Command (USSOUTHCOM) Quarry Heights, Panama
US Atlantic Command (USATLANTCOM) Norfolk, Virginia

US Central Command (USCENTCOM) Macdill AFB, Florida
US Special Operations Command (USSOCOM) Macdill AFB, Florida
US Space Command (USSPACOM) Peterson AFB, Colorado
US Transportation Command (USTRANSCOM) Scott AFB, Illinois

HEADQUARTERS SPECIFIED COMMANDS

Strategic Air Command (SAC) Offutt AFB, Nebraska
Forces Command (FORSCOM) Fort MacPherson, Georgia

PACIFIC COMMAND (USPACOM):

HQ: Hawaii. Controls two subordinate unified
commands; US Forces, Korea, and US Forces, Japan.

HAWAII:
ARMY: 19,000. HQ US Army Pacific (USARPAC).
1 lt inf div.
1 ARNG inf bde.
AIR FORCE: 5,800. HQ Pacific Air Forces (PACAF).
1 air div, 1 airlift div (MAC), 1 air base wing, 1
AWACS sqn, 1 tac tpt sqn (ANG), 1 AD sqn
with F-15 (ANG).
NAVY: 12,500. HQ US Pacific Fleet, HQ US
Third Fleet. Homeport for some 19
submarines, 9 PSC and 10 spt and misc ships.
MARINES: 9,400. 1 MEB (from MEF in Okinawa).§
PHILIPPINES:
ARMY: 600.
AIR FORCE: 9,200.
1 air force HQ, 1 air div, 48 cbt ac.
1 wing: 2 ftr sqn (1 with F-4E, 1 with F-4E/G).
1 special ops sqn (MAC) with 3 MC-130E.
1 tac tpt wing (MAC) with 16 C-130.
1 SAR sqn (MAC) with 3 H/CH-3.
NAVY: 5,500. Subic Bay base. Maintenance and
logistic facilities. Naval air station.
MARINES: 2,000; 1 MEU (SOC)§ may be deployed.
JAPAN:
ARMY: 2,000.
1 corps HQ, base and spt units.
AIR FORCE: 16,500: 1 air force HQ; 1 air div:
120 cbt ac.
3 wings (6 sqn) with 72 F-15C/D, 48 F-16, 16
RF-4C; 6 C-12F, 3 C-21A ac, UH-1E/F/N hel.
1 sqn (TAC) with 3 E-3 AWACS.
1 tac tpt gp with 16 C-130.
1 strategic det with KC-135 tkr.
1 SAR sqn (MAC) with 6 HC-130 ac, 3 HH-3 hel.
NAVY: 8,300: Bases: Yokosuka (HQ 7th Fleet).
Homeport for 1 CV, 8 surface combatants.
Sasebo. Homeport for 3 submarines, 3 amph ships.
MARINES: 23,700: 1 MEF§ (Okinawa with elm
in Hawaii).
SOUTH KOREA:
ARMY: 31,600.
1 Army HQ (UN command).
1 inf div, 1 *Lance* SSM bty.
AIR FORCE: 11,600: 1 air div: 2 wings, 84 cbt ac.
4 sqn (3 with 72 F-16, 1 with 12 A-10).
1 det with 8 RF-4C.
1 tac control gp with 12 OA-10.
1 SAR sqn (MAC) with 6 H/CH-3 hel.
GUAM:
AIR FORCE: 4,200: 1 air div HQ (SAC):
14 cbt ac.
1 bbr wing (SAC) with 1 sqn B-52
(non-nuclear role).

1 wing (SAC) with KC-135 tkr.
NAVY: 4,000. Naval air station, comms and
spt facilities.
AUSTRALIA:
AIR FORCE: 290.
NAVY: 450: comms facility at NW Cape,
SEWS/SIGINT station at Pine Gap, and SEWS
station at Nurrungar.
DIEGO GARCIA:
NAVY: 1,400, 5 MPS (equipment for 1 MEB§).
Naval air station, spt facilities.
US WEST COAST:
MARINES: 1 MEF.§
AT SEA:
PACIFIC FLEET: (HQ Pearl Harbor).
Submarines: 8 *Ohio* SSBN, 3 SSGN, 37 SSN, 3 SS.
Surface Combatants: 7 CV/CVN, 2 BB, 22
CG/CGN, 14 DDG, 15 DD, 21 FFG, 26 FF.
Amphibious: 1 comd, 3 LHA, 3 LPH, 7 LPD, 7
LSD, 10 LST, 3 LKA.
Surface Combatants divided among two fleets:
Third Fleet (HQ Pearl Harbor): covers Eastern
and Central Pacific, Aleutians, Bering Sea, etc.
Typically 5 CVBG, 1–2 Battleship Surface
Attack Gp, 4 URG. Amph Gp.
Seventh Fleet (HQ Yokosuka, Japan): covers
Western Pacific, Japan, Philippines, ANZUS
responsibilities, Indian Ocean. Typically 2
CVBG, 0–1 Battleship Surface Attack Gp, 1
URG, Amph Gp (1 MEU embarked).
INDIAN OCEAN: (det from Seventh/Second Fleets).

CENTRAL COMMAND (USCENTCOM):

Takes command of deployed forces in its region.
HQ USCENTCOM. MacDill AFB, Florida.

AT SEA:
Joint Task Force Middle East.
1 comd ship, 1 LPD, 6 principal surface
combatants, 3 MCO.
1 CVBG in N. Arabian Sea. (Maritime forces are
provided from both Atlantic and Pacific fleets.)
EGYPT:
ARMY: 1,350 (MFO Sinai).

SOUTHERN COMMAND (USSOCOM):

HQ USSOCOM: Quarry Heights, Panama.
HQ US Southern Air Force (12th Air Force):
Bergstrom, Texas.

PANAMA:
ARMY: HQ US Army South, Fort Clayton
Panama: 6,800.
1 inf bde (2 inf, 1 avn bn, 1 bty 105mm).
NAVY: HQ US Naval Forces Southern
Command, Fort Amador, Panama: 500.
Special boat unit, fleet support.

MARINES: 600.
AIR FORCE: 2,800.
1 air div: A-7, OA-37, C-130 ac.
HONDURAS:
ARMY: 1,500.

ATLANTIC COMMAND (USLANTCOM):
HQ: Norfolk, Virginia (Commander is SACLANT).
US EAST COAST:
MARINES:
1 MEF.§
1 Reserve div.
BERMUDA:
NAVY: 1,700.
CUBA:
NAVY: 1,900 (Guantánamo).
MARINES: 500 (Guantánamo).
ICELAND:
NAVY: 1,800 1 MR sqn with 9 P-3.
AIR FORCE: 1,300.
1 ftr sqn with F-15.
PORTUGAL (AZORES):
NAVY: 400.
Facilities at Lajes.
1 MR ac det with 3 P-3C (from Rota).
AIR FORCE: 1,800.
1 AD sqn with 18 F-15, 1–3 E-3 AWACS.
1 SAR det (MAC).
AT SEA:
ATLANTIC FLEET: (HQ Norfolk, Virginia).
Submarines: 1 *Ohio*, 26 other SSBN, 7 SSGN, 46 SSN.
Surface Combatants: 7 CV/CVN, 2 BB 19 CG/CGN, 23 DDG, 16 DD, 30 FFG, 25 FF.
Amphibious: 1 LCC, 3 LHA, 4 LPH, 6 LPD, 6 LSD, 10 LST, 2 LKA.
Surface Forces divided into two Fleets:
Second Fleet (HQ Norfolk): covers Atlantic, both north and south. Typically 6–7 CVBG, 1–2 Battleship Surface Attack Gps, Amph Gp, 4 URG.
Sixth Fleet (HQ Gaeta, Italy): Mediterranean. Under op comd of EUCOM. See EUCOM entry for typical force levels.

CONTINENTAL UNITED STATES (CONUS):
Major units/formations only listed.

FORCES COMMAND: (FORSCOM): (Army)
provides general reserve of cbt-ready ground forces for other comd.
Active: 6 Army HQ, 3 Corps HQ, 2 armd, 5 mech, 3 lt inf (1 in Alaska), 1 AB, 1 air aslt div; 1 armd, 1 mech, 1 inf, 3 arty bde; 1 armd cav regt.

Reserve: ARNG: 2 armd, 2 mech, 5 inf, 1 lt inf div; 19 indep bde, 2 armd cav regt. AR: 3 indep bde.

STRATEGIC AIR COMMAND (SAC):
See entry on p. 16.

TACTICAL AIR COMMAND (TAC):
Responsible for provision of strategic Air Defence units and of cbt-ready Air Force units for rapid deployment.
AIR DEFENCE:
2 USAF sqn, 12 ANG sqn
FIGHTER/FGA:
34 USAF sqn, 31 ANG sqn, 12 AFR sqn.
ALASKAN AIR COMMAND: 2 USAF sqn F-15; 1 USAF sqn A-10.

US SPECIAL OPERATIONS COMMAND (USSOCOM):
Has under command all active, reserve and National Guard special operations forces of all services based in CONUS. See p. 23.

US TRANSPORTATION COMMAND (USTRANSCOM):
Responsible for providing all common-user airlift, sealift and land transportation to deploy and maintain US forces on a global basis.

MILITARY AIRLIFT COMMAND (MAC):
Responsible for providing strategic, tactical and special operations airlift, aero medical evacuation, SAR and weather recce.

MILITARY SEALIFT COMMAND.
See entry for Strategic Sealift, p. 22.

MILITARY TRAFFIC MANAGEMENT COMMAND

PARA-MILITARY:

CIVIL AIR PATROL (CAP): 68,000 (27,500 cadets); HQ, 8 geographical regions, 52 wings, 1,881 units, 579 CAP ac plus 8,465 private ac.

---

* Figures are for Total Obligational Authority. This includes Budget Authority (BA), obligations from previous fiscal years and other receipts (such as earned income, interest, etc.).
† Manpower incl in Army, Navy and Air Force totals.
§ An MEF is normally based on a marine div supported by an air wing with logistic support. Typically 55,000 men with 70 tk, 200 APC, 120 arty pieces, 156 cbt ac, 24 armed hel. An MEB has approximately one-third the ground combat element and half the aviation element of an MEF. An MEU (SOC) is a reinforced battalion landing team that has been specially configured, trained and certified as special operations capable for 18 distinct missions.

The Soviet Union

The last twelve months have seen very significant developments in Soviet policy, which hold the promise of transition to a much less threatening and confrontational approach – at least in the conventional field – to what are now described as issues of common security.

Since President Gorbachev's impressive speech at the United Nations General Assembly on 7 December 1988, when he announced a wide range of unilateral conventional force reductions, there have been a series of statements amplifying and detailing both unilateral reductions and force withdrawals from allied countries to be made by Soviet Armed Forces. In January 1989 Warsaw Pact Defence Ministers also made an unprecedented statement giving details of the strength of non-Soviet Warsaw Pact armed forces and of Soviet forces west of the Urals. Details of the Soviet defence budget have begun to emerge, together with statements of intent concerning its reduction. The WP has adopted a defensive doctrine, and the policy of 'reasonable sufficiency' has been enunciated, although not elaborated with any clarity. Detailed initial proposals have been made at both the negotiations on Conventional Forces in Europe (CFE) and on Confidence-Building and Security Measures (CBSM), and a response to the Western proposals at CFE has been tabled. Although there are many issues, including verification measures, counting rules and definitions, still to be settled, there are good grounds for optimism that the gaps between the two sides on key matters such as overall force ceilings, numbers of forces permitted to be stationed outside national borders, and national force limits can be bridged. In all these areas the USSR appears to be willing to make very large asymmetrical cuts to its forces. Once the unilateral cuts are implemented, and if the negotiations on CFE lead to results on the basis of the existing negotiating positions, the Soviet Union's military capabilities will have been fundamentally altered. During the first six months of 1989, however, these changes were still only in their opening stages.

Nuclear Forces

Strategic Systems
While 20 SS-11 ICBM have been withdrawn, the numbers of both mobile ICBM systems have increased substantially. The number of rail-mobile ten-warhead SS-24 *Scalpel* has risen from ten to over 30, and there are now over 165 mobile single-warhead SS-25 *Sickle*, as opposed to last year's count of some 100 in service.

A fifth *Delta*-IV SSBN with 16 SS-N-23 *Skiff* SLBM has been commissioned while one *Yankee*-1 with 16 SS-N-6 *Serb* has been retired. Six *Golf* SSB, each with three SS-N-5 *Sark* (non-SALT accountable) SLBM have also been decommissioned.

The Tu-160 *Blackjack* bomber, shown to US Secretary of Defense Carlucci in 1988, is now operational with a regiment of some 20 aircraft in service. The medium-range Tu-16 *Badger* force has been reduced from 272 to 140 aircraft, and the Mya-4 *Bison* finally retired as a bomber. We no longer believe any short-range nuclear-capable bombers to be held with the Strategic Aviation force; we now show all Su-24 *Fencer* as being under Theatre (TVD) command. These aircraft are dual capable but most probably, as with comparable NATO aircraft, only a percentage of pilots are trained in the nuclear delivery role.

Intermediate Nuclear Forces
By 1 June 1989, the Soviet Union had eliminated 945, or 51% of the missiles covered by the terms of the Intermediate-Range Nuclear Force (INF) Treaty. The numbers of missiles and launchers which have been destroyed and, in parentheses, remaining are: SS-20 192 missiles (462) and 169 launchers (340); SS-12 600 missiles (128) and all launchers; SS-23 none of the 239 missiles and 30 (76) launchers; SS-4 72 missiles (77) and 29 launchers (43), and all 80 SSC-X-4 GLCM and six launchers. We are unable to give accurate figures for INF weapons still operationally deployed.

Short-Range Nuclear Forces
The Soviet Union has offered to remove all nuclear warheads from the territories of its allies if the US would do the same and has also proposed negotiations on the elimination of all short-range nuclear weapons (i.e., not solely short-range missiles). It has announced a unilateral reduction of 500 short-range nuclear warheads in Europe, of which 284 would be SSM warheads, 50 artillery projectiles and 166 air-delivered warheads. We are not in a position to estimate the total Soviet holding of SNF warheads from which these reductions will be taken, but figures of some 5,000 have appeared in Western journals.

The Warsaw Pact has also given details of its SSM launcher holdings which revealed a much larger holding of SS-21 than previously estimated. The Western Group of Forces (WGF) (formerly the Group of Soviet Forces Germany (GSFG)), is now fully equipped with SS-21 in place of *FROG*, and has withdrawn SS-21 battalions from divisions and concentrated them in brigades at Army level. A similar reorganization can be expected elsewhere and may be underway. It is possible that the reorganization reflects the increased range of SS-21 over *FROG* (120 *vice* 70 km) and the scope this provides for enhancing flexibility of employment by more centralized control.

Conventional Forces – General

Unilateral Reductions
In his UN speech President Gorbachev pledged to reduce Soviet armed forces by 500,000 men and to eliminate a total of 10,000 tanks, 8,500 artillery pieces and 800 combat aircraft from forces now located in Eastern Europe, including European Russia, by 1991. Of the 500,000 men to be reduced 200,000 would come from the Far East, including Mongolia, 240,000 from west of the Urals, and 60,000 from the Southern borders.

Fifty thousand men and 5,300 tanks will come from forces now stationed in the non-Soviet Warsaw Pact countries. Four tank divisions (328 tanks each) and three tank training regiments (94 tanks each) in the GDR, one tank division in Czechoslovakia, and one tank division and one tank training regiment in Hungary will be withdrawn and disbanded. Divisions remaining in Czechoslovakia, the GDR, Hungary and Poland will be reorganized. Tank and motor rifle divisions will all lose one tank regiment (94 tanks) and motor rifle divisions will also lose their independent tank battalions (51 tanks); the divisions will receive additional anti-tank and air defence assets. Air Assault (airborne) units (of which there are currently one brigade and five battalions in the GDR, one battalion each in Czechoslovakia and Hungary) and Assault Crossing (engineer) units (currently six battalions in the GDR and one each in Czechoslovakia and Hungary) will be withdrawn to the Soviet Union. It is not clear, however, whether all such units are to be withdrawn nor whether they will then be disbanded. The Northern Group of Forces in Poland is to lose one SAM regiment and one helicopter regiment (as well as one tank regiment from each division). Withdrawals from all four countries have already begun; Tass claimed on 1 June 1989 that nearly 9,000 men had been withdrawn from the GDR, Poland and Hungary, together with 2,100 tanks and 300 artillery pieces. As no complete divisions had been withdrawn by 1 June 1989 nor, we believe, had any tanks been destroyed, we have not altered our entries to take account of these partial withdrawals. Listings therefore reflect the position immediately before the first unilateral withdrawal.

East of the Urals two tank and one motor rifle division (leaving one motor rifle division) and two air force divisions are being withdrawn from Mongolia and some units will be disbanded. The first moves back to the Soviet Union took place on 15 May 1989. By 1 June 1989 some 2,800 men with 200 tanks and 170 artillery pieces had reportedly been withdrawn, and by the end of 1989 it is expected that one quarter of the planned withdrawals will have been effected.

During his visit to China in May 1989, President Gorbachev announced that forces along the Far East borders would be reduced by 120,000 men, and that 12 army divisions and 11 air force regiments would be disbanded. Sixteen warships would be withdrawn from the Pacific Fleet. He proposed a reorganization of remaining forces and said that some divisions would become defensive 'machine gun' divisions. On 2 June 1989 it was announced that the Central

Asian Military District (MD) had been disbanded; some of its units are to be reduced or disbanded, meanwhile troops and territory have been transferred to the Turkestan MD. This move alters somewhat the split of forces between the Far Eastern and Southern TVD as the Central Asian MD had been held as part of the Far Eastern TVD since 1969.

Afghanistan
The Soviet withdrawal from Afghanistan was completed, on schedule, on 15 February 1989. We believe that the formations withdrawn have returned to their original military districts, with the airborne division going to the Belorussia MD, and the remainder to the now enlarged Turkestan MD where they are likely to be reduced to a lower state of readiness and manning than Category A. The USSR admits to having lost some 15,000 men killed during the occupation; equipment losses are impossible to estimate.

Negotiations on Conventional Forces in Europe (CFE)
The Warsaw Pact has tabled several proposals at the CFE talks in Vienna. For 'stationed forces' (i.e Soviet forces outside Soviet borders), the limits proposed are 350,000 men, 4,500 (4,630) tanks, 4,000 (4,780) artillery and mortar pieces, 7,500 (10,000) APC, 350 strike aircraft (there is no agreed definition for strike aircraft) and 600 combat helicopters. The figures in parentheses show IISS estimates (as no WP figures have been released) of Soviet equipment holdings after the announced unilateral reductions have taken place. The WP has also tabled figures for national limits which, if agreed to, would require the USSR to reduce its forces west of the Urals to 920,000 men, 14,000 (31,280) tanks, 17,000 artillery and mortar pieces, 18,000 (45,000) APC, 1,200 strike aircraft and 1,350 combat helicopters. In this case, the figures given in parentheses represent Soviet equipment strengths after announced unilateral reductions have been effected and are based on Soviet data, and hence also on Soviet definitions and counting rules (see pp. 226–31).

Manpower
There have been various WP statements concerning the breakdown of the unilateral reduction of 500,000 men between and within the armed forces. The cuts will include 100,000 officers and 50,000 warrant officers, the remainder being conscripts. Air Defence forces will lose 50,000 men, 60,000 will be cut from southern Russia, mainly from units withdrawn from Afghanistan and 20,000 from the Leningrad MD and Northern Fleet.

Speaking at the Guildhall in London, on 8 April 1989 President Gorbachev gave figures for the strength of the Soviet Armed Forces – 4,258,000 overall, of which 1,596,000 were in the ground forces and 437,000 in the Navy. The WP data release gave manpower figures in the Atlantic to Urals area, including overall conventional force manpower of 2,458,000, of which 1,187,000 were Army and 289,000 Navy personnel. In the light of a subsequent assertion by Defence Minister Yazov that Soviet construction and railway troops do not undergo military training, we assume that this manpower (estimated at up to 490,000) was excluded from the Gorbachev figures and from the WP data document. We also assume that these figures, like those tabled by the WP in Vienna, exclude para-military forces such as the KGB and MVD (some 570,000). While analysis reveals some anomalies, we have no reason to challenge published Soviet manpower figures. We have also decided to follow the WP practice of separating centrally controlled staffs (Ministry of Defence, reconnaissance, electronic warfare, training and logistics) from the five branches of the armed forces and this is reflected in the figures given on p. 32 and subsequently throughout the Soviet entry.

Some changes have been made to the conditions for conscript service for those graduating from higher education. The length of service for all services has been reduced to one year. Deferment of call-up will now be granted until students complete their studies (or until they reach the age of 27). After their conscript service and special training these men become reserve officers.

Ground Forces

One of the two unified Corps established, we believe, on an experimental basis, has been disbanded and its units reformed into divisions. The remaining Corps, now called 'independent', may also be disbanded. The number of divisions has been revised to show an increase of one tank division and three motor rifle divisions and a decrease of two mobilization divisions. The overall total (counting the Corps as two division equivalents) has not therefore changed.

We have always had difficulty in estimating Soviet stockpile equipment holdings. Analysis of President Gorbachev's 8 April 1989 assertion of WP global holdings of 80,000 tanks and of the WP published data for holdings West of the Urals, together with the counting rules and conventions these reveal, suggest the existence of some 6,700 tanks above those held by units – some 2,700 west of the Urals and 4,000 to the east. Such a holding, which would imply reserves of about 13% of the number held in units, is wholly plausible. However, we cannot identify either the type or location of the tanks concerned. We have therefore included them with the equipment holdings listed on p. 34 and in the NATO and Warsaw Pact Conventional Force data in Table A at pp. 232–3 but cannot attribute them to specific Strategic Directions in our analysis of the deployment of Soviet forces at pp. 37 to 41; these deployment figures only include equipments held by units.

Production of modern equipment has continued, with the Army receiving some 1,000 T-72L/-M and 500 T-80 tanks with some older models being withdrawn. Artillery holdings have hardly altered, but holdings of modern SAM including SA-11, SA-12A and SA-13 have increased. No new equipment type has been introduced into service.

For the first time our listings specifically identify the nuclear-capable heavy artillery brigades of which we believe there are 12, probably held at front level. The brigades are equipped with the 203mm SP gun 2S7 and some also have the 240mm SP mortar 2S4. It is not clear whether the brigade in GSFG is independent or subordinate to the artillery division.

Naval Forces

The Soviet Aircraft Carrier programme continues, albeit slowly. We now show the *Baku* as a separate class from the *Kiev*, because of her different weapon and sensor fit. The *Tbilisi*, the first of a new class of two 65,000-tonne carriers is expected to start trials this year, while the second was launched in November 1988. A third, rather larger ship, was laid down in the same yard at the same time. There is still no firm information regarding the aircraft destined to operate from these large V/STOL platforms.

The tactical submarine force shows a slight overall increase – possibly due to a lack of information on retirements – with four new units: an *Oscar* SSGN, a *Sierra* and a *Victor*-III and a *Kilo*-class SS entering the force against the loss of the experimental *Mike*-class, *Komsomolets*, in the Norwegian Sea on 7 April 1989. The slight reduction in surface forces conceals a substantial increase in quality. In addition to the third units of both *Kirov* and *Slava* classes, new *Sovremennyy* and *Udaloy* destroyers have joined the operational fleet. The number of frigates has increased by five, largely since the new smaller classes joining the fleet displace more than 1,000 tonnes and hence qualify for this category, while those they are replacing fell below this tonnage. It should be noted in this context that our figures include 113 frigates between 1,000 and 1,200 tonnes full load displacement which are not counted by the WP in its data category of large surface ships.

This shift in emphasis from quantity to quality is underlined by the decommissioning of a *Sverdlov*-class cruiser and 12 old destroyers, and the sale to Western commercial interests of one *Sverdlov*, a number of old destroyers and over 20 submarines for scrapping.

Air Defence Troops

The programme to install 100 ABM around Moscow has been completed, the missiles being a mix of ABM-1B *Galosh*, SH-11 modified *Galosh*, and SH-08 *Gazelle*.

The total number of SAM deployed is slightly reduced with some SA-1, SA-2 and SA-3 having been withdrawn and replaced by smaller numbers of SA-5 and SA-10. Air defence fighter holdings show only marginal changes.

Air Forces
Overall aircraft numbers (including strategic base defence aircraft, Air Defence Troops and Air Force) have only altered slightly with numbers of the newer models increasing marginally faster than older models are retired. No new models have been introduced in the last twelve months.

Defence Spending

The Military Balance 1988/89 argued that the most significant savings in the defence budget could be made only by reducing manpower strengths; in December 1988 President Gorbachev announced cuts of 500,000 men over the next two years, and the forthcoming Soviet attitude at the CFE negotiations offers the prospect of more. The conversion of defence production plants to the civilian economy, especially for consumer goods, has also got under way, some with Western technical and financial assistance. The Deputy Chairman of the Council of Ministers, Igor Belousov, claimed that 345 plants had already been converted, and that, by 1995, 60% of military industry would be available for civilian use. In addition, not only are INF missile launcher vehicles and some of the unilaterally reduced tanks being converted for civilian use, but other equipments such as heavy trucks and petrol bowsers, as well as vacated buildings and real estate are to be handed over by the military.

At the end of May 1989, the Soviet leadership revealed some details of its revised defence budget; that for the current year is given as 77.3 bn roubles (around $120 bn at prevailing exchange rates). It also claimed that the defence budget had been frozen for the last two years and that savings of 10 bn roubles will be made in 1990 and 1991. This budget represents about 12% of national income or roughly twice what the US spends on defence, but comes at the lower end of Western estimates. While the government claims that the figure includes the costs of personnel, research and development, procurement and construction, some Western observers argue that expenditure on military space (officially stated to be 3.9 bn roubles) and nuclear programmes are still excluded. It is doubtful whether the full costs of the Afghanistan operation, revealed by the USSR as having amounted to some 45 bn roubles, was included in past budgets, or whether existing military assistance programmes are included in the present budget. Uncertainty about the true level of Soviet defence expenditure appears likely to continue for some time, and, in the absence of any detailed disaggregated data, Soviet figures for defence spending should be treated with caution.

THE SOVIET UNION

| NMP | 1987: r 599.6 bn |
| | 1988: r 625.0 bn |

Growth	1987: 2.3%	1988: 4.2%
GNP	1987ε: $1,800–2,387 bn
	1988ε: $1,900–2,487 bn
Inflation	1987: 1.6%	1988: 2%
Debt	1987: $36.5 bn	1988: $38.0 bn
Official	1988: r 20.5 bn ($32.08 bn)
def exp*	1989: r 77.3 bn ($119.253 bn)

Official rate:
$1 = r   (1987): 0.6435   (1988): 0.6390
           (1989): 0.6482

r = roubles
*See text above

Population: 287,776,000

	13–17	18–22	23–32
Men	10,984,000	10,379,000	24,357,000
Women	10,516,000	10,028,000	23,480,000

TOTAL ARMED FORCES:

ACTIVE: 4,258,000 (perhaps 2,700,000 conscripts) (incl some 988,000 Ministry of Defence staff, centrally controlled units for EW, trg, log and civil (territorial) defence. Tps not listed below, but excl some 490,000 railway and construction tps and 570,000 KGB and MVD).

Terms of Service: 2 years (3 years for sea-going naval personnel, about 50% of Naval conscripts, 1 year deferred for higher education graduates). Women with medical and other special skills may volunteer.

RESERVES: some 5,560,000 with service within last 5 years: Strategic Rocket Forces ε 537,000; Army 3,000,000; AD 750,000; Air Force 775,000; Navy 540,000. Reserve obligation to age 50; total: some 55,000,000. (Regular retirees could add to the above totals.)

STRATEGIC NUCLEAR FORCES: 287,000
(plus 123,500 assigned from Air and Navy).
(70–75% conscripts ε 215,000); under direct op
comd of the Supreme High Command (VGK).

NAVY: (15,500). 960 msl in 69 submarines (942
msl in 62 SSBN count under SALT rules; 18
theatre SLBM, 1 SSBN and 6 SSB do not count).
SSBN: 63:

5 *Typhoon* with 20 SS-N-20 *Sturgeon*	(100 msl).	
5 *Delta-IV* with 16 SS-N-23 *Skiff*	(80 msl)	
14 *Delta-III* with 16 SS-N-18 *Stingray*	(224 msl).	
4 *Delta-II* with 16 SS-N-8 *Sawfly*	(64 msl).	
18 *Delta-I* with 12 SS-N-8	(216 msl).	
1 *Yankee-II* with 12 SS-N-17 *Snipe*	(12 msl).	
15 *Yankee-I* with 16 SS-N-6 *Serb*	(240 msl).	
1 *Hotel-III* with 6 SS-N-8 *Sawfly* (msl, but not submarine, under SALT)	(6 msl).	

SSB: 6:
6 *Golf-II* with 3 SS-N-5 *Sark* (18 non-SALT
accountable theatre msl).

STRATEGIC ROCKET FORCES: (287,000): 6
rocket armies, org in div, regt, bn and bty of 1
msl launcher; 28 'fields', 300 launch control HQ,
3 msl test centres.
ICBM: 1,451+.
SS-11 *Sego*: 400 mod 2/3 (at some 8 fields; SS-25
is replacing).
SS-13 *Savage*: 60 (at 1 field, SS-25 may replace).
SS-17 *Spanker* (RS-16): 138 (at 2 fields; mod
3/4 MIRV).
SS-18 *Satan* (RS-20): 308 (at 6 fields; mostly mod
4/10 MIRV).
SS-19 *Stiletto* (RS-18): 350 (at 4 fields; mostly
mod 3, 6 MIRV).
SS-24 *Scalpel*: some 30+ (deployment in progress;
rail-mobile, 10 MIRV).
SS-25 *Sickle* (RS-12M): some 165+ (mobile,
single-warhead msl replacing SS-11 and may
replace SS-13; has been reported in gp of 9 on
former SS-7 sites, 20+ bases, each for 9 msl,
reported under conversion).
IRBM/MRBM: 383 launchers still to be eliminated
in accordance with INF Treaty.
SS-20 *Saber* (RSD-10): 340 mobile IRBM (3 MIRV).
SS-4 *Sandal* (R-12): 43.

STRATEGIC AVIATION: (108,000) 5 Armies;
about 890 cbt ac.
Moscow: 1 army (for intercontinental roles).
Western TVD: 1 army (Smolensk).
Far East TVD: 1 army (Irkutsk).
BOMBERS: 630.
LONG-RANGE: 195.

175 Tu-95 (some 60 B/G have AS-3/-4 ASM,
some 75 H have up to 8 AS-15 ALCM);
20 Tu-160 *Blackjack* (ALCM capable).
MEDIUM-RANGE: 435.
175 Tu-26 (AS-4 ASM).
140 Tu-16 (AS-6 ASM).
120 Tu-22.
RECCE: 130.
STRATEGIC: 20 Tu-16, 20 Tu-22.
TACTICAL: 40 MiG-25, 50 Su-24.
FIGHTER (base defence): 260:
45 MiG-21, 135 MiG-23, 80 Su-27.
ECM: 170:
100 Tu-16, 30 Il-20/-22, 40 Yak-28.
TANKERS: 74:
40 Mya-4, 20 Tu-16, 14 Il-78.
ASM/ALCM: AS-3 *Kangaroo*, AS-4 *Kitchen*, AS-5
Kelt, AS-6 *Kingfish*, AS-15 *Kent*, AS-16 *Kickback*.

GROUND FORCES: 1,596,000 (perhaps
1,200,000 conscripts).
15 Military Districts (MD), 4 Groups of Forces.
1 indep Army Corps (equivalent to about 2 div).
53 TD (Type: 3 tk, 1 motor rifle, 1 arty, 1 SAM
regt; 1 SSM, 1 MRL bn; spt units).
153 MRD (Type: 3 motor rifle, 1 tk, 1 arty, 1
SAM regt; 1 SSM, 1 ATK, 1 MRL bn; spt units).
7 ABD (each 3 para, 1 arty regt; 1 AA bn).
ε 3 mob div (type, location n.k.).
18 arty div, Front: (No standard org: perhaps 4
bde (12 bn): 152mm SP, 152mm towed and
MRL: some will have older eqpt).
Arty bde, Army: No standard org: perhaps 4 bn:
2 each of 24 152mm towed guns, 2 each of 24
152mm SP guns.
Some 12 indep hy arty bde (up to 4 bn of 12
203mm SP guns some with 240mm SP mor).
Some 10 air aslt bde, Front (each 4 inf bn (1 with
BMD); arty, SAM, ATK; spt tps). Most armies
have indep air aslt bn.
Front and Army tps:
Tk, arty, SSM, ATK, AD (SAM and arty), engr bde;
sigs, EW, hy tk tpt regt; CW def bn; spt services.
Special forces (*Spetsnaz*): 27–30,000: 16 bde (each
3–4 para bn), 3 regt (org in 6–8-man teams).
Avn: regt and bn assigned to div and above;
some 20 attack regt with 24 Mi-8 and 40
Mi-24 armed hel.
[NATO defines 4 categories of combat readiness,
which parallel to some extent the Soviet system:
Category A: 75% to full strength, eqpt complete,
combat ready. Incl both Soviet units at wartime
establishment and at reduced wartime
establishment;
Category B: 50–75% strength, eqpt normally
complete, full manning planned to take 3 days.
Soviet units at peacetime establishment. NATO
considers combat ready;

Category C: some 20–50% strength, eqpt possibly complete with older models, planned to be fully manned in 7 days and retrained in less than 60 days. Soviet units at reduced peacetime establishment.

Category D/E or mob div, with max of 5% manning and stockpile of much older eqpt. Soviet 'invisible' (shadow) div. Will take some months to become combat ready. Over past years have progressively been upgraded to Cat C.

To bring all these divisions up to war establishment could require up to 2,000,000 men.

For a broad assessment of the 213 Cat A/B/C div by categories see pp. 37–8 below.]

EQUIPMENT:

MBT: some 53,350: some 350 T-10/-10M, some 19,000 T-54/-55, 11,300 T-62, some 9,700 T-64A/-B, 10,000 T-72L/-M and 3,000 T-80.

LIGHT TANKS: 1,200 PT-76.

OTHER TANKS: Some 6,700 types unknown in store.

RECCE: 8,000: incl some 3,500 BRDM-2.

AIFV: some 28,500: some 26,000 BMP-1 (73mm gun/AT-3 ATGW), BMP-2 (30mm gun/AT-5 ATGW); some 2,500 BMD (AB).

APC: some 30,000: some 26,000 BTR-50P/-60P/-70/-80/-152; 4,000 MT-LB.

TOWED ARTY: 22,500: 122mm: D-74, M-1938, D-30; 130mm: M-46; 152mm: 500 M-1937, 2,000 D-20 (M-1955), ε 1,000 M-1976; 180mm: ε 180 S23;

SP ARTY: some 9,000: 120mm: 2S9 (BMD chassis); 122mm: ε 3,200 2S1; 152mm: 3,500+ 2S3, ε 2,100 2S5; 203mm: ε 200 2S7.

MRL: 7,100:
122mm: BM-21, RM-70 40-tube; M-1975 12-tube; M-1976 36-tube;
140mm: BM-14-16, RPU-14 16 tube;
220mm: BM-22 16-tube;
240mm: BM-24 12-tube.

MORTARS: 120mm: 10,500+; 240mm 400 2S4.

SSM (nuclear-capable): some 1,636 launchers, incl some 630 FROG (Luna), 300 SS-21 Scarab (Tochka), 630 Scud B (R-17), 76 SS-23 (OTR-23) Spider, SS-23 being eliminated in accordance with INF Treaty.

ATGW: AT-2 Swatter, AT-3 Sagger, AT-4 Spigot, AT-5 Spandrel, AT-6 Spiral, BRDM AT-5, AT-7 Saxhorn.

ATK GUNS: 8,000: 57mm: ASU-57 SP; 76mm: 85mm: D-44/SD-44, ASU-85 SP; 100mm: T-12/-12A/M-55 towed.

AD GUNS: some 12,000; 23mm: ZU-23, ZSU-23-4 SP; 30mm: ZSU-30-2 SP with 4 SAM; 37mm; 57mm: S-60, ZSU-57-2 SP; 85mm: M-1939; 100mm: KS-19; 130mm: KS-30.

SAM: about 4,700+ crew-served field mobile systems; (some 440 units):
SA-4 A/B Ganef (twin): 1,350 (Army/Front weapon, being replaced by SA-11 and SA-12A).
SA-6 Gainful (triple): 800 (at div).
SA-7 Grail (man-portable): perhaps 18,500 (unit weapon, being replaced by SA-14 and SA-16).
SA-8 Gecko (2 twin or 2 triple): some 900 (at div).
SA-9 Gaskin (2 twin): 425 (at regt).
SA-11 Gadfly (quad): 250 (replacing SA-4/-6).
SA-12A Gladiator: 45+ (replacing SA-4).
SA-X-12B Giant: under development (possible ATBM role).
SA-13 Gopher (2 twin): 930 (replacing SA-9).
SA-14 Gremlin: 2,500 (replacing SA-7).
SA-16: 3,500 (replacing SA-7 and some SA-14).

HELICOPTERS: some 4,500:
  ARMED: some 2,050 incl 340 Mi-8, 290 Mi-17, 1,420 Mi-24; Mi-28 under development.
  TRANSPORT: some 1,510 incl 1,010 Mi-8, 435 Mi-6, 55 Mi-26 (hy), 10 Mi-10 (hy).
  EW/ECM: 200 Mi-8.
  GENERAL-PURPOSE: 680: incl 600 Mi-2, 80 Mi-8 (comms).

AIR DEFENCE TROOPS (VPVO): 502,000

(ε 300,000 conscripts).

5 Air Defence Armies: air regt and indep sqn; AD regt; 14 specialist schools.

ABM: 100: ABM-1B Galosh, SH-11 (mod Galosh), SH-08 Gazelle.

AIRCRAFT: (Aviation of Air Defence – APVO):

FIGHTER: some 2,225: incl 45 MiG-21 (4 AAM), 900 MiG-23 (6 AAM); 350 MiG-25 (4 AAM); 250 MiG-31 (4 AA-9); 500 Su-15 (2 AAM); 160 Su-27 (up to 10 AAM); 20 Yak-28 (2 AA-5).

AEW AND CONTROL: ε 17: ε 3 Tu-126; 14 Il-76 (replacing Tu-126).

AAM: AA-2 Atoll, AA-3 Anab, AA-5 Ash, AA-6 Acrid, AA-7 Apex, AA-8 Aphid, AA-9 Amos, AA-10 Alamo, AA-11 Archer.

SAM: strategic role; some 8,500 launchers in some 1,200 sites:
SA-1 Guild: 1,600 (being replaced by SA-10).
SA-2 Guideline: 2,400 (being replaced by SA-10).
SA-3 Goa: 1,000 (2 or 4 launcher rails, over 300 sites, low- to med-altitude intercept).
SA-5 Gammon: 2,000 launchers (130 complexes, long-range intercept).
SA-10 Grumble: some 1,500 quad (theatre/strategic role).

WARNING SYSTEMS:

SATELLITES: 9 with ICBM/SLBM launch detection capability. Others incl 9 warning, 6 ELINT, 2–4 recce, 1 launch detection.

RADARS:

  OVER-THE-HORIZON (backscatter) OTH(B): 3: 2 near Kiev and Komsomolsk (Ukraine), covering US and polar areas; 1 near Nikolayev-na-Amur, covering China.

  LONG-RANGE EARLY-WARNING:

    ABM-ASSOCIATED:

      9 long-range phased-array systems at Baranovichi, Skrunda (Belorussia),

Mukachevo (Ukraine), Olnegorsk (Kola),
Krasnoyarsk (construction suspended),
Lyaki (Caucasus), Sary-shagan
(Kazakhstan), Pechora (Urals), Mishelevka
(Irkutsk).
11 *Hen House*-series; range 6,000 km, 6
locations covering approaches from the
west and south-west, north-east and
south-east and (partially) south. Linked to
intermediate-range *Dog House* (range
2,800 km), *Cat House* and *Try Add* msl
control radar.
Engagement, guidance, battle management: 1
Pillbox phased-array at Pushkino (Moscow).

AIR FORCE: 448,000 (some 310,000 conscripts)
incl 108,000 with Strategic Aviation.

AIR FORCES OF THE SOVIET UNION: 16
MD and Groups of Forces Air Forces.
Some 4,595 cbt ac. Forces' strengths vary, mostly
org in div of 3 regt of 3 sqn, total 135 ac. Regt
roles incl AD, interdiction, recce, tac air spt; div
roles may be mixed.
FGA: some 2,900: incl 180 MiG-21, 855 MiG-27,
810 Su-17, 830 Su-24 (incl 480 dual-capable
under TVD control), 225 Su-25.
FIGHTER: some 1,695: incl 260 MiG-21, 800
MiG-23, 25 MiG-25, 500 MiG-29, 110 Su-27.
RECCE: some 505: incl 50 MiG-21, 120 MiG-25,
135 Su-17, 100 Su-24, 100 Yak-28.
ECM: some 30 Yak-28.
TRAINING: some 2,000 ac (none counted as cbt ac).
AAM: AA-2 *Atoll*, AA-7 *Apex*, AA-8 *Aphid*, AA-9
Amos, AA-10 *Alamo*, AA-11 *Archer*.
ASM: AS-7 *Kerry*, AS-10 *Karen*.

MILITARY TRANSPORT AVIATION (VTA):
40,000; 5 div, each 3 regt, each 30 ac; some
indep regt.
EQUIPMENT: some 577 ac: 125 An-12, 385
Il-76M/MD *Candid* B (replacing An-12), 55
An-22, 12 An-124.
Additional ac (VTA augmentation force): Tpt ac in
comd other than VTA: org in indep regt and sqn:
1,200+: Tu-134, Tu-154, An-12, An-24, An-26 , Il-14.
Civilian Aeroflot fleet: 1,700 med- and long-range
passenger ac, incl some 220 An-12 and Il-76.

NAVY: 437,000, (ε 260,000 conscripts) Ashore
and Afloat Forces: 344,500.
SUBMARINES: 368:
STRATEGIC SUBMARINES: 69 (see p. 33).
TACTICAL SUBMARINES: 280:
SSGN: 53:
5 *Oscar* with 24 × SS-N-19 *Shipwreck* USGW
(VLS); plus T-65 HWT.

1 *Papa* with 10 × SS-N-9 *Siren* USGW; plus
T-53 HWT.
6 *Charlie-II* with 8 × SS-N-9; plus T-53 HWT.
10 *Charlie-I* with 8 × SS-N-7 *Starbright* USGW;
plus T-53 HWT.
28 *Echo-II* ε 16 with 8 × SS-N-3A *Shaddock*, ε
12 with SS-N-12 *Sandbox* SSM; plus T-53 HWT.
2 *Yankee* 'Notch' with 20+ SS-N-21 *Sampson* SLCM.
1 *Yankee* (trials) with SS-NX-24 SLCM.
SSN: 94:
4 *Akula* with T-65 HWT; plus SS-N-21.
3 *Sierra* with T-65 HWT; plus SS-N-21.
5 *Alfa* with T-53 HWT; plus SS-N-15 *Starfish* or
SS-N-16 *Stallion* UUGW.
23 *Victor-III* with T-65 HWT; plus SS-N-15 or -16.
7 *Victor-II* with T-53 HWT; plus SS-N-15 or -16.
16 *Victor-I* with T-53 HWT.
5 *Echo-I* with T-53 HWT.
12 *November* with T-53 HWT.
About 5 *Hotel* and *Yankee* ex-SSBN converted
to SSN.
12 *Yankee-I*, 2 *Hotel-II* converting from SSBN.
SSG: 16 *Juliet* with 4 × SS-N-3A *Shaddock* SSM.
SS: 117 (all with T-53 HWT):
12 *Kilo*, 18 *Tango*, 39 *Foxtrot*, 3 *Romeo*, 45
Whiskey.
OTHER ROLES: 19:
SSN: 4: 1 *Uniform*, 1 *X-Ray*
experimental/trials, 1 *Hotel-II* comms, 1
Echo-II auxiliary.
SS: 15: 1 *Beluga*, 4 *Bravo* wpn targets, 3 *Golf-I*
research, 3 *Golf-II* comms, 1 *Lima*, 1
Golf-V (SLBM trials), 2 *India* rescue.
IN STORE: 55: 10 *Foxtrot*, 2 *Zulu*, 43 *Whiskey*
(not counted in totals).
PRINCIPAL SURFACE COMBATANTS: 264. (See
also 'additional in store' and KGB (Para-Military).)
CARRIERS: 4:
1 *Baku* (CVV) (38,000 tonnes) with 13 Yak-38
V/STOL ac, 16 Ka-25/-27 hel (ASW with
E-45-75 LWT/AEW/OTHT/SAR); plus 6 × 2
SS-N-12 *Sandbox* SSM, 4 × 8 SA-N-6 *Grumble*
SAM. 2 × 100mm guns.
3 *Kiev* (CVV) (38,000 tonnes) with 13 Yak-38
V/STOL ac, 16 Ka-25/-27 hel; plus 4 × 2
SS-N-12 *Sandbox* SSM, 2 × 2 SA-N-3 SAM, 1 ×
2 SUW-N-1.
CRUISERS: 37:
CGN: 3 *Kirov* (AAW/ASUW) with 12 × 8 SA-N-6
Grumble, 20 SS-N-19 *Shipwreck* SSM, 3
Ka-25/-27 hel for OTHT/AEW/ASW; plus 1 with
1 × 2 130mm guns, 1 with 1 × 2 SS-N-14 *Silex*
SUGW (LWT or nuc payload), 10 × 533mm TT.
CG: 30:
2 *Moskva* (CGH) (ASW) with 18 Ka-25 hel
(E45-75 LWT), 1 × 2 SUW-N-1; plus 2 × 2
SA-N-3 SAM.
3 *Slava* (AAW/ASUW) with 8 × 8 SA-N-6
Grumble, 8 × 2 SS-N-12 *Sandbox* SSM, 1

Ka-25/-27 hel; (AEW/ASW); plus 8 × 533mm TT, 1 × 2 130mm guns.

7 *Nikolayev (Kara)* (ASW) with 2 × 4 SS-N-14 *Silex* SUGW, 10 × 533mm TT, 1 Ka-25 hel; plus 2 × 2 SA-N-3 *Goblet*; (1 (*Azov*) with 3 × 8 SA-N-6, only 1 × SA-N-3 and other differences).

10 *Kronshtadt (Kresta-II)* (ASW) with 2 × 4 SS-N-14 SUGW, 1 Ka-25 hel, 10 × 533mm TT; plus 2 × 2 SA-N-3 SAM.

4 *Admiral Zozulya (Kresta-I)* (ASUW/ASW) with 2 × 2 SS-N-3b *Shaddock* SSM, 1 Ka-25 hel (OTHT), 10 × 533mm TT.

4 *Grozny (Kynda)* (ASUW) with 2 × 4 SS-N-3b plus 1 × 2 SA-N-1 *Goa* SAM 6 × 533mm TT.

CC: 4 *Sverdlov* with 4 × 3 152mm guns (2 converted to comd role with hel pad and hangar replacing 1/2 152mm mounts.

DESTROYERS: 52:
DDG: 31:
AAW/ASUW: 15:
10 *Sovremennyy* with 2 × 4 SS-N-22 *Sunburn* SSM, 2 × 1 SA-N-7 *Gadfly* SAM, 2 × 2 130mm guns, 1 Ka-25 (B) hel (OTHT); plus 4 × 533mm TT.

5 *Sderzhannyy* (mod *Kashin*) with 4 SS-N-2C *Styx* SSM, 2 × 2 SA-N-1 SAM; plus 5 × 533mm TT.

ASW: 16:
12 *Komsomolets Ukrainyy (Kashin)* with 2 × 12 ASW RL, 5 × 533mm TT; plus 2 × 2 SA-N-1 SAM, (1 with trials fit 1 × SA-N-7).

4 *Skromnyy (SAM Kotlin)* with 2 × 12 ASW RL, 5 × 533mm TT; plus 1 × 2 SA-N-1, 1 × 2 130mm guns.

DD: 21:
10 *Udaloy* (ASW) with 2 × 4 SS-N-14 SUGW, 2 × 12 ASW RL, 8 × 533mm TT, 2 Ka-27 hel; plus 2 × 100mm guns.

3 *Bedovyy* (mod *Kildin*) (ASUW) with 4 *Styx* SSM; plus 4 × 533mm TT.

4 *Svedushchiy* (*Kotlin*, mod *Kotlin*) (ASUW) with 2 × 16 ASW RL, 10 × 533mm TT, 4 × 130mm guns.

4 *Skory* with 10 × 533mm TT, 4 × 130mm guns.

FRIGATES: 171:
11 *Rezvyy (Krivak-II)* with 1 × 4 SS-N-14 *Silex* SUGW, 8 × 533mm TT, 2 × 12 ASW RL; plus 2 × 100mm guns.

21 *Bditelnyy (Krivak-I)* (weapons as *Rezvyy* minus guns).

1 *Ulyantsev (Koni)* with 2 × 12 ASW RL.

25 '*Riga*' with 2 × 16 ASW RL, 2 or 3 × 533mm TT, 3 × 100mm guns.

Note: Frigates listed below lie between 1,000 and 1,200 tonnes full load displacement and are not counted in WP official releases.

59 '*Grisha-I, -III, -V*', with 2 × 12 ASW RL, 4 × 533mm TT.

8 '*Parchim-II*' (ASW) with 2 × ASW RL, 4 × 406mm ASTT.

18 '*Mirka-I, -II*', with 4 × 12 ASW RL, 5 or 10 × 406mm ASTT.

28 '*Petya*' with ASW RL, 5 or 10 × 406mm ASTT.

ADDITIONAL IN STORE: 4 *Sverdlov* CC; 2 *Skromnyy* DDG; 17 *Svedushchiy*, 5 *Skory* DD; 15 *Riga* FF; 8 *Petya* FF.

PATROL AND COASTAL COMBATANTS: 400:
CORVETTES: 64:
34 *Tarantul* (ASUW), 22 -*I*, -*II*, with 2 × 2 SS-N-2C *Styx*; 12 -*III* with 2 × 2 SS-N-22 *Sunburn*.

30 *Nanuchka* (ASUW) -*I* and -*III*, with 2 × 3 SS-N-9 *Siren*.

MISSILE CRAFT: 86:
70 *Osa* PFM (40 -*I*, 30 -*II*) with 4 × SS-N-2C.
1 *Sarancha* PHM with 2 × 2 SS-N-9.
15 *Matka* PHM with 2 × 1 SS-N-2C.

TORPEDO CRAFT: 30:
25 *Turya* PHT with 4 × 533mm TT.
5 *Shershen* PFT with 4 × 533mm TT.

PATROL CRAFT: 220:
OFFSHORE: 15 T-58.
COASTAL: 83:
32 *Pauk* (ASW) with 2 × ASW RL, 4 × ASTT.
50 *Poti* (ASW) with 2 × ASW RL, 4 × ASTT.
1 *Babochka* PH (ASW) with 8 × ASTT.

INSHORE: 11:
10 SO-1 with 2 × ASTT.
1 *Slepen* PFI.

RIVERINE AND CASPIAN: 111:
20 *Yaz* with 2 × 115mm gun.
10 *Piyavka*, 8 *Vosh*, 73 misc⟨.

MINE WARFARE: About 374:
MINELAYERS: 3 *Pripyat* (*Alesha*), capacity 300 mines.
Note: All Soviet submarines and many surface combatants are equipped for minelaying.

MINE COUNTERMEASURES: About 370:
OFFSHORE: 70:
35 *Natya-I* and -*II* MSO.
35 T-43 MSO.
COASTAL: About 110:
45 *Yurka* MSC.
3 *Andyusha* MSC (trials).
About 60 *Sonya* MSC
3 *Zhenya* MSC.
INSHORE: About 190:
65 *Vanya*, 10 *Sasha*, about 115 MSI⟨.

AMPHIBIOUS: 76:
LPD: 2 *Ivan Rogov* with 4–5 Ka-27 hel: capacity 520 tps, 20 tk;
LST: 38:
24 *Ropucha*: capacity 225 tps, 9 tk.
14 *Alligator*: capacity 300 tps, 20 tk.
LSM: 36 *Polnocny* (3 types): capacity 180 tps, 6 tk: (some adapted for mine warfare but retain amph primary role).

Plus CRAFT: about 140:
  LCU: 15: 10 *Vydra*, 5 SMB-1.
  LCM: 40 *Ondatra*.
  LCAC and SES: about 85, incl 3 *Pomornik*, 20 *Aist*,
    5 *Tsaplya*, 20 *Lebed*, 2 *Utenok*, 31 *Gus*.
    1 *Orlan* 'wing-in-ground-effect' (WIG)
    experimental.

SUPPORT AND MISCELLANEOUS: about 698:
UNDERWAY SUPPORT: 44:
  1 *Berezina*, 6 *Chilikin*, 23 other AO, 14 AOS.
MAINTENANCE AND LOGISTICS: about 260:
  18 AS, 38 AR, 12 general maint/spt, 27 AOT, 18
    missile spt/resupply, 70 tugs, 14 special liquid
    carriers, 13 water carriers, 50 AK.
SPECIAL PURPOSES: about 143:
  67 AGI (some armed), 7 msl range
    instrumentation, 12 trg, about 55 icebreakers
    (civil manned), 2 AH.
SURVEY/RESEARCH: about 251:
  40 naval, 60 civil AGOR.
  100 naval, 40 civil AGHS.
  11 space-associated ships (civil manned).
MERCHANT FLEET (auxiliary/augmentation):
  2,500 ocean-going vessels (17 in Arctic service),
    incl 90 ramp-fitted and roll-on/roll-off (ro-ro),
    some with rails for rolling stock, 3
    roll-on/float-off, 7 barge carriers, 78 passenger
    liners, 500 coastal and river ships.

NAVAL AVIATION: (68,000).
  739 cbt ac; 300 cbt hel.
  Four Fleet Air Forces; org in air div, each with
    2–3 regt of HQ elm and 2 bn of 9–10 ac each;
    recce, ASW, tpt/utility org in indep regt or sqn.
BOMBERS: 355:
  6 regt with some 180 Tu-26 (AS-4 ASM).
  6 regt with some 135 Tu-16 (AS-5/-6 ASM).
  2 bn with 40 Tu-22.
FGA: 189:
  104 Yak-38 V/STOL (in carriers).
  75 Su-17.
  10 MiG-23.
ASW: 195 ac, 270 hel:
  AIRCRAFT: 60 Tu-142, 45 Il-38, 90 Be-12.
  HELICOPTERS: 95 Mi-14, 100 Ka-25, 75 Ka-27.
MR/EW: some 185 ac, 30 hel:
  AIRCRAFT: incl 40 Tu-95, 40 Tu-16 (MR), 55
    Tu-16 (ECM), 20 Tu-22, 10 Su-24, 20 An-12.
  HELICOPTERS: 30 Ka-25 hel.
MCM: 25 Mi-14 hel.
CBT ASLT: 25 Ka-27 hel.
TANKERS: 46 Tu-16.
TRANSPORT/TRAINING: 445 ac and hel.
  AIRCRAFT: An-12, An-24, An-26, Il-14.
  HELICOPTERS: Mi-6/-8.
ASM: AS-2 *Kipper*, AS-4 *Kitchen*, AS-5 *Kelt*, AS-6
  Kingfish, AS-7 *Kerry*.

NAVAL INFANTRY (Marines): (some 17,000).
  1 div (7,000: 3 inf, 1 tk, 1 arty regt).
  3 indep bde (type: 3,000: 3 inf, 1 tk (1 med, 3 lt
    tk coy), arty, MRL, AD, ATK bn; with 10 MBT,
    31 lt tk, ε 90 APC, 18 SP how, 18 MRL, 6 SP
    ATK, 4 AA guns, 4 SP SAM.)
  4 fleet Special Forces (*Spetsnaz*) bde: 2–3
    underwater, 1 para bn, spt elm.
EQUIPMENT:
MBT: 230 T-54/-55.
LIGHT TANKS: 150 PT-76.
RECCE: 30 BRDM-2/*Sagger* ATGW.
AIFV: some BMP-1/-2.
APC: 1,045: BTR-60P/PA/PB/-70/-80, some MT-LB.
SP ARTY: 122mm: 90 2S1; 152mm: 2S3.
MRL: 122mm: 150 BM-21.
MORTARS: 120mm: 125 .
ATGW: 50 AT-3/-5.
AD GUNS: 23mm: 60 ZSU-23-4 SP.
SAM: 250 SA-7, 10 SA-8, 35 SA-9/-13.

COASTAL ARTILLERY AND ROCKET TROOPS: (7,500).
  1 coastal arty div (role: protects approaches to
    naval bases and major ports).
EQUIPMENT:
ARTILLERY: incl SM-4-1 130mm.
SSM: 40 SS-C-1b *Sepal* (similar to SS-N-3), SS-C-3,
  Styx, SS-C-4 reported.

DEPLOYMENT (all Services):
Soviet strategic planning divides the world into a
number of continental and maritime TVD (*Teatr
Voennykh Deistvii*) for which the latest Soviet
title appears to be Strategic Direction
(*Napravlenie*). These do not necessarily have any
operational command function but are for
staff-planning and intelligence purposes. In
peacetime all forces are located in Military
Districts (MD) or Fleets (some of which have a
wartime command role) or in non-Soviet Warsaw
Pact countries. We have listed forces
geographically and, where possible, grouped them
as they might be commanded in war. We have
listed elements of Strategic Nuclear Forces, Air
Defence Troops and the ABD according to their
physical location, although they are directly
controlled by the Supreme High Command
(VGK). Levels of command between the VGK and
fronts can be established and are known as High
Commands (GK).
Determining the manning category of Soviet div is
difficult. The following assessment is based on a
number of recent statements.
Category A. (Above 75%) Incl all div in the Groups
of Forces, 6 of the 7 ABD, all air aslt bde, div
withdrawn from Afghanistan, div in Mongolia.

Possibly amounting to 24 TD, 6 ABD and 24 MRD and the Indep Corps.

Category B. (50–75%) Most TD in Western Military Districts, about 50% of MRD in Southern and Far East TVD. Possibly 20 TD, 1 ABD and 32 MRD.

Category C. (20–50%) Most MRD other than in Groups of Forces. Possibly 9 TD and 97 MRD.

NORTHERN FLEET: (Arctic and Atlantic)
(HQ Severomorsk): (126,000).

BASES: Kola Inlet, Motovskiy Gulf, Gremikha, Polyarny, Litsa Gulf.

SUBMARINES: 171: strategic: 39 SSBN; tactical: 116: 29 SSGN, 49 SSN, 7 SSG, 31 SS. (4–5 normally deployed to Mediterranean) 16 other roles.

PRINCIPAL SURFACE COMBATANTS: 70: 2 CVV, 13 cruisers, 13 destroyers, 42 frigates; det to Mediterranean sqn. (See Mediterranean Squadron on p. 39.)

OTHER SURFACE SHIPS: 40 patrol and coastal combatants, 64 mine warfare, 15 amph, some 190 spt and misc.

NAVAL AVIATION:
175 cbt ac; 75 cbt hel.

BOMBERS: 65: 40 Tu-26, 25 Tu-16.

FIGHTER/FGA: 30 Yak-38.

ASW:
  AIRCRAFT: 80: 30 Tu-142, 20 Il-38, 30 Be-12;
  HELICOPTERS: 65: (afloat): Ka-25; Ka-27; (ashore): Mi-14.

MR/EW:
  AIRCRAFT: 68: 25 Tu-95, 33 Tu-16, 10 An-12;
  HELICOPTERS: 5 Ka-25.

MCM: 8 Mi-14 hel.

CBT ASLT HEL: 10 Ka-27.

COMMUNICATIONS: Tu-142.

TANKERS: 18 Tu-16.

NAVAL INFANTRY:
  1 bde: 4 bn: 3,000.

NORTHERN FRONT (indep HQ with Leningrad MD).

STRATEGIC FORCES (under central comd):

SLBM: 594: Northern Fleet: 39 SSBN (SLBM numbers in parentheses): 5 *Typhoon* (100); 9 *D-I* (108); 4 *D-II* (64); 6 *D-III* (96); 5 *D-IV* (80); 8 *Y-I* (128); 1 *Y-II* (12); 1 *H-III* (6).

ICBM: Plesetsk test centre.

AIR DEFENCE TROOPS (under VPVO comd):

EARLY WARNING: major site near Kovdov, W. Kola, detailed deployments unknown.

FIGHTER: 350: 12 regt with MiG-23, MiG-25, MiG-31, Su-15, Su-27.

ELINT: 5 Il-20.

AEW: ε 17: ε 3 Tu-126, 14 Il-76 (replacing Tu-126).

SAM: over 100 complexes: SA-2/-3/-5/-10.

LENINGRAD MD (HQ Leningrad):

1 Army, 2 Corps HQ, 11 MRD, 1 ABD; plus 1 arty div, 4 *Scud* and 1 air aslt bde.

FGA: 135: 3 regt MiG-21, MiG-27, Su-17.

RECCE: 25: MiG-25, Su-17.

Mob could field some 2 armies.

EQUIPMENT: up to 1,200 MBT; 2,900 arty/MRL/mor, 44 *FROG*/SS-21, 42 *Scud* SSM; 40 armed hel.

TACTICAL AVIATION: 135 cbt ac.

WESTERN STRATEGIC DIRECTION (TVD): (HQ Legnica)

3 Groups of Soviet Forces, Baltic, Belorussian, Carpathian MD, 1 Indep Corps, 64 div (31 TD, 30 MRD, 3 AB), plus 6 arty div, 4 air aslt bde.

STRATEGIC FORCES (under central comd):

SLBM: 12: Baltic Fleet: 4 *G-II* SSB.

ICBM:* 90: SS-19 (1 field).

IRBM: SS-20 (number deployed n.k., being withdrawn).

MRBM: SS-4 (number deployed n.k., being withdrawn).

ELINT: 5 Il-20/-22.

AIR DEFENCE TROOPS (under VPVO comd):

EARLY WARNING: 2 OTH(B) near Minsk, 1 major complex near Tallinn; details unknown.

FIGHTER: 325: Su-15, MiG-23, MiG-25.

SAM: SA-2/-3/-5/-10; 200+ complexes and sites.

UNDER TVD CONTROL:

STRIKE/FGA: 1 air army (HQ Legnica), 300 Su-24.

FRONTAL FORCES:

WESTERN GROUP OF FORCES (GDR) (HQ Zossen-Wünsdorf): (380,000):

1 Gp, 5 Army HQ; 11 TD, 8 MRD plus 1 arty div; 5 indep tk regt, 3 tk trg regt; 1 air aslt, 5 SS-21, 7 *Scud*, 5 arty bde; 6 attack hel regt: some 100 Mi-8; some 250 Mi-24; 25 Mi-8 ECM, some 20 tpt.

FGA: 400: 12 regt: Su-17, Su-24, Su-25, MiG-27.

FIGHTER: 305: 8 regt: MiG-21, MiG-23, MiG-25, MiG-29.

RECCE: 65 Su-17, Su-24, MiG-25.

ECM: 15 Yak-28.

NORTHERN GROUP OF FORCES (Poland) (HQ Legnica): (40,000):

1 Gp HQ; 1 TD, 1 MRD; 1 *Scud* bde; 1 SAM, 1 tk trg, 1 attack hel regt: 80 Mi-8/-24 hel.

CENTRAL GROUP OF FORCES (Czechoslovakia) (HQ Milovice): (70,000):

1 Gp, 1 Corps HQ; 2 TD, 3 MRD; 1 air aslt bn; 2 *Scud*, 1 arty bde; 2 attack hel regt: 180 Mi-8/-24 hel.

FGA: 45: 1 regt MiG-27.

FIGHTER: 45: 1 regt MiG-23.

RECCE: 15 Su-17.

BALTIC MD (HQ Kaliningrad):

1 Army HQ; 3 TD, 7 MRD, 2 ABD plus 2 arty div, 1 air aslt bde: 120 Mi-8/-24 hel.

FIGHTER: 45: 1 regt MiG-29.

RECCE: 35: Su-17, Su-24, MiG-25.

ECM: 15 Yak-28.

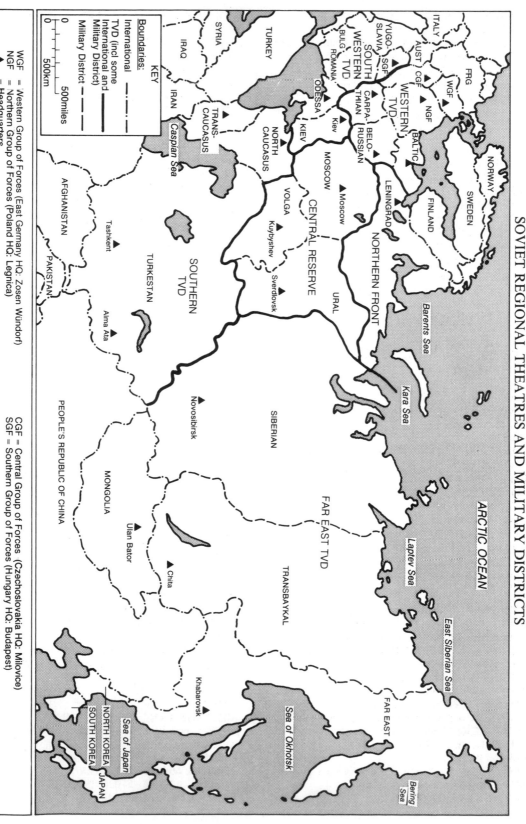

SOVIET REGIONAL THEATRES AND MILITARY DISTRICTS

KEY

Boundaries:
International — ·—·—·
TVD (incl some International and Military District) ————
Military District ————

▲ = Headquarters

WGF = Western Group of Forces (East Germany HQ: Zossen Wünsdorf)
NGF = Northern Group of Forces (Poland HQ: Legnica)
CGF = Central Group of Forces (Czechoslovakia HQ: Milovice)
SGF = Southern Group of Forces (Hungary HQ: Budapest)

BELORUSSIAN MD (HQ Minsk):
  1 Indep Army Corps, 10 TD, 2 MRD, 1 ABD, plus 1 arty div, 1 air aslt, 4 *Scud*, 150 Mi-8/-24 hel.
  FGA: 165: 3 regt MiG-27, 1 regt Su-25.
  FIGHTER: 120: 2 regt MiG-23, 1 regt MiG-29.
  RECCE: 40: MiG-21 *Fishbed* H, MiG-25.
CARPATHIAN MD (HQ Lvov):
  3 Army HQ; 4 TD, 9 MRD, plus 2 arty div, 1 air aslt, 3 *Scud* bde; 150 Mi-8/-24 hel.
  FGA: 165: 4 regt: MiG-27, Su-17, Su-25.
  FIGHTER: 115: 3 regt: MiG-21, MiG-23, MiG-29.
  RECCE: 25: 10 MiG-25, 15 Su-17.
On mob TVD could produce five Fronts, with a total of 103 div (incl non-Soviet WP).
EQUIPMENT (Soviet): up to 18,800 MBT; 16,000 arty/MRL/mor, 252 *FROG*/SS-21, 300 *Scud*, SSM; some 1,850 hel, perhaps 700 armed.
  TACTICAL AVIATION: some 1,885 cbt ac.
BALTIC FLEET (HQ Kaliningrad): 87,000.
  BASES: Kronshtadt, Liepaya, Baltiysk, Talinn.
  SUBMARINES: 47; strategic: 4 SSB; tactical: 3 SSG, 35 SS; other roles: 5 SS.
  PRINCIPAL SURFACE COMBATANTS: 47: 3 cruisers, 13 destroyers, 31 frigates.
  OTHER SURFACE SHIPS: 155 patrol and coastal combatants, 119 mine warfare, 20 amph, some 120 spt and misc.
  NAVAL AVIATION:
    150 cbt ac, 35 cbt hel.
  BOMBERS: 100: 3 regt with 60 Tu-26; 1 with 25 Tu-16; 1 with 15 Tu-22.
  FGA: 35: 1 regt Su-17.
  ASW:
    AIRCRAFT: 15: 5 Il-38, 10 Be-12;
    HELICOPTERS: 30: Ka-25, Ka-27, Mi-14.
  MR/EW:
    AIRCRAFT 42: 20 Tu-16, 10 Tu-22, 10 Su-24, 2 An-12.
    HELICOPTERS: 5 Ka-25.
  MCM: 5 Mi-14 hel.
  CBT ASLT HEL: 5 Ka-27.
  TANKER: 10 Tu-16.
  NAVAL INFANTRY:
    1 bde: 5 bn; 3,000.
  COAST DEFENCE:
  SSM: 1 regt: some 8 SS-C-1b *Sepal*.
  ARTY: 11 bn: some 72 130mm guns.

SOUTH-WESTERN STRATEGIC DIRECTION (TVD) (HQ Beltsy, Ukraine).
  1 Group of Forces, Kiev, Odessa MD. 29 div (10 TD, 18 MRD, 1 ABD), plus 3 arty div, 2 air aslt bde.
STRATEGIC FORCES: (under central comd)
ICBM*: 90 SS-19 (1 field).
ELINT: 5 Il-20/-22.
FIGHTER: 75: 3 regt: MiG-25, Su-27.
SAM: 120 SA-2/-3/-5/-10 sites.
UNDER TVD CONTROL:

STRIKE/FGA: 1 air army (HQ Vinnitsa): 180 Su-24.
FRONTAL FORCES:
SOUTHERN GROUP OF FORCES (Hungary) (HQ Budapest): (65,000):
  2 TD, 2 MRD, 1 air aslt bde; 50 Mi-8/-24 hel.
  FGA: 210: 5 regt: MiG-21, Su-17, Su-24.
  FIGHTER: 135: 3 regt: MiG-23, MiG-29.
  RECCE 20 Su-17, Yak-28.
  ECM: 5 ac.
KIEV MD (HQ Kiev):
  8 TD, 7 MRD plus 2 arty div; 180 Mi-8/-24 hel.
  FGA: 30 Su-24.
  FIGHTER: 45 MiG-23.
ODESSA MD (HQ Odessa):
  1 Army HQ, 1 corps HQ, 9 MRD, 1 ABD, plus 1 arty div, 1 air aslt bde: 170 Mi-8/-24 armed hel; some Mi-2, Mi-6 tpt hel.
  FGA: 90: 3 regt: MiG-27, Su-25.
  FIGHTER: 135: 3 regt: MiG-21, MiG-23.
  RECCE: 10 Su-17 *Fitter* H.
Mob of these forces (with 3 corps from Hungary plus the 3 tk and 16 motor rifle div of Bulgaria and Romania) could produce 4 Fronts, each of some 5 all-arms Armies.
EQUIPMENT (Soviet): some 8,200 MBT; 7,200 arty/MRL/mor; 112 *FROG*/SS-21, 114 *Scud* SSM; 190 armed, perhaps 160 other hel.
  TACTICAL AVIATION: 645 cbt ac.
BLACK SEA FLEET: (HQ Sevastopol): (97,000).
  BASES: Sevastopol, Balaclava, Poti, Odessa.
  SUBMARINES: 28: tactical 26: 2 SSG, 24 SS; other roles: 2.
  PRINCIPAL SURFACE COMBATANTS: 65: 10 cruisers, 18 destroyers, 37 frigates.
  OTHER SURFACE SHIPS: 80 patrol and coastal combatants, 63 mine warfare, 15 amph, some 150 spt and misc.
  NAVAL AVIATION:
    105 cbt ac; 80 cbt hel.
  BOMBERS: 80: 2 regt with 40 Tu-26; 1 with 25 Tu-16; 1 with 15 Tu-22.
  ASW:
    AIRCRAFT: 25 Be-12.
    HELICOPTERS: 80: Ka-25, Ka-27, Mi-14.
  MR/EW:
    AIRCRAFT: 40: 25 Tu-16, 10 Tu-22, 5 An-12;
    HELICOPTERS: 5 Ka-25.
  MCM: 5 Mi-14 hel.
  TANKERS: 5 Tu-16.
  NAVAL INFANTRY:
    1 bde: 5 bn; 3,000.

MEDITERRANEAN SQUADRON (HQ afloat): elm of North, Baltic and Black Sea Fleets.
Average composition:
SUBMARINES (from Northern Fleet): 4–5.
PRINCIPAL SURFACE COMBATANTS (from all European Fleets): 3–6: 1 cruiser, 2–3 destroyers, 1–2 frigates and periodically, CVV or CGH.

AMPHIBIOUS: 1
MCMV: 2.
SUPPORT AND MISC: some 20–24, incl 2+ AGI.

SOUTHERN STRATEGIC DIRECTION (TVD) (HQ Baku).

North Caucasus, Trans-Caucasus, Turkestan MD, 39 div (2 TD, 36 MRD, 1 AB) plus 3 arty div; 2 indep motor rifle, 2 air aslt bde.
AIR DEFENCE TROOPS: (under VPVO comd)
EARLY WARNING: phased-array radar system: 1 site: Lyaki (Trans-Caucasus).
FIGHTER: 265: 7 regt with MiG-23, MiG-25, Su-15, Su-27, Yak-28.
ELINT: 5 Il-20/-22.
FRONTAL FORCES: 3 MD:
NORTH CAUCASUS MD (HQ Rostov):
    1 TD, 8 MRD, 1 arty div; 1 *Scud* bde; 100 Mi-8/-24 hel.
TRANS-CAUCASUS MD (HQ Tbilisi):
    12 MRD, 1 ABD, 1 arty div, 620 hel incl 150 Mi-8/-24, 20 Mi-6, Mi-2.
    FGA: 240: 6 regt: Su-17, MiG-27, Su-24, Su-25.
    FIGHTER: 80: 2 regt: MiG-23, MiG-29.
    RECCE: 30: Su-17, MiG-25.
TURKESTAN MD (HQ Tashkent):
    1 Army HQ, 1 TD, 16 MRD, 1 arty div; 2 motor rifle, 2 air aslt, 1 arty, 1 *Scud* bde, 170 Mi-8/-24 hel.
    FGA: 240: 2 regt: MiG-27, Su-24, 4 regt with Su-17, Su-24, Su-25.
    FIGHTER: 180: 4 regt with MiG-21, MiG-23.
    RECCE: 80: MiG-25, Su-17, MiG-21, Yak-28.
On mob the TVD could put 2–3 Fronts, perhaps 9 all-arms armies, in the field.
EQUIPMENT: perhaps 8,600 MBT; 10,000 arty/MRL/mor, 152 *FROG*, 66 *Scud*, some 400 cbt hel.
    TACTICAL AVIATION: 560 cbt ac.
NAVY: (Caspian Flotilla) (HQ Baku): (4,000). 5 frigates, 25 patrol and coastal combatants, 26 mine warfare, 15 amph, 10 spt.

CENTRAL STRATEGIC REGION (HQ Moscow): Moscow, Volga, Urals MD; 20 div (3 TD, 16 MRD, 1 ABD) plus 1 arty div.

STRATEGIC FORCES (under central comd):
ICBM*: some 668: SS-11 (150 msl), SS-13 (converting to SS-25; 1 field, 60 msl), SS-17 (1 field, ε 100 msl), SS-18 (2 fields, ε 188 msl), SS-19 (2 fields, 170 msl).
BOMBERS: 415: 1 Air Army (HQ Smolensk): 130 Tu-95, 20 Tu-160 *Blackjack*, 115 Tu-26, 90 Tu-16, 60 Tu-22.
RECCE/ECM: 130: 110 Tu-16, 20 Tu-22.
ELINT: 5 Il-20/-22.
TANKER: 65: 40 Mya-4, 11 Tu-16, 14 Il-78.

AIR DEFENCE TROOPS (under VPVO comd):
FIGHTER: 475: 12 regt: MiG-23, MiG-25, MiG-31, Su-15.
ABM: Moscow complexes: 9 with *Galosh*, SH-11 mod *Galosh, Gazelle*.
SAM: 135 SA-1/-2/-3/-5, 40 SA-10 complexes and sites.
FRONTAL FORCES:
MOSCOW MD (HQ Moscow):
    2 TD, 7 MRD, 1 ABD, plus 1 arty div; 130 Mi-8/-24 hel (50 armed).
    FGA: 45: 1 regt Su-17.
    FIGHTER: 90: 2 regt: MiG-23, MiG-29.
URAL MD (HQ Sverdlovsk):
    1 TD, 5 MRD.
VOLGA MD (HQ Kuybyshev):
    4 MRD.
On mob could possibly field up to 4 armies.
EQUIPMENT: 4,500 MBT; 4,700 arty/MRL/mor; 76 *FROG*, 18 *Scud* SSM; 900 SAM; 225 hel.
    TACTICAL AVIATION: 135 cbt ac.

FAR EASTERN STRATEGIC DIRECTION (TVD): (HQ Transbaykal MD).

Transbaykal, Siberian, Far Eastern MD, Forces in Mongolia: 50 div (7 TD, 42 MRD, 1 coastal defence) plus 4 arty div; 1 air aslt bde.
STRATEGIC FORCES (under central comd):
SLBM: 354: Pacific Fleet: 26 submarines (msl in parentheses): 9 *D-I* (108), 8 *D-III* (128), 7 *Y-I* (112), 2 *G-II* (6).
ICBM*: 408: SS-11 (4 fields, ε 250 msl, could have theatre role), SS-17 (ε 38 msl), SS-18 (4 fields, ε 120 msl).
IRBM: SS-20 (number deployed n.k., to be withdrawn).
BOMBERS: 215: 1 Air Army (HQ Irkutsk): 45 Tu-95, 60 Tu-26, 50 Tu-16, 60 Tu-22.
RECCE/ECM: ε 60 Tu-16.
ELINT: 5 Il-20/-22.
TANKERS: some 9 Tu-16.
AIR DEFENCE TROOPS (under VPVO comd):
FIGHTER: 590: 15 regt with MiG-21, MiG-23, MiG-25, Su-15, Su-27.
SAM: 215 SA-2/-3/-5, 10 SA-10 complexes and sites.
FRONTAL FORCES:
SIBERIAN MD (HQ Novosibirsk):
    8 MRD, 1 arty div.
TRANSBAYKAL MD (HQ Chita):
    2 TD, 11 MRD, 1 arty div; 225 hel incl Mi-8/-24.
    FGA: 240: 6 regt: MiG-27, Su-17, Su-24.
    FIGHTER: 135: 3 regt: MiG-21, MiG-23.
    RECCE: 75: Su-17, Su-24, MiG-25.
FAR EASTERN MD (HQ Khabarovsk):
    3 TD, 21 MRD, 1 coastal defence, 2 arty div; 1 air aslt bde, some 670 hel.
    FGA: 390: 10 regt: MiG-27, Su-17, Su-24, Su-25.
    FIGHTER: 125: 3 regt MiG-23, Su-27.
    RECCE: 65: Yak-28, Su-17, MiG-25.
    ECM: 10 Yak-28.
MONGOLIA (HQ Ulan Bator):

1 Army HQ, 2 TD, 2 MRD div. All are at Cat A.
(See also Forces Abroad, below.)
On mob could put 4 Fronts, perhaps 12 Armies,
into the field.
EQUIPMENT: perhaps 11,500 MBT; 12,500
arty/MRL/mor; ε 149 *FROG*, 90 *Scud*, some
1,100 hel.
TACTICAL AVIATION: 890 cbt ac.

PACIFIC FLEET (Pacific and Indian Ocean)
(HQ Vladivostok): (160,000).
BASES: Vladivostok, Petropavlovsk, Sovyetskaya
Gavan; abroad: Cam Ranh Bay (Vietnam),
Aden (South Yemen).
SUBMARINES: 120: strategic: 24 SSBN, 2 SSB;
tactical: 84: 22 SSGN, 31 SSN, 4 SSG, 27 SS;
other roles: 10 SS.
PRINCIPAL SURFACE COMBATANTS: 77: 2 carriers,
11 cruisers, 8 destroyers, 56 frigates.
OTHER SURFACE SHIPS: 100 patrol and coastal
combatants, 102 mine warfare, 21 amph, some
230 spt and misc.
Regular deployments:
To the Indian Ocean and South Yemen (Aden,
Socotra, Persian Gulf) and Ethiopia (Dahlak
Is, Mits'iwa): average 1–2 submarines, 2–3
principal surface combatants, 1–3 mine
warfare, 1 amph, 8–10 spt ships.
To Vietnam (Cam Ranh Bay) and the South
China Sea: average 1–2 submarines, principal
surface combatants, 1 patrol, 2 mine warfare,
0–1 amph, 9–12 spt vessels.
NAVAL AIR (Pacific Fleet Air Force) (HQ
Vladivostok): 245 cbt ac, 100 hel.
BOMBERS: 65: 2 regt with 40 Tu-26, 1 with 25
Tu-16 *Badger* A/C/G.
FGA: 105: afloat: 4 flt Yak-38; (ashore): 1 regt
Su-17, 1 sqn MiG-23MF.
ASW:
  AIRCRAFT 75: 30 Tu-142, 20 Il-38; 25 Be-12.
  HELICOPTERS: 90: (afloat): Ka-25, Ka-27;
  (ashore): Mi-14.
MR/EW:
  AIRCRAFT: 74: 20 Tu-95, 50 Tu-16, 4 An-12 *Cub* B;
  HELICOPTERS: 10 Ka-25.
MCM: 5 Mi-14 hel.

CBT ASLT HEL: 10 Ka-27.
COMMUNICATION: Tu-142.
TANKERS: 20 Tu-16.
NAVAL INFANTRY:
1 div HQ, 3 inf, 1 tk and 1 arty regt: 7,000.

FORCES ABROAD:
MONGOLIA: ε 60,000 (50,000 to be withdrawn).
VIETNAM: (2,800); naval base (as above);
composite air unit (drawn from Far East
TVD/Pacific Fleet Air Forces): 6 Tu-95/-142, 16
Tu-16 *Badger* A/C/E/J MR or ASW, 1 sqn
MiG-23 ftr ac, AA, SAM, electronic monitoring
station.
OTHER: Afghanistan, some advisers; Algeria 700;
Angola 1,000, plus 4–8 ships, MR ac; Congo 75;
Cuba some 7,700 (1 bde (2,800), advisers (ε
2,800) plus some 2,100 SIGINT and other
technicians); Ethiopia 1,600 (plus, dry-dock,
naval inf det); India 500; Iraq 1,000; Kampuchea
500; Laos 500; Libya 1,500; Mali 75;
Mozambique 700; Nicaragua 100; Peru 50; Syria
2,000; South Yemen 1,000; Africa (remainder) 600.

PARA-MILITARY: 570,000.
KGB (*Komitet Gosudarstvennoy Bezopasnosti*):
230,000 (70–75% conscripts: ε 167,000): border
tps (incl Maritime Border Guards, 23,000),
Kremlin Guard; Special Guard.
EQUIPMENT: tk, SP guns, AFV, ac and ships.
PATROL AND COASTAL COMBATANTS: About 213:
  OFFSHORE PATROL: 23:
    4 *Krivak-III* with 1 × Ka-27 hel, 1 × 100mm gun.
    12 *Grisha-II*, 1 *Purga* with 4 × 100mm gun, 6 T-58.
  COASTAL PATROL: 25: 15 *Pauk*, 10 T-43
  INSHORE PATROL: About 165: 120 *Stenka*, 10
    Murayev, 30 *Zhuk*, some SO-1.
SUPPORT AND MISCELLANEOUS: About 20:
  10 river patrol, 8 icebreakers, some tugs.

MVD (*Ministerstvo Vnutrennikh Del*): 340,000: internal
security tps; some 30 div with tk and AFV. By law
part of armed forces of USSR and operationally
capable at least of rear area security tasks.

---

* Mobile ICBM, SS-24 and SS-25 have not been incl
in deployment.

The Alliances and Europe

(1) THE WARSAW PACT

Military Developments

Following President Gorbachev's announcement of unilateral Soviet force reductions, all members of the Warsaw Pact (WP), except Romania, have announced measures to reduce the size of their armed forces. These are described below. The publication of force data by both NATO and the WP has allowed us to reassess WP force structure and equipment holding; not all changes therefore reflect reorganization or procurement in the last 12 months.

The **Bulgarian** armed forces strengths have been reassessed, and we show a drop in man-power of some 40,000, mainly from the army. Further reductions announced by the Bulgarian Defence Minister include a motor rifle division, a tank brigade and an air force regiment and would reduce strengths by 10,000 men, 200 tanks, 200 artillery pieces and 20 aircraft. The Navy is to dispose of five unspecified units. The length of military service is not being altered but the opportunity will be taken to retire older officers and NCO.

While we now show the Bulgarian Army with fewer tanks and artillery than previously assessed, they have received additional BMP and 122mm 2S1 SP guns. We had previously overestimated the holding of SSM. The air force no longer operates MiG-17 or MiG-23 in the FGA role; combat aircraft holdings are therefore down by some 60 aircraft. Naval strength has been increased by three Soviet *Poti*-class corvettes.

Fresh information has now established that the **Czechoslovak** Army contains five mobiliz-ation divisions; one tank and four motor rifle, in addition to its active divisions. Announced Czech force reductions include 12,000 men from combat units (but some 20,000 more will be conscripted into construction units), 850 tanks and 51 combat aircraft. Restructuring will reduce the number of both tank and air force regiments. The Czech Army will also place three divisions on a mobilization basis with sufficient manpower only for security and equipment maintenance; no details of which divisions are affected have been given.

We now assess Czech tank holdings at some 4,580; holdings of this size would be needed to maintain an army of 16 divisions and allow for some reserve pool. We have substantially reduced our estimate of Czech 122mm 2S1 SP gun holdings, and now believe only 230 to be held.

The Czech Air Force has retired its 45 Su-7 *Fitter* FGA from service. We had expected these to be replaced by Su-22 but none have been received, and we now believe the Su-25, first brought into service in 1987, to be their replacement. Overall combat aircraft holdings are down by some 70 aircraft.

Further information indicates that the **GDR** holds five mobilization divisions, rather than the four we listed last year. All are motor rifle divisions and are largely based on the principal NCO schools.

Unilateral reductions announced for the National People's Army (NVA) will amount to 10,000 men, the scrapping or conversion to industrial use of 600 tanks and the decommissioning of 50 fighter aircraft. These reductions are to be achieved by disbanding six tank regiments, one in each of the six divisions, and one air force regiment. Implementation started on 28 April 1989.

We have reassessed our listing of tanks to 3,140, an increase of 290, sufficient to equip an army of 12 divisions. The number will decline as unilaterally reduced tanks are destroyed or converted. Equipment holdings show modest increases in T-72 tanks, BMP-1, and 122mm 2S1 SP guns. A second SSM battalion has received SS-21 in place of *FROG*.

The air force have formed two air defence squadrons with 20 MiG-29 *Fulcrum*, the first non-Soviet WP force to receive these. The East German Navy has commissioned a new miss-ile craft tentatively classified 'S-1' which mounts 4 SSM. We have reclassified the 18 *Kondor I*-class minesweepers as naval rather than Frontier Troops.

Further information on the **Hungarian** Army reorganization shows that the three corps have a standard organization of one tank, four motor rifle and one artillery brigade and an SA-6 regiment. The remaining tank brigade is held at Army level, with a further artillery brigade and the *Scud* SSM brigade.

Hungarian unilateral reductions in 1989–90 will amount to 9,300 men (of which 2,000 are to be career soldiers and some, we assume, will be Border Guards), 251 tanks, 430 artillery and mortar pieces, six SSM launchers and nine air defence aircraft. In a further reorganization one tank brigade and an air force 'division' will be disbanded and other streamlining measures taken. The length of conscript service is to be reduced from 18 months to one year.

We had previously overestimated the holding of *FROG* SSM of which only 18 are held; the announced reduction of six launchers suggests that each corps will have a battalion of four launchers. Holdings of T-72 tanks, BMP-1 and 122mm 2S1 SP guns have all been increased, the last by 64 guns.

The Hungarian Air Force has reduced its air defence force by two squadrons with 34 MiG-23MF.

In an interview in January 1989 the Polish Defence Minister claimed that during 1987–88 **Polish** armed forces had disbanded two divisions, cut strength by 15,000 men and destroyed many older equipments. It is now known that the two divisions were two Category C motor rifle divisions in the Warsaw Military District (MD). Polish Army manpower has dropped by 13,000 men. In 1989–90 two further motor rifle divisions (one each in the Pomeranian and Silesian MD) will be disbanded, and the manning level of two Category A tank divisions (again one each in the Pomeranian and Silesian MD) will be 'substantially reduced' probably to Category C status. The remaining divisions are to be reorganized to a standard pattern. These moves will reduce armed forces strength by 40,000 men, 850 tanks, 900 artillery and mortar pieces, 700 APC and 80 aircraft. Internal Defence Troops (WOW) and Border Troops (WOP) are also to be reduced in strength, and a number of units including construction, engineering, road and railway units, and other military projects will be handed over to civil ministries. The first reductions were claimed to have taken place on 3–4 March 1989, with two tank units and an SSM brigade being disbanded, but we have received no confirmation of this.

We now believe the Polish Army to include two mobilization divisions, one tank and one motor rifle, but we do not know their location nor how long they have been in existence. Polish Army equipment holdings, particularly of tanks and artillery, have been considerably reduced with the destruction of older, stored equipments. However, modern SP artillery holdings have increased to reach 425 122mm 2S1 and 40 152mm *Dana* SP guns. T-72 tank holdings have increased slightly and some 350 more BMP-1 are now in service.

The Polish Navy received a second Soviet *Foxtrot*-class submarine and retired a *Whiskey*-class. A fourth *Gornik* (Soviet *Tarantul* 1) corvette has joined the fleet. Polish Air Force aircraft holdings have been reduced with the retirement of 25 LIM-6 FGA and 35 MiG-21 fighters. Polish Naval Aviation now only operates helicopters; the MiG-17 regiment has been disbanded.

Romania is the only Warsaw Pact member not to have announced unilateral force reductions but President Ceausescu has claimed that forces were cut in 1987 by some 10,000 men, 250 tanks, 130 artillery pieces and 26 combat aircraft. We have seen nothing to support this claim. Indeed, in the light of the WP data document we have reassessed tank and artillery holdings which now show a considerable increase over last year's estimates. In particular, we now credit Romania with holding some 250 122mm SP guns; ATGW, anti-tank gun and SAM holdings have also been increased.

The Romanian Air Force, like all WP members, has reduced the numbers of its older aircraft, with some 55 MiG-17 FGA retired from service.

Defence Spending

In addition to announcing cuts to their armed forces, non-Soviet WP members have announced cuts in defence spending. Bulgaria claims it has cut the 1989 defence budget by 12%, Czechoslovakia proposes 15% reductions over 1989 and 1990, while the GDR will have cut defence expenditure by 10% by the end of 1990. In Hungary a 17% cut in defence spending in real terms has been approved by Parliament (but new budget accounting procedures make precise interpretation a matter for debate), Polish budget cuts will amount to approximately 4% in real terms. Finally Romania has announced no new cuts in defence spending but claims to have cut spending by 5% between 1985 and 1988.

These announcements of reduced spending were made after details of the 1989 defence budgets had been released. Bulgarian, GDR and Romanian defence budgets show modest increases but certainly no more, and possibly somewhat less, than would be needed to cover inflation. Czechoslovakia and Hungary reduced their defence budgets in real terms which will probably translate into significant decreases when inflation is taken into account, and this before unilateral cuts are made. Only the Polish defence budget shows a large increase, probably sufficient to offset 1988's inflation but perhaps not all of the anticipated 1989 inflation.

As Hungary, Poland and Romania report on their economies to the International Monetary Fund (IMF) we have decided to use IMF data when reporting details of NMP, GNP/GDP, local currency and dollar equivalents for these countries. The effect will be to lower dollar values, as fixed official exchange rates may have overvalued domestic currency.

BULGARIA

NMP	1987ε: leva 29.00 bn	
	1988ε: leva 30.80 bn	
Growth	1987: 5.1%	1988: 6.2%
GNP	1986ε: $26.4–58.9 bn	
	1987ε: $30.4–67.8 bn	
Inflation	1986: 3.5%	1987: 3.0%
Debt	1987: $6.2 bn	1988: $6.9 bn
Def exp*	1988ε: leva 1.405 bn ($2.465 bn)	
Def bdgt	1989ε: leva 1.53 bn ($1.75 bn)	
$1 = leva	1987: 0.864 (off) 0.54 (adj)	
	1988: 0.905 (off) 0.57 (adj)	
	1989: 0.873 (off)	

Population: 8,985,000

	13–17	18–22	23–32
Men	338,000	317,000	621,000
Women	319,000	301,000	599,000

TOTAL ARMED FORCES:
ACTIVE: 117,500 (91,000 conscripts).
Terms of service: 2 years (3 years for sea-going naval conscripts).
RESERVES: 472,500. Army 420,000; Navy (to age 55, officers 60 or 65) 7,500; Air (to age 60) 45,000.

ARMY: 81,900 (70,000 conscripts).
3 Military Districts/Army HQ:
  1 with 2 MRD, 1 tk bde;
  2 with 3 MRD, 2 tk bde;
  (Cat A/B: 5 MRD, 5 tk bde; Cat C: 3 MRD).
Army tps: 4 *Scud*, 1 SAM bde, 3 arty, 3 AD arty regt, 1 cdo coy.
1 AB regt (manned by Air Force).
EQUIPMENT:

MBT: 2,200: 1,200 T-54/-55, 125 T-62, some 200 T-72; (some 675 T-34 in store).
RECCE: 420 BRDM-1/-2.
AIFV: some 280 BMP-1.
APC: 1,100 BTR-50/-60, 35 OT-62, 500 MT-LB.
ARTY: ε 830:
  TOWED: 100mm: 80+ M-1944; 122mm: 400+ M-1938 (M-30), D-30; 130mm: 40 M-46; 152mm: 170 M-1937, D-20.
  SP: 122mm: 120 2S1; 152mm: ε 20 2S3.
MRL: 122mm: 130 BM-21; 130mm: 120 M-51.
MORTARS: 120mm: 450.
SSM: launchers: 36 *FROG*-7, 36 *Scud*.
ATGW: 360 AT-3 *Sagger*.
ATK GUNS: 76mm: 150 M-1942; 100mm: 150 T-12.
AD GUNS: 400: 23mm: ZU-23, ZSU-23-4 SP; 57mm: S-60; 85mm: KS-12; 100mm: KS-19.
SAM: 50 SA-4/-6/-13.

NAVY: 8,800 (3,000 conscripts).
BASES: coastal: Varna (HQ), Atiya, Sozopol, Balchik. **Danube:** Vidin (HQ).
SUBMARINES: 4 *Pobeda* (Sov *Romeo*) class with 533mm TT.
FRIGATES: 3 *Druzki* (Sov *Riga*) with 4 × 5 ASW RL, plus 3 × 533mm TT, 3 × 100mm guns.
PATROL AND COASTAL COMBATANTS: 21:
CORVETTES: 6 *Poti* ASW with 2 × ASW RL, 4 × ASTT.
MISSILE CRAFT: 6 *Osa* PFM with 4 × SS-N-2A/B *Styx* SSM.
TORPEDO CRAFT: 6 *Shershen* PFT with 4 × 533mm TT.
PATROL INSHORE: 3 Sov *SO-1*.
MINE WARFARE: 33:
MINELAYERS: None but SS and FF have capability.
MCMV: 33:
  1 Sov T-43 MSC.
  4 *Sonya* MSC.
  28 MSI: 6 *Vanya*, 4 *Yevgenya*, 18⟨.
AMPHIBIOUS: 2:

2 Sov *Polnocny* LSM, capacity 150 tps, 6 tk;
Plus 23 craft: 19 *Vydra* LCM, 4 LCU.
SUPPORT AND MISCELLANEOUS: 6:
2 AOT, 2 AGOR, 1 AGI, 1 trg.

NAVAL AVIATION: ε 3 armed hel.
HELICOPTERS: 1 SAR/ASW sqn with 9 Mi-14, Mi-8, Mi-4.

COASTAL ARTY:
2 regt, 20 bty:
GUNS: 100mm: ε 150; 130mm: SM-4-1.
SSM: SS-C-1b *Sepal*, SSC-3 *Styx*.

NAVAL GUARD: 3 coy.

AIR FORCE: 26,800 (18,000 conscripts), incl
AB regt listed under Army;
193 cbt ac, 65 armed hel.
2 air div: 7 cbt regt:
FGA: 1 regt with 45 Su-25.
FIGHTER: 4 regt with some 40 MiG-23MF *Flogger*
B/G; 108 MiG-21PFM.
RECCE: 1 regt with 35 MiG-17/-21/-25, Su-22.
TRANSPORT: 1 regt with 5 An-12, 5 Il-14, 4 An-24,
4 An-2.
HELICOPTERS: 1 regt with 10 Mi-2, 10 Mi-4, 20
Mi-8, 45 Mi-24 (attack).
TRAINING: 170+ incl 18 L-39, 80 L-29, Yak-11/-18.
AAM: AA-1 *Alkali*, AA-2 *Atoll*, AA-7 *Apex*.
ASM: AS-7 *Kerry*.
AD: 1 div: 30 SAM sites; some 280 SA-2/-3/-4.

PARA-MILITARY:
BORDER GUARDS (Ministry of Interior): 15,000;
16 regt.
SECURITY POLICE: 7,500.
PEOPLE'S TERRITORIAL MILITIA (R): 150,000.

---

* Incl police and internal security budget. Defence
expenditures estimated, since budgets have not been
available for over ten years.

CZECHOSLOVAKIA

NMP1987ε:		Kcs 582.60 bn	
Growth	1987:	1.8%	1988: 1.6%
GNP	1987:	Kcs 71.0 bn ($142.0 bn)	
	1988:	Kcs 72.0 bn ($144.0 bn)	
Inflation	1987:	0.2%	1988: 0.2%
Debt	1987:	$5.2 bn	1988: $5.5 bn
Def bdgt*	1988ε:	Kcs 29.50 bn ($5.36 bn)	
	1989:	Kcs 28.40 bn ($2.94 bn)	
$1 = Kcs	1987:	5.40 (off)	4.35 (adj)
	1988:	5.50 (off)	4.40 (adj)
	1989:	9.67 (off)	

Kcs = koruny

Population: 15,624,000

	13–17	18–22	23–32
Men	610,000	562,000	1,147,000
Women	583,000	532,000	1,101,000

TOTAL ARMED FORCES:
ACTIVE: 199,700 (118,000 conscripts).
Terms of service: 2 years
RESERVES: 295,000. Army 250,000 (295,000
more with liability to age 50 (men) or 60
(officers)); Air Force 45,000.

ARMY: 148,600 (100,000 conscripts).
2 Military Districts (MD):
Western MD with 2 Army HQ:
1 with 1 TD, 3 MRD; 1 arty, 1 *Scud*, 1 engr
bde; 1 ATK regt.
1 with 2 TD, 2 MRD; 1 arty, 1 *Scud*, 1 engr
bde; 1 ATK regt.
1 arty div.
Eastern MD with 1 Corps HQ, 2 TD (trg role)
(Cat A: 1 TD, 3 MRD. Cat B: 2 TD, 1 MRD. Cat C:
2 TD, 1 MRD.)
1 *Scud* bde,
1 AB recce bde,
4 engr (2 bridge, 2 road construction) bde.
RESERVES: 5 mob div: 1 TD, 2 MRD (West); 2
TD (East).
EQUIPMENT:
MBT: 4,585: T-54/-55, T-72.
RECCE: 1,250: 280 OT-65A, 970 BRDM.
AIFV: 1,150: 1,100 BVP-1 (BMP-1), 50 BMP-2.
APC: 2,500: OT-62A/B, OT-64A/C, OT-810.
ARTY: some 2,100
TOWED: 1,600: incl 122mm: 840 M-1931/37,
D-30/M-30; 130mm: M-46; 152mm: M-1937.
SP: 500: incl 122mm: 230 2S1; 152mm: 260
Dana (M-77, Tatra 815 chassis); 203mm: 12 2S7.
MRL: 500: incl 122mm: 200 RM-70; 130mm: 120
M-51 (being replaced).
MORTARS: 120mm: 60; 240mm: 12 2S4.
SSM: launchers: 36 *FROG*, 8 SS-21, 30 *Scud*.
ATGW: 540: AT-3 *Sagger* (220 on BRDM-2 SP),
AT-4 *Spigot*, 80 AT-5 *Spandrel*.
ATK GUNS: 100mm: 250 M-53.
AD GUNS: 575: 30mm: M-53/-59 SP; 57mm: S-60.
SAM: SA-7, 210: SA-4/-6/-8/-9/-13.

AIR FORCE: 51,100 (18,000 conscripts);
377 cbt ac, 50 armed hel.
2 air armies: 4 air div: 12 cbt regt.
FGA: 3 regt:
1 with 40 MiG-23BN/UM;
1 with 20 MiG-21SMT/U;

1 with 40 Su-25.
1 with 32 Su-22.
FIGHTER: 6 regt:
5 with 200 MiG-21/-21U;
1 with 45 MiG-23MF.
RECCE: 1 regt with 16 MiG-21RF, 10 Su-22, 15 L-29.
TRANSPORT: 2 regt with 2 An-12, 16 An-24, 5 Il-14, 1 Tu-134, 30 L-410M.
HELICOPTERS: 3 regt:
ATTACK: 50 Mi-24.
ASSAULT TPT: (med) 75 Mi-8; (lt): 60 Mi-2.
TRAINING: L-29, 24 L-39, Z-42.
LIAISON: ac incl Z-43.
AAM: AA-2 *Atoll*, AA-7 *Apex*, AA-8 *Aphid*.
AD: 3 div: 6 SAM regt:
some 40 sites; 250 SA-2/-3.

FORCES ABROAD:
ADVISERS: Iraq 40, Libya 500, Mozambique 50, Syria 110.
UNITED NATIONS: Angola (UNAVM) 7.

PARA-MILITARY:
BORDER TROOPS: (Ministry of Interior) 11,000; 7 bde (each 3 bn); BVP-1, OT-62/-64 AFV, ATK weapons.
NATIONAL SECURITY CORPS: (SNB) (Ministry of Interior): 12,500.
PEOPLE'S MILITIA (R): 120,000; OT-64/-65 AFV, mor, ATK, AA weapons.
CIVIL DEFENCE TROOPS: 7,000. 5 regt.

FOREIGN FORCES:
USSR: Central Group of Forces: Army: 1 Gp, 1 corps HQ; 2 TD, 3 MRD; Air: 1 Gp HQ; 1 FGA, 1 ftr regt, 1 recce sqn.

---

* Incl police and security budget.

GERMAN DEMOCRATIC REPUBLIC

NMP	1987ε:	DMO 262.0 bn ($146.01 bn)
	1988ε:	DMO 269.20 bn ($158.58 bn)
Growth	1987: 3.6%	1988: 3.0%
GNP	1987:	$94.0–182.0 bn
	1988:	$97.0–187.5 bn
Inflation	1987: 0.1%	1988: 1.2%
Debt	1988: $19.5 bn	1989: $20.9 bn
Def exp*	1988:	DMO 21.647 bn ($12.75 bn)
	1989:	DMO 22.430 bn ($12.01 bn)
$1 = DMO	1987:	1.7944 (off) 2.41 (adj)
	1988:	1.6976 (off) 2.27 (adj)
	1989:	1.8671 (off)
DMO = ostmarks		

Population: 16,616,000

	13–17	18–22	23–32
Men	475,000	609,000	1,390,000
Women	425,000	579,000	1,324,000

TOTAL ARMED FORCES:
ACTIVE: 173,100 (92,500 conscripts).
Terms of service: 18 months (3 years for sea-going naval conscripts).
RESERVES: 323,500. Army 250,000, up to 6 months call-up per year to total 24 months (250,000 more have Reserve commitment to 50 (men) or 60 (officers)); Navy 21,000; Air 52,500.

ARMY: 120,000 (71,500 conscripts).
2 Military Districts each 1 Army HQ, 2 MRD, 1 TD (5 with SA-6, 1 with SA-8 regt). (All divs Cat A.)
MOD tps: 1 arty bde, 1 AB bn.
Army tps: 2 *Scud*, 2 arty, 2 SA-4, 1 AD arty, 5 engr (incl 2 pontoon bridge) regt. 2 ATK bn.
RESERVES:
5 mob div: MRD (based on NCO trg schools).
EQUIPMENT:
MBT: 3,140: ε 2,100 T-54/-55, 400 T-72, ε 640 T-34 (in store).
RECCE: 1,050 BRDM-1/-2.
AIFV: 1,000 BMP-1/-2.
APC: 4,350: 2,500 BTR-60P, 1,000 BTR-70, 150 MT-LB, 700 BTR-50P/-152 (in store).
ARTY: 1,260.
TOWED: 870: 122mm: 400 D-30, 200 M-1938 (M-30); 130mm: 90 M-46; 152mm: 180 D-20.
SP: 390: 122mm: 300 2S1; 152mm: 90 2S3.
MRL: 220: 122mm: 200: Cz RM-70; 240mm: 20 BM-24.
MORTARS: 82mm: ε 100; 120mm: 550.
SSM: launchers: 44 *FROG*-7, 8 SS-21, 28 *Scud* B.
ATGW: 620: AT-3 *Sagger* (incl BRDM-2 SP), AT-4 *Spigot*, AT-5 *Spandrel*.
ATK GUNS: 300: 85mm: 100 D-48; 100mm: 200 T-12.
AD GUNS: 300: 23mm: ZU-23, 96 ZSU-23-4 SP; 57mm: ZSU-57-2.
SAM: SA-7, 300: SA-4/-6/-8/-9.

NAVY: 16,000 (6,000 conscripts).
BASES: Peenemünde, Warnemünde, Dranske-Bug, Sassnitz, Wolgast.
FRIGATES: 19:
3 *Rostock* (Sov *Koni*) with 2 × 12 ASW RL.
16 *Bützow* (*Parchim I*) with 2 × 12 ASW RL, 4 × ASTT.
PATROL AND COASTAL COMBATANTS: 38:
CORVETTES: 5 *Albin Koebis* (Sov *Tarantul* I) with 4 × SS-N-2C *Styx* SSM.
MISSILE CRAFT: 13:
1 S-1 '*BAL-COM 10*' with 2 × 4 SSM.
12 Sov *Osa -I* PFM with 4 × SS-N-2A *Styx*.
TORPEDO CRAFT: 20 PFT:

6 Sov *Shershen* with 4 × 533mm TT.
14 *Libelle* with 2 × 533mm TT.
MINE WARFARE: 42.
24 *Kondor* II MSC.
18 *Kondor* I MSC.
AMPHIBIOUS: 12 *Hoyerswerda* (*Frosch*) LSM,
capacity 180 tps, 10 tk, (some with 2 × 40
122mm MRL).
SUPPORT AND MISCELLANEOUS: 15:
3 AOT, 3 AGI, 2 *Frosch* combat spt, 6 log spt, 1
training.
NAVAL AVIATION: (1,000);
25 cbt ac, 12 armed hel.
FGA: 1 sqn with 25 Su-22.
HELICOPTERS: 1 sqn with 12 Mi-14 ASW.
COASTAL ARTILLERY: 3 bty SS-C-3 *Styx*.

AIR FORCE: 37,100 (15,000 conscripts);
335 cbt ac, 100 armed hel.
2 air div:
FGA: 2 regt: 5 sqn:
2 with 25 MiG-23BN;
3 with 35 Su-22.
TRANSPORT: 1 regt: 3 sqn:
An-2/-14, 18 An-26, 15 Tu-134, L-410.
HELICOPTERS: 3 regt:
ATTACK: 2 with 65 Mi-24, 35 Mi-8 (armed);
ASSAULT TPT: 1 with 40 Mi-8.
AD COMMAND:
FIGHTER: 6 regt:
14 sqn with 210 MiG-21F/MF/PF/U;
3 sqn with 45 MiG-23.
2 sqn with 20 MiG-29.
SAM: 7 regt: some 30 sites with 205 SA-2/-3/-5.
RADAR: 2 regt.
TRAINING: incl Yak-18, 16 L-29, L-39, Z-226,
MiG-15UTI, MiG-21U, MiG-23U, Su-22U.
LIAISON: incl Z-43 ac, Mi-4 hel.
AAM: AA-2 *Atoll*, AA -8 *Aphid*.
ASM: AT-3 *Sagger* ATGW.

FORCES ABROAD:
ADVISERS:
Algeria 250, Angola 500, Ethiopia 550, Guinea 125,
Iraq 160, Libya 400, Mozambique 100, S. Yemen
75, Syria 210, Zambia (some reported).

PARA-MILITARY: 89,500 Regulars, perhaps
1 million in an emergency.
FRONTIER TROOPS: Ministry of Defence (47,000):
6 sectors incl coast, 2 'commandos' (Polish,
Czech borders), 1 coast bde, 1 arty regt, 18
border, 4 indep coast, 2 boat bn, 1 MRL unit, 6
trg regt; Arty: 85mm: 50 D-44; 122mm: 36
M-1938; 130mm: 18 M-46. MRL: 122mm.
PATROL CRAFT: 15 inshore and riverine⟨.
BERLIN GUARD REGIMENT: (Ministry for State
Security) 7,000: 6 motor rifle, 1 arty, 1 trg bn;

PSZH-IV APC, 120mm mor, 85mm, 100mm
ATK, ZU-23 AA guns, hel.
PEOPLE'S POLICE ALERT UNITS: (Ministry of
Interior) 12,000; 21 bn; BTR-40/-152 APC,
82mm mor.
TRANSPORT POLICE: 8,500: 16 coy; small arms,
RPG-7 RL.
WORKERS' MILITIA (R): (Ministry of Defence) ε
500,000 incl 3,000 active; 15,000 cbt gp.
CIVIL DEFENCE: 15,000; 14 bn; light weapons.

FOREIGN FORCES:
USSR: Western Group of Forces: Army: 1 Gp, 5
Army HQ; 11 TD, 8 MRD. Air: 1 Gp HQ; 12
FGA, 8 ftr regt.

* Incl. DMO 6.0 bn (1988) and DMO 5.9 bn (1989)
for internal and border security.

HUNGARY

| NMP | 1987: f 999.60 bn ($19.83 bn) |
| | 1988: f 1,165.53 bn ($23.12 bn) |

| Growth | 1987: 3.0% | 1988: 1.6% |

| GDP | 1986: f 1,088.8 bn ($23.18 bn) |
| | 1987: f 1,226.4 bn ($24.33 bn) |

Inflation	1987: 8.8%	1988: 15.6%
Debt	1987: $17.7 bn	1988: $18.6 bn
Def bdgt*	1988ε: f 47.00 bn ($932.30 m)
	1989: f 45.50 bn ($827.47 m)
$1 = f	1987: 46.971	1988: 50.413
	1989: 54.987

f = forint

Population: 10,590,000

	13–17	18–22	23–32
Men	412,000	368,000	719,000
Women	389,000	346,000	688,000

TOTAL ARMED FORCES:
ACTIVE: 91,000 (48,000 conscripts).
Terms of service: 18 months.
RESERVES: 168,000: Army: 140,000; Air:
28,000 (to age 55).

ARMY: 68,000 (40,000 conscripts) incl Danube
Flotilla.
1 Army, 3 Corps HQ:
each Corps with 1 tk, 4 MR, 1 arty bde, 1 SA-6 regt.
Army tps: 1 tk, 1 arty, 1 *Scud*, 1 SA-4, bde; 1
ATK, 1 AD arty, 1 AB bn.
(Cat of bde not known, but 2 corps at Cat B or above.)
EQUIPMENT:
MBT: some 1,435: some 1,300 T-54/-55, 135 T-72.

RECCE: 750: some 410 BRDM-2, 340 FUG-65 (OT-65).
AIFV: 490 BMP-1.
APC: 1,070 PSZH-IV (FUG-70).
ARTY: 866:
  TOWED: 590: 122mm: 225 M-1938; 152mm: 50 M-1943 (D-1), 315 D-20.
  SP: 276: 76mm: 104 SU-76; 122mm: 154 2S1; 152mm: 18 2S3.
MRL: 122mm: 60 BM-21.
MORTARS: 82mm: 560; 120mm: 260.
SSM: launchers: 18 *FROG*-7, 9 *Scud*.
ATGW: 270: 180 AT-3 *Sagger* (incl BRDM-2 SP), 90 AT-4 *Spigot*, AT-5 *Spandrel* reported.
ATK GUNS: 85mm: 110 D-44; 100mm: 60 T-12.
AD GUNS: 23mm: 14 ZSU-23-4 SP; 57mm: 189 S-60.
SAM: 25 SA-4, 50 SA-6, 150 SA-7, 50 SA-9, SA-13 reported.
DANUBE FLOTILLA:
MCMV: 10 *Nestin* MSI (riverine); boats.

AIR FORCE: 23,000 (8,000 conscripts);
  101 cbt ac, 40 armed hel.
  1 air div:
FIGHTER:
  2 regt with 90 MiG-21bis.
  1 sqn with 11 MiG-23MF.
RECCE: 1 sqn with 11 Su-22.
TRANSPORT: 1 regt: 2 sqn:
  1 with 12 An-26;
  1 with 4 An-24 ac; 4 Mi-8, 4 Ka-26 hel.
HELICOPTERS: 2 regt.
  1 ATK/tpt:
    2 sqn with 40 Mi-24;
    3 sqn with 25 Mi-8/-17;
    1 liaison: 3 sqn with 10 Ka-26, 3 Mi-2.
TRAINING: incl Yak-11/-18, L-29, MiG-15UTI.
AAM: AA-2 *Atoll*.
AD: 1 div: 3 SAM regt, some 20 sites: 120 SA-2/-3.

FORCES ABROAD:
ADVISERS:
Mozambique 75, Syria 55, S. Yemen 60.

PARA-MILITARY:
BORDER GUARDS: (Ministry of Interior) 16,000 (11,000 conscripts); 11 districts.
WORKERS' GUARDS (R): (Ministry of Interior) 60,000.

FOREIGN FORCES:
USSR: Southern Group of Forces: Army: 2 TD, 2 MRD. Air: 5 FGA, 3 ftr regt.

* Incl. internal police and security budget.

POLAND

NMP	1987:	z 14,013 bn	
	1988ε:	z 22,561 bn	
Growth	1987:	1.7%	1988ε: 4.5%
GDP	1986:	z 12,953 bn ($73.89 bn)	
	1987:	z 16,940 bn ($63.91 bn)	
Inflation	1987:	25.3%	1988: 57.7%
Debt	1987:	$39.2 bn	1988: $39.2 bn
Def bdgt	1988:	z 545.85 bn ($1.27 bn)	
	1989:	z 954.00 bn ($1.68 bn)	
$1 = z	1987:	265.08 (off)	
	1988:	430.55 (off)	
	1989:	566.18 (off)	

z = zlotys

Population: 38,105,000

	13–17	18–22	23–32
Men	1,481,000	1,281,000	3,033,000
Women	1,418,000	1,227,000	2,899,000

TOTAL ARMED FORCES:
ACTIVE: 412,000 (231,000 conscripts) incl Internal Defence troops (see Para-Military).
  Terms of service: 2 years (3 years, for sea-going naval conscripts).
RESERVES: 505,000. Army 420,000; Navy 10,000 (to age 50); Air Force 75,000 (to age 60).

ARMY: 217,000 (168,000 conscripts).
  3 Military Districts/Army HQ:
    1 with 3 TD, 2 MRD;
    1 with 2 TD, 3 MRD;
    1 with 1 MRD.
  (Cat A: 5 TD (2 to be Cat C:), 3 MRD.
    Cat C: 3 MRD (2 to be disbanded)).
  Army tps:
  1 AB bde ((Cat A) 4 AB, 1 arty bn).
  1 amph aslt bde ((Cat A) 3 amph regt, 1 lt tk, 1 MRL, 1 *FROG*, 1 engr bn).
  5 arty bde (each 4 bn).
  4 *Scud* bde.
  1 SA-4 bde.
  1 SA-8, 2 SA-6 regt.
  3 ATK regt.
  Div tps: 3 SA-6, 2 SA-8 regt.
RESERVES: 2 mob div: 1 MRD, 1 TD.
EQUIPMENT:
MBT: 3,300: 270 T-34, 2,700 T-54/-55, 360 T-72.
LIGHT TANKS: 100 PT-76.
RECCE: 900 FUG/BRDM-2.
AIFV: 1,250 BMP-1.
APC: 2,700 OT-64A (SKOT), OT-64B (SKOT-2), OT-64C(1)(SKOT-2A), OT-64C(2)(SKOT-2AP), 200 OT-62A (TOPAS), OT-62C (TOPAS-2AP).
ARTY: 2,090:

TOWED: 1,625: 122mm: some 400 M-1931/37, 850 M-1938; 152mm: 230 M-1937, 145 D-1.
SP: 465: 122mm: 425 2S1; 152mm: 40 *Dana* ((M-77) Tatra 815 chassis).
MRL: 260: 122mm: BM-21; 140mm: BM-14, ε 30 WP-8.
MORTARS: 82mm; 120mm: ε 550.
SSM: launchers: 52 *FROG*, 30 *Scud* B.
ATGW: 435: AT-1 *Snapper*, AT-3 *Sagger* (incl BRDM-2 SP), AT-4 *Spigot*, AT-5 *Spandrel*, AT-7 *Saxhorn*.
ATK GUNS: 85mm: 380 D-44; 100mm: some 15 T-12.
AD GUNS: 1,000: 23mm: ZU-23, 150 ZSU-23-4 SP; 57mm: S-60.
SAM: SA-7, 400 SA-4/-6/-8/-9/-13.

NAVY: 25,000 incl coast defence. (6,000 conscripts).
BASES: Gdynia, Hel, Swinoujscie, Gdansk; Kolobrzeg (border/coast guard).
SUBMARINES: 4:
  1 *Orzel* SS (Sov *Kilo*) with 533mm.
  2 Sov *Foxtrot* with 533mm TT.
  1 *Sokol* SS (Sov *Whiskey*) with 533mm TT.
PRINCIPAL SURFACE COMBATANTS: 2:
DESTROYERS: 1 *Warszawa* DDG (Sov mod *Kashin*) with 2 × 2 SA-N-1 *Goa* SAM, 4 × SS-N-2C *Styx* SSM, 5 × 533mm TT, 2 × ASW RL.
FRIGATES: 1 *Kaszub* with 2 × ASW RL, 4 × 533mm TT.
PATROL AND COASTAL COMBATANTS: 25:
CORVETTES: 4 *Gornik* (Sov *Tarantul I*) with 2 × 2 SS-N-2C *Styx* SSM.
MISSILE CRAFT: 12 Sov *Osa*-I PFM with 4 SS-N-2A SSM.
PATROL: 9:
  8 *Obluze* PCI
  1 T-43 PCI (radar).
MINE WARFARE: 32:
MINELAYERS: None, but submarines and *Krogulec* MSC have capability.
MINE COUNTERMEASURES: 32:
  12 *Krogulec* MSC.
  9 *Tur* (Sov *T.43*) MSC.
  9 *Notec* MSI.
  2 *Leniwka* MSI.
AMPHIBIOUS: 23 Sov *Polnocny*: capacity 180 tps, 6 tk, some with 2 × 140mm MRL.
Plus craft: 1 LCU, 15 LCP.
SUPPORT AND MISCELLANEOUS: 10:
  2 AGI, 3 spt tankers, 3 survey, 2 trg.

NAVAL AVIATION: 1 div (2,300);
  11 armed hel.
ASW: hel: 11 Mi-14.
HELICOPTERS: 1 regt: 3 sqn with 10 Mi-2, 10 Mi-4, 5 Mi-8.

COAST DEFENCE:
  6 arty bn with M-1937 152mm.
  3 SSM bn with SS-C-2B.

AIR FORCE: 105,000 (30,000 conscripts); 565 cbt ac, ε 80 armed hel.
6 air div:
FGA: 200: 3 div: 5 regt:
  1 with some 30 Su-7B/-7U;
  3 with some 50 Su-20, 75 Su-22;
  1 with 45 LIM-6.
FIGHTER: 4 div: 11 regt: 33 sqn with 325 MiG-21/U; 40 MiG-23MF.
RECCE: 3 sqn with 35 MiG-21RF.
TRANSPORT: 2 regt with 9 An-2, 20 An-12, 12 An-26, 12 Il-14.
VIP: 1 VIP tpt sqn with 2 Tu-134A, 12 Yak-40, 1 Il-18; 25 PZL-130.
HELICOPTERS: 3 regt with 130 Mi-2, 50 Mi-8 (may be armed), 8 Ka-26, 30 Mi-24 (attack).
TRAINING: 300 ac: TS-8/-11, LIM-1, MiG-21UT1, Su-7U, PZL-130.
AAM: AA-1 *Alkali*, AA-2 *Atoll*.
ASM: AS-7 *Kerry*.
SAM: 10 regt with 300 SA-2/-3/-5.

FORCES ABROAD:
UNITED NATIONS: SYRIA (UNDOF): 50
ADVISERS: Libya 200.

PARA-MILITARY:
INTERNAL DEFENCE TROOPS: (WOW) (Ministry of Defence), 65,000 (27,000 conscripts); (incl construction tps) tk, APC, ATK guns.
BORDER TROOPS AND COAST GUARD (WOP) (Ministry of Interior): 22,000: 3 Provincial Comd: 8 bde (incl 1 mtn); 18 PCI: 5 *Obluze*, 2 *Gdansk*, 11 *Pilica*.
VOLUNTARY MILITIA RESERVE: (ORMO): 350,000
RIOT POLICE: (ZOMO): 28,000.

FOREIGN FORCES:
USSR: Northern Group of Forces: Army: 1 Gp HQ; 1 TD, 1 MRD, Air Force; 1 air army 300 Su-24.

ROMANIA

NMP	1987ε: lei 799.20 bn	
	1988ε: lei 822.30 bn	
Growth	1987: 3.5%	1988ε: 2.9%
GNP	1986: lei 917.5 bn ($56.80 bn)	
	1987ε: lei 949.1 bn ($65.20 bn)	
Debt	1987: $4.6 bn	1988: $3.2 bn
Def exp	1988: lei 11.552 bn ($811.98 m)	
	1989: lei 11.753 bn ($797.48 m)	
$1 = lei	1987: 14.557	1988: 14.227
	1989: 14.738	

Population: 23,583,000

	13–17	*18–22*	*23–32*
Men	987,000	935,000	1,679,000
Women	943,000	890,000	1,612,000

TOTAL ARMED FORCES:
ACTIVE: 171,000 (107,500 conscripts).
Terms of service: Army, Air Force 16 months; Navy 24 months.
RESERVES: 203,000: Army 178,000; Navy 6,000; Air 19,000.

ARMY: 128,000 (95,000 conscripts).
4 Army Areas:
  1 with 1 TD, 2 MRD;
  1 with 1 TD, 1 MRD;
  1 with 3 MRD;
  1 with 2 MRD.
(Cat A: 1 TD, 1 MRD. Cat B: 1 TD, 3 MRD. Cat C: 4 MRD.)
Army tps:
  4 mtn bde/regt.
  4 arty bde/regt.
  1 ATK bde (5 regt).
  4 AA bde; 2 AA, 3 SA-6 regt.
  2 *Scud* bde.
  4 AB regt.
EQUIPMENT:
MBT: 3,200 incl T-34, T-54/-55, M-77, T-72.
ASSAULT GUN: 270 SU-76/-100 SP.
RECCE: 650 BRDM-1/-2.
APC: 3,500 BTR-50/-60 and TAB-72, TAB-77.
ARTY: 1,130.
  TOWED: 880: 100mm: 55 M-1944; 122mm: 525 M-1938; 152mm: 300: M-1937, D-20, M-1938.
  SP: 250: 122mm.
MRL: 325: 122mm: 175 BM-21/RO; 130mm: 150 M-51 (ZIL).
MORTARS: 82mm: 140; 120mm: 225.
SSM: launchers: 32 *FROG*-3, 18 *Scud*.
ATGW: 400: AT-1 *Snapper*, AT-3 *Sagger* (incl BRDM-2 SP).
ATK GUNS: 300: 57mm: M-1943; 85mm: D-44; 100mm: T-12.
AD GUNS: 400: 30mm; 37mm; 57mm; 85mm; 100mm.
SAM: SA-7, 160 SA-6.

NAVY: 9,000 (2,500 conscripts). Black Sea Fleet, Danube Sqn, Coastal Defence.
BASES: coastal: Mangalia, Constanţa;
  Danube: Braila, Giurgiu, Sulina, Tulcea.
SUBMARINE: 1 Sov *Kilo* SS with 533mm TT.
PRINCIPAL SURFACE COMBATANTS: 5:
DESTROYER: 1 *Muntenia* DDG with SA-N-7 *Gadfly* SAM, plus 4 × 2 SS-N-2C *Styx* SSM, 2 *Alouette* III hel, 2 × 3 533mm TT.
FRIGATES: 4 '*Tetal*' with 2 × ASW RL, 4 × ASTT.
PATROL AND COASTAL COMBATANTS: 83:
CORVETTES: 3 Sov *Poti* ASW with 2 × ASW RL, 4 × 533mm TT.
MISSILE CRAFT: 6 Sov *Osa* PFM with 4 × SS-N-2A *Styx*.
TORPEDO: 42:
  12 *Epitrop* PFT with 4 × 533mm TT.
  26 Ch *Huchuan* PHT with 2 × 533mm TT.
  4 Ch P-4 PFT⟨, with 2 × 457mm TT.
PATROL: 32:
  OFFSHORE: 4 *Democratia* (GDR M-40) PCO.
  COASTAL: 3 Sov *Kronshtadt* PCC.
  INSHORE: 4 Ch *Shanghai* PFI.
  RIVERINE: 21: 3 '*Brutar*' with 1 × 100mm gun, 18⟨.
MINE WARFARE: 42:
MINELAYERS: 2 '*Cosar*', capacity 200 mines.
MCM: 40:
  2 *Musca* MSC.
  12 T.301 MSI.
  26 VD141 MSI⟨.
SUPPORT AND MISCELLANEOUS: 10:
2 '*Croitor*' log spt/tenders (hel deck), 3 spt tankers, 2 AGOR, 1 trg, 2 tugs.

COASTAL DEFENCE (2,000): HQ Constanţa.
4 sectors:
10 coastal arty bty with some 100 130mm, 150mm and 152mm guns.
Some 8 bty of AA arty reported; eqpt unknown.
Would get 1 regt of naval inf on mob.

AIR FORCE: 34,000 (10,000 conscripts);
295 cbt ac, no armed hel.
3 air div: 7 cbt regt:
FGA: 6 sqn with 30 MiG-17, 35 *Orao*.
FIGHTER: 15 sqn:
  3 with 45 MiG-23;
  12 with 185 MiG-21F/PF/U.
RECCE/ECM: 1 sqn with 15 Il-28.
TRANSPORT: 1 regt with 10 An-2, 3 Il-14, 2 Il-18, 1 Tu-154, 11 An-24, 8 An-26, 4 Li-2, 2 Boeing 707.
HELICOPTERS: 2 regt; plus 3 sqn with 10 Mi-4, 15 Mi-8, 55 IAR-316B, 40 IAR-330.
TRAINING: 10 MiG-15UTI, 40 L-29, 20 L-39; 40 IAR-823, 10 IAR-28MA lt.
AAM: AA-2 *Atoll*.
AD: 1 div: 20 SAM sites with 135 SA-2.

PARA-MILITARY:
BORDER GUARDS: ε 20,000; 12 bde; 26 Ch *Shanghai* II PFI.
SECURITY TROOPS (Ministry of Defence): ε 20,000; AFV, ATK guns.
PATRIOTIC GUARD (R): some 250,000 (perhaps 12,000 active).

(2) NATO

Nuclear Forces

In the nuclear field much political attention has focused on the future of the Theatre Nuclear Force (TNF) arsenal (currently comprising artillery fired atomic projectiles (AFAP), *Lance* SSM and air-delivered gravity bombs). While it has been agreed that the force is to be kept up to date, both its qualitative and quantitative make-up have been under debate and review, and the May 1989 NATO summit agreed that the *partial* reduction of land-based missile forces could become the subject of arms-control negotiations once the implementation of conventional reductions agreed at the negotiations on Conventional Armed Forces in Europe (CFE) was under way. Meanwhile, in the context of keeping the force up to date, US production and delivery to Europe of M-753 AFAP (which incorporate a rocket motor to increase range) for the 203mm M-110 SP howitzer continues; the US Congress is expected to authorize funds for the early research and development for a follow-on to *Lance* (FOTL) – although the question of introduction and deployment will not be decided until 1992; and development of new tactical air to surface missiles (TASM) to replace gravity bombs continues in the US. On the question of quantities, SACEUR has completed a nuclear weapons requirement study, understood to confirm a continued requirement for all three elements of the arsenal (artillery, missile and air delivered) but to judge a substantial reduction in AFAP to be possible, given the introduction of FOTL with a range substantially greater than that of *Lance*.

France has re-commissioned the second SSBN to be modified for the M-4 SLBM. We have revised our listing of SSBN to show more accurately the composition of the force. There is one SSBN, *L'Inflexible*, built especially for M-4. Two of the *Le Redoutable*-class have now been modified to take M-4 and of the remaining three, one is now in refit being modified, one more will be modified starting in 1991 but it is not currently planned to modify the final submarine as this should be replaced by the first of the new generation SSBN, *Le Triomphant*. This is to be armed with M-45 SLBM but will not enter service until 1994 at the earliest. There have been, as yet, no other changes to French nuclear forces. It has been announced that, for budgetary reasons, two of the five 'sub-strategic' strike squadrons (which were to have been re-equipped with *Mirage* 2000N mounting *ASMP*), will be eliminated. Other nuclear modernization projects have not been affected by the defence spending cuts although there is increasing uncertainty about the future of the S-4 IRBM. The development of the replacement SSM, *Hadès*, is on schedule for introduction in 1992 and successful test firings took place in November 1988 and February 1989.

The **United Kingdom** *Trident* SLBM programme continues to make progress but there are some concerns with the warhead production programme. The construction of the first two *Vanguard*-class SSBN is on schedule despite a shipyard strike, and it is planned to order the third (of four) submarines before the end of 1989. British interest in procurement of a stand-off air-to-surface missile armed with a UK-manufactured warhead continues, and a memorandum of understanding has been signed with the US for the acquisition of a new TASM.

Conventional Forces

In **Belgium**, parliament has accepted broad plans for restructuring the armed forces, designed to achieve savings of 2% in the national defence budget. Which detailed recommendations will be implemented is not yet clear but a number of units now stationed in the FRG, including an armoured and an artillery battalion and three aviation squadrons will be withdrawn to Belgium. However, an order has been placed for 46 Agusta A-109 helicopters for delivery between the end of 1990 and mid-1993. Twenty-eight will be in the ATGW role, armed with *TOW*-2 (Belgium's first armed helicopters) and the remaining 18 will be for reconnaissance and will have a night capability. During the year two FGA squadrons have been re-equipped with F-16A/B in place of their *Mirage* aircraft which have been put in store.

The bold provisions of the **Canadian** 1987 Defence White Paper have been severely blunted by the 1989 defence budget which looks to save $C 2,740 m over the next five years. The main casualty has been the nuclear-powered submarine project. Other programmes to be cancelled or modified include the cancellation of six additional CP-140 long-range maritime patrol aircraft and further procurement of CF-18 fighters. The procurement of a replacement for *Leopard* I MBT has been deferred and only the replacement of the 77 tanks stationed in the FRG is being considered. Plans to reinforce Canadian troops in the FRG in the event of war to a full division of some 16,500 men have been modified to a strength of 11–12,000. During the year some improvements to the Air Force have been achieved with all squadrons for the air division now having CF-18 and the CF-116 being retired. Helicopters holdings have increased, with eight more CH-135 and 27 more CH-136 coming into service.

All **Denmark's** 155mm M-109 SP howitzers have now been upgraded to A3 standard. The Navy has retired two *Delfinen* submarines and has taken into service the first of three *Tumleren* submarines which are modified Norwegian *Kobben*-class.

A number of **French** conventional weapon procurement plans will be stretched over time and some may be cancelled. While construction of the hull of the *Charles de Gaulle* nuclear-powered aircraft carrier was started in April 1989 it is now unlikely to enter service before 1998. A study on the restructuring of the three services, *Armées 2000* provides for the reduction of the number of military regions and greater inter-service co-operation, as well as the elimination of one of the corps in the 1st Army while maintaining and resubordinating its divisions. Developments in the past 12 months include the continuation of the upgrading AMX-30 tanks to B2 standard with a further 75 modified (it has been decided to stop this programme pending the deployment of the *Leclerc* MBT from 1992). Some 160 additional AMX-10 variants and 13 155mm AU-F-1 SP guns were brought into service. The first of some 30 *Super Puma* AS-322M to be used by the *Force d'action rapide* (FAR) for logistics and surveillance have been delivered. The Navy has commissioned a sixth *Georges Leygues* frigate.

There have been few developments in the **FRG** where the ground forces are planning the implementation of the restructuring required by the plan *Heeresstruktur 2000*. Four brigades are now testing the new organization which involves brigades comprising two active and two equipment holding, reservist manned, battalions as opposed to the current organization of three active battalions each with one equipment holding company. The Navy has retired two *Köln*-class frigates which have been transferred to the Turkish Navy. The Air Force has formed a fifth *Tornado* FGA wing and the first *Patriot* air defence systems (of a total procurement of 192 by 1994) have been delivered.

In the **Greek** Army we have been listing one infantry division too many, due to a misunderstanding of an earlier reorganization. A lengthy reorganization of the Territorial Army has now been completed barring some redeployment of equipment from the Field Army. Our listing reflects the revised order of battle. The Air Force has taken delivery of its first F-16 FGA; no squadrons are yet operational, but delivery of 40 aircraft should be complete by the end of the year. *Mirage* 2000 E/D are also being delivered and the first fighter squadron is already operational; no older aircraft have yet been retired from squadron service other than the RF-84F, which is being withdrawn piecemeal as aircraft reach the end of their service lives. The length of conscript service for all services has been reduced by one month.

The **Italian** armed forces are to reduce the conscript entry by 20,000 in 1989 for budgetary reasons, but without reducing the length of conscript service. Army APC holdings have risen by some 350 with more M-113 and VCC1/-2 in service. Although the law was changed in January 1989 to allow the Navy aircraft for its carrier, no orders for V/STOL aircraft have yet been placed. The Navy has commissioned one new *Pelosi*-class submarine, which is an improved version of the *Sauro* (last year we incorrectly listed an earlier *Pelosi* as a *Sauro*). The *Romeo Romei* has been decommissioned.

The **Netherlands** Navy has commissioned the first of four *Zeeleuw* submarines, which are armed with Mark 48 torpedoes and *Harpoon* underwater-to-surface guided weapons.

During the year both Portugal and Spain have joined the Western European Union (WEU). The **Spanish** Navy's new 16,200-tonne aircraft carrier *Príncipe de Asturias* has been accepted into service, having completed its sea-trials and work-up. The *Dédalo* has now been decommissioned, as have three destroyers. Naval Aviation has received ten additional AV-8 aircraft to form a second carrier capable squadron, and six SH-60B (with LAMPS-III fit) to form a fourth ASW helicopter squadron. The Spanish Air Force's holding of EF-18 A/B FGA has increased by nine.

Fresh information has allowed us to revise our listing for the **Turkish** Army; there are now one armoured, two mechanized and 12 infantry divisions. Four of the infantry divisions contain an armoured brigade, the remainder have only one armoured battalion. With the exception of one of the four infantry divisions with an armoured brigade, all the heavy divisions are deployed in the 1st Army which has responsibility for the defence of north-west Turkey. In the last 12 months the Army has taken delivery of a further 150 *Leopard* I tanks. The Navy has completed the fourth *Yavuz*-class frigate and two more *Doğan* missile craft and, additionally, has received two further *Gelibolu* (ex T-120 *Köln*-class) from the FRG. The Air Force has received its first F-16 FGA; two squadrons have been formed with a third still forming. F-100D/-F and F-104D FGA have now all been retired.

In the **United Kingdom** two further armoured regiments have re-equipped with *Challenger* tanks and, while a decision on whether to replace the remaining *Chieftain* tanks with a UK tank or a purchase of M-1A1 *Abrams* has been deferred, a contract has been placed with Vickers for nine prototype *Challenger* 2 for comparative trials. A third battalion is being equipped with *Warrior* AIFV and two more battalions have received *Saxon* wheeled APC. An order has been placed for 155mm AS90 SP guns to replace 105mm *Abbot*. A decision has been taken to retain the Brigade of Gurkhas after the withdrawal from Hong Kong in 1997 but the final strength of the force will depend on circumstances then.

Naval active carrier strength has been reduced to two, with *Illustrious* having recently been placed in store following completion of the refit of HMS *Invincible*. Two Type 22 *Cornwall* frigates have been commissioned and last of the this type is nearing completion. The second and third Type 23 frigates have been launched and four more are on order, the first of this class is starting sea-trials. Two *Leander*-class frigates have been decommissioned. Two mine countermeasures ships have been commissioned – the last *Brecon*-class and HMS *Sandown*, the first of a new class of minehunter. Four more *Sandown* have been ordered by the RN and six by Saudi Arabia.

In the Royal Air Force a third air defence squadron has converted to *Tornado* (from *Phantom*), and the first *Tornado* recce variant (GR-1A) squadron has formed and deployed to the FRG.

Defence Spending

During the past year NATO's overall defence expenditure showed only a marginal growth of less than 1%. Only two of the poorest NATO members achieved significant increases in real terms: Greece (10%) and Portugal (4%). Of the industrialized nations only Canada (1%) and Denmark (3%) increased their expenditure; all others either remained at around last year's level or recorded significant reductions, such as Turkey where defence spending dropped by over 10%, and US (4.5%) and Norway (4.5%). In France the long-term defence spending plan has been radically reduced, bringing the phased rate of increase in defence investment (R&D, procurement and infrastructure) down to 1.8% in 1990 and to 4% for each of the following two years. Despite this trend NATO declared at the June Defence Planning Council meeting that it would continue to adhere to the principle of 3% annual increases.

The conflict between the 3% goal and actual levels of national defence investment within NATO appears likely to become more acute given the unilateral force reductions announced by the Warsaw Pact, Soviet plans for sizeable defence budget reductions, hopeful prospects for a satisfactory outcome to the CFE negotiations – the whole leading to a public perception of an improving East–West relationship and a much reduced military threat to Europe.

The debate over NATO burden-sharing intensified in 1988/9 and appears likely to persist, although the Bush Administration, like its predecessor, can be expected strongly to resist consequential domestic pressures for US troop withdrawals beyond those required by arms-control measures. A NATO study, *Enhancing Alliance Collective Security: Shared Roles, Risks and Responsibilities by the Alliance*, brought some perspective to the debate by broadening it beyond a focus on purely monetary inputs to embrace measures of output and consideration of the less easily quantifiable elements of 'burden', such as conscription and the ecological and quality-of-life penalties resulting from the concentrated troop presence in Europe. Some inequalities of burden-sharing undoubtedly persist, however, and are unlikely to be rectified by greater investment of resources on the part of the European nations concerned. A satisfactory CFE agreement could considerably ameliorate the problem, provided a suitable arrangement for apportionment of any reductions can be devised.

BELGIUM

GDP	1987:	fr 5,323 bn ($142.58 bn)	
	1988:	fr 5,608 bn ($152.52 bn)	
Growth	1987:	2.4%	1988: 3.9%
Inflation	1987:	1.6%	1988: 1.2%
Debt	1987:	$29.4 bn	1988: $29.7 bn
Def exp	1988:	fr 103.10 bn ($2.80 bn);	
		NATO defn $4.22 bn	
Def bdgt	1989:	fr 99.00 bn ($2.53 bn);	
		NATO defn $3.86 bn	
$1 = fr	(1987):	37.334	(1988): 36.768
	(1989):	39.084	

fr = Belgian francs

Population: 9,938,000

	13–17	18–22	23–32
Men	329,000	366,000	808,000
Women	315,000	353,000	778,000

TOTAL ARMED FORCES:
ACTIVE: 92,400 (3,500 women, 36,700 conscripts).
  Terms of service: 10 months in FRG or 12 months in Belgium.
RESERVES: Total Reserve Status: 411,500. With service in past 5 years: ε 146,500 (Army 109,000; Medical Service 16,500; Navy 4,500; Air Force 16,500).

ARMY: 67,800 (30,100 conscripts). Both figures incl Medical Service.
  1 Corps HQ, 2 Div HQ.
  1 armd bde (2 tk, 2 mech inf, 1 SP arty bn, 1 ATK coy).
  3 mech inf bde (each 1 tk, 2 mech inf, 1 SP arty bn, 1 ATK coy).
  1 para-cdo regt (3 para-cdo bn, armd recce sqn, ATK coy, arty bty).
  Recce Comd (2 recce, 1 tk bn).
  1 indep tk bn.
  3 SP arty bn.
  1 SSM bn: 2 bty, each with 2 *Lance*.
  4 AD bn: 2 *HAWK*; 2 *Gepard* AA.
  4 engr bn (2 fd, 1 bridge, 1 eqpt).
  3 lt avn sqn.
RESERVES: some on immediate recall status; 2 mech inf bde; 2 inf, 1 SP arty bn, cbt spt, log spt tp. Territorial defence: 11 mot inf regt, 4 inf bn.
EQUIPMENT:
MBT: 334 *Leopard* 1 (14 in store).
LIGHT TANKS: 133 *Scorpion* (23 in store).
RECCE: 153 *Scimitar* (20 in store).
AIFV: 520 AIFV-B (46 in store).
APC: 1,267 (209 in store): incl 535 M-113 (68 in store), 266 *Spartan* (29 in store), AMX-VCI (to Reserves).
TOWED ARTY: 105mm: 22 (14 in store).
SP ARTY: 176: 155mm; 41 M-109A3 (1 in store), 124 M-109A2 (4 in store); 203mm: 11 M-110A2 (3 in store).
MORTARS: 81mm: 296 (113 in store); 107mm: 133 (61 in store).
SSM: 5 *Lance* launchers (1 in store).
ATGW: 420 *Milan* (320 veh-mounted) (10 in store), 43 *Striker* AFV with *Swingfire* (7 in store).
ATK GUNS: 80 JPK-90mm SP (8 in store).
AD GUNS: 20mm: 36 HS-804 (12 in store), 100 M-167 *Vulcan* (21 in store); 35mm: 54 *Gepard* SP.
SAM: 39 *Improved HAWK* (3 in store).
AIRCRAFT: 10 BN-2A *Islander*.
HELICOPTERS: 59 SA-313/-318.

NAVY: 4,700 (1,550 conscripts).
BASES: Ostend, Zeebrugge, Kallo.
FRIGATES: 4 *Wielingen* with 2 × ASTT (Fr L-5 LWT), 1 × 6 ASW mor; plus 4 × MM-38 *Exocet* SSM, 1 × 100mm gun.
MINE WARFARE: 27 MCMV:
  6 *Van Haverbeke* (US *Aggressive* MSO).
  7 *Aster* (tripartite) MHC.
  4 *Stavelot* (US *Adjutant*) MSC.

10 *Herstal* MSI.

SUPPORT AND MISCELLANEOUS: 3:
2 log spt/comd, 1 research/survey vessels.
HELICOPTERS: 2 SA-318.

AIR FORCE: 19,900 (5,100 conscripts).
FGA: 5 sqn: 1 with *Mirage* 5BA/BD; 4 (1 converting)
with F-16A/B.
FIGHTER: 2 sqn with F-16A/B.
SAM: 4 sqn with *Nike Hercules* (modernized). To be
withdrawn, 1989–90.
RECCE: 1 sqn with *Mirage* 5BR.
TRANSPORT: 2 sqn: 1 with 12 C-130H; 1 with 2
Boeing 727QC, 3 HS-748, 5 *Merlin* IIIA, 2
Mystère-Falcon 20.
LIAISON: 1 sqn with CM-170.
TRAINING: 3 sqn: 2 with *Alpha Jet*; 1 with SF-260.
SAR: 1 sqn with *Sea King* Mk 48.
EQUIPMENT: 126 cbt ac (plus 43 in store), no
armed hel.
AIRCRAFT:
 Mirage: 36: **5BA/BD:** 18 (FGA). **5BR:** 18 (recce);
  plus 29 in store.
 F-16: 108: **A/B:** 72 (FGA), 36 (FTR); plus 14 in store.
 C-130: 12 (tpt).
 Boeing 727: 2 (tpt). **HS-748:** 3 (tpt). **Merlin IIIA:** 5
  (tpt). **Mystère-Falcon 20:** 2 (tpt). **CM-170:** 18
  (liaison). **SF-260:** 30 (trg). **Alpha Jet:** 31 (trg).
HELICOPTERS:
 Sea King: 5 (SAR).
MISSILES:
 SAM: 36 *Nike Hercules*.
 AAM: AIM-9 *Sidewinder*.

FORCES ABROAD:
FRG: 26,600 (to reduce by 1,400 1989–94);
1 corps HQ, 1 div HQ, 1 armd, 1 mech inf bde;
COMRECCE; 1 indep tk, 3 arty, 1 SSM, 2 *Gepard*
AA, 2 SAM, 3 engr bn, 200 MBT; 3 hel sqn; 4
Nike SAM sqn (to be withdrawn 1989–90).

PARA-MILITARY:
GENDARMERIE 15,900; 62 FN, 4 RM/62F armd
cars, 5 *Alouette* II, 3 *Puma* hel.

FOREIGN FORCES:
NATO:
 HQ NATO Brussels.
 HQ SHAPE Mons.
US: 3,100.

CANADA

| GDP | 1987: | $C 549.69 bn ($US 414.55 bn) |
| | 1988: | $C 598.70 bn ($US 494.06 bn) |

Growth	1987:	4.0%	1988:	4.5%
Inflation	1987:	4.3%	1988:	4.0%
Debt	1987ε:	$US 122.0 bn		
	1988ε:	$US 125.0 bn		

Def exp 1988/90: $C 10.70 bn ($US 8.83 bn);
                NATO defn* $US 10.176 bn
Def bdgt 1989/90: $C 11.10 bn ($US 9.29 bn);
                NATO defn* n.a.

$ 1 = $C	(1987/8):	1.3107	(1988/9):	1.2118
	(1989):	1.1953		

Population: 26,065,000

	13–17	18–22	23–32
Men	943,000	1,030,000	2,340,000
Women	895,000	965,000	2,351,000

Canadian Armed Forces are unified and are
organized in functional commands (Mobile,
Maritime, Air, Communications and Training).
This entry is set out in the traditional single
service manner.†

TOTAL ARMED FORCES:
ACTIVE: 89,000 (planned 90,000 by end 1989;
7,700 women; of the total strength some 24,200
are not identified by service).
Terms of service: voluntary.
RESERVES: Primary 26,100. Army (Militia)
18,800; Navy 4,000; Air 1,300. Comms 2,000;
Supplementary 28,500.

ARMY (Land Forces): 23,500.†
 1 div HQ:
  1 mech bde gp with 1 armd regt, 2 mech inf bn,
   1 arty, 1 engr regt.
  2 bde gp each with 1 armd regt, 3 mech inf bn,
   1 arty (2 close spt, 1 AD bty), 1 engr regt.
 1 AD regt (4 bty).
 1 special service force (4,000): 1 armd regt, 1 inf
  bn, 1 AB, 1 arty, 1 engr regt.
RESERVES: Militia: 8 armd, 18 arty, 52 inf, 11
engr, 20 spt bn level units, 11 med coy.
 Canadian Rangers: Northern region: 750: 37
 patrols (to increase). Newfoundland: 900.
EQUIPMENT:
MBT: 114 *Leopard* C-1.
RECCE: 174 *Lynx*, 195 *Cougar*.
APC: 881 M-113 (136 in store), 55 M-577, 269 *Grizzly*.
TOWED ARTY: 248: 105mm: 12 Model 44 (L-5) pack,
 179 C1 (M-101); 155mm: 57 M-114 (in store).
SP ARTY: 155mm: 76 M-109.
MOR: 81mm: 150.
ATGW: 215 *TOW* (incl 64 M-113 SP).
AD GUNS: 35mm: 20 GDF-005; 40mm: 57 L-40/60.
SAM: some ADATS, 111 *Blowpipe*.

NAVY (Maritime Forces): 17,100.†
SUBMARINES: 3 *Ojibwa* (UK *Oberon*) SS with Mk 48 HWT; plus *Harpoon* USGW.
FRIGATES: 19:
FFH: 11:
  4 *Iroquois* (incl 2 in conversion refit to DDG) with 2 CH-124 *Sea King* ASW hel (Mk 46 LWT), 2 × 3 ASTT, 1 × 3 ASW mor; plus 1 × 127mm gun.
  2 *Annapolis*, 5 *St Laurent* with 1 *Sea King* hel, 2 × 3 ASTT, 1 × 3 ASW mor.
FF: 8:
  4 Improved *Restigouche* with 1 × 8 *ASROC*, 2 × 3 ASTT, 1 × 3 ASW mor.
  4 *Mackenzie* with 2 × 3 ASTT, 2 × 3 ASW mor.
  Plus 1 FFH in store.
PATROL AND COASTAL COMBATANTS: 12:
  6 *Fundy* (ex MSC) PCC (trg).
  5 *Porte St Jean* PCC, 1 PCI⟨ (reserve trg).
MINE WARFARE: 2:
  2 *Anticosti* MSO (converted offshore spt vessels) (reserve trg).
SUPPORT AND MISCELLANEOUS: 7:
  2 *Protecteur* AO with 3 *Sea King*, 1 *Provider* AO with 2 *Sea King*, 3 AGOR, 1 diver spt.

DEPLOYMENT AND BASES:
ATLANTIC: Halifax (HQ) (Maritime Commander is also COMCANLANT): 3 SS, 10 FFH, 1 FF, 2 AGOR. 2 MR sqn each with 7 CP-140, 1 MR sqn with 12 CP-121, 3 ASW hel sqn with 32 CH-124 hel.
PACIFIC: Esquimalt (HQ): 1 FFH, 7 FF, 1 AGOR, 6 PCC. 1 MR sqn with 4 CP-140, 1 MR sqn with 3 CP-121.
RESERVES: 4,000 in 24 divisions: Patrol craft, MCM, Naval Control of Shipping, augmentation of regular units.

AIR FORCE: 24,200.†
CANADIAN AIR DIVISION (Lahr AB, FRG): 3 sqn with CF-18; plus 2 NATO-assigned sqn with CF-18 based in Canada.
FIGHTER GROUP:
FGA: 3 sqn (2 NATO-assigned) with CF-18.
FIGHTER: 2 sqn with CF-18 (trg sqn to augment).
EW: 1 trg sqn with CC-144 (CL-601), CT-133.
EARLY WARNING: 13 North Warning System sites, supplemented by 39 short-range radar sites; Region Operational Control Centre (ROCC). 1 space tracking and identification site.
MARITIME AIR GROUP:
MR: 6 sqn:
  4 (1 trg) with CP-140 (P-3 mod);
  2 (1 with twinned reserve sqn) with CP-121.
ASW: 3 hel sqn (1 trg) with CH-124, some afloat.
LIAISON: 2 utility sqn with T-33, CP-121 ac; CH-135 (Bell 212) hel.
TACTICAL AIR GROUP (TAG):

HELICOPTERS: 10 sqn: 4 with CH-135, CH-136; 2 with CH-47; 4 reserve sqn with CH-136.
AIR TRANSPORT GROUP:
TRANSPORT: 6 sqn:
  4 (1 trg) with CC-130E/H *Hercules*.
  1 with CC-137 (Boeing 707).
  1 with CC-109, CC-144, CC-142.
SAR: 4 tpt/SAR sqn (1 with twinned reserve sqn) with CC-115, CC-138 ac; CH-113/-113A hel.
LIAISON: 3 base hel flt with CH-118, CH-135.
TRAINING GROUP:
TRAINING: 3 flying schools with CF-116, CT-133, CT-134, CT-114, CC-142 ac; CH-139 hel. 1 demonstration unit with CT-114.
EQUIPMENT: 151 cbt ac (plus 26 in store); 131 armed hel.
AIRCRAFT:
  CF-18: 118. **-A:** 98 (78 FGA, 20 ftr); **-B:** 20 (trg); plus 15 in store.
  CP-140: 18 (MR).
  CP-121: 18 (15 MR, 3 liaison); plus 15 in store.
  CC-130E/H: 27 (tpt).
  CC-137: 5 (3 tpt, 2 tkr/ tpt).
  CC-109: 7 (tpt). **CC/E-144:** 16 (7 EW trg, 1 trials, 4 VIP, 4 tpt). **CC-132:** 1 (tpt). **CC-138:** 8 (SAR/tpt). **CC-115:** 14 (SAR/tpt). **T-33:** 9 (liaison). **CT-133:** 50 (trg, liaison). **CT-114:** 108 (trg). **CT-134:** 20 (trg). **CC/T-142:** 8 (2 tpt, 6 trg).
HELICOPTERS:
  CH-124: 35 (32 ASW afloat, 3 reserve). **CH-135:** 46 (36 tac, 6 SAR, 4 liaison). **CH-136:** 63 (tac). **CH-147:** 7 (tac). **CH-113:** 14 (SAR/tpt). **CH-118:** 9 (liaison). **CH-139:** 13 (trg).

FORCES ABROAD:
FRG:
  1 mech bde gp (4,400) (assigned to CENTAG); 77 *Leopard* 1 MBT, 26 M-109 155mm SP how, 48 *TOW* ATGW, 1 tac hel sqn with 13 CH-136.
  1 air div: (2,700). 3 FGA sqn with 51 CF-18, plus 3 in store. 1 det; 1 CC-132 and 4 CT-133 liaison ac.
UN AND PEACE-KEEPING:
  CYPRUS (UNFICYP): 575: 1 inf bn.
  EGYPT (MFO): 136.
  IRAN/IRAQ (UNIIMOG): observers.
  SYRIA/ISRAEL (UNDOF): 226 (log).
  OTHER MIDDLE EAST (UNTSO): 22.
  NAMIBIA (UNTAG): 262 (log).

PARA-MILITARY:
COAST GUARD: 6,600 (civilian-manned); 1 arctic, 7 large, 5 med, 2 lt icebreakers, 44 SAR vessels, 27 tenders, 2 DHC-7R ac, 37 hel, 5 hovercraft.

---

* Canadian fiscal year is 1 April–31 March. NATO data refer to calendar year.

† Mobile Command commands land combat forces, and Maritime Command all naval forces. Air Command commands all air forces, but Maritime Command has operational control of maritime air forces. Mobile Command has operational control of TAG. HQ 4 ATAF in Europe has operational control of 1 Canadian Air Division.

DENMARK

GDP	1987:	kr 693.03 bn ($101.32 bn)
	1988:	kr 724.64 bn ($107.64 bn)
Growth	1987: −1.0%	1988: 0.3%
Inflation	1987: 4.0%	1988: 4.5%
Debt	1987: $40.4 bn	1988: $44.0 bn
Def bdgt	1988: kr 13.50 bn ($2.01 bn);	
	NATO defn $2.34 bn	
	1989: kr 13.50 bn ($1.86 bn);	
	NATO defn $2.19 bn	
$1 = kr	(1987): 6.840 (1988): 6.732	
	(1989): 7.270	

kr = Danish kroner

Population: 5,141,000

	13–17	18–22	23–32
Men	187,000	199,000	400,960
Women	179,447	188,787	379,051

TOTAL ARMED FORCES:
ACTIVE: 31,600 (9,215 conscripts, 800 women).
Terms of service: 9–12 months (up to 27 months in certain ranks).
RESERVES: 74,700: Army 55,000; Navy 7,600; Air Force 12,100. Home Guard (*Hjemmevaernet*) (volunteers to age 50): Army 58,400; Naval 4,900; Air Force, 11,700.

ARMY: some 17,000 (7,600 conscripts):
Covering Force (peacetime units requiring some reinforcement to be combat ready and mob of some reserve units):
2 geographical comd, 2 div HQ.
5 mech inf bde, each with 1 tk, 2 mech (incl 1 Reserve), 1 arty bn, spt units.
1 inf bde (−).
2 recce bn.
1 avn unit, some 8 pl.
Regional Defence (cadre basis until mob):
7 Regional HQ.
1 inf bde
4 regt cbt teams (each 2–3 inf bn, 1 arty bn, 1 tk coy).
9 inf bn.
1 inf bn (UN).
EQUIPMENT:

MBT: 210: 120 *Leopard* 1A3, 90 *Centurion*.
LIGHT TANKS: 52 M-41 DK-1.
APC: 530 M-113.
TOWED ARTY: 314: 105mm: 182 M-101; 155mm: 24 M-59, 96 M-114 (being upgraded); 203mm: 12 M-115.
SP ARTY: 155mm: 76 M-109A3.
MORTARS: 81mm: 300 (incl 56 M-106); 120mm: 152.
ATGW: 140 *TOW* (incl 56 SP).
RCL: 106mm: 144.
ATK GUNS: 84mm/105mm: 126 KVGKN (ex-*Centurion* tk).
AD GUNS: 40mm: 36 L/60.
SAM: *Hamlet* (*Redeye*).
AIRCRAFT: 8 SAAB T-17.
HELICOPTERS: 14 Hughes 500M.

NAVY: 7,700 (900 conscripts).
BASES: Copenhagen, Korsør, Frederikshavn.
SUBMARINES: 3:
1 *Tumleren* (mod No *Kobben*) SSC with Sw FFV Type 61 HWT.
2 *Narhvalen*, SSC with FFV Type 61 and 41 HWT
FRIGATES: 3:
3 *Niels Juel* with 2 × 4 *Harpoon* SSM.
PATROL AND COASTAL COMBATANTS: 40:
MISSILE CRAFT: 10 *Willemoes* PFM with 2 × 4 *Harpoon*.
TORPEDO CRAFT: 6 *Søløven* PFT with 4 × 533mm
PATROL: 24:
  OFFSHORE: 5:
    1 *Thetis* with 1 *Lynx* hel.
    1 *Beskytteren*, 3 *Hvidbjørnen* PCO with 1 *Lynx* hel.
  COASTAL: 4:
    1 *Flyvefisken* (Stanflex 300) PFC.
    3 *Agdlek* PCC.
  INSHORE: 15: 4 *Daphné*, 2 *Magen*, 9 *Barsø*.
MINE WARFARE: 9:
MINELAYERS: 6: 4 *Falster* (400 mines), 2 *Lindormen* (50 mines).
MCMV: 3 *Alssund* (US MSC-128) MSC.
SUPPORT AND MISCELLANEOUS: 7:
2 AOT (small), 4 icebreakers (civilian-manned), 1 Royal Yacht.
IN STORE: 2 *Peder Skram* FF.
HELICOPTERS: 8 *Lynx* (up to 4 embarked).

COAST DEFENCE: 2 coastal fortresses; 150mm guns; 40mm AA guns. Coastal radar.
RESERVES (Home Guard): 37 inshore patrol craft.

AIR FORCE: 6,900 (700 conscripts).
TACTICAL AIR COMMAND:
FGA/FIGHTER: 5 sqn: 4 with F-16A/B; 1 with F-35 *Draken*.
FGA/RECCE: 1 sqn with RF-35 *Draken*.

TRANSPORT: 1 sqn, 3 comms flt with C-130H, *Gulfstream* III, SAAB T-17.
SAR: 1 sqn with S-61A hel.
TRAINING: 1 flying school with T-17.
AIR DEFENCE GROUP:
AD: 2 SAM bn: 8 bty with *Improved HAWK*.
CONTROL/REPORTING GROUP: 5 radar stations.
EQUIPMENT: 89 cbt ac, no armed hel.
AIRCRAFT:
F-16A/B: 57 (FGA/ftr).
F-35: 41. 16 (FGA/ftr); **RF-35:** 16 (FGA/recce); **TF-35:** 9 (trg).
C-130H: 3 (tpt). *Gulfstream* III: 3 (tpt). **SAAB T-17:** 22 (6 tpt, 16 trg).
HELICOPTERS:
S-61: 8 (SAR).
MISSILES:
AAM: *Sidewinder*.
SAM: 36 *Improved HAWK*.

FORCES ABROAD:
CYPRUS (UNFICYP): 1 bn: 320.
NAMIBIA (UNTAG): 1 log coy: 132.

FRANCE

GDP	1987: fr 5,282.90 bn ($878.92 bn)		
	1988: fr 5,660.00 bn ($950.16 bn)		
Growth	1987: 2.1%	1988:	2.3%
Inflation	1987: 3.3%	1988:	2.7%
Debt	1987: $63.5 bn	1988:	$63.5 bn
Def exp*	1988: fr 182.88 bn ($30.70 bn); NATO defn $35.95 bn		
Def bdgt	1989: fr 182.36 bn ($28.83 bn); NATO defn $35.07 bn		
$1 = fr	(1987): 6.0107	(1988):	5.9569
	(1989): 6.3248		

Population: 55,784,000

	13–17	18–22	23–32
Men	2,051,000	2,174,000	4,262,000
Women	1,947,000	2,084,000	4,240,000

TOTAL ARMED FORCES:
ACTIVE: some 466,300 (13,300 women, 240,100 conscripts) incl 3,600 Central Staff, 8,700 (2,000 conscripts) Service de santé, 2,000 Service des essences not listed below.
Terms of service: 12 months (can be voluntarily extended to 16–24 months).
RESERVES: Earmarked for mob: 353,000; Army 267,000, Navy 28,000, Air 58,000. Potential: 1,190,500, Army 915,000, Navy 96,000, Air 179,500.

STRATEGIC NUCLEAR FORCES:
(18,700; some 2,800 Army, 5,000 Navy, 10,200 Air Force, 700 Gendarmerie).

NAVY: 96 SLBM in 6 SSBN.
SSBN: 6:
1 *L'Inflexible* with 16 M-4/TN-70 or -71; plus SM-39 *Exocet* USGW.
2 modernized *Le Redoutable* with 16 M-4; plus SM-39.
3 *Le Redoutable* with 16 M-20/TN-60 msl (1 in long refit and conversion to M-4).

AIR FORCE:
IRBM: 18 SSBS S-3D/TN-61 msl in 2 sqn. (Test centre: 4 silos.)
BOMBERS: 2 sqn with 16 *Mirage* IVP (*ASMP*: Air-Sol, Moyenne-Porteé nuclear ASM); plus 2 in store.
TRAINING: 7 *Mirage* IIIB, 1 *Mystère-Falcon* 20P.
TANKERS: 1 wing:
3 sqn with 11 KC-135F/FR.
COMMUNICATIONS: 2 C-160 *ASTARTE* airborne comms centres.
RECCE: 6 *Mirage* IVA (in store).

'PRESTRATEGIC' NUCLEAR FORCES: (8,450).
ARMY (6,100): 32 *Pluton* SSM launchers.
NAVY (150): 40 *Super Etendard* strike ac (to get *ASMP* nuc ASM); plus 24 in store.
AIR (2,200): 6 sqn:
3 with 43 *Jaguar* (AN-52 bombs); 1 with 15 *Mirage* III E; 2 with 30 *Mirage* 2000N (with *ASMP*).
Eqpt also listed with Service sections.

ARMY: 292,500, (6,000 women, 183,000 conscripts).
Note: regiments are normally of bn size.
1 army (continental ops).
3 corps (1 of 2 armd, 1 of 3 armd and 1 inf, 1 of 1 armd and 1 inf div).
(Armd div with 2 or 3 armd, 2 mech, 1 APC inf, 2 arty, 1 engr regt; inf div with 3 inf, 1 armd cavalry, 1 arty regt).
Army/corps units: 3 armd recce, 1 special ops, 1 para, 2 inf, 1 hy arty, 5 SSM with *Pluton* (each of 3 bty, 2 launchers each), 5 *Roland* SAM (each of 4 bty), 3 *HAWK* SAM regt, 3 cbt hel (each 10 SA-330, 24 SA-341/-342 ATK, 10 SA-341 gunships), 5 engr regt.
Rapid Action Force (FAR: 47,000).
1 para div: 6 para inf, 1 armd cavalry, 1 arty, 1 engr regt.
1 air portable marine div: 2 inf, 2 lt armd, 1 arty, 1 engr regt.
1 lt armd div: 2 armd cavalry, 2 APC inf, 1 arty, 1 engr regt.

1 mtn div: 6 mtn inf, 1 lt armd, 1 arty regt; 1
engr bn.
1 air-mobile div: 1 inf regt, 3 cbt, 1 comd, 1 spt
hel regt. (Total 241 hel: 84 SA-330, 90
SA-342/*HOT*, 67 SA-341 (30 gun, 27 recce,
10 liaison).)
1 Franco/German bde (still forming).
Indep: 1 para, 6 arty, 4 engr, 1 EW regt.
Foreign Legion (8,500):
1 armd, 1 para, 4 inf, 2 engr regt.
12 Marine inf regt (overseas).

RESERVES::
2 lt armd div (based on Inf and Armd schools).
1 territorial div (Rhine) (active: 1 engr regt;
reserve: 5 engr, 1 AD regt, 3 inf bn).
Individual reinforcements for 1st Army and FAR.
Territorial Defence Army: 6 Military Regions
each with 1 (1 with 2) Defence Zone bde
(normally 2 inf, 1 armd regt: AML-90, *Milan*,
120mm mor); 22 Military Territorial Div
(geographical), each 1 (2 in Corsica)
combined-arms territorial regt (900–1,300).

EQUIPMENT:
MBT: 1,340 AMX-30 (475 -B2);
LIGHT TANKS: some 230 AMX-13 (140 in store).
RECCE: 284 AMX-10RC, 147 ERC-90F4 *Sagaïe*, 640
AML-60/90 (perhaps 300 in store), 36 VBL M-11.
AIFV: 960 AMX-10P/PC.
APC: 150 AMX-13 VTT, 3,125 VAB.
TOWED ARTY: 556: 105mm: 159 HM-2, 50 AU-50
(140 in store); 155mm: 130 BF-50, some 12
TR-F-1, 205 (80 in store) F-3.
SP ARTY: 155mm: 208 AU-F-1.
MORTARS: 81mm; 120mm: 630 incl 370 RT-F1,
some 260 M-51 (in store).
SSM: 32 *Pluton* launchers.
ATGW: 113 AMX-13/SS-11, 1,440 *Milan*, *HOT* (incl
135 VAB SP).
RL: 89mm: 11,575; 112mm: *APILAS*.
AD GUNS: 1,305: 20mm: 140 53T1, 706 53T2;
30mm: 390 towed, 69 AMX-13 DCA twin SP.
SAM: 272: 69 *HAWK*, 183 *Roland* I/II, 20 *Mistral*.
HELICOPTERS 610: 135 SA-313/-318, 59 SA-316/-319,
113 SA-330, 143 SA-341F/M (12 with *HOT*, 65
gun-armed, 27 recce, 39 utility), 160 SA-342M
(144 with *HOT*; more being delivered).
AIRCRAFT: 2 L-19, 10 MH-1521, 2 Reims-Cessna 406.

NAVY: 65,500 incl 11,000 Naval Air, 2,600
Marines (1,400 women; 19,200 conscripts).
COMMANDS: 1 strategic sub (ALFOST), 2 home
(CECLANT, CECMED), 2 overseas: Indian Ocean
(ALINDIEN), Pacific Ocean (ALPACI).
BASES: France: Cherbourg, Brest (HQ), Lorient,
Toulon (HQ). Overseas: Papeete (HQ), La
Réunion, Noumea, Fort de France (Martinique).
SUBMARINES: 21.
STRATEGIC SUBMARINES: 6 SSBN (see p. 59).

TACTICAL SUBMARINES: 14:
SSN: 4 *Rubis* ASW/ASUW with F-17 HWT, SM-39
Exocet USGW.
SS: 10:
4 *Agosta* with F-17 HWT; plus *Exocet* USGW.
6 *Daphné*, with E-15 HWT; (plus 2 in store).
OTHER ROLES: 1 *Narval* (trials).
PRINCIPAL SURFACE COMBATANTS: 43.
CARRIERS: 2:
2 *Clemenceau* CVS, (33,300 tonnes) capacity 40 ac
(typically 2 flt with 16 *Super Etendard*, 1 with 7
F-8E *Crusader*, 1 with 6 *Alizé*; 1 det with 2
Etendard IVP, 2 *Super Frelon*, 2 *Lynx* hel).
CRUISERS: 2:
1 *Colbert* CG with 1 × 2 *Masurca* SAM, 4 ×
MM-38 *Exocet*, 2 × 100mm guns.
1 *Jeanne d'Arc* CCH (trg/ASW) with 6 MM-38
Exocet SSM, 4 × 100mm guns, capacity 8 ×
Lynx hel.
DESTROYERS: 4 DDG:
1 *Cassard* with 1 × 1 *Standard* SM-1 MR; plus 8 ×
MM-40 *Exocet*, 1 × 100mm gun, 2 × ASTT, 1
SA-365 hel (ASW/OTHT).
2 *Suffren* with 1 × 2 *Masurca* SAM; plus 1
Malafon SUGW, 4 ASTT, 4 MM-38 *Exocet*, 2 ×
100mm guns.
1 *Du Chayla* with 1 × 1 *Standard* SM-1 MR SAM;
plus 2 × 3 ASTT.
FRIGATES: 36:
6 *Georges Leygues* with 2 *Lynx* hel (Mk 46 LWT),
2 × ASTT; plus 4 with 8 MM-40, 2 with 4
MM-38 *Exocet*, all with 1 × 100mm gun.
3 *Tourville* with 2 × *Lynx* hel, 1 *Malafon* SUGW, 2 ×
ASTT; plus 6 × MM-38 *Exocet*, 2 × 100mm guns.
2 T-56/T-53 weapons varied.
1 *Aconit* with *Malafon*, 2 × ASTT; plus 4 MM-38
Exocet, 2 × 100mm guns.
7 *Commandant Rivière* with 2 × 3 ASTT, 1 × 12
ASW mor; plus 6 with 4 × MM-38 *Exocet*, all
with 2 × 100mm guns.
17 *D'Estienne d'Orves* with 4 × ASTT, 1 × 6 ASW
mor; plus 3 with 2 × MM-38, 6 with 4 ×
MM-40 *Exocet*, all with 1 × 100mm gun.
PATROL AND COASTAL COMBATANTS: 24:
PATROL OFFSHORE:
1 *Albatros* PCO (Public Service Force)
COASTAL: 21:
10 *L'Audacieuse.*
8 *Léopard* PCC (trg).
2 *Sterne* PCC (Public Service Force).
1 *Mercure* PCC.
INSHORE: 2 *Athos* PCI.
MINE WARFARE: 24:
MINELAYERS: Nil, but submarines have capability.
MINE COUNTERMEASURES: 24:
10 *Eridan* tripartite MHC.
5 *Circé* MHC.
4 *Ouistreham* (US *Aggressive*) MSO.

1 *Cantho* (US *Aggressive*) MCO.
4 *Vulcain* MCM diver spt.

AMPHIBIOUS: 8:

2 *Ouragan* LPD: capacity 350 tps, 25 tk, 3 *Super Frelon* hel.
1 *Bougainville* LSD: capacity 500 men, 6 tk, 2 AS-332 hel: (assigned to spt DIRCEN nuclear test centre South Pacific).
5 *Champlain* LSM (*BATRAL*): capacity 140 tps, 7 tk. Plus craft: 8 LCT, 20 LCM.

SUPPORT AND MISCELLANEOUS: 38:

UNDERWAY SUPPORT: 7:
5 *Durance* AOR, 2 AO.

MAINTENANCE/LOGISTIC: 19:
1 AOT, 2 AOT (small), 1 *Jules Verne*, 5 *Rhin* maint/spt, 3 tpt, 7 tugs (4 civil charter).

SPECIAL PURPOSES: 5:
2 msl trials, 1 sonar trials, 1 mine warfare trials, 1 underwater trials.

SURVEY/RESEARCH: 5 AGHS, 2 AGOR

NAVAL AIR FORCE: (11,000).

NUCLEAR STRIKE: 3 flt with *Super Etendard* (AN-52 nuclear weapons).
FIGHTER: 1 flt with F-8E (FN) *Crusader*.
ASW: 2 flt with *Alizé* (mod).
MR: 6 flt, 4 with *Atlantic*, 2 with *Gardian*.
RECCE: 1 flt with *Etendard* IVP.
OCU: *Etendard* IVM; *Alizé*; *Zéphir*.
TRAINING: 5 units with N-262 *Frégate*, Piper *Navajo*, EMB-121 *Xingu*, MS-760 *Paris*, *Mystère-Falcon* 10MER, *Rallye* 880.
MISCELLANEOUS: 3 comms/liaison units (1 VIP) with *Falcon* 10MER, *Alizé*, N-262, *Xingu*, *Navajo*.
1 trial unit with N-2504.
2 lt ac units with 12 *Rallye* 880, 6 CAP-10.
ASW: 3 sqn with *Lynx*.
COMMANDO: 2 aslt sqn with SA-321.
TRAINING: *Alouette* II/III.
MISCELLANEOUS: 2 comms/SAR units with *Alouette* II/III, 1 trials unit with *Alouette* II/III, *Lynx* SA-321.
EQUIPMENT: 104 cbt ac (plus 40 in store); 24 armed hel.
AIRCRAFT:
Super Etendard: 40 (strike); 24 in store. Total of 53 to be mod for *ASMP*.
Etendard: 20. IVP: 8 (recce); IVM: 12 (trg). 12 in store (3 -P, 9 -M).
Crusader: 8 (ftr). 3 in store
Alizé: 28 (20 ASW, 8 trg). 6 in store.
Atlantic: 28 (MR); 2 -NG on trials.
Gardian: 5 (MR).
Zéphir: 12 (trg). **Nord 262:** 22 (12 trg, 10 misc). **Navajo:** 12 (2 trg, 10 misc). **Xingu:** 18 (13 trg, 5 misc). **Rallye 880:** 16 (4 trg, 12 misc). **CAP-10:** 10 (misc). **MS-760:** 8 (trg). **Falcon 10MER:** 8 (misc, trg).
HELICOPTERS:
Lynx: 38 (24 ASW, 14 SAR).
SA-321: 16 (13 cdo, 3 misc).
SA-313: 10 (2 trg, 8 misc).
SA-316/-319: 38 (10 trg, 28 misc).
ASM: AS-12/-20/-30, *Martel* AS-37, AM-39 *Exocet*.
AAM: R-530, R-550 *Magic, Sidewinder*.

MARINES: 2,600 (Fusiliers-Marins).
COMMANDO UNITS: (600).
4 Assault gp.
1 Attack Swimmer unit.
1 HQ section.
NAVAL BASE PROTECTION: 2,000.

PUBLIC SERVICE FORCE: Naval personnel, performing general coast guard, fishery, SAR and traffic surveillance duties; 2 *Sterne*, 1 *Mercure* patrol craft, 1 *Albatros* PCO, 3 N-262 ac, 1 SA-360 hel (ships included in naval patrol and coastal totals). Command exercised through 'Maritime Prefectures': No. 1 at Cherbourg, No. 2 at Brest, No. 3 at Toulon.

AIR FORCE: 94,100 (5,600 women, 35,900 conscripts), incl strategic and prestrategic forces.

AIR DEFENCE COMMAND (CAFDA): (7,150).
FIGHTER: 13 sqn:
8 with *Mirage* F-1C;
1 (OCU) with *Mirage* F-1C/B;
3 with *Mirage* 2000C.
1 (OCU) with *Mirage* 2000C/B.
TRAINING: 4 flt with CM-170,
CONTROL: automatic *STRIDA* II, 10 radar stations.
SAM: 12 sqn (1 trg) with 24 *Crotale* bty (48 fire, 24 radar units).
AA GUNS: 300 bty (20mm).

TACTICAL AIR FORCE (FATAC): (19,200).
FGA: 9 sqn plus 2 flt:
3 with *Mirage* IIIE;
2 flt with *Mirage* IIIE/B/BE.
2 with *Mirage* 5F;
4 with *Jaguar* A.
RECCE: 3 sqn with *Mirage* F-1CR.
TRAINING: 1 OCU sqn with *Jaguar* A/E; 6 trg flt with CM-170.
(Attached to Air Transport Command – see below):
EW: 2 sqn: 1 with C-160 ELINT/ESM ac, AS-330 hel; 1 with DC-8 ELINT.
LIAISON: 3 sqn with CM-170.
HELICOPTERS: 1 sqn with *Alouette* II/III.

AIR TRANSPORT COMMAND (COTAM): (4,000).
TRANSPORT: 19 sqn:
1 hy with DC-8F;
5 tac with C-160/-160NG/C-130H;
13 lt tpt/trg/SAR with C-160, N-262, *Falcon* 20, *Falcon* 50, *Falcon* 900, MS-760, DH-6, EMB-121.

TRAINING: 1 OCU with N-262, C-160.
MISCELLANEOUS: 4 sqn with DC-8, C-160, *Falcon* 20.
HELICOPTERS: 5 sqn with *Alouette* II/III, SA-330, AS-332, SA-365, AS-350.
TRAINING: 1 OCU with *Alouette* II/III, SA-330, AS-350.
TRAINING COMMAND (CEAA): (5,000).
TRAINING: *Alpha Jet*, CM-170, EMB-121, TB-30, CAP-10B/-20.
TRIALS (trials units): 1 sqn with *Mirage* F-1, *Mirage* 2000, *Jaguar;* 1 sqn with N-262.
EQUIPMENT: 598 cbt ac, (plus 30 in store), no armed hel.
AIRCRAFT:
Mirage: 413: **F-1B:** 14 (OCU); **F-1C:** 121 (ftr); **F-1CR:** 45 (recce); **IIIE:** 60 (45 FGA); **IIIB/BE:** 15 (trg); **-5F:** 30 (FGA); **IVA:** 5; **IVP:** 18 (bbr); **-2000B/C:** 75 (60 -C, 15 -B); **-2000N:** 30.
Jaguar: 122: **-A:** 102 (43 strike, 57 FGA, 2 trg); **-E:** 20 (trg).
Alpha Jet: 106 (trg).
DC-8: 6 (5 tpt, 1 EW).
C-130: 8. **-H:** 3 (tpt); **-H-30:** 5 (tpt).
C-135F/FR: 11 (tkr).
C-160: 68 (4 *Gabriel* ELINT/ESM, 2 *ASTARTE* comms, 35 tac tpt, 8 OCU, 22 -NG tac tpt).
N-262: 23 (20 lt tpt, 2 trg, 1 trials).
C-212: 5 (Flt Test Centre spt).
Falcon: 17. **-20:** 15 (misc), **-50:** 2 (misc). **MS-760:** 25 (misc). **DHC-6:** 10. **EMB-121:** 8 (6 tpt, 2 misc). **EMB-312:** 25 (6 lt tpt, 17 trg, 2 misc). **CM-170:** 188 (liaison, trg). **TB-30:** 98 (trg): **CAP-10B/20:** 55 (trg).
HELICOPTERS:
SA-313: 29 (incl 9 OCU).
SA-316: 33 (incl 9 OCU).
SA-330: 23 (20 tpt, 3 OCU).
AS-332: 5 (tpt).
SA-365: 3 (tpt). **AS-350:** 19 (tpt).
AAM: R-530, *Super* 530F, R-550 *Magic* 1/11, *Sidewinder.*
ASM: AS-30/-30L, *Martel* AS-37.

DEPLOYMENT:
NAVY:
Atlantic Fleet: (HQ, Brest): 6 SSBN, 7 SS, 1 CCH, 18 DD/FF, 10 MCM, 3 amph.
Channel Flotilla: (HQ, Cherbourg): 3 FF, 6 MCMV.
Mediterranean Fleet: (HQ, Toulon): 4 SSN, 4 SS, 2 carriers, 1 CG, 13 DD/FF, 8 MCMV.

FORCES ABROAD:
FRG: 52,700; 3 armd div (570 MBT, 150 155mm SP, 180 ATGW). Berlin: (2,700); 1 armd regt, 1 inf regt.
ANTILLES-GUYANA (HQ Cayenne): 8,200; 3 marine inf, 1 Foreign Legion regt, 3 ships (incl 1 amph), 1 *Atlantic* ac (Dakar, Senegal), 1 air tpt unit (C-160 ac, SA-330, SA-316/318, AS-350 hel).

INDIAN OCEAN (Mayotte, La Réunion): 3,300; incl 3 marine inf regt, 1 Foreign Legion coy, 1 air tpt unit (C-160 ac, *Alouette* III, SA-330 hel).
NAVY: Indian Ocean Squadron, Comd ALINDIEN (HQ afloat): (1,500); 3 FF, 4 patrol combatants, 1 amph, 3 spt (1 comd).
NEW CALEDONIA (HQ Noumea): 9,500; 1 marine inf regt, 2 inf gp, 3 inf coy, 1 air tpt unit (C-160 ac, *Alouette* III hel). Gendarmerie (3,200)
POLYNESIA (HQ Papeete): 5,400 (incl ALPACI); 1 marine, 1 Foreign Legion regt, 1 air tpt unit (*Caravelle, Gardian* ac; AS-332, *Alouette* III hel), Gendarmerie.
PACIFIC NAVAL SQUADRON (comd, ALPACI, HQ Noumea) (1,300); 3 FF, 4 patrol and coastal, 3 amph, some 6 spt, 4 *Gardian* MR ac.
CENTRAL AFRICAN REPUBLIC: 1,200:
GARRISON: 1 bn gp incl 1 motor coy; 1 pl AML armd cars (6); spt coy with O-1E lt ac, 120mm mor, *Milan* ATGW.
FROM FRANCE: 1 AML armd car sqn and 1 tp, 2 inf coy, 1 arty bty (105mm), 1 avn det (3 med tpt hel); air elm with cbt and tpt ac and hel;
CHAD: 1,700; 3 inf coy; AA arty units; cbt and tpt ac and hel.
DJIBOUTI: 3,650; 1 marine inf, 1 Foreign Legion, 1 arty regt; 1 ALAT det (5 med tpt hel); 1 sqn with 11 *Mirage* IIIC, 1 C-160 ac, 2 *Alouette* II, 1 *Alouette* III hel.
GABON: 550; 1 marine inf regt; *Jaguar,* 1 C-160, *Atlantic* ac, 1 *Alouette* III hel.
COTE D'IVOIRE: 920; 1 marine inf regt; 1 AS-350 hel.
SENEGAL: 1,150; 1 marine inf regt; Atlantic MR ac; 1 air tpt unit (C-160 tpt ac; *Alouette* II/III hel).
UN AND PEACE-KEEPING:
LEBANON (UNIFIL): 530; 1 log bn.
EGYPT (MFO): 40; incl 2 DHC-6, 1 C-160 tpt ac.

PARA-MILITARY:
GENDARMERIE: 87,200 (incl 1,400 women, 10,100 conscripts, 1,000 civilians); *Territorial* (52,800); *Mobile* (17,500), *Schools* (7,000); *Special Duties* (5,000), *Overseas* (3,200+); *Maritime* (1,200); *Air* (1,100). *Reserves* (130,000).
EQUIPMENT: 121 AML, 28 VBC-90 armd cars; 33 AMX-VTT, 155 VBRG-170 APC; 288 81mm mor; 15 PCI; 6 Cessna 206C ac; 8 *Alouette* II, 12 *Alouette* III, 22 AS-350 hel.

* A 5-year military development plan for 1988–92, totalling fr 850 bn, is being implemented.

GERMANY: FEDERAL REPUBLIC

GDP	1987:	DM 2,009.1 bn ($1,117.8 bn)
	1988:	DM 2,117.4 bn ($1,205.7 bn)
Growth	1987:	1.8% 1988: 3.5%

Inflation	1987:	0.3%	1988:	1.1%
Debt	1987:	$22.5 bn	1988:	$17.4 bn

Def bdgt* 1988: DM 51.22 bn ($29.17 bn);
NATO defn $35.40 bn
1989: DM 53.29 bn ($28.57 bn);
NATO defn $34.2 bn

$1 = DM (1987): 1.7974 (1988): 1.7562
(1989): 1.8653

DM = Deutschmark

Population: 61,214,000

	13–17	*18–22*	*23–32*
Men	1,568,000	2,318,000	5,336,000
Women	1,509,000	2,201,000	5,041,000

TOTAL ARMED FORCES:
ACTIVE: 494,300 (222,300 conscripts; 7,000
active Reserve trg posts, all Services) incl 11,600
inter-service staff, not listed below.
Terms of service: 15 months.
RESERVES: 852,000 (men to age 45,
officers/NCO to 60): Army 717,000, Navy 26,000,
Air 106,000, others 4,000.

ARMY: 340,700 (175,900 conscripts).
FIELD ARMY: 3 Corps, 12 div.
I Corps (NORTHAG):
3 armd, 1 armd inf div.
II Corps (CENTAG):
1 armd, 1 armd inf, 1 AB, 1 mtn div.
III Corps (CENTAG):
2 armd, 1 armd inf div.
1 armd inf div (LANDJUT).
(Armd div with 2 armd and 1 armd inf bde;
armd inf div with 2 armd inf and 1 armd bde;
mtn div with 1 armd, 1 armd inf and 1 mtn
bde; all with 1 armd recce bn, 1 arty regt (1 bn
each: 18 FH-70, 18 203mm, 16 110mm MRL),
1 AD regt (with 35mm *Gepard*), 1 avn sqn; AB
div with 3 AB bde.)
Corps Tps: 4 SSM bn each with 6 *Lance*;
3 AD comd (each 1 regt with 36 *Roland* and 2
eqpt holding bn 40mm L/70).
1 *Roland* SAM bn.
1 AD arty bn with *Gepard* 35mm.
3 avn bde each 1 lt (48 UH-1D), 1 med tpt (32
CH-539), 1 ATGW hel (56 Bo-105 *HOT*) regt.
TERRITORIAL ARMY (cadre): 41,700 in
peacetime;
Command Structure: 3 Territorial Comd (linked
with NATO cmd) 5 Military Districts, 29
Military Regions, 80 Sub-regions: Units (eqpt
holding only unless stated).
6 Home Defence bde with 2 armd, 2 armd inf,
1 arty bn plus full log spt (at 50–60% in
peacetime) (two assigned to field army div).

6 Home Defence bde with 1 armd, 2 armd inf,
1 arty bn.
1 German/French bde (still forming).
15 Home Defence regt with 3 mot inf bn, 18
120mm mor.
150 Home Defence coy, 300 Security pl.

EQUIPMENT:
MBT: 5,005: 650 M-48A2G (Territorial bn), 225
M-48 (in store), 2,130 *Leopard* 1A1 (1,339 to be
upgraded to A5), 2,000 *Leopard* 2.
RECCE: 410 SPz-2 *Luchs*, 140 TPz-1 *Fuchs* (NBC).
AIFV: 2,136 *Marder* A1 (2,100 to upgrade to A3).
APC: 856 TPz-1 *Fuchs*, 2,560 M-113, 220 M-577.
TOWED ARTY: 460: 105mm: 244 M-101; 155mm:
216 FH-70.
SP ARTY: 812: 155mm: 586 M-109A3; 203mm:
226 M-110A2.
MRL: 110mm: 209 *LARS*; 227mm: 6 MLRS (trg).
MORTARS: 120mm: 406 Brandt, 600 Tampella on
M-113.
SSM: 26 *Lance* launchers (incl 2 in store).
ATGW: 1,975 *Milan*, 205 *TOW*, 316 RJPz-(*HOT*)
Jaguar 1, 162 RJPz-(*TOW*) SP.
RCL: 106mm: 99 (in store).
ATK GUNS: 90mm: 120 JPz-4-5 SP.
AD GUNS: 2,396: 20mm: 1,762 Rh 202 towed;
35mm: 432 *Gepard* SP; 40mm: 202 L/70.
SAM: 658 *Fliegerfaust* 1 (*Redeye*), 143 *Roland* SP.
HELICOPTERS:
210 PAH-1 (Bo-105 with *HOT*), 87 UH-1D, 108
CH-53G, 97 Bo-105M, 138 SA-313.
MARINE: (River Engineers): 36 LCM, 12 PCI (river)⟨.

NAVY: 36,000 incl naval air (9,900 conscripts).
BASES: Glücksburg (Maritime HQ). Baltic:
Eckernförde, Flensburg, Kiel, Olpenitz, Neustadt.
North Sea: Borkum, Bremerhaven, Cuxhaven,
Emden, Wilhelmshaven.
SUBMARINES: 24:
18 Type 206/206A SSC with *Seal* DM2 533mm
HWT (2 conversions to T-206A complete).
6 Type 205 SSC with DM3 HWT.
PRINCIPAL SURFACE COMBATANTS: 14:
DESTROYERS: 7:
DDG: 3 *Lütjens* (mod US *Adams*) with 1 × 1 SM-1
MR SAM/*Harpoon* SSM launcher, 2 × 127mm
guns; plus 1 × 8 *ASROC* (Mk 46 LWT), 2 × 3 ASTT.
DD: 4 *Hamburg* (ASUW) with 2 × 2 MM-38 *Exocet*,
4 × 533mm TT (SUT), 3 × 100mm guns.
FRIGATES: 7:
6 *Bremen* with 2 *Lynx* hel (ASW/OTHT), 2 × 2
ASTT; plus 2 × 4 *Harpoon*.
1 *Deutschland* (trg) with 4 × 533mm TT, 2 × 4
ASW mor, 4 × 100mm guns.
PATROL AND COASTAL COMBATANTS: 45:
CORVETTES: 5 *Thetis* (ASW) with 1 × 4 ASW RL, 4 ×
533mm TT.
MISSILE CRAFT: 40:

20 *Albatros/Gepard* (Type 143/143A) PFM with 2 × 2 *Exocet*, 10 (T-143) with 2 × 533mm TT.

20 *Tiger* (Type 148) PFM with 2 × 2 MM-38 *Exocet*.

MINE WARFARE: 56:

MINELAYERS 2 *Sachsenwald* (600+ mines).

MINE COUNTERMEASURES: 54:

2 *Hameln* (T-343) comb ML/MCC.

6 *Lindau* 'Troika' MSC control and guidance, each with 3 unmanned sweep craft.

12 converted *Lindau* (T-331) MHC.

14 *Schütze* (T-340/-341) comb ML/MSC.

18 *Ariadne/Frauenlob* MSI.

2 MCM diver spt ships.

AMPHIBIOUS: Craft only; some 20 LCU.

SUPPORT AND MISCELLANEOUS: 51:

UNDERWAY SUPPORT: 4:

2 *Spessart*, 2 *Eifel* AO.

MAINTENANCE/LOGISTIC: 35:

2 AR, 9 *Rhein* SS/MCMV spt, 5 small (2,000-tonne) AOT, 8 *Lüneburg* logistic spt, 2 AE, 8 tugs, 1 icebreaker (civil).

SPECIAL PURPOSE: 9:

3 AGI, 2 trials, 3 multi-purpose (T-748), 1 trg.

RESEARCH AND SURVEY: 3:

1 AGOR, 2 AGHS (civil-manned for Ministry of Transport).

NAVAL AIR ARM:

4 wings, 9 sqn:

2 wings with *Tornado*.

1 MR/ASW wing with *Atlantic, Lynx*.

1 SAR/liaison wing with Do-28, *Sea King*.

FGA: 3 sqn with *Tornado*.

FGA/RECCE: 1 sqn with *Tornado*.

MR/ELINT: 2 sqn with *Atlantic*.

LIAISON: 1 sqn with Do-28-D2.

ASW: 1 sqn with *Sea Lynx* Mk 88 hel.

SAR: 1 sqn with *Sea King* Mk 41 hel.

EQUIPMENT: 109 cbt ac, 19 armed hel.

AIRCRAFT:

Tornado: 95 (69 FGA, 18 FGA/recce, 8 trg).

Atlantic: 19 (14 MR, 5 ELINT).

Do-28: 19 (17 SAR, liaison; 2 environmental protection).

HELICOPTERS:

Sea Lynx: 19 (ASW).

Sea King: 22 (SAR).

ASM: *Kormoran*.

AIR FORCE: 106,000 (36,500 conscripts).

TACTICAL COMMAND (GAFTAC).

4 air div: 2 tac, 2 AD.

FGA: 11 wings, 21 sqn:

5 wings with *Tornado*.

2 with F-4F.

4 with *Alpha Jet*.

FIGHTER: 2 wings with F-4F.

RECCE: 2 wings with RF-4E.

EW: 1 trg sqn with HFB-320 *Hansa Jet*.

SSM: 8 sqn with *Pershing* IA.

SAM: 4 wing (each 6 sqn) *Patriot*, being deployed; 9 wing (each 4 sqn) *HAWK*; 11 sqn *Roland* being deployed.

RADAR: 2 tac Air Control Commands: 10 sites; 3 remote radars.

AAM: *Sidewinder*.

ASM: AS-20.

TRANSPORT COMMAND (GAFTC).

TRANSPORT: 3 wings: 6 sqn with Transall C-160, incl 1 (OCU) with C-160, Do-28.

1 special air mission wing with Boeing 707-320C, VFW-614, CL-601, Do-28 ac; UH-1D hel (VIP).

HELICOPTERS: 1 wing: 3 sqn; plus 1 det with UH-1D (liaison/SAR).

TRAINING COMMAND:

FGA: 1 det (Cottesmore, UK) with *Tornado*; 1 OCU (Beja, Portugal) with *Alpha Jet*.

FIGHTER: OCU (George AFB, US) with F-4E.

TRAINING: NATO joint pilot trg (Sheppard AFB, US) with T-37B, T-38A; primary trg sqn with P-149D.

LIAISON: base flt with Do-28D.

EQUIPMENT: 507 cbt ac (plus 8 trg (overseas), 21 in store), no armed hel.

AIRCRAFT:

F-4: 224. **-F:** 144 (FGA, ftr); **-E:** 8 (OCU, in US); **RF-4E:** 72 (recce).

Tornado: 198 (176 FGA, 22 in tri-national trg sqn, (in UK)); plus 18 in store.

Alpha Jet: 165 (147 FGA, 18 wpn trg (in Portugal)); plus 3 in store.

Transall C-160: 84 (tpt, trg).

Boeing 707: 4 (VIP). **VFW-614:** 3 (VIP). **CL-601:** 7 (VIP). **Do-28-D2:** 60 (6 VIP, 54 tpt, liaison).

T-37B: 35. **T-38A:** 41. **P-149D:** 31 (trg).

HELICOPTERS:

UH-1D: 110 (106 SAR, tpt, liaison; 4 VIP).

MISSILES:

SSM: 72 *Pershing* IA.

ASM: *Maverick*.

SAM: 216 *HAWK* launchers; ε 34 *Roland* (68 by 1991).

FORCES ABROAD:

NAVY: 1 DDG, 1 FF, 1 AO in Mediterranean on 3-month roulement with some gaps (about 70% cover).

PARA-MILITARY:

FEDERAL BORDER GUARD (Ministry of Interior): 20,000; 5 cmd (constitutionally has no combat status). Eqpt: *MOWAG* SW-1/-2 APC; 2 P-149D, 1 Do-27 ac; Bo-105M, 32 *Alouette* II, 13 UH-1D, 10 Bell 212, 22 *Puma* hel.

COAST GUARD: 1,000; 1 inshore tug, 8 PCI.

FOREIGN FORCES:

NATO:

HQ Northern Army Gp (NORTHAG).

HQ Central Army Gp (CENTAG).

HQ Allied Air Forces Central Europe.

HQ 2 Allied Tactical Air Force (2 ATAF).

HQ 4 Allied Tactical Air Force (4 ATAF).

BELGIUM: 26,600; 1 corps HQ, 1 div HQ; 1 armd, 1 mech inf bde (NORTHAG).

CANADA: 7,100; 1 mech bde gp. 1 tac hel sqn. 1 Air Group with 3 FGA sqn (CENTAG/4 ATAF).

FRANCE: 52,700; 1 corps HQ, 3 armd div. Berlin: (2,700), 1 armd, 1 inf regt.

NETHERLANDS: 5,700; 1 armd bde (NORTHAG)

UNITED KINGDOM: 69,700; 1 corps HQ, 3 armd div, 13 ac sqn (NORTHAG/2 ATAF). Berlin: (3,000), 1 inf bde.

US: 239,200. 1 army HQ, 2 corps HQ; 2 armd, 2 mech div; 1 armd, 1 mech bde. 1 Air Force HQ; 2 air div (CENTAG/4 ATAF). Berlin: 4,300, 1 inf bde.

---

* Excl Berlin support costs, which amounted to DM 16.7 bn in 1988, and an ε DM 17.2 bn in 1989.

GREECE

GDP	1987:	dr 6,389.5 bn ($47.18 bn)	
	1988:	dr 7,347.9 bn ($51.8 bn)	
Growth	1987:	−0.4%	1988: 1.2%
Inflation	1987:	16.4%	1988: 13.5%
Debt	1987:	$18.0 bn	1988: $20.5 bn
Def bdgt	1988:	dr 353 bn ($2.49 bn)	
		NATO defn $3.47 bn	
	1989:	dr 611 bn ($3.89 bn)	
		NATO defn n.a.	
FMA	1988:	$382.95 m (US, FRG)	
$1 = dr	(1987):	135.43	(1988): 141.86
	(1989):	157.50	
dr = drachmas			

Population: 10,105,000

	13–17	18–22	23–32
Men	313,000	602,000	722,000
Women	360,000	381,000	708,000

TOTAL ARMED FORCES:

ACTIVE: 208,500 (143,500 conscripts, 1,800 women).

Terms of service: Army 20, Navy 24, Air Force 22 months.

RESERVES: some 406,000 (to age 50). Army some 350,000 (Field Army 230,000, Territorial Army/National Guard 120,000); Navy about 24,000; Air about 32,000.

ARMY: 160,000 (115,000 conscripts, 1,400 women).

FIELD ARMY 135,500: 3 Military Regions.

4 corps HQ.

1 armd div (3 armd bde, 1 SP arty regt) Cat A.

1 mech div (2 mech, 1 armd bde, 1 SP arty regt) Cat A.

10 inf div (3 inf bde, 1 arty regt, 1 armd bn) 2 Cat A, 3 Cat B, 5 Cat C.

1 para-cdo div (1 para (2 bn), 2 cdo regt (6 bn), 1 raider bn) Cat A.

4 indep armd bde (each 2 armd, 1 mech inf, 1 SP arty bn, 1 armd recce sqn) Cat A.

1 indep mech bde (2 mech, 1 armd, 1 SP arty bn, 1 armd recce sqn) Cat A.

1 marine bde (3 inf, 1 lt arty bn, 1 armd sqn) Cat A.

4 armd bn.

15 fd arty bn (12 corps, 3 indep).

8 AD arty bn.

2 SAM bn with *Improved HAWK*.

3 army avn bn.

1 indep avn coy.

Units are manned at 3 different levels: Cat A 85% fully ready, Cat B 60% ready in 24 hours, Cat C 20% ready in 48 hours.

TERRITORIAL ARMY: 24,500 (incl 13,250 National Guard cadre, plus 5,000 reservists on refresher trg). 2 Territorial, 17 Sub-Commands.

ACTIVE: 1 lt inf bde (3 inf, 1 mtn arty bn) Cat A.

5 lt inf regt (each 2 inf, 1 mtn arty bn) 1 Cat A, 4 Cat B.

RESERVES (National Guard): 120,000. Role: coastal and island def. All Cat C.

28 inf bde (each 3 inf, 1 lt arty bn).

5 lt inf bde (each 3 inf, 1 mtn arty bn).

EQUIPMENT:

MBT: 1,941: 108 M-26, 359 M-47, 1,175 M-48 (300 -A2, 600 -A3, 275 -A5), 190 AMX-30, 109 *Leopard* 1A3.

LIGHT TANKS: 278: 170 M-24, 108 M-41A3.

RECCE: 210: 180 M-8, 30 M-20.

AIFV: 180 AMX-10P.

APC: 2,283: 300 *Leonidas*, 114 M-2, 403 M-3 half-track, 432 M-59, 1,034 M-113.

TOWED ARTY: 1,050: 105mm: 150 M-56 pack, 306 M-101, 180 M-102; 155mm: 72 M-59, 240 M-114, 58 M-198; 203mm: 44 M-115 (4 in store).

SP ARTY: 334: 105mm: 108 M-52; 155mm: 36 M-44, 90 M-109, 36 M-53; 175mm: 36 M-107; 203mm: 24 M-110, 4 M-55.

MORTARS: 81mm, 107mm: M-2, M-30, M-84 SP (M-59 APC), M-106A1 SP; 120mm: EBO Type E-56, *Leonidas* Gr W.2 SP.

ATGW: 82 M-113A2 SP *TOW*, 54 M-901 SP *Improved TOW*, SS-11, *Cobra*, *TOW*, 84 *Milan* (incl 12 AMX-10 SP).

RCL: 57mm: 900 M-18; 75mm: 400 M-20; 90mm: 1,080 EM-67; 106mm: 672 M-40A1; 112mm: some EBO ARIS-4.

AD GUNS: 995: 20mm: 100 Rh-202 twin; 30mm: 24 *Artemis* 30 twin; 40mm: 400 M-1, 150 L/70, 101 M-42A twin SP; 75mm: 110 M-51; 90mm: 110 M-117/-118.

SAM: 42 *Improved HAWK*, 37 M-48 *Chaparral*, *Redeye*.

AIRCRAFT: 2 *Super King Air*, 2 *Aero Commander*, 1 DHC-2, 50 U-17A.

HELICOPTERS: 10 AH-1 with *TOW*, 5 Bell 47G, 64 UH-1 (14 -D, 50 -H), 3 AB-204B, 43 AB-205A, 15 AB-206A, 1 AB-212, 1 A-109, 8 CH-47C, 20 NH-300.

NAVY: 20,500 (12,000 conscripts, 200 women);
BASES: Salamis, Patras, Soudha Bay.
SUBMARINES: 10:
    8 *Glavkos* (FRG T-209/1100) with 533mm TT.
    2 *Katsonis* (US *Guppy*) with 533mm TT.
PRINCIPAL SURFACE COMBATANTS: 21:
DESTROYERS: 14:
    7 *Themistocles* (US *Gearing*) with 1 × 8 *ASROC*, 2 × 3 ASTT, 1 with AB-212 hel; plus 3 × 2 127mm guns (2 being refitted to incl 2 × 4 *Harpoon* SSM).
    1 *Miaoulis* (US *Sumner*) with AB-212 hel, 2 × 3 ASTT; plus 3 × 2 127mm guns.
    6 *Aspis* (US *Fletcher*) with 2 × 3 ASTT; plus 4 × 127mm guns.
FRIGATES: 7:
    2 *Elli* (Nl *Kortenaer*) with 2 AB-212 hel, 2 × 3 ASTT; plus 2 × 4 *Harpoon*
    4 *Aetos* (US *Cannon*) with 2 × 3 ASTT.
    1 *Aegeon* (FRG *Rhein* AD) with 2 × 3 ASTT, 2 × 100mm gun.
PATROL AND COASTAL COMBATANTS: 35:
MISSILE CRAFT: 16:
    14 *Laskos* (Fr *Combattante*) PFM, 8 with 4 × MM-38 *Exocet*, 6 with 6 *Penguin* 2 SSM, all with 2 × 533mm TT.
    2 *Stamou*⟨, with 4 × SS-12 SSM.
TORPEDO CRAFT: 9:
    5 *Hesperos* (FRG *Jaguar*) PFT with 4 × 533mm TT.
    4 No '*Nasty*' PFT⟨ with 4 × 533mm TT.
PATROL: 10 PCI⟨.
MINE WARFARE: 16:
MINELAYERS: 2 *Aktion* (US LSM-1) (100–130 mines).
MINE COUNTERMEASURES: 14:
    9 *Alkyon* (US MSC-294) MSC.
    5 *Atalanti* (US *Adjutant*) MSC.
AMPHIBIOUS: 13:
    1 *Nafkratoussa* (US *Cabildo*) LSD: capacity 200 tps, 18 tk, 1 hel.
    2 *Inouse* (US *County*) LST: capacity 400 tps, 18 tk.
    5 *Ikaria* (US LST-510): capacity 200 tps, 16 tk.
    5 *Ipopliarhos Grigoropoulos* (US LSM-1) LSM, capacity 50 tps, 4 tk.
    Plus about 70 craft: 2 LCT, 6 LCU, 13 LCM, some 50 LCVP.

SUPPORT AND MISCELLANEOUS: 5:
    2 AOT, 1 watercarrier, 1 trg, 1 AE.
NAVAL AIR: 15 armed hel.
ASW: 1 hel div: 3 sqn:
    2 with 14 AB-212 (11 ASW, 3 ECM);
    1 with 4 SA-319 (with ASM).

AIR FORCE: 28,000 (16,000 conscripts, 200 women).
TACTICAL AIR FORCE: 7 cbt wings, 1 tpt wing.
FGA: 10 sqn:
    3 with A-7H.
    3 with F-104G.
    2 with F-5A/B (to convert to F-16C/D).
    2 with F-4E.
    Deliveries of 40 F-16 to be complete by end 1989.
FIGHTER: 5 sqn:
    1 with F-4E.
    1 with F-5A/B.
    2 with *Mirage* F-1CG.
    1 with *Mirage* 2000E/D.
    Deliveries of *Mirage* 2000 continue.
RECCE: 3 sqn:
    1 with RF-84F, RF-4E.
    1 with RF-5A.
    1 with RF-104G/F-104G/TF-104G.
MR: 1 sqn with HU-16B.
TRANSPORT: 3 sqn with C-130H, YS-11, N-2501, C-47, Do-28, *Gulfstream*.
LIAISON: T-33A.
HELICOPTERS: 3 sqn with AB-205A, AB-206A, Bell 47G, UH-1D, AB-212, CH-47C.
AD: 1 bn with *Nike Hercules* SAM (36 launchers). 20 bty with *Skyguard/Sparrow* SAM, twin 35mm guns.
AIR TRAINING COMMAND:
TRAINING: 4 sqn:
    1 with T-41A; 1 with T-37B/C; 2 with T-2E.
HELICOPTERS: 2 NH-300.
EQUIPMENT: 330 cbt ac (plus 35 in store), no armed hel.
AIRCRAFT:
A-7H: 54. 49 (FGA); plus 4 in store; **TA-7H:** 5 (FGA).
F-104: 80. **F-104G:** 60 (FGA); plus 6 in store; **TF-104G:** 8 (FGA); **RF-104G:** 12 (recce).
F-5: 68; plus 13 in store: **-A:** 60 (36 FGA, 24 ftr); **-B:** 8 (4 FGA, 4 ftr); plus 13 (10 -A, 3 -B) in store.
F-4: 57. **-E:** 45 (30 FGA, 15 ftr; plus 4 in store); **RF-4E:** 12 (recce).
F-16: some, delivery started Nov 1988.
***Mirage* F-1GC:** 33 (ftr); plus 4 in store.
***Mirage* 2000 E/D:** some.
RF-84: 8 (recce).
HU-16B: 12 (8 MR; 4 being updated). **C-130H:** 14 (tpt). **YS-11-200:** 5 (tpt). **C-47:** 16 (tpt). **CL-215:** 14 (tpt, fire-fighting). **Do-28:** 11 (lt tpt). ***Gulfstream* I:** 1 (VIP tpt). **T-33A:** 58 (liaison). **T-41:** 20 (trg). **T-37:** 25 (trg). **T-2:** 36 (trg).
HELICOPTERS:

AB-205A: 11 (tpt). **AB-206A:** 2 (tpt). **Bell 47G:** 15 (tpt). **AB-212:** 4 (tpt). **CH-47C:** 8 (tpt). **NH-300:** 2 (trg).

MISSILES:

AAM: AIM-7 *Sparrow*, AIM-9 *Sidewinder*, R-550 *Magic*.

ASM: AGM-65 *Maverick*.

SAM: 36 *Nike Hercules*; 40 *Sparrow*.

FORCES ABROAD:

CYPRUS: 3,950. 1 inf bn, 1 cdo bn, spt elm; officers/NCO seconded to Greek-Cypriot forces.

PARA-MILITARY:

GENDARMERIE: 26,500; MOWAG *Roland*, 15 UR-416 APC.

COAST GUARD AND CUSTOMS: 4,000; some 100 patrol craft, 2 Cessna *Cutlass*, 2 TB-20 *Trinidad* ac.

FOREIGN FORCES:

US: 3,300 incl 2 air base gp.

ICELAND

GDP	1987:	K 207.46 bn ($5.364 bn)	
	1988:	K 253.34 bn ($5.890 bn)	
Growth	1987:	8.7%	1988: −2.4%
Inflation	1987:	18.7%	1988: 37.5%
Debt	1987:	$1.0 bn	1988: $1.1 bn
$1 = K	1987:	38.677	1988: 43.014
K = Kronur			

Population: 250,000

	13–17	*18–22*	*23–32*
Men	11,000	11,000	22,000
Women	10,000	11,000	21,000

ARMED FORCES: None.

PARA-MILITARY: 150

COAST GUARD: 150:

BASE: Reykjavik

PATROL CRAFT: 4:

2 *Gyr*, 1 *Odinn* PCO with hel deck, 1 *Arvakur* PCO.

AVIATION: 1 F-27 ac, 1 SA-360.

FOREIGN FORCES:

NATO: Island Commander Iceland (ISCOMICE).

US:

NAVY: 1,800

MR: 1 sqn with 9 P-3C.

Comms facilities

AIR FORCE: 1,300

FIGHTER: 1 sqn with 18 F-15

NETHERLANDS:

NAVY: 30, 1 P-3C.

ITALY

GDP	1987:	L 982.59 bn ($758.11 bn)		
	1988:	L 1061.20 bn ($815.30 bn)		
Growth	1987:	3.1%	1988:	2.5%
Inflation	1987:	4.7%	1988:	5.0%
Debt	1987:	$97.5 bn	1988:	$105 bn
Def bdgt*	1988:	L 21,000 bn ($16.13 bn);		
		NATO defn $19.17 bn		
	1989:	L 23,000 bn ($16.22 bn);		
		NATO defn n.a.		
$1 = L	(1987):	1,296.1	(1988):	1,301.6
	(1989):	1,412.3		
L = lire				

Population: 57,587,000

	13–17	*18–22*	*23–32*
Men	2,147,000	2,364,000	4,481,000
Women	2,042,000	2,268,000	4,365,000

TOTAL ARMED FORCES:

ACTIVE: 390,000 (272,500 conscripts).

Terms of service: All services 12 months

RESERVES: 584,000. Army 520,000 (obligation to age 45), immediate mob 240,000.

Navy 36,000 (to age 39 for men, variable for officers to 73). Air 28,000 (to age 25 or 45 (specialists)).

ARMY: 265,000 (215,000 conscripts).

7 Military Regions.

FIELD ARMY:

3 Corps HQ (1 mtn):

1 with 4 mech, 3 armd bde, 1 hy corps spt bde (1 *Lance* SSM, 1 hy arty bn).

1 with 4 mech, 1 armd, 1 mot bde, 1 arty bn.

1 with 5 mtn bde, 1 arty bn.

1 armd cav bn.

1 AD gp: 6 AD arty (1 trg), 4 *HAWK* SAM bn.

Avn: 4 wings org in sqn and flt (flt usually has 6 ac/hel):

9 lt ac flt with SM-1019/Cessna O-1E.

12 hel sqn, 14 flt with AB-206.

Multi-role: 15 hel sqn: 1 with AB-204B; 12 with AB-205; 2 with AB-212B.

Med tpt: 4 hel sqn with CH-47.

TERRITORIAL DEFENCE:

2 indep mech bde (each 3 mech, 1 tk bn).

2 indep mot bde.

Rapid Intervention Force (*FIR*):

1 AB bde (incl 1 SF bn), 1 mot bde, 1 Marine bn (see Navy), 1

hel unit (Army), 1 air tpt unit (Air Force).

1 amph regt (2 *Lagunari* bn).

1 armd bn.

3 inf bn.

3 engr bn.

29 inf trg bn.

RESERVES: Immediate recall, formed from schools; 1 mtn, 1 mech, 1 armd bde.

On mob: 1 inf bde, 1 armd, 3 inf, 7 arty bn.

EQUIPMENT:

MBT: 1,720: 500 M-47 (incl 200 in reserve), 300 M-60A1, 920 *Leopard*.

APC: 4,786: 421 M-106, 2,486 M-113, 211 M-548, 199 M-577, 1,469 VCC1/-2.

TOWED ARTY: 970: 105mm: 360 Model 56 pack; 155mm: 164 FH-70, 423 M-114; 203mm: 23 M-115.

SP ARTY: 278: 155mm: 260 M-109G/-L; 203mm: 18 M-110A2.

MRL: 122mm: 7 FIROS-30; 227mm: 2 MLRS.

MORTARS: 81mm: 1,205; 120mm: 1,950 M-20.

SSM: 6 *Lance* launchers.

ATGW: 432 *TOW*, 270 M-113 with *TOW*, 1,000 *Milan*.

RL: 500 *APILAS*.

RCL: 80mm: 800 *Folgore*.

AD GUNS: 25mm: 35 SP (M-113); 40mm: 252.

SAM: 126 *HAWK*, 150 *Stinger*.

AIRCRAFT: 91: 59 SM-1019, 32 O-1E (target acquisition/utility).

HELICOPTERS: 326: 22 A-47G/J, 21 A-109, 92 AB-205A, 136 AB-206 (observation), 14 AB-212, 11 AB-412, 30 CH-47C.

NAVY: 52,000 incl 1,500 air arm, 600 special forces and 800 marines; (27,500 conscripts).

BASES: La Spezia (HQ), Taranto (HQ), Ancona, Brindisi, Augusta, Messina, La Maddalena, Cagliari, Naples, Venice.

SUBMARINES: 10:

2 *Pelosi* (imp *Sauro*) with Type 184 HWT.

4 *Sauro* with Type 184 HWT.

4 *Toti* SSC with Type 184 HWT.

PRINCIPAL SURFACE COMBATANTS: 30:

CARRIER: 1:

1 *G. Garibaldi* CVV with 16 SH-3 *Sea King* hel, 4 *Teseo* SSM, 2 × 3 ASTT (has capability to operate V/STOL ac not yet acquired).

CRUISERS: 3:

1 *Vittorio Veneto* CGH with 1 × 2 SM-1 MR SAM, 6 AB-212 ASW hel (Mk 46 LWT); plus 4 *Teseo* SSM, 2 × 3 ASTT.

2 *Andrea Doria* CGH, with 1 × 2 SM-1 MR SAM, 3 AB-212 hel; plus 2 × 3 ASTT.

DESTROYERS: 4:

2 *Audace* DDGH, with 1 × SM-1 MR SAM, 4 *Teseo* SSM, plus 2 × AB-212 hel, 1 × 127mm gun, 2 × 3 ASTT.

2 *Impavido* DDG with 1 SM-1 MR SAM; plus 1 × 2 127mm guns, 2 × 3 ASTT.

FRIGATES: 22:

8 *Maestrale* FFH with 2 AB-212 hel, 2 × 533mm DP TT; plus 4 *Teseo* SSM, 1 × 127mm gun.

4 *Lupo* FF with 1 AB-212 hel, 2 × 3 ASTT; plus 8 *Teseo* SSM, 1 × 127mm gun.

2 *Alpino* with 1 AB-212 hel, 2 × 3 ASTT, 1 × ASW mor.

4 *Minerva* with 2 × 3 ASTT.

4 *De Cristofaro* with 2 × 3 ASTT, 1 ASW mor.

PATROL AND COASTAL COMBATANTS: 13:

CORVETTES: 3:

3 *Albatros* with 2 × 3 ASTT.

MISSILE CRAFT: 7 *Sparviero* PHM with 2 *Teseo* SSM.

PATROL OFFSHORE: 3 *Cassiopea* with 1 AB-212 hel.

MINE WARFARE: 15:

MCMV: 15:

4 *Storione* (US *Aggressive*) MSO.

4 *Lerici* MHC.

2 *Castagno* (US *Adjutant*) MHC.

5 *Agave* MSC.

AMPHIBIOUS: 2:

2 *San Giorgio* LPD: capacity 500 tps, 10 tk, 5 CH-47 hel.

Plus 33 craft: 4 LCU, 21 LCVP, 8 LCVP.

SUPPORT AND MISCELLANEOUS: 24:

2 *Stromboli* AOR, 9 tugs, 5 water tankers, 3 trials, 2 trg, 3 AGOR.

SPECIAL FORCES (600) (*Comando Subacquei Incursori* – COMSUBIN):

6 gp; 2 assigned aslt swimmer craft; 2 raiding ops; 1 underwater ops; 1 SF; 1 school; 1 research.

MARINES (San Marco gp) (800):

1 bn gp.

1 trg gp.

1 log gp.

EQUIPMENT: 30 VCC-1, 10 LVTP-7 APC, 16 81mm mor, 8 106mm RCL, 6 *Milan* ATGW.

NAVAL AIR ARM (1,500); 98 armed hel.

ASW: 5 hel sqn with 36 SH-3D, 62 AB-212.

ASM: *Marte* Mk 2.

AIR FORCE: 73,000 (30,000 conscripts).

FGA: 7 FGA/recce sqn:

3 with *Tornado*;

2 with F-104S (being modernized);

2 with G-91Y.

CAS: 3 sqn:

1 lt attack with MB-339;

2 lt attack/recce with G-91R/R1/R1A (to be replaced).

FIGHTER: 7 sqn with F-104S.

RECCE: 2 sqn with F/RF-104G.

MR: 2 sqn with *Atlantic* (Navy-assigned; to be modernized).

EW: 1 ECM/recce sqn with G-222VS, PD-808.
CALIBRATION: 1 navigation-aid calibration sqn with
G-222RM, PD-808, MB-339.
TRANSPORT: 3 sqn: 2 with G-222; 1 with C-130H.
COMMUNICATIONS: 1 sqn with *Gulfstream* III,
Falcon 50, P-166M, SIAI-208M, PD-808,
MB-326, DC-9 ac; SH-3D hel.
TRAINING: 1 OCU with TF-104G;
1 det (Cottesmore, UK) with *Tornado*;
6 sqn with G-91, MB-339A, SF-260M ac;
AB-47 hel.
SAR: 1 sqn and 3 det with HH-3F.
6 det with AB-212.
AD: 8 SAM gp with *Nike Hercules*;
5 SAM bty with *Spada*.
EQUIPMENT: 390 cbt ac (plus 78 in store), no
armed hel.
AIRCRAFT:
Tornado: 64 (54 FGA, 10 in tri-national trg sqn);
plus 34 in store.
F-104: 156. **-S:** 102 (18 FGA, 84 ftr); **RF-104G:**
30 (recce); **TF-104G:** 24 (OCU); plus 19 in store.
G-91: 116. **-Y:** 35 (FGA); **-R:** 36 (lt attack/recce); **-T:**
45 (trg); plus 25 in store.
MB-339: 85 (15 tac, 65 trg, 5 calibration).
Atlantic: 18 (MR).
MB-326: 30 (liaison).
C-130: 10 (tpt); **G-222:** 38 (34 tpt, 4 calibration);
-VS: 2 (ECM); **DC-9:** 2 (VIP); *Gulfstream* **III:** 2
(VIP); *Falcon* **50:** 2 (VIP); **P-166:** 42: **-M:** 36
(liaison, trg); **-DL3:** 6 (survey); **PD-808:** 22 (8
ECM, 6 calibration, 8 VIP tpt); **SF-260:** 30 (trg).
SIAI-208: 36 (liaison).
HELICOPTERS:
HH-3F: 30 (SAR).
SH-3D: 2 (liaison).
AB-212: 35 (SAR).
AB-412: 4.
AB-47: 20 (trg).
MISSILES:
AAM: AIM-7E *Sparrow*, AIM-9B/L *Sidewinder*.
ASM: AS-20, *Kormoran*, AGM-65 *Maverick*.
SAM: 96 *Nike Hercules*, *Spada*.

FORCES ABROAD:
EGYPT (Sinai MFO): (90); 3 minesweepers.
LEBANON (UNIFIL): (51).
NAMIBIA (UNTAG): (94).

PARA-MILITARY:
CARABINIERI 105,000: Territorial: 9 bde, 24
legions, 100 gp. Mobile def: 1 mech bde, 13 bn, 1
AB bn, 2 cav sqn, avn and naval units.
EQUIPMENT: 37 M-47 MBT; Fiat 6616, 80 M-6, M-8
armd cars; 470 Fiat 242/18AD, 240 M-113 APC;
23 AB-47, 2 A-109, 5 AB-205, 23 AB-206 hel.
PUBLIC SECURITY GUARD (Ministry of Interior):
80,400: 11 mobile units; 40 Fiat 6614 APC, 3

P-64B, 5 P-68 ac; 1 AB-47, 12 A-109, 20 AB-206,
9 AB-212 hel.
FINANCE GUARDS (Treasury Department):
53,000; 11 Zones, 20 Legions, 120 Gps; 10
A-109, 68 Nardi-Hughes (40 NH-500C, 16 -D, 12
-M) hel; 3 PCI, 65⟨; plus about 300 boats.
HARBOUR CONTROL (*Capitanerie di Porto*)
(Subordinated to Navy in emergencies):
Some 25 PCI⟨, 100 + boats.

FOREIGN FORCES:
NATO:
HQ Allied Forces Southern Europe, Naples.
US: 15,000. Army (3,900); 1 AB bn gp; Navy
(5,200); Air (5,800); 1 tac, 1 air base gp.

* Excl budget for Carabinieri.

LUXEMBOURG

GDP	1987:	fr 222.52 ($6.05 bn)		
	1988:	fr 240.99 bn ($6.17 bn)		
Growth	1987:	3.7%	1988:	3.0%
Inflation	1987:	−0.14%	1988:	1.6%
Debt	1987:	$485 m	1988:	$421 m
Def exp	1988:	fr 2,729 bn ($74.22 m)		
		NATO defn $81.38 m		
Def bdgt	1989:	fr 3.163 bn ($80.39 m)		
		NATO defn n.a.		
$1 = fr	(1987):	37.334	(1988):	36.768
	(1989):	39.084		

fr = Luxembourg francs

Population: 369,000

	13–17	18–22	23–32
Men	12,000	14,000	30,500
Women	11,000	13,000	30,400

TOTAL ARMED FORCES:
ACTIVE: 800.
Terms of service: voluntary, minimum 3 years.

ARMY: 800.
1 lt inf bn.
EQUIPMENT:
APC: 5 *Commando*.
ATGW: *TOW* some 6 SP (*Hummer*).
RL: *LAW*.

AIR FORCE: (None, but for legal purposes NATO's
E-3A AEW ac have Luxembourg registration.)
1 sqn with 18 E-3A *Sentry* (NATO Standard), 2
Boeing 707 (trg).

PARA-MILITARY:
GENDARMERIE: 500.

NETHERLANDS

GDP	1987:	gld 431.82 bn ($213.17 bn)
	1988:	gld 449.65 bn ($227.48 bn)
Growth	1987: 1.7%	1988: 2.1%
Inflation	1987: -0.7%	1988: 0.7%
Debt	1987: $16.5 bn	
Def bdgt	1988:	gld 13.93 bn ($7.05 bn)
		NATO defn $6.75 bn
	1989:	gld 13.99 bn ($6.64 bn)
		NATO defn $6.37 bn
$1 = gld	(1987): 2.0257	(1988): 1.9766
	(1989): 2.1050	

gld = guilders

Population: 14,800,000

	13–17	18–22	23–32
Men	560,000	638,000	1,273,000
Women	536,000	613,000	1,222,000

TOTAL ARMED FORCES:
ACTIVE: 103,600 (incl 3,700 Royal Military Constabulary, 1,100 Inter-Service Organization); 1,700 women; 49,600 conscripts.
Terms of service: Army 14–16, Navy and Air Force 14–17 months.
RESERVES: 158,400 (men to age 35, NCO to 40, officers to 45). Army 143,000 (some – at the end of their conscription period – on short leave, immediate recall), Navy some 9,400 (7,000 on immediate recall); Air Force 6,000 (immediate recall).

ARMY: 63,700 (43,000 conscripts).
1 Corps HQ, 3 mech div HQ.
3 armd bde (incl 1 cadre).
6 mech inf bde (incl 2 cadre).
1 indep inf bn (cadre).
1 SSM bn with *Lance*.
3 AD bn.
3 hel sqn (Air Force-manned).
RESERVES: cadre bde and corps tps completed by call-up of reservists; 2 inf bde could be mobilized for territorial defence.
Home Guard: 3 sectors; inf weapons.
EQUIPMENT:
MBT: 913 (incl 163 in store): 468 *Leopard* 1A4, 445 *Leopard* 2.
AIFV: 973 (incl 142 in store): 708 YPR-765, 265 M-113C/-R all with 25mm.

APC: 1,916: 484 M-113, 1,432 YPR-765.
TOWED ARTY: 182: 105mm: 42 M-101; 155mm: 140 M-114.
SP ARTY: 298: 155mm: 222 M-109A2; 203mm: 76 M-110A2.
MORTARS: 81mm; 107mm: 194; 120mm: 145 (incl 10 in store).
SSM: 7 *Lance* launchers, (incl 1 in store).
ATGW: 753 (incl 207 in store): 427 *Dragon*, 326 *TOW*.
RCL: 106mm: 185.
AD GUNS: 35mm: 95 *Gepard* SP; 40mm: 131 L/70 towed.
SAM: 479 *Stinger*.
HELICOPTERS: 64 *Alouette* III (to be replaced), 29 Bo-105. (Air Force-manned).
MARINE: 1 tk tpt, 3 coastal, 15 river patrol boats.

NAVY: 16,900, incl naval air arm and marines (1,400 conscripts).
BASES: Netherlands: Den Helder (HQ); Vlissingen. Overseas: Willemstad (Curaçao), Oranjestad (Aruba).
SUBMARINES: 6:
1 *Zeeleuw* with Mk 48 HWT; plus *Harpoon* USGW.
2 *Zwaardvis* with Mk 37 HWT; plus *Harpoon* USGW.
3 *Dolfijn* with Mk 37 HWT.
PRINCIPAL SURFACE COMBATANTS: 15:
DESTROYERS: 4 DDG:
2 *Tromp* with 1 SM-1 MR SAM; plus 2 × 4 *Harpoon* SSM, 1 × 2 120mm guns, 1 *Lynx* hel (ASW/OTHT), 2 × 3 ASTT (Mk 46 LWT).
2 *Van Heemskerck* with 1 SM-1 MR SAM; plus 2 × 4 *Harpoon*, 2 × 2 ASTT.
FRIGATES: 11:
10 *Kortenaer* with 2 *Lynx* (ASW/OTHT) hel, 2 × 2 ASTT; plus 2 × 4 *Harpoon*.
1 *Van Speijk* with 1 *Lynx* hel, 2 × 3 ASTT; plus 2 × 4 *Harpoon*.
MINE WARFARE: 26:
MINELAYERS: none, but *Mercuur*, listed under spt and misc, has capability.
MINE COUNTERMEASURES: 26:
15 *Alkmaar* (tripartite) MHC.
11 *Dokkum* MSC.
AMPHIBIOUS: craft only; LCA/LCVP: 12⟨.
SUPPORT AND MISCELLANEOUS: 8:
2 *Poolster* AOR (1–3 *Lynx* hel), 3 survey, 1 *Mercuur* torpedo tender, 2 trg.
IN STORE: 1 *Van Speijk* FF awaiting transfer to Indonesia late 1989.

NAVAL AIR ARM: (1,400);
MR: 1 sqn with F-27M (see Air Force).
MR/ASW: 3 sqn (1 trg) with P-3C.
ASW: 1 sqn with *Lynx* SH-14B/C.
SAR: 1 (SAR/trg) sqn with *Lynx* UH-14A.

EQUIPMENT: 13 cbt ac, 17 armed hel.
AIRCRAFT:
P-3: 13 (MR).
HELICOPTERS:
Lynx: 22: **UH-14A:** 5 (SAR/trg); **SH-14B:** 9 (ASW);
SH-14C: 8 (ASW).

MARINES: (2,800).
2 cdo gp.
1 mtn/arctic warfare coy.
RESERVE: 1 cdo gp.

AIR FORCE: 18,200 (4,800 conscripts).
FGA: 4 sqn:
2 with F-16A/B;
2 with NF-5A (converting to F-16).
FIGHTER: 4 sqn with F-16A/B (3 ftr/FGA, 1 ftr).
RECCE: 1 sqn with RF-16A.
MR: 2 F-27M (assigned to Navy).
TRANSPORT: 1 sqn with F-27.
OCU: 1 sqn with F-16B (temporarily integrated with
1 F-16A ftr sqn).
SAR: 1 flt with SA-319.
AD: 9 bty with *HAWK* SAM (5 in FRG).
3 bty with *Patriot* SAM (op 1989, in FRG).
EQUIPMENT: 189 cbt ac, no armed hel.
AIRCRAFT:
NF-5: 46. **-A:** 31 (FGA); **-B:** 15 (OCU).
F-16: 161. **-A:** 109 (36 FGA, 73 ftr); **-B:** 32 (trg);
RF-16A: 20.
F-27: 14 (12 tpt, 2 MR).
HELICOPTERS:
SA-319: 4 (SAR).
AAM: AIM-9J/L/M/N *Sidewinder.*
SAM: 54 *HAWK,* 15 *Patriot,* 100 *Stinger.*
AD: GUNS: 25 VL 4/41 *Flycatcher* radar, 75 L/70
40mm systems.

FORCES ABROAD:
FRG: 5,700. 1 armd bde, 1 recce sqn, 1
engr bn, spt elm (122 MBT, 18 155mm SP, 30
ATGW).
NETHERLANDS ANTILLES: 1 frigate, 1 amph
cbt det, 1 MR det with 2 F-27MPA ac.
ICELAND: 30: 1 P-3C (at Keflavik).
EGYPT (Sinai MFO): 105: 1 sigs det.
NAMIBIA (UNTAG): 33 (Royal Military Constabulary).

PARA-MILITARY:
ROYAL MILITARY CONSTABULARY:
(*Koninklijke Marechaussee*): 3,700 (400
conscripts); 3 'div' comprising 10 districts with
72 'bde'.
CIVIL DEFENCE: (*Corps Mobiele Colonnes*):
4,750: 22,000 on mob; disaster relief
under Army comd.

FOREIGN FORCES:
NATO:
HQ Allied Forces Central Europe (AFCENT).
US: 2,800. Army 800; Air 2,000
1 tac ftr sqn.

NORWAY

GDP	1987:	kr 562.94 bn ($83.55 bn)
	1988:	kr 589.32 bn ($90.43 bn)
Growth	1987: 0.9%	1988: 1.5%
Inflation	1987: 8.7%	1988: 0.7%
Debt	1987: $56.4 bn	1988: $50.0 bn
Def bdgt	1988:	kr 19.121 bn ($2.934 bn)
		NATO defn $2.919 bn
	1989:	kr 20.407 bn ($3.01 bn)
		NATO defn n.a.
$1 = kr	(1987): 6.7375	(1988): 6.5170
	(1989): 6.7902	

kr = kroner

Population: 4,210,900

	13–17	18–22	23–32
Men	163,000	173,700	326,300
Women	155,700	164,800	309,700

TOTAL ARMED FORCES:
ACTIVE: some 34,100 (21,800 conscripts) incl 400
Joint Services org, 300 Home Guard permanent staff.
Terms of service: Army, Navy coast arty, Air
Force AD elm, 12 months plus 4 to 5 refresher
trg periods; Navy, Air Force 15 months.
RESERVES: 285,000 mobilizable in 24–72 hours;
obligation to 44 (conscripts remain with fd army
units to age 35); (officers to age 55; regulars: 60).
Army: 146,000; Navy: 26,000; Air: 28,000.
Home Guard: War some 85,000.
Second-line reserves: 60,000 (all services).

ARMY: 19,000 (13,000 conscripts).
4 Land, 4 Regional, 16 subordinate comd.
STANDING FORCES:
North Norway:
1 reinforced mech bde: 2 inf, 1 tk, 1 SP fd arty,
1 engr bn, 1 AD bty, spt units.
1 border garrison bn.
1 reinforced inf bn task force: inf, tk coy, fd
arty, AD bty.
South Norway:
1 inf bn (Royal Guard).
Indep units.
RESERVES: cadre units for mob: 3 div HQ, 3
armd, 4 mech, 6 lt inf bde, 5 mech, 23 inf, 7 arty

bn; 55 indep inf coy, tk sqn, arty bty, engr coy, sigs units, spt.

LAND HOME GUARD 75,000

18 districts each divided into 2–6 sub-districts and some 470 sub-units (pl). *Carl Gustav* 84mm, L-18 57mm RCL.

EQUIPMENT:

MBT: 80 *Leopard* 1, 37 M-48A5.
LIGHT TANKS: 70 NM-116 (M-24/90).
AIFV: ε 100 NM-135 (M-113/20mm).
APC: 150 M-113.
TOWED ARTY: 105mm: 120 M-101; 155mm: 155 M-114.
SP ARTY: 155mm: 130 M-109G SP (to be upgraded to A3GN).
MORTARS: 81mm, 107mm: ε 117 M-30F1, M-106A1 SP.
ATGW: *TOW*-1/-2, some NM-142 (M-113/*TOW*-2).
RCL: 106mm: M-40A1.
AD GUNS: 20mm: Rh-202; 40mm: L/60 and L/70.
SAM: 108 RBS-70.
AIRCRAFT: 17 O-1A (Air Force ac, Army crews).

NAVY: 5,300, incl 2,000 coast artillery (3,500 conscripts).

8 Naval/Coast defence cmd (9 on mob).
BASES: Horten, Haakonsvern (Bergen), Ramsund, Olavsvern (Tromsø).
SUBMARINES: 12:
  1 *Ula* with FRG *Seeal* DM2A3 HWT.
  11 *Kobben* SSC (1 modernized with Swe T-61) others US Mk 37 HWT.
FRIGATES: 5 *Oslo* with 2 × 3 ASTT, 1 × 6 *Terne* ASW RL; plus 6 × *Penguin* 2 SSM.
PATROL AND COASTAL COMBATANTS: 38:
CORVETTES: 2 *Sleipner* with 2 × 3 ASTT, 1 × 6 *Terne*.
MISSILE CRAFT: 36:
  14 *Hauk* PFM with 6 × *Penguin* 2, 2 × 533mm TT.
  16 *Storm* PFM with 6 × *Penguin* 2.
  6 *Snøgg* PFM with 4 × *Penguin* 2, 4 × 533mm TT.
MINE WARFARE: 10:
MINELAYERS: 2:
  2 *Vidar*, coastal (300–400 mines).
  Note: Amph craft also fitted for minelaying.
MINE COUNTERMEASURES: 8:
  5 *Sauda* MSC, 1 *Tana* MHC.
  2 diver spt.
AMPHIBIOUS: craft only; 5 LCT
SUPPORT AND MISCELLANEOUS: 2:
  1 MCM/PF depot ship.
  1 Royal Yacht.
NAVAL HOME GUARD: 7,000. On mob assigned to the 9 naval/coast defence comd.
  2 LCT, some 400 fishing craft.
COAST DEFENCE: 32 fortresses:
  34 arty bty: 75mm; 105mm; 120mm; 127mm; 150mm guns.
  Some cable mine and torpedo bty.

AIR FORCE: 9,100 (5,300 conscripts).

FGA: 4 sqn with F-16 (incl 1 OCU).
FIGHTER: 1 trg sqn with F-5A/B (has AD role).
MR: 1 sqn with P-3C *Orion* (2 assigned to coast guard).
TRANSPORT: 2 sqn:
  1 with C-130;
  1 with DHC-6 ac, UH-1B hel.
TRAINING: MFI-15.
SAR: 1 sqn with *Sea King* Mk 43.
COAST GUARD: 1 sqn with *Lynx* Mk 86.
TAC HEL: 2 utility sqn with Bell 412 SP.
AD: 22 lt AA arty bty; 1 SAM bn (3 bty *Nike Hercules*). (Being delivered: 6 bty NOAH SAM (Norwegian-adapted *HAWK*)).
EQUIPMENT: 83 cbt ac (plus 14 in store), no armed hel.
AIRCRAFT:
  F-5A/B: 16 (trg); plus 14 in store.
  F-16: 63. **-A:** 53 (FGA), **-B:** 10 (FGA).
  P-3: -C: 4 (MR); **-B:** 2 (coast guard).
  C-130H: 6 (tpt).
  ***Falcon* 20C:** 3 (EW/tpt).
  DHC-6: 4 (tpt); **MFI-15:** 16 (trg).
HELICOPTERS:
  Sea King: 8 (SAR).
  Lynx Mk 86: 5 (coast guard).
  Bell: 412 SP: 18 (tpt).
MISSILES:
  AAM: AIM-9L/N *Sidewinder*.
  ASM: CVR (AGM-12B *Bullpup*).
AD:
  GUNS: 40mm: 32 L/60, 64 L/70.
  SAM: 128 *Nike Hercules*; NOAH (Norwegian-adapted *HAWK*).
ANTI-AIRCRAFT HOME GUARD (on mob under comd of Air Force): 3,000; 2 bn (9 bty) lt AA; some Rh-202 20mm, 72 L-60 40mm guns (being replaced by Rh-202).

FORCES ABROAD:

LEBANON: (UNIFIL): 887; 1 inf bn, 1 service coy, plus HQ personnel.

PARA-MILITARY:

COAST GUARD: 680:
PATROL OFFSHORE: 13:
  3 *Nordkapp* with 1 × *Lynx* hel (SAR/recce), 2 × 3 ASTT, fitted for 6 *Penguin* Mk 2 SSM.
  1 *Nornen*, 2 *Farm*, 7 chartered.
AIRCRAFT: 2 P-3B *Orion* ac, 6 *Lynx* hel (Air Force-manned).

FOREIGN FORCES:

NATO:
  HQ Allied Forces Northern Europe (HQ AFNORTH).

US: Prepositioned eqpt for 1 MEB.

PORTUGAL

GDP	1987:	esc 4,986.8 bn ($35.398 bn)	
	1988ε:	esc 5,684.9 bn ($36.965 bn)	
Growth	1987:	5.0%	1988: 3.5%
Inflation	1987:	9.4%	1988: 9.6%
Debt	1987:	$16.2 bn	1988: $18.5 bn
Def bdgt	1988:	esc 173.59 bn ($1.27 m);	
		NATO defn $1.37 bn	
	1989ε:	esc 192.0 bn ($1.25 m);	
		NATO defn n.a.	
FMA	1988:	$125.21 m (US, FRG)	
$1 = esc	(1986):	149.59	(1987): 140.88
	(1988):	136.63	(1989): 153.79

esc = escudos

Population: 10,373,000

	13–17	18–22	23–32
Men	437,000	438,000	784,000
Women	420,000	426,000	780,000

TOTAL ARMED FORCES:
ACTIVE: 75,300 (47,200 conscripts).
Terms of service: Army 16, Navy 24, Air Force 21–24 months.
RESERVES: 190,000 (all services) (obligation: men to age 45; officers to 70).

ARMY: 44,000 (35,000 conscripts).
6 Territorial Commands (4 military regions, 2 military zones).
3 composite bde (1 mech, 2 mot inf, 1 tk, 1 fd arty bn).
1 AB/lt inf bde (1 cdo regt, 3 AB, 1 log bn).
1 AB bde (Air Force-manned).
3 cav regt.
12 inf regt, each 1 armd, 3 inf bn.
1 fd, 1 AD, 1 coast arty regt.
2 engr regt.
EQUIPMENT:
MBT: 86 M-48A5.
RECCE: 30 *Saladin*, 56 AML-60/-90, 32 *Ferret* Mk 4.
APC: 132 M-113 (incl -A2 *TOW*), 19 M-577A2, 81 *Chaimite*.
TOWED ARTY: 141: 105mm: 42 M-101A1, 18 M-101, 18 pack; 140mm: 23 5.5-in; 155mm: 40 M-114.
SP ARTY: 155mm: 6 M-109A2.
COAST ARTY: 150mm: 27; 152mm; 234mm.
MORTARS: 136: incl 81mm, 107mm: 20 M-2/M-30; 120mm: 81.
ATGW: 46 *TOW*, 31 SS-11, 45 *Milan*.
RCL: 240: 90mm; 106mm.

AD GUNS: 20mm: 34 M-163A1 *Vulcan* SP, 30 Rh-202; 40mm: 322 L/60.
SAM: 57 *Blowpipe*.

DEPLOYMENT:
3 inf regt, 2 coast arty bn, 2 AA bty in Azores and Madeira.

NAVY: 16,100 incl 2,800 marines (5,900 conscripts) 3 comd: Continental, Azores, Madeira.
BASES: Lisbon (Alfeite), Portimâo (HQ Continental comd), Punta Delgado (HQ Azores), Funchal (HQ Madeira).
SUBMARINES: 3 *Albacora* (Fr *Daphne*) SS with EL-5 HWT.
FRIGATES: 14:
4 *Commandante Joâo Belo* (Fr *Cdt Rivière*) with 2 × 3 ASTT, 1 × 4 ASW mor; plus 3 × 100mm gun.
4 *Baptista de Andrade* with 2 × 3 ASTT; plus 1 × 100mm gun.
6 *Joâo Coutinho*.
PATROL AND COASTAL COMBATANTS: 21:
PATROL COASTAL: 14:
10 *Cacine*, 4 *São Roque* ex-MSC.
INSHORE: 7⟨.
AMPHIBIOUS: Craft only; 3 LCU, 3 LCM
SUPPORT AND MISCELLANEOUS: 5:
1 AOR, 1 AK, 1 AGHS, 1 trg, 1 tug.

MARINES: (2,800) (1,400 conscripts).
3 bn (2 inf, 1 police), spt units.
EQUIPMENT: *Chaimite* APC, mor, 7 LCM.

AIR FORCE: 15,200 (6,300 conscripts) incl 2,000 AB tps listed with Army.
1 operational air command (COFA).
FGA: 4 sqn:
2 with A-7P;
1 with G-91R3/T1;
1 with G-91R4/T1.
SURVEY: 1 sqn with C-212B.
MR: 1 sqn with P-3P.
TRANSPORT: 6 sqn:
1 with C-130;
2 with C-212;
1 with *Falcon* 20.
2 hel with SA-316.
SAR: 2 sqn with SA-330 hel.
LIAISON: 2 sqn with Reims-Cessna FTB-337G.
OCU: 1 sqn with T-33, T-38.
TRAINING: 3 sqn:
1 with C-212 ac, SA-316 hel;
1 with T-37C;
1 with *Chipmunk*, TB-30, Cessna 337.
EQUIPMENT: 99 cbt ac, no armed hel.
AIRCRAFT:

A-7: 40. -7P: 34 (FGA); TA-7P: 6 (trg).
G-91: 53. -R3: 25 (FGA); R4: 18 (FGA); -T1:
   10 (trg).
P-3P: 6 (MR).
T-38: 12 (trg).
T-33: 18 (trg).
T-37: 23 (trg).
C-130: 5 (SAR, tpt).
C-212: 22. -A: 18 (12 tpt/SAR, 4 OCU, 2 ECM trg);
   -B: 4 (survey).
Falcon 20: 3 (tpt, calibration).
Cessna 337: 31 (23 liaison, 8 trg).
Chipmunk: 5 (trg).
TB-30: 18 (trg).
HELICOPTERS:
SA-330: 10 (SAR/tpt).
SA-316: 24 (trg, utility).

PARA-MILITARY:
NATIONAL REPUBLICAN GUARD: 19,000;
   Commando Mk III APC, 12 SA-313 hel .
PUBLIC SECURITY POLICE: 17,000.
BORDER SECURITY GUARD: 8,500.

FOREIGN FORCES:
NATO:
   NATO HQ for IBERLANT area at Lisbon (Oeiras).
US: 3,800. Navy (800). Air (3,000) (incl Azores).

SPAIN

GDP	1987:	pts 35,741 bn ($289.23 bn)	
	1988:	pts 39,618 bn ($340.10 bn)	
Growth	1987:	5.5%	1988: 7.9%
Inflation	1987:	5.2%	1988: 4.8%
Debt	1987:	$30.2 bn	1988: $32.3 bn
Def bdgt	1988:	pts 762.06 bn ($6.54 bn);	
		NATO defn $7.32 bn.	
	1989:	pts 794.9 bn ($6.84 bn);	
		NATO defn $7.04 bn	
FMA	1988:	$2.4 m (US)	
$1 = pts	(1987):	123.48	(1988): 116.49
	(1989):	116.20	

pts = pesetas

Population: 39,263,000

	13–17	18–22	23–32
Men	1,720,000	1,707,000	3,087,000
Women	1,600,000	1,617,000	3,015,000

TOTAL ARMED FORCES:
ACTIVE: 285,000 (210,000 conscripts (to be
   reduced), some 200 women) .
   Terms of service: volunteers 16, 18, 24 or 36
   months, conscripts 12 months.

RESERVES: 2,400,000 (all services to age 38);
   1,030,000 (service in past 5 years): Army:
   820,000; Navy: 135,000; Air Force: 35,000.

ARMY: 210,000 (164,000 conscripts);
   Plan META, a modernization and reorganization
   programme, is in progress incl strength
   reduction. Due to be completed in 1990.
   8 Regional Operational Commands incl 2 Overseas:
      1 armd div (1 armd, 1 mech bde, 1 arty, 1 lt
         armd cav, 1 engr regt).
      1 mech div (2 mech bde, 1 arty, 1 lt armd cav,
         1 engr regt).
      1 mot div (2 mot, 1 mech bde, 1 arty, 1 lt
         armd cav, 1 engr regt).
      2 mtn div (each 2 bde, 1 arty, 1 engr regt).
      2 armd cav bde.
      1 air portable bde.
      1 inf regt.
      1 coast arty comd (6 mixed arty regt; 1 coast
         arty gp).
      6 special ops bn.
      5 regional engr bn.
      1 Spanish Legion (7,000): 3 regt;
         2 with 1 mech, 1 mot bn, 1 ATK coy; 1 with
         2 mot bn; 1 lt inf bn.
   General Reserve Force:
      1 AB bde (3 bn) (also Army elm of Rapid
         Deployment Force).
      1 AD comd (6 AD regt incl 1 HAWK SAM gp, 1
         Nike Hercules bty, 1 Roland gp).
      1 fd arty comd (1 fd, 1 locating, 1 MRL regt).
      1 engr comd (4 engr regt incl 2 railway).
   Royal Guard Regt (incl inf, naval, air force coy
      and escort cav sqn).
   Aviation (FAMET): 40 armed hel.
      HQ with 1 hel, 1 spt, 1 trg sqn.
      1 attack bn.
      1 tpt bn (1 med, 1 hy coy).
      3 utility units.
EQUIPMENT:
MBT: 838: 299 AMX-30, 329 M-47E1, 46 M-47E2,
   164 M-48A5E.
LIGHT TANKS: 36 M-41.
RECCE: 138 VEC.
APC: 2,565: 1,195 M-113, 1,370 BMR-600 (incl
   variants).
TOWED ARTY: 684: 105mm: 359 M-26 (215 in store),
   150 Model-56 pack; 122mm: 85 390-1; 155mm:
   84 M-114, 6 M-44.
SP ARTY: 180: 105mm: 48 M-108; 155mm: 96
   M-109A; 203mm: 24 203/25, 12 M-110.
COAST ARTY: 6-in: 113; 203mm: 24; 305mm: 14;
   381mm: 7.
MRL: 140mm: 12 Teruel.
MORTARS: 81mm: 1,200 (incl 767 SP); 120mm: 400
   M-40 (incl 190 SP).
ATGW: 442 Milan, 28 HOT.

RCL: 106mm: 654.
AD GUNS: 20mm: 365 GAI-BO1; 35mm: 92
GDF-002 twin; 40mm: 274 L/70.
SAM: 4 *Nike Hercules*, 24 *Improved HAWK*, 16
Roland, some *Skyguard/Aspide*.
HELICOPTERS: 59 HU-8/-10B (UH-1B/H), 71 HA-15
(19 with 20mm guns, 28 with *HOT*), 6 AB-212,
17 HR-12B, 6 HT-21, 18 HT-17.

DEPLOYMENT:
CEUTA AND MELILLA: 15,800;
2 armd cav, 2 Spanish Legion, 2 mixed arty regt;
2 lt AD bn, 2 engr, 1 coast arty gp.
BALEARIC ISLANDS: 5,600;
1 inf regt: 2 inf bn. 1 arty regt: 2 fd arty, 1 coast
arty, 1 engr bn, 1 special ops coy.
CANARY ISLANDS: 10,000;
2 inf bn. 1 Spanish Legion, 2 coast arty regt, 2
engr bn, 2 special ops coy.

NAVY: 39,000, incl marines (24,500 conscripts).
5 Commands (Fleet, plus 4 Naval Regions:
Cantabria (Atlantic), Mediterranean, Straits,
Canaries).
BASES: Ferrol (HQ Cantabria), Rota (HQ Fleet),
Cadiz (HQ Straits), Cartagena (HQ Mediterranean
and submarine base), Palma de Mallorca, Mahón,
Las Palmas (HQ Canaries).
SUBMARINES: 8:
4 *Galerna* (Fr *Agosta*) with F-17 and L.5 HWT
4 *Delfin* (Fr *Daphné*) with F-17 and L.5 HWT.
PRINCIPAL SURFACE COMBATANTS: 19:
CARRIERS: 1 (CVV):
1 *Príncipe de Asturias* (16,200 tonnes). Air gp
about 21 ac: typically 8 AV-8B, 8 *Sea King*
(Mk 46 LWT), 4 AB-212, 1 *Sea King* AEW.
DESTROYERS: 4:
4 *Churruca* (US *Gearing*) with 1 × 8 *ASROC*, 2 ×
3 ASTT, 2 × 2 127mm guns, 1 Hughes 500 hel;
FRIGATES: 14:
FFG: 8 (AAW/ASW):
3 *Santa María* (US *Perry*) with 1 × 1 SM-1
MR/*Harpoon* launcher, 1 × SH-60B hel, 2 ×
3 ASTT.
5 *Baleares* with 1 × 1 SM-1 MR SAM, 1 × 8
ASROC, 2 × 533mm, 4 × 324mm ASTT; plus
2 × 4 *Harpoon*, 1 × 127mm gun.
FF: 6 *Descubierta* with 2 × 3 ASTT, 1 × 2 ASW RL;
plus 2 × 2 *Harpoon* SSM.
PATROL AND COASTAL COMBATANTS: 59:
PATROL OFFSHORE: 4 *Atrevida* PCO.
COASTAL: 18 PCC:
6 *Lazaga*, 10 *Anaga*, 2 *Nalón* (ex MSC).
INSHORE: 37:
6 *Barceló* PFI; 1 *Sálvora* PCI, 30 PCI⟨.
MINE WARFARE: 12:
MCMV: 12:

4 *Guadalete* (US *Aggressive*) MSO.
8 *Júcar* (US *Adjutant*) MSC.
AMPHIBIOUS: 5:
2 *Castilla* (US *Paul Revere*) amph tpt, capacity:
1,600 tps.
3 *Velasco* (US *Terrebonne Parish*) LST, capacity:
400 tps, 18 tk.
Plus 11 craft: 3 LCT, 2 LCU, 6 LCM.
SUPPORT AND MISCELLANEOUS: 19:
1 tpt, 5 ocean tugs, 1 Royal Yacht, 4 water
carriers, 6 AGHS, 2 trg.

NAVAL AIR:
FGA: 2 sqn:
1 with AV-8A *Matador* (*Harrier* II), TAV-8A.
1 with AV-8B.
LIAISON: 1 sqn with 6 *Comanche*, *Citation*.
HELICOPTERS: 6 sqn:
ASW: 4 sqn:
1 with Hughes 500.
1 with AB-212 ASW.
1 with SH-3D/G *Sea King* (mod to SH-3H
standard).
1 with SH-60B (LAMPS-III fit).
AEW: 1 flt with SH-3D (*Searchwater* radar).
COMMAND/RECCE: 1 sqn with AB-212.
TRAINING: 1 sqn with Bell 47G.
EQUIPMENT: 23 cbt ac, 39 armed hel.
AIRCRAFT:
AV-8: 23. **-A:** 7 (FGA); **-B:** 12 (FGA); **TAV-8A:** 4 (trg).
Comanche: 2 (liaison). ***Twin Comanche:*** 2
(liaison). ***Citation*** II: 2 (liaison).
HELICOPTERS:
AB-212: 12 (ASW/SAR).
Sea King: 13 (10 ASW, 3 AEW).
Hughes 500M: 11 (ASW).
SH-60B: 6 (ASW).
Bell 47G: 8 (trg).

MARINES: (8,500).
1 marine regt (3,500): 2 inf, 1 spt bn; 3 arty bty.
5 marine garrison regt.
EQUIPMENT:
MBT: 18 M-48E.
AFV: 17 *Scorpion* lt tk, 19 LVTP-7 amph.
TOWED ARTY: 105mm: 12 Oto Melara M-56 pack.
SP ARTY: 105 mm: 8 M-52A1; 155mm: 6 M-109A.
ATGW: 18 *TOW*, 18 *Dragon*.
RL: 88mm: M-65; 90mm: C-90C.
RCL: 106mm: 66.

AIR FORCE: 36,000 (21,500 conscripts).
COMBAT AIR COMMAND (MACOM): 4 wings.
FIGHTER: 8 sqn:
2 with EF-18 (F-18 *Hornet*);
2 with F-4C/RF-4C (F-4C to retire 1989);
2 with *Mirage* IIIEE/ED.

2 with *Mirage* F-1CE/BE.

TACTICAL AIR COMMAND (MATAC): 3 wings.
FGA: 2 sqn with F-5A, F-5B, RF-5A.
OCU: 2 sqn with F-5B.
MR: 1 sqn with P-3A.
LIAISON: 1 sqn with Do-27.
AAM: *Sparrow*, *Sidewinder*, R-550 *Magic*.

AIR COMMAND, CANARY ISLANDS
(MACAN):
FGA: 1 sqn with *Mirage* F-1EE.
TRANSPORT: 1 sqn with C-212 *Aviocar*, Do-27.
SAR: 1 sqn with F-27 ac, AS-332 hel.

TRANSPORT COMMAND (MATRA): 3 wings.
TRANSPORT: 6 sqn.
1 with C-130H/H-30;
1 tkr/tpt with KC-130H;
2 with C-212;
2 with DHC-4.

TRAINING COMMAND (MAPER):
TRAINING:
11 ac sqn with Piper (*Aztec, Navajo*), Beech
(*Bonanza, Baron*), C-101 *Aviojet*, C-212, T-34
(to be replaced by E-26 *Támiz*).
2 hel sqn: 1 with AB-205A, UH-1H; 1 with
Hughes 269, Bell-47G/OH-13.

MATERIEL COMMAND (MAMAT): 1 wing.
TRIALS: 1 sqn with C-101, C-212.

AIR FORCE HQ GROUP (ACGA):
TRANSPORT: 1 hel sqn with SA-330, AS-332.
1 ac sqn with Boeing 707 (tkr/tpt), *Falcon* 900,
Falcon-50, *Falcon*-20, 1 DC-8 (to be replaced). (VIP)
SAR: 3 sqn (incl 1 under MACAN):
1 with C-212 ac, AS-332 hel;
1 with C-212 ac, AS-332, SA-319 hel;
1 (MACAN) with F-27 ac, AS-332 hel.
SUPPORT: 2 sqn with CL-215, Do-27/C-127.
LIAISON: 1 ac sqn with C-212, Do-27/C-127;
1 hel sqn with SA-330, AS-332.
EQUIPMENT: 217 cbt ac (plus 12 in store), no
armed hel.
AIRCRAFT:
EF-18 A/B: 55 (ftr, OCU).
F-5: 51. **-A:** 14 (FGA); **-B:** 25 (3 FGA, 22 OCU);
RF-5A: 12 (recce); plus 12 in store.
Mirage: 85. **F-1CE:** 36 (FGA); **F-1BE:** 5 (ftr);
F-1EE: 21 (ftr); **IIIEE:** 18 (ftr); **IIIDE:** 5 (ftr).
F-4C: 32 (ftr); **RF-4C:** 12 (recce).
P-3A: 6 (MR).
Boeing 707: 2 (tkr/tpt).
C-130H: 12. 7 (tpt); **KC-130H:** 5 (tkr).
C-212: 83 (27 tpt, 11 SAR, 5 liaison, 24 trg); **-E:** 14
trg; **TR-12D:** 2 (EW).
C-101: 85 (trg).
CL-215: 13 (spt).
DHC-4: 21 (tpt).
Falcon 20: 5 (VIP tpt); **Falcon 50:** 1 (VIP tpt);
Falcon 900: 1 (VIP tpt).
F-27: 3 (SAR).

Do-27/CASA C-127: 58 (liaison).
T-34: 21 (trg).
Other: 68 (6 *Aztec*, 2 *Navajo*, 43 *Bonanza*, 17 *Baron*).
HELICOPTERS:
AB-205/UH-1H: 13 (trg). **AB-206:** 4 (trg). **SA-319:** 6
(SAR). **SA-330:** 6 (tpt). **AS-332:** 11 (9 SAR, 2
tpt). **Hughes 269A (TH-55A):** 17 (trg). **Bell
47/OH-13:** 25 (trg).

FORCES ABROAD:
NAMIBIA (UNTAG): 85. 8 C-212 tpt ac.

PARA-MILITARY:
GUARDIA CIVIL: 64,000 (3,000 auxiliary); 20 inf
tercios (regt), 56 rural bn, 6 traffic security gp, 1
anti-terrorist special gp; BLR APC, 1 B-11T
(BK-117) hel.
POLICIA NACIONAL: 47,000; 26 inf bn, 2 cav sqn
gp, 3 cav tp, 1 special ops cdo gp (GEO), civil
security gp.
MARITIME SURVEILLANCE FORCE: (Ministry of
Transportation and Communications): some 54
patrol craft, many armed.

FOREIGN FORCES:
US: 8,600. Navy (3,700). Air (4,900):
1 tac wing with 72 cbt ac.

TURKEY

GDP	1987ε:	TL 53,642 bn ($62.58 bn)		
	1988ε:	TL 90,000 bn ($62.23 bn)		
Growth	1987:	6.8%	1988:	3.4%
Inflation	1987:	30.0%	1988:	75.0%
Debt	1987:	$38.3 bn	1988:	$36.44 bn
Def bdgt	1988ε:	TL 2,903 bn ($2.04 bn);		
		NATO defn $2.66 bn.		
	1989ε:	TL 5,856 bn ($2.93 bn)		
		NATO defn n.a.		
FMA	1988:	$568.87 m (US, FRG)		
$1 = TL	(1987):	857.17	(1988):	1,422.30
	(1989):	2,000.00		
TL = Turkish liras				

Population: 55,541,000

	13–17	*18–22*	*23–32*
Men	3,259,000	2,870,000	4,628,000
Women	3,043,000	2,633,000	4,471,000

TOTAL ARMED FORCES:
ACTIVE: 650,900 (575,800 conscripts).
Terms of service: 18 months.
RESERVES: 951,000 to age 46 (all). Army
808,000, Navy 73,000, Air 70,000.

ARMY: 528,500 (497,000 conscripts).

4 army HQ: 10 corps HQ.

1 armd div (3 armd bde, 1 arty regt, 1 recce bn).

2 mech div (each 1 armd, 2 mech bde, 1 arty regt, 1 recce bn).

12 inf div (4 with 1 armd, 2 inf bde, 1 arty regt; 8 with 3 inf bde, 1 arty regt, 1 armd bn).

6 indep armd bde (each 2 armd, 1 mech inf, 1 arty bn, 1 recce sqn).

4 indep mech bde (each 1 armd, 2 mech inf, 1 arty bn, 1 recce sqn).

11 indep inf bde (each 3 inf, 1 mtn arty bn, 1 recce sqn).

1 AB bde (3 AB, 1 mtn arty bn).

2 cdo bde (each 3 cdo, 1 arty bn).

5 coastal def bn.

Corps units: 10 tk, 50 (30 fd 20 AD) arty bn.

Note: some div and bde may be understrength.

EQUIPMENT:

MBT: some 3,727: 800 M-47 (500 in reserve), 1,100 M-48A1/A2 (to be -A5), 1,600 M-48A5, some 227 *Leopard* 1A3.

LIGHT TANKS: 114 M-24 in store.

RECCE: M-8 in store.

APC: 3,300: 500 M-59, 2,000 M-113, some 800 M-2/-3 (incl perhaps 150 in store).

TOWED ARTY: 1,428: 75mm: 108 M-116; 105mm: 618 M-101A1, 108 M-102; 155mm: 402 M-114A1, 144 M-59; 203mm: 48 M-115.

SP ARTY: 739: 105mm: 90 M-108, 108 M-7, 162 M-52; 155mm: 168 M-44 (some in store), 42 M-109A1, 36 M-53; 175mm: 36 M-107; 203mm: 81 M-55 in store, 16 M-110A2.

COAST ARTY: 240mm: 20.

MRL: 12 MLRS.

MORTARS: 81mm: M-1, M-4A1 (M-2/-3 APC), UT1, M-29, M-125A1 SP; 107mm (incl 4.2-in): M-2, M-30, M-84 (M-59 APC) SP, M-106A1 SP; 120mm: 100: Soltam, TOSAM Mk E HY12-DI.

ATGW: 85 *Cobra*, SS-11, *TOW* incl M-113 SP, 162 *Milan*.

RCL: 57mm: 1,200 M-18; 75mm: 400 M-40A1; 106mm: 1,000+.

AD GUNS: 20mm: 88 GAI-DO1, Mk 20 Rh-202 twin; 35mm: 84 Oerlikon twin; 40mm: 900 M-1A1, L/70, 153 M-42A1; 75mm: M-51; 90mm: M-117/-118.

SAM: 12 *Rapier*, *Redeye*.

AIRCRAFT: 1 DHC-2 *Beaver*, 20 U-17 (Cessna 185), 50 O-1E, 8 Cessna 206, 4 Cessna 421, 5 Do-27A, 19 Do-28D, 15 T-42A (Beech *Baron*), 1 Piper *Cherokee*, 40 *Citabria* 150S trg.

HELICOPTERS: 20 AB-204, 85 AB-205, 20 AB-206A, 3 AB-212, 30 UH-1D, 70 UH-1H, 60 SA-313, 30 TH-55, 15 OH-13H.

NAVY: 55,000, incl marines (42,000 conscripts).

BASES: Ankara (Navy HQ and COMEDNOREAST), Gölcük (HQ Fleet), Istanbul (HQ Black Sea area), Izmir, (HQ Mediterranean coast area), Eregli, Iskenderun, Kara Mursel, Aksaz Bay.

SUBMARINES: 15 SS:

6 *Atilay* (FRG Type 209/1200) with SST-4 HWT.

7 *Burakreis* (US *Guppy*) with Mk 37 HWT.

2 *Hizirreis* (US *Tang*) with Mk 37 HWT.

PRINCIPAL SURFACE COMBATANTS: 22:

DESTROYERS: 12:

8 *Yücetepe* (US *Gearing*) (ASW/ASUW) with 2 × 3 ASTT (Mk 46 LWT); 5 with 1 × 8 *ASROC*, 2 with *Harpoon* SSM, all with 2 × 2 127mm guns.

2 *Alcitepe* (US *Carpenter*) with 1 × 8 *ASROC*, 2 × 3 ASTT, 1 × 2 127mm guns.

1 *Zafer* (US *Sumner*) with 2 × 3 ASTT, 3 × 2 127mm guns.

1 *Muavenet* (mod *Sumner*), weapons as *Zafer*; plus 80 mines.

FRIGATES: 10:

4 *Yavuz* (FRG *MEKO* 200) with 1 × AB-212 hel (ASW/OTHT), 2 × 3 ASTT; plus 2 × 4 *Harpoon* SSM, 1 × 127mm gun.

4 *Gelibolu* (FRG T-120 *Köln*) with 4 × 533mm ASTT, 2 × 4 ASW mor; plus 2 × 100mm gun.

2 *Berk* with 2 × 3 ASTT.

PATROL AND COASTAL COMBATANTS: 48:

MISSILE CRAFT: 16:

8 *Doğan* (FRG Lürssen-57) (PFM) with 2 × 4 *Harpoon* SSM.

8 *Kartal* (FRG *Jaguar*) (PFM) with 4 × *Penguin* 2 SSM, 2 × 533mm TT.

TORPEDO CRAFT: 4:

4 *Turfan* (FRG *Jaguar*) PFT with 4 × 533mm TT.

PATROL: 28:

COASTAL: 7: 1 *Girne* PFC, 6 *Sultanhisar* PCC.

INSHORE: 21: 1 *Bora* (US *Asheville*) PFI, 12 AB-27 PCI, 4 AB-21, 4⟨.

MINE WARFARE: 39:

MINELAYERS: 6:

1 *Nusret* (400 mines).

5 *Mordoğan* (US LSM) coastal (400 mines).

Note: *Bayraktar*, *Sarucabey* and *Çacabey* LST have dual amph/minelaying role.

MINE COUNTERMEASURES: 33:

12 *Seymen* (US *Adjutant*) MSC.

4 *Trabzon* (Cdn *Bay*) MSC.

6 *Karamürsel* (FRG *Vegesack*) MSC.

4 *Foça* (US *Cape*) MSI.

7 MSI⟨.

AMPHIBIOUS: 7 LST:

2 *Ertuğrul* (US *Terrebonne Parish*): capacity 400 tps, 18 tk.

2 *Bayraktar* (US LST-512): capacity 200 tps, 16 tk.

2 *Sarucabey*: capacity 600 tps, 11 tk.

1 *Çakabey*: capacity 400 tps, 9 tk.

Plus about 73 craft: 40 LCT, 13 LCU, 20 LCM.

SUPPORT AND MISCELLANEOUS: 17:

1 *Akar* AO, 6 spt tankers, 5 depot ships, 3 salvage/rescue, 1 survey, 1 trg.

NAVAL AVIATION: 22 combat ac, 9 armed hel.
ASW: 1 sqn with 22 S-2A/E/TS-2A *Tracker* ac (Air
Force owned, Air Force and Navy crews); 3
AB-204AS, 6 AB-212 ASW hel.

MARINES: 1 bde (4,000).
HQ, 3 bn, 1 arty bn (18 guns), spt units.

AIR FORCE: 67,400 (36,800 conscripts).
2 tac air forces, 1 tpt, 1 air trg comd.
FGA: 18 sqn:
  3 (1 OCU) with F-5A/B;
  7 (1 OCU) with F-4E;
  3 with F-16 (1 OCU, 1 converting)
  5 (1 OCU) with F/TF-104G.
FIGHTER: 2 sqn with F-104S/G, TF-104G.
RECCE: 2 sqn:
  1 with RF-5A/F-5B/RT-33;
  1 with RF-4E.
ASW: 1 sqn with S-2A/E *Tracker* (see Navy).
TRANSPORT: 4 sqn:
  1 with C-130H and C-47;
  1 with C-160D;
  1 with C-47, *Viscount* 794 (VIP) ac; UH-1H hel.
  1 with C-47 (ECM/ELINT/SAR/calibration).
LIAISON:
  3 HQ flt with C-47, Beech AT-11, T-33 ac;
    UH-1H hel;
  10 base flt with C-47, T-33 ac; UH-1H, UH-19B
    (Sikorsky S-55) hel.
TRAINING: 3 sqn: 1 with T-34, T-41; 1 with T-33,
  T-38; 1 with T-37; trg schools with C-47 ac,
  UH-1H hel.
SAM: 8 sqn with *Nike Hercules*; 2 *Rapier* sqn.
EQUIPMENT: 366 cbt ac (plus 110 in store), no
  armed hel.
AIRCRAFT:
  F-16C/D: 33 (FGA, OCU).
  F-5: 104. **-A:** 54 (FGA); **-B:** 7 (6 FGA, 1 recce);
    RF-5A: 19 (recce); **NF-5A/B:** 24; plus 15 in store.
  F-4E: 108. 90 (FGA); 10 (OCU); **RF-4E:** 8 (recce).
  F-104: 140. **-G:** 108 (90 FGA, 18 ftr); **TF-104G:** 14
    (10 FGA, 4 ftr); **-S:** 18 (ftr); plus 95 in store.
  S-2 *Tracker*: 22. **-A:** 10 (8 ASW, 2 TS-2A trg); **-E:**
    12 (ASW). With Navy.
  C-130: 7 (tpt). **C-160D:** 20 (tpt). *Viscount:* 2 (VIP).
    C-47: 40+ (22 tpt, 2 VIP, 12 comms flt, trg
    school ac). *Citation:* 4 (VIP tpt). **T-33:** 94 (60
    trg/OCU, 34 liaison/OCU). **T-38:** 29 (trg). **T-37:**
    42 (30 trg, 12 store). **T-34:** 12 (trg). **T-41:** 20 (trg).
HELICOPTERS:
  UH-1H: 45+ (tpt, liaison, base flt, trg schools).
SAM: 128 *Nike Hercules*, 24 *Rapier*.

FORCES ABROAD:
CYPRUS: 1 corps of 2 inf div, 1 indep armd bde
  (27,000); 275 M-47, M-48A2/-A5 MBT; 100

M-113, 100 M-59 APC; 144 105mm, 36 155mm,
8 203mm towed; 18 105mm, 6 155mm SP; 114
107mm mor; 84 40mm AA guns; 8 ac, 12 hel.

PARA-MILITARY:
GENDARMERIE/NATIONAL GUARD: (Ministry of
  Interior, Ministry of Defence in War) 75,000
  active, 50,000 reserve (incl 3 mobile bde, 67 regt,
  plus 5 cdo regt with V-150, UR-416, *Condor* APC;
  AB-204, AB-205, AB-206, S-70A hel).
COAST GUARD: 1,100: 28 PCI plus boats, 4 tpt.

FOREIGN FORCES:
US: 4,900. Army (1,300). Air (3,600): 1 tac, 1 air
  base gp.

UNITED KINGDOM

GDP	1986:	£377.46 bn ($519.99 bn)	
	1987	£408.55 bn ($609.69 bn)	
Growth	1987:	3.6%	1988: 4.4%
Inflation	1987:	4.2%	1988: 4.9%
Debt	1986:	$90.2 bn	1987: $ ε $101 bn
Def bdgt	1988/9:	£19.22 bn ($33.76 bn);	
		NATO defn $34.49 bn.	
	1989/9:	£20.153 bn ($34.56 bn);	
		NATO defn $35.25 bn.	
$1 = £	(1987/8): 0.5873	(1988/9): 0.5652	
	(1989/90): 0.5831		

Population: 57,013,000

	13–17	18–22	23–32
Men	1,897,000	2,297,000	5,042,000
Women	1,796,000	2,190,000	4,910,000

TOTAL ARMED FORCES:
ACTIVE: 311,650 incl 16,250 women and some
  9,200 enlisted outside the UK.
  Terms of service: voluntary.
RESERVES: 325,000.
  Army: 255,200. Regular 173,100; Territorial
    Army (TA) 72,800; Home Service Force some
    3,000. Ulster Defence Regt (UDR) 6,300 (3,400
    part time).
  Navy: 30,300. Regular 24,700; Volunteers and
    Auxiliary Service 8,800.
  Marines: 3,700. Regular 2,400; Volunteers and
    Auxiliary Forces 1,300.
  Air Force: 35,700. Regular 34,100; Volunteers
    and Auxiliary Forces 1,600.

STRATEGIC FORCES: 2,100:
SLBM: 64 msl in 4 SSBN:

4 *Resolution* SSBN each with 16 *Polaris* A-3TK msl (1 in refit).
Ballistic Missile Early Warning System (BMEWS) station at Fylingdales (to be upgraded).

ARMY: 155,500 (incl 6,500 women and 8,900 enlisted outside the UK, of whom some 7,600 are Gurkhas).

(Note: regt are normally of bn size).
1 corps HQ.
3 armd div (2 with 3 armd bde, 1 with 2 armd, 1 mech bde, all 3 arty, 1 engr, 1 avn regt, 1 AD bty).
corps tps: 1 arty bde (1 SSM, 3 hy, 2 AD regt), 2 armd recce, 4 engr regt.
1 inf div (1 air-mobile bde, 2 inf bde (reserve), 1 arty regt).
2 mech bde (*Saxon*).
1 AB bde.
3 inf bde (incl 1 air-mobile).
9 inf bde (mixed regular and TA for trg/administrative purposes only).
3 engr bde HQ.
Summary Combat Arm Units:
  13 armd regt.
  5 armd recce regt.
  20 mech inf bn (10 FV 432, 10 *Saxon*).
  3 armd inf bn (*Warrior*).
  29 inf bn (incl 5 Gurkha).
  3 AB bn (2 only in para role).
  1 SF (SAS) regt.
  18 arty regt (1 SSM with 12 *Lance* launchers, 3 hy, 8 SP, 6 fd incl 1 cdo, 1 AB).
  3 AD regt (*Rapier*).
  13 engr regt (incl 1 Gurkha, 1 amph, 1 armd).
  4 avn regt.

RESERVES:
Territorial Army: 2 armd recce, 3 lt recce regt, 41 inf bn, 2 SAS, 2 fd, 1 arty recce, 4 AD (*Blowpipe/Javelin*), 8 engr regt, 1 avn sqn.
Home Service Force: some 43 coy (to be 47).
Ulster Defence Regiment (UDR): 9 bn (internal security role in Northern Ireland only).

EQUIPMENT:
MBT: 1,290 some 420 *Challenger*, 870 *Chieftain* (incl 400 in store).
LIGHT TANKS: 271 FV 101 *Scorpion*.
RECCE: 290 FV 107 *Scimitar*, 500 *Ferret*, some 200 *Fox*.
AIFV: some 200 *Warrior* (MCV-80).
APC: 3,437: 2,338 FV 432 (incl variants), some 60 FV 603 *Saracen*, 12 FV 601 *Saladin*, 500 FV 103 *Spartan*, some 527 AT-105 *Saxon*.
TOWED ARTY: 229: 105mm: 150 L-118; 155mm: 79 FH-70.
SP ARTY: 321: 105mm: 159 FV 32 *Abbot;* 155mm: 110 M-109/A2/A3 SP; 175mm: 36 M-107; 203mm: 16 M-110 (to be withdrawn).
MRL: 4 MLRS 227mm (trials).
MORTARS: 81mm: some 500.

SSM: 14 *Lance* launchers (incl 2 in store).
ATGW: ε 1,100 *Milan* (incl 72 FV 103 *Spartan* SP), 48 *Swingfire* (FV 102 *Striker* SP).
SAM: *Blowpipe*, 12 *Javelin*; 120 *Rapier* (some 50 SP).
AIRCRAFT: 5 BN-2, 7 DHC-2, 21 *Chipmunk* trg.
HELICOPTERS: 30 *Scout*, 159 SA-341, 120 *Lynx* AH-1/-7/-9 (some with *TOW*), 4 A-109.
LANDING CRAFT:
2 *Ardennes*, 9 *Arromanches* log; 4 *Avon*, LCVP‹; 3 tugs, 28 other service vessels.

NAVY (RN): 64,650 (incl Air, Marines, 3,450 women and 400 enlisted outside the UK).

ROYAL FLEET AUXILIARY (RFA): (2,350 civilians) man major spt vessels.
ROYAL MARITIME AUXILIARY SERVICE (RMAS): (2,900 civilians) provides harbour/coastal services.
RESERVES:
ROYAL FLEET RESERVE: (24,700) Ex-regulars, no trg commitment.
ROYAL NAVAL RESERVE (RNR): (5,600) 6 HQ units, 11 Sea Trg Centres (STC), 12 Comms Trg Centres (CTC), 1 MCM sqn: 10 MCMV, 19 PCI.
ROYAL NAVAL AUXILIARY SERVICE (RNXS): (3,200) 72 auxiliary service units; Port HQ, patrols, etc.
BASES: UK: Northwood (HQ Fleet, CINCHAN/ CINCEASTLANT), Devonport (HQ), Faslane, Portland, Portsmouth, Rosyth (HQ). Overseas: Gibraltar, Hong Kong.
SUBMARINES: 31:
STRATEGIC SUBMARINES: 4 SSBN (see p. 78)
TACTICAL SUBMARINES: 27:
  SSN: 16 (incl 3 in refit):
    5 *Trafalgar*, 6 *Swiftsure* all with Mk 24 HWT and *Harpoon* USGW.
    2 *Valiant*, 3 *Churchill* with Mk 24 HWT and *Harpoon* .
  SS: 11 (incl 2 in refit):
    11 *Oberon* with Mk 24 HWT (incl 2 in refit).
PRINCIPAL SURFACE COMBATANTS: 49:
CARRIERS: 2 *Invincible* CVV (plus 1 in store); each with ac: 8 *Sea Harrier* V/STOL; hel: 12 *Sea King*: 9 ASW, 3 AEW; plus 1 × 2 *Sea Dart* SAM.
DESTROYERS: 13 DDG (incl 3 in refit):
  12 *Birmingham* with 1 × 2 *Sea Dart* SAM; plus 1 *Lynx* hel, 2 × 3 ASTT, 1 × 114mm gun.
  1 *Bristol* (trg) with 1 × 2 *Sea Dart* SAM; plus 1 × 114mm gun.
FRIGATES: 34 (incl 5 in refit)
  3 *Cornwall* (Type 22 Batch 3) with 1 *Sea King* hel (*Sting Ray* LWT), 2 × 3 ASTT; plus 2 × 4 *Harpoon* SSM, 1 × 114mm gun.
  10 *Broadsword* (Type 22 Batch 1/2) with 2 *Lynx* hel (2 with 1 × *Sea King*), 2 × 3 ASTT; plus 4 × MM-38 *Exocet* SSM.
  6 *Amazon* with 1 *Lynx* hel, 2 × 3 ASTT; plus 4 × MM-38 *Exocet*, 1 × 114mm gun.

15 *Leander:*
  12 (Batch 2/3A) with 1 *Lynx* hel, 2 × 3 ASTT;
    plus 4 × MM-38 *Exocet.*
  2 (Batch 3B) with 1 × 3 ASW mor; plus 2 ×
    114mm guns.
  1 trg with 2 × 3 ASTT.

PATROL AND COASTAL COMBATANTS: 44:
OFFSHORE: 14 PCO: 1 *Endurance,* 1 *Sentinel,* 2
  Castle, 7 *Jersey,* 3 *Peacock.*
INSHORE: 30 PCI: 5 *Kingfisher,* 4 *Manly,* 21⟨.

MINE WARFARE: 38:
MINELAYER: No dedicated minelayer, but all
  submarines have limited minelaying capability.

MINE COUNTERMEASURES: 38:
  13 *Brecon* MCO.
  1 *Sandown* MHC.
  12 *Waveney* MSO (11 with RNR).
  9 '*Ton*' MHC, 3 '*Ton*' MSC.

AMPHIBIOUS: 7:
  2 *Fearless* LPD with 4 LCU, 4 LCVP; capacity 400
    tps, 15 tk, 3 hel. (1 in refit).
  1 *Sir Galahad,* 4 *Sir Lancelot* LST: capacity 340
    tps, 16 tk (*Sir G.* 18), 1 hel (RFA manned).
  Plus 32 craft: 15 LCU, 17 LCVP.
  Note: See Army for additional amph lift capability.

SUPPORT AND MISCELLANEOUS: 38:
UNDERWAY SUPPORT: 13:
  3 *Olwen,* 1 *Tidespring,* 5 *Green Rover* AO, 4 AEF.
MAINTENANCE/LOGISTIC: 11:
  2 AR (1 chartered), 5 AOT, 1 AK, 3 AT.
SPECIAL PURPOSE: 7:
  1 AVT, 1 trg (chartered), 1 seabed ops, 3
    trials/research, 1 Royal Yacht.
SURVEY: 7 AGHS.
(29 of above civilian manned, either RFA or RMAS).

FLEET AIR ARM (FAA):
FIGHTER/ATTACK: 3 ac sqn with *Sea Harrier* FRS-1.
ASW: 7 hel sqn with *Sea King* HAS-5;
ASW/ATTACK: 2 sqn with *Lynx* HAS-2/-3 (in indep flt).
AEW: 1 hel sqn with *Sea King* AEW-2.
COMMANDO SUPPORT: 3 hel sqn with *Sea King* HC-4.
SAR: 1 hel sqn with *Sea King* HC-4.
TRAINING: 3 sqn: 1 with *Jetstream* ac; 1 with SA-341
  Gazelle HT-2 hel; 1 with *Wessex* HU-5 hel,
  Chipmunk T-10, *Sea Devon* C-20 ac.
FLEET SUPPORT: *Canberra* T-18/-22, *Hunter* T-7/-8,
  GA-11, PR-11, 3 *Mystère-Falcon* 20 (civil
  registration, operated under contract).
LIAISON: HS-125 (VIP, operated by RAF), *Sea
  Heron, Sea Devon.*
EQUIPMENT: 44 cbt ac, 134 armed hel.
AIRCRAFT:
  Sea Harrier/Harrier: 46. *Sea Harrier* **FRS-1:**
    42 (some being mod to FRS-2). **T-4N:** 2 (trg).
    Harrier **T-4A:** 2 (trg).
  Canberra: 10 (3 spt, 7 store).
  Hunter: 26 (spt, trg).

HS-125: 2 (VIP tpt); ***Mystère-Falcon* 20:** 8 (spt);
Jetstream: 19; **T-2:** 15 (trg); **T-3:** 4 (trg); ***Sea
  Heron:*** 4 (liaison). ***Heron:*** 1 (liaison). ***Sea Devon:***
  2 (liaison). 1 in store. ***Chipmunk:*** 14 (trg).
HELICOPTERS:
  SH-3: 120. **HAS-5:** 76 (56 ASW, 20 trg). **HC-4:** 34
    (cdo). **AEW-2:** 10.
  Lynx: 78. **HAS-2:** 55. **HAS-3:** 23.
  ***Gazelle* HT-2/-3:** 22 (trg).
ASM: *Sea Skua, Sea Eagle.* **AAM:** AIM-9 *Sidewinder.*

MARINES (RM): (7,700).
  1 cdo bde: 3 cdo; 1 cdo arty regt (Army) + 1 bty
    (TA); 2 cdo engr sqn (1 Army, 1 TA), 1 log regt
    (tri-Service); 1 lt hel sqn.
  1 mtn and arctic warfare cadre.
  Special Boat Service (SF): HQ: 5 sqn.
  1 aslt sqn (6 landing craft).

EQUIPMENT:
ATGW: *Milan.*
SAM: *Javelin, Blowpipe.*
HELICOPTERS: 8 SA-341, 6 *Lynx* AH-1.

AIR FORCE (RAF): 91,450 (incl 6,300 women).
FGA/BOMBER: 11 sqn: (nuclear capable)
  9 with *Tornado* GR-1;
  2 with *Buccaneer* S-2A/B (maritime strike, with
    Sea Eagle ASM).
FGA: 5 sqn:
  3 with *Harrier* GR-3/T-4, GR-5 being delivered;
  2 with *Jaguar.*
FIGHTER: 9 sqn:
  5 with *Phantom;* (to be replaced with *Tornado*
    F-3 and European Fighter Aircraft).
  4 with *Tornado* F-3.
RECCE: 1 sqn with *Tornado* GR-1A; 1 sqn with *Jaguar*
  GR-1; 1 photo-recce unit with *Canberra* PR-9.
MR: 4 sqn with *Nimrod* MR-2.
AEW: 1 sqn with *Shackleton* AEW-2.
ECM/ELINT: 2 sqn: 1 ECM with *Canberra,* 1 ELINT
  with *Nimrod* R-1.
TANKER: 3 sqn: 1 with *Victor* K-2; 1 with VC-10
  K-2/-3; 1 with *Tristar* K-1/KC-1.
TRANSPORT: 5 sqn:
  1 strategic with VC-10 C-1.
  4 tac with *Hercules* C-1/-1K/-1P/-3P.
LIAISON: 2 comms sqn with HS-125, *Andover* ac;
  SA-341E hel.
  Queen's Flt: BAe -146-100, *Andover* ac; *Wessex* hel.
CALIBRATION: 2 sqn: 1 with *Andover* E-3/-3A;
  1 calibration/target facility with *Canberra*
  B-2/E-15/T-4/TT-18.
OCU: 11: *Tornado* GR-1, *Tornado* F-3, *Buccaneer* S
  Mk 2, *Phantom* FGR-2, *Jaguar* GR-1/T-2,
  Harrier GR-3/5, T-4 *Nimrod, Canberra* B-2/T-4,
  Hercules, VC-10, SA-330/CH-47.
  1 weapons conversion unit with *Tornado* GR-1.

2 tac weapons units with *Hawk* T-1A.

TRAINING: *Hawk* T-1, *Jet Provost*, *Jetstream* T-1,
Bulldog T-1, *Chipmunk* T-10, HS-125 *Dominie*
T-1. *Tucano* in service, 1989.

TACTICAL HELICOPTERS: 5 sqn: 1 with *Wessex*; 2
with SA-330 HC-1; 2 with CH-47 HC-1.

SAR: 2 hel sqn; 9 flt: 4 with *Wessex* HC-2;
5 with *Sea King* HAR-3.

TRAINING: *Wessex*, SA-341.

AD: 2 SAM sqn with *Bloodhound* 2.

EQUIPMENT: 570 cbt ac (plus 251 in store), no
armed hel.

AIRCRAFT:
  Tornado: some 221: **GR-1:** 161 (108 strike, 12
    recce, 20 in tri-national trg sqn (Cottesmore),
    21 in weapons conversion unit); **F-2/3:** 66 (48
    ftr, 18 OCU); plus 51 GR-1, 59 F-2/-3 in store.
  Buccaneer: 34 (25 attack, 9 OCU), plus 25 in store.
  Jaguar: 87 (24 FGA, 24 close spt, 24 recce,
    15 OCU); plus 55 in store.
  Harrier: 51 (36 close spt, 15 OCU); plus 18 in store.
  Phantom: 90. **FG-1:** 18 (ftr); **F-3** (F-4J): 12 (ftr);
    FGR-2: 60 (42 ftr, 18 OCU); plus 55 in store.
  Hawk: 117 (72 tac weapons unit (*Sidewinder*-
    capable), 45 trg).
  Canberra: 48. **B2:** 5 (trg); **T4:** 9 (trg); **PR7:** 4
    (recce); **PR9:** 5 (recce); **T-17:** 12 (ECM); **TT-18:** 9
    (target towing); **E15:** 4 (calibration).
  Nimrod: 37. **R-1:** 3 (ECM); **MR-2:** 34 (MR); plus 2
    MR-2 in store.
  Shackleton: 6 (AEW); plus 5 in store.
  Victor: 14 (tanker/OCU).
  Tristar: 9. **K-1:** 4 (tanker/tpt); **KC-1:** 2 (tanker/cgo);
    K-2: 3 (tpt, to be mod to tanker/tpt).
  VC-10: 22. **C-1:** 13 (strategic tpt); **K-2:** 5 (tanker);
    K-3: 4 (tanker).
  Hercules: 60 C-130H (mod): **C-1:** 8 (OCU); **C-1K:** 6
    (tpt/tkr); **C-1P:** 16 (tac tpt, air-refuelled); **C-3P:**
    30 (tac tpt).
  Andover: 12 (6 calibration, 6 comms).
  HS-125: 31; **T-1:** 19 (trg); **CC-1/-2/3:** 12 (comms).
  BAe-146: 2 (comms).
  Jet Provost: 144 (trg).
  Jetstream: 11 (trg).
  Chieftain: 3 (comms).
  Bulldog: 122 (trg).
  Chipmunk: 65 (trg).

HELICOPTERS:
  Wessex: 64 (28 tac tpt, 18 SAR, 4 OCU, 2 VIP,
    12 trg).
  CH-47: 32 (27 tac tpt, 5 OCU).
  SA-330: 31 (26 tac tpt, 5 OCU).
  Sea King: 19 (SAR).
  SA-341: 22 (liaison, trg).

MISSILES:
  AAM: *Sidewinder, Sparrow, Red Top, Firestreak,
    Sky Flash.*
  ASM: *Martel, Harpoon, Sea Eagle.*

SAM: 64 *Bloodhound.*

ROYAL AIR FORCE REGIMENT:
5 wing HQ.
5 lt armd sqn.
1 lt inf wpn sqn.
6 SAM sqn (*Rapier*).
36 *Scorpion* lt tk; 90 *Spartan* APC; 72 *Rapier* SAM.

RESERVES (Royal Auxiliary Air Force Regiment):
6 fd def sqn; 1 lt AA gun sqn with 12 × twin
35mm *Oerlikon* and *Skyguard.*

DEPLOYMENT:
ARMY:
United Kingdom Land Forces (UKLF):
Reinforcements for 1 (BR) Corps (declared to
  NORTHAG).
  1 inf div (regular: 1 air-mobile bde, 1 arty regt, 1
  avn sqn. TA: 2 inf bde, 2 arty regt).
  1 mech bde (for armd div).
  Additional TA units incl 18 inf bn, 2 SAS, 1 arty
  recce, 4 AD (*Blowpipe*) regt.
United Kingdom Mobile Force (UKMF): (declared
  to COMLANDJUT, based on 1 mech bde, would
  be reinforced by 5,000 TA/reservists):
  1 air portable inf bde: 4 inf bn, 1 armd recce, 1
  arty regt, 1 armd sqn, 1+ SAM bty; log spt gp.
Allied Command Europe Mobile Force (*Land*)
  (AMF(L)): (some 2,300):
  UK contribution 1 inf bn, 1 armd recce, 1 sigs, 1
  engr sqn, 1 arty bty, 1 log bn; 1 avn flt.
HQ Northern Ireland: (some 9,200 excl UDR): 3 inf
  bde HQ, up to 10 major units in inf role (6
  resident, 4 roulement inf bn), 1 SAS, 1 engr sqn, 2
  avn sqn. 9 UDR bn.
Remainder of Army regular and TA units for
  Home Defence.

NAVY:
FLEET: (CinC is also CINCCHAN and
  CINCEASTLANT).
  Regular Forces, with the exception of most Patrol
  and Coastal Combatants, Mine Warfare and
  Support forces are declared to ACCHAN or
  EASTLANT.

MARINES: 1 cdo bde (declared to AFNORTH).

AIR FORCE:
STRIKE COMMAND: (CinC is also CINCUKAIR).
  Commands all combat air operations other than
  for RAF (Germany), Belize and Falklands: 3
  Groups: No. 1 (Strike, Attack, Transport), No 11
  (Air Defence), No 18 (Maritime).

SUPPORT COMMAND: trg, supply and maint spt of
  other comd.

OVERSEAS:
ANTARCTICA: 1 ice patrol ship (in summer).
ASCENSION ISLAND: RAF: *Hercules* C-1K det.

BELIZE: 1,500. Army: some 1,200; 1 inf bn, 1 armd recce tp, 1 fd arty bty, 1 engr sqn, 1 hel flt (3 *Gazelle* AH-1). RAF: 300; 1 flt (4 *Harrier* GR-3 FGA, 4 *Puma* hel), 1 *Rapier* AD det (4 fire units) RAF Regt.

BRUNEI: Army: some 900: 1 Gurkha inf bn, 1 hel flt (3 hel).

CANADA: Army: trg and liaison unit. RAF: *Tornado* det.

CYPRUS: 3,900. Army: 2,300
1 inf bn plus 2 inf coy, 1 armd recce, 1 engr spt sqn, 1 hel flt. RAF: 1,600: 1 hel sqn (*Wessex*), det of *Phantom*, *Tornado* ac, 1 lt armd sqn RAF Regt. Navy/Marines: 20.

FALKLAND ISLANDS: some 1,600. Army: 1 inf bn gp (incl AD bty, engr sqn), 1–4 engr sqn (fd, plant). RN: 1 DD/FF, 2 patrol, spt and auxiliary ships. RAF: 1 *Phantom* flt, 6 *Hercules* C-1K, 3 *Sea King* HAR-3, 6 CH-47 hel, 1 sqn RAF regt (*Rapier* SAM).

(Garrison may vary through the year.)

FRG: 69,700. Army (BAOR declared to NORTHAG): 55,700; 1 corps HQ; 3 armd div; 1 arty bde, 2 armd recce, 4 engr regt. Berlin Inf Bde: (3,000); 3 inf bn, 1 armd sqn. RAF: 11,000 (declared to 2 ATAF); 13 ac, 2 hel sqn: 7 *Tornado*, 2 *Harrier*, 2 *Phantom* FGR-2, 1 *Tornado* recce, 1 *Andover* (comms); 1 SA-330, 1 CH-47 (tpt). RAF regt: 2 Wing HQ; 4 *Rapier* SAM, 1 lt armd sqn.

GIBRALTAR: 1,800. Army: 700; 1 inf bn, Gibraltar regt (reserve), 1 engr team, 1 arty surveillance tps. Navy/Marines: 700; 2 PCI, Marine det, 2 twin *Exocet* launchers (coast defence), base unit. RAF: 400; periodic *Jaguar* ac det.

HONG KONG: 8,200. Army: 5,900 (British 1,700, Gurkha 4,200, Hong Kong regt (reserve) 1,200). Gurkha inf bde with 1 UK, 3 Gurkha inf bn, 1 Gurkha engr, regt, 1 hel sqn (–) with 10 *Scout* AH-1, 3 small landing craft, 3 other vessels. Navy/Marines: 700 (400 locally enlisted); 3 *Peacock* PCC, (12 patrol boats in local service). RAF: 300; 1 *Wessex* hel sqn (10 HC-2).

INDIAN OCEAN (Operation Armilla): 3 DD/FF, 1 spt ship. Diego Garcia: 1 naval party, 1 Marine det.

WEST INDIES (see also Belize): 1 DD/FF.

MILITARY ADVISERS: 550 in 30 countries.

PEACE-KEEPING:

CYPRUS (UNFICYP): 700: 1 inf bn(-), 1 armd recce sqn, 1 hel flt, engr and log spt.

EGYPT (Sinai MFO): 38 admin and spt.

NAMIBIA (UNTAG): Army: 175; (comms).

FOREIGN FORCES:

US: 27,900. Navy (2,500). Air (25,400):
1 Air Force HQ, 292 cbt ac trg.

FRG/ITALY: Tri-national *Tornado* trg sqn.

(3) OTHER EUROPEAN COUNTRIES

European neutral and non-aligned nations have contributed to the four United Nations peace-keeping and observer groups established during the year. Finland has supplied an infantry battalion and Switzerland the medical support in Namibia (UNTAG), with Ireland and Yugoslavia providing observers. Yugoslavia also provides observers in Angola (UNAVM) and in Iran/Iraq (UNIIMOG). Austria, Finland, Ireland and Sweden provide observers both for UNIIMOG and in Afghanistan/Pakistan (UNGOMAP).

There have been only minor developments in the size and shape of the armed forces listed in this section over the last twelve months. Fresh information has allowed us to reassess the organization of the **Cypriot** National Guard. Rather than two active formed brigades we now believe that there are merely two active level HQ each with an area responsibility and a number of active force battalions. We now list cadre infantry brigades as reserves and the Militia of 60 Home Guard battalions as a para-military force. It is proposed to raise an additional force of militia companies consisting of men over the age of 50 to support the Home Guard. Equipment developments include: the equipping of 18 VAB APC to carry *HOT* ATGW and 28 EE-3 recce vehicles with *Milan*, the delivery of eight Oerlikon twin 35mm AA guns and *Skyguard* mobile radar units, eight Yugoslav-made 128mm tube MRL, and two more *Gazelle* helicopters mounting *HOT* ATGW.

By the mid-1990s the **Swiss** Army's reservist strength will be cut by some 100,000 as military service for non-commissioned ranks is to end at age 42 (instead of 50) and for officers at age 50 (instead of 55). There are plans to enhance Swiss artillery by the procurement of additional 155mm M-109 SP howitzers for three battalions. A referendum on the possible disbandment of the army will be held in November 1989; current assessments are that this will be clearly rejected.

Naval developments include the **Irish** Navy's purchase of two *Peacock* offshore patrol craft from the UK. **Sweden** has retired four *Draken* submarines, commissioned a third *Västergötland*, with a fourth under construction, and modernized one *Näcken* submarine with an air-independent propulsion system which greatly increases its ability to remain submerged for long periods. New information has enabled us to revise our assessment of the **Yugoslav** frigate force which now comprises two Soviet *Koni*-class (Yugoslav *Split*) and two very similar but Yugoslav-built, *Kotor*-class ships, one *Kotor* was commissioned in the last twelve months.

There have been few Air Force developments. The **Austrian** Air Force has a squadron of eight J-350e *Draken* fighters now operational, which have replaced the SAAB 105e. Last year we overestimated **Yugoslav** holdings of MiG-29, the current holding is 16 not 26.

ALBANIA

GNP	1986ε:	lekë 23.97 bn ($2.12 bn)	
	1987ε:	lekë 25.17 bn ($4.03 bn)	
Growth	1986:	7.2%	1987: 5.0%
Debt*	1984:	$5.4 bn	1985: $5.6 bn
Def bdgt	1987:	lekë 1,055.0 m ($168.80 m)	
	1988:	lekë 1,080.0 m ($196.36 m)	
$1 = lekë	(1986):	8.56	(1987): 6.25
	(1988):	5.50	

Population: 3,185,000

	13–17	18–22	23–32
Men	173,000	161,000	293,000
Women	163,000	155,000	282,000

TOTAL ARMED FORCES:
ACTIVE: 40,700 (22,400 conscripts).
  Terms of service: Army 2 years; Air Force, Navy and special units 3 years.
RESERVES: 155,000 (to age 56): Army 150,000, Navy/Air Force 5,000.

ARMY: 31,500 (20,000 conscripts).
  1 tk bde.
  4 inf bde.
  3 arty regt.
  6 lt coastal arty bn.
  1 engr regt.
EQUIPMENT:†
MBT: 190: T-34, T-54.

RECCE: 13 BRDM-1.
APC: 80: BTR-40/-50/-152, Ch Type-531.
TOWED ARTY: 122mm: M-1931/37, M-1938, Ch
    Type-60; 130mm: Ch Type-59-1; 152mm:
    M-1937, Ch Type-66, D-1.
MRL: 107mm: Ch Type-63.
MORTARS: 82mm, 120mm, 160mm.
RCL: 82mm: T-21.
ATK GUNS: 45mm: M-1942; 57mm: M-1943; 85mm:
    D-44, Ch Type-56.
AD GUNS: 80: 23mm: ZU-23 twin; 37mm: M-1939;
    57mm: S-60; 85mm: KS-12.

NAVY: 2,000 (1,000 conscripts). 400 may serve in
    coast defence.†
BASES: Durres, Valona, Sazan Island, Pasha Liman.
SUBMARINES: 2 Sov *Whiskey* with 533mm TT
    (plus 1 trg, unserviceable).
PATROL AND COASTAL COMBATANTS: 40:
TORPEDO CRAFT: 32 Ch *Huchwan* PHT with 2 ×
    533mm TT.
PATROL: 8:
    2 Sov *Kronshtadt* PCO; 6 Ch *Shanghai*-II PFI.
MINE WARFARE: 1 Sov T-301 MSI;
SUPPORT: 1 Sov *Khobi* harbour tanker.

AIR FORCE: 7,200 (1,400 conscripts);
    95 cbt ac, no armed hel.†
FGA: 3 sqn:
    1 with 10 Ch J-2;
    2 with 35 J-4.
FIGHTER: 3 sqn:
    2 with 30 J-6;
    1 with 20 J-7.
TRANSPORT: 1 sqn with 3 Il-14M, 6 Li-2, 10 Y-5.
HELICOPTERS: 2 sqn with 20 Ch Z-5.
TRAINING: 6 MiG-15UTI, 8 CJ-5, 6 Yak-11.
SAM: some 4 SA-2 sites, 22 launchers.

PARA-MILITARY: 12,000.
INTERNAL SECURITY FORCE: (5,000).
FRONTIER GUARD: (7,000).

---

* Est total since 1949.
† Spares are short; some eqpt may be unserviceable.

AUSTRIA

GDP	1987: OS 1,487.50 bn ($117.65 bn)
	1988: OS 1,567.00 bn ($126.90 bn)
Growth	1987: 1.3% 1988: 4.2%
Inflation	1987: 1.4% 1988: 1.9%
Debt	1987: $12.0 bn 1988: $15.0 bn
Def bdgt	1988: OS 17.65 bn ($1.43 bn)
	1989: OS 17.26 bn ($1.31 bn)
FMA	1988: $0.03 m (US)

$1 = OS	(1987):	12.64	(1988):	12.35
	(1989):	13.13		

OS = schilling

Population: 7,564,000

	13–17	18–22	23–32
Men	244,000	308,000	637,000
Women	234,000	294,000	629,000

TOTAL ARMED FORCES: (Air Service
    forms part of the Army):
ACTIVE: 42,500 (20,500 conscripts; some 80,000
    reservists a year undergo refresher training, a
    proportion at a time).
Terms of service: 6 months recruit trg, 60 days
    reservist refresher trg during 15 years (or 8
    months trg, no refresher); 30–90 days
    additional for officers, NCO and specialists.
RESERVES: 242,000 ready (72 hrs) reserves;
    1,200,000 with reserve trg but no commitment
    (men to age 51, specialists, NCO, officers to 65).

ARMY: 38,000 (ε 20,000 conscripts).
Army HQ.
Standing Alert Force: (some 15,000):
    1 mech div of 3 mech bde (each 1 tk, 1 mech inf,
    1 SP arty, 1 SP ATK bn); 1 recce bn (cadre), 1
    AA, 1 engr bn.
    1 air-mobile, 1 mtn bn.
Field Units:
    Army: 1 HQ, 1 arty (cadre), 1 SF bn.
    Corps: 2 HQ, 1 guard, 2 arty, 1 SP ATK, 2 AA, 2
    engr bn (cadre), 2 log regt (cadre).
    9 Provincial Commands.
        Peacetime: trg and maint.
        On mob: equates to div HQ (with 1 inf bde, 1 or
        more territorial defence regt and indep units).
    30 *Landwehrstammregimente* (trg regt, no war role):
RESERVES:
8 inf bde HQ: with 24 inf, 8 arty, 3 engr/ATK/recce bn.
Territorial Tps: (82,000):
    26 inf regt, 90 inf coy, 42 guard coy;
    16 hy, 15 lt inf, 11 inf/ATK bn,
    5 hy arty bty (static), 13 engr, 6 ATK coy.
EQUIPMENT:
MBT: 56 M-60A3, 114 M-60A1 (to be A3).
APC: 460 Saurer 4K4E/F.
TOWED ARTY: 105mm: 144 IFH (M-2A1);
    155mm: 24 M-114, 6 GHN-45 (trials).
SP ARTY: 155mm: 59 M-109 A2.
MRL: 128mm: 18 M-51.
MORTARS: 81mm: 551; 107mm: 105; 120mm: 82.
RL: 400 *LAW*.
RCL: 74mm: *Miniman*; 84mm: *Carl Gustav*;
    106mm: 397 M-40A1.
ATK GUNS:

SP: 105mm: 284 *Kuerassier* JPz SK.
TOWED: 85mm: 240 M-52/M-55;
STATIC: 84mm: 60 20-pdr tk turrets;
90mm: some 130 M-47 tk turrets;
105mm: some 300 L7A2 (*Centurion* tk);
155mm: 24 SFKM2 fortress.
AD GUNS: 20mm: 512; 35mm: 74 Oerlikon twin
towed; 40mm: 38 M-42 twin SP.
MARINE WING (under School of Military Engineering):
1 river patrol craft⟨; 10 boats.

AIR FORCE: 4,500 (500 conscripts)
24 cbt ac, no armed hel.
1 air div HQ; 3 air regt; 1 AD regt:
FGA: 2 sqn with 16 SAAB J-35Oe.
FIGHTER: 1 sqn with 8 J-35Oe.
RECCE: 15 O-1E (arty fire control).
HELICOPTERS: 7 sqn:
  RECCE: 12 OH-58B, 8 AB-204 (9 in store).
  TRANSPORT: (med): 23 AB-212; (lt): 11 AB-206A.
  SAR: 24 *Alouette* III.
LIAISON: 1 sqn with 2 *Skyvan* 3M, 11 PC-6B.
TRAINING: 6 SAAB 105Oe, 14 SAAB 91D, 16
  PC-7, O-1A/-E.
AD: 3 bn with 36 20mm, 18 M-65 twin 35mm AA
guns; *Super-Bat* and *Skyguard* AD, *Goldhaube*,
Selenia MR(S-403) 3-D radar systems.

FORCES ABROAD:
AFGHANISTAN (UNGOMAP): 5.
CYPRUS (UNFICYP): 1 inf bn (410).
SYRIA (UNDOF): 1 inf bn (532).
MIDDLE EAST (UNTSO): 17.
IRAN/IRAQ (UNIIMOG): Observers.

CYPRUS

GDP	1987: £C 1.79 bn ($3.73 bn)		
	1988: £C 1.98 bn ($4.24 bn)		
Growth	1987: 7.2%	1988:	6.9%
Inflation	1987: 2.8%	1988:	3.5%
Debt	1987: $1.2 bn	1988:	$1.4 bn
Def bdgt	1987: £C 58.17 m ($121.01 m)		
$1 = £C	(1987): 0.4807	(1988):	0.4663

Population: 694,000

	13–17	*18–22*	*23–32*
Men	26,000	27,000	60,000
Women	25,000	26,000	56,000

TOTAL ARMED FORCES:
ACTIVE: 13,000.
Terms of service: conscription, 29 months, then
reserve to age 50 (officers 65).

RESERVE: 50,000 (have yearly refresher trg):
20,000 first-line; 30,000 second-line.

NATIONAL GUARD: 13,000.*
1 Army, 2 div HQ.
2 bde HQ.
2 mech bn.
1 armd bn.
1 arty bn.
1 cdo bn.
RESERVES: 6 inf bde (each with 3 inf, 1 lt arty
bn, 1 armd recce sqn) (all at cadre strength).
EQUIPMENT:
MBT: 8 T-34 (static defence), 16 AMX-30 B-2.
RECCE: 40 EE-9 *Cascavel*, 24 Marmon-Harrington
armd cars.
AIFV: 27 VAB-VCI.
APC: 16 *Leonidas*, 81 VAB-VTT; 15 EE-11 *Urutu*,
17 BTR-50P.
TOWED ARTY: 75mm: 4 M-116A1 pack; 76mm: 18
M-42; 88mm: 52 25-pdr; 100mm: 18 M-1944;
105mm: 18 M-101, 18 M-56.
MRL: 128mm: 8 Yug M-77 (YMRL-32).
MORTARS: 81mm: 71 incl SP; 82mm: M-41/-43
some SP; 107mm: 12 M-2.
ATGW: *Milan*, *HOT* (incl 18 VAB).
RL: 89mm: 540 M-20.
RCL: 57mm: 189 M-18; 106mm: 126 M-40.
AD GUNS: 100: 20mm: M-55; 35mm: 8 GDF-003;
40mm; 94mm: 3.7-in.
SAM: 20+ SA-7.
MARINE: 1 PCI⟨.
AIRCRAFT: 1 BN-2A *Maritime Defender*.
HELICOPTERS: ε 6 SA-342 *Gazelle* (with *HOT*).

PARA-MILITARY:
**NATIONAL GUARD TERRITORIAL DEFENCE
FORCE:** some 30,000, 60 Home Guard bn.
ARMED POLICE: 3,700 Shorland armd cars, 2 17m
patrol boats.

FOREIGN FORCES:
GREECE (ELDYK): 950: (Army) 1 inf, 1 cdo bn, spt
elm, plus 3,000 officers/NCO seconded to
Greek-Cypriot forces.
UNITED KINGDOM: (in Sovereign Base areas)
4,200: Army: 1 inf bn plus 2 coy, 1 armd recce
sqn. Air Force: 1 hel sqn plus ac on det.

UNITED NATIONS:
UNFICYP: some 2,300; 3 inf bn (Austria, Canada,
Denmark) 1 inf bn, armd recce sqn (UK).

---

* Mainly Greek-Cypriot conscripts, but some 3,000
seconded Greek Army officers and NCO.

NORTHERN CYPRUS

Data presented here represents the *de facto* situation in the island. It in no way implies recognition, or IISS approval.

Def bdgt* 1987ε: TL 5.20 bn ($6.07 m)
        1988: TL 8.00 bn ($5.62 m)
$1 = TL (1987): 857   (1988): 1,422
TL = Turkish lira

TOTAL ARMED FORCES:
ACTIVE: some 3,000.
   Terms of service: conscription, 24 months, then reserve to age 50.
RESERVES: 5,000 first-line, 10,000 second-line.

ARMY:
   7 inf bn.
   spt arty reported.
EQUIPMENT:
MBT: 5 T-34 (operability questionable).
MORTARS: 107mm: 10 4.2-in.; 120mm: 30.
MARITIME: 1 patrol boat.

FOREIGN FORCES:
TURKEY: 27,000; 1 corps of 2 inf div, 1 indep armd bde.

* Officially reported figures.

FINLAND

GDP	1987: m 393.60 bn ($89.54 bn)		
	1988ε: m 437.51 bn ($104.6 bn)		
Growth	1987: 3.8%	1988: 4.5%	
Inflation	1987: 4.1%	1988: 5.1%	
Debt	1986: $28.9 bn	1987: $30.3 bn	
Def bdgt	1988: m 6.34 bn ($1.52 bn)		
	1989: m 7.90 bn ($1.81 bn)		
FMA	1988: $0.04 m (US)		
$1 = m	(1987): 4.3956	(1988): 4.1828	
	(1989): 4.3569		

m = markka

Population: 4,980,000

	13–17	18–22	23–32
Men	157,000	174,000	387,000
Women	150,000	167,000	369,000

TOTAL ARMED FORCES:
ACTIVE: 31,000 (23,700 conscripts).
   Terms of service: 8–11 months (11 months for officers and NCO).

RESERVES (all services): some 700,000 (31,000 a year do conscript trg; some 50,000 reservists a year do refresher trg: total obligation 40 days (75 for NCO, 100 for officers) between conscript service and age 50 (NCO and officers to age 60)).
Total strength on mob some 500,000, with 300,000 in general forces (bde etc) and 200,000 in local defence forces, (Army 460,000, Navy 12,000, Air Force 30,000) plus 200,000 unallocated as replacements etc.

ARMY: 27,800 (22,300 conscripts).
7 Military Areas; 23 Military Districts:
   1 armd bde (1 armd, 1 mech inf, 1 ATK, 1 arty bn, 1 AA bty).
   7 inf trg bde (each 3 inf bn (1 cadre), some with 1 arty bn).
   5 indep inf bn (incl 1 cdo, 1 para).
   Field arty: 3 regt, 1 indep bn.
   Coast arty: 2 regt; 3 indep bn (1 mobile).
   3 AA arty regt (incl 1 SAM bn with SAM-79).
   1 indep AD arty bn.
   2 engr bn.
RESERVES:
   2 armd bde.
   25 inf bde (11 Type 90, 14 Type 80).
   Some 50 indep bn.
   200 local defence units.
EQUIPMENT:
MBT: 100 T-54/-55, 80 T-72.
LIGHT TANKS: 15 PT-76.
AIFV: 30 BMP-1, 6 BMP-2.
APC: 90 BTR-50P, some 60 BTR-60, some 80 A-180 *Sisu*, 10 MT-LB.
TOWED ARTY: 105mm: 70+ M-37/-61; 122mm: M-38/D-30; 130mm: 170 M-54 (M-46); 150mm: M-40; 152mm: 240 M-38; 155mm: 12 M-74 (K-83).
COAST ARTY: 100mm: D-10T (tank turrets); 122mm: M-60; 130mm: 170 K-87; 152mm: 240.
COAST SSM: some RBS-15.
MORTARS: 81mm: 880; 120mm: 550.
ATGW: 24 M-82 (AT-4 *Spigot*), 12 M-83 (BGM-71C *Improved TOW*), AT-5 *Spandrel*.
RL: 112mm: some *APILAS*.
RCL: 55mm: M-55; 74mm: *Miniman*; 95mm: 100 SM-58-61.
AD GUNS: 20mm; 23mm: ZU-23; 30mm; 35mm: GDF-002; 40mm: 100+ L-60/L-70; 57mm: 12 S-60 towed, 12 ZSU-57-2 SP.
SAM: SAM-79 (SA-3), SAM-78 (SA-7), SAM-86 (SA-14).

NAVY: 1,400 (600 conscripts).
BASES: Upinniemi (Helsinki), Turku.
4 functional sqn (gunboat, missile, patrol, mine warfare). Approx 50% of units kept fully manned. Others in short-notice storage, rotated regularly.

PATROL AND COASTAL COMBATANTS: 21:
CORVETTES: 2 *Turunmaa* with 1 × 120mm gun, 2 × 5 ASW RL.
MISSILE CRAFT: 8:
4 *Helsinki I* PFM with 2 × 2 RBS-15SF SSM;
4 *Tuima* (Sov *Osa-II*) with 4 MTO-74 (Sov SS-N-2B) SSM.
PATROL CRAFT: inshore: 11:
2 *Rihtriemi* with 2 ASW RL.
3 *Ruissalo* with 2 ASW RL.
6 *Nuoli* PFI⟨.
MINE WARFARE: 8:
MINELAYERS: 2:
1 *Pohjanmaa* (trg), 120 mines; plus 1 × 120mm gun.
1 *Keihässalmi*, 100 mines.
MCM: 6 *Kuha* MSI⟨.
AMPHIBIOUS: craft only; 3 *Kampela* LCU tpt, 6 *Kala* LCU, 5 *Kave* LCU.
SUPPORT AND MISCELLANEOUS:
5 *Valas* coastal tpt (can be used for minelaying).
9 icebreakers (civil, Board of Navigation Control).

AIR FORCE: 1,800 (800 conscripts);
75 cbt ac, no armed hel.
3 AD districts: 3 fighter wings.
FIGHTER: 3 sqn:
1 with 25 MiG-21bis;
2 with 41 SAAB J-35.
OCU: 5 MiG-21U/UM, 4 SAAB SK-35C.
RECCE: 1 flt with 8 *Hawk* Mk 51.
SURVEY: 3 Learjet 35A (survey, ECM trg, target-towing).
TRANSPORT: 1 ac sqn with 3 F-27.
1 hel flt with 7 Mi-8 (also SAR), 2 Hughes 500.
TRAINING: 38 *Hawk* Mk 51, 30 L-70 *Vinka*.
LIAISON: 6 CM-170 *Magister*, 15 Piper (9 *Cherokee Arrow*, 6 *Chieftain*).
AAM: AA-2 *Atoll*, RB-27, RB-28 (*Falcon*), AIM-9 *Sidewinder*.

FORCES ABROAD:
AFGHANISTAN (UNGOMAP): 3.
CYPRUS (UNFICYP): 8.
INDIA/PAKISTAN (UNMOGIP): 4.
IRAN/IRAQ (UNIIMOG): 15.
LEBANON (UNIFIL): 1 bn (550).
MIDDLE EAST (UNTSO): 23.
NAMIBIA (UNTAG): 1 bn (890).
SYRIA (UNDOF): 1 bn (410).

PARA-MILITARY:
FRONTIER GUARD (Ministry of Interior): 4,400 (on mob 24,000); 4 frontier, 3 coast guard districts, 1 air comd; 5 offshore, 1 coastal, 9 inshore patrol craft; 3 Mi-8 (SAR), 2 AS-332, 3 AB 412, 7 AB-206 hel; 4 lt ac.

IRELAND

GDP	1987:	£I 19.78 bn ($29.43 bn)		
	1988ε:	£I 20.66 bn ($31.50 bn)		
Growth	1987:	4.1%	1988ε:	2.5%
Inflation	1987:	3.2%	1988:	2.1%
Debt	1987:	$26.3 bn	1988:	$29.2 bn
Def bdgt	1988:	£I 253.09 m ($386.24 m)		
	1989:	£I 264.50 m ($379.05 m)		
FMA	1988:	$0.03 m (US)		
$1 = £I	(1987):	0.6720	(1988):	0.6553
	(1989):	0.6978		

Population: 3,599,000

	13–17	18–22	23–32
Men	178,000	169,000	285,000
Women	169,000	161,000	275,000

TOTAL ARMED FORCES:
ACTIVE: 13,000 incl 60 women.
Terms of service: voluntary, 3-year terms to age 60, officers 56–65.
RESERVES: 16,100 (obligation to age 60, officers 57–65). Army: first-line 950, second-line 14,800. Navy 350.

ARMY: 11,200.
4 cmd.
1 inf force (2 inf bn).
4 inf bde:
2 with 2 inf bn, 1 with 3, all with 1 fd arty regt, 1 cav recce sqn, 1 engr coy;
1 with 2 inf bn, 1 armd recce sqn, 1 fd arty bty.
Army tps: 1 lt tk sqn, 1 AD regt, 1 Ranger coy.
(Total units: 11 inf bn; 1 UNIFIL bn *ad hoc* with elm from other bn, 1 tk sqn, 4 recce sqn (1 armd), 3 fd arty regt (each of 2 bty); 1 indep bty, 1 AD regt (1 regular, 3 reserve bty), 3 fd engr coy, 1 Ranger coy).
RESERVES:
4 Army Gp (garrisons), 18 inf bn, 6 fd arty regt, 3 cav sqn, 3 engr sqn, 3 AA bty.
EQUIPMENT:
LIGHT TANKS: 14 *Scorpion*.
RECCE: 19 AML-90, 32 AML-60.
APC: 60 Panhard VTT/M3, 10 *Timoney*.
TOWED ARTY: 88mm: 48 25-pdr; 105mm: 12 lt.
MORTARS: 81mm: 400; 120mm: 72.
ATGW: 21 *Milan*.
RCL: 84mm: 444 *Carl Gustav*; 90mm: 96 PV-1110.
AD GUNS: 40mm: 24 L/60, 2 L/70.
SAM: 7 RBS-70.

NAVY: 1,000.
BASE: Cork.

PATROL AND COASTAL COMBATANTS: 7:
7 PCO:
1 *Eithne* with 1 *Dauphin* hel;
3 *Emer*, 1 *Deirdre*.
2 *Orla* (UK *Peacock*).

AIR FORCE: 800.
14 cbt ac, no armed hel.
3 wings (1 trg):
COIN: 1 sqn with 6 CM-170-2 *Super Magister*.
COIN/TRAINING: 1 sqn with 8 SF-260WE, 1 SF-260
MC ac, 2 SA-342L trg hel.
MR: 2 *Super King Air* 200.
TRANSPORT: 1 HS-125, 1 *Super King Air* 200.
LIAISON: 1 sqn with 7 Reims Cessna F-172H,
1 F-172K.
HELICOPTERS: 3 sqn.
1 Army spt with 8 *Alouette* III.
1 Navy spt with 2 SA-365.
1 SAR with 3 SA-365.

FORCES ABROAD:
AFGHANISTAN (UNGOMAP): 5.
CYPRUS (UNFICYP): 8.
INDIA/PAKISTAN (UNMOGIP): 1
IRAN/IRAQ (UNIIMOG): 52.
LEBANON (UNIFIL): 1 bn+ (748); 4 AML-90 armd
cars, 13 VTT/M3 APC, 4 120mm mor.
MIDDLE EAST (UNTSO): 21.
NAMIBIA (UNTAG): 20.

MALTA

GDP	1987: LM 546.50 m ($1.58 bn)		
	1988: LM 587.00 m ($1.78 bn)		
Growth	1987: 4.2%	1988: 4.8%	
Inflation	1987: 0.5%	1988: 1.0%	
Debt	1987: $86.7 m	1988: $85.0 m	
Def bdgt	1988: LM 7.40 m ($22.39 m)		
	1989: LM 8.20 m ($23.64 m)		
FMA	1988: $0.03 m (US)		
$1 = LM	(1987): 0.3451	(1988): 0.3306	
	(1989): 0.3468		
LM = lira			

Population: 393,800

	13–17	18–22	23–32
Men	13,800	12,600	27,700
Women	12,900	11,900	26,300

TOTAL ARMED FORCES:
ACTIVE: 1,500.
Terms of service: voluntary.

'ARMED FORCES OF MALTA':
Comd HQ, spt tps.
No. 1 Regt with:
1 inf coy; RPG-7 RL, 81mm and 82mm mor.
1 marine sqn; 8 inshore patrol craft.
1 airport coy; 1 airport security coy.
1 hel flt; 2 AB-204, 1 AB-206A, 1 AB-47G, 1
Bell-47G. (3 SA-316 in store).
No. 2 Regt with:
1 AD bty; 50 ZPU-4 14.5mm AA guns.
1 general duties coy.
1 security coy.
1 electrical and mechanical engr coy.

PARA-MILITARY:
'ID DEJMA' (R): 700 (being phased out).

FOREIGN FORCES:
ITALY: 2 AB-212 (SAR) hel.

SWEDEN

GDP	1987: S kr 1,005.23 bn ($158.54 bn)		
	1988ε: S kr 1,083.64 bn ($176.86 bn)		
Growth	1987: 2.4%	1988: 2.0%	
Inflation	1987: 4.2%	1988: 5.8%	
Debt	1987: $50.0 bn	1988ε: $41.7 bn	
Def bdgt	1987/8: S kr 29.77 bn ($4.86 bn)		
	1988/9: S kr 30.17 bn ($4.78 bn)		
$1 = kr	(1987): 6.3404	(1988): 6.1272	
kr = kronor			

Population: 8,391,000

	13–17	18–22	23–32
Men	279,000	295,000	590,000
Women	266,000	281,000	564,000

TOTAL ARMED FORCES:
ACTIVE: 64,500 (49,000 conscripts);
Terms of Service: Army and Navy 7½–15 months,
Air Force 8–12 months.
RESERVES* (obligation to age 47): 709,000:
Army (incl Local Defence and Home Guard)
550,000; Navy 102,000; Air Force 57,000.

ARMY: 44,500 (37,700 conscripts).
6 Military comd; 26 Defence districts (*Laens*).
PEACE ESTABLISHMENT:
44 armd, cav, inf, arty, AA, engr, sig, spt regt
(local defence, cadre for mob, basic conscript
plus refresher trg).
WAR ESTABLISHMENT: (725,000 on mob)
Field Army: (300,000).

4 armd bde.
1 mech bde.
18 inf, 5 *Norrland*, 1 *Gotland* bde.
100 indep armd, inf, arty and AA arty bn.
1 avn bn.
9 arty avn pl.
Local Defence Units: (300,000)
90 indep bn, 400–500 indep coy.
Home Guard: (125,000)
incl inf, arty, static arty, AD
EQUIPMENT:
MBT: 340 Strv-101, 110 Strv-102/-104 (*Centurion*), 335 Strv-103B.
LIGHT TANKS: 200 Ikv-91.
APC: 600 Pbv-302.
TOWED ARTY: 105mm: 550 Type-40; 150mm: 140 M-39; 155mm: 300 FH-77A/-B.
SP ARTY: 155mm: 30 BK-1A.
MORTARS: 81mm: 1,000; 120mm: 500.
ATGW: RB-53 (*Bantam*), RB-55 (*TOW*, incl Pvrbv 551 SP).
RCL: 74mm: *Miniman*; 84mm: AT-4, *Carl Gustav*; 90mm: PV-1110.
AD GUNS: 20mm: 114; 40mm: 600.
SAM: RB-69 (*Redeye*), RBS-70 (incl Lvrbv SP), RB-77 (*Improved HAWK*).
AIRCRAFT: 17 SK-61C (BAe *Bulldog*) observation, 2 Dornier Do-27 tpt.
HELICOPTERS: 20 HKP-9A ATK, 14 HKP-3 tpt, 26 HKP-5B trg, 19 HKP-6A utility.

NAVY: 12,000, incl coast arty and naval air (6,300 conscripts); some vessels with Coast Defence.
BASES: Muskö, Härnösand, Karlskrona, Göteborg (spt only).
SUBMARINES: 11:
3 *Västergötland* with TP-617 HWT and TP-42 LWT.
1 modernized *Näcken* (AIP) with TP-617 and TP-42.
2 *Näcken*, 5 *Sjöormen*, with TP-61 and TP-42.
PATROL AND COASTAL COMBATANTS: 45:
MISSILE CRAFT: 30 PFM:
2 *Stockholm* with 4 × 2 RBS-15 SSM; plus 2 × 533mm TT or 4 × 400mm TT.
16 *Hugin* with 6 RB-12 (No *Penguin*) SSM; plus 4 *Elma* ASW launchers.
12 *Norrköping* with 2 RBS-15 SSM or up to 6 × 533mm TT.
PATROL: 15:
1 PFC, 3 PCC, 11 PCI⟨.
MINE WARFARE: 31:
MINELAYERS: 3:
1 *Carlskrona* (105 mines) trg.
2 *Älvsborg* (300 mines).
MINE COUNTERMEASURES: 28:
6 *Landsort* MCC.
4 *Arkö* MSC.
18 other MSI
AMPHIBIOUS: craft only; 12 LCM.

SUPPORT AND MISCELLANEOUS: 12:
1 AGI, 1 salvage ship, 1 survey, 6 icebreakers, 2 tugs, 1 MCM spt ship.

COAST DEFENCE: (2,650; 1,700 conscripts).
5 arty bde: 60 units incl arty, barrier bn, coast ranger coy, minelayer sqn.
EQUIPMENT:
GUNS: 40mm incl L/70 AA, 75mm, 120mm incl CD-80 *Karin* (mobile); 75mm, 120mm (static).
SSM: RBS-17 *Hellfire*, RBS-08A, RB-52.
MINELAYERS: 9 coastal, 16 inshore.
PATROL CRAFT: 18 PCI⟨.
AMPHIBIOUS: 9 LCM, 80 LCU, 55 LCA.

NAVAL AIR: 1 cbt ac, 14 armed hel.
ASW: 1 C-212 ac.
HELICOPTERS: 3 sqn with 14 HKP-4B/C (KV-107) ASW, 9 HKP-6 (AB-206) liaison.

AIR FORCE: 8,000 (5,000 conscripts);
417 cbt ac, no armed hel.
1 attack gp.
4 AD districts.
9 wings liaison ac: 42 SK-50 (SAAB 91 *Safir*).
FGA: 6 sqn:
5 with 82 AJ-37 *Viggen*;
1 (OCU) with 18 SK-37.
FIGHTER: 11 sqn:
3 with 68 J-35F/J, 4 SK-35C *Draken*;
8 with 139 JA-37 *Viggen*.
RECCE: 3 sqn with 48 SH/SF-37 *Viggen*.
ECM: 2 *Caravelle* (ECM/ELINT).
TRANSPORT: 1 sqn with 8 C-130E/H.
COMMUNICATIONS: SK-60, 3 *King Air* 200, 2 *Metro* III (VIP).
TRAINING: incl 106 SK-60A/B/C (also have lt attack/recce role), 50 SK-61, 22 J-32 *Lansen* (14 -32E ECM trg, 8 -32D target towing).
SAR: 1 sqn with 6 HKP-4, 4 HKP-9B, 2 HKP-10.
UTILITY: 6 HKP-3 hel.
AAM: RB-24 (AIM-9J/L *Sidewinder*), RB-27 (*Falcon*), RB-28 (*Improved Falcon*), RB-71 (*Skyflash*).
ASM: RB-04E, RB-05A, RB-15F, RB-75 (*Maverick*).
AD: Semi-automatic control and surveillance system, *Stril* 60, co-ordinates all AD components.

FORCES ABROAD:
AFGHANISTAN (UNGOMAP): 6.
LEBANON (UNIFIL): 770 log bn and medical tps.
IRAN/IRAQ (UNIIMOG): Observers.

PARA-MILITARY:
COAST GUARD: (550); 2 TV-171 fishery protection vessels, 70 PCI⟨; (Air Arm:) 2 C-212 MR, 1 Cessna 337G, 1 402C ac.

CIVIL DEFENCE: shelters for 6,300,000. All between age 16–25 liable for civil defence duty.

VOLUNTARY AUXILIARY ORGANIZATIONS: Some 35,000 volunteers for army units from: Motor Cycle Corps, Radio Organization, Women's Motor Transport Corps, Women's Auxiliary Defence Services, Red Cross.

---

* Each year some 100,000 reservists carry out refresher trg; length of trg depends on rank (officers up to 31 days, NCO and specialists, 24 days, others 17 days). Commitment is 5 exercises during reserve service period, plus mob call-outs.

SWITZERLAND

GDP	1987:	fr 255.10 bn ($171.07 bn)	
	1988ε:	fr 267.34 bn ($182.70 bn)	
Growth	1987: 2.3%		1988: 3.0%
Inflation	1987: 1.4%		1988: 1.9%
Debt	1986: $32.0 bn		1987: $31.0 bn
Def bdgt	1988:	fr 4.78 bn ($3.26 bn)	
	1989:	fr 5.23 bn ($3.27 bn)	
$1 = fr	(1987):	1.4912	(1988): 1.4633
	(1989):	1.5970	

fr = francs

Population: 6,586,000

	13–17	18–22	23–32
Men	206,000	247,000	510,000
Women	196,000	236,000	502,000

TOTAL ARMED FORCES: (Air Corps forms part of the Army):

ACTIVE: about 3,500 regular, plus recruits (2 intakes of 18,000 each for 17 weeks only).

Terms of service: 17 weeks compulsory recruit trg at age 20, followed by reservist refresher trg of 3 weeks over an 8-year period between ages 21–32 for *Auszug* (call out), 39 days over a 3-year period (33–42) for *Landwehr* (militia), 13 days over 2-year period (43–50) for *Landsturm* (Home Guard/last reserve). Some 438,500 attend trg each year.

RESERVES (all services): 625,000.

ARMY: 565,000 on mob.

3 corps, each 1 mech, 2 inf div, 1 inf, 1 cyclist, 1 SAM, 1 engr regt, 1 arty bn, 1 hel sqn, 1 lt ac flt.

1 mtn corps with 3 mtn div (each 1 inf, 1 fortification, 1 redoubt bde), 1 mtn, 7 inf, 1 engr, 5 pack horse bn, 1 hel sqn.

Corps Tps:

6 Territorial Zones: each with log, medical and civil defence regt.

11 border bde.

Army Tps:

1 inf, 3 engr regt, 3 sigs (EW) bn.

1 airport guard regt, 1 indep airport bn.

20 fortress guard coy.

EQUIPMENT:

MBT: some 820: some 130 Pz-87 (*Leopard* 2), 150 Pz-55/-57 (*Centurion*), 150 Pz-61, 390 Pz-68 (195 to be mod).

APC: 1,350 M-63/-73/-64 (M-113).

TOWED ARTY: 105mm: some 360 Model-35, 468 Model-46.

SP ARTY: 155mm: 473 PzHb-66/-74 (M-109U).

MRL: 81mm: RWK-014 30-tube.

MORTARS: 2,750: 81mm: M-33, M-72; 120mm: 110 M-64/-74.

ATGW: 6 MOWAG *Piranha* with *TOW*-2; 800 B/B-65 (*Bantam*), B/B-77 (*Dragon*).

RL: 83mm: 5,500 M-80.

RCL: 106mm: 600 M-58.

ATK GUNS: 90mm: 850 Model-50/-57.

AD GUNS: 20mm: 1,700; 35mm: 260 GDF-002.

SAM: 60 B/L-84 (*Rapier*).

MARINE: 11 *Aquarius* patrol boats.

AIR CORPS: 60,000 on mob; (incl military airfield guard units).

272 cbt ac, no armed hel.

1 Air Force bde: 3 air regt (1 lt ac wing, 1 long-range recce patrol coy).

FGA: 8 sqn with 127 *Hunter* F-58, 7 T-68.

FIGHTER: 8 sqn:

6 with 92 F-5E, 12 F-5F;

2 with 30 *Mirage* IIIS.

RECCE: 1 sqn with 18 *Mirage* IIIRS.

LIAISON/SAR: 1 sqn with 2 Learjet 36, 18 PC-6 *Turbo-Porter*.

HELICOPTERS: 7 sqn with 26 SA-315, 70 SA-316, 3 AS-332.

TRAINING: incl 40 PC-7, 32 *Vampire* T-55, 20 *Vampire* Mk 6 (plus 40 in store), 4 *Mirage* IIIBS, 64 Pilatus P-3, 4 PC-9.

AAM: AIM-9 *Sidewinder*, AIM-26B *Falcon*.

ASM: AGM-65A/B *Maverick*, AS-30.

1 airbase bde:

3 regt × 4 bn, each with 4 bty of 20mm and twin 35mm guns with *Skyguard* fire-control radar.

1 AD bde:

1 SAM regt (2 bn, each of 2 bty; 64 *Bloodhound*);

7 AD arty regt (each of 3 bty; 35mm guns, *Skyguard* fire control).

PARA-MILITARY:

CIVIL DEFENCE: 480,000 (300,000 fully trained). Shelter programme for 5,500,000; emergency supplies and medical facilities.

YUGOSLAVIA

GMP	1986:	YD 25,083 bn ($66.14 bn)		
	1987:	YD 55,936 bn ($75.90 bn)		
Growth	1986:	3.5%	1987:	1.5%
Inflation	1987:	120.8%	1988:	260.0%
Debt	1987:	$20.2 bn	1988:	$19.8 bn
Def bdgt	1988:	YD 5,247.0 bn ($2.08 bn)		
	1989:	YD 34,920.0 bn ($4.41 bn)		
FMA	1988:	$0.10 m (US)		
$1 = YD	(1986):	379.22	(1987):	737.00
	(1988):	2,522.60	(1989):	7,915.00
YD = dinar				

Population: 23,571,000

	13–17	18–22	23–32
Men	951,000	924,000	1,909,000
Women	899,000	875,000	1,820,000

TOTAL ARMED FORCES:
ACTIVE: 180,000 (101,400 conscripts).
Terms of service: 12 months.
RESERVES: 510,000: Army 440,000; Navy 43,000; Air 27,000 (to age 55, officers 60).

ARMY: 138,000 (93,000 conscripts);
4 Military Regions; incl 1 coastal.
10 Corps HQ.
2 inf div.
29 armd/mech inf/mtn/arty bde reported following recent re-org.
1 AB bde.
RESERVES:
Territorial Defence Force (militia): 860,000 in wartime; mobile inf bde, arty, AA bn; (eqpt mainly obsolescent).
EQUIPMENT:
MBT: 1,635: 750 T-54/-55, some 290 M-84 (T-74; mod T-72) and T-72, 45 M-47, some 250 T-34 (in store), 300 M-4 (in store).
LIGHT TANKS: 13 PT-76.
RECCE: 92 M-3A1, 18 M-8, some 40 BRDM-2.
AIFV: 410 M-80.
APC: 200 BTR-40/-50, 300 M-60P.
TOWED ARTY: 2,137: 105mm: 516: M-101, M-56, M-18; 122mm: 241 M-1931/37, 378 M-1938/D-30; 130mm: 186 M-46; 152mm: 240: M-1937, D-20/M-84; 155mm: 150 M-59, 426 M-65, M-114.
SP ARTY: 105mm: M-7; 122mm: 2S1.
MRL: 128mm: 160 M-77 (YMRL-32), M-63.
MORTARS: 82mm: 3,400; 120mm: 3,000.
SSM: 4 FROG-7.
ATGW: BOV-1 veh with AT-1 *Snapper*, AT-3 *Sagger*.
RCL: 57mm: 1,550; 82mm: 2,000 M-60PB SP; 105mm: 650 M-65.

ATK GUNS: 75mm: 748: M-1943, PAL-40; 90mm: 540: M-63B2 (incl SP); 100mm: 511 T-12.
AD GUNS: 20mm: 2,300: M-55/-75, BOV-3 SP triple; 30mm: 620: M-53, M-53/-59, BOV-3 SP; 37mm: 418 M-1939; 40mm: 128: M-1, L/70; 57mm: 304: S-60, ZSU-57-2 SP; 85mm: 260 M-1944; 90mm: 210 M-117; 3.7-in. (94mm): 46.
SAM: SA-6/-7/-9.

NAVY: 10,000 incl 900 marines, 2,300 coast defence (4,400 conscripts).
BASES: Split, Pula, Sibenik, Kardeljevo, Kotor.
SUBMARINES: 5:
3 *Heroj* SS with 533mm TT.
2 *Sutjeska* SSC (trg) with 533mm TT.
plus 4 *Una* SSI for SF ops.
FRIGATES: 4:
2 *Kotor* with 4 × SS-N-2B *Styx* SSM, 2 × 12 ASW RL, 2 × 3 ASTT.
2 *Split* (Sov *Koni*) with 4 SS-N-2B *Styx* SSM, 2 × 12 ASW RL.
PATROL AND COASTAL COMBATANTS: 71:
MISSILE CRAFT: 16:
6 *Rade Koncar* PFM with 2 × SS-N-2B *Styx*.
10 *Mitar Acev* (Sov *Osa-I*) PFM with 4 × SS-N-2A.
TORPEDO CRAFT: 15:
15 *Topcider* (Sov *Shershen*) with 4 × 533mm TT.
PATROL: 40:
COASTAL: 3 *Mornar* ASW with 4 × ASW RL.
INSHORE: 27: 10 *Kraljevica*, 17 *Mirna*
RIVERINE: 10⟨.
MINE WARFARE: 14
MINELAYERS: None, but DTM-211 LCT can lay 100 mines - see amph forces.
MCM: 14:
4 *Vukov Klanac* MHC
4 UK '*Ham*' MSI.
6 *M-117* MSI
(plus 6 riverine MSI⟨).
AMPHIBIOUS: craft only; 35: 10 DTM-211 LCT, 25 DJC-601 LCM.
SUPPORT AND MISCELLANEOUS: 7:
3 PO-91 *Lubin* tpt, 1 salvage, 1 Sov *Moma* survey, 1 trg, 1 flagship.

MARINES:
2 marine bde (2 regt each of 2 bn).

COAST DEFENCE:
25 coast arty bty.
GUNS: 85mm: 45 M-44; 88mm: 55 M-36; 122mm: 75 M-37; 130mm: 85 M-54; 152mm: 85 D-20.
SSM: SS-C-3 *Shaddock*, *Brom* (truck-mounted SS-N-2).

AIR FORCE: 32,000 (4,000 conscripts);

421 cbt ac, some 200 armed hel.

3 air corps each 1 AD div, incl ac, AD arty, SAM.

FGA: 12 sqn with 25 P-2 *Kraguj*, 60 *Jastreb*, 30 *Super Galeb*, 50 *Orao* 2.

FIGHTER: 9 sqn with 112 MiG-21F/PF/M/bis, 18 MiG-21U, 16 MiG-29.

RECCE: 4 sqn with 25 *Galeb*, 20 *Jastreb* RJ-1, 25 *Orao*-1.

ARMED HEL: 70 Mi-8 (aslt); 120 *Gazela* (attack).

ASW: 1 hel sqn with 8 Ka-25, 2 Ka-28 (Navy-assigned).

TRANSPORT: 2 ac sqn with 6 Yak-40, 12 An-12, 15 An-26, 2 *Falcon* 50 (VIP), 2 *Learjet*, 4 CL-215 (SAR/fire-fighting), 9 PC-6.

7 hel sqn with *Gazela*, Mi-8 (Army-assigned).

1 sqn with 10 Mi-8, 15 *Gazela* (Navy-assigned).

LIAISON: 50 UTVA-66 ac, 14 *Gazela* hel.

TRAINING: ac: 110 *Galeb/Jastreb,* 80 UTVA-75/-76; **hel:** 20 *Gazela*.

AAM: AA-2 *Atoll*, AA-8 *Aphid*.

ASM: AGM-65 *Maverick*, AS-7 *Kerry*, AS-9 *Kyle*.

AD: 14 SAM bn (8 SA-2, 6 SA-3).

15 regt AD arty.

FORCES ABROAD:
ANGOLA (UNAVM): 7.

IRAN/IRAQ (UNIIMOG): Observers.

NAMIBIA (UNTAG): 25.

PARA-MILITARY:
FRONTIER GUARDS: Ministry of Defence (15,000); 10 *Mirna*, 6 Type-131 PCI.

MILICIJA (Police): BRDM-2 recce; TAB-71/-72, BTR-50, M-60P APC; SA-341/-342 hel.

CIVIL DEFENCE: 2 m on mob (not under Army).

The Middle East and North Africa

Military Developments

Weapon Proliferation

Concern over the proliferation of chemical weapons (CW) and SSM continues. Despite denials, **Libya** is widely believed to have been constructing a CW plant at Rabta some 35 miles inland from Tripoli. Following press allegations **Egypt** has also denied that it has a CW production capability. Allegations have also been made of the existence of an **Israeli** CW plant in the Negev.

While the year has seen no new operational deployments of ballistic missiles in the region, co-operative development of them involving Middle East and other Third-world partners has continued apace. Joint **Egyptian–Iraqi** development of the *Badr* 2000, based on the Argentinian *Condor* 2, with a claimed capability of accurate delivery to 400 km and maximum range of 1,200 km remains of concern. **Iraq** also continues to extend the range of its Soviet-supplied *Scud* B. Israel has again tested the *Jericho* 2, this time to a range of 850 km; it is assessed that the missile will have an eventual maximum range of 1,500 km. **Israel** also launched its first satellite, the *Ofek* 1, which went into low orbit on 19 September 1988 with a 75-kg test payload. Although the next launch is not expected for two to three years, it is already being suggested that the launch rocket, the *Shavit*, might provide a basis for a *Jericho* 3 with a potential range of up to 7,000 km. Another worrying development in the region is the delivery to **Libya** of some six Su-24 fighter-bombers coupled with the possibility that the Soviet Union would convert a Libyan transport to the tanker role.

The Gulf War

After eight years of bitter fighting the UN-brokered cease-fire between **Iraq** and **Iran** came into force on 20 August 1988. The UN Iran Iraq Military Observer Group (UNIIMOG), to which 26 countries have contributed some 600 military personnel, was quickly deployed. There have been relatively few cease-fire violations even though neither side has withdrawn all troops into their own territory. A limited exchange of sick and injured prisoners of war has taken place. Though both sides need to rebuild and re-equip their armed forces there is little evidence as yet of any new large-scale arms imports. Indeed, at the Baghdad Military Fair in April/May 1989, Iraq revealed the extent to which it has managed to establish, with Egyptian assistance, its own armaments industry. Amongst equipments unveiled at the exhibition were two new 6 × 6 wheeled SP guns, of 155mm and 210mm calibre, for which maximum ranges of 38 and 57 km are claimed. Other developments noted were the successful integration of equipments from different sources, such as a French *Mirage* aircraft armed with a Soviet ASM, and Soviet transport aircraft equipped for AEW with both French and British radar equipment. Apart from a requirement for advanced combat aircraft, which has led to the procurement of further Chinese J-6 FGA aircraft, Iraq is more in the market for industrial technology, components and production licences. Iran has also procured more J-6 aircraft but, although it held an arms trade fair in Teheran in November 1988, at which were notably displayed various types of Iranian-made free-flight rockets copied from other models, no other major acquisitions to restore the Iranian armoury have yet been reported. The visit to Moscow by Hashemi-Rafsanjani Speaker of the Iranian *Majlis* was widely believed to include a request for Soviet arms. Moscow is thought to have assured Iraq that only items of a defensive nature such as SAM and ATGW would be supplied to Iran. Gulf naval forces, remain substantially unchanged. The major portion of the Iraqi fleet remains in the Mediterranean whilst negotiations between Italy and Iraq continue on the terms of payment for the undelivered ships. Improvements in the Khawr Abd'Allah waterway to Umm Qasr mean that Iraq would not be dependent on the use of the Shatt al'Arab to berth the ships.

International naval forces in the Gulf have continued to draw down since the cease-fire. Belgium, Italy and the Netherlands have brought their ships home: the US has cut its escort force from nine to six combatants and reduced the MCM group to three vessels, while maintaining a

Carrier Battle Group on station in the Western Indian Ocean but at longer notice for intervention thus allowing it a wider field of operations. The UK has withdrawn its MCM group but retains the *Armilla* patrol, and the French and Soviet navies are covering the area from normal on-station forces.

Regional Diplomacy

Saudi Arabia and Iraq signed a non-aggression pact in March 1989 during a visit by King Fahd to Baghdad. In February 1989 the Arab Cooperation Council was formed with Iraq, Egypt, North Yemen and Jordan as members. Its stated aim is to foster economic co-operation but it seems unlikely to be able to avoid becoming involved in political and military affairs. The final outstanding element of the Egyptian–Israeli peace treaty was resolved in September 1988, when international arbitrators ruled on the line of the border in Sinai and determined that the disputed Tabah area, on the Gulf of Aqaba coast, was Egyptian territory. Israel withdrew from the area on 15 March 1989 after compensation terms had been agreed.

Lebanon

Inter-factional fighting continued in **Lebanon**, mainly between Syrian-backed Muslim groups and General Aoun's Christian army units, now backed to some extent by Iraq, which is rumoured to have supplied the Lebanese forces with *Frog* SSM. The Arab League took measures aimed at resolving the civil war. An Arab League Observer Force some 300 strong is to be established with officers provided by Algeria, Jordan, Kuwait, Sudan and Tunisia, but despite a visit by the Arab League Secretary General and two Arab generals, no observers have yet deployed to Lebanon. The Arab League has also set up a committee, comprising King Fahd of Saudi Arabia, King Hassan of Morocco and President Chadli Bendjedid of Algeria to assist the Lebanese parliament to make constitutional changes that would lead to the election of a Lebanese President.

Israel

The *intifada* in the West Bank and Gaza Strip continues unabated but without the anticipated rise in the use by the Palestinians of fire-arms and explosives which remains at a very low level. Implications for the Israeli Defence Forces include: loss of conventional training, problems of morale, increased periods of duty for reservists, the growing militancy of Jewish settlers and, additional expenditure.

Forces and Armaments

Ground force inventories in the region show little change. **Algeria** and **Kuwait** have taken delivery of Soviet BMP-2, their first AIFV, and Kuwait has received 100 Egyptian *Fahd* APC. The **UAE** now includes MRL in its artillery (Belgian LAU-97 and Italian FIROS-25) and has also procured some 45 *Milan* firing posts. **Oman** has acquired *Javelin* SAM from the UK. **Saudi Arabian** acquisitions include further M-113 APC, some 460 V-150 *Commando* APC for the National Guard and we have been able to reassess holdings of AM-10P which show an increase of 150 AIFV. The upgrading programme for M-60A1 tanks continues with 100 more tanks upgraded to A3 standard, but no decision (despite hard lobbying) has yet been taken on the next generation MBT. **Jordan's** tank holding has been increased with a gift from Iraq of 90 *Chieftain* MBT and 19 *Scorpion* light tanks captured from Iran, some in the final stages of the war. **Israel** added some 50 *Merkava* 2 tanks to its holding.

There have been some minor naval developments. We have revised the **Moroccan** naval entry so as to show the correct class names. New deliveries in the year have been a fourth *LV Rabhi* from Spain and two *El Wacil* patrol craft from France. In November 1988 **Djibouti** took delivery of three inshore patrol craft from the UK. **Egypt** has retired two Soviet *Whiskey*-class submarines. **Oman** has commissioned a fourth *Dhofar* missile craft armed with *Exocet* SSM. **Saudi Arabia** is reported to have placed an order for two, possibly three French frigates. **Israel** has commissioned four *Super-Dvora* inshore patrol craft and retired two *Sa'ar* missile craft which have been sold and delivered to Chile. Although the order for new multi-purpose corvettes is going ahead, the decision to order replacement submarines remains in the balance.

Most other changes to last year's air force listings are a result of re-assessment. **Syria** has formed two more squadrons with additional MiG-29 aircraft. The **YAR** has added a squadron of MiG-17 FGA. Egypt has introduced the F-16C into operational service.

Defence Spending

United States aid still goes predominantly to Egypt and Israel. For FY 1990 the Administration has requested $2.3 bn in combined military, economic and food assistance for Egypt; of this $1.3 bn is for foreign military sales financing (FMSF) and will be focused on modernization programmes for armour and air force requirements. The FY 1990 request for Israel is for $1.8 bn in FMSF and $1.2 bn in economic assistance, both to be provided on a grant basis. Israel's FMSF is mainly associated with F-15 and F-16 aircraft purchases, financing the Israeli-designed and manufactured *Merkava* tank (of which a number of Mark 3 prototypes were recently unveiled) and for naval modernization; $400 m would be authorized for procurement costs within Israel. Additionally, the US will provide $120 m for continued joint research of the *Arrow* ATBM programme, as part of the SDI programme.

Economic problems, as forecast in earlier editions of *The Military Balance*, have led to political disorder with potential implications for internal security in several countries in the region. Algiers was the scene of uprisings in autumn 1988, caused by rising food prices and shortages, housing shortages and unemployment; similar riots and protests took place in Jordan in spring 1989. Throughout the year Egypt also witnessed social unrest which strengthened the government's resolve (unlike Jordan) not to implement proposed IMF fiscal reforms (and so reduce food subsidies) for fear of major disturbances. Tunisia, too, saw sporadic anti-government demonstrations. Syria, with debts of over $20 bn is on the brink of economic disaster aggravated by its involvement in Lebanon.

Even the oil-producers face major economic problems. Iran, whose acceptance of UN Resolution 598 was provoked mainly by economic pressure, now faces major programmes for social and industrial reconstruction as well as the rearmament of the forces for which $2.4 bn has been allocated, all to be paid for by very limited hard currency resources, which amounted to less than $10 bn in 1988. At least Iran has no major debt problem, however, unlike Iraq which owes some $50 bn to Western and Eastern Bloc countries (and around a further $40 bn to its Arab neighbours which may well be forgiven). However, Iraq's armed forces are in better shape than Iran's (and are stronger and better trained than they were in 1980 when the Gulf War started). It also has a higher oil revenue – some $14 bn in 1988.

Despite continued shortfalls in oil revenues the Gulf States, especially Saudi Arabia, nevertheless continue to expand and modernize their military inventories. These programmes, however, tend not to be reflected in official budgets, but instead are set against complex barter, counter, offset and net back agreements whose precise values are not known. In the region as a whole only Israel shows a significant increase in budgeted defence spending, to some extent caused by the *Intifida* in the West Bank and Gaza Strip.

ALGERIA

GDP	1987ε: D 307.9 bn ($62.90 bn)
	1988ε: D 320.0 bn ($54.10 bn)
Growth	1987: 0.8% 1988: −2.0%
Inflation	1987: 7.4% 1988: 6.0%
Debt	1987: $22.2 bn 1988: $21.5 bn
Def bdgt*	1988ε: D 6.20 bn ($1.05 bn)
	1989ε: D 6.60 bn ($949.5 m)
FMA	1988: $0.15 m (US)

$1 = D (1987): 4.849 (1988): 5.915
(1989): 6.951

D = dinar

Population: 24,550,000

	13–17	18–22	23–32
Men	1,480,000	1,272,600	2,098,000
Women	1,426,000	1,225,000	2,022,000

TOTAL ARMED FORCES:
ACTIVE: 138,500 (70,000 conscripts).
Terms of service: 18 months Army only; 6 months basic, 1 year civil projects.
RESERVES: Army: some 150,000, to age 50.

ARMY: 120,000 (70,000 conscripts).
6 Military Regions.
3 armd bde (3 tk, 1 mech, 1 arty, 1 engr bn, recce coy, ATK, log bn).
5 mech bde (3 mech, 1 tk, 1 arty, 1 engr recce, ATK, log bn).
12 mot inf bde (3 inf, 1 tk, 1 arty, 1 engr bn).
1 AB/SF bde.
31 indep inf, 4 para bn.
5 indep arty, 5 AD bn.
4 engr bn.
12 coy desert troops.
EQUIPMENT:
MBT: some 900: 113 T-34 (in store), 390 T-54/-55, 300 T-62, 100 T-72.
LIGHT TANKS: 50 PT-76.
RECCE: 140 BRDM-2.
AIFV: 780: 690 BMP-1, 90 BMP-2.
APC: 860: 460 BTR-50/-60, 400 BTR-152.
TOWED ARTY: 440: 122mm: 100 M-1931/37, 70 M-1974, 40 M-30, M-1938, 170 D-30; 152mm: 60 M-1937.
SP ARTY: 152mm: 50 ISU-152.
MRL: 78: 122mm: 48 BM-21; 240mm: 30 BM-24.
MORTARS: 120mm: M-43.
ATGW: AT-3 *Sagger* (some SP/BRDM-2), *Milan*.
RCL: 168: 82mm: 110 T-21; 107mm: 58 B-11.
ATK GUNS: 206: 57mm: 156 ZIS-2; 100mm: 50 SU-100 SP.
AD GUNS: 855: 14.5mm: 65 ZPU-2/-4; 20mm: 100; 23mm: 65 ZU-23; 37mm: 150; 57mm: 75; 85mm: 20; 100mm: 150; 130mm: 20 towed; 210 ZSU-23-4 and ZSU-57-2 SP.
SAM: SA-7/-8/-9.

NAVY: 6,500.
BASES: Mers el Kebir, Algiers, Annaba.
SUBMARINES: 4:
2 Sov *Kilo* with 533mm TT.
2 Sov *Romeo* with 533mm TT.
FRIGATES: 3 *Mourad Reis* (Sov *Koni*) with 2 × 12 ASW RL.
PATROL AND COASTAL COMBATANTS: 25:
CORVETTES: 3 *Rais Hamidou* (Sov *Nanuchka*) with 4 × SS-N-2C *Styx* SSM.
MISSILE CRAFT: 11 *Osa* with 4 × SS-N-2 SSM.
PATROL: 11.
OFFSHORE: 1 local-built PFO.
INSHORE: 9 *El Yadekh* PCI, 1⟨.
MINE WARFARE: 2 Sov T-43 MSC.
AMPHIBIOUS: 3:

2 *Kalaat beni Hammad* LST, capacity 240 tps, 10 tk, 1 hel.
1 *Polnocny* LSM, capacity 100 tps, 5 tk.

COAST GUARD (under naval control): 550; 16 PFI⟨.

AIR FORCE: 12,000; 299 cbt ac, 48 armed hel.
FGA: 5 sqn:
1 with 18 Su-7BM;
3 with some 54 MiG-23BN/MF;
1 with some 12 Su-20.
FIGHTER: 9 sqn:
8 with 98 MiG-21MF/bis;
1 with 18 MiG-25.
COIN: 2 sqn with 21 CM-170.
RECCE: 1 sqn with 7 MiG-25R.
MR: 1 sqn with 3 F-27-400 (Navy-assigned, may not be operational), 2 *Super King Air* B-200T.
TRANSPORT: 1 sqn with 6 An-12, 2 An-26, 10 C-130H, 3 C-130H-30, 3 SE-210, 1 *Aero Commander* 680 (survey);
VIP: 1 Il-18, 2 *Falcon* 20, 4 *Gulfstream* (1 -II, 3 -III), 4 *Super King Air*.
HELICOPTERS: 9 sqn:
ATTACK: 4 sqn with 48 Mi-24.
TRANSPORT: (hy): 3 sqn with 38 Mi-8 (some may be armed), 4 Mi-6; (med): 2 sqn with 42 Mi-4, 5 SA-330; (lt): 6 Hughes 269A, 4 SA-313, 6 SA-316.
TRAINING: 10 MiG-15, 4 MiG-15U, 55 MiG-17, 9 MiG-21U, 9 MiG-23U, 3 MiG-25U, 19 Yak-11, 6 T-34C.
AD: GUNS: 3 bde+: 85mm, 100mm, 130mm.
SAM: 3 regt: 1 with 30 SA-2, 2 with SA-6, 21 SA-3.

PARA-MILITARY:
GENDARMERIE: (Ministry of Interior): 23,000; 44 Panhard AML-60/M-3 APC.

* Excl eqpt and internal security costs.

BAHRAIN

GDP	1987:	D 1.250 bn ($3.324 bn)	
	1988ε:	D 1.200 bn ($3.191 bn)	
Growth	1987:	−10.5%	1988: −4%
Inflation	1987:	−0.3%	1988: 0.0%
Debt	1987:	$325 m	1988: $365 m
Def exp*	1989:	D 69.4 m ($184.574 m)	
Def bdgt	1990:	D 72.9 m ($193.883 m)	
$1 = D	(1987/8/9):	0.376	
D = dinar			

Population: 458,000 (incl some 155,000 expatriates)

	13–17†	18–22†	23–32†
Men	20,800	19,300	61,800
Women	20,700	18,700	33,600

TOTAL ARMED FORCES:
ACTIVE: 3,350.
Terms of service: voluntary.

ARMY: 2,300.
1 bde: 2 inf bn, 1 tk, 1 SF bn, 1 armd car sqn, 2
arty, 2 mor bty.
EQUIPMENT:
MBT: 54 M-60A3.
RECCE: 8 *Saladin*, 22 AML-90, 8 *Ferret*.
APC: some 10 AT-105 *Saxon*, 93 Panhard M-3.
TOWED ARTY: 105mm: 8 lt; 155mm: 12 M-198.
MORTARS: 81mm:
ATGW: 60 BGM-71A *TOW*.
RCL: 106mm: 30 M-40A1, 120mm: 6 MOBAT.
SAM: 40+ RBS-70, 60+ *Stinger*.

NAVY: 600.
BASE: Jufair (Manama).
PATROL AND COASTAL COMBATANTS: 13:
CORVETTES: 2 *Al Manama* (FRG Lürssen 62-m)
with 2 × 2 MM-40 *Exocet* SSM, 1 × *Dauphin* II
hel (AS-15 ASM).
MISSILE CRAFT: 4 *Ahmad el Fateh* (FRG Lürssen
45-m) with 2 × 2 MM-40 *Exocet*.
PATROL: 2 *Al Riffa* (FRG Lürssen 38-mPFI).
5 PFI⟨.

AIR FORCE: 450; 12 cbt ac, 12 armed hel.
FGA: 1 sqn with 8 F-5E, 4 F-5F.
TRANSPORT: 2 *Gulfstream* (1 -II, 1 -III; VIP).
HELICOPTERS: 1 sqn with 12 AB-212 (8 armed), 4
Bo-105 (armed).
AAM: AIM-9P3 *Sidewinder*.
ASM: AS-11, AS-12.

PARA-MILITARY: (Ministry of Interior):
COAST GUARD 250; 6 PCI⟨, plus boats; 3 landing
craft, 1 hovercraft.
POLICE 2,000; 2 Sikorsky S-76, 2 Hughes 500, 2
Bell 412, 1 Bell 205 hel.

* Excl a subsidy from the Gulf Cooperation Council
(GCC) of $1.8 bn (1984–94) shared between
Bahrain and Oman.
† Total population

DJIBOUTI

GDP	1985ε: frD 62.0 bn ($348.86 m)
	1986: frD 59.17 bn ($332.94 m)
Debt	1986ε: frD 125 m 1987: $145 m
Def exp	1987: frD 6.10 m ($34.323 m)
	1988ε: frD 6.35 m ($35.730 m)
FMA	1988: $10.64 m (US, Fr)
$1 =	fr 1985/6/7/8: 177.72
frD = Djibouti francs	

Population: ε 404,000

	13–17	18–22	23–32
Men	26,000	22,000	33,000
Women	25,000	21,000	33,000

TOTAL ARMED FORCES: (all services, incl
Gendarmerie, form part of the Army):
ACTIVE: 4,230, incl 1,200 Gendarmerie.
Terms of service: voluntary.

ARMY: 2,870.
1 inf bn, incl mor, ATK pl.
1 armd sqn.
1 spt bn.
1 border cdo bn.
1 AB coy.
EQUIPMENT:
RECCE: some 10 BRDM-2, 4 AML-60, 16 AML-90,
15 M-11 VBL.
APC: 18 BTR-60.
MORTARS: 81mm; 120mm: 9.
RL: 70: 73mm, 89mm.
RCL: 106mm: 18.
AD GUNS: 20mm: M-693 SP; 23mm: 4 ZSU-23-2.

NAVY: 60.
BASE: Djibouti.
PATROL CRAFT, INSHORE: 5⟨.·

AIR FORCE: 100; no cbt ac or armed hel.
TRANSPORT: 2 N-2501, 2 C-212. lt: 1 Cessna 206G,
1 SOCATA 235GT.
HELICOPTERS: 1 SA-330, 2 SA-313, 3 AS-355.

PARA-MILITARY: 1,200.
GENDARMERIE: 1 bn, 1 patrol boat.

FOREIGN FORCES:
FRANCE: 3,900, incl 1 inf, 1 Foreign Legion regt, 1
FGA sqn.

EGYPT

GDP	1986/7: £E 44.05 bn ($62.94 bn)
	1987/8: £E 52.86 bn ($76.61 bn)
Growth	1987: 3.5% 1988: 2.7%
Inflation	1987: 19.7% 1988: 17.6%
Debt*	1987: $43.9 bn 1988: $45.6 bn
Def exp	1988/9: £E 3.95 bn ($5.64 bn)
	1989/90: £E 4.70 bn ($6.80 bn)
FMA	1988: $1.301 bn (US)
$1 = £E	(1986/7/8/9): 0.69†

Population: 54,115,000

	13–17	18–22	23–32
Men	3,102,000	3,004,000	4,169,000
Women	2,876,000	2,687,000	3,934,000

TOTAL ARMED FORCES:
ACTIVE: 448,000 (some 250,000 conscripts).
Terms of service: 3 years (selective).
RESERVES: 604,000. Army 500,000; Navy 14,000; Air Force 20,000; AD 70,000.

ARMY: 320,000 (perhaps 180,000 conscripts).
2 Army HQ:
   4 armd div (each with 2 armd, 1 mech bde).
   6 mech inf div (type: 2 mech, 1 armd bde).
   2 inf div (each with 2 inf, 1 mech bde).
1 Republican Guard armd bde.
1 indep armd bde.
4 indep inf bde.
3 indep mech bde.
2 airmobile, 1 para bde.
14 indep arty bde (2 more to form).
2 hy mor bde.
7 cdo gp.
2 SSM regt (1 with *FROG*-7, 1 with *Scud* B).
EQUIPMENT:‡
MBT: 2,425: 1,040 T-54/-55, 600 T-62, 785 M-60A3.
LIGHT TANKS: 15 PT-76.
RECCE: 300 BRDM-2.
AIFV: 470: 220 BMP-1, some 250 BMR-600P.
APC: 2,925: 650 *Walid*, 200 *Fahd*, 1,075 BTR-50/OT-62, 1,000 M-113A2.
TOWED ARTY: 1,120: 122mm: 48 M-31/37, 400 M-1938, 220 D-30; 130mm: 440 M-46; 152mm: 12 M-1937 (ML-20).
SP ARTY: 122mm: some mod D-30; 155mm: 140 M-109A2.
MRL: about 300: 80mm: VAP-80-12; 122mm: BM-21/*as-Saqr*-18/-30; 130mm: M-51/Praga V3S; 132mm: BM-13-16; 140mm: BM-14-16; 240mm: BM-24.
MORTARS: 82mm (some 50 SP); 120mm: 450 M-43; 160mm: 100 M-43; 240mm: 24 M-1953.

SSM (launchers): 12 *FROG*-7, 9 *Scud* B.
ATGW: 1,000 AT-1 *Snapper*, AT-2 *Swatter*, 1,400 AT-3 *Sagger* (incl BRDM-2); 220 *Milan*; 200 *Swingfire*; 520 *TOW* (incl 52 on M-901 (M-113) SP).
RCL: 107mm: B-11.
AD GUNS: 14.5mm: ZPU-2/-4; 23mm: 460 ZU-23-2, 110 ZSU-23-4 SP, 45 *Sinai*; 37mm: 150 M-1939; 57mm: 300 S-60, 40 ZSU-57-2 SP.
SAM: 1,200 SA-7/*'Ayn as-Saqr*, SA-9, some M-54 SP *Chaparral*.

NAVY: 18,000 (10,000 conscripts).
BASES: Alexandria (HQ, Mediterranean), Port Said, Mersa Matruh, Safaqa, Port Tewfig; Hurghada (HQ, Red Sea).
SUBMARINES: 10:
   10 Sov *Romeo* (4 Ch Type-033) with 533mm TT (some to be modernized).
PRINCIPAL SURFACE COMBATANTS: 6:
DESTROYER: 1: *El Fateh* (UK 'Z') (trg), with 4 × 114mm guns, 5 × 533mm TT.
FRIGATES: 5:
   2 *El Suez* (Sp *Descubierta*) with 2 × 3 ASTT, 1 × 2 ASW RL; plus 2 × 4 *Harpoon* SSM.
   2 *Al Zaffir* (Ch *Jianghu*) with 2 × ASW RL; plus 2 × CSS-N-2 (HY-2) SSM.
   1 *Tariq* (UK *Black Swan*) (trg) with 3 × 2 102mm guns.
PATROL AND COASTAL COMBATANTS: 43:
MISSILE CRAFT: 25:
   6 *Ramadan* with 4 *Otomat* SSM.
   7 Sov *Osa-I* with 4 × SS-N-2A *Styx* SSM.
   6 *October*⟨ with 2 *Otomat* SSM.
   6 Ch *Hegu* (*Komar*-type)⟨ with 2 HY-2 SSM.
PATROL: 18:
   8 Ch *Hainan* PFC with 4 × ASW RL.
   6 Sov *Shershen* PFI with BM-21 (8-tube) 122mm or 1 BM-24 (12-tube) 240mm MRL, or 4 × 533mm TT.
   4 Ch *Shanghai* II PFI.
MINE WARFARE: 9:
MINELAYERS: 3 SRN-6 hovercraft.
MINE COUNTERMEASURES: 6:
   4 *Aswan* (Sov *Yurka*) MSC.
   2 *El Fayoum* (Sov T-301) MSI.
AMPHIBIOUS: 3 Sov *Polnocny* LSM, capacity 100 tps, 5 tk.
SUPPORT AND MISCELLANEOUS: 7:
   1 submarine spt, 2 trg, 4 tugs.

NAVAL AVIATION:
HELICOPTERS: 5 *Sea King* Mk 47 (ASW, anti-ship); 12 SA-342 (anti-ship).

COASTAL DEFENCE: (Army tps, Navy control):
GUNS: 130mm: SM-4-1.
SSM: 30 *Otomat* and *Samlet*.

AIR FORCE: 30,000 (10,000 conscripts); (incl AD comd).‡
517 cbt ac, 72 armed hel.
BOMBERS: 1 bde (sqn): 9 Tu-16.
FGA: 10 sqn:
　1 with 16 *Mirage* 5E2.
　2 with 33 F-4E.
　4 with 76 Ch J-6.
　1 with 15 *Alpha Jet*.
　2 with 30 MiG-17.
FIGHTER: 6 bde (16 sqn):
　5 sqn with 83 MiG-21.
　3 with 52 Ch J-7.
　2 with 33 F-16A.
　2 with 34 F-16C.
　3 with 54 *Mirage* 5E.
　1 with 16 *Mirage* 2000C.
RECCE: 20: 1 bde (2 sqn) with 6 *Mirage* 5SDR, 14 MiG-21.
EW: 2 EC-130H (ELINT), 4 Beech 1900 (ELINT) ac; 4 *Commando* 2E hel (ECM).
AEW: 5 E-2C.
MR: 1 Beech 1900C. One more due, late 1989.
HELICOPTERS: 15 sqn:
　ATTACK: 2 bde (4 sqn) with 72 SA-342L (42 with *HOT*, 30 with 20mm gun).
　TACTICAL TRANSPORT: 3 bde: **hy:** 6 Mi-6, 15 CH-47C; **med:** 27 Mi-8, 24 *Commando* (5 -1 tpt, 17 -2 tpt, 2 -2B VIP); **lt:** 12 Mi-4, 17 UH-12E (trg).
TRANSPORT: 2 bde (3 sqn) with 19 C-130H, 5 An-12, 5 DHC-5D, 1 C-123B.
TRAINING: incl 29 *Alpha Jet* MS-1, 20 L-29, 36 *Gumhuria*, 10 PZL-104, 5 *Mirage* 5SDD, 7 F-16B, 6 F-16D, 3 *Mirage* 2000B, 40 EMB-312, 4 DHC-5, 16 JJ-6.
AAM: AA-2 *Atoll*, Matra R-530, AIM-7F *Sparrow*, R-550 *Magic*, AIM-9P3/-9L *Sidewinder*.
ASM: AS-1 *Kennel*, AS-5 *Kelt*, AGM-65 *Maverick*, AS-30, AS-30 Laser, *HOT*.

AIR DEFENCE COMMAND: 80,000
(50,000 conscripts).
5 div: regional bde.
100 AD arty bn.
65 SA-2, 60 SA-3 bn.
12 bty *Improved HAWK*
12 bty *Crotale*
EQUIPMENT:
AD GUNS: some 2,500: 20mm, 23mm, 37mm, 40mm, 57mm, 85mm; 100mm.
SAM: 858+: some 400 SA-2, 240 SA-3, 60 SA-6, 108 *Improved HAWK*, ε 50 *Crotale*, SA-9.
AD SYSTEMS: some 18 *Amoun* (*Skyguard*/RIM-7F *Sparrow* – some 36 twin 35mm guns, some 36 quad SAM). *Sinai*-23 short-range AD: Dassault 6SD-20S radar, 23mm guns, *'Ayn as-Saqr* SAM.

FORCES ABROAD: Advisers in Iraq, Kuwait, Oman, Saudi Arabia, Sudan, Somalia, Zaire.

PARA-MILITARY:
COAST GUARD: ε 2,000.
　PATROL, INSHORE: 20:
　　9 *Swiftships*, 5 *Nisr*, 6 *Crestitalia* PFI⟨, plus boats.
CENTRAL SECURITY FORCES: 300,000.
NATIONAL GUARD: 60,000: *Walid* APC.
FRONTIER CORPS: 12,000.

FOREIGN FORCES:
PEACE-KEEPING (MFO): some 2,600. Contingents from the US, Canada, UK, Colombia, Fiji, France, Italy, Netherlands, New Zealand and Uruguay.

---

* Est military debt of $11–12 bn, of which some $3 bn is owed to the USSR and $4.6 bn to the US.
† Egypt operates five exchange rates; for consistency, the official rate is used here.
‡ Most Soviet eqpt now in store, incl MBT and some cbt ac.

IRAN

GDP	1986/7:	r 21,121 bn ($268.71 bn)
	1987/8ε:	r 25,345 bn ($362.18 bn)
Growth	1986/7: −8.0%	1987/8: −11%
Inflation	1987: 50%	1988: 40%
Debt	1987: $2.5 bn	1988: ε $3.6 bn
Def bdgt*	1988/9ε:	r 680.00 bn ($9.90 bn)
	1989/90:	r 410.00 bn ($5.77 bn)
$1 = r	(1986/7): 78.76	(1987/8): 69.9
	(1988/9): 68.683	(1989/90):71.011
r = rial		

Population: 54,370,000†

	13–17	18–22	23–32
Men	2,832,000	2,406,000	3,202,000
Women	2,642,000	2,254,000	3,575,000

TOTAL ARMED FORCES:
ACTIVE: 604,500.
　Terms of service: 24–30 months.
RESERVES: Army: 350,000, ex-service volunteers.

ARMY: 305,000 (perhaps 250,000 conscripts).
ε 3 Army HQ.
4 mech div (each 3 bde: 9 armd, 18 mech bn).
6 inf div.
1 AB bde.
1 SF div (4 bde).
Some indep armd, inf bde (incl 'coastal force').

12 SAM bn with *Improved HAWK*.

RESERVES: '*Qods*' bn (ex-service).

EQUIPMENT:‡

MBT: perhaps 500: T-54/-55, Ch T-59, T-62, some T-72, *Chieftain* Mk 3/5, M-47/-48, M-60A1.

LIGHT TANKS: 30 *Scorpion*.

RECCE: 130 EE-9 *Cascavel*.

AIFV: 100+ BMP-1.

APC: perhaps 500: BTR-50, BTR-60, M-113.

ARTY: perhaps 800.

TOWED: 105mm: M-101, 36 Oto Melara; 130mm: 125 M-46/Type-59; 155mm: 50 M-71, 18 FH-77B, ε 130 GHN-45, G-5 reported; 203mm: some 30 M-115.

SP: 155mm: some 100 M-109A1; 175mm: 30 M-107; 203mm: 10 M-110.

MRL: 107mm: Ch Type-63; 122mm: 65 BM-21; 122mm: BM-11.

MORTARS: 81mm; 107mm: M-30 4.2-in.; 120mm: 3,000.

SSM: *Scud*; local manufacture msl reported incl ε 50 *Oghab*, *Nazeat*, *Shahin* 2.

ATGW: *ENTAC*, SS-11/-12, *Dragon*, *TOW*.

RCL: 57mm; 75mm; 106mm: M-40A/C.

AD GUNS: 1,500: 23mm: ZU-23 towed, ZSU-23-4 SP; 35mm: 92; 37mm; 57mm: ZSU-57-2 SP.

SAM: 30 *Improved HAWK*, SA-7, some 200 RBS-70.

AIRCRAFT: incl 40+ Cessna (185, 310, O-2A), 2 F-27, 5 *Shrike Commander*, 2 *Falcon* 20.

HELICOPTERS: ε 100 AH-1J (attack); ε 10 CH-47C (hy tpt); ε 250 Bell 214A; ε 35 AB-205A; ε 15 AB-206.

REVOLUTIONARY GUARD CORPS

(*Pasdaran Inqilab*):

GROUND FORCES: some 250,000; 11 Regional Commands: loosely org in bn of no fixed size, grouped into perhaps 40 inf, 5 armd div and many indep bde, incl inf, armd, para, SF, arty incl SSM, engr, AD and border defence units, serve indep or with Army; small arms, spt weapons from Army; controls *Basij* (see Para-military) when mob.

NAVAL FORCES: strength unknown, five island bases (Al Farsiyah, Halul (oil platform), Sirri, Abu Musa, Larak); some 40 Swedish Boghammar Marin boats armed with ATGW, RCL, machine guns. Italian SSM reported. Controls coast defence elm incl arty and CSS-N-2 (HY-2) *Silkworm* SSM in at least 3 sites, each 3–6 msl.

MARINES: 3 bde reported.

AIR FORCES: forming. 60 Ch J-7 (AD), 10 J-6 (trg) reported. Also to have AD role in static defence of major installations.

NAVY: 14,500, incl naval air and marines.‡

BASES: Bandar Abbas (HQ), Bushehr, Kharg, Bandar-e-Anzelli, Bandar-e-Khomeini, Chah Bahar (building).

PRINCIPAL SURFACE COMBATANTS: 8:

DESTROYERS: 3:

1 *Damavand* (UK *Battle*) with 4 × 2 SM-1 (boxed) SSM, 2 × 2 114mm guns; plus 1 × 3 AS mor.

2 *Babr* (US *Sumner*) with 4 × 2 SM-1 SSM (boxed), 2 × 2 127mm guns; plus 2 × 3 ASTT.

FRIGATES: 5:

3 *Alvand* (UK Vosper Mk 5) with 1 × 5 *Sea Killer* SSM, 1 × 3 AS mor, 1 × 114mm gun.

2 *Bayandor* (US PF-103).

PATROL AND COASTAL COMBATANTS: 34:

MISSILE CRAFT: 10 *Kaman* (Fr *Combattante* II) PFM fitted for *Harpoon* SSM.

PATROL INSHORE: 24:

3 *Kaivan*, 3 *Parvin* PCI, 3 Ch *Chaho* PFI, plus some 15 hovercraft⟨ (about half serviceable).

MINE WARFARE: 3:

2 *Shahrokh* MSC, 1 *Harischi* MSI.

AMPHIBIOUS: 7:

4 *Hengam* LST, capacity 9 tk, 225 tps, 1 hel.

3 *Iran Hormuz 24* (Korean) LST, capacity 8 tk, 140 tps.

Plus craft: 4 LCT.

SUPPORT AND MISCELLANEOUS: 8:

1 *Kharg* AOR, 2 *Bandar Abbas* AOR, 1 repair, 2 water tankers, 2 accommodation vessels.

MARINES: 3 bn.

NAVAL AIR: 11 armed hel.

ASW: 1 hel sqn with ε 3 SH-3D, 6 AB-212 ASW.

MCM: 1 hel sqn with 2 RH-53D.

TRANSPORT: 1 sqn with 4 *Commander*, 4 F-27, 1 *Mystère-Falcon* 20 ac; AB-205, AB-206 hel.

AIR FORCE: 35,000;

Some 121 cbt ac (est numbers serviceable in brackets; total 70); no armed hel.‡

FGA: 8 sqn:

4 with some 35 (20) F-4D/E;

4 with some 45 (20) F-5E/F.

24 Ch J-6 reported.

FIGHTER: 1 sqn with 15 (5) F-14.

MR: 2 (1) P-3F.

RECCE: 1 sqn (det) with some 5 F-5, 3 RF-4E.

TANKER/TRANSPORT: 1 sqn with 4 Boeing 707.

TRANSPORT: 5 sqn: 9 Boeing 747F, 10 Boeing 707, ε 20 C-130E/H, 9 F-27, 3 *Commander* 690, 3 *Falcon* 20.

HELICOPTERS: 2 AB-206A, 39 Bell 214C, 10 CH-47, 2 S-61A.

TRAINING: incl 26 F-33A/C *Bonanza*, 7 T-33, 46 PC-7. 5–6 EMB-312 (15 on delivery).

SAM: 5 sqn with 30 *Rapier*, 25 *Tigercat*, 50 HQ-2J (Ch version of SA-2).

AAM: AIM-54 *Phoenix*, AIM-9 *Sidewinder*, AIM-7 *Sparrow*.

ASM: AS-12 *Bullpup*, AGM-84 *Harpoon*.

FORCES ABROAD:
LEBANON: Revolutionary Guard 2,000 reported.

PARA-MILITARY:
BASIJ 'Popular Mobilization Army' volunteers, mostly youths: strength has been as high as 1 million during periods of offensive operations. Org in up to 500 300–350-man 'bn' of 3 coy, each 4 pl and spt; small arms only. Not currently embodied for mil ops.

GENDARMERIE: (45,000 incl border guard elm); Cessna 185/310 lt ac, AB-205/-206 hel, patrol boats, 96 coastal, 40 harbour craft.‡

HOME GUARD: some 2.5 million reported. controlled by Revolutionary Guard Corps.

TRIBAL GUARDS: some 40 units reported forming.

KURDS: Kurdish Democratic Party armed wing *Pesh Merga*, ε 12,000.

OPPOSITION:
KURDISH COMMUNIST PARTY OF IRAN (KOMALA): strength unknown.

DEMOCRATIC PARTY OF IRANIAN KURDISTAN (DPIK): perhaps 10,500.

NATIONAL LIBERATION ARMY (NLA): ε4,500. Org in bde, armed with captured eqpt. Iraq based.

FOREIGN FORCES:
UNITED NATIONS (UNIIMOG): Observers from 26 countries.

* Defence costs are highly tentative. Excl also barter, countertrade agreements. Value unknown.
† Population estimates tentative due to unknown casualties in Iraq–Iran War.
‡ State or operability of all eqpt unknown.

IRAQ

GDP*	1987ε:	12.144 bn ($39.061 bn)	
	1988ε:	14.00 bn ($45.0 bn)	
Growth	1987ε:	–10.5	1988ε: –4.0%
Inflation	1987:	17%	1988: 22%
Debt	1987ε:	$75.0 bn	1988ε: $75–80 bn
Def exp	1987ε:	D 4.35 bn ($13.99 bn)	
	1988ε:	D 4.0 bn ($12.87 bn)	
$1 = D	(1987/8/9):	0.3109	
D = dinar			

Population: 17,840,000†

	13–17	18–22	23–32
Men	1,071,000	873,000	1,313,000
Women	1,022,000	856,000	1,215,000

TOTAL ARMED FORCES:
ACTIVE: 1,000,000.
Terms of service: 21–24 months.
RESERVES: People's Army (Para-military) ε 850,000

ARMY: 955,000 (incl perhaps 480,000 recalled reserves).
7 corps HQ.
7 armd/mech div.
42 inf div.
6 Presidential Guard Force div (3 armd, 1 inf, 1 cdo bde).
20+ SF bde.
2 SSM bde.

EQUIPMENT:
MBT: some 5,500: 2,500 T-54/-55/M-77, 1,500 Ch T-59/-69, 1,000 T-62, ε500 T-72, 30 *Chieftain* Mk 3/5, M-60, M-47.

LIGHT TANKS: 100 PT-76.

RECCE: incl BRDM-2, 300 AML-60/-90, FUG-70, ERC-90, MOWAG *Roland*, EE-9 *Cascavel*, 300 EE-3 *Jararaca*.

AIFV: 1,000 BMP.

APC: ε 7,100: BTR-50/-60/-152, OT-62/-64, M-113A1, Panhard M-3, EE-11 *Urutu*.

TOWED ARTY: some 3,000: 105mm: M-56 pack; 122mm: D-74, D-30, M-1938; 130mm: M-46, Type 59-1; 152mm: M-1937, M-1943; 155mm: 100 G-5, 200 GHN-45, M-114.

SP ARTY: ε 500: 122mm: 2S1; 152mm: 2S3; 155mm: M-109, 85 AUF-1 (GCT).

MRL: 200: incl 122mm: BM-21; 127mm: 60 *ASTROS* II; 128mm: *Ababil*; 132mm: BM-13/-16; 180mm: *ASTROS* SS-40; 300mm: *ASTROS* SS-60.

MORTARS: 81mm; 120mm; 160mm.

SSM (launchers): 30 *FROG*-7; *Sijil*; 36 *Scud* B; *Abbas*; *Husayn*.

ATGW: AT-3 *Sagger* (incl BRDM-2), AT-4 *Spigot* reported, SS-11, *Milan*, *HOT* (incl 100 VC-TH).

RCL: 73mm: SPG-9; 82mm: B-10; 107mm.

ATK GUNS: 85mm; 100mm towed; 105mm: 100 JPz SK-105 SP.

HELICOPTERS: some 160 armed hel.
ATTACK: ε 40 Mi-24 with AT-2 *Swatter*; 20 SA-342; 13 SA-321, some with *Exocet* ASM; some 30 SA-316B with AS-12 ASM; some 56 Bo-105 with AS-11 ATGW.
TRANSPORT: hy: 15 Mi-6; **med:** 100 Mi-8/-17, 6 AS-61, 10 SA-330, 20 Mi-4; **lt:** 3 A-109, 5 AB-212, 40 Bell 214 ST, Hughes 300C/500D/530F (30/30/26), 30 SA-342.

AD GUNS: 4,000: 23mm: ZSU-23-4 SP; 37mm: M-1939 and twin; 57mm: incl ZSU-57-2 SP; 85mm; 100mm; 130mm.

SAM: 120 SA-2, 150 SA-3, SA-6, SA-7, SA-9, SA-13, SA-14, 60 *Roland*.

NAVY: 5,000.
BASES: Basra, Umm Qasr.
FRIGATES: 5:
    4 *Hittin* (It *Lupo*) with 1 AB-212 hel (ASW), 2 × 3
    ASTT; plus 8 × *Otomat* SSM, 1 × 127mm gun.‡
    1 *Khaldoum* (trg) with 2 × ASTT.

PATROL AND COASTAL COMBATANTS: 38:
CORVETTES: 4:
    2 *Hussa el Hussair* (It *Assad*, hel version) 1 ×
    AB-212 hel, 2 × *Otomat* SSM.
    2 *Hussa el Hussair* (It *Assad*) with 6 × *Otomat*, 2
    × 3 ASTT.‡
MISSILE CRAFT: 8 *Nisan 7* (Sov *Osa*) with 4 ×
    SS-N-2 *Styx* SSM.
TORPEDO CRAFT: 6 Sov P-6⟨ with 2 × 533mm TT.
PATROL, INSHORE: 20:
    3 SO-1, 4 *Nyryat* II, 13⟨.
MINE WARFARE: 8:
MCM: 2 Sov T-43 MSC, 6 MSI⟨.
AMPHIBIOUS: 6:
    3 *Al Zahraa* LST, capacity 250 tps, 20 tk, 1 hel.
    3 Sov *Polnocny* LSM, capacity 180 tps, 6 tk.
SUPPORT AND MISCELLANEOUS: 3:
    1 *Agnadeen* (It *Stromboli*) AOR‡, 2 Presidential yachts.

AIR FORCE: 40,000 incl 10,000 AD personnel;
    some 513 cbt ac, no armed hel.
BOMBERS: 2 sqn:
    1 with 8 Tu-22; 1 with 8 Tu-16, 4 Ch H-6D.
FGA: 17 sqn:
    4 with 70 MiG-23BN;
    4 with 64 *Mirage* F-1EQ5/EQ5-200 (EQ5 with
    Exocet; -200 with in-flight refuelling);
    2 with 30 Su-7;
    3 with 50 Su-20;
    2 with 30 Su-25;
    2 with 40 Ch J-6.
FIGHTER: ε 16 sqn with some 25 MiG-25, some 80
    Ch J-7, 70 MiG-21, 30 *Mirage* F-1EQ, 18 MiG-29.
RECCE: 1 sqn with 8 MiG-25.
TRANSPORT: 2 sqn: 10 An-2; 6 An-12, 6 An-24; 2
    An-26, 19 Il-76, 19 Il-14.
TRAINING: incl MiG-15/-17/-21/-23U, Su-7U, 16
    Mirage F-1BQ, 50 L-29, 40 L-39, 50 PC-7, 15
    PC-9, 88 EMB-312, 35 AS-202.
AAM: R-530, R-550 *Magic*, AA-2/-6/-7/-8.
ASM: AS-30 Laser, *Armat*, *Exocet* AM-39, C-601,
    AS-4, AS-5.

PARA-MILITARY:
FRONTIER GUARDS.
SECURITY TROOPS: 4,800.

OPPOSITION:

KURDISH DEMOCRATIC PARTY (KDP): 15,000
    (30,000 more in militia); small arms, some
    Iranian lt arty, MRL, mor, SAM-7.
KURDISH WORKERS' PARTY: strength unknown;
    breakaway from KDP, anti-Iran, Syria-based.
PATRIOTIC UNION OF KURDISTAN (PUK): 4,000
    cbt (plus 6,000 spt). 11 T-54/-55 MBT; 450 mor
    (60mm, 82mm, 120mm); 106mm RCL; some 200
    12.5mm AA guns; SA-7 SAM.
SOCIALIST PARTY OF KURDISTAN: ε 1,500.
**SUPREME ASSEMBLY OF THE ISLAMIC
    REVOLUTION** (SAIRI): claims 3 div; Iran based;
    Iraqi dissidents, ex prisoners of war.

FOREIGN FORCES:
EGYPT: some 2,000 advisers and technicians
UNITED NATIONS (UNIIMOG): Observers from
    26 countries.

* Based on official information; previous editions of *The
Military Balance* used commercial banking estimates.
† Population estimates tentative due to unknown
casualties in Iraq–Iran War.
‡ Remain in Mediterranean awaiting delivery.

ISRAEL

GDP	1987:	NS 55.336 bn ($34.69 bn)	
	1988:	NS 65.241 bn ($40.801 bn)	
Growth	1987:	4%	1988: 1.6%
Inflation	1987:	19.8%	1988: 16.3%
Debt	1987:	$24.2 bn	1988: $24.4 bn
Def bdgt	1988:	NS 8.945 bn ($5.71 bn)	
	1989:	NS 11.528 bn ($6.37 bn)	
FMA	1988:	$1.8 bn (US)	
$1 = NS	(1987):	1.595	(1988): 1.599
	(1989):	1.810	
NS = new sheqalim			

Population: 4,542,000

	13–17	18–22	23–32
Men	226,000	198,000	344,000
Women	215,000	188,000	330,000

TOTAL ARMED FORCES:
ACTIVE: 141,000 (110,000 conscripts).
    Terms of Service: officers 48 months, men 36
    months, women 24 months (Jews and Druze
    only; Christians, Circassians and Muslims may
    volunteer). Annual trg as reservists thereafter
    to age 54 for men, 24 (or marriage) for women.
RESERVES: 504,000: Army 494,000; Navy
    1,000; Air Force 9,000. Most serve at least one
    month a year, ideally 2 weeks trg and 2 weeks op
    duty (border def, security at military installations
    or administrative duties). Male commitment

until 54 in reserve op units may be followed by voluntary service in the Civil Guard or Civil Defence.

STRATEGIC:
It is widely believed that Israel has a nuclear capability. Delivery means could include ac, *Jericho* 1 SSM (range up to 450 km), *Jericho* 2 (tested in 1987 and 1988, range ε 1,500 km) and *Lance*, with up to 100 warheads.

ARMY: 104,000 (88,000 conscripts, male and female); some 598,000 on mob.
2 corps HQ
3 armd div (2 armd, 1 arty bde, plus 1 armd, 1 mech inf bde on mob).
5 mech inf bde (incl 1 para trained, 1 based on NCO school, 1 Nahal (*Noar Halutzi Lohen* Pioneer Fighting Youth, combines military duty with establishing agricultural settlements).
3 Regional inf div HQ (border def).
1 *Lance* SSM bn.
3 arty bn with 203mm M-110 SP.
RESERVES:
9 armd div (2 or 3 armd, 1 mech inf, 1 arty bde).
1 airmobile/mech inf div (3 bde manned by para trained reservists).
10 regional inf bde (each with own border sector).
4 arty bde.
EQUIPMENT:
MBT: 3,794 incl 1,080 *Centurion*, 561 M-48A5, 1,300 M-60/A1/A3, 138 T-54/-55 mod, 115 T-62, 600 *Merkava* I/II.
RECCE: about 400 incl *Ramta* RBY, M-2/-3, BRDM-2.
APC: 5,900 M-113, ε 80 *Nagmashot*, BTR-50P, 4,400 M2/-3 half track.
TOWED ARTY: 579: 105mm: 70 M-101; 130mm: 109 M-46; 122mm: 100 D-30; 155mm: 300 Soltam M-68/-71, M-839P/-845P.
SP ARTY: 781: 155mm: L-33, 75 M-50, 530 M-109A1/A2; 175mm: 140 M-107; 203mm: 36 M-110.
MRL: 122mm: BM-21; 160mm: LAR-160; 240mm: BM-24; 290mm: MAR-290.
MORTARS: 81mm; 120mm: ε 230; 160mm (some SP).
SSM: 12 *Lance*, *Jericho* 1.
ATGW: *TOW* (incl *Ramta* (M-113) SP), *Dragon*, *Picket* 81mm, *Mapats*.
RL: 82mm: B-300.
RCL: 84mm: *Carl Gustav*; 106mm: 250.
AD GUNS: 20mm: 850; 30 M-163 *Vulcan*/M-48 *Chaparral* gun/msl systems; 23mm: ZU-23-2 and 50 ZSU-23-4 SP; 37mm and 40mm: L-70.
SAM: *Redeye*.

NAVY: 9,000 (3,000 conscripts), 10,000 on mob.
BASES: Haifa, Ashdod, Eilat.

SUBMARINES: 3 *Gal* (UK Vickers) SSC with Mk 37 HWT, *Harpoon* USGW.
PATROL AND COASTAL COMBATANTS: 61:
MISSILE CRAFT: 26 PFM:
2 *Aliya* with 4 *Harpoon*, 4 *Gabriel* SSM, 1 AB-206 *Kiowa* hel (OTHT).
2 *Romat* with 8 *Harpoon*, 8 *Gabriel*.
8 *Reshef* with 2–4 *Harpoon* 4–6 *Gabriel*,
10 *Mivtach/Sa'ar* with 2 *Harpoon*, 3–5 *Gabriel*.
3 *Shimrit* (US *Flagstaff* 2) PHM with 4 *Harpoon*, 2 *Gabriel*.
1 *Dvora*⟨ with 2 *Gabriel*.
PATROL, INSHORE: 35:
4 *Super-Dvora* PFI⟨
31 *Dabur* PFI⟨.
AMPHIBIOUS: Craft only; 6 LCT, 3 LCM.
SUPPORT AND MISCELLANEOUS: 2:
1 patrol craft depot ship, 1 tpt.

MARINES: Naval cdo: 300.

AIR FORCE: 28,000 (19,000 conscripts, mainly in AD), 37,000 on mob; 574 cbt ac (plus perhaps 102 stored), 77 armed hel.
FGA/FIGHTER: 16 sqn:
2 with 53 F-15 (35 -A, 2 -B, 11 -C, 5 -D);
4 with 112 F-4E (plus 13 in store);
4 with 95 *Kfir* C2/C7 (plus 75 in store);
6 with 145 F-16 (62 -A, 8 -B, 51 -C, 24 -D).
FGA: 4 sqn with 121 A-4H/N, plus 14 in store.
RECCE: 14 RF-4E, plus 10 in store.
AEW: 4 E-2C.
EW: 6 Boeing 707 (ELINT/ECM), 9 *King Air* (3 RU-21A, 6 RC-21D; ELINT), 2 EV-1E (ECM), 4 IAI 201 (ELINT).
MR: 5 IAI-1124 *Seascan*.
TANKER: 5 Boeing-707, 2 KC-130H.
TRANSPORT: 1 wing: incl 3 Boeing 707, 24 C-130H, 10 1A1-201, 3 IAI-1124, 20 C-47.
LIAISON: 4 *Islander*, 16 Dornier (6 Do-27, 10 Do-28D); 45 Cessna (41 U-206C, 2 172, 2 180); 12 *Queen Air* 80.
TRAINING: incl 27 TA-4H/J, 5 *Kfir* TC2/7, 16 F-4E, 80 *Magister/Tzugit*, 35 *Super Cub*, 6 Cessna 152.
HELICOPTERS:
  ATTACK: 3 sqn: 2 with 42 AH-1G/S, 1 with 35 Hughes 500MD;
  SAR: 1 sqn with 2 HH-65A;
  TRANSPORT: hy: 35 CH-53 (2 -A, 33 -D); **med:** 9 SA-321, 17 UH-1D; **lt:** 58 Bell 212, 40 Bell 206A.
SAM: 15 bn with MIM-23 *HAWK/Improved HAWK*.
AAM: AIM-9/-9L *Sidewinder*, AIM-7E/F/M *Sparrow*, R-530, *Shafrir*, *Python* III.
ASM: AGM-45 *Shrike*, AGM-62A *Walleye*, AGM-65 *Maverick*, AGM-78D *Standard*, *Luz*, *Gabriel* III (mod).

PARA-MILITARY:
BORDER POLICE: 6,000; BTR-152 APC.
COAST GUARD: 3 US PBR, 3 other patrol craft.

JORDAN

GDP	1987:	D 1.686 bn ($4.978 bn)	
	1988:	D 1.630 bn ($4.388 bn)	
Growth	1987:	3.1%	1988: −2.5%
Inflation	1987:	−0.3%	1988: 3.2%
Debt	1987:	$4.20 bn	1988: $8.1 bn
Def bdgt*	1988:	D 256 m ($689.1 m)	
	1989:	D 251.5 m ($465.7 m)	
FMA	1988:	$11.75 m (US)	
$1 = D	(1987):	0.3387 (1988):	0.3715
	(1989):	0.5400	

D = dinar

Population: 3,109,000

	13–17	18–22	23–32
Men	208,000	175,000	231,000
Women	183,000	156,000	207,000

TOTAL ARMED FORCES:
ACTIVE: 85,250.
Terms of service: voluntary; conscription, 2 years authorized.
RESERVES: 35,000 (all services): Army 30,000 (obligation to age 40).

ARMY: 74,000.
2 armd div (each 2 tk, 1 mech inf, 1 AD bde).
2 mech inf div (each 2 mech inf, 1 tk, 1 AD bde).
1 indep Royal Guards bde.
1 SF bde (3 AB bn).
16 arty bn.
EQUIPMENT:
MBT: some 1,131: 260 M-47/-48A5 (in store), 218 M-60A1/A3, 360 *Khalid/Chieftain*, 293 *Tariq (Centurion)*.
LIGHT TANKS: 19 *Scorpion*.
RECCE: 144 *Ferret*.
APC: 1,235 M-113, 34 *Saracen*, some EE-11 *Urutu*.
TOWED ARTY: 95: 105mm: 36 M-101A1; 155mm: 38 M-114 towed, 17 M-59; 203mm: 4 M-115 towed (in store).
SP ARTY: 152: 155mm: 20 M-44, 108 M-109A2; 203mm: 24 M-110.
MORTARS: 81mm, 107mm, 120mm.
ATGW: 330 *TOW* (incl 50 SP), 310 *Dragon*.
RL: 112mm: *APILAS*.
RCL: 106mm: 330.
AD GUNS: 408: 20mm: 100 M-163 *Vulcan*; 23mm: 44 ZSU-23-4 SP; 40mm: 264 M-42 SP.

SAM: SA-7B2, 20 SA-8, 20 SA-13, SA-14, *Redeye*.

NAVY (Coast guard): 250.
BASE: Aqaba.
PATROL: boats only.

AIR FORCE: 11,000; 111 cbt ac, 24 armed hel.
FGA: 4 sqn with 59 F-5 (52 -E, 7 -F).
FIGHTER: 2 sqn with 34 *Mirage* F-1 (15 -CJ, 17 -EJ, 2 -BJ).
OCU: 1 sqn with 14 F-5A, 4 F-5B.
TRANSPORT: 1 sqn with 6 C-130 (2 -B, 4 -H), 3 C-212A.
VIP: 1 sqn with 2 Boeing 727, 2 *Gulfstream* III (VIP) ac; 4 S-76 hel.
HELICOPTERS: 5 sqn:
  ATTACK: 2 with 24 AH-1S (with *TOW* ASM; for eventual transfer to Army);
  TRANSPORT: 1 with 14 S-76, 3 S-70; 1 with 12 AS-332M. 1 with 8 Hughes 500D.
TRAINING: 16 C-101, 18 *Bulldog*, 18 Piper (12 *Warrior*-II, 6 *Seneca*-II).
AD: 2 bde: 14 bty with 126 *Improved HAWK*.
AAM: AIM-9 *Sidewinder*, R-550 *Magic*.
ASM: *TOW*.

PARA-MILITARY:
PUBLIC SECURITY FORCE: 4,000.
CIVIL MILITIA 'PEOPLE'S ARMY': 15,000+; men 16–65, women 16–45.
PALESTINE LIBERATION ARMY (PLA): 1,200; 1 bde (PLO but firmly supervised by Jordanian Army).

* Excl some D 25 m for 'internal security, civil defence and Islamic Justice'.

KUWAIT

GDP	1986/7:	D 5.444 bn ($19.540 bn)	
	1987/8ε:	D 5.600 bn ($20.071 bn)	
Growth	1987:	5.4%	1988: 1.3%
Inflation	1987:	1.1%	1988: 1.5%
Def bdgt*	1988/9ε:	D 425 m ($1.55 bn)	
	1989/90ε:	D 450 m ($1.556 bn)	
$1 = D	(1987):	0.2786 (1988):	0.2790
	(1989):	0.2892	

D = dinar

Population: 2,039,000 (incl 1.1 m expatriates)

	13–17	18–22	23–32
Men	92,500	76,400	185,000
Women	89,100	75,600	145,100

TOTAL ARMED FORCES:
ACTIVE: 20,300.
Terms of service: conscription, 2 years (university students, 1 year).

RESERVES: Obligation for 14 years following regular/conscript service. 1 month annual trg.

ARMY: 16,000.
2 armd bde (each with 2 armd regt, 1 arty bn; 1 with 1 mech inf, 1 with 2 mech inf regt).
1 mech inf bde (with 1 armd, 3 mech inf/cdo regt, 1 arty bn).
1 arty bde with 1 SP arty regt, 1 SSM bn.
EQUIPMENT:
MBT: 275: 70 Vickers Mk 1, 40 *Centurion*, 165 *Chieftain*.
RECCE: 100 *Saladin*, 90 *Ferret*.
AIFV: 50 BMP-2.
APC: 200 M-113, 130 *Saracen*, 100 *Fahd*.
TOWED ARTY: 105mm: 16 M-101; 155mm: 40 AMX Mk F-3.
SP ARTY: 155mm: 36 M-109A2.
MORTARS: 81mm; 120mm: 40.
SSM: 12 *FROG*-7 launchers.
ATGW: 20 *HOT, TOW/Improved TOW* (incl 56 M-901 SP), 200 *Vigilant*.
RCL: 84mm: *Carl Gustav*; 106mm: 24.
SAM: SA-7.

NAVY: 2,100.
BASES: El Adami (HQ), Shuwaikh.
PATROL AND COASTAL COMBATANTS: 23:
MISSILE CRAFT: 8:
2 *Istiqlal* (FRG Lürssen FPB-57) PFM with 2 × MM-40 *Exocet* SSM.
6 *Al Boom* (FRG Lürssen TNC-45) with 2 × MM-40 *Exocet*.
PATROL: 15 inshore⟨.
AMPHIBIOUS: Craft only; 4 LCM.
SUPPORT SHIPS: 3 coastal transports.
MARINES: 2 bn cdo.

AIR FORCE: 2,200 (excl foreign personnel);
36 cbt ac, 18 armed hel.
FGA: 24 A-4KU, 3 TA-4KU in store. To be replaced by F-18.
FIGHTER: 2 sqn with 20 *Mirage* F-1CK, 4 F-1BK.
12 *Lightning*, 4 *Hunter* in store.
COIN/TRAINING: 1 sqn with 12 *Hawk* Mk 64.
TRANSPORT: 2 DC-9, 4 L-100-30, 2 DHC-4; used also in civil role.
HELICOPTERS: 3 sqn:
ATTACK: 12 SA-342K (with HOT), 6 AS-332 (with *Exocet*; anti-ship).
TRANSPORT: 10 SA-330.
TRAINING: 8 SA-342 hel.
AD: KAFAD (Kuwait Air Forces and Air Defence): integrated AD control system plus; 1 SAM bn (6 bty each 2 × 12 *Improved HAWK*) SA-6 reported.
AAM: R-550 *Magic*, Super R-530, AIM-9 *Sidewinder*.
ASM: AS-11/-12, *HOT*, AM-39 *Exocet*.

PARA-MILITARY:
NATIONAL GUARD: 1,500: Palace, Border Guard; 20 V-150, 62 V-300 *Commando* APC.
CIVIL DEFENCE: forming.

* Excl eqpt and internal security budget.

LEBANON

No worthwhile economic or demographic data is available. However, the government announced a defence budget of some $26 m in 1988.

Despite the apparent break-up of the Lebanese Armed Forces all units are still paid from national funds and we continue to list these under national Armed Forces. Only the main Militia groups have been listed.

NATIONAL ARMED FORCES:

ARMY: some 21,000.
10 nominal bde.
Christian: (12,000): 6 bde, 1 Ranger, 1 SF bn.
Muslim: (8,000): 3 bde (2 Sunni, 1 Shi'a (AMAL)).
Druze: (1,000): 1 bde (may be divided amongst militia units).
EQUIPMENT:
MBT: some 105 M-48 A1/A5.
LIGHT TANKS: 32 AMX-13 (with 75mm or 105mm guns).
RECCE: 65 *Saladin*, 5 *Ferret*.
APC: 300 M-113, *Saracen*, 20 VAB-VTT.
TOWED ARTY: 105mm: 15 M-101A1;
122mm: 18 M-102, M-1938/D-30; 130mm: M-46; 155mm: 36 M-50, M-114, M-198.
MORTARS: 81mm; 120mm: 25.
ATGW: *ENTAC, Milan*, 20 BGM-71A *TOW*.
RL: 85mm: RPG-7; 89mm: M-65.
RCL: 106mm: M-40A1.
AD GUNS: 20mm; 23mm: ZU-23; 30mm: towed; 40mm: 15 M-42 SP.

NAVY: some 500 (Christian controlled)
BASE: Juniye.
PATROL CRAFT: Inshore: 4
1 *Tarablous*, 3 *Byblos*⟨.
AMPHIBIOUS: Craft only; 2 Fr LCT.

AIR FORCE: Some 800 (mainly Christian).
1 operational base (Juniye–Jubayl highway strip).
EQUIPMENT (operational status doubtful):
FIGHTERS: 6 *Hunter* (5 F-70, 1 T-66); (5 operational).
HELICOPTERS: 1 sqn:
ATTACK: 4 SA-342 with SS-11/-12 ASM;
TRANSPORT: (med): 7 AB-212, 9 SA-330;

(lt): 2 SA-313, 7 SA-316.
TRAINING: 5 *Bulldog*, 3 CM-170.
TRANSPORT: 1 *Dove*, 1 *Turbo-Commander* 690A.

PARA-MILITARY:
INTERNAL SECURITY FORCE (Ministry of
Interior): 8,000 (largely ineffective: some law
courts closed); 30 *Chaimite* APC.
CUSTOMS: 2 *Tracker*, inshore patrol craft⟨.

MILITIAS:
CHRISTIAN:
LEBANESE FORCES MILITIA: 6,000 active,
35,000 all told.
EQUIPMENT:
MBT: some 150 T-55, M-48.
LIGHT TANKS: some 5 AMX-13.
APC: M-113.
ARTY: some 100: 105mm, 122mm: 25; 130mm;
155mm: 10.
MORTARS: 60mm, 81mm, 120mm.
SSM: *FROG*-7 reported.
RL: RPG-7.
AD: 12.7mm, 14.5mm, 23mm guns.
PATROL CRAFT: 1 *Tracker*, 2 *Dvora* PFI⟨.
THE PHALANGE: 800–1,000 active, 6,000 all told.
EQUIPMENT:
APC: some M-113
MORTARS: some 120mm
RL: RPG-7.

MUSLIM:
AMAL (Shi'a, pro-Syria): ε 5,000 active; some
15,000 all told.
EQUIPMENT:
MBT: M-48, 50 T-54/-55.
RECCE: *Saladin.*
APC: 25 VAB, BTR, M-113.
TOWED ARTY: 105mm, 122mm, 130mm, 155mm.
MRL: 107mm, 122mm.
MORTARS: 81mm, 120mm.
ATGW: AT-3 *Sagger.*
RCL: 107mm.
ATK GUNS: 85mm, 100mm.
AD GUNS: 23mm ZU-23.
SAM: SA-7.
HIZBOLLAH ('The Party of God'; Shi'a,
fundamentalist, pro-Iranian): ε 3,500 active;
some 15,000 all told.
EQUIPMENT incl:
APC, arty, RL, RCL, ATGW, (AT-3 *Sagger*) AA guns.

DRUZE:
PROGRESSIVE SOCIALIST PARTY (PSP): ε 5,000
active; perhaps 12,000 all told.
EQUIPMENT:

MBT: 70 T-34, T-54/-55.
APC: BTR-60/-152.

SOUTH LEBANESE ARMY (SLA): ε 1,200
active, 1,500 militia; (mainly Christian, some
Shi'a and Druze, trained, equipped and supported
by Israel, occupies the 'Security Zone' between
Israeli border and area controlled by UNIFIL)
EQUIPMENT:
MBT: 40 M-4, 30 T-54/-55.
APC: M-113.
TOWED ARTY: 122mm: M-1938; 130mm: M-46;
150mm: Fr; 155mm: M-198.

FOREIGN FORCES:
UNITED NATIONS (UNIFIL): some 5,500;
Contingents from France, Fiji, Finland, Ghana,
Ireland, Italy, Nepal, Norway and Sweden.

SYRIA: 30,000.
BEIRUT: 1 armd bde, 5 SF regt.
METN: 1 mech inf bde.
BEKAA: Div HQ, 1 inf bde, 1 mech inf bde.
TRIPOLI: 3 SF regt, elm PLA.

IRAN: Revolutionary Guards: some 2,000
including locally recruited Shi'ia Lebanese.

PALESTINE LIBERATION
ORGANIZATION (PLO):*
All significant factions of the PLO and other
Palestinian military groups are listed here
irrespective of the country in which they are
mainly based. Strengths are estimates of the
number of active 'fighters', these could be trebled
perhaps to give an all-told figure.
FATAH: 4,500.
PLF (Palestine Liberation Front, Al-Abas): ε 300.
FATAH (dissidents, Abu Musa): 1,000.
PFLP (Popular Front for Liberation of Palestine,
Habash): 900.
PFLP (GC) (Popular Front for Liberation of
Palestine, (General Command), Jibril): 500.
SAIQA (al-Khadi): 600.
PSF (Popular Struggle Front, Ghisha): ε 500.
DFLP (Democratic Front for Liberation of
Palestine, Hawatmah): ε 1,000.
FRC (Fatah Revolutionary Council, Abu Nidal): ε 500.

---

* The Palestine Liberation Army is not part of the
PLO but is the name for Palestinian units either
forming part of, or closely monitored by, host nation
armed forces, 3–4 bde (Jordan, 2–3 Syria, possibly Iraq).

LIBYA

GDP	1987:	D 6.683 bn ($24.697 bn)
	1988ε:	D 6.000 bn ($21.04 bn)
Growth	1987: −2.7%	1988: −9%

Inflation 1987: 11% 1988: 9%
Debt* 1987: $6.0 bn 1988: $4.8 bn
Def exp(ε) 1987: D 375 m ($1.39 bn)
          1988: D 405 m ($1.420 bn)
$1 = D (1987): 0.2706 (1988): 0.2852
D = dinar

Population: 4,390,000

	13–17	18–22	23–32
Men	242,000	198,000	293,000
Women	234,000	189,000	268,000

TOTAL ARMED FORCES:
ACTIVE: 85,000.
  Terms of service: selective conscription, term
    varies: 2 to 4 years.
RESERVES: People's Militia, some 40,000.

ARMY: 55,000.
  1 tk div (2 tk, 1 mech bde, 1 arty regt).
  2 mech inf div (each 2 mech, 1 tk bde, 1 arty
    regt).
  38 tk bn.
  54 mech inf bn.
  1 National Guard bde.
  41 arty, 2 AD arty bn.
  12 para/cdo bn.
  7 SSM bde.
  3 SAM bde.
EQUIPMENT:
MBT: 1,800 T-54/-55/-62 (incl 1,200 in store), 180 T-72.
RECCE: 240 BRDM-2, 380 EE-9 *Cascavel*.
AIFV: 520 BMP.
APC: 690 BTR-50/-60, OT-62/-64, 100 EE-11 *Urutu*,
  Fiat 6614.
TOWED ARTY: some 800: 105mm: some 60 M-101;
  122mm: 60 D-74, 330 D-30; 130mm: 350 M-46.
SP ARTY: some 382: 122mm: 126 2S1; 152mm: 48
  2S3, *DANA*; 155mm: 190 *Palmaria*, 18 M-109.
MRL: some 540: 107mm: Type 63; 122mm:
  BM-21/RM-70; 130mm: 36 M-51.
MORTARS: 82mm, 120mm, 160mm, 240mm.
SSM launchers: 30 *FROG*-7, 75 *Scud* B.
ATGW: 3,000: *Vigilant*, *Milan*, AT-3 *Sagger* (incl
  BRDM SP).
RCL: 106mm: 220.
AD GUNS: 600: 23mm: ZSU-23-2, ZSU-23-4 SP,
  30mm: M-53/59 SP; 40mm: L/70; 57mm: 92 S-60.
SAM: SA-7/-9/-13, 24 quad *Crotale*.
HELICOPTERS:
  TRANSPORT: 13 CH-47.
  LIAISON: 5 AB-206, 11 SA-316.
DEPLOYMENT:
Aouzou Strip: ε 2,000; 2 mech bn, 2 tk bn: T-55 tk,
  BMP-1 MICV, MRL, AD guns, SAM, 5 SF-260W
  ac, 3 Mi-24 hel.

NAVY: 8,000 incl Coast Guard.
BASES: Tarabulus, Benghazi, Darnah, Tubruq,
  Sidi Bilal, Al Khums.
SUBMARINES: 6 *Al Badr* (Sov *Foxtrot*) with
  533mm and 406mm TT.
FRIGATES: 3:
  1 *Dat Assawari* (UK Vosper Mk 7) with 2 × 3
    ASTT; plus 4 *Otomat* SSM, 1 × 114mm gun.
  2 *Al Hani* (Sov *Koni*) with 4 × ASTT, 2 × ASW
    RL; plus 4 SS-N-2C SSM.
PATROL AND COASTAL COMBATANTS: 55:
CORVETTES: 7:
  4 *Assad al Tadjer* (It *Assad*) with 4 *Otomat* SSM;
    plus 2 × 3 ASTT (A244S LWT).
  3 *Ean al Gazala* (Sov *Nanuchka*) with 2 × 2
    SS-N-2C *Styx* SSM,
MISSILE CRAFT: 24
  9 *Sharara* (Fr *La Combattante-II*) with 4 *Otomat* SSM;
  12 *Al Katum* (Sov *Osa-II*) with 4 SS-N-2C SSM;
  3 *Susa*⟨ with 8 SS-12M SSM.
PATROL CRAFT: 24:
  COASTAL: 1 *Tobruk* with 1 × 102mm gun.
  INSHORE: 23: 4 *Garian*, 14 Tu *SAR-33*, 3 *Benina*, 2⟨.
MINE WARFARE: 8 *Ras al Gelais* (Sov *Natya* MSO).
AMPHIBIOUS: 5:
  2 *Ibn Ouf* LST, capacity 240 tps, 6 tk, 1 hel.
  3 Sov *Polnocny* LSM, capacity 180 tps, 6 tk.
  Plus craft; 16 LCT.
SUPPORT AND MISCELLANEOUS: 4:
  1 log spt, 1 tpt, 1 salvage, 1 diving spt.

NAVAL AVIATION:
HELICOPTERS: 2 sqn:
  1 with 25 Mi-14 (ASW);
  1 with 12 SA-321 (ASW, SAR).

AIR FORCE: 22,000 (incl Air Defence); (some
  Syrian pilots, Soviet, North Korean and
  Pakistani instructors);
  515 cbt ac, 16 armed hel (many ac in store,
  number nk)
BOMBERS: 1 sqn with 4 Tu-22.
FGA: 5 sqn and 1 OCU:
  45 *Mirage* 5D/DE, 10 *Mirage* 5DD, 12 *Mirage*
  F-1AD, 28 MiG-23BN, 8 MiG-23U, 90 Su-20,
  ε 6 Su-24.
FIGHTER: 3 sqn and 1 OCU:
  12 *Mirage* F-1ED, 6 F-1BD, 75 MiG-21, 131
  MiG-23 *Flogger* E, 55 MiG-25
  Foxbat A, 3 MiG-25U.
COIN: 1 sqn with 30 J-1 *Jastreb*.
RECCE: 1 sqn with 6 *Mirage* 5DR, 7 MiG-25R.
TRANSPORT: 2 sqn:
  16 An-26, 12 Lockheed (7 C-130H, 2 L-100-20, 3
  L-100-30), 20 G-222, 5 Il-76, 18 L-410.
HELICOPTERS: 9 sqn:

ATTACK: 2 with 16 Mi-24.
TRANSPORT: hy: 1 with 6 CH-47C; **med:** 1 with 7 Mi-8, 1 AS-61 (VIP); **lt:** 1 with 4 SA-316.
TRAINING: 4 sqn:
2 with 89 *Galeb* G-2 ac;
2 with 20 Mi-2 hel;
trg units with 2 Tu-22, 70 L-39ZO, 77 SF-260WL.
AAM: AA-2 *Atoll*, AA-6 *Acrid*, AA-7 *Apex*, AA-8 *Aphid*, R-550 *Magic*.
ASM: AT-2 *Swatter* ATGW (hel-borne).

AIR DEFENCE COMMAND:
'Senezh' AD comd and control system.
3 SA-5A bde: each 2 bn of 6 launchers, some 4 AD arty gun bn; radar coy.
3 Regions: 2 bde each 18 SA-2; 2–3 bde each 12 twin SA-3; ε 3 bde each 20–24 SA-6/-8.
Some 2,000 Soviet personnel reportedly man the SA-5 complexes. Expatriates form a large proportion of the technical support staff.

PARA-MILITARY:
LIWA HARIS AL-JAMAHIRIYA (Revolution Guard Corps). T-54/-55/-62, armd cars, APC, MRL, ZSU-23-4, SA-8 (Army inventory).
ISLAMIC PAN-AFRICAN LEGION, some 2,500: reports of 1 armd, 1 inf, 1 para/cdo bde. Some 75 T-54/-55, EE-9 AIFV, BTR-50/-60 (Army inventory).
PEOPLE'S CAVALRY FORCE: parade unit.
CUSTOMS/COAST GUARD (Naval control):
14 PFI, 7 PCI; counted in naval totals.

OPPOSITION:
National Front for the Salvation of Libya: 2,000:
(bases in Chad and Cameroon reported).

* Excl ε $5.0 bn military and commercial debt to the USSR.

MAURITANIA

GDP	1985ε: OM 55.04 ($714.00 m)		
	1986ε: OM 61.6 bn ($828.29 m)		
Growth	1987ε: 2%	1988ε: 4%	
Inflation	1987ε: 8.0%	1988ε: 8%	
Debt	1986: $1.76 bn	1987: $2.0 bn	
FMA	1988: $10.13 m (US, Fr)		
$1 = OM	(1986): 74.37	(1987): 73.87	
	(1988): 72.78		
OM = ouguiyas			

Population: 2,125,000

	13–17	18–22	23–32
Men	108,000	107,000	143,000
Women	105,000	99,000	140,000

TOTAL ARMED FORCES:
ACTIVE: 11,000.
Terms of service: conscription (2 years) authorized.

ARMY: 10,400.
6 Military Regions; 2 indep sectors.
2 inf bn.
1 para bn.
1 arty bn.
1 Camel Corps.
3 armd recce sqn.
4 AD arty bty.
1 engr coy.
EQUIPMENT:
RECCE: 15 EBR-75 hy, 39 AML-60, 14 -90, 12 M-3A1.
APC: 40 M-3 half-track.
TOWED ARTY: 105mm: 18 LH-105, 10 M-101A1/HM-2; **122mm:** 12 D-74, 18 D-30.
MORTARS: 81mm; 120mm: 30 AR-51/-EC1A-L/SL.
ATGW: 4 *Milan.*
RCL: 57mm: M-18; **75mm:** M-20; **106mm:** 45 M-40.
ATK GUNS: 85mm: 12 D-44.
AD GUNS: 14.5mm; 23mm: 50 ZU-23-2; **37mm:** 25 M-1939; **100mm:** 12 KS-19.
SAM: SA-7.

NAVY: 350.
BASES: Nouadhibou.
PATROL CRAFT, INSHORE: 8:
1 *Dix Juillet* (Fr *Patra*) PCI.
3 *El Vaiz* (FRG Lürssen 36-m) PFI.
2 PFI, 2 PCI⟨.

AIR FORCE: 250; 5 cbt ac, no armed hel.
COIN: 5 BN-2 *Defender.*
MR: 2 *Cheyenne* II.
TRANSPORT: 1 *Gulfstream* II, 1 DHC-5D, 2 *Skyvan* 3M, 1 Cessna F-337.

PARA-MILITARY:
GENDARMERIE 2,200; 6 regional coy (Defence Ministry).
NATIONAL GUARD: 2,800.
BORDER GUARD: 100.
AUXILIARIES: 1,000 (Interior Ministry).

MOROCCO

GDP	1987: D 142.40 bn ($17.838 bn)		
	1988ε: D 155.0 bn ($18.88 bn)		
Growth	1987: 1.0%	1988: 4.8%	
Inflation	1987: 2.7%	1988: 2.3%	
Debt	1987: $16.81 bn	1988ε: $19.5 bn	
Def exp*	1988: D 9.329 bn ($1.136 m)		

1989: D 10.235 bn ($1.216 bn)
FMA 1988: $53 m (US)
$1 = D (1987): 8.359 (1988): 8.209
(1989): 8.418

D = dirham

Population: 24,039,000

	13–17	18–22	23–32
Men	1,459,000	1,279,000	1,878,000
Women	1,402,000	1,232,000	1,908,000

TOTAL ARMED FORCES:
ACTIVE: 192,500.
 Terms of service: conscription 18 months authorized;
 most enlisted personnel are volunteers.
RESERVES: 100,000: obligation to age 50.

ARMY: 170,000.
 3 Comd (South, Northwest Atlas, Border).
 1 mech inf bde HQ.
 2 mot inf bde HQ.
 1 lt sy bde.
 2 para bde.
 6 mech inf regt.
 2 mot inf regt.
 Independent units:

11 arty gp.	3 mot (camel corps) bn.
1 AD gp.	3 cav bn.
7 armd sqn gp.	1 mtn bn.
41 inf bn.	5 engr bn.

ROYAL GUARD: 1,500,
 1 Royal Guard bn.
 1 Royal Guard cav sqn.
EQUIPMENT:
MBT: 224 M-48A5.
LIGHT TANKS: 50 AMX-13.
RECCE: 16 EBR-75, 80 AMX-10RC, 190 AML-90,
 38 AML-60-7, 40 *Eland* 90mm.
AIFV: 30 *Ratel* 20, some 30-90, 30 VAB-VCI.
APC: 420 M-113, 360 VAB-VTT, 70 UR-416, 29
 M-3; some 45 OT-62/-64 may be operational.
TOWED ARTY: 105mm: 30 lt (L-118), 40 M-101,
 36 HM2 (Fr M-101A1); 130mm: 18 M-46;
 155mm: 20 M-114;
SP ARTY: 155mm: 98 AMX-F3, 44 M-109.
MRL: 122mm: 40 BM-21.
MORTARS: 81mm; 120mm: 680 (incl 20 VAB SP).
ATGW: *Dragon,* 80 *Milan, TOW.*
RL: 66mm: *LAW*; 88mm: M-20 3.5-in.,
 STRIM-89.
RCL: 75mm: 260 M-20; 90mm: 30 M-67; 106mm:
 350 M-40.
ATK GUNS: 90mm: 28 M-56; 100mm: 8 SU-100 SP;
 105mm: 90 Steyr SK-105 *Kuerassier* SP.
AD GUNS: 14.5mm: 180 ZPU-2, 20 ZPU-4;
 20mm: 40 towed, 60 M-163 *Vulcan* SP;

23mm: 90 ZU-23-2; 37mm: 25 M-38/-39;
 100mm: 12 KS-19 towed.
SAM: 37 M-54 SP *Chaparral,* SA-7.

NAVY: 6,500 incl 1,500 naval infantry.
BASES: Casablanca, Agadir, Al Hoceima, Dakhla.
FRIGATE: 1 *Lt Col. Errhamani* (Sp *Descubierta*)
 with 2 × 3 ASTT (Mk 46 LWT), 1 × 2 375mm AS
 mor; plus 4 × MM-40 *Exocet* SSM.
PATROL AND COASTAL COMBATANTS: 23:
MISSILE CRAFT: 4 *Cdt El Khattabi* (Sp *Lazaga*) PFM
 with 4 × MM-38 *Exocet* SSM.
PATROL: 19:
 COASTAL: 9:
 2 *Okba* (Fr PR-72) PFC.
 4 *LV Rabhi* (Sp 58m B-200D) PCC.
 1 *Riffi* PCC.
 2 *El Lahik* (Dk '*Osprey*') PCC.
 INSHORE: 10 *El Wacil* (Fr P-32) PFI⟨.
AMPHIBIOUS: 3: *Ben Aicha* (Fr *Champlain*
 BATRAL) LSM, capacity 140 tps, 7 tk.
 Plus craft; 1 LCT
SUPPORT: 2 tpt, 1 ro-ro ferry.

MARINES: 1,500.
 1 naval inf bn.

AIR FORCE: 16,000; 109 cbt ac, 24 armed hel.
FGA: 3 sqn:
 1 with 17 *Mirage* F-1EH;
 1 with 7 F-5A, 2 F-5B;
 1 with 13 F-5E, 4 F-5F.
FIGHTER: 1 sqn with 21 *Mirage* F-1CH.
COIN: 2 sqn:
 1 with 23 *Alpha Jet*;
 1 with 22 CM-170.
RECCE: 1 sqn with 1 RF-5A, 2 F-5E, 4 OV-10.
 2 C-130H with side-looking radar.
EW: 1 C-130 (ELINT), 1 *Falcon* 20 (ELINT).
TANKER: 1 Boeing 707, 2 KC-130H.
TRANSPORT: 1 Boeing 707, 11 C-130H, 1 *Falcon* 50
 (VIP), 1 *Falcon* 20, 1 *Gulfstream* II (VIP), 5 *King*
 Air A100, 1 *King Air* A200, 3 Do-28.
HELICOPTERS:
 ATTACK: 24 SA-342 (12 with *HOT,* 12 with cannon).
 TRANSPORT: hy: 7 CH-47; **med:** 27 SA-330, 24
 AB-205A; **lt:** 20 AB-206, 5 AB-212.
TRAINING: 10 AS-202, 2 CAP-10, 4 CAP-230, 10 T-34C.
LIAISON: 2 *King Air* 200.
AAM: AIM-9B/D/J *Sidewinder,* R-530, R-550 *Magic.*
ASM: AGM-65B *Maverick* (for F-5E).

DEPLOYMENT:
ARMY:
 Northwest Atlas: 1 Royal Guard, 1 mtn bn; 1
 armd sqn, 1 mech sqn, 1 cav sqn, 1 arty gp.

South: 1 mech inf, 2 motor inf bde: 1 mech inf, 2 motor inf regt; 25 inf, 2 para, 2 Camel Corps bn; 3 lt sy, 4 armd sqn, 1 mech sqn gp; 4 mech sqn gp (UR-416 APC); 7 arty gp.

Border: 2 mech inf regt; 3 inf, 1 Camel Corps bn; 2 armd sqn, 1 arty gp.

FORCES ABROAD:
EQUATORIAL GUINEA: 360: 1 bn.

PARA-MILITARY: 40,000.
GENDARMERIE ROYALE: 10,000;
1 bde, 2 mobile gp, air sqn, coast guard unit; 18 boats, 2 *Rallye* ac; 2 SA-318, 3 SA-315, 3 SA-316, 6 *Gazelle*, 2 SA-360 SA-330, 6 *Puma* hel.
FORCE AUXILIAIRE: 30,000 incl Mobile Intervention Corps (5,000).

OPPOSITION:
POLISARIO: Military Wing: Sahrawi People's Liberation Army: 15,000 (perhaps 4,000 active) org in bn.
EQUIPMENT: T-55, T-62 tk; BMP-1, 20–30 EE-9 *Cascavel* MICV; M-1931/37 122mm how; BM-21 122mm MRL; 120mm, 160mm mor; AT-4 *Spigot* ATGW; ZSU-23-2 23mm SP AA guns; SA-6/-7/-9 SAM.
(Captured Moroccan eqpt incl AML-90, *Eland* AFV, *Ratel* 20, Panhard APC, Steyr SK-105 105mm SP ATK guns.)

---

* Incl border and internal security costs.

OMAN

GDP	1987:	R 2.40 bn ($6.24 bn)	
	1988:	R 2.45 bn ($6.37 bn)	
Growth	1987:	6.5%	1988: 0%
Inflation	1987:	0.0%	1988: 1%
Debt	1987:	$3.45 bn	1988: $3.70 bn
Def bdgt*	1988:	R 532.6 m ($1.385 bn)	
	1989ε:	R 510.0 m ($1.326 bn)	
FMA	1988:	$0.1 m (US)	
$1 = R	(1987/8/9):	0.3845	
R = rial			

Population: ε 1,472,900 (incl expatriates, number nk)			
	13–17	*18–22*	*23–32*
Men	72,800	60,200	102,800
Women	70,000	56,400	87,800

TOTAL ARMED FORCES:
ACTIVE: 25,500 (excl Royal Household tps, but incl some 3,700 foreign personnel).

Terms of service: voluntary.

ARMY: 20,000. (Regt are of bn size.)
1 div HQ.
2 bde HQ.
1 armd regt (2 tk sqn).
2 arty regt, 1 AD bty.
1 armd recce regt (3 armd car sqn).
8 inf regt (incl 3 Baluch).
1 inf recce regt (3 recce coy), 2 indep recce coy.
1 fd engr regt (3 sqn).
1 AB regt.
Musandam Security Force (indep rifle coy).
EQUIPMENT:
MBT: 6 M-60A1, 33 *Qayid al-Ardh* (*Chieftain*).
LIGHT TANKS: 30 *Scorpion*, 6 VBC-90.
AIFV: 2 VAB PC.
APC: 6 VAB VCI, 15 AT-105 *Saxon*, *Fahd* reported.
TOWED ARTY: 63: 105mm: 39 ROF lt; 130mm: 12 M-1946; 155mm: 12 FH-70.
SP ARTY: 155mm: 12 M-109A2.
MORTARS: 81mm; 107mm: 12 M-30 4.2-in.; 120mm: 12.
ATGW: 10 *TOW*, 50 *Milan* (incl 2 VCAC).
AD GUNS: 20mm (incl 2 VAB VD); 23mm: 4 ZU-23-2; 40mm: 12 *Bofors* L/60.
SAM: *Blowpipe*, 28 *Javelin*, SA-7.

NAVY: 2,500.
BASES: Seeb (HQ), Wudam (main base), Raysut, Ghanam Island, Alwi.
PATROL AND COASTAL COMBATANTS: 12:
MISSILE CRAFT: 4 *Dhofar*, 1 with 2 × 3 MM-40, 3 with 2 × 4 MM-40 *Exocet* SSM.
PATROL: 8:
4 *Wafi* (UK 37-m) PCC, 4 *Seeb* (UK 25-m) PCI.
AMPHIBIOUS: 2:
1 *Nasr el Bahr* LST, capacity 240 tps, 7 tk, hel deck.
1 *Al Munassir* LST, capacity 200 tps, 8 tk, hel deck.
Plus craft; 3 LCM.
SUPPORT: 1 tpt.

AIR FORCE: 3,000; 63 cbt ac, no armed hel.
FGA: 2 sqn with 18 *Jaguar* S(O) Mk 1, 1 GR1, 4 T-2.
FGA/RECCE: 1 sqn with 13 *Hunter* FGA-73, 4 T-7.
COIN/TRAINING: 1 sqn with 12 BAC-167 Mk 82, 4 AS-202.
TRANSPORT: 3 sqn:
1 with 3 BAC-111; 2 with 7 BN-2 *Defender/Islander*, 15 *Skyvan* 3M (7 radar-equipped, for MR), 3 C-130H.
HELICOPTERS: 2 med tpt sqn with 20 AB-205, 3 AB-206.
AD: 2 sqn with 28 *Rapier* SAM, *Martello* radar.
AAM: AIM-9P *Sidewinder*, R-550 *Magic*.

ROYAL HOUSEHOLD:
Royal Guard bde.
1 Special Force regt.
Royal Yacht Squadron (based Muscat):
  1 Royal Yacht, 3,800 tonnes.
  1 Royal Yacht spt ship, 11,000 tonnes, 1 hel.
Royal Flight: 1 Boeing-747 SP, 1 DC-8, 2
  Gulfstream, 1 *Falcon* 20 ac; 2 AS-332, 4 SA-330 hel.

PARA-MILITARY:
TRIBAL HOME GUARD (*Firqat*): 3,500.
POLICE COAST GUARD: 400: 15 AT-105 APC, 11
  inshore patrol craft.
POLICE AIR WING: 100: 1 *Learjet*, 2 Do-228-100,
  2 *Merlin* IVA, 3 DHC-5 *Buffalo*, 1 *Learjet* ac, 5
  AB-205, 3 AB-206, 6 Bell 214 ST, 1 Hughes 369 hel.

* Excl $1.8 bn military subsidy from GCC between
1984 and 1991, shared with Bahrain.

QATAR

GDP   1987: R 17.500 bn ($4.808 bn)
         1988: R 17.00 bn ($4.67 bn)
Growth   1987: −4%   1988: −3%
Inflation 1987: 0%   1988: 0.5%
Def bdgt 1987: R 561.2 m ($154.2 m)
$1 =R   (1986/8): 3.640
R = rial

Population: 397,000 (incl some 300,000 expatriates)

	13–17	18–22	23–32
Men	13,000	12,200	31,100
Women	12,800	10,700	17,700

TOTAL ARMED FORCES:
ACTIVE: 7,000.
  Terms of service: voluntary.

ARMY: 6,000.
  1 Royal Guard regt.
  1 tk bn.
  3 mech inf bn.
  1 fd arty regt.
  1 SAM bty with *Rapier*.
EQUIPMENT:
MBT: 24 AMX-30.
RECCE: 10 *Ferret* (in store).
AIFV: 30 AMX-10P.
APC: 160 VAB, 8 *Commando* Mk 3.
TOWED ARTY: 88mm: 8 25-pdr.
SP ARTY: 155mm: 6 Mk F-3.
MORTARS: 81mm.
ATGW: 100 *Milan*, *HOT* (incl 24 VAB SP).

RCL: 84mm: *Carl Gustav*.
SAM: 12 *Rapier*, *Blowpipe*, some 12 *Stinger* reported.

NAVY: 700 incl Marine Police.
BASE: Doha.
PATROL AND COASTAL COMBATANTS: 9:
MISSILE CRAFT: 3 *Damsah* (Fr *Combattante* III)
  with 2 × 4 MM-40 *Exocet* SSM.
PATROL, INSHORE: 6:
  6 *Barzan* (UK 33-m) PCI.
COAST DEFENCE: 3 × 4 MM-40 *Exocet*.

AIR FORCE: 300; 13 cbt ac, 20 armed hel.
FGA: Tac spt unit with 6 *Alpha Jet*.
FIGHTER: 1 AD sqn with 13 *Mirage* F1 (11 -E, 2 -D).
TRANSPORT: 1 sqn with 1 Boeing 727, 2 Boeing 707.
HELICOPTERS:
  ATTACK: 12 SA-342L (with *HOT*), 8 *Commando*
    Mk 3 (AM-39 *Exocet*).
  TRANSPORT: 4 *Commando* (3 -2A tpt, 1 -2C VIP).
  LIAISON: 2 SA-341G.
ASM: AM-39 *Exocet*.
SAM: 6 *Roland*.

SAUDI ARABIA

GDP   1987: R 267.6 bn ($71.146 bn)
         1988ε: R 274.8 bn ($73.385 bn)
Growth   1987: −2.4%   1988: 1.7%
Inflation 1987: −1%   1988: 1%
Def bdgt 1988: R 50.8 bn ($13.57 bn)
         1989ε: R 55.0 bn ($14.69 bn)
$1 = R   (1987/8/9): 3.745
R = rial

Population: 13,489,000 (incl some 5 m expatriates)

	13–17*	18–22*	23–32*
Men	727,000	627,000	1,233,000
Women	722,000	550,000	810,000

TOTAL ARMED FORCES:
ACTIVE: 65,700.
  Terms of service: voluntary; conscription, males
    aged 18–35, authorized.

ARMY: 38,000.
  2 armd bde.
  4 mech bde.
  1 inf bde.
  1 AB bde (2 AB bn, 3 SF coy).
  1 Royal Guard regt (3 bn).
  5 arty bn.
  18 AD arty bty.

EQUIPMENT:
MBT: 550: 300 AMX-30, 50 M-60A1 (to be A3), 200 M-60A3.
RECCE: 250 AML-60/-90.
AIFV: 500+ AMX-10P.
APC: 1,100 M-113 (incl *TOW*/comd/spt variants), 30 EE-11 *Urutu*, 170 Panhard M-3.
TOWED ARTY: 105mm: some 24 Model 56 pack, 40 M-101/-102 (in store); 155mm: 70 FH-70, 34 M-198.
SP ARTY: 275: 155mm: 224 M-109, 51 GCT.
MRL: 127mm: 6 *ASTROS II*.
MORTARS: 107mm: 360 M-30 4.2-in.
SSM: ε 9 Ch CSS-2.
ATGW: BGM-71A *TOW* (incl 200 VCC-1 SP), M-47 *Dragon*, *HOT* (incl AMX-10P SP).
RCL: 75mm; 84mm: 450 *Carl Gustav*; 90mm; 106mm.
AD GUNS: 40mm: M-42 SP; 90mm: 15 M-117.
SAM: *Stinger*, 500 *Redeye*.

NAVY: 7,200 (incl 1,200 marines);
BASES: Riyadh (HQ Naval Forces). Western Fleet: Jiddah (HQ), Al Wajh, Yanbu. Eastern Fleet: Jabayl (HQ), Al Qatif, Ras Tanura, Al Dammam, Ras al Mishab.
FRIGATES: 8:
    4 *Madina* (Fr F.2000) with 4 × 533mm, 2 × 406mm ASTT, 1 × AS-365N hel (AS 15 ASM) plus 8 *Otomat-2* SSM, 1 × 100mm gun.
    4 *Badr* (US Tacoma) (ASUW) with 2 × 4 *Harpoon* SSM, 2 × 3 ASTT (Mk 46 LWT).
PATROL AND COASTAL COMBATANTS: 13:
MISSILE CRAFT: 9 *As Siddiq* (US 58m) PFM with 2 × 2 *Harpoon*.
TORPEDO CRAFT: 3 *Dammam* (FRG *Jaguar*) with 4 × 533mm TT.
PATROL, INSHORE: 1 US *Pegasus* PHI, 9 PCI in store.
MINE WARFARE: 4 *Addriyah* (US MSC-322) MCC
AMPHIBIOUS: Craft only; 4 LCU, 12 LCM.
SUPPORT AND MISCELLANEOUS: 6:
    2 *Boraida* (mod Fr *Durance*) AOR, 3 ocean tugs, 1 Royal Yacht.

NAVAL AVIATION:
HELICOPTERS: 24 AS-365N, (4 SAR, 20 with AS-15TT ASM).

MARINES: (1,200): 1 inf regt, with 140 BMR-600P.

AIR FORCE: 16,500; 179 cbt ac, no armed hel.
FGA: 5 sqn:
    3 with 63 F-5E;
    2 with 20 *Tornado* IDS.
FIGHTER: 3 sqn with 42 F-15C. *Tornado* ADV being delivered.
RECCE: 1 sqn with 10 RF-5E.
AEW: 1 sqn with 5 E-3A.

TANKER: 8 KE-3A, 8 KC-130H.
OCU: 2 with 15 F-5B, 22 F-5F, 17 F-15D.
TRANSPORT: 3 sqn:
    35 C-130 (10 -E, 25 -H), 9 L-100-30HS (hospital ac), 35 C-212.
HELICOPTERS: 2 sqn: 1 AB-204, 14 AB-205, 25 AB-206B, 29 AB-212, 17 KV-107 (SAR, tpt).
TRAINING: 30 *Hawk* Mk 60, 30 BAC-167 Mk 80, 30 PC-9, 2 *Jetstream* 31, 13 Cessna 172.
ROYAL FLIGHT:
    ac: 2 BAe 125-800, 2 C-140, 4 CN-235, 1 *Gulfstream* III, 2 *Learjet* 35, 2 VC-130H.
    hel: 5 AS-61, AB-212.
AAM: AIM-9J/L/P *Sidewinder*, AIM-7F *Sparrow*.
ASM: AGM-65 *Maverick*.

AIR DEFENCE FORCES: (4,000):
    33 SAM bty:
    16 with 128 *Improved HAWK*;
    17 with 68 *Shahine* (*Crotale*) fire units and AMX-30SA 30mm SP AA guns.
    73 static *Shahine* fire units as static defence.
EQUIPMENT:
AD GUNS: 20mm: 100 M-163 *Vulcan*; 30mm: 53 AMX-30SA; 35mm: 180; 40mm: 120 L70 (in store).
SAM: 141 *Shahine*, 128 MIM-23B *Improved HAWK*.

PARA-MILITARY:
NATIONAL GUARD: (Ministry of Interior) 56,000 (10,000 active, 20,000 reserve; 26,000 tribal levies):
    2 mech inf bde each 4 all arms bn.
    1 ceremonial cav sqn.
EQUIPMENT:
APC: 700+ V-150 *Commando*.
TOWED ARTY: 105mm: 50 M-102.
RCL: 106mm.
ATGW: *TOW*.
AD GUNS: 20mm: 30 M-40 *Vulcan*.
FRONTIER FORCE: 8,500.
COAST GUARD: about 40 PCI⟨, 24 hovercraft, about 400 boats.
GENERAL CIVIL DEFENCE ADMINISTRATION UNITS: 10 KV-107 hel.

FOREIGN FORCES:
PENINSULAR SHIELD FORCE: ε 2,000; 1 inf bde (understrength with elm from all GCC states), also incl 1 Saudi bde.

---

* Indigenous population only.

SOMALI REPUBLIC

GDP	1986:	S sh 54.60 bn ($758.3 m)	
Growth	1987:	−1.5%	1988: −2%
Inflation	1987:	40%	1988: 70%

Debt   1987: $1.4 bn   1988: $1.75 bn
Def exp   1986ε: S sh 6.00 bn ($3.33 m)
FMA   1988: $4.65 m (US)
$1 = S sh (1986):   72.00   (1987):   105.20
             (1988):   170.45
S sh = Somali shillings

Population: 5,226,000

	13–17	18–22	23–32
Men	332,000	291,000	440,000
Women	320,000	277,000	433,000

TOTAL ARMED FORCES:
ACTIVE: 65,000.
> *Terms of service:* conscription (males 18–40), 18
> months selective.

ARMY: 61,300 (ε 30,000 conscripts).
4 corps, 12 div HQ (formations in name only;
   below establishment in units, men and eqpt.
   Bde of bn size).
4 tk bde.
45 mech and inf bde.
4 cdo bde.
1 SAM bde.
3 fd arty bde.
30 fd, 1 AD arty bn.
EQUIPMENT:*
MBT: 293: 30 *Centurion*, 123 M-47, 30 T-34, 110
   T-54/-55.
LIGHT TANKS: 10 M-41.
RECCE: 30 BRDM-2, 15 AML-90.
APC: 474: 64 BTR-40/-50/-60, 100 BTR-152, 310
   Fiat 6614/6616; BMR-600 reported.
TOWED ARTY: 210: 100mm: 8 M-1944; 105mm: 100
   M-56; 122mm: 84 M-1938; 155mm: 18 M-198.
MORTARS: 82mm: 100 M-41; 120mm: 50 M-1943.
ATGW: 100 *Milan, TOW* (incl 22 SP).
RL: 89mm: 300 LRAC.
RCL: 106mm: 60 M-40.
AD GUNS: 20mm; 23mm: 50 ZU-23-2, 4 ZSU-23-4
   SP; 37mm: 180 M-1939/Type 63; 40mm; 57mm:
   20 S-60; 100mm: 24 KS-19.
SAM: 40 SA-2 (operational status uncertain), 10
   SA-3, 20 SA-7.

NAVY:* 1,200.
BASES: Berbera, Mogadishu, Kismayu.
PATROL AND COASTAL COMBATANTS: 12:
MISSILE CRAFT: 2 Sov *Osa-II* PFM with SS-N-2A
   Styx SSM.
TORPEDO CRAFT: 4 Sov *Mol* PFT with 4 × 533mm TT.
PATROL INSHORE: 1 US Swiftships 32-m, 5 Sov
   Poluchat⟨.
AMPHIBIOUS: 1 Sov *Polnocny* LSM, capacity 120
   tps, 5 tk. Plus craft; 4 LCM.

AIR FORCE: 2,500; 63 cbt ac, no armed hel.*
FGA: 3 sqn with 12 MiG-17, 6 *Hunter* (5 FGA-76,
   1 T-77).
FIGHTER: 3 sqn with 8 MiG-21MF, 30 J-6.
COIN: 1 sqn with 5 SF-260W.
FIGHTER/RECCE: 2 *Hunter* FR76.
TRANSPORT: 1 sqn with 3 An-2, 3 An-24, 1 An-26, 4
   BN-2, 6 C-212 (2 VIP), 2 G-222.
HELICOPTERS: 1 sqn with 6 Mi-4, 2 Mi-8, 5
   Agusta-Bell (1 204, 4 212 (2 VIP)).
TRAINING: incl 2 MiG-15UTI, 3 SF-260W, 2 Cessna
   150, 10 Yak-11.
AAM: AA-2 *Atoll*.

PARA-MILITARY: 29,500.
POLICE: 8,000; 2 Do-28, 2 Cessna (1 185, 1 150) ac.
BORDER GUARDS: 1,500.
PEOPLE'S MILITIA: 20,000.

OPPOSITION:
**DEMOCRATIC FRONT FOR THE SALVATION OF
   SOMALIA** (DFSS): perhaps 1,200; mainly central
   Somalia from Mjerten tribe.
SOMALI NATIONAL MOVEMENT (SNM); some
   10,000 Northern Somalia from Issaq tribe.

* Much eqpt is unserviceable.

SUDAN

GDP   1985/6: £S 22.009 bn
             1986/7: £S 31.57 bn
Growth   1987:   –2%   1988:   –1%
Inflation   1987:   30.0%   1988:   40%
Debt   1987: $11.5 bn   1988: $13.8 bn
Def exp* 1986/7: £S 1.10 bn ($391.2 m)
             1987/8: £S 2.15 bn ($478.2 m)
FMA   1988: $0.9 m (US)
$1 = £S   (1986): 2.5   (1987): 2.812
             (1988): 4.5

Population: 24,278,000

	13–17	18–22	23–32
Men	1,333,000	1,182,000	1,848,000
Women	1,400,000	1,149,000	1,810,000

TOTAL ARMED FORCES:
ACTIVE: 72,800.
> *Terms of Service:* voluntary.

ARMY: 65,000.
1 Military District.

5 Regional Commands ('infantry divisions').
1 armd div HQ.
1 Republican Guard bde.
2 armd bde.
1 mech inf bde.
12 inf bde.
1 AB bde.
1 air aslt bde.
3 arty regt.
1 engr regt.
2 AD arty bde.

EQUIPMENT:†
MBT: 175: 155 T-54/-55, 20 M-60A3.
LIGHT TANKS: 70 Ch Type-62.
RECCE: 6 AML-90, 15 *Saladin*, 50 *Ferret*, BRDM-1/-2.
APC: 286: 40 BTR-50/-152, 30 OT-62/-64, 36 M-113, 80 V-100/-150, 100 *Walid*.
TOWED ARTY: 159: 100mm: 20 M-1944; 105mm: 18 M-101 pack; 122mm: 26 Type-60, 24 M-1938, 12 Type-54/D-30; 130mm: 36 M-46 and Ch Type 59-1; 155mm: 11 Mk F-3, 12 M-114A1.
MRL: 122mm: 6 *Al Saqr*-30, 4 BM-21.
MORTARS: 81mm (some SP); 82mm; 120mm: 50 RT-61, 50 M-38/-43.
ATGW: 18 *Swingfire*.
ATK GUNS: 76 mm: 18 M-1942; 100mm: some M-1944.
AD GUNS: 20mm: M-167 towed, M-163 SP; 23mm: ZU-23-2; 37mm: 120 M-1939/Type-63; 40mm: 60 L/60; 85mm: KS-12; 100mm: KS-19 towed.
SAM: SA-7.

NAVY:† 1,800.
BASE: Port Sudan.
PATROL CRAFT: 6:
3 *Gihad* (Yug 35m) PCI.
3 PCI⟨.
AMPHIBIOUS: Craft only; 2 *Sobat* (Yug DTM-221) LCT.

AIR FORCE: 6,000 (incl Air Defence).
45 cbt ac, no armed hel.†
FGA: 2 sqn: 1 with 3 F-5 (1 -E, 2 -F); 1 with 10 J-5.
FIGHTER: 2 sqn: 1 with some 8 MiG-21, 4 MiG-23; 1 with 6 J-6.
COIN: 1 sqn with 3 BAC-167, 3 *Jet Provost* Mk 55.
MR: 2 C-212.
TRANSPORT: 1 sqn with 4 C-130H, 4 C-212, 1 F-27, 2 *Falcon* 20, 2 DHC-5D, 6 EMB-110.
HELICOPTERS: 1 sqn with 15 IAR/SA-330, 10 Mi-8, 9 Bo-105 (police), 10 Mi-4, 11 AB-212.
TRAINING: incl 4 MiG-15UTI, 4 MiG-21U, 2 JJ-5, 2 JJ-6.
AD: 5 bty SA-2 SAM.
AAM: AIM-9 *Sidewinder*, AA-2 *Atoll*.

PARA-MILITARY:
NATIONAL GUARD: 500.

BORDER GUARD: 2,500.

OPPOSITION:
SUDANESE PEOPLE'S LIBERATION ARMY
(SPLA): ε 30,000 org in bn; mainly small arms plus 60mm mor, 14.5mm AA, SA-7 SAM; arty reported; operating only in southern Sudan.

* Excl £S 450 m for internal security.
† Eqpt serviceability questionable.

SYRIA

GDP	1987: £S 126.33 bn ($32.19 bn)		
	1988ε: £S 203.39 bn ($18.12 bn)		
Growth	1987: −9.3%	1988: 2%	
Inflation	1987: 59.4%	1988: 60%	
Debt*	1987: $4.60 bn	1988: $4.9 bn	
Def bdgt	1988ε: £S 18.0 bn ($1.60 bn)		
	1989ε: £S 28.0 bn ($2.49 bn)		
$1 = £S	(1987): 3.925	(1988): 11.225	
	(1989): 11.225		

Population: 11,724,000

	13–17	18–22	23–32
Men	743,000	515,000	683,000
Women	673,000	489,000	592,000

TOTAL ARMED FORCES:
ACTIVE: 404,000.
Terms of service: conscription, 30 months.
RESERVES (to age 45): 400,000. Army 392,000 active; Navy 8,000.

ARMY: 300,000 (130,000 conscripts, 50,000 reservists).
2 corps HQ:
5 armd div (each 3 armd, 1 mech, 1 arty bde).
3 mech div (each 2 armd, 2 mech, 1 arty bde).
1 SF div (5 para/cdo regt).
(1 bde in each div at cadre strength).
2 indep mech inf bde.
2 arty bde.
7 indep SF regt.
3 SSM bde:
2 (each 3 bn) with *FROG, Scud*; 1 (3 bn) with SS-21.
1 coastal def SSM bde with SS-C-1B *Sepal* and SS-C-3.
2 coastal def bde.
RESERVES: 9 mech and inf bde.
EQUIPMENT:
MBT: 4,050: 2,100 T-54/-55, 1,000 T-62M/K, 950 T-72/-72M (some 1,100 in static positions and in store).
RECCE: 500 BRDM-2.

AIFV: 2,350 BMP-1.
APC: 1,450 BTR-40/-50/-60/-152, OT-64.
TOWED ARTY: some 2,000; 122mm: 100 M-1931/-37 (in store), ISU-122; M-1938, 500 D-30; 130mm: 650 M-46; 152mm: D-1, M-1937, M-1943; 180mm: S23.
SP ARTY: 122mm: 72 2S1, 36 T-34/D-30; 152mm: ISU-152, 42 2S3.
MRL: 122mm: 250 BM-21; 220mm: BM-27; 240mm: BM-24.
MORTARS: 82mm; 120mm, 160mm, 240mm.
SSM launchers: 18 *FROG*-7, some 18 SS-21, 18 *Scud*-B; SS-C-1B *Sepal*, SS-C-3 coastal.
ATGW: 1,300 AT-3 *Sagger* (incl BRDM-2 SP), AT-4 *Spigot* and *Milan*.
ATK GUNS: 100mm: T-12.
AD GUNS: 1,700: 23mm: ZU-23-2 towed, ZSU-23-4 SP; 37mm: M-1939; 57mm: S-60, ZSU-57-2 SP; 85mm: M-1939/-44; 100mm: KS-19.
SAM: SA-7/-9/-13.

NAVY: 4,000.
BASES: Latakia, Tartus, Minet el-Baida.
SUBMARINES: 3: Sov *Romeo* with 533mm TT.
FRIGATES: 2 Sov *Petya* II with 4 × ASW RL, 3 × 533mm TT.
PATROL AND COASTAL COMBATANTS: 18:
MISSILE CRAFT: 12 Sov *Osa* PFM with 4 SS-N-2 *Styx* SSM.
PATROL: 6 Sov *Zhuk* PFI⟨.
MINE COUNTERMEASURES: 9:
   1 Sov *Natya* MSO
   1 Sov T-43, 1 *Sonya* MSC.
   2 Sov *Vanya*, 4 *Yevgenya* MSI.
AMPHIBIOUS: 3 *Polnocny* LSM, capacity 100 tps, 5 tk.

NAVAL AVIATION:
ASW: 12 Mi-14, 5 Ka-25 hel.

AIR FORCE: 40,000; 499 cbt ac; 110 armed hel.†
FGA: 9 sqn:
   2 with 38 MiG-17 (FGA/trg);
   1 with 15 Su-7;
   2 with 35 Su-20;
   4 with 60 MiG-23BN.
FIGHTERS: 17 sqn:
   2 with 30 MiG-25, 5 MiG-25U;
   8 with 172 MiG-21PF/PFMA/bis;
   5 with 80 MiG-23MF;
   2 with 24 MiG-29.
RECCE: 6 MiG-25R.
TRANSPORT: 6 An-12, 4 An-24, civil-registered ac incl: 4 An-26, 2 *Falcon* 20, 4 Il-76, 7 Yak-40.
HELICOPTERS:
   ATTACK: 25 Mi-24, 35 Mi-25, 50 SA-342L (ATK).
   TRANSPORT: 10 Mi-6 (hy), 60 Mi-8, 45 Mi-17, 10 Mi-4, 10 Mi-2.

ASW (Navy-assigned): 5 Ka-25, 20 Mi-14.
TRAINING: incl 90 L-39, 70 L-29, 20 MBB-223, 10 MiG-17, 20 MiG-21U, 10 Su-7U, Yak-11.
AAM: AA-2 *Atoll*, AA-6 *Acrid*, AA-7 *Apex*, AA-8 *Aphid*.
ASM: ATGW: AT-2 *Swatter*, AS-12, *HOT*.

AIR DEFENCE COMMAND: ε 60,000;
   21 AD bde (some 95 SAM bty):
      11 (some 60 bty) with some 392 SA-2/-3;
      10 (27 bty) with some 200 SA-6 and AD arty.
      2 SAM regt (each 2 bn of 2 bty) with some 48 SA-5, 60 SA-8.

FORCES ABROAD:
LEBANON: 30,000: 1 div HQ, 1 armd, 2 mech, 1 inf bde, 8 SF regt.

PARA-MILITARY:
REPUBLICAN GUARD (Internal Security Force): 10,000: 1 armd bde (3 armd, 1 mech inf, 1 arty bn) plus some 5 indep units.
DESERT GUARD (Frontier Force): 1,800.
PALESTINE LIBERATION ARMY: 4,500; 2 or 3 bde (in Syria/Lebanon, some Syrian officers); 90 T-54/-55 MBT; 105mm, 122mm, 152mm how; MRL; AT-3 *Sagger* ATGW; SA-7 SAM.
GENDARMERIE (Ministry of Interior): 8,000.
BA'ATH PARTY: Workers Militia (People's Army).

FOREIGN FORCES:
UNITED NATIONS (UNDOF): some 1,400, contingents from Austria, Canada, Finland and Poland.
SOVIET UNION: Some 3,000 advisers, mainly in Air Defence.

* Excl some $14–15 bn owed to USSR and Eastern-bloc countries, probably half for military eqpt.
† Some ac may be in store.

TUNISIA

GDP	1987: D 8.013 bn ($9.575 bn)		
	1988ε: D 8.838 bn ($9.377 bn)		
Growth	1987: 5.5%	1988: 4%	
Inflation	1987: 7.2%	1988: 6.3%	
Debt	1987: $7.4 bn	1988: $8.1 bn	
Def bdgt	1988: D ε 445.0 m ($545.47 m)		
FMA	1988: $31.4 m (US)		
$1 = D	(1987): 0.8287	(1988): 0.8158	
	(1989): 0.9426		

D = dinar

Population: 7,635,000

	13–17	18–22	23–32
Men	443,000	410,000	664,000
Women	421,000	395,000	655,000

TOTAL ARMED FORCES:
ACTIVE: 38,000 (26,400 conscripts).
Terms of service: 12 months selective.

ARMY: 30,000 (25,000 conscripts).
2 mech bde (each with 1 armd, 2 mech inf bn).
1 Sahara bde.
1 para-cdo bde.
1 armd recce regt.
1 ATK regt.
1 fd arty regt.
1 AD bde (2 AD regt).
1 engr regt.
EQUIPMENT:
MBT: 68: 14 M-48A3, 54 M-60A3.
LIGHT TANKS: 104: 40 AMX-13, 10 M-41, 54 Steyr SK-105 *Kuerassier*.
RECCE: 24 *Saladin*, 23 AML-90.
APC: 208: 100 M-113A1/-2, 18 EE-11 *Urutu*, 90 Fiat F-6614.
TOWED ARTY: 123: 105mm: 48 M-101A1/A2; 155mm: 18 M-114A1, 57 M-198.
SP ARTY: 28: 105mm: 10 M-108; 155mm: 18 M-109.
MORTARS: 81mm; 107mm: 12 M-30 SP; 120mm: 18.
ATGW: *TOW* (incl 35 M-901), *Milan*, SS-11.
RL: STRIM-89.
AD GUNS: 20mm: 26 M-163 *Vulcan* SP; 37mm: 10 M-1939/Type-55; 40mm: 12 M-42.
SAM: 48 RBS-70, 25 MIM-72 *Chaparral*.

NAVY: 4,500 (700 conscripts).
BASES: Bizerte, Sfax, Kelibia.
FRIGATE: 1 *Pres Bourguiba* (US *Savage*) with 2 × 3 ASTT.
PATROL AND COASTAL COMBATANTS: 23:
MISSILE CRAFT: 6:
3 *La Galite* (Fr *Combattante* III) PFM with 8 MM-40 *Exocet* SSM;
3 *Bizerte* (Fr P-48) with 8 × SS-12 SSM.
PATROL: 17:
COASTAL: 3: 1 *Youssef*, 2 *Hannibal* (US *Adjutant* ex-MSC).
INSHORE: 14: 2 *Gafsa* (Ch *Shanghai*) PFI, 2 *Tazarka* (UK Vosper 31-m) PCI, 10⟨.

AIR FORCE: 3,500 (700 conscripts);
43 cbt aircraft, no armed hel.
FGA: 8 F-5E, 4 F-5F.
COIN: 1 sqn with 7 MB-326K, 4 MB-326L.
TRANSPORT: 2 C-130H.
LIAISON: 2 S-208M.
TRAINING: 21 SF-260 (9 -C, 12 -W), 8 MB-326B.
HELICOPTERS: 1 wing with 6 SA-313, 5 SA-316, 6 UH-1 (4 -H, 2 -N), 18 AB-205, 6 AS-350B, 1 AS-365F.
AAM: AIM-9J *Sidewinder*.

PARA-MILITARY:
PUBLIC ORDER BRIGADE: 3,500: (Ministry of Interior); army trained; 3 bn; EBR-75 AFV; 110 Fiat 6614, V-150 Commando APC.
NATIONAL GUARD: 10,000; incl Coastal Patrol with some 13 craft⟨.

UNITED ARAB EMIRATES (UAE)

GDP	1987:	Dh 85.0 bn ($23.15 bn)	
	1988:	Dh 84.0 bn ($22.88 bn)	
Growth	1987:	−8%	1988: 1%
Inflation	1987:	−1%	1988: −1%
Def bdgt	1988:	Dh 5.826 bn ($1.59 bn)	
	1989ε:	Dh 5.40 bn ($1.47 bn)	
$1 = Dh	(1986/7/8): 3.671		
Dh = dirham			

Population: 1,681,000 (incl some 800,000 expatriates)

	13–17	18–22	23–32
Men	74,000	58,000	136,000
Women	71,000	53,000	73,000

TOTAL ARMED FORCES:*
ACTIVE: 43,000 (perhaps 30% expatriates).
Terms of service: voluntary.

ARMY: 40,000.
MoD (Dubai); GHQ (Abu Dhabi).
INTEGRATED:
1 Royal Guard 'bde'.
1 armd bde.
1 mech inf bde.
2 inf bde.
1 arty, 1 AD bde (each 3 bn).
NOT INTEGRATED:
1 inf bde (Dubai)
EQUIPMENT:
MBT: 131: 95 AMX-30, 36 OF-40 Mk 2 (*Lion*).
LIGHT TANKS: 76 *Scorpion*.
RECCE: 90 AML-90, VBC-40, 70 *Saladin* (in store), 60 *Ferret* (in store).
AIFV: 30 AMX-10P.
APC: 428: 30 AMX VCI, VCRTT, 300 Panhard M-3, 20 VAB, 66 EE-11 *Urutu*; 12 *Saracen* (in store).
TOWED ARTY: 77: 105mm: 59 ROF lt, 18 M-56 pack.
SP ARTY: 155mm: 20 Mk F-3.
MRL: 70mm: 18 LAU-97; 122mm: 40 FIROS-25.
MORTARS: 81mm: 80; 120mm: 21.
ATGW: 45 *Milan*, *Vigilant*, 25 *TOW* (incl EE-11 SP), *HOT* (incl 20 SP).
RCL: 84mm: *Carl Gustav*; 120mm: BAT L-4.

AD GUNS: 20mm: 48 M-3VDA SP; 30mm: 12 GCF-BM2.
SAM: 12 *Rapier*, 8 *Crotale*, 140 RBS-70.

NAVY: 1,500.
BASES: Abu Dhabi: Dalma, Mina Zayed; **Ajman; Dubai:** Mina Rashid, Mina Jabal 'Ali; **Fujairah; Ras al Khaimah:** Mina Sakr; **Sharjah:** Mina Khalid, Khor Fakkan; Taweela (under construction).
PATROL AND COASTAL COMBATANTS: 15:
MISSILE CRAFT: 6 *Ban Yas* (FRG Lürssen TNC-45) PFM with 2 × 2 MM-40 *Exocet* SSM.
PATROL, INSHORE: 9: 6 *Ardhana* (UK Vosper 33-m) PFI, 3⟨.
AMPHIBIOUS: Craft only, 2 *Jananah* LCT.
SUPPORT AND MISCELLANEOUS: 1 maint ship.

AIR FORCE: (incl Police Air Wing): 1,500; 61 cbt ac, 19 armed hel.
FGA: 2 sqn:
 1 with 14 *Mirage* IIIEAD;
 1 with 12 *Hawk* Mk 63 (FGA/trg).
FIGHTER: 1 sqn with 12 *Mirage* 5AD.
 Mirage 2000 being delivered.
COIN: 1 sqn with 6 MB-326 (4 -KD, 2 -LD), 5 MB-339A.
RECCE: 3 *Mirage* 5RAD.
EW: 4 C-212.
TRANSPORT: incl 5 BN-2, 4 C-130H, 2 L-100-30, 5 DHC-5D, 1 G-222, 2 Cessna 182.
HELICOPTERS:
 ATTACK: 2 AS-332F (anti-ship, with *Exocet* AM-39), 10 SA-342K (with *HOT*), 7 SA-316/-319 (with AS-11/-12).
 TRANSPORT: 8 AS-332 (2 VIP), 1 AS-350, 13 Bell (3 -205, 5 -206A, 1 -206L, 4 -214), 11 SA-330.
TRAINING: 2 *Mirage* 5DAD, some 20 PC-7, 8 *Hawk* Mk 61, 6 SF-260TP, 2 MB-339A.
AAM: R-550 *Magic*.
ASM: *HOT*, AS-11/-12, AS-15TT, AM-39 *Exocet*.
AD: AN/TPS-70 radar.
 5 bty *Improved Hawk* (still forming).

PARA-MILITARY:
COAST GUARD (Ministry of the Interior): 28 PCI⟨, about 32 boats.

---

* The Union Defence Force and the armed forces of the UAE (Abu Dhabi, Dubai, Ras Al Khaimah and Sharjah) were formally merged in 1976; Abu Dhabi and Dubai still maintain a degree of independence.

YEMEN ARAB REPUBLIC (NORTH)

GDP	1986:	R 38.389 bn ($3.98 bn)		
	1987:	R 43.559 bn ($4.22 bn)		
Growth	1987:	4.7%	1988:	3.5%

Inflation	1987:	22%	1988:	20.0%
Debt	1987:	$3.0 bn	1988:	$3.4 bn
Def exp	1987:	R 4.72 bn ($530.04 m)		
	1988:	R 5.2 bn ($532.2 m)		
FMA	1988:	$1.5 m (US)		
$1 = R	(1986):	9.6392	(1987):	10.3417
	(1988):	9.7717		
R = rial				

Population: 7,620,000

	13–17	18–22	23–32
Men	559,000	518,000	788,000
Women	544,000	503,000	790,000

TOTAL ARMED FORCES:
ACTIVE: 36,500 (perhaps 25,000 conscripts).
 Terms of service: conscription, 3 years.
RESERVES: Army: perhaps 40,000.

ARMY: 35,000 (perhaps 25,000 conscripts).
 3 armd 'bde' (bn).
 9 inf bde.
 1 mech bde.
 1 SF bde.
 2 AB/cdo bde.
 1 central guard force.
 5 arty bde.
 3 AD arty bn, 2 AD bn (1 with SA-2 SAM).
EQUIPMENT:
MBT: 664: 100 T-34, 480 T-54/-55, 20 T-62, 64 M-60A1.
RECCE: 50 *Saladin*, Ferret.
AIFV: 120 BMP-1.
APC: 370: 70 M-113, 300 BTR-40/-50/-60.
TOWED ARTY: 332: 76mm: 200 M-1942; 105mm: 90 M-101; 122mm: 30 M-1931/37; 155mm: 12 M-114.
ASSAULT GUNS: 100mm: 30 SU-100.
MRL: 122mm: 65 BM-21.
MORTARS: 81mm; 82mm; 120mm: 50 M-43.
ATGW: 20 *Vigilant*, 12 *TOW*, 24 *Dragon*.
RL: 66mm M72 *LAW*.
RCL: 75mm: M-20; 82mm.
AD GUNS: 20mm: 52 M-167, 20 M-163 *Vulcan* SP; 23mm: 30 ZU-23, ZSU-23-4; 37mm: 150 M-1939; 57mm: 120 S-60.
SAM: SA-2, SA-9.

NAVY: 500.
BASE: Hodeida.
PATROL CRAFT, INSHORE: 8:
 3 *Sana'a* (US *Broadsword* 32-m) PFI, 5 Sov *Zhuk*⟨.
MINE COUNTERMEASURES: 3 Sov *Yevgenya* MSI.
AMPHIBIOUS: Craft only; 2 Sov *Ondatra* LCU, 2 T-4 LCU.

AIR FORCE: 1,000;

83 cbt ac (plus some 40 in store), no armed hel.
FGA: 3 sqn:
1 with 11 F-5E;
1 with 10 MiG-17;
1 with 22 Su-20.
FIGHTER: 2 sqn with 30 MiG-21.
TRANSPORT: 3 An-24, 3 An-26, 2 C-130H, 2 F-27, 2 *Skyvan* 3M.
TRAINING: 2 F-5B, 2 MiG-15, 4 MiG-21U, 4 Su-22U, Yak-11.
HELICOPTERS: 2 AB-204, 6 AB-206, 6 AB-212, 1 Mi-4, 23 Mi-8, 2 SA-316.
AD: 12 SAM bty: 4 with SA-2; 3 with SA-3; 5 with SA-6.
AAM: AA-2 *Atoll*, AIM-9 *Sidewinder*.

PARA-MILITARY:
MINISTRY OF NATIONAL SECURITY FORCE: 5,000.
TRIBAL LEVIES: at least 20,000.

YEMEN: PEOPLE'S DEMOCRATIC REPUBLIC (SOUTH)

GDP	1987ε: D 423.5 m ($1.226 bn)		
	1988ε: D 479.5 m ($1.388 bn)		
Growth	1987: 5%	1988: 8.9%	
Debt	1984: $2.9 bn	1985: $3.4 bn	
Def exp	1984: D 67.0 m ($193.978 m)		
$1 = D	(1985/6/7/8): 0.3454		
D = dinar			

Population: 2,364,000

	13–17	18–22	23–32
Men	210,000	153,000	175,000
Women	205,000	149,000	170,000

TOTAL ARMED FORCES:
ACTIVE: 27,500 (perhaps 18,000 conscripts).
Terms of service: 2 years.
RESERVES: Army: 45,000.

ARMY: 24,000 (perhaps 18,000 conscripts).
1 armd bde.
3 mech bde (status uncertain).
9 inf regt (some being mech).
3 arty bde.
10 arty bn.
2 SSM bde with *FROG*-7 and *Scud* B.
EQUIPMENT:*
MBT: 480 T-34/-54/-55/-62.
RECCE: 130 BRDM-2.

AIFV: some 150 BMP-1.
APC: 325 BTR-40/-60/-152.
TOWED ARTY: 225: 122mm: 40 M-1938, 120 D-30; 130mm: 65 M-46.
COAST ARTY: 130mm: 36 SM-4-1.
MRL: 155: 122mm: 140 BM-21; 140mm: 15 BM-14.
MORTARS: 82mm; 120mm: 50 M-43; 160mm.
SSM: launchers: 12 *FROG*-7, 6 *Scud* B.
ATGW: AT-3 *Sagger* (incl 36 BRDM SP).
RCL: 82mm: 20 B-10; 107mm: B-11.
ATK GUNS: 70: 85mm: 30 D-44; 100mm: 40.
AD GUNS: 200: 23mm: ZU-23, ZSU-23-4 SP; 37mm: 30 M-1939; 57mm: S-60; 85mm: 20 KS-12.
SAM: SA-7/-9.

NAVY:* 1,000.
BASES: Aden, Perim Island, Al Mukalla.
PATROL AND COASTAL COMBATANTS: 10:
MISSILE CRAFT: 6 Sov *Osa*-II with 4 × SSN-2B *Styx* SSM.
TORPEDO CRAFT: 2 Sov P-6⟨ with 2 × 533mm TT.
PATROL: 2 Sov *Zhuk* PFI⟨.
AMPHIBIOUS: 5:
1 Sov *Ropucha* LST, capacity 200 tps, 9 tk.
4 Sov *Polnocny* LSM, capacity 100 tps, 5 tk.

AIR FORCE: 2,500 (may be some Soviet and Cuban aircrew). 114 cbt ac, 12 armed hel.*
BOMBERS: 5 Il-28.
FGA: 4 sqn:
1 with 25 MiG-17;
1 with 12 MiG-21;
1 with 25 Su-20;
1 with 15 MiG-23BN.
FIGHTER: 3 sqn with 30 MiG-21.
TRANSPORT: 1 sqn with 2 An-12, 6 An-24, 2 An-26, 4 Il-14.
HELICOPTERS: 1 sqn with 12 Mi-24, 30 Mi-8, 4 Mi-4, 2 Ka-26.
TRAINING: 3 MiG-15UTI, 2 MiG-21U.
AD: 1 SAM regt: 6 bty SA-2, 3 bty SA-3, SA-6 reported.
AAM: AA-2 *Atoll*.
ASM: AT-2 *Swatter*, AT-6 *Spiral*.

PARA-MILITARY:
PEOPLE'S MILITIA: 15,000.
PUBLIC SECURITY FORCE: 30,000 (increasing); 6 PFI⟨.

FOREIGN FORCES:
Cuba: 500.

* Eqpt totals are of doubtful reliability, as is serviceability.

Sub-Saharan Africa

Peace Processes

Angola/Namibia

The most significant development in the year has been the conclusion of treaties between Angola, Cuba and South Africa designed to produce an **Angolan/Namibian** settlement based on the implementation of UN Resolution 435 in conjunction with a phased withdrawal of Cuban troops from Angola. The settlement has required a pull-out of South African troops from Angolan territory and, as a preliminary to their eventual complete withdrawal, a reduction of South African forces in Namibia to 1,500, confined to two bases at Oshivelo and Grootfontein, by 1 July 1989. Both these have been effected. Cuban troops in Angola were required both to withdraw progressively northwards and, in a phased programme, to pull out altogether by 1 July 1991. By 1 June 1989 most, if not all, Cuban troops were believed to have redeployed north of the 13th Parallel and total Cuban strength in Angola had been reduced by some 10,000 to about 40,000 men.

Two UN groups have been established: the UN Angolan Verification Mission (UNAVM), with military observers from ten countries, is monitoring the Cuban withdrawal; and the UN Transition Assistance Group (UNTAG) is tasked with supervising a demilitarized zone along the Namibia–Angola border and monitoring the transition to Namibian independence – including elections currently scheduled for 1 November 1989. The UNTAG force, originally planned to be 7,500 strong, was implemented at a strength of only 4,600 because of budgetary pressures and comprises infantry battalions from Finland, Kenya and Malaysia, supported by British signal troops and Australian engineers.

Delays in setting-up and deploying the force meant that only the support contingents were in place by the implementation date of 1 April. Shortly after this, some 500 armed SWAPO guerrillas crossed into Namibia from Angola, contrary to the agreement, for purposes which remain obscure. This disrupted the transition process by provoking the deployment of South African troops from the camps to which they had withdrawn prior to returning to South Africa. After some fighting, in which SWAPO suffered casualties, UN troops established 'safe' rendezvous to which a few SWAPO forces reported, while the remainder withdrew to Angola. The programme now appears to be back on track, although some concerns remain about the role of former members of the *Koevoet* the South West African counter-insurgency unit, who appear to be taking an active part in policing although the unit has nominally been disbanded. UNITA was not involved in the peace process, but in June 1989 at a meeting organized by President Mobuto of Zaire it met the Angolan government and established the basis for a reconciliation.

Mozambique

In **Mozambique**, however, while there are grounds for some optimism regarding settlement of the internal struggle, resolution may still remain distant. South Africa has reaffirmed the Nkomati Accord and thus, at least officially distanced itself from any support of the RENAMO rebels; there are reported contacts between the Mozambican government and RENAMO; and the Bush Administration is keen to follow up its success in Angola-Namibia by similarly brokering a settlement in Mozambique. As yet, however, RENAMO remains active. Zimbabwean and Malawian forces are still deployed in Mozambique keeping lines of communication open, but the Tanzanian detachment has been withdrawn.

The Horn of Africa

There are also prospects of progress towards peace in the Horn of Africa. In **Ethiopia** the Eritrean People's Liberation Front (EPLF), after considerable success in wresting territory from government control, and the Tigre People's Liberation Front (TPLF) have agreed to hold talks with the government which survived an attempted army coup in May 1989 and the subsequent purge of the higher echelons of the armed forces. In **Sudan** a bloodless military coup succeeded in June 1989. The new regime has instituted a cease-fire and seems more determined to negotiate a settlement of the SPLA revolt in the southern provinces than its predecessor, but dialogue with the rebels has not been taken up as quickly as expected.

Military Developments
There have been few developments in the armed forces of the Sub-Saharan region. While some new aircraft have been delivered, most of the changes noted in this edition could have been effected more than twelve months ago and represent revisions rather than acquisitions. The **South African** Air Force now has some 27 *Cheetah* (locally modified *Mirage*) in service. A further South African development with considerable potential significance is the successful test of the booster stage of a rocket, thought to be part of the development of an IRBM (possibly in co-operation with Israel). **Angolan** aircraft holdings now include MiG-17 FGA and additional MiG-21 fighters. The **Nigerian** Air Force's MB-339AN trainers have a COIN capability, as do some 16 Bo-105D helicopters shown in the SAR role last year. **Burkina Faso's** SF/260 aircraft also have a COIN capability. **Botswana** has acquired nine BAC-167 Mk 83 COIN aircraft. **Togo** now has eight CM-170, four in the COIN role and four trainers.

Defence Spending
There has been an overall downwards trend for defence expenditure in the region over the last two years, both in local currency terms and, more markedly, in dollar terms, the latter emphasized by the continuing depreciation of currencies in the region against the dollar. The sole exceptions have been South Africa and Zimbabwe. While **South Africa's** increasing isolation affected its economy, which registered only limited growth, defence spending has continued to rise – by 9% in real terms in 1988 and with an 8% increase planned for 1989. The cost of replacing equipment, however, is becoming prohibitive, though the 1977 arms embargo has led to the establishment of a broad-based arms industry which has gained a foothold in the export market. **Zimbabwe** has curbed its defence allocations in real terms in the current fiscal year. The more significant defence spenders have either kept a check on, or reduced, allocations. **Mozambique** has allocated some $115 m to defence in 1989, about half what it spent three years earlier, while **Nigeria** kept defence allocations for 1989 level with 1988 in local currency terms, but this represents almost a 30% reduction when converted to nominal dollar terms. A similar pattern is to be found in **Uganda**. Information for other major countries is insufficient to draw firm conclusions, but **Ethiopia**, which is under some pressure from its principal ally, the USSR, will nevertheless attempt to maintain a high level of defence spending.

ANGOLA

GDP	1987ε:	K 140.61 bn ($4.70 bn)	
Growth	1987ε:	0.0%	
Debt*	1986:	$4.0 bn	1987: $4.7 bn
Def exp†	1986:	K 32.76 bn ($1.09 bn)	
	1988:	K 24.79 bn ($819.0 m)	
$1 = K	(1986/7):	29.918	(1988): 30.248
	(1989):	30.433	
K = kwanza			

Population: 9,560,000

	13–17	17–22	23–32
Men:	529,000	430,000	674,000
Women:	534,000	436,000	690,000

TOTAL ARMED FORCES:

ACTIVE: ε 100,000 (incl some 10,000 recalled ODP militia, 24,000 conscripts).
Terms of service: conscription, 2 years.
RESERVES: Militia (ODP): 50,000.

ARMY: ε 91,500 (ε 24,000 conscripts, 10,000 ODP).
10 Military Regions, (some may be fd HQ).
70 + bde (each with inf, tk, APC, arty and AA units as required. Bde = ε 1,000 men).
EQUIPMENT:‡
MBT: 500: 100 T-34, 300 T-54/-55, 100+ T-62.
LIGHT TANKS: some 50 PT-76.
RECCE: 200+ BRDM-2.
APC: 255 BTR-40/-50/-60/-152.
TOWED ARTY: 500: incl 76mm, 85mm, 100mm, 122mm, 130mm, 152mm.
ASSAULT GUNS: SU-100.
MRL: 122mm: 75 BM-21, BM-24.
MORTARS: 82mm; 120mm: 40+.

ATGW: AT-3 *Sagger.*
RCL: 900: 75mm, 82mm, 107mm.
AD GUNS: 300+: 14.5mm: ZPU-4; 20mm: M-55;
23mm: M-1939, ZU-23-2, 20 ZSU-23-4 SP;
37mm; 57mm: 70 S-60 towed, 40 ZSU-57-2 SP.
SAM: SA-7/-14.
RESERVES:
PEOPLE'S DEFENCE ORGANIZATION (ODP):
50,000; 11+ 'bde'. 10,000 serving with the
Regular Army at any one time.

NAVY:‡ 1,500.
BASES: Luanda (HQ), Lobito, Namibe.
PATROL AND COASTAL COMBATANTS: 24:
MISSILE CRAFT: 6 Sov *Osa*-II with 4 × SS-N-2 *Styx* SSM.
TORPEDO CRAFT: 5 *Shershen* with 4 × 533mm HWT.
PATROL, INSHORE 13: 4 Port *Argos*, 2 Sov *Poluchat*, 7⟨.
MINE WARFARE: 2 Sov *Yevgenya* MHI.
AMPHIBIOUS: 3 Sov *Polnocny* LSM, capacity 100
tps. 6 tk.
Plus craft; 1 LCT, 10 LCM.
COASTAL DEFENCE: SS-C-1 *Sepal* at Luanda.

AIR FORCE/AIR DEFENCE: ε 7,000;
179 cbt ac, 22 armed hel.‡
FGA: 25 MiG-17, 53 MiG-23; 10 Su-22;
FIGHTER: 75 MiG-21 MF/bis.
COIN/RECCE: 1 sqn with 8 PC-7.
MR: 1 F-27MPA, 2 EMB-111.
ATTACK HELICOPTERS: 16 Mi-25, 6 SA-365M.
TRANSPORT: 2 sqn with 3 C-47, 12 CASA C-212, 12
An-12 (Sov), 30 An-26, 4 PC-6B, 13 BN-2 *Islander.*
HELICOPTERS: 2 sqn with 13 Mi-17, 49 Mi-8, 30
IAR-316, 1 SA-315, 10 SA-316, 6 SA-342, 10 SA-365.
LIAISON: 10 An-2, 5 Do-27.
TRAINING: 3 MiG-15UTI, 6 MiG-21U, 2 Su-22, 11
PC-7, 6 Yak-11, 3 Cessna 172.
AD: 5 SAM bn. 10 bty; with 12 SA-2, 40 SA-3, 72
SA-6, 48 SA-8, SA-9, SA-13.
AAM: AA-2 *Atoll.*

FORCES ABROAD:
SAO TOME: some 500; 1 bn.

PARA-MILITARY:
BORDER GUARD (TGFA): 7,000.

OPPOSITION:
UNITA (Union for the Total Independence of
Angola): some 28,000 'regulars' (1–2 years
service), 37,000 'militia' (spt and log);
EQUIPMENT: captured T-34/85, 70 T-55 MBT
reported, misc APC (not in service); BM-21
122mm MRL; 75mm, 76mm, 122mm fd guns;
81mm, 82mm, 120mm mor; 85mm RPG-7 RL;
75mm RCL; 12.7mm hy machine guns; 14.5mm,

20mm and ZU-23-2 23mm AA guns; *Stinger,*
SAM-7;
FNLA (*National Front for the Liberation of
Angola*): (Bakongo tribesmen) claims up to 5,000,
actual strength ε 250; small arms only.
FLEC (*Front for the Liberation of the Cabinda
Enclave*): (200–300); small arms only.

FOREIGN FORCES:
CUBA: 40,000 (plus 8,000 civilian instructors/
advisers); 5 'Div Comds', 1 inf div, some 13 inf
regt in security and in field roles, cbt ac pilots,
technicians, advisers. To be progressively
withdrawn by 1 July 1991.
GDR: 500; intelligence and security advisers.
USSR: 1,200 advisers and technicians; ship
repair facilities Luanda; *Bear* D MR ac.
ANC: African National Congress, up to 1,400.
SWAPO: (South West African People's
Organization) 9,000.
UNITED NATIONS: (UNAVM) observers from
Algeria, Argentina, Brazil, Congo, Czechoslovakia,
India, Jordan, Norway, Spain, Yugoslavia.

* Incl some $1.5 bn owed to the USSR, mostly for arms.
† Angola is reported to have received up to $2 bn in
Soviet military material between 1983 and 1986. US
State Dept reported that Angola received some $1 bn
in military assistance in 1987.
‡ Delivery and loss data incomplete; eqpt totals
uncertain, as is serviceability.

BENIN

GDP	1986:	fr 502.80 bn ($1.45 bn)	
	1987:	fr 533.08 bn ($1.84 bn)	
Debt	1987:	$840.0 m	1988: $960.0 m
Def bdgt	1988:	fr 11.42 bn ($38.36 m)	
FMA	1988:	$2.58 m (US, Fr)	
$1 = fr	(1986):	346.30	(1987): 300.54
	(1988):	297.85	(1989): 316.94

fr = francs CFA (Communauté financière africaine)

Population: 4,335,000

	13–17	18–22	23–32
Men:	244,000	204,000	280,000
Women:	261,000	219,000	335,000

TOTAL ARMED FORCES: (all services
form part of the Army):
ACTIVE: 4,350.
Terms of service: conscription (selective), 18 months.

ARMY 3,800.
3 inf, 1 AB/cdo, 1 engr bn, 1 armd sqn, 1 arty bty.

EQUIPMENT:
LIGHT TANKS: 20 PT-76.
RECCE: 9 M-8, 14 BRDM-2.
TOWED ARTY: 105mm: 4 M-101.
MORTARS: 81mm.
RL: 89mm: LRAC.

NAVY: 200.
BASE: Cotonou.
PATROL AND COASTAL COMBATANTS: 7:
TORPEDO CRAFT: 2 Sov P-4⟨ with 2 × 533mm TT.
PATROL, INSHORE: 1 *Patriote* PFI (Fr 38m), 4⟨.
Note: All except *Patriote*, which is new, probably non-operational.

AIR FORCE: 350; no cbt ac, 1 armed hel.
AIRCRAFT: 3 An-2, 2 An-26, 2 C-47, 1 *Commander* 500B, 2 Do-128.
HELICOPTERS: 2 AS-350B, 1 Ka-26, 1 SE-3130, 1 SA-355 (armed).

PARA-MILITARY:
GENDARMERIE: 2,000; 4 mobile coy.
PUBLIC SECURITY FORCE.
PEOPLE'S MILITIA: 1,500–2,000.

BOTSWANA

GDP	1986/7: P 2.75 bn ($1.48 bn)		
	1987/8: P 3.27 bn ($1.97 bn)		
Growth	1986/7: 14.8%	1987/8: −1.3%	
Inflation	1987: 9.8%	1988: 8.4%	
Debt	1986: $410.0 m	1987: $510.0 m	
Def bdgt	1988/9ε: P 73.00 m ($38.10 m)		
	1989/90: P 93.00 m ($45.77 m)		
FMA	1988: $0.35 m (US)		
$1 = P	(1986/7): 1.8503	(1987/8): 1.6593	
	(1988/9): 1.9163	(1989): 2.0317	

P = pula

Population: 1,210,000

	13–17	18–22	23–32
Men:	69,000	58,000	78,000
Women:	69,000	60,000	96,000

TOTAL ARMED FORCES: (both services form part of the Army):
ACTIVE: 4,500.
Terms of service: voluntary.

ARMY:
5 inf, 1 armd car, 1 recce, 1 engr coy.
EQUIPMENT:

RECCE: 10 *Shorland*, 12 V-150 *Commando* (11 with 90mm gun).
APC: 30 BTR-60 (unserviceable).
TOWED ARTY: 105mm: 6 lt, 4 Model 56 pack.
MORTARS: 81mm; 120mm: 10.
ATGW: *TOW* reported.
RCL: 84mm: 20 *Carl Gustav*.
AD GUNS: 20mm: M-167 reported.
SAM: some 10 SA-7.

AIR FORCE: 14 cbt ac, no armed hel.
COIN: 1 sqn with 5 BN-2 *Defender*, 9 BAC-167 Mk 83.
TRANSPORT: 1 sqn with 2 BN *Trislander*, 2 CN-235, 2 *Skyvan* 3M.
LIAISON/TRAINING: 1 sqn with 1 Cessna 152, 5 *Bulldog* 120.
HELICOPTERS: 2 AS-350L, 3 Bell 212.

PARA-MILITARY:
POLICE MOBILE UNIT: 1,000.

BURKINA FASO

GDP	1986: fr 503.50 bn ($1.45 bn)		
Inflation	1987: −2.9%	1988: 4.2%	
Debt	1986: $664.7 m	1987: $720.0 m	
Def bdgt	1986: fr 14.28 bn ($41.24 m)		
	1987: fr 15.34 bn ($51.03 m)		
FMA	1988: $1.40 m (US, Fr)		
$1 = fr	(1986): 346.30	(1987): 300.54	
	(1988): 297.85	(1989): 316.28	

fr = francs CFA (Communauté financière africaine)

Population: 7,030,000

	13–17	18–22	23–32
Men:	418,000	355,000	540,000
Women:	409,000	382,000	497,000

TOTAL ARMED FORCES: (all services incl Gendarmerie form part of the Army):
ACTIVE: 8,700.
Terms of service: voluntary.

ARMY: 7,000.
6 Military Regions.
  5 inf 'regt': HQ, 3 'bn' (each 1 coy of 5 pl).
  1 AB 'regt': HQ, 1 'bn', 2 coy.
  1 tk 'bn': 2 pl.
  1 arty 'bn': 2 tps.
  1 engr 'bn'.
EQUIPMENT:
RECCE: 83: 15 AML-60/-90, 24 EE-9 *Cascavel*, 10 M-8, 4 M-20, 30 *Ferret*.

APC: 13 M-3.
TOWED ARTY: 105mm: 8 M-101.
MRL: 107mm: Ch Type-63.
MORTARS: 81mm.
RL: 89mm: LRAC, M-20.
RCL: 75mm: Ch Type-52.
AD GUNS: 14.5mm: 30
SAM: SA-7.

AIR FORCE: 200;

18 cbt ac, no armed hel.
FIGHTER: 1 sqn with 8 MiG-21.
COIN: 4 SF-260W, 6 SF-260WP.
TRANSPORT: 2 C-47, 1 *Commander* 500B, 2 HS-748, 2 N-262.
LIAISON: 3 MH-1521M.
HELICOPTERS: 2 SA-316B, 2 SA-365N.

===

PARA-MILITARY: 1,750:

GENDARMERIE: 1,500; 6 coy (2 mobile).
PEOPLE'S MILITIA: 45,000 trained; 2 years part-time; men and women 20–35 (military and civil duties).
SECURITY COMPANY (CRG): 250.

BURUNDI

GDP	1986:	fr 140.84 bn ($1.23 bn)	
	1987:	fr 143.59 bn ($1.16 bn)	
Growth	1986:	3.8%	1987: 6.4%
Inflation	1987:	7.3%	1988: 4.3%
Debt	1986:	$550.7 m	1987: $710.0 m
Def exp	1986:	fr 4.78 bn ($41.87 m)	
Def bdgt	1987ε:	fr 3.91 bn ($31.64 m)	
FMA	1988:	$3.14 m (US, Fr)	
$1 = fr	(1986):	114.17 (1987):	123.56
	(1988):	140.40 (1989):	153.90
fr = Burundi francs			

Population: 5,303,000

	13–17	18–22	23–32
Men:	276,000	236,000	428,000
Women:	282,000	238,000	448,000

===

TOTAL ARMED FORCES: (all services incl Gendarmerie form part of the Army):

ACTIVE: ε 7,200 (incl Gendarmerie).
Terms of service: voluntary.

ARMY: 5,500.

2 inf, 1 AB, 1 cdo bn.
1 armd car coy.
EQUIPMENT:

RECCE: 6 AML-60, 12 -90, 7 *Shorland.*
APC: 29: 9 M-3, 20 BTR-40 and *Walid.*
MORTARS: 82mm: 18.
RL: 83mm: *Blindicide.*
RCL: 75mm: 15 Ch Type-52.
AD GUNS: 14.5mm: 15 ZPU-4.

NAVY: 50.

BASE: Bujumbura.
PATROL BOATS: river: 3⟨

AIR: 150. 3 cbt ac, no armed hel.

COIN: 3 SF-260W.
TRANSPORT: 1 C-47.
HELICOPTERS: 3 SA-316B, 4 SA-342L.
LIAISON: 3 Reims-Cessna 150, 1 Do-27Q.
TRAINING: 3 SF-260C, 4 SF-260TP.

===

PARA-MILITARY:

GENDARMERIE: ε 1,500.

CAMEROON

GDP	1986/7: fr 4,004.90 bn ($12.56 bn)		
	1987/8: fr 3,769.90 bn ($12.92 bn)		
Inflation	1987: 9.7%	1988: 8.6%	
Debt	1986: $3.5 bn	1987: $3.9 bn	
Def bdgt	1987/8: fr 44.72 bn ($153.29 m)		
	1988/9: fr 45.52 bn ($147.67 m)		
FMA	1988: $8.28 m (US, Fr)		
$1 = fr	(1986/7): 318.79	(1987/8): 291.71	
	(1988/9): 312.49	(1989): 316.24	
fr = francs CFA (Coopération financière en Afrique centrale)			

Population: 11,373,000

	13–17	18–22	23–32
Men:	624,000	524,000	840,000
Women:	617,000	523,000	835,000

===

TOTAL ARMED FORCES:

ACTIVE: 11,600 (incl Gendarmerie).
Terms of service: voluntary (pre-military compulsory trg programme in force).

===

ARMY: 6,600.

3 Military Regions; 7 Military Sectors: coy gp under command.
Presidential Guard: 1 guard, 1 armd recce bn, 3 inf coy.
1 AB/cdo bn.

5 inf bn (1 trg).
1 engr bn.
1 arty bn (5 bty).
1 AA bn (6 bty).
EQUIPMENT:
RECCE: 8 M-8, *Ferret*, 8 V-150 *Commando* (20mm gun).
AIFV: 12 V-150 *Commando* (90mm gun).
APC: 29 V-150 *Commando*, 12 M-3 half-track.
TOWED ARTY: 22: 75mm: 6 M-116 pack; 105mm:
16 M-101.
MORTARS: 81mm; 120mm: 16.
ATGW: *Milan*.
RL: 89mm: LRAC.
RCL: 57mm: 13 Ch Type-52; 106mm: 40 M-40.
AD GUNS: 14.5mm: 18 Ch Type-58; 35mm: 18 twin
Oerlikon; 37mm: 18 Ch Type-63.

NAVY: 700.
BASES: Douala (HQ), Limbe, Kribi.
PATROL AND COASTAL COMBATANTS: 4:
MISSILE CRAFT: 1 *Bakasi* (Fr P.48) PFM with 8
MM-40 *Exocet* SSM.
PATROL: INSHORE: 3:
1 *L'Audacieux* (Fr P. 48m) PFI, 2⟨.
AMPHIBIOUS: craft only: 2 LCM, 5 LCVP.

AIR FORCE: 300;
16 cbt ac, 4 armed hel.
1 composite sqn.
1 Presidential flt.
FGA/COIN: 5 *Alpha Jet*, 11 *Magister*.
MR: 2 Do-128D-6.
ATTACK HELICOPTERS: 4 SA-342L (with HOT).
TRANSPORT: 3 C-130H/-H-30, 1 DHC-4, 4
DHC-5D, 1 IAI-201, 2 PA-23.
HELICOPTERS: 3 SE-3130, 1 SA-318, 4 SA-319.

PARA-MILITARY:
GENDARMERIE: 4,000:
10 regional groups.
PATROL CRAFT: 1 PCC, 12 PCI.

CAPE VERDE

GDP	1986ε:	CV E 13.93 bn ($156.00 m)	
Inflation	1986:	16.0%	
Debt	1986:	$112.0 m	1987: $113.0 m
FMA	1988	$0.08 m (US, Fr)	

$1 = CV E (1986): 89.27   (1987): 75.51
CV E = Cape Verde escudos

Population: 350,000

	13–17	18–22	23–32
Men:	23,000	21,000	26,000
Women:	23,000	22,000	33,000

TOTAL ARMED FORCES:
ACTIVE: 1,200.
Terms of service: conscription (selective).

ARMY: 1,000 (Popular Militia).
4 inf coy.
EQUIPMENT:
RECCE: 8 BRDM-2.
MORTARS: 82mm; 120mm: 8 M-1943.
RL: 89mm: 3.5-in.

NAVY: 200.
BASE: Praia.
PATROL AND COASTAL COMBATANTS: 5:
2 Sov *Shershen* PFI (no TT), 3⟨.
SUPPORT AND MISCELLANEOUS:
1 survey.

AIR FORCE: under 100; no cbt ac.
TRANSPORT: 2 An-26.

CENTRAL AFRICAN REPUBLIC

GDP	1986:	fr 330.90 bn ($955.53 m)	
	1987:	fr 323.70 bn ($1.08 bn)	
Inflation	1986:	7.6%	1987: 8.0%
Debt	1986:	$452.7 m	1987: $640.0 m
Def exp	1987:	fr 5.61 bn ($18.67 m)	
FMA	1988	$10.18 m (US, Fr)	

$1 = fr (1986):   346.30   (1987):   300.54
          (1988):   297.85   (1989):   316.24
fr = francs CFA (Coopération financière en Afrique
centrale)

Population: 2,946,000

	13–17	18–22	23–32
Men:	151,000	127,000	204,000
Women:	157,000	133,000	217,000

TOTAL ARMED FORCES:
ACTIVE: 6,500 incl Gendarmerie.
Terms of service: conscription (selective),
2 years; Reserve obligation thereafter, term
unknown.

ARMY: 3,500.
1 Republican Guard regt (2 bn).
1 territorial defence regt (bn).
1 combined arms regt (1 mech, 1 inf bn).
1 spt/HQ regt.
1 Presidential Guard bn.
EQUIPMENT:*

MBT: 4 T-55.
RECCE: 10 *Ferret*.
APC: 4 BTR-152, some 10 VAB, 25+ ACMAT.
MORTARS: 81mm; 120mm: 12 M-1943.
RL: 89mm: LRAC.
RCL: 106mm: 14.
RIVER PATROL CRAFT: 9⟨.

AIR FORCE: 300;
No cbt ac, no armed hel.
TRANSPORT: 2 C-47, 2 Cessna 337, 1 DC-4.
LIAISON: 8 AL-60, 6 MH-1521.
HELICOPTERS: 1 AS-350, 1 SE-3130.

PARA-MILITARY:
GENDARMERIE: 2,700;
3 Regional Legions, 8 'bde'.

FOREIGN FORCES:
FRANCE: 1,100. 1 inf bn gp, 1 armd cav sqn, 1 arty bty. Cbt and tpt ac/hel.

---

* All Soviet eqpt probably unserviceable.

CHAD

GDP	1986ε: fr 278.86 bn ($805.27 m)		
Growth	1986ε: −2.0%		
Inflation	1986: −13.0%	1987: −2.8%	
Debt	1986: $187.4 m	1987: $270.0 m	
Def bdgt	1988ε: fr 23.20 bn ($77.89 m)		
FMA	1988: $28.25 m (US, Fr)		
$1 = fr	(1986): 346.30	(1987): 300.54	
	(1988): 297.85	(1989): 316.24	

fr = francs CFA (Coopération financière en Afrique centrale).

Population: 5,443,000

	13–17	18–22	23–32
Men:	279,000	244,000	483,000
Women:	278,000	238,000	402,000

TOTAL ARMED FORCES:
ACTIVE: some 17,000.
Terms of service: conscription, 3 years.

ARMY: ε 17,000; comprises regular and rejoined rebel groups.
1 armd bn.
3 inf bn and 16 inf coy.
Presidential Guard regt.
1 recce sqn and 2 recce tp.
2 arty bty.

EQUIPMENT:
AFV: some 65: 4 Panhard ERC-90, some 50 AML-60/-90, 9 V-150 with 90mm.
TOWED ARTY: 105mm: 5 M-101.
MORTARS: 81mm; 120mm: AM-50.
ATGW: *Milan*.
RL: 68mm; 89mm.
RCL: 106mm: M-40; 112mm: *APILAS*.
AD GUNS: 20mm, 30mm.
SAM: 10 *Stinger* launchers.

AIR FORCE: 200;
4 cbt ac, no armed hel.
COIN: 2 PC-7, 2 SF-260W.
TRANSPORT: 3 C-47, 3 C-130 (1 -A, 2 -B), 1 C-212, 2 DC-4.
HELICOPTERS: 4 SA-330, 1 SA-341.
LIAISON: 2 PC-6B, 5 Reims-Cessna FTB 337.

PARA-MILITARY: perhaps 5,700:
NATIONAL MILITARY POLICE (PMN).
TERRITORIAL MILITARY POLICE (PMT).
SURETÉ (Police): 800.

OPPOSITION:
CONSEIL DEMOCRATIQUE DE LA REVOLUTION (CDR): ε 1,000 (Libyan-backed).

FOREIGN FORCES:
FRANCE: 1,400. 3 inf coy, AD arty units; cbt and tpt ac/hel.

CONGO

GDP	1987ε: fr 656.70 bn ($2.19 bn)		
	1988ε: fr 638.20 bn ($2.14 bn)		
Growth	1987ε: −3.0%	1988ε: −2.8%	
Inflation	1987: 2.2%	1988: 5.9%	
Debt	1987: $3.5 bn	1988: $3.8 bn	
FMA	1988 $2.53 m (US, Fr)		
$1 = fr	(1987): 300.54	(1988): 297.85	
	(1989): 316.24		

fr = francs CFA (Coopération financière en Afrique centrale)

Population: 1,907,000

	13–17	18–22	23–32
Men:	128,000	109,000	157,000
Women:	128,000	114,000	169,000

TOTAL ARMED FORCES:
ACTIVE: 8,800.
Terms of service: voluntary (2 years).

ARMY: 8,000.
2 armd bn.
2 inf bn gp (each with lt tk tp, 76mm gun bty).
1 inf bn.
1 arty gp (how, MRL).
1 engr bn.
1 AB/cdo bn.

EQUIPMENT:*
MBT: 35 T-54/-55, 15 Ch Type-59. (Some T-34 in store.)
LIGHT TANKS: 14 Ch Type-62, 3 PT-76.
RECCE: 25 BRDM-1/-2.
APC: M-3, 104 BTR (30 -50, 30 -60, 44 -152).
TOWED ARTY: 75mm: 6 M-116 pack; 76mm: 8
  M-1942; 100mm: 10 M-1944; 122mm: 8 M-1938.
MRL: 122mm: 8 BM-21.
MORTARS: 82mm; 120mm: 10 M-1943.
RCL: 57mm: M-18.
ATK GUNS: 57mm: 5 M-1943.
AD GUNS: 14.5mm: ZPU-2/-4; 23mm: ZSU-23-4 SP;
  37mm: 28 M-1939; 57mm: S-60.

NAVY:* 300.
BASE: Point Noire.
PATROL AND COASTAL COMBATANTS: 13:
PATROL, INSHORE: 13:
  3 *Marien N'gouabi* PFI (Sp *Barcelo* 33m).
  3 Ch *Shanghai*-II, 1 Sov *Shershen* (no TT),
  6 Sov *Zhuk* PFI⟨.

AIR FORCE: 500.
20 cbt ac, no armed hel.*
FGA: 20 MiG-17. MiG-21 reported.
TRANSPORT: 5 An-24, 1 An-26, 2 C-47, 2 Il-14, 1 N-2501.
TRAINING: 4 L-39, 1 MiG-15UTI.
HELICOPTERS: 2 SA-316, 2 SA-318, 1 SA-365.

FORCES ABROAD
ANGOLA (UNAVM): observers.

PARA-MILITARY: 6,100:
GENDARMERIE: 1,400; 20 coy.
PEOPLE'S MILITIA: 4,700.

FOREIGN FORCES:
CUBA: 500.

* Spares are short; much eqpt may be non-operational.

CÔTE D'IVOIRE

GDP	1987ε: fr 2,839.20 bn ($9.45 bn)	
	1988ε: fr 3,072.70 bn ($10.32 bn)	
Growth	1987ε: −3.7%	1988ε: 0.2%
Inflation	1987: 5.2%	1988ε: 8.0%
Debt	1987: $13.5 bn	1988: $14.2 bn

Def bdgt	1986: fr 32.42 bn ($93.62 m)		
FMA	1988: $11.15 m (US, Fr)		
$1 = fr	(1986): 346.30	(1987):	300.54
	(1988): 297.85	(1989):	316.24
fr = francs CFA (Communauté financière africaine)			

Population: 11,122,000

	13–17	18–22	23–32
Men:	597,000	479,000	820,000
Women:	591,000	470,000	720,000

TOTAL ARMED FORCES:
ACTIVE: 7,100.
  Terms of service: conscription (selective),
    6 months.
RESERVES: 12,000.

ARMY: 5,500.
4 Military Regions:
  1 armd, 3 inf bn, 1 arty gp.
  1 AB, 1 AA, 1 engr coy.

EQUIPMENT:
LIGHT TANKS: 5 AMX-13.
RECCE: 7 ERC-90, ε 16 AML-60/-90.
APC: 16 M-3, 13 VAB.
TOWED ARTY: 105mm: 4 M-1950.
MORTARS: 81mm; 120mm: 16 AM-50.
RL: 89mm: LRAC.
RCL: 106mm: M-40.
AD GUNS: 20mm: 16 incl 6 M-3 VDA SP; 40mm: 5 L/60.

NAVY: 700.
BASE: Locodjo (Abidjan).
PATROL AND COASTAL COMBATANTS: 10:
MISSILE CRAFT: 2:
  2 *L'Ardent* (Fr Auroux 37m) with 4 × SS-12 SSM.
PATROL: 2 *Le Vigilant* (Fr SFCN 47-m), 6 PCI⟨.
AMPHIBIOUS: 1 *L'Eléphant* (Fr *BATRAL*) LSM,
  capacity 140 tps, 7 tk, hel deck.

AIR FORCE: 900;
6 cbt ac, no armed hel.
FGA: 1 sqn with 6 *Alpha Jet.*
TRANSPORT: 1 hel sqn with 1 SA-318, 1 SA-319, 1
  SA-330, 4 SA-365C.
PRESIDENTIAL FLIGHT:
  AIRCRAFT: 1 F-28, 1 *Gulfstream* IV.
  HELICOPTERS: 1 SA-330.
TRAINING: 6 *Bonanza* F-33C, 2 Reims Cessna 150H.
LIAISON: 1 Cessna 421, 2 *Super King Air* 200.

PARA-MILITARY: 7,800:
PRESIDENTIAL GUARD: 1,100.
GENDARMERIE: 4,400; VAB APC, 4 patrol boats.
MILITIA: 1,500.

MILITARY FIRE SERVICE: 800.

FOREIGN FORCES:
FRANCE: 500: 1 marine inf regt.

EQUATORIAL GUINEA

GDP   1987: fr 42.00 bn ($139.75 m)
Inflation 1987: −12.2%   1988: 8.3%
Debt   1986: $151.6 m   1987: $141.3 m
FMA   1988: $0.15 m (US, Fr)
$1 = fr   (1987): 300.54   (1988): 297.85
           (1989): 316.24
fr = francs CFA (Coopération financière en Afrique centrale)

Population: 424,000

	13–17	18–22	23–32
Men:	20,000	18,000	30,000
Women:	21,000	18,000	31,000

TOTAL ARMED FORCES:
ACTIVE: 1,400.
Terms of service: voluntary.

ARMY: 1,100.
3 inf bn.
EQUIPMENT:
RECCE: 6 BRDM-2.
APC: 10 BTR-152.

NAVY: 100.
BASES: Malabo (Santa Isabel), Bata.
PATROL COMBATANTS: 2 PFI⟨.

AIR FORCE: 100; no cbt ac or armed hel.
TRANSPORT: 1 Yak-40. 3 C-212 on loan from Spain.

PARA-MILITARY: some 2,000.
GUARDIA CIVIL: 2 coy.

FOREIGN FORCES:
MOROCCO: 360: 1 bn.

ETHIOPIA

GDP   1985/6: EB 10.82 bn ($5.23 bn)
           1986/7: EB 11.13 bn ($5.38 bn)
Growth   1985/6: 9.7%   1986/7: 2.7%
Inflation 1987: −2.4%   1988: 7.0%
Debt*   1987: $2.6 bn   1988: $2.9 bn

Def bdgt   1986/7: EB 922.97 m ($445.86 m)
           1987/8ε: EB 976.20 m ($471.59 m)
$1 = EB   (1985/6/7/8): 2.07
EB = birr

Population: 47,944,000

	13–17	18–22	23–32
Men:	2,831,000	2,027,000	2,738,000
Women:	2,634,000	1,898,000	3,192,000

TOTAL ARMED FORCES:
ACTIVE: 315,800 (not incl foreign personnel).
Terms of service: conscription, 30 months, incl police, border guard.
RESERVES: People's Militia. All citizens 18–50 do 6 months trg. Assigned to Army, Police and Border Guard.

ARMY: 313,000: (incl ε 150,000 People's Militia).
22 inf div (incl 3 mot, 4 mtn, 3 lt) with some 32 tk bn.
8 AB/cdo bde.
37 arty bn (assignment to div varies).
12 AD bn (incl 3 bn each of SA-2, SA-3 SAM).
EQUIPMENT:†
MBT: ε 750: 30 M-47, 20 T-34, ε 600 T-54/-55, 100 T-62.
LIGHT TANKS: 15 M-41.
RECCE: 200 BRDM-1/-2.
AIFV: 40 BMP-1.
APC: some 30 M-113, 600 BTR-40/-60/-152.
TOWED ARTY: some 700 incl: 75mm: M-116 pack; 105mm: 40; 122mm: 370: 180 D-30, M-1938; 130mm: 48 M-46; 152mm: 12 D-20.
SP ARTY: 122mm: some; 155mm: 6 M-109.
MRL: 122mm: BM-21.
MORTARS: 107mm: 200 M-2/-30; 120mm: 100 M-38.
ATGW: AT-3 *Sagger*.
RCL: 82mm: B-10.
ATK GUNS: 100mm: M-1955.
AD GUNS: 23mm: ZU-23, ZSU-23-4 SP; 37mm: M-1939; 57mm: M-1950, ZSU-57-2 SP.
SAM: 18 SA-2, 18 SA-3, SA-7.
AIRCRAFT: 3 DHC-6, 4 DHC-3, 1 U-17.
HELICOPTERS: 6 UH-1H.

NAVY: 1,800.†
BASES: Massawa, Assab.
FRIGATES: 2 *Zerai Deres* (Sov *Petya* II) with 2 × ASW RL, 10 × 406mm TT.
PATROL AND COASTAL COMBATANTS: 21:
MISSILE CRAFT: 8 Sov *Osa* with 4 × SS-N-2 *Styx* SSM.
TORPEDO CRAFT: 6: 2 Sov *Turya* PHT, 4 *Mol* PFT all with 4 × 533mm TT.
PATROL: 7:
COASTAL: 1 Nl ex-MSC.
INSHORE: 6 PFI: 3 US Swiftships 32m, 3⟨.

AMPHIBIOUS: 2 Sov *Polnocny* LSM, capacity 100 tps, 6 tk.
Plus craft; 2 LCT, 4 LCM.
SUPPORT AND MISCELLANEOUS: 2:
1 tpt, 1 trg.

AIR FORCE: 4,000;
143 cbt ac; 22 armed hel.
FGA: 8 sqn:
1 with 20 MiG-17F;
6 with 78 MiG-21MF;
1 with 40 MiG-23BN.
TRANSPORT: 1 sqn with 11 An-12, 2 An-26, 2 L-100-30, 1 Yak-40 (VIP).
TRAINING: 11 L-39, 5 MiG-21U, 21 SF-260TP.
HELICOPTERS:
TRANSPORT: 32 Mi-8, 1 IAR-330.
LIAISON: 10 IAR-316, 10 *Chetak*.

PARA-MILITARY: 169,000.
BORDER GUARD.
MOBILE EMERGENCY POLICE FORCE: 9,000. 2 Do-28, 1 Cessna 337 ac.

OPPOSITION:
Main groups only listed:
ERITREAN PEOPLE'S LIBERATION FRONT (EPLF): some 30,000: Captured eqpt incl T-54/-55 and artillery. Has absorbed ELF (Eritrean Liberation Front).
TIGRE PEOPLE'S LIBERATION FRONT (TPLF): some 20,000.
WESTERN SOMALI LIBERATION FRONT (WSLF): some 1,000. In Ogaden region.

FOREIGN FORCES:
CUBA: 2,800: possibly 1 inf bde, advisers and technicians.
SOVIET UNION: Some 1,700 advisers and technicians.
GDR: 550 advisers and technicians.
NORTH KOREA: 200 advisers.

* Excl debt to the Soviet Union.
† War situation makes eqpt data suspect; older US eqpt probably unserviceable.

GABON

GDP	1986:	fr 1,176.30 bn ($3.40 bn)
	1987ε:	fr 1,019.30 bn ($3.39 bn)
Growth	1986ε: −12.0%	1987ε: −3.5%
Inflation	1986: 6.3%	1987: −0.9%
Debt	1987: $2.0 bn	1988: $2.2 bn
Def bdgt*	1988: fr 45.8 bn ($153.77 m)	
FMA	1988 $0.55 m (US, Fr)	

$1 = fr	(1986):	346.30	(1987):	300.54
	(1988):	297.85	(1989):	316.24

fr = francs CFA (Communauté financière africaine)

Population: 1,220,000			
	13–17	*18–22*	*23–32*
Men:	41,000	37,000	62,000
Women:	43,000	38,000	65,000

TOTAL ARMED FORCES:
ACTIVE: 4,700.
Terms of service: voluntary.

ARMY: 3,200.
Presidential Guard bn gp (1 recce/armd, 3 inf coy, arty, AA bty) (under direct Presidential control).
8 inf, 1 AB/cdo, 1 engr coy.
EQUIPMENT:
RECCE: 16 EE-9 *Cascavel*, 24 AML-90, 12 EE-3 *Jararaca*, some VBL M-11.
AIFV: 12 EE-11 *Urutu* with 20mm gun.
APC: 6 V-150 *Commando*, Panhard M-3, 12 VXB-170.
TOWED ARTY: 105mm: 4 M-101.
MRL: 140mm: 8.
MORTARS: 81mm; 120mm: 20.
RL: 89mm: LRAC.
RCL: 106mm: M40.
AD GUNS: 23mm: 24 ZU-23-2; 37mm: 10 M-1939; 40mm: 2.

NAVY: 500.
BASE: Port Gentil (HQ).
PATROL AND COASTAL COMBATANTS: 6:
MISSILE CRAFT: 1 *General Nazaire Boulingi Kounba* PFM (Fr 42m) with 4 SS-12 SSM.
PATROL: 5.
COASTAL: 1 *General Ba'Oumar* (Fr P.400 55m).
INSHORE: 4: 1 *Nguene* (US Swiftships 32m), 3⟨.
AMPHIBIOUS: 1 *President Omar Bongo* (Fr BATRAL) LSM, capacity 140 tps, 7 tk.
Plus craft; 2 LCT, 1 LCM.

AIR FORCE: 1,000. 19 cbt ac, 7 armed hel.
FGA: 9 *Mirage* 5 (2 -G, 4 -GII, 3 -DG).
MR: 1 EMB-111P1.
TRANSPORT: 1 C-130H, 1 L-100-20, 2 L-100-30, EMB-110, 1 *Falcon* 50, 1 *Gulfstream III*, 2 YS-11A.
HELICOPTERS:
ATTACK: 2 AS-350, 5 SA-342.
TRANSPORT: 3 SA-330C/-H.
LIAISON: 3 SA-316/-319.
PRESIDENTIAL GUARD:
COIN: 6 CM-170, 4 T-34.
TRANSPORT: 1 EMB-110.

PARA-MILITARY:
COAST GUARD: 2,800; boats only.
GENDARMERIE: 2,000; 3 'bdes', 11 coy, 2 armd sqn, air unit.

FOREIGN FORCES:
FRANCE: 550: marine inf regt.

* Incl internal security.

GHANA

GDP	1987:	C 746.00 bn ($5.07 bn)		
	1988ε:	C 1,014.56 bn ($5.07 bn)		
Growth	1987:	4.8%	1988ε: 6.0%	
Inflation	1987:	39.8%	1988ε: 29.7%	
Debt	1987:	$2.8 bn	1988: $2.9 bn	
Def bdgt	1987:	C 6.66 bn ($45.28 m)		
	1989:	C 11.20 bn ($42.56 m)		
FMA	1988:	$0.18 m (US)		
$1 = C	(1987):	147.06	(1988):	200.00
	(1989):	263.16		

C = cedi

Population: 15,253,000

	13–17	18–22	23–32
Men:	902,000	671,000	1,119,000
Women:	885,000	676,000	1,099,000

TOTAL ARMED FORCES:
ACTIVE: 11,600.
Terms of service: voluntary.

ARMY: 10,000.
2 Command HQ:
  2 bde (comprising 6 inf bn (incl 1 trg, 1 UNIFIL), spt units).
  1 recce bn (2 sqn).
  1 AB force (incl 1 para coy).
  1 indep inf bn.
  1 arty 'regt' (mor bn).
  1 fd engr regt (bn).
EQUIPMENT:
RECCE: 3 *Saladin*, 3 EE-9 *Cascavel*.
APC: 50 MOWAG *Piranha*.
MORTARS: 81mm: 50; 120mm: 28 Tampella.
RCL: 84mm: 50 *Carl Gustav*.

NAVY: 800.
2 Commands, Western and Eastern.
BASES: Sekondi, (HQ, West) Tema (HQ, East).
PATROL AND COASTAL COMBATANTS: 8:
COASTAL: 4:

2 *Kromantse* PCC (ASW) with 1 × 3 *Squid* ASW mor, 1 × 102mm gun.
2 *Achimota* (FRG Lürssen 57m) PFC.
INSHORE: 4
  2 *Dzata* (FRG Lürssen 45m) PCI.
  2 *Dela* PFI.
Note: all unserviceable; except 1 × PFC, 1 × PFI recently refitted in UK.

AIR FORCE: 800.
6 cbt ac, no armed hel.
COIN: 1 sqn with 4 MB-326K (serviceability doubtful), 2 MB-339.
TRANSPORT: 3 sqn:
  1 VIP with 3 Fokker (2 F-27, 1 F-28);
  1 with 3 F-27, 1 C-212.
  1 with 6 *Skyvan*.
HELICOPTERS: 2 Bell 212 (VIP), 2 Mi-2, 4 SA-318.
TRAINING: 1 sqn with 10 *Bulldog* 122 (serviceability doubtful).

FORCES ABROAD:
LEBANON (UNIFIL): 1 bn (850).
IRAN/IRAQ (UNIIMOG) observers.

PARA-MILITARY:
PEOPLE'S MILITIA: 5,000.

GUINEA

GDP	1985ε: G fr 47.83 bn ($1.98 bn)	
Growth	1985: 3.0%	
Inflation	1986: 78.0%	1987: 33.0%
Debt	1986: $1.5 bn	1987: $1.6 bn
FMA	1988: $3.65 m (US, Fr)	
$1 = G fr* (1985):	24.11	(1986): 276.88

G fr = Guinean franc

Population: 6,593,000

	13–17	18–22	23–32
Men:	379,000	335,000	498,000
Women:	360,000	303,000	484,000

TOTAL ARMED FORCES:
ACTIVE: 9,900 (perhaps 7,500 conscripts).
Terms of service: conscription, 2 years.

ARMY: 8,500.
  1 armd bn.
  5 inf bn.
  1 arty bn.
  1 engr bn.
  1 cdo bn.

1 SF bn.
1 AD bn.

EQUIPMENT:†
MBT: 30 T-34, 8 T-54.
LIGHT TANKS: 20 PT-76.
RECCE: 25 BRDM-1/-2.
APC: 40 BTR (16 -40, 10 -50, 8 -60, 6 -152).
TOWED ARTY: 76mm: 8 M-1942; 85mm: 6 D-44;
   122mm: 12 M-1931/38.
MORTARS: 82mm: M-43; 120mm: 20 M-1938/43.
RCL: 82mm: B-10.
ATK GUNS: 57mm: M-1943.
AD GUNS: 30mm: twin M-53; 37mm: 8 M-1939;
   57mm: 12 S-60, Ch Type-59; 100mm: 4 KS-19.
SAM: SA-7.

NAVY: 400.
BASES: Conakry, Kakanda.
PATROL AND COASTAL COMBATANTS: 9:
INSHORE: 9:
   1 *Vigilante*, 1 *Intrepide*, 1 Sov. *Matka*, 6 other PCI⟨.
AMPHIBIOUS: Craft only; LCU: 2.

AIR FORCE: 800; 12 cbt ac, no armed hel.†
FGA: 4 MiG-17F, 8 MiG-21.
TRANSPORT: 2 An-12, 4 An-14.
TRAINING: 3 L-29, 2 MiG-15UTI, 6 Yak-18.
HELICOPTERS: 4 Mi-4, 1 SA-316B, 1 SA-330, 1
   IAR-330, 1 SA-342K.

PARA-MILITARY:.
PEOPLE'S MILITIA: 7,000.
GENDARMERIE: 1,000.
REPUBLICAN GUARD: 1,600.

* In January 1986 the Guinean franc replaced the
Syli at par, followed by a major devaluation.
† Operational status of Soviet supplied eqpt uncertain.

GUINEA-BISSAU

GDP	1986ε:	pG 26.37 bn ($129.31 m)	
Growth	1986:	4.0%	
Debt	1987:	$360.0 m	1988: $408.1 m
Def bdgt	1986:	pG 1,250.50 m ($6.13 m)	
	1987:	pG 2,168.00 m ($3.88 m)	
FMA	1988:	$0.10 m (US, Fr)	
$1 = pG	(1986):	203.95	(1987): 559.33
	(1988):	596.51	(1989): 652.27
pG = Guinea pesos			

Population: 950,000

	13–17	*18–22*	*23–32*
Men:	63,000	48,000	62,000
Women:	63,000	42,000	74,000

TOTAL ARMED FORCES: (all services incl
   Gendarmerie are part of the Army):
ACTIVE: 9,200.
   Terms of service: conscription (selective).

ARMY: 6,800.
   1 armd 'bn' (sqn).
   5 inf, 1 arty bn, 1 recce, 1 engr coy.
EQUIPMENT:
MBT: 10 T-34.
LIGHT TANKS: 20 PT-76.
RECCE: 10 BRDM-2.
APC: 35 BTR-40/-60/-152, 20 Ch Type-56.
TOWED ARTY: 85mm: 8 D-44; 122mm: 18
   M-1938/D-30.
MORTARS: 82mm: M-43; 120mm: 8 M-1943.
RL: 89mm.
RCL: 75mm: Ch Type-52; 82mm: B-10.
AD GUNS: 23mm: 18 ZU-23; 37mm: 6 M-1939;
   57mm: 10 S-60.
SAM: SA-7.

NAVY: 300.
BASE: Bissau.
PATROL AND COASTAL COMBATANTS: 12:
PATROL INSHORE: 12:
   1 Sov *Shershen* (no TT), 1 Sov *Matka*, 2 Ch
   Shantou PFI.
   8 PCI⟨.
AMPHIBIOUS: Craft only; 2 Sov T4 LCVP.

AIR FORCE: 100.
   4 cbt ac, no armed hel.
FIGHTER: 3 MiG-17.
MR: 1 Reims-Cessna FTB 337.
HELICOPTERS: 1 SA-318, 2 SA-319.

PARA-MILITARY:
GENDARMERIE: 2,000.

KENYA

GDP	1987:	sh 132.29 bn ($8.04 bn)	
	1988ε:	sh 149.75 bn ($8.44 bn)	
Growth	1987:	5.9%	1988: 5.0%
Inflation	1987:	5.2%	1988: 8.2%
Debt	1987:	$4.6 bn	1988: $4.8 bn
FMA	1988:	$16.03 m (US)	
$1 = sh	(1987):	16.454	(1988): 17.747
	(1989):	19.393	
sh = Kenyan shillings			

Population: 23,389,000

	13–17	*18–22*	*23–32*
Men:	1,398,000	1,112,000	1,482,000
Women:	1,373,000	1,106,000	1,503,000

TOTAL ARMED FORCES:
ACTIVE: 23,600.
Terms of service: voluntary.

ARMY: 19,000.
1 armd bde (2 armd bn).
2 inf bde (1 with 2, 1 with 3 inf bn; 1 armd recce, 2 arty bn).
1 engr bde.
2 engr bn.
1 indep air cav bn.
5 inf bn (cadre).
1 AB bn.
1 AA bn.
EQUIPMENT:
MBT: 76 Vickers Mk 3.
RECCE: 40 AML-60/-90, 8 *Shorland*.
APC: 30 UR-416, 10 Panhard M-3.
TOWED ARTY: 105mm; 40 lt; 16 pack.
MORTARS: 81mm: 20 L16; 120mm: 10.
ATGW: *Milan*, 8 *Swingfire*.
RCL: 84mm: 80 *Carl Gustav*; 120mm: *Wombat*.
AD GUNS: 20mm: 50 TCM-20.

NAVY: 1,100.
BASE: Mombasa.
PATROL AND COASTAL COMBATANTS: 8:
MISSILE CRAFT 6:
2 *Nyayo* (UK Vosper 56m) PFM, with 4 *Otomat* II SSM.
1 *Mamba*, 3 *Madaraka* (UK Brooke Marine 37m/32m) PCM with 4 × *Gabriel* II SSM.
PATROL, INSHORE: 2⟨.

AIR FORCE: 3,500:
28 cbt ac, 38 armed hel.
FGA: 11 F-5 (9 -E, 2 -F).
COIN: 17 BAe (5 *Strikemaster* Mk 87, 12 *Hawk* T-62).
TRANSPORT: 1 *Commander* 680, 8 DHC-5D, 7 Do-28D, 1 PA-32.
TRAINING: 8 *Bulldog* 103/127.
HELICOPTERS:
ATTACK: 15 Hughes 500MD (with *TOW*), 8 Hughes 500ME, 15 Hughes 500M.
TRANSPORT: 9 IAR-330, 3 SA-330, 1 SA-342.
TRAINING: 2 Hughes 500D.
AAM: AIM-9 *Sidewinder*.
ASM: AGM-65 *Maverick*.

PARA-MILITARY:
POLICE GENERAL SERVICE UNIT: 4,000.

POLICE AIR WING: 7 Cessna lt ac, 3 Bell hel (1 206L, 2 47G).
POLICE NAVAL SQN: Some boats.

FORCES ABROAD:
NAMIBIA (UNTAG): 889: 1 inf bn plus HQ staff.
IRAN/IRAQ (UNIIMOG): observers.

LESOTHO

GDP	1986:	M 647.2 m ($285.29 m)
	1987:	M 762.9 m ($374.89 m)
Growth	1986:	0.0%
Debt	1986:	$186.0 m
Def bdgt	1985:	M 25.3 m ($11.55 m)
FMA	1988	$0.07 m (US)

$1 = M (1986): 2.27 (1987): 2.04
M = maloti

Population: 1,660,000

	13–17	*18–22*	*23–32*
Men:	88,000	74,000	118,000
Women:	87,000	74,000	120,000

TOTAL ARMED FORCES:
ACTIVE: 2,000.
Terms of service: voluntary.

ARMY:
7 inf coy.
1 spt coy (incl recce/AB, 81mm mor).
1 air sqn.
EQUIPMENT:
RECCE: 10 Is *Rabta*.
HELICOPTERS: 2 Bo-105, 3 Bell 412.

LIBERIA

GDP	1986:	$L 1,034.80 m ($US 1,034.80 m)
Growth	1986:	−1.2%
Inflation	1986:	3.6% 1987: 5.0%
Debt	1988:	$US 1.7 bn
Def bdgt	1988:	$L 28.07 m ($US 28.07 m)
FMA	1988:	$0.5 m (US)

$1 = $L (1986/7/8/9): 1.00

Population: 2,400,000

	13–17	*18–22*	*23–32*
Men:	122,000	105,000	167,000
Women:	122,000	105,000	171,000

TOTAL ARMED FORCES:
ACTIVE: 5,800.
Terms of service: voluntary.
RESERVES: ε 50,000 males 16–45.

ARMY: 5,300.
1 Executive Mansion Guard bn.
6 inf bn.
1 arty bn.
1 engr bn.
1 armd recce sqn.
1 air recce bn.
EQUIPMENT:
APC: 10 MOWAG *Piranha*.
TOWED ARTY: 75mm 3 M-116 pack; 105mm: 8 M-101.
MRL: 122mm: BM-21.
MORTARS: 82mm: M-37; 107mm; 120mm: M-43.
RL: 89mm: LRAC.
RCL: 106mm: M-40.
AVIATION:
LIAISON/RECCE: 2 Cessna 172, 1 Cessna 208.

NAVY: (Coast Guard): 500.
BASES: Monrovia, Bassa, Sinoe, Cape Palmas.
PATROL CRAFT: 5 PCI⟨.

PARA-MILITARY:
NATIONAL POLICE: 2,000.

FOREIGN FORCES:
NORTH KOREA: 100.

MADAGASCAR

GDP	1986:	fr 1,806.90 bn ($2.67 bn)		
	1987ε:	fr 2,123.11 bn ($1.99 bn)		
Growth	1986:	0.3%	1987:	2.5%
Inflation	1986:	14.5%	1987:	15.0%
Debt	1987:	$3.1 bn	1988:	$3.5 bn
Def bdgt	1986:	fr 39.80 bn ($58.85 m)		
	1987:	fr 39.20 bn ($36.66 m)		
FMA	1988:	$2.88 m (US, Fr)		
$1 = fr	(1986):	676.34	(1987):	1,069.21
	(1988):	1,407.10	(1989):	1,586.20
fr = Malagasy francs				

Population: 11,050,000

	13–17	18–22	23–32
Men:	622,000	540,000	809,000
Women:	617,000	521,000	804,000

TOTAL ARMED FORCES:

ACTIVE: 21,000.
Terms of service: conscription (incl for civil purposes), 18 months.

ARMY: some 20,000.
2 bn gp.
1 engr regt.
1 sigs regt.
1 service regt.
7 construction regt.
EQUIPMENT:
LIGHT TANKS: 12 PT-76.
RECCE: 8 M-8, ε 20 M-3A1, 10 *Ferret*, ε 35 BRDM-2.
APC: ε 30 M-3A1 half-track.
TOWED ARTY: 76mm: 12 ZIS-3; 105mm: some M-101; 122mm: 12 D-30.
MORTARS: 81mm: M-29; 120mm: 8.
RL: 89mm: M-20.
RCL: 106mm: M-40.
AD GUNS: 14.5mm: 50 ZPU-4; 37mm: 20 Type 55.

NAVY: 500 (incl some 100 marines).
BASE: Diégo-Suarez.
PATROL CRAFT: 1 *Malaika* (Fr PR-48m) PCI.
AMPHIBIOUS: 1 *Toky* (Fr BATRAM) LSM, with 8 × SS-12 SSM, capacity 30 tps, 4 tk.
Plus craft; 1 LCT, 1 LCA.
SUPPORT AND MISCELLANEOUS: 1 tpt/trg.

AIR FORCE: 500; 12 cbt ac, no armed hel.
FGA: 1 sqn with 4 MiG-17F, 8 MiG-21FL.
TRANSPORT: 4 An-26, 2 Yak-40 (VIP).
HELICOPTERS: 1 sqn with 6 Mi-8.
LIAISON: 3 BN-2, 1 Cessna 310, 1 PA-23.
TRAINING: 4 Cessna 172.

PARA-MILITARY:
GENDARMERIE: 7,500, incl maritime police with 5 PCI⟨.

MALAWI

GDP	1987:	K 2.76 bn ($1.25 bn)		
	1988:	K 3.70 bn ($1.44 bn)		
Growth	1987:	0.1%	1988:	3.8%
Inflation	1987:	25.1%	1988ε:	30.0%
Debt	1986:	$1.1 bn	1987:	$1.3 bn
Def bdgt	1986/7:	K 49.26 m ($26.47 m)		
FMA	1988	$0.75 m (US)		
$1 = K	(1986):	1.861	(1987):	2.209
	(1988):	2.561	(1989):	2.703
K = kwacha				

Population: 7,983,000

	13–17	18–22	23–32
Men:	439,000	359,000	527,000
Women:	446,000	370,000	574,000

TOTAL ARMED FORCES: (all services form part of the Army):
ACTIVE: 7,250.
Terms of service: voluntary, 7 years.
RESERVES: Army: some 1,000; ex-soldiers have a 5-year obligation.

ARMY: 7,000.
3 inf bn.
1 spt bn (incl 1 recce sqn).
EQUIPMENT:
RECCE: 20 *Fox*, 10 *Ferret*, 4 *Eland*.
TOWED ARTY: 12 105mm lt.
MORTARS: 81mm: L16.
RL: 89mm: M-20.
RCL: 57mm.
SAM: 12 *Blowpipe*.

MARINE: 100.
BASE: Chilumba. (Lake Nyasa).
PATROL CRAFT: 1 PCI 〈, some boats.

AIR: 150;
No cbt ac, 2 armed hel.
TRANSPORT: 1 sqn with 6 Dornier (3 Do-28, 3 Do-228), 1 HS-125-800 (VIP).
HELICOPTERS: 1 sqn with 1 SA-316B, 2 SA-330J, 2 AS-350 (COIN).

FORCES ABROAD:
MOZAMBIQUE: ε 600; elm of 1 inf bn.

PARA-MILITARY: 500.
POLICE: 3 BN-2T *Defender* (border patrol), 1 *Skyvan* 3M ac; 1 AS-350 hel.

MALI

GDP	1986:	fr 510.00 bn ($1.47 bn)	
	1987:	fr 596.60 bn ($1.99 bn)	
Debt	1986:	$1.7 bn	1987: $2.0 bn
Def bdgt	1986:	fr 12.90 bn ($37.25 m)	
	1987:	fr 18.31 bn ($60.94 m)	
FMA	1988:	$3.15 m (US, Fr)	
$1 = fr	(1986):	346.30	(1987): 300.54
	(1988):	297.85	(1989): 316.24
fr = francs CFA (Communauté financière africaine)			

Population: 9,072,000

	13–17	18–22	23–32
Men:	470,000	436,000	654,000
Women:	485,000	421,000	674,000

TOTAL ARMED FORCES: (all services form part of the Army):
ACTIVE: 7,300.
Terms of service: conscription (incl for civil purposes), 2 years (selective).

ARMY: 6,900.
2 tk, 4 inf, 1 AB, 2 arty, 1 engr, 1 SF bn, 2 AD, 1 SAM bty.
EQUIPMENT:*
MBT: 21 T-34.
LIGHT TANKS: 18 Type 62.
RECCE: 20 BRDM-2.
APC: 30 BTR-40, 10 BTR-152, 10 BTR-60.
TOWED ARTY: 85mm: 6 D-44; 100mm: 6 M-1944; 122mm: 8 D-30.
MRL: 122mm: 2 BM-21.
MORTARS: 81mm; 120mm: 30 M-43.
AD GUNS: 37mm: 6 M-1939; 57mm: 6 S-60.
SAM: 12 SA-3.

NAVY: About 50.
BASES: Bamako, Mopti, Segou, Timbuktu.
PATROL CRAFT: 3 river PCI〈.

AIR FORCE: 400;
27 cbt ac, no armed hel.*
FGA: 5 MiG-17F, 8 MiG-19.
FIGHTER: 14 MiG-21.
TRANSPORT: 2 An-2, 2 An-24, 2 An-26.
TRAINING: 6 L-29, 1 MiG-15UTI, 6 Yak (4 -11, 2 -18).
HELICOPTERS: 2 Mi-4, 1 Mi-8.

PARA-MILITARY:
GENDARMERIE: 1,800; 8 coy.
REPUBLICAN GUARD: 2,000.
MILITIA: 3,000.
NATIONAL POLICE: 1,000.

MOZAMBIQUE

GDP	1986ε:	M 111.65 bn ($2.75 bn)	
Growth	1986:	1.5%	1987: 4.0%
Debt	1986:	$3.2 bn	1987: $3.6 bn
Def bdgt	1988:	M 52.00 bn ($97.57 m)	
	1989:	M 80.00 bn ($115.74 m)	
$1 = M	(1986):	40.610	(1987): 278.995
	(1988):	532.970	(1989): 691.233
M = meticais			

Population: 15,375,000

	13–17	18–22	23–32
Men:	940,000	813,000	1,041,000
Women:	970,000	977,000	1,148,000

TOTAL ARMED FORCES:
ACTIVE: 71,000 (some 10,500 conscripts) incl Border Guard.

Terms of service: conscription (selective), 2 years (incl women), extended during emergency.

ARMY: ε 60,000 (perhaps 75% conscripts; most units well under strength.)
10 Provincial Commands.
1 tk bde (Presidential Guard).
7 inf bde (each 1 tk, 3 inf, 2 mot, 2 arty, 1 AD bn).
Many indep cbt and cbt spt bn and sy units.
6 AA arty bn.

EQUIPMENT:*
MBT: 150: some 50 T-34, some 100 T-54/-55.
RECCE: 48: 30 BRDM-1/-2.
AIFV: 16 BMP-1.
APC: 100+ BTR-60, 100 BTR-152.
TOWED ARTY: 200: 76mm: M-1942; 85mm: D-44; 100mm: 24 M-1944; 105mm: M-101; 122mm: M-1938, D-30; 130mm: 24 M-46; 152mm: 20 D-1.
MRL: 122mm: 30 BM-21.
MORTARS: 82mm: M-43; 120mm: M-43.
ATGW: AT-3 *Sagger*.
RCL: 75mm; 82mm: B-10; 107mm: B-11.
AD GUNS: 400: 20mm: M-55; 23mm: ZU-23-2; 37mm: M-1939; 57mm: S-60 towed, ZSU-57-2 SP.
SAM: SA-7.

NAVY: 750.*
BASES: Maputo (HQ), Beira, Nacala, Pemba, Inhambane, Quelimane (ocean); Metangula (Lake Nyasa) where about 4 PCI⟨ are based.
PATROL AND COASTAL COMBATANTS: 26:
INSHORE: 26:
    5 Sov SO-1, 5 other PFI⟨.
    1 Sov *Poluchat*, some 15 other PCI⟨.
MINE WARFARE: 3 Sov *Yevgenya* MSI.
AMPHIBIOUS: craft only; 2 LCU.

AIR FORCE: 4,250 (incl AD units);
66 cbt ac, 12 armed hel.*
FGA: 5 sqn with some 21 MiG-17, 45 MiG-21.
TRANSPORT: 1 sqn with 8 An-26 (some equipped for COIN operations), 3 Cessna (2 152, 1 172).
HELICOPTERS: 2 sqn with 8 Mi-8, 12 Mi-24/-25.
TRAINING: 1 Cessna 180, 4 Cessna 182, 3 MiG-15UTI, 4 PA-32.
AD SAM: SA-2, 10 SA-3.

PARA-MILITARY:
BORDER GUARD: 6,000; 5 bde.
PROVINCIAL (some 10 bn per province as required), People's Militias, Local Militias (village self-defence force): to be 100,000 in 1989.

OPPOSITION:
MOZAMBIQUE NATIONAL RESISTANCE: (MNR or RENAMO): 20,000 reported, ε 10,000 trained. 4 bn (active).
Special Forces (ε 200) in small teams.
EQUIPMENT: RCL: 82mm B-10, RPG-7. **MORTARS:** 60mm, 82mm, 120mm M-1943. **AD GUNS:** 12.7mm and 14.5mm.

FOREIGN FORCES:
ZIMBABWE: Some 3,000–8,000 (varies).
MALAWI: ε 600 (varies).
MILITARY ADVISERS: USSR 650; Cuba 600; North Korea 10, Zimbabwe ε 200.
SECURITY ADVISERS: GDR 50.

* Eqpt serviceability questionable; perhaps only 50–60% operational. Some eqpt in store.

NAMIBIA

GDP	1986: R 2.93 bn ($1.30 bn)	
	1987: R 3.13 bn ($1.54 bn)	
Growth	1986: 3.1%	1987: 2.9%
Inflation	1986: 13.4%	1987: 12.6%
Def exp	1987/8: R 327.9 m ($161.7 m)	
Def bdgt	1988/9: R 212.74 m ($89.77 m)	
$1 = R	(1986/7): 2.25 (1987/8): 2.028	
	(1988/9): 2.37	

R = rand
Population: 1,711,000

Joint Transition Administration headed by South African Administrator-General and UN Special representative. UN-monitored election due in November 1989 for an assembly which is to agree the constitution, after which independence will be achieved.

ARMED FORCES:
Nil. (South West Africa Territory Forces incl Standing Force, Reaction Force, Area Force claimed to be disbanded.)

PARA MILITARY:
Status of Police COIN unit (*Koevoet*) uncertain, but claimed to have been disbanded.

FOREIGN FORCES:

SOUTH AFRICA: 1,500 (to remain until independence).

UNITED NATIONS (UNTAG) 4,470: 3 inf bn (Finland, Kenya, Malaysia), engr (Australia), sigs (UK), medical (Switzerland), log (Poland, Canada), avn (Italy, Spain), observers (Bangladesh, Czechoslovakia, India, Ireland, Pakistan, Panama, Peru, Sudan, Togo, Yugoslavia).

NIGER

GDP	1986ε:	fr 662.00 bn ($1.91 bn)	
	1987ε:	fr 654.72 bn ($2.18 bn)	
Growth	1986: −2.0%	1987: −4.6%	
Inflation	1987: −6.7%	1988: −1.4%	
Debt	1987: $1.7 bn	1988: $1.9 bn	
Def bdgt	1987/8:	fr 5.24 bn ($17.58 m)	
	1988/9:	fr 5.49 bn ($17.37 m)	
FMA	1988:	$7.68 m (US, Fr)	
$1 = fr	(1986): 346.30	(1987):	300.54
	(1988): 297.85	(1989):	316.24

fr = francs CFA (Communauté financière africaine)

Population: 6,755,000

	13–17	18–22	23–32
Men:	378,000	323,000	503,000
Women:	387,000	329,000	514,000

TOTAL ARMED FORCES:
ACTIVE: 3,300.
Terms of service: selective conscription (2 years).

ARMY: 3,200.
3 Military Districts.
2 armd recce sqn.
6 inf, 1 AB, 1 engr coy.
EQUIPMENT:
RECCE: 50+: 10 M-8, 18 AML-90, 18 AML-60-7, some AML-60-20.
APC: 14 M-3.
MORTARS: 81mm: 30; 120mm: 15.
RL: 89mm: LRAC.
RCL: 57mm: 8 M-18; 75mm: 6 M-20.
AD GUNS: 20mm: 10 M-3 VDA SP.

AIR FORCE: 100+; no cbt ac or armed hel.
TRANSPORT: 1 C-54, 2 C-130H, 2 Do-228, 3 N-2501.
LIAISON: 2 Cessna 337D, 3 Do-28D.

PARA-MILITARY:
GENDARMERIE: 900; 7 groups.
PRESIDENTIAL GUARD: 200.
REPUBLICAN GUARD: 1,900.

NATIONAL POLICE: 1,500.

NIGERIA

GDP	1987:	N 110.58 bn ($27.60 bn)	
	1988:	N 136.96 bn ($30.56 bn)	
Growth	1987: 1.8%	1988: 5.0%	
Inflation	1987: 10.2%	1988: 38.2%	
Debt	1987: $26.7 bn	1988: $29.9 bn	
Def bdgt*	1988:	N 1.27 bn ($283.34 m)	
	1989:	N 1.27 bn ($167.16 m)	
FMA	1988:	$0.1 m (US)	
$1 = N	(1987): 4.0064	(1988):	4.4823
	(1989): 7.5815		

N = naira

Population: 112,258,000

	13–17	18–22	23–32
Men:	6,308,000	5,184,000	7,685,000
Women:	6,318,000	5,215,000	7,835,000

TOTAL ARMED FORCES:
ACTIVE: 94,500.
Terms of service: voluntary.
RESERVES: planned; none organized.

ARMY: 80,000.
1 armd div (4 armd, 1 mech bde).
1 composite div (incl 1 AB, 1 air portable, 1 amph bde).
2 mech div (each 3 mech bde).
Div tps: each div 1 arty, 1 engr bde, 1 recce bn.
EQUIPMENT:
MBT: 132: 60 T-55, 72 Vickers Mk 3.
LIGHT TANKS: 100 *Scorpion*.
RECCE: 20 *Saladin*, ε 120 AML-60, 60 AML-90, 55 *Fox*.
APC: 10 *Saracen*, 300 Steyr 4K-7FA.
TOWED ARTY: 105mm: 200 M-56; 122mm: 200 D-30/-74; 155mm: 25 FH-77B.
SP ARTY: 155mm: 25 *Palmaria*.
MORTARS: 81mm: 200.
RCL: 84mm: *Carl Gustav*; 106mm: M-40.
AD GUNS: 20mm: some 60; 23mm: 30 ZSU-23-4 SP; 40mm: L/60.
SAM: 48 *Blowpipe*, 16 *Roland*.

NAVY: 5,000.
BASES: Apapa (Lagos; HQ Western Command), Calabar (HQ Eastern Command), Warri.
FRIGATES: 2:
1 *Aradu* (FRG *Meko*-360) with 1 *Lynx* hel, 2 × 3 ASTT; plus 8 × *Otomat* SSM, 1 × 127mm gun.
1 *Obuma* (trg) with hel deck; plus 1 × 2 102mm guns.
PATROL AND COASTAL COMBATANTS: 51:
CORVETTES: 3:

2 *Erinomi* (UK Vosper Mk 9) with 1 × 2 ASW mor.

1 *Otobo* (UK Vosper Mk 3) (in Italy, refitting to PCO).

MISSILE CRAFT: 6:

3 *Ekpe* (FRG Lürssen-57) PFM with 4 × *Otomat* SSM.

3 *Siri* (Fr *Combattante*) with 2 × 2 MM-38 *Exocet* SSM.

PATROL, INSHORE: 42:

4 *Makurdi* (UK Brooke Marine 33m), some 38 PCI⟨.

MINE WARFARE: 2 *Ohue* (mod It *Lerici*) MCC.

AMPHIBIOUS: 2 *Ambe* (FRG) LST, capacity 200 tps, 5 tk.

SUPPORT AND MISCELLANEOUS: 1 survey.

NAVAL AVIATION:

HELICOPTERS: 3 Westland *Lynx* Mk 89 MR/SAR.

AIR FORCE: 9,500;

95 cbt ac (plus 12 being mod), 16 armed hel.

FGA/FIGHTER: 3 sqn:

1 with 22 *Alpha Jet* (FGA/trg);

1 with 11 MiG-21 MF, 6 MiG-21U (plus 12 MiG-21MF being mod);

1 with 18 *Jaguar* (14 -SN, 4 -BN).

COIN/TRAINING: 24 L-39, 12 MB-339AN.

ATTACK HELICOPTERS: 16 Bo-105D.

MR/SAR: 1 sqn with:

AIRCRAFT: 2 F-27MR (armed);

HELICOPTERS: 4 Bo-105D.

TRANSPORT: 2 sqn with 9 C-130 (6 -H, 3 -H-30), 3 Do-228 (VIP), 3 F-27, 5 G-222.

LIGHT TPT: 3 sqn with 18 Do-28D, 18 Do-128-6.

HELICOPTERS: incl 2 SA-330, 12 AS-332 (being delivered), 4 Bo-105C.

TRAINING:

AIRCRAFT: 2 MiG-21U, 25 *Bulldog*;

HELICOPTERS: 14 Hughes 300.

AAM: AA-2 *Atoll*.

PARA-MILITARY:

COAST GUARD: 15 *Abeokuta*, 3 other patrol craft.

PORT SECURITY POLICE: 12,000.

SECURITY AND CIVIL DEFENCE CORPS

(Ministry of Internal Affairs): Police: UR- 416 APC; 1 Cessna 500, 3 Piper (2 *Navajo*, 1 *Chieftain*) ac, 4 Bell (2 -212, 2 -222) hel; 68 small craft, 7 hovercraft (5 AV *Tiger*).

---

* Excl Police and Police Affairs Dept, and Internal Affairs Ministry.

RWANDA

GDP	1986: fr 161.90 bn ($1.85 bn)	
	1987: fr 166.50 bn ($2.09 bn)	
Growth	1986ε: −1.0%	1987ε: 2.0%
Inflation	1987: 4.1%	1988: 2.9%
Debt	1987: $947.7 m	1988ε: $1.0 bn

Def bdgt*	1987: fr 3.00 bn ($37.66 m)	
	1988: fr 2.80 bn ($36.63 m)	
FMA	1988: $3.1 m (US, Fr)	

$1 = fr	(1986):	87.64	(1987):	79.67
	(1988):	76.45	(1989):	79.07

fr = Rwanda francs

Population: 6,815,000

	13–17	18–22	23–32
Men:	353,000	309,000	548,000
Women:	357,000	310,000	540,000

TOTAL ARMED FORCES: (all services form part of the Army):

ACTIVE: 5,200.

Terms of service: voluntary.

ARMY: 5,000.

1 cdo bn.

1 recce, 8 inf, 1 engr coy.

EQUIPMENT:

RECCE: 12 AML-60.

APC: 16 M-3.

MORTARS: 81mm: 8.

RL: 83mm: *Blindicide*.

ATK GUNS: 57mm: 6.

AVIATION:

TRANSPORT: 2 C-47, 2 Do-27Q-4.

HELICOPTERS: 2 SE-3160.

AIR: 200; 2 cbt ac, no armed hel.

COIN: 2 R-235 *Guerrier*.

TRANSPORT: 2 BN-2, 1 N-2501.

LIAISON: 5 SA-316, 6 SA-342L hel.

PARA-MILITARY:

GENDARMERIE: 1,200.

---

* Recurrent budget only

SENEGAMBIA

In December 1983 a confederal budget was introduced. In 1988/9 it was fr CFA 3.4 bn. The Federal Armed Forces consist of 1 inf bn located in The Gambia. One coy is manned by Gambian troops, the remainder by Senegal.

SENEGAL

GDP	1986ε: fr 1,216.94 bn ($3.82 bn)	
Growth	1986: 4.3%	1987: 4.0%

Inflation	1987: −4.3%	1988: −1.9%
Debt	1987: $3.5 bn	1988: $3.9 bn

Def bdgt 1987/8: fr 28.97 bn ($99.30 m)
1988/9: fr 30.29 bn ($96.94 m)
FMA 1988: $8.98 m (US, Fr)
$1 = fr (1986/7): 318.79 (1987/8): 291.71
(1988/9): 312.49 (1989): 316.24
fr = francs CFA (Communauté financière africaine)

Population: 7,138,000

	13–17	18–22	23–32
Men:	399,000	336,000	530,000
Women:	401,000	338,000	534,000

TOTAL ARMED FORCES: (incl Federal):
ACTIVE: 9,700.
Terms of service: conscription, 2 years selective.
RESERVE: exists, no details known.

ARMY: 8,500 (mostly conscripts).
4 Military Zone HQ.
1 armd bn.
5 inf bn.
1 inf bn (−) with confederal force.
1 AB bn.
1 cdo bn.
1 arty bn.
1 engr bn.
1 Presidential Guard (horsed).
3 construction coy.
EQUIPMENT:
RECCE: 10 M-8, 4 M-20, 30 AML-60, 27 -90.
APC: some 16 Panhard M-3, 12 M-3 half-track.
TOWED ARTY: 18: 75mm: 6 M-116 pack; 105mm: 6 M-101; 155mm: ε 6 Fr Model-50.
MORTARS: 81mm: 8; 120mm: 8.
ATGW: *Milan.*
RL: 89mm: LRAC.
AD GUNS: 20mm: 21 M-693; 40mm: 12 L/60.

NAVY: 700.
BASES: Dakar, Casamance (Senegal).
PATROL AND COASTAL COMBATANTS: 8:
PATROL COASTAL: 2:
1 *Fouta* (Dk '*Osprey*') PCC.
1 *Njambuur* (Fr SFCN 59m) PFC.
INSHORE: 6:
3 *Saint Louis* (Fr 48m) PCI, 3⟨.
AMPHIBIOUS: craft only; 2 LCT, 2 LCM.

AIR FORCE: 500;
9 cbt ac, no armed hel.
COIN: 1 sqn with 5 CM-170, 4 R-235 *Guerrier.*
MR/SAR: 1 DHC-6-300M, 1 EMB-111.
TRANSPORT: 1 sqn with 6 F-27-400M, 2 MH-1521.
1 PA-23 (liaison).

TRAINING: 4 *Rallye* (2 235A, 2 160).
HELICOPTERS: 2 SA-318C, 2 SA-330, 1 SA-341H.

FORCES ABROAD
IRAN/IRAQ (UNIIMOG): observers.

PARA-MILITARY:
GENDARMERIE: 12 VXB-170 APC.
CUSTOMS: 2 PCI⟨, boats.

FOREIGN FORCES:
FRANCE: 1,100: 1 marine inf regt, MR and tpt ac/hel.

THE GAMBIA

GDP 1986/7: D 1,078.10 m ($148.00 m)
1987/8ε: D 1,282.95 m ($190.58 m)
Growth 1986/7: 6.0% 1987/8: 5.4%
Inflation 1987: 23.5% 1988: 19.0%
Debt 1986: $273.0 m
FMA 1988: $0.12 m (US, Fr)
$1 = D (1986/7): 7.2846 (1987/8): 6.7317
(1988/9): 6.8201 (1989): 6.5228
D = dalasi

Population: 681,000

	13–17	18–22	23–32
Men:	45,000	33,000	56,000
Women:	43,000	34,000	65,000

TOTAL ARMED FORCES:
ACTIVE: (900).
Terms of service: voluntary; some compulsory conditions authorized.

GAMBIAN NATIONAL ARMY (GNA):
1 inf bn (3 coy), engr sqn.
1 inf coy with Confederal bn.
MARINE BRANCH: About 100.
BASE: Banjul.
PATROL, INSHORE: 6:
2 Ch *Shanghai-II* PFI, 4 PFI⟨.

PARA-MILITARY:
GENDARMERIE: 600+.

SEYCHELLES

GDP 1986: SR 1,311.40 bn ($212.31 m)
Growth 1986ε: 8.5%
Inflation 1987: 2.6% 1988: 1.7%

Debt   1986: $106.0 m   1987: $130.0 m
Def bdgt   1989: SR 70.00 m ($12.57 m)
FMA   1988: $0.05 m (US)
$1 = SR   (1986):   6.177   (1987):   5.600
            (1988):   5.384   (1989):   5.567
SR = Seychelles rupees

Population: 67,700

	13–17	18–22	23–32
Men:	3,900	3,700	7,300
Women:	3,800	3,700	6,500

TOTAL ARMED FORCES: (all services
form part of the Army):
ACTIVE: 1,300.
Terms of service: conscription: 2 years.

ARMY: 1,000.
1 inf bn (3 coy).
2 arty tps.
Spt coy.
EQUIPMENT:
RECCE: 6 BRDM-2, ε 8 *Shorland*.
APC: 4 BTR-152.
TOWED ARTY: 122mm: 3 D-30.
MRL: 122mm: 2 BM-21.
MORTARS: 82mm: 6 M-43.
RL: RPG-7.
SAM: 10 SA-7.

MARINE: 200.
BASE: Port Victoria.
PATROL AND COASTAL COMBATANTS: 5:
INSHORE: 5:
   1 *Andromache* (It Pichiotti 42m) PFI
   1 *Zoroaster* (Sov *Turya*, no foils) PFI.
   2 PFI⟨, 1 PCI⟨.
AMPHIBIOUS: craft only; 1 LCT.

AIR: 100
1 cbt ac, no armed hel.
MR: 1 BN-2 *Defender*.
LIAISON: 1 *Merlin* IIIB, 1 R-235E.
HELICOPTERS: 2 *Chetak*.

PARA-MILITARY:
PEOPLE'S MILITIA: 800.

SIERRA LEONE

GDP   1985/6: Le 6.35 bn ($1.22 bn)
Inflation   1987:   178.7%
Debt   1986: $589.8 m   1987: $660.0 m

Def bdgt   1985/6: Le 26.80 m ($5.13 m)
FMA   1988: $0.07 m (US)
$1 = Le   (1985/6): 5.221   (1986/7): 31.847
            (1987/8): 25.141
Le = leones

Population: 3,839,000

	13–17	18–22	23–32
Men:	196,000	166,000	265,000
Women:	199,000	169,000	273,000

TOTAL ARMED FORCES:
ACTIVE: 3,100.
Terms of service: voluntary.

ARMY: 3,000.
2 inf bn.
2 arty bty.
1 engr sqn.
EQUIPMENT:
RECCE: 4 *Saladin*.
APC: 10 MOWAG *Piranha*.
MORTARS: 81mm.
RCL: 84mm: *Carl Gustav*.
SAM: SA-7.

NAVY: 150.
BASE: Freetown.
PATROL AND COASTAL COMBATANTS: 2:
2 Ch *Shanghai-II* PFI.
AMPHIBIOUS: craft only; 3 LCU⟨.

PARA-MILITARY: 800.
STATE SECURITY DIVISION: 1 SF bn.

SOUTH AFRICA

GDP   1987: R 164.46 bn ($81.10 bn)
            1988ε: R 191.26 bn ($80.70 bn)
Growth   1987: 2.6%   1988: 3.2%
Inflation   1987: 16.1%   1988: 12.9%
Debt   1986: $24.6 bn   1987: $20.5 bn
Def bdgt*   1988/9: R 8.09 bn ($3.41 bn)
            1989/90: R 9.94 bn ($3.91 bn)
$1 = R   (1987/8): 2.0278   (1988/9): 2.3699
            (1989):   2.5432
R = rand

Population: 35,364,000, incl Homelands 6,360,000.
   (Black: 24,719,000; White: 6,295,000;
   Coloured: 3,324,000; Asian: 1,026,000)

	13–17	18–22	23–32
Men:	1,621,000	1,427,000	2,667,000
Women:	1,611,000	1,421,000	2,523,000

TOTAL ARMED FORCES:

ACTIVE: (Full Time Force and National Service) 103,000 (incl 64,000 white conscripts; 3,200 women).

Terms of service: 24 months National Service for whites, followed by 12 years part-time service in Citizen Force (CF) (in any 2 years periods of call-up for op duty not to exceed 90 days, plus 30 days trg). Thereafter continued voluntary service in Citizen Force (to age 55) or 5 years with no commitment in Active Citizen Force Reserve. Then may be allocated to Commandos to age 55 with annual commitment of 12 days. Races other than whites volunteer for Full Time Force, National Service and Commandos but are not conscripted.

RESERVES: 425,000.

Citizen Force 380,000: Active Citizen Force Reserve: 150,000: Commandos ε 140,000.

ARMY: ε 77,500. Full Time Force 19,900 (12,000 White, 5,400 Black and Coloured; ε 2,500 women). National Service: ε 58,500.

FULL TIME FORCE (FT):

Army tps
  1 AB bde (1 FT, 1 trg, 2 CF AB bn, 1 CF arty bn with 120mm mor).
  SF: 5 recce coy (4 FT, 1 CF)
  State President's Guard bn.
Territorial Forces
  11 Territorial comd
  7 inf bn (2 coloured, 5 black)
Training Units (all with cbt capability)
  2 armd bn
  9 inf bn (8 white, 1 black)
  2 arty regt
  1 AD arty regt
  1 engr regt.

RESERVES:

CITIZEN FORCE (CF):

1 Corps HQ. (FT administered)
  2 div (each 1 armd, 2 mech bde) (bdes: armd: 2 armd regt, 2 mech inf bn; mech: 3 inf bn; all 1 armd recce, 1 arty, 1 engr regt).
  1 indep mot inf bde
  2-3 arty regt
Territorial Forces
  2 armd recce regt
  16 inf bn
  2 arty regt
  2 AD regt
  3 engr regt

COMMANDOS:

Some 150 inf bn home defence units.

EQUIPMENT:

MBT: some 250 *Centurion/Olifant* 2B.
RECCE: 1,600 *Eland* (90mm gun, 60mm mor), some *Rooikat*.

AIFV: 1,500 *Ratel* (20mm/60mm/90mm gun; 81mm mor).
APC: 1,500 incl *Buffalo, Bulldog, Hippo, Casspir, Rhino, Hyena, Lynx* (wheeled).
TOWED ARTY: 145: 25-pdr (88mm): 30; 5.5-in (140mm): 75 G-2; 155mm: 40+ G-5.
SP ARTY: 155mm: 10+ G-6.
MRL: 127mm: 120 *Valkiri* 22 SP; some *Valkiri* 5 towed.
MORTARS: 81mm: 4,000; 120mm: + 120.
ATGW: SS-11, 120 *ENTAC*.
RCL: 84mm; 106mm.
ATK GUNS: 6-pdr (57mm); 17-pdr (76mm); 90mm: M-67.
AD GUNS: 20mm: some SP; 35mm: 55 K-63 twin; 40mm: 25 L/70; 3.7-in (94mm): 15.
SAM: 20 *Cactus* (*Crotale*), 54 *Tigercat*.
Some captured SA-7/-8/-9/-13/-14 SAM and ZU-23-2 AA guns may be in service.

NAVY: 6,500, (incl 900 marines, 1,500 conscripts; ε 300 women).

Two Commands: Western (HQ, Cape Town); Eastern (HQ, Durban).
BASES: Simonstown, Durban.
SUBMARINES: 3 *Maria Van Riebeek* (Fr *Daphné*) with 550mm TT.
PATROL AND COASTAL COMBATANTS: 9:
MISSILE CRAFT: 9:
  9 *Jan Smuts* (Is *Reshef*) with 6 *Skerpioen* (Is *Gabriel*) SSM.
MINE WARFARE: 9:
  1 *Kimberley* (UK 'Ton') MHC.
  3 *Walvisbaai* (UK 'Ton') MSC.
  4 *Umximkulu* MHC.
  1 diving spt.
SUPPORT AND MISCELLANEOUS: 3:
  2 AOR, each with 2 hel and extempore amph capability (perhaps 200 tps), 1 survey.
ADDITIONAL IN STORE:
  1 *President Pretorius* (UK *Rothesay*) FF.

MARINES: (900; 600 conscripts).

1 Bde HQ.
9 local harbour/base defence units.
1 amph coy.
EQUIPMENT:
81mm mortars, some 30 boats.

AIR FORCE: 11,000 (4,000 conscripts; ε 400 women);

338 cbt ac (incl 116 with Citizen Force), 14+ armed hel.
2 Territorial Area Comds Air Defence, Tac Spt, Log, Trg Comd.
BOMBERS: 2 sqn:
  1 with 5 *Canberra* B(I)12, 2 T-4;
  1 with 5 *Buccaneer* S-50.
FGA/FIGHTER: 8 sqn.
  1 with 29 *Mirage* F-1AZ;

1 with 14 *Mirage* F-1CZ;
1 with 16 *Mirage* III CZ/BZ, plus recce flt
  (below);
1 with 13 *Cheetah*;
4 (Citizen Force) with 92 *Impala* II, 14 *Cheetah*.
RECCE: 1 flt with 7 *Mirage* III (4 RZ, 3 R2Z).
EW: 1 sqn with 4 Boeing 707 (ELINT/tkr).
MR: 2 sqn:
  1 with some 8 C-47;
  1 with 19 P-166S (COIN/SAR roles, also).
  (Some C-130 have a MR role).
ASW: 1 hel sqn: 8 *Wasp* HAS-1, 6 SA-316.
TRANSPORT: 3 sqn:
  1 with 7 C-130B, 9 C-160Z;
  1 (VIP) with 4 HS-125 (civil registration).
  1 with 1 *Viscount* 781 (civil registration), 19
  C-47, 4 DC-4.
HELICOPTERS: 5 sqn with 14 SA-321,
  65 SA-330, 57 SA-316 (some armed).
LIAISON/FAC: 3 sqn with 34 AM-3C, 35 C-4M, 10
  Cessna 185.
TRAINING COMMAND (incl OCU): 6 schools:
  AIRCRAFT: 130 T-6G *Harvard* IIA/III (80 to be
    updated), 120 *Impala* I, 12 C-47;
  HELICOPTERS: 30 SE-3130, 7 SA-316.
AAM: R-530, R-550 *Magic*, AIM-9 *Sidewinder*,
  Kukri V-3.
ASM: AS-11/-20/-30.
RPV: *Meteor* P1, IAI *Scout*, Armscor *Seeker*.
RESERVES:
CITIZEN FORCE: 4 sqn, see FGA/FIGHTER above.
  Sqn are available for day-to-day ops.

MEDICAL SERVICE: 8,000. A separate
service within SADF, organized territorially to
support all three services.

PARA-MILITARY:
SOUTH AFRICAN POLICE: 55,000 (to be
  increased); Police Reserves: 37,000.
Coast guard to form; 7 MR ac planned.

OPPOSITION:
AFRICAN NATIONAL CONGRESS (ANC): combat
  wing *Umkhonto we Sizwe*: perhaps 10,000
  trained; up to 1,400 based in Angola.
PAN AFRICANIST CONGRESS (PAC): Azanian
  People's Liberation Army: possibly inactive.

HOMELANDS

Each homeland has its own armed forces, not
included in South African data. Currency in all
cases is the South African Rand.

BOPHUTHATSWANA
Population: 1,855,000.
ARMED FORCES: ε 3,100
Terms of service: voluntary; conscription authorized.
  6 Military Regions.
  1 inf bn.
  1 AB/SF unit (coy-).
  2–3 indep inf coy gp.
  Air Wing: 1 recce, 1 lt tpt, 1 hel flt.
EQUIPMENT:
APC: *Buffalo.*
MORTARS: 81mm.
AIRCRAFT: 2 P-68, 2 C-212–200.
HELICOPTERS: 1 AS-355, 2 BK-117, 2 SA-316.

CISKEI
Population: 831,000.
ARMED FORCES: ε 1,000:
  Terms of service: voluntary; conscription authorized.
    1 inf bn (2nd forming).
    1 AB/SF coy
AIRCRAFT: 2 BN-2, 2 *Skyvan*, 1 IAI-1124 (VIP).
HELICOPTERS: 3 BK-117, 1 Bo-105.

TRANSKEI
Def bdgt 1985/86: R 203 m.
Population: 3,221,000.
ARMED FORCES: ε 2,000:
  Terms of service: voluntary; conscription authorized.
    1 lt inf/COIN bn.
  1 SF regt: 1 SF coy, AB coy, mounted sqn, marine gp.
Air wing.
AIRCRAFT: 2 C-212.
HELICOPTERS: 2 BK-117.

VENDA
Def bdgt 1984/5: R 257.19 m.
Population: 453,000.
ARMED FORCES: ε 1,500:
  Terms of service: voluntary.
    2 inf bn.
    Engr tp.
    Air wing.
EQUIPMENT:
APC: *Buffalo.*
MORTARS: 81mm.
HELICOPTERS: 2 BK-117, 1 SA-316B.

---

* Excl Intelligence and Police (internal sy) bdgt
which in 1988/9 amounted to R 1.8 bn and
Namibian expenditure.

TANZANIA

| GDP | 1986: sh 149.47 bn ($4.57 bn) |
| | 1987ε: sh 311.66 bn ($4.85 bn) |

Growth	1986ε: 1.0%	1987ε: 3.5%
Inflation	1987: 30.0%	1988: 28.0%
Debt	1987: $4.0 bn	1988: $4.3 bn
Def bdgt	1985/6ε: sh 4.17 bn ($223.42 m)	
FMA	1988: $0.05 m (US)	
$1 = sh	(1986): 32.698	(1987): 64.260
	(1988): 99.292	(1989): 135.878

sh = Tanzanian shilling

Population: 24,333,000

	13–17	18–22	23–32
Men:	1,415,000	1,172,000	1,573,000
Women:	1,412,000	1,213,000	1,705,000

TOTAL ARMED FORCES:
ACTIVE: 46,700 (perhaps 20,000 conscripts).
Terms of service: national service incl civil duties, 2 years.
RESERVE: 10,000: armed elm of Citizen's Militia.

ARMY: 45,000 (some 20,000 conscripts).
3 div HQ.
8 inf bde.
1 tk bde.
2 fd arty bn, 2 AA arty bn (6 bty).
2 mor bn.
1 SAM bn with SA-3, SA-6.
2 ATK bn.
2 sigs bn.
EQUIPMENT:†
MBT: 30 Ch Type-59, 30 T-62.
LIGHT TANKS: 30 Ch Type-62, 36 *Scorpion*.
RECCE: 20 BRDM-2.
APC: 45 BTR-40/-152, 30 Ch Type-56.
TOWED ARTY: 76mm: 45 ZIS-3; 85mm: 80 Ch Type-56; 122mm: 200 D-30, 20 Ch Type-54; 130mm: 50 Type-59.
MRL: 122mm: 50 BM-21.
MORTARS: 82mm: 300 M-43; 120mm: 50 M-43.
RCL: 75mm: 540 Ch Type-52.
AD GUNS: 14.5mm: 280 ZPU-2/-4; 23mm: 40 ZU-23; 37mm: 120 Ch Type-55.
SAM: 9 SA-3, 12 SA-6, SA-7.

NAVY: 700.
BASES: Dar es Salaam, Zanzibar, Mwanza (Lake Victoria – 4 boats).
PATROL AND COASTAL COMBATANTS: 18:
TORPEDO CRAFT: 4 Ch *Huchuan* PHT⟨ with 2 × 533mm TT.
PATROL, INSHORE: 14:
6 Ch *Shanghai* II PFI, 8 PCI⟨, (4 in Zanzibar).
AMPHIBIOUS: craft only; 4 LCA⟨.
Note: Spares are short; some vessels are not operational.

AIR FORCE: 1,000;
24 cbt ac, no armed hel†.
FIGHTER: 3 sqn with 11 Ch J-7, 3 J-5, 10 J-6.
TRANSPORT: 1 sqn with 5 DHC-5D, 1 Ch Y-5.
HELICOPTERS: 4 AB-205.
LIAISON: 9 Cessna (7 310, 2 404), 5 PA-28, 1 PA-32 ac; 2 Bell 206B hel.
TRAINING: 2 MiG-15UTI.

PARA-MILITARY:
POLICE FIELD FORCE: 1,400.
POLICE AIR WING: 1 Cessna U206 ac; 2 Bell 206 L, 4 AB 206 (2 -A, 2 -L), 2 Bell 47G hel.
POLICE MARINE UNIT: (100).
CITIZEN'S MILITIA: 100,000.

TOGO

GDP	1987: fr 371.70 bn ($1.24 bn)	
	1988ε: fr 402.80 bn ($1.35 bn)	
Growth	1986: 3.4%	1987: 1.4%
Inflation	1986: 4.1%	1987: 0.1%
Debt	1986: $1.1 bn	1987: $1.2 bn
Def bdgt	1986: fr 10.39 bn ($30.01 m)	
FMA	1988: $11.1 m (US, Fr)	
$1 = fr	(1986): 346.30	(1987): 300.54
	(1988): 297.85	(1989): 316.24

fr = francs CFA (Communauté financière africaine)

Population: 3,290,000

	13–17	18–22	23–32
Men:	183,000	153,000	201,000
Women:	194,000	163,000	249,000

TOTAL ARMED FORCES: (all services, incl Gendarmerie, form part of the Army):
ACTIVE: 5,900.
Terms of service: conscription, 2 years (selective).

ARMY: 4,000.
2 inf regt:
1 with 1 mech bn, 1 mot bn;
1 with 2 armd sqn, 3 inf coy; spt units (trg).
1 Presidential Guard regt: 2 bn (1 cdo), 2 coy.
1 para cdo regt: 3 coy.
1 spt regt: 1 fd arty bty; 2 AD arty bty; 1 log/tpt/engr bn.
EQUIPMENT:
MBT: 2 T-54/-55.
LIGHT TANKS: 9 *Scorpion*.
RECCE: 6 M-8, 3 M-20, 3 AML-60, 7 -90, 36 EE-9 *Cascavel*.
APC: 4 M-3A1, 30 UR-416.
TOWED ARTY: 105mm: 4 HM-2.

MORTARS: 82mm: 20 M-43.
RCL: 57mm: 5 ZIS-2; 75mm: 12 Ch Type-52/-56;
  85mm: 10 Ch Type-65.
AD GUNS: 14.5mm: 38 ZPU-4; 37mm: 5 M-39.

NAVY: 100.
BASE: Lomé.
PATROL AND COASTAL COMBATANTS: 2
INSHORE: 2 *Mono* PFI⟨.

AIR FORCE: 250;
  18 cbt ac, no armed hel.
COIN/TRAINING: 5 *Alpha Jet*, 4 CM-170, 6
  EMB-326G, 3 TB-30.
TRANSPORT: 2 *Baron*, 2 DHC-5D, 1 Do-27, 1
  F-28-1000 (VIP), 1 *Falcon* 10 (VIP), 2
  Reims-Cessna 337.
HELICOPTERS: 2 SA-313B, 2 SA-315, 1 SA-330.

FORCES ABROAD:
NAMIBIA (UNTAG): 25 observers.

PARA-MILITARY:
GENDARMERIE: 750; 1 trg school, 2 regional
  sections, 1 mobile sqn.
PRESIDENTIAL HONOUR GUARD: 800.

UGANDA

GDP	1986:	N sh 30.42 bn ($2.17 bn)		
	1987ε:	N sh 102.50 bn ($2.39 bn)		
Growth	1986:	−0.2%	1987:	6.0%
Inflation	1986:	169.0%	1987:	237.5%
Debt	1987:	$1.8 bn	1988:	$2.1 bn
Def bdgt*	1987/8ε:	N sh 8.50 bn ($141.67 m)		
	1988/9:	N sh 6.90 bn ($40.68 m)		
FMA	1988:	$11.15 m (US, Fr)		

$1 = N sh (1987/8): 60.000   (1988/9): 169.608
N sh = Ugandan shillings

Population: 17,396,000

	13–17	*18–22*	*23–32*
Men:	943,000	780,000	1,093,000
Women:	963,000	794,000	1,122,000

TOTAL ARMED FORCES:
ACTIVE: ε 70,000
  Terms of service: voluntary.

NATIONAL RESISTANCE ARMY (NRA):

(now incorporates surrendered Uganda People's
Democratic Army and Uganda National
Liberation Army).
6 bde.
Some bn.

EQUIPMENT:†
APC: some BTR-60, 4 OT-64 SKOT.
TOWED ARTY: 76mm: 60; 122mm: 20.
MORTARS: 82mm; 120mm.
ATGW: 40 AT-3 *Sagger*.
AD GUNS: 40: 23mm, 37mm.
SAM: SA-7.
AVIATION: 13 cbt ac no armed hel.
  FGA: 8 MiG-17F.
  FIGHTER: 5 MiG-21MF.
  TRANSPORT: 1 *Commander* 112, 1 N-2501.
  TRAINING: 5 L-29, 5 P-149D, 4 S-211, 6
  SF-260, SF-260W.
  HELICOPTERS:
    ATTACK: 2 AB-412.
    TRANSPORT: 3 Bell 205, 5 Bell 206, 3 Bell 214,
    2 Mi-8, 1 *Sioux*.
  LIAISON: 2 PA-23, 11 *Super Cub*.
POLICE AIR WING:
  AIRCRAFT: 1 DHC-2, 1 DHC-4, 1 DHC-6.
  HELICOPTERS: 2 Bell 206, 4 Bell 212.

OPPOSITION:
HOLY SPIRIT MOVEMENT: ε 500, small arms only.

---

* Recurrent budget only.
† Serviceability doubtful.

ZAIRE

GDP	1987:	Z 326.95 bn ($2.91 bn)		
	1988:	Z 595.60 bn ($3.18 bn)		
Growth	1987:	2.6%	1988:	2.7%
Inflation	1987:	79.2%	1988:	85.0%
Debt	1987:	$6.3 bn	1988:	$7.1 bn
Def bdgt*	1986:	Z 10.11 bn ($169.55 m)		
	1987:	Z 5.23 bn ($46.56 m)		
FMA	1988:	$2.0 m (US)		

$1 = Z (1986): 59.625   (1987): 112.403
     (1988): 187.070   (1989): 349.620
Z = zaires

Population: 32,922,000

	13–17	*18–22*	*23–32*
Men:	2,074,000	1,705,000	2,612,000
Women:	2,030,000	1,690,000	2,647,000

TOTAL ARMED FORCES:
ACTIVE: 51,000 (incl Gendarmerie).
  Terms of service: voluntary.

ARMY: 22,000.
  3 Military Regions.
  1 inf div (3 inf bde).
  1 SF div:
    1 para bde (3 para, 1 spt bn) (2nd forming).
    1 SF (cdo/COIN) bde.
    1 Presidential Guard bde.
  1 indep armd bde.
  2 indep inf bde (each 3 inf bn, 1 spt bn).
EQUIPMENT:
MBT: some 50 Ch Type-62.
RECCE: 95 AML-60, 60 -90.
APC: 12 M-113, 12 YW-531, 60 M-3.
TOWED ARTY: 75mm: 30 M-116 pack; 85mm: 20
  Type 56; 122mm: 20 M-1938/D-30, 30 Type 60;
  130mm: 8 Type 59.
MRL: 107mm: 20 Type 63.
MORTARS: 81mm; 107mm: M-30; 120mm: 50.
RCL: 57mm: M-18; 75mm: M-20; 106mm: M-40;
  107mm.
AD GUNS: 12.7mm; 14.5mm; 20mm; 37mm:
  M-1939; 40mm: L/60.

NAVY: 1,500 incl marines.
BASES: Banana, Boma, Matadi (coast), Kinshasa
  (river), Kalémié (lake (4 boats)).
PATROL AND COASTAL COMBATANTS: 4:
INSHORE: 4 Ch *Shanghai-II* PFI.

MARINES: 600.

AIR FORCE: 2,500;
  28 cbt ac, no armed hel.
FGA/FIGHTER: 1 sqn with 8 *Mirage* (7 -5M, 1 -5DM).
COIN: 1 sqn with 6 MB-326K, 6 AT-6G.
TRANSPORT: 1 wing with 1 BN-2, 8 C-47, 5
  C-130H, 3 DHC-5, 2 MU-2J (VIP).
  HELICOPTERS: 1 sqn with 1 AS-332, 7 SA-316, 1
  SA-321 (VIP), 9 SA-330.
TRAINING: incl 21 Cessna (12 150, 9 310), 8
  MB-326GB, 9 SF-260C ac; 6 Bell 47 hel.

PARA-MILITARY:
GENDARMERIE: 25,000 (to be 27,000); 40 bn.
CIVIL GUARD: 25,000.

* Excl capital expenditure.

ZAMBIA

GDP	1987:	K 19.63 bn ($2.21 bn)		
	1988:	K 21.46 bn ($2.61 bn)		
Growth	1986:	0.6%	1987:	−0.2%
Inflation	1987:	43.1%	1988:	55.7%
Debt	1987:	$6.5 bn	1988:	$6.9 bn

Def exp	1986ε:	$100.6 m	1987ε:	$126.8 m
$1 = K	(1987):	8.889	(1988):	8.224
	(1989):	10.101		

K = kwacha

Population: 7,396,000			
	13–17	*18–22*	*23–32*
Men:	433,000	360,000	505,000
Women:	425,000	353,000	539,000

TOTAL ARMED FORCES:
ACTIVE: 16,200.
Terms of service: voluntary.

ARMY: 15,000.
  1 armd regt (incl 1 armd recce bn).
  9 inf bn (3 Reserve).
  3 arty bty, 2 AA arty bty.
  1 engr bn.
EQUIPMENT:
MBT: 10 T-54/-55, 20 Ch Type-59.
LIGHT TANKS: 30 PT-76.
RECCE: 88 BRDM-1/-2.
APC: 13 BTR-60.
TOWED ARTY: 76mm: 35 M-1942;
  105mm: 18 Model 56 pack;
  122mm: 25 D-30;
  130mm: 25 M-46.
MRL: 122mm: 50 BM-21.
ATGW: AT-3 *Sagger*.
RCL: 57mm: 12 M-18; 75mm: M-20;
  84mm: *Carl Gustav*.
AD GUNS: 20mm: 50 M-55 triple; 37mm: 40
  M-1939; 57mm: 55 S-60; 85mm: 16 KS-12.
SAM: SA-7.

AIR FORCE: 1,200;
  68 cbt ac, some armed hel.
FGA: 1 sqn with 12 Ch J-6;
FIGHTER: 1 sqn with 13 MiG-21 MF.
COIN/TRAINING:
  5 *Galeb* G-2, 18 *Jastreb* J-1, 18 MB-326GB.
TRANSPORT: 1 sqn with 4 An-26, 6 C-47, 2 DC-6B;
  VIP: 1 flt with 1 HS-748, 3 Yak-40.
LIAISON: 9 Do-28.
TRAINING: 10 CJ-6, 20 MFI-17, 2 MiG-21U, 8
  SF-260MZ.
HELICOPTERS: 1 sqn with 13 AB-205A, 2 AB-212, 7 Mi-8.
LIAISON HELICOPTERS: 15 AB-47G.
SAM: 1 bn; 3 bty: SA-3 *Goa*.

PARA-MILITARY:
POLICE MOBILE UNIT (PMU): 700;
  1 bn of 4 coy.
POLICE PARA-MILITARY UNIT (PPMU): 500;
  1 bn of 3 coy.

ZIMBABWE

| GDP* | 1987ε: $Z 9.10 bn ($US 5.48 bn) |
| | 1988ε: $Z 10.51 bn ($US 5.83 bn) |

Growth	1987: −2.5%		1988: 5.8%	
Inflation	1987: 12.5%		1988: 12.8%	
Debt	1987: $US 2.8 bn	1988: $US 3.6 bn		
Def bdgt	1987/8: $Z 720.00 m ($US 423.74 m)			
	1988/9: $Z 768.00 m ($US 396.84 m)			
FMA	1988: $0.2 m (US)			
$1 = $Z	(1987/8): 1.6992	(1988/9ε): 1.9353		
	(1989): 2.0125			

Population: 9,528,000

	13–17	18–22	23–32
Men:	591,000	500,000	667,000
Women:	594,000	500,000	756,000

TOTAL ARMED FORCES:
ACTIVE: 49,500.

Terms of service: conscription; length unknown.

ARMY: 47,000.
7 bde HQ (incl 1 Presidential Guard).
1 armd regt.
26 inf bn (incl 3 Guard, 1 mech, 1 cdo, 2 para, 1 mounted).
1 arty regt (incl 2 AD bty).
1 engr spt regt.
EQUIPMENT:
MBT: 8 T-54, 35 Ch T-59/Ch T-62.
RECCE: 90 EE-9 *Cascavel* (90mm gun),
28 AML-90 *Eland*.
APC: 10 YW-531, ε 40 UR-416, 50+ *Crocodile*.

TOWED ARTY: 76mm: M-1942; 88mm: 24 25-pdr;
122mm: 18 Ch Type-60, Ch Type-54.
MRL: 107mm: Ch Type-63.
MORTARS: 81mm: L16; 120mm: 4.
RCL: 107mm: 12.
AD GUNS: 14.5mm; 23mm: ZU-23; 37mm: M-1939.
SAM: SA-7.

AIR FORCE: 2,500;
81 (65) cbt ac, no armed hel; (est number op in parentheses).
FGA/COIN: 2 sqn:
1 with 9 *Hunter* FGA-90, 1 T-81 (7);
1 with 7 *Hawk* Mk 60 (3).
FIGHTER: 3 sqn with 48 Ch J-7 (48).
COIN/RECCE: 1 sqn with 16 Reims-Cessna 337 *Lynx* (7).
TRAINING/RECCE/LIAISON: 1 sqn with 13 SF-260C/W *Genet*, 5 SF-260TP (10).
TRANSPORT: 7 BN-2, 11 C-212-200 (1 VIP), 7 C-47.
HELICOPTERS: 2 sqn:
1 with 6 AB-205, 10 SA-316 (4 all types);
1 with 10 AB-412 (VIP) (4).
SECURITY: 2 sqn.

FORCES ABROAD:
MOZAMBIQUE: some 3,000–8,000 (varies).

PARA-MILITARY:
ZIMBABWE REPUBLIC POLICE FORCE, incl Air Wing: 15,000.
POLICE SUPPORT UNIT: 3,000.
NATIONAL MILITIA: 20,000.

* Calendar year exchange rate average used to calculate $US GDP: 1 $US = $Z 1.6611 (1987); $Z 1.8018 (1988)

Asia and Australasia

(1) CHINA

General

Events in Tiananmen Square, culminating on 4 June 1989 in the action by the People's Liberation Army (PLA) to reassert government control, have had a profound effect on the world's attitude to relations with China. Most Western nations immediately banned all trade in the defence sector and cancelled high-level official visits. These moves will adversely affect the modernization programme of the Chinese armed forces but may not impact much on China's growing arms export business. The events themselves showed the PLA to be generally unprepared and inappropriately trained and equipped for internal security operations. While there was some evidence indicating a difference in approach to the task between forces based around Beijing and those brought in from other military districts, media reports of a possible break-up of the PLA into contending factions appear to have been much exaggerated.

The events coincided with a visit to Beijing by President Gorbachev. The degree of Sino-Soviet *rapprochement* the visit signalled, together with the announced withdrawals and reductions of Soviet forces in Mongolia and in the Far East Military District, and the continuing negotiations on the disputed border issues may permit further reductions and more rapid progress with the reorganization of the PLA. Some redeployment from the border areas may also be possible.

Nuclear Forces

The 60 CSS-1 (DF-2) MRBM of the Strategic Rocket Forces have been retired. The CSS-1 was first introduced in 1970; it had a range of 1,200 km and was assessed as carrying a 20-KT warhead. No replacement weapon has yet been noted. There have been no other developments in the nuclear field.

Conventional Forces

Information has allowed us to revise the organization of Chinese military districts (MD); there are now 28 MD (shown on the map on p. 147) reinstating the South Xinjiang MD and deleting the Sanxia MD (in Chengdu Region). We have also revised the number of Group Armies (GA), up by two, to 24 and their deployment by Military Region (MR). As forecast last year, helicopter groups have been formed in two GA.

The Chinese Navy continues to be slimmed down. The only new completions we can confirm are the commissioning of a fourth *Han*-class SSN and a new mine countermeasures vessel. The second *Xia*-class SSBN is still not operational. The 20 *Whiskey*-class submarines built some 30 years ago are no longer in service; we show them as in store, but like other elderly submarines they are unlikely to be made operational again.

We have no new information on Air Force aircraft holdings (but we have corrected last year's inadvertent error which showed the combat aircraft total at 6,000 instead of 5,000).

Defence Spending

Although growth continued at over 11% in real terms, it was uneven; inflation reached a new high of over 20%. Gross external debt also rose to $35 bn, about 10% of GDP. The government was forced to make urgent price reforms, to introduce subsidies as well as price ceilings on certain commodities.

After accepting years of manpower contraction, a significantly reduced defence budget and a much lower political profile, the military was brought back into prominence as a result of the civil disturbances of May and early June. The defence establishment had made up its reduced defence expenditures by large-scale arms exports (especially to Iran and other Middle Eastern states) in recent years. In the wake of the Peking confrontation it seems probable that its budget will once again increase.

CHINA

GNP	1987:	Y 1,117.90 bn	
		($300.34 bn)	
	1988:	Y 1,369.40 bn	
		($367.91 bn)	
Growth	1987:	10.3%	1988: 11.2%
Inflation	1987:	8.8%	1988: 20.7%
Debt	1987:	$31.0 bn	1988: $35.0 bn
Def exp	1987:	Y 20.98 bn ($5.64 bn)	
	1988:	Y 21.80 bn ($5.86 bn)	
Def bdgt	1989:	Y 24.55 bn ($6.60 bn)	
$1 = yuan	(1987/8/9): 3.7221		
Y = yuan			

Population: 1,104,872,000

	13–17	18–22	23–32
Men:	61,351,000	66,225,000	95,261,000
Women:	57,815,000	63,009,000	91,347,000

TOTAL ARMED FORCES:*
ACTIVE: some 3,030,000 (perhaps 1,350,000 conscripts – men and women aged 18–22), being reduced.
Terms of Service: selective conscription; Army, Marines 3 years; Navy, Air Force 4 years.
RESERVES: 1,200,000+ incl military and militia reserves. National Defence Reserve being formed on a province-wide basis.

STRATEGIC MISSILE FORCES:
OFFENSIVE (Strategic Rocket Units): (90,000).
MISSILES: org in 6 (perhaps 7) div with regt or bde and bn; org varies by msl type.
 ICBM: 8:
  2 CSS-4 (DF-5); mod tested with MIRV.
  6 CSS-3 (DF-4).
 IRBM: 60 CSS-2 (DF-3), some updated.
SUBMARINES: 1:
 SSBN: 1 *Xia* with 12 CSS-N-3 (J-1).
 (Note: Production of Chinese SSBN is continuing, but extremely slowly. A further 3 *Xia*-class are believed under construction.)
DEFENSIVE:
(a) Tracking stations: Xinjiang (covers central Asia) and Shanxi (northern border).
(b) Phased-array radar complex. Ballistic missile early warning.

ARMY: 2,300,000 (perhaps 1,075,000 conscripts), (reductions continue).
 7 Military Regions (MR), 28 Military Districts, 3 Garrison Comd.
 24 Integrated Group Armies (GA, equivalent to Western corps) comprising:
  80 inf div (some being mech 'all arms').
  10 armd div (normally 3 regt, 323 MBT).
  5–6 field and AD arty div.
  Some indep arty, AD regt.
  50 indep engr regt.
  Avn: 2 group hel.
 AB (manned by Air Force):
  1 corps of 3 div.
  1 indep div.
  Spt tps.
EQUIPMENT:
MBT: some 7,500–8,000: T-54, 6,000 Type-59, 200 T-69 (mod Type-59), some Type-79, Type-80 reported.
LIGHT TANKS: 1,200 Type-62, 800 Type-63 amph.
AIFV: YW-307/-309.
APC: 2,800 Type-531 C/-D/-E, YW-534, Type-85 (YW-531H), Type-55 (BTR-40), -56 (BTR-152), -63, Type-77-1/-2 (Sov BTR-50PK amph); Type-523, Type-551.
TOWED ARTY: 14,500:
 100mm: Type-59 (fd/ATK), Type-86;
 122mm: Type-54, Type-60, Type-83, D-30;
 130mm: Types-59/-59-1;
 152mm: Type-54, Type-66, Type-83.
SP ARTY: 122mm: Type-54-1 (Type-531 chassis), YW-302; 152mm: Type-83.
MRL: 3,800: 107mm: Types-63 towed /-81 SP (being replaced by 122mm);
 122mm: Type-81, Type-83; 130mm: Type-63, Type-70 SP, Type-82; 132mm: BM-13-16;
 140mm: BM-14-16; 273mm: Type-83; 284mm: Type-74 minelayer; 320mm: WS-1; 425mm: Type-762 mine clearance.
MORTARS: 82mm: Type-53, Type-W84, YW-304 SP; 120mm: Type-55, Type-W86, YW-381 SP; 160mm: Type-56.
SSM: M-9 (range 600 km); M-11 (range 120–150 km; under development – in service ε 1989/90).
ATGW: HJ-73 (*Sagger*-type), HJ-8 (*TOW/Milan*-type).
RCL: 75mm: Type-52, Type-56, 82mm: Type-65.
RL: 90mm: Type-51.
ATK GUNS: 57mm: Type-55; 76mm: Type-54; 100mm: Type-73, Type-86.

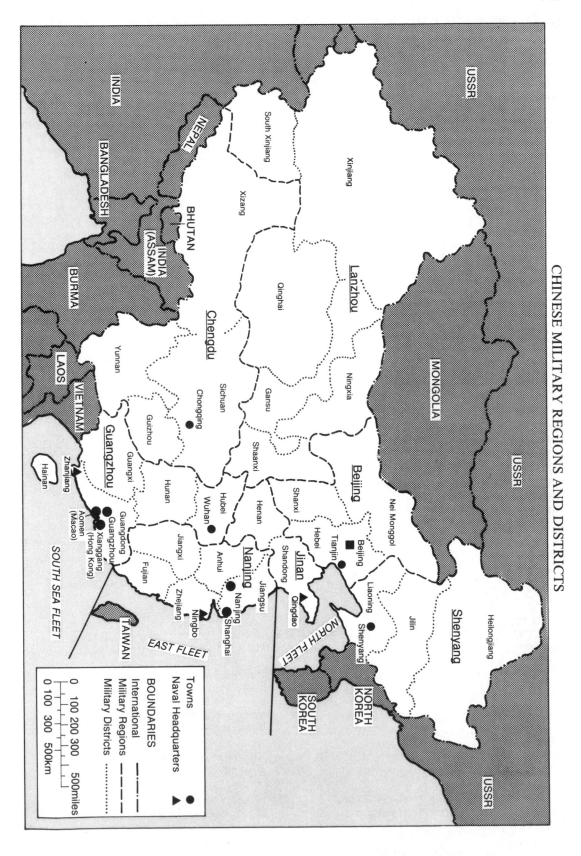

CHINESE MILITARY REGIONS AND DISTRICTS

AD: GUNS: 15,000: incl 23mm: (ZSU-23 type); 37mm: Types-55/-65/-74, -63 twin SP; 57mm: Types-59, -80 SP; 85mm: Type-56; 100mm: Type-59.

SAM: HN-5, HN-5A/-C (SA-7 type); HQ-61 twin SP.

HELICOPTERS: Some hel transferred from Air Force. Details not yet known.

RESERVES: (undergoing radical reorganization on a provincial basis) 30+ inf div, cbt spt div.

DEPLOYMENT:

North-East: Shenyang MR (Heilongjiang, Jilin, Liaoning MD): 5 GA, 2 msl, 4 armd, 16 inf div;†

North: Beijing MR (Beijing, Tianjin Garrison Comds; Nei Monggol, Hebei, Shanxi MD): 6 GA, 1 msl, 3 armd, 17 inf; 1 AB (Air Force div);

West: Lanzhou MR (incl Ningxia, Shaanxi, Gansu, Qinghai, Xinjiang, South Xinjiang MD): 2 GA, 2 msl, 1 armd, 9 inf div;†

South-West: Chengdu MR (incl Sichuan, Guizhou, Yunnan, Xizang MD): 2 GA, 1 msl, 10 inf div;†

South: Guangzhou MR (Hubei, Hunan, Guangdong, Guangxi, Hainan): 2 GA, ε 10 inf div;†

Centre: Jinan MR (Shandong, Henan, MD): 4 GA, 1 armd, 7 inf, 3 AB (Air Force) div;

East: Nanjing MR (Shanghai Garrison Comd; Jiangsu, Zhejiang, Fujian, Jiangxi, Anhui MD): 3 GA, 1 armd, 11 inf div.

NAVY: 260,000 incl Coast Defence (27,000), Marines (6,000) and Naval Air (25,000) (some 35,000 conscripts);

SUBMARINES: 93:

STRATEGIC SUBMARINES: 1 SSBN: (see p. 146).

TACTICAL SUBMARINES: 92

SSN: 4 *Han* with 533mm TT.

SSG: 1 modified *Romeo* (Type ES5G), with 6 C-801 (YJ-6, *Exocet* derivative) SSM; plus 533mm TT.

SS: 87:
3 *Improved Ming* (Type ES5E) with 533mm TT.
84 *Romeo* (Type ES3B) with 533mm TT.
(Note: probably only about half the *Romeo*-class op plus 20 *Whiskey* in store.)

OTHER ROLES: 1 *Golf* (SLBM trials)

PRINCIPAL SURFACE COMBATANTS: 56:

DESTROYERS: 19:
1 modified *Luda* (Type EF-4) with 1 × 3 CSS-N-2 *Hai Ying-2* (HY-2 *Styx* derivative) SSM, 1 × 2 130mm guns, 1 Z-9A (Fr *Dauphin*) hel (OTHT), 2 × 3 ASTT.
16 *Luda* (Type-051) (ASUW) with 2 × 3 HY-2 SSM, 2 × 2 130mm guns; plus 2 × 12 ASW RL
2 *Anshan* (Sov *Gordy*) with 2 × SSM, 2 × 2 130mm guns.

FRIGATES: 37:
26 *Jianghu*; 4 variants:
About 13 Type I, with 4 × 5 ASW RL, plus 2 × 2 HY-2 SSM, 2 × 100mm guns.

About 9 Type II, with 2 × 5 ASW RL, plus 2 × 2 HY-2, 2 × 2 100mm guns.
About 2 Type III, with 2 × 3 ASTT, plus 8 × C-801 SSM, 2 × 2 100mm guns.
About 2 Type IV, with 1 Z-9A hel, 2 × 5 ASW RL, 2 × HY-2 SSM, 1 × 100mm gun.
2 *Jiangdong* with 2 × 5 ASW RL, 2 × 2 100mm guns.
5 *Jiangnan* with 2 × 5 ASW RL, 3 × 100mm guns.
4 *Chengdu* with 1 × 2 HY-2 SSM, 3 × 100mm guns.

PATROL AND COASTAL COMBATANTS: About 915:

MISSILE CRAFT: 215:
125 *Huangfeng/Hola* (Sov *Osa*-type) with 4 × HY-2 or 8 × C-801 SSM.
90 *Hegu/Hema* (*Komar*-Type) with 2 × HY-2 or 4 × C-801 SSM.

TORPEDO CRAFT: About 160:
100 *Huchuan*, 60 P-6, all 〈 with 2 × 533mm TT.

PATROL: About 540:
COASTAL: 110:
10 *Hairui* with 3 × 5 ASW RL
90 *Hainan* with 4 × ASW RL.
10 Sov *Kronshtadt* with 2 × ASW RL.
INSHORE: 380:
290 *Shanghai* PFI, about 90〈.
RIVERINE: about 50〈.

(Note: some minor combatants are reportedly being assigned to para-military forces – People's Armed Police, border guards and the militia – or into store. Continuing reductions in manpower means craft totals may be high).

MINE WARFARE: 56:

MINELAYERS: None dedicated, but *Luda, Anshan, Jiangnan* and *Chengdu* class DD/FF, *Hainan, Kronshtadt* and *Shanghai* PC and T-43 MSO have minelaying capability.

MCM: 56:
35 Sov T-43 MSO.
1 new construction MSI Hull No 4422.
20 *Fushun* MSI; plus about 60 unmanned drone MSI〈.

AMPHIBIOUS: 58:
3 *Yukan* LST, capacity about 200 tps, 10 tk.
13 *Shan* (US LST-1) LST, capacity about 150 tps, 16 tk.
30 *Yuliang*, 1 *Yuling*, 1 *Yudao* LSM, capacity about 100 tps, 3 tk.
10 *Hua* (US LSM-1), capacity 50 tps, 4 tk.
Plus about 400 craft: 320 LCU, 40 LCP, 10 LCT and some hovercraft.

SUPPORT AND MISCELLANEOUS: 118:
3 *Fuqing* AO, 25 AOT, 1 AFS, 8 submarine spt, 2 repair, 6 *Qiong Sha* tp tpt, 11 tpt, 35 survey/research/experimental, 3 icebreakers, 23 ocean tugs, 1 trg.

COASTAL REGIONAL DEFENCE FORCES: (27,000).

ε 35 indep arty and SSM regt deployed in 25 coastal defence regions to protect naval bases, offshore islands and other vulnerable points.

GUNS: 85mm, 100mm, 130mm.
SSM: CSS-C-2 (*Hai Ying 2* variant, *'Silkworm'*).

MARINES: (Naval Infantry): (some 6,000).
1 bde.
Special recce units.
RESERVES: On mob to total 8 div (24 inf, 8 tk, 8 arty regt), 2 indep tk regt.
(3 Army div also have an amph role.)
EQUIPMENT:
MBT: T-59.
LIGHT TANKS: T-60/-63, PT-76.
APC: Type-531, LVT; some Type-77.
ARTY: how: 122mm: Type-54 (incl -54-1 SP).
MRL: Type-63.

NAVAL AIR FORCE: (25,000);
894 shore-based cbt ac, 55 armed hel.
Org in 3 bbr, 6 ftr div, incl:
BOMBERS: some 50 H-6, some H-6D reported with C-601 anti-ship ALCM.
About 130 H-5 torpedo-carrying lt bbr.
FGA: some 100 Q-5.
FIGHTER: some 600, incl J-5/-6/-7.
RECCE: H-5.
MR/ASW: 10 ex-Sov Be-6 *Madge*, 4 PS-5 (Y-8 mod).
HELICOPTERS: 50 Z-5, 12 SA-321 ASW, 6 Z-9.
MISCELLANEOUS: some 60 lt tpt ac; JJ-5/-6 trg ac.
ALCM: FL-1/C-601.
Naval fighters are integrated into the national AD system.

DEPLOYMENT AND BASES:
NORTH SEA FLEET: Coastal defence from Korean border (Yalu River) to south of Lianyungang (approx 35°10′N); equates to Shenyang, Beijing and Jinan Military Regions; and to seaward:
BASES: Qingdao (HQ), Dalian (Luda), Huludao, Weihai, Chengshan.
9 Coastal defence districts.
FORCES: 2 submarine, 3 escort, 1 mine warfare, 1 amph sqn; plus Bohai Gulf trg flotillas. About 325 patrol and coastal combatants.
EAST SEA FLEET: Coastal defence from south of Lianyungang to Dongshan (35°10′N to 23°30′N approx); equates to Nanjing Military Region, and to seaward:
BASES: Shanghai (HQ), Wusong, Dinghai, Hangzhou.
7 coastal defence districts.
FORCES: 2 submarine, 2 escort, 1 mine warfare, 1 amph sqn. About 270 patrol and coastal combatants. Marines: 1 cadre div.
Coastal Defence Regional Forces: Nanjing Coastal District.

SOUTH SEA FLEET: Coastal defence from Dongshan (approx 23°30′N) to Vietnam border; equates to Guangzhou Military Region, and to seaward (including Paracel and Spratly Islands).
BASES: Zhanjiang (HQ), Shantou, Guangzhou, Haikou, Yulin, Beihai. Huangpu; plus outposts on Paracel and Spratly Is.
9 Coastal Defence districts.
FORCES: 2 submarine, 2 escort, 1 mine warfare, 1 amph sqn. About 320 patrol and coastal combatants. Marines: 1 bde.

AIR FORCE: 470,000, incl strategic forces and 220,000 AD personnel (160,000 conscripts); some 5,000 cbt ac, few armed hel.
7 Military Air Regions, HQ Beijing.
Combat elm org in armies of varying numbers of air div (each with 3 regt of 3 sqn of 3 flt of 4–5 ac, 1 maint unit, some tpt and trg ac).
Tpt ac in regt only.
BOMBERS:
  MEDIUM: 120 H-6 (some may be nuclear-capable). Some carry C-601 ASM; some others to be converted to tkr.
  LIGHT: Some 250-300 H-5 (some with C-801 ASM).
FGA: 500 Q-5.
FIGHTER: ε 4,000, incl 400 J-5, some 60 regt with about 3,000 J-6/B/D/E, 300 J-7, 200 J-8.
RECCE: ε 150 JZ-5, 100 JZ-6, 40 HZ-5 ac.
TRANSPORT: some 420, incl 18 BAe *Trident* 1E/2E, 30 Il-14, 10 Il-18, 50 Li-2, 300 Y-5, 20 Y-7, 25 Y-8, Y-11, Y-12.
HELICOPTERS: 400: incl 6 AS-332, 4 Bell 214, 30 Mi-8, 24 S-70, 300 Z-5, Z-6, 10 Z-9. 8 SA-342 (with HOT) on trial.
TRAINERS: (some OCU) incl CJ-5/-6 (mod CJ-5), J-2, JJ-2, JJ-4/-5/-6, HJ-5.
MISSILES:
  AAM: PL-2/-2A, PL-5B *Atoll*-type, PL-7.
  ASM (anti-ship): C-601 subsonic ALCM (perhaps HY-2 SSM derivative); C-801 surface skimmer.
AD ARTY:
16 div: 16,000 35mm, 57mm, 85mm and 100mm guns;
28 indep AD regts (100 SAM units with HQ-2/-2B, -2J (CSA-1), -61 SAM).

PARA-MILITARY: some 12,000,000,
Ministry of Public Security: People's Armed Police: (1,830,000).
29 div, 1,029 bn border/mtn/internal defence.

---

* The term 'People's Liberation Army' comprises all services.

(2) OTHER ASIAN AND AUSTRALASIAN COUNTRIES

Military Developments

The Soviet withdrawal from **Afghanistan** has been reported at p. 30. As it withdrew the Soviet Army handed over a good deal of its equipment stocks to the Afghan Army and has continued to supply arms and ammunition since then. Few details of the types and quantities involved are available, however, although *Scud* B SSM and large stocks of missiles were included and have been used against the *Mujaheddin* guerrillas. FGA aircraft (including MiG-23 and Su-7B) and armed helicopters are also known to have been supplied. The opposition factions based in Peshawar have continued to be supplied with US armaments channelled through Pakistan. Since the Soviet withdrawal the *Mujaheddin* campaign has not had the success forecast by some observers. The Kabul government has, if anything, strengthened its position and has not yet lost any major town, despite major *Mujaheddin* efforts, particularly at Jalalabad. The *Mujaheddin* are now suffering the traditional fate of guerrilla movements forced to engage in conventional set-piece warfare and there are already signs of serious dissension between some of the main groups and between the Peshawar-based group of seven and those based in Iran.

Soviet forces are also withdrawing from **Mongolia** where only one motor rifle division will remain by the end of 1990. Mongolia is to reduce the strength of its armed forces by 13,000 men and to cut defence spending in 1990 by 10%.

Despite improved political relations between **India** and **Pakistan**, both countries continue to invest heavily in their armed forces. Prime Minister Gandhi has visited Pakistan twice; on the first occasion in December 1988 he and Prime Minister Bhutto initialled an agreement pledging that neither side would attack the other's nuclear facilities. The two countries have clashed, however, on several occasions during the year in the disputed Siachen Glacier region but, after a meeting of defence ministers, a cease-fire has been agreed and talks between senior military officers are under way to resolve the long-standing border dispute. India has continued its missile development programme: both the *Privthi* 250-km range SSM and *Agni* 2,000-km range IRBM have been successfully tested. The *Trishul* SAM has been tested and is expected in service within two years. Pakistan has also tested SSM and SAM. The *Haft*-I SSM has a range of 80 km and is probably in service, while *Haft*-II with a range of some 300 km is under development. The *Anza* 5,000-m range SAM has been tested and displayed on parade; it may now be in service. Both countries are expanding their defence industries; for example, India plans to manufacture 1,500 *Arjun* MBT between the early 1990s and the year 2000, while Pakistan plans to produce an improved version of the Chinese T-69 tank.

During the year both countries have brought new equipments into service. The growth of the Indian Navy continues. The year saw the completion of a number of separate purchases of Soviet vessels. The last three of the six *Sindhughosh* (*Kilo*)-class SS joined the fleet as did the last three *Veer* (*Tarantul*)-class corvettes and three *Pondicherry* (*Natya*) off-shore minesweepers. In the home yards the first Indian-built submarine, a *Shishumar* (FRG T-209/1500) class SS is expected to commence trials at the end of the year, which should also see the completion of the *Vikrant* carrier's conversion to operate only V/STOL aircraft. The Pakistani Navy, too, has enjoyed a dramatic increase in size during the year. The acquisition, by purchase and/or lease of two *Shamsher* (UK *Leander*), four *Khyber* (US *Brooke*) and four *Saif* (US *Garcia*) frigates has more than doubled the combat tonnage of the fleet. In addition, the destroyer *Babur* has completed a conversion refit enabling her to embark four *Sea King* ASW helicopters. Both Indian and Pakistani Air Forces have increased their combat strength. India has added over 100 aircraft to the inventory including *Mirage 2000* fighters and a maritime attack squadron with eight *Jaguar* armed with *Sea Eagle*. Indian Army helicopter holdings have increased by some 80 *Chetak* (SA-319) and 40 *Cheetah* (SA-315). Pakistani Air Force acquisitions include a further 90 Chinese Q-5 FGA and some 20 J-6 and 20 J-7 fighter aircraft. The Pakistan Army has added more 155mm M-109A2 SP guns and some 100 Chinese Type-59 tanks to its holding.

Despite continuing violence in **Sri Lanka** instigated both by the *Janatha Vimukthi Peramuna* (JVP) and the Tamil separatist movements, President Premadasa has campaigned actively to achieve the withdrawal of the Indian Peace Keeping Force (IPKF). The force was reduced by some 8,000 in May 1989 but since then India has adamantly refused to be rushed into further reductions – until the eleventh hour – when at the end of July a token battalion of 600 was withdrawn. India also intervened to forestall an attempted coup launched by mercenaries against the government of The Maldives. The Indian Army despatched airborne forces, which landed within 24 hours of the alert being given. Some 1,500 men were deployed and the coup was put down within 12 hours. About 150 Indian troops remain on the islands.

There has been growing co-operation between **Indonesia**, **Malaysia** and **Singapore** in defence matters. Singapore and Indonesia signed a Memorandum of Understanding in February 1989 which included arrangements for Singaporean armed forces to train in Indonesia. Malaysia and Singapore have also reached agreement on joint army training and the use of each other's training facilities; arrangements for joint air force training were already in effect. Meanwhile, **New Zealand** has withdrawn its infantry battalion from Singapore, leaving only a small support unit. We have revised our holdings of Indonesian Naval Patrol and Coastal Combatants: last year we listed two *Andou* FRG Lürssen torpedo craft; there is only one torpedo craft – the *Singa* – and there are a total of seven *Andou* coastal patrol craft which have been delivered over the last three years. It has been confirmed that the Navy is to acquire a further two ex-Netherlands *Van Speijk* frigates, the first to be delivered in late 1989. The delivery of six *Wasp* HAS-1 helicopters to the Malaysian Navy has been completed. Malaysia has concluded a major arms deal with the United Kingdom said to total £1 bn, to be financed mainly through counter trade. Few details are available but it has been speculated that arms to be supplied will include both ground attack and air defence *Tornado*, *Rapier* SAM and possibly a refurbished submarine. The Singaporean Navy has commissioned its first FRG-designed, Lürssen 62m corvette armed with *Harpoon* SSM and ASTT. The first eight F-16 aircraft have been delivered but are not yet operational.

The **Vietnamese** Army has continued its withdrawal from both Laos, where some 10–15,000 (mainly construction) troops remain, and Cambodia. Vietnam is committed to a complete withdrawal from Cambodia by 27 September 1989, but at 1 June still had some 60–65,000 troops there. A month-long international conference on the Cambodian situation began as we went to press.

In **Thailand** the army has introduced the Corps HQ to improve operational command following the poorly executed operations along the Laotian border in 1987–8. There are Corps HQ in the Central and North East Regions. The first of three divisions has been converted to a new mechanized organization. Equipment acquisitions include some 300 Chinese Type-88 and 100 Type-63 APC, while holdings of Chinese Type-69 tanks have doubled to 60. Some Chinese 130mm Type-82 MRL may also have been delivered.

There has been only minimal progress towards improved relations between the two Koreas. A proposed prime ministerial meeting foundered over the continuance of the annual major US-Korean military exercise 'Team Spirit'. The **North Korean** Navy has taken into service two additional Chinese Type-031 submarines, while the Air Force inventory has increased by some 34 MiG-29 fighters. We have reassessed our listing of army formations and now show 31 (rather than 26) active infantry divisions and 26 reserve infantry divisions (rather than 2 divisions and 18 independent brigades). The main changes in **South Korean** forces are the start of the replacement of F-5 FGA aircraft by smaller numbers of F-16, Air Force holdings of F-16 have doubled to 48 aircraft in the last twelve months.

The **Japanese** Self-Defense Forces have continued to expand their armoury. The Maritime Self-Defense Force has commissioned a tenth *Yuushio*-class submarine, three more *Asagiri*-class frigates and two *Hatsushima*-class mine countermeasure vessels. The first of six improved *Yubari*-class frigates was launched in December 1988 and the second *Towada*-class tanker (AO) in March 1989. Fabrication of the first *Aegis*-equipped guided missile destroyer is expected to start during 1989. We have recategorized a number of Japanese ship classes as frigates to reflect their primarily ASW role. The Naval Air Arm has withdrawn the PS-1 maritime reconnaissance aircraft from service while increasing its holding of P-3C, and has taken delivery of the first two (of ten) S-80 MCM helicopters.

The first of two indigenously-built *Adelaide*-class FFG was finally launched for the **Australian** Navy in May 1989, over two years behind schedule, and is not now due to complete before 1991. To date no decision has been reached on the design for the new ANZAC frigate. The Australian Air Force has acquired a further 15 F-18 fighter/FGA aircraft and has formed a squadron, in the joint training/attack role with 16 M3-326H. There have been no developments in the New Zealand Armed Forces other than the withdrawal of the infantry battalion from Singapore.

Defence Spending

In general, defence expenditures have continued to increase in real terms. In **Japan** increased commitments to play a wider security role and decisions on major acquisition programmes have led to major increases in defence budgets which rose by some 4.2% and 4.8%, in real terms, in fiscal years 1989 and 1990 but are unlikely to excede 1% of GDP. If NATO defence budget definitions are applied, Japan has been the second largest defence spender amongst the industrialized countries.

Both **South Korea** and **Taiwan** have increased their defence spending, but, because of their fast rate of economic growth, these increases represent a smaller percentage of national resources. **North Korea**, whose economy has not expanded, also increased defence spending. Both **Sri Lanka** and **The Philippines** have internal security problems which required additional defence expenditure.

India's defence budget decreased in real terms in 1989 but the official figure excluded the cost of operations in Sri Lanka, The Maldives and on the Siachen Glacier, as well as much of the R&D programme which is largely funded by the Department of Science and Technology. The Indian Space Research Organisation, which carries out work of a defence nature, is not funded by the Defence Ministry, nor is a significant portion of foreign arms procurement which is financed by special allocations from the Finance Ministry. **Pakistan's** defence expenditure rose some 5% in real terms in FY 1989/90, assisted by a generous US FMA allocation which is in some jeopardy as a result of Congressional concerns over Pakistan's nuclear aspirations.

There is little economic data available for either Afghanistan or the Indochina region, where **Vietnam** is in acute economic difficulties but should be able to make savings in defence spending once the withdrawal from Cambodia is completed (although the reabsorption of substantial numbers of demobilized servicemen into the domestic economy may itself cause problems).

Finally **Australia**, **Malaysia** and **Thailand** have announced ambitious modernization programmes for their armed forces which have been reflected in increased defence allocations.

AFGHANISTAN

GDP   1986/7: Afs 198.31 bn ($3.92 bn)
           1987/8ε: Afs 187.22 bn ($3.70 bn)
Growth   1986/7: 3.3%   1987/8: 2.3%
Inflation 1986:   20.0%
Debt   1986ε: +$30 bn
Def bdgt* 1985: Afs 14.50 bn ($286.56 m)
$1 = Afs (1986/7/8): 50.60
Afs = afghanis

Population: ε 16,362,000

	13–17	18–22	23–32
Men:	921,000	680,000	1,060,000
Women:	831,000	731,000	1,130,000

TOTAL ARMED FORCES:
ACTIVE: 55,000.
  Terms of service: Males 15–55: volunteers 2 years, conscription 3 years+, non-combatants 4–5 years.
RESERVES: No formal force identified; call-up from ex-servicemen, Youth League and tribesmen from age 20 to age 40.

ARMY: 50,000 (mostly conscripts).†
4 corps HQ.
3 armd div
14 inf div } (understrength bde).
1 Special Guard div (6 bde incl presidential guard, cdo units).
1 mtn div (2 mtn regt).
1 mech inf div/bde.
2 cdo bde.
1 arty bde.
1 AD arty bde.
EQUIPMENT:
MBT: 620: 50 T-34, 400 T-54/-55, 170 T-62.
LIGHT TANKS: 60 PT-76.
AIFV: 250 BMP-1/-2.
APC: 850 BTR-40/-50/-60/-70/-80/-152.
TOWED ARTY: 1,000+: 100mm: M-1944; 122mm: M-30, D-30; 130mm: M-46; 152mm: D-1.
MRL: 122mm: BM-21; 132mm: 50 BM-13-16. 220mm: BM-27 reported.
MORTARS: 1,000+: 82mm: M-37; 107mm; 120mm: 100 M-43; 160mm: M-43.
SSM: 2+ *Scud* launchers.
RCL: 73mm: SPG-9; 82mm: B-10.
ATK GUNS: 76mm; 100mm.
AD GUNS: 600+ 14.5mm; 23mm: 20 ZSU-23-4 SP; 37mm, 57mm, 85mm and 100mm towed.

AIR FORCE: 5,000 (incl AD comd);
193 cbt ac, 74 armed hel.†
FGA: 10 sqn (3 regt):
3 with 40 MiG-17;
1 with 15 MiG-23;
4 with 60 Su-7B;
2 with 30 Su-22.
FIGHTER:
1 regt with 30 MiG-21F.
ATTACK HELICOPTERS: 8 sqn with 25 Mi-8, 35 Mi-17, 14 Mi-25.
TRANSPORT:
  AIRCRAFT:
    1 VIP sqn with 2 Il-18D, 1 An-24;
    2 sqn with 10 An-2, 12 An-12, 40 An-26, 12 Il-14.
  HELICOPTERS: 12 Mi-4.
TRAINING: 18 L-29, 6 MiG-15UTI, 20 MiG-19, 18 MiG-21, Yak-11, Yak-18.
AD: 1 div:
2 SAM bde (each 3 bn) with 115 SA-2, 110 SA-3;
1 AD arty bde (2 bn) with 37mm, 85mm, 100mm guns;
1 radar bde (3 bn).

PARA-MILITARY:
BORDER GUARD (under Army): some 7,000; 7 'bde'.

WAD (KHAD) (Ministry of State Security): 70,000; some 27,000 in cbt units.
REGIONAL MILITIAS: 100,000+. incl Defence of the Revolution (GPS), Village militia, Pioneers, Afghan Communist Party Guards, Khalqi Youth, tribal bde (Ministry of Tribes and Nationalities), National Fatherland Front.

SARANDOY (Ministry of Interior): ε 30,000.

OPPOSITION:‡
Afghan resistance is a broad national movement. The military elements, 'mujahedin' fighters, comprise numerous groups affiliated to either one of the seven parties of the Peshawar-based Resistance Alliance or one of the predominantly Shia groups based in Iran. It is not possible to give accurate strengths; however of the Peshawar groups some 40,000 are reported to be active, supported by a further 120,000.
Peshawar groups, leaders names in parentheses:-

TRADITIONALIST MODERATE:
NATIONAL LIBERATION FRONT (*Jabhāt-Nijāt-Millī*): Sibghatullah Modjaddi: ε35,000.
NATIONAL ISLAMIC FRONT (*Mahaz-Millin Islami*): Sayyed Amhad Gailani: ε 20,000.
ISLAMIC REVOLUTIONARY MOVEMENT (*Harakāt-Inqilāb-Islāmi*): Mohammed Nabi Mohammed: ε 20,000.

ISLAMIC FUNDAMENTALIST:
ISLAMIC PARTY (*Hizbi-Islāmi-Khālis*): Yūnis Khālis: ε 10,000.
ISLAMIC PARTY (*Hizbi-Islāmi-Gulbaddin*): Gulbaddin Hekmatyar: ε 35,000.
ISLAMIC UNION (*Ittihād-Islāmi*): Abdul Rasul Sayyaf: ε 15,000.
ISLAMIC SOCIETY (*Jamiāt Islāmi*): Burhanuddin Rabāni: ε 20,000.

IRAN-BASED:
SAZMAVE NASR (50,000).
HARAKAT-E-ISLAMI (20,000).
PASDARAV-E-JEHAD (8,000).
HEZBOLLAH (4,000).
NEHZAT (4,000).
SHOORA-E-ITTEFAQ (30,000+).
EQUIPMENT: (predominantly captured): T-34, T-55 MBT; BMP MICV, BTR-40/-60 APC; 76mm guns, 122mm D-30 how; 107mm, 122mm MRL; 82mm M-41, 120mm mor; RPG-7 RL; 12.7mm, 14.5mm, 20mm AA guns incl 40 GAI-BOI; *Blowpipe, Stinger*, SA-7 SAM.

* No details of Soviet military aid known; but economic assistance from CMEA officially est at $223 m in 1988.
† Actual strength suspect. Divisions reported to average 2,500 (about quarter strength). Desertion is common.

‡ US, Western and friendly Islamic states' assistance to Afghan rebels ε $500 m in 1986.

AUSTRALIA

GDP   1987/8: $A 307.08 bn ($223.89 bn)
            1988/9ε: $A 315.79 bn ($260.68 bn)
Growth   1986/7:   2.7%   1987/8:   4.2%
Inflation   1987:   8.3%   1988:   7.6%
Debt   1987: $US 71.8 bn 1988: $US 87.0 bn
Def bdgt   1987/8: $A 7.41 bn ($5.40 bn)
            1988/9: $A 7.66 bn ($6.32 bn)
$US 1 = $A (1987/8):   1.3716 (1988/9):   1.2114
           (1989):   1.2258
$A = Australian dollars

Population: 16,510,000

	13–17	18–22	23–32
Men:	667,000	674,000	1,330,000
Women:	638,000	645,000	1,292,000

TOTAL ARMED FORCES:
ACTIVE: 69,600.
Terms of Service: voluntary.
RESERVES: 27,580 (increasing). Army: 25,000; Navy: 1,220; Air: 1,360.

ARMY: 31,300.
LAND COMD: 7 military districts
   Comd tps:
      1 AD regt +
      1 engr regt (construction)
      1 avn regt.
      1 Special Air Service regt (3 sqn)
   1 inf div
      1 mech bde (1 armd, 1 mech, 1 para inf bn)
      2 inf bde (each 2 inf bn)
      1 recce regt +
      1 APC regt
      4 arty regt (1 med, 3 fd (1 reserve))
      1 engr regt +
      1 avn regt (3 hel, 1 ac sqn).
      2 avn sqn forming as hel transferred from Air Force.
      (2 reserve inf bde see below)
RESERVES:
   2 div HQ, 7 bde HQ, 3 recce regt, 3 APC sqn, 17 inf bn, 1 cdo, 6 arty (1 med, 5 fd) regt, 3 fd arty bty, 4 engr (2 fd, 2 construction) regt, 3 regional surveillance units.
EQUIPMENT:
MBT: 103 *Leopard* 1A3, 42 *Centurion* (in store).
AIFV: 40 M-113 with 76mm gun.
APC: 725 M-113 (incl variants).
TOWED ARTY: 105mm: 142 M2A2/L5, 18 *Hamel*. 155mm: 35 M-198.

MORTARS: 81mm: 284.
ATGW: 10 *Milan*.
RCL: 84mm: 574 *Carl Gustav*; 106mm: 73 M-40.
SAM: 19 *Rapier*, 19 RBS-70.
AIRCRAFT: 14 PC-6 *Turbo-Porter*, 22 GAF N-22B *Missionmaster*.
HELICOPTERS: 14 S-70 (Army/Air Force crews), 47 OH-58 *Kiowa*, 47 Bell 206B.
MARINE: 16 LCM, 85 LARC-5 amph craft.

NAVY: 15,700 (incl Fleet Air Arm).
Maritime Command, Support Command, 6 Naval Area cmd.
BASES: Sydney, NSW. (Maritime Command HQ). Base for: 4 SS, 3 DDG, 6 FF, 2 patrol, LST, AOR, AD, AGT, 1 survey, 2 LCT. Cockburn Sound, WA. Base for: 2 SS, 3 FF, 3 patrol, 1 survey. Cairns, Qld: 5 patrol. 1 survey, 1 LCT Darwin, NT: 5 patrol.
SUBMARINES: 6 *Oxley* (mod UK *Oberon*) with Mk 48 HWT and *Harpoon* SSM.
PRINCIPAL SURFACE COMBATANTS: 12.
DESTROYERS: 3 *Perth* (US *Adams*) DDG (2 in refit) with 1 SM-1 MR SAM/*Harpoon* SSM launcher; plus 2 × *Ikara* SUGW, 2 × 3 ASTT (Mk 46 LWT), 2 × 127mm guns.
FRIGATES: 9:
   4 *Adelaide* (US *Perry*) FFG with 1 AS-350 *Squirrel* hel, 2 × 3 ASTT; plus 1 × SM-1 MR SAM/*Harpoon* SSM launcher.
   2 *Swan*, 3 *Paramatta* FF with 1 *Ikara* SUGW, 2 × 3 ASTT; plus 2 × 114mm guns.
PATROL AND COASTAL COMBATANTS: 22:
INSHORE: 22:
   15 *Fremantle* PFI, 5 *Attack* PCI (Reserve trg).
   2 *Banks* PCC (Reserve trg).
MINE WARFARE: 3:
   1 *Curlew* (UK '*Ton*') MHC.
   2 *Rushcutter* MHI.
AMPHIBIOUS: 1:
   1 *Tobruk* LST, capacity 14 tk, 350 tps, hel deck.
   Plus craft; 3 LCT, capacity 3 tk (3 more in store).
SUPPORT AND MISCELLANEOUS: 6:
   1 *Success* (mod Fr *Durance*) AO, 1 *Stalwart* AD/comd, 1 trg/log spt (ex-ferry), 1 AGOR, 2 AGHS.

FLEET AIR ARM: (1,200);
   no cbt ac, 10 armed hel.
ASW: 1 hel sqn with 7 *Sea King* Mk 50A (ASW), 3 S-70B-2.
UTILITY/SAR: 1 sqn with 6 AS-350B, 3 Bell 206B, 4 UH-1B, 3 *Wessex* 31B; 1 with 2 BAe-748.

AIR FORCE: 22,600;
   116 cbt ac, no armed hel.
FGA/RECCE: 2 sqn with 18 F-111C, 4 RF-111C.

FIGHTER/FGA: 3 sqn with 48 F-18 (45 -A, 3 -B).
ATTACK/TRAINING: 1 sqn with 16 MB-326H.
MR: 2 sqn with 20 P-3C.
OCU: 1 with 14 F-18B.
FAC: 1 flt with 4 CA-25 *Winjeel*.
TRANSPORT: 6 sqn:
  2 with 24 C-130 (12 -E, 12 -H);
  1 with 6 Boeing 707 (4 to be tanker ac);
  1 with 15 DHC-4;
  1 with 4 DHC-4, 16 UH-1H;
  1 VIP with 4 BAe (2 BAC-111, 2 BAe-748), 3
  Falcon 20.
HELICOPTERS:
  TRANSPORT: 1 med hel sqn with 8 CH-47 (plus 3
  in store). To be withdrawn in 1989.
  UTILITY: 1 hel sqn with 12 UH-1H (to be
  transferred to Army 1989–91).
TRAINING: 55 MB-326H (life-extended), 8
  BAe-748T2, 12 PC-9 (more being delivered), 48
  CT-4/4A ac. 18 *Squirrel* (AS-350) hel being
  transferred to Army.
AAM: *Sparrow* AIM-7M, *Sidewinder* AIM-9L, -9M.
ASM: AGM-84 *Harpoon*.
AD: *Jindalee* OTH radar: 1 experimental, 3 planned.
3 Control and Reporting units (1 mobile).

FORCES ABROAD:
MALAYSIA/SINGAPORE: 1 inf coy, det with PC-3 ac.
IRAN/IRAQ (UNIIMOG): 15.
NAMIBIA (UNTAG): 304 (engr).
PAPUA NEW GUINEA: 100; trg unit, 1 engr unit,
  30 advisers.
Advisers in Solomon Is., Vanuatu, Tonga, W.
Samoa and Kiribati.

PARA-MILITARY:
BUREAU OF CUSTOMS: 10 GAF N-22B
Searchmaster MR ac; 6 boats.

FOREIGN FORCES:
US: Air Force: 290; Navy: 450, joint facilities at
NW Cape, Pine Gap and Nurrungar.

BANGLADESH

GDP	1986/7: Tk 539.17 bn ($17.60 bn)	
	1987/8: Tk 594.10 bn ($19.01 bn)	
Growth	1986/7: 4.0%	1987/8: 2.6%
Inflation	1987: 9.6%	1988: 9.4%
Debt	1986: $7.9 bn	1987: $8.4 bn
Def bdgt	1985/6: Tk 5.06 bn ($169.17 m)	
	1986/7: Tk 6.64 bn ($216.75 m)	
FMA	1988: $0.3 m (US)	
$1 = Tk	(1985/6/7): 30.635	(1987/8): 31.246
Tk = Taka		

Population: 106,039,000

	13–17	18–22	23–32
Men:	6,762,000	6,520,000	8,502,000
Women:	6,707,000	5,966,000	8,039,000

TOTAL ARMED FORCES:
ACTIVE: 103,000.
Terms of service: voluntary.

ARMY: 90,000.
  6 inf div HQ.
  14 inf bde (some 26 bn).
  1 armd bde (2 armd regt).
  6 arty regt.
  6 engr bn.
EQUIPMENT:*
MBT: 20 Ch Type-59, 30 T-54/-55.
LIGHT TANKS: some 40 Ch Type-62.
TOWED ARTY: 105mm: 30 Model 56 pack,
  50 M-101; 122mm: 20 Ch Type-54.
MORTARS: 81mm; 82mm: Ch Type-53; 120mm: 50
  Ch Type-53.
RCL: 106mm: 30 M-40.
ATK GUNS: 57mm: 18 6-pdr; 76mm: 50 Ch Type-54.

NAVY:* 7,000.
BASES: Chittagong (HQ), Dhaka, Khulna, Kaptai.
FRIGATES: 3:
  1 *Umar Farooq* (UK *Salisbury*) with 1 × 3 *Squid*
  ASW mor, 1 × 2 114mm guns.
  2 *Abu Bakr* (UK *Leopard*) with 2 × 2 114mm guns.
PATROL AND COASTAL COMBATANTS: 37:
MISSILE CRAFT: 4 *Durbar* (Ch *Hegu*) PFM with 2 ×
  CSS-N-2 (HY-2) SSM.
TORPEDO CRAFT: 4 Ch Type-123K PFI⟨ with 2 ×
  450mm TT.
PATROL: COASTAL: 11:
  8 *Durjoy* (Ch *Hainan*) with 4 × 5 ASW RL.
  2 *Meghna* fishery protection,
  1 *Shahjalal*.
PATROL, INSHORE: 13:
  8 *Shahead Daulat* PFI (Ch *Shanghai*)
  2 *Karnaphuli*, 2 *Padma*, 1 *Bishkali* PCI.
RIVERINE: 5⟨.
SUPPORT AND MISCELLANEOUS: 4:
  1 coastal tanker, 1 repair, 1 ocean tug, 1 tpt/trg.

AIR FORCE:* 6,000;
  61 cbt ac, no armed hel.
FGA: 2 sqn with 25 J-6/JJ-6, 16 Q-5.
FIGHTER: 1 sqn with 16 MiG-21MF,
  2 MiG-21U.
TRANSPORT: 1 sqn with 1 An-24, 4 An-26, 2 DHC-3.
HELICOPTERS: 3 sqn with 2 Bell 206L, 13 -212,
  12 Mi-8.

TRAINING: 20 Ch CJ-6, 14 CM-170, 2 JJ-5, 4 MiG-15UTI.

FORCES ABROAD:
NAMIBIA (UNTAG): 25 observers.

PARA-MILITARY:
BANGLADESH RIFLES: 30,000 (border guard).
PRESIDENTIAL SECURITY FORCE:
ARMED POLICE: 5,000.
ANSARS (Security Guards): 20,000.

OPPOSITION:
SHANTI BAHINI (Peace Force), Chakma tribe Chittagong Hills, ε 5,000.

* Spares are short; some eqpt unserviceable.

BRUNEI

GDP   1985: $B 7.53 bn ($US 3.42 bn)
            1986: $B 6.98 bn ($US 3.21 bn)
Growth 1985: −6.2%   1986ε: −7.0%
Inflation 1985: 4.0%
Def bdgt 1986: $B 505.00 m ($US 232.42 m)
          1987ε: $B 410.00 m ($US 193.21 m)
$US 1 = $B (1985): 2.200   (1986): 2.173
           (1987): 2.106   (1988): 2.143
$B = Brunei dollars

Population: 272,000

	13–17	18–22	23–32
Men:	14,000	12,000	24,000
Women:	13,000	11,000	21,000

TOTAL ARMED FORCES: (all services form part of the Army):
ACTIVE: 4,200 incl 250 women.
Terms of service: voluntary.
RESERVES: Army: to be 900.

ARMY: 3,400.
2 inf bn.
1 armd recce sqn.
1 SAM bty: 2 tps with *Rapier*.
1 engr sqn.
EQUIPMENT:
LIGHT TANKS: 16 *Scorpion*.
APC: 24 Sankey AT-104.
MORTARS: 81mm.
SAM: 12 *Rapier* (with *Blindfire*).
RESERVES: 1 bn (forming).

NAVY: 500.
BASE: Muara.
PATROL AND COASTAL COMBATANTS: 6:
MISSILE CRAFT: 3 *Waspada* PFM with 2 × MM-38 *Exocet* SSM.
PATROL: 3 *Perwira* PFI⟨.
RIVERINE: Boats only.
AMPHIBIOUS: Craft only; 2 LCM⟨.

AIR FORCE: 300;
4 cbt ac, 7 armed hel.
COIN: 1 sqn with 7 Bo-105 armed hel.
HELICOPTERS: 1 sqn with 10 Bell 212, 1 -214 (SAR).
VIP tpt: 2 S-70 hel.
TRAINING: 4 SF-260W ac, 2 Bell 206B hel.

PARA-MILITARY:
GURKHA RESERVE UNIT: 900+.
ROYAL BRUNEI POLICE: 1,750, 2 PCI⟨, boats.

FOREIGN FORCES:
UK: some 900. (Army) 1 Gurkha inf bn, 1 hel flt.
SINGAPORE: some 500: trg school incl hel det (5 UH-1).

BURMA

GDP   1986/7: K 58.45 bn ($8.20 bn)
          1987/8ε: K 60.06 bn ($9.31 bn)
Growth 1986/7: 3.7%   1987/8ε: 0.2%
Inflation 1986:   9.2%   1987:   23.4%
Debt   1987: $4.5 bn 1988: $4.9 bn
Def bdgt 1987/8: K 1.90 bn ($291.60 m)
         1988/9: K 2.24 bn ($347.16 m)
FMA   1988: $0.26 m (US)
$1 = K   (1986/7): 7.127   (1987/8): 6.516
        (1988/9): 6.458
K = kyats

Population: 40,356,000

	13–17	18–22	23–32
Men:	2,368,000	2,145,000	3,702,000
Women:	2,336,000	2,124,000	3,674,000

TOTAL ARMED FORCES:
ACTIVE: 200,000.
Terms of service: voluntary.

ARMY: 182,000.
9 lt inf div (each 3 Tac op comd (TOC)
9 Regional Comd (8 with 3 TOC, 1 with 4 TOC)

28 TOC with 85 garrison inf bn.
Summary of cbt units:
  175 inf bn.
  2 armd bn.
  4 arty bn.
  1 AA arty bn.

EQUIPMENT:*
MBT: 26 *Comet.*
RECCE: 45 *Ferret.*
APC: 40 *Humber.*
TOWED ARTY: 76mm: 120 M-1948; 88mm: 50
  25-pdr; 105mm: 96 M-101; 140mm: 5.5-in.
MRL: 122mm: reported.
MORTARS: 120mm: 80.
RCL: 84mm: 500 *Carl Gustav*; 106mm: M40A1.
ATK GUNS: 60: 57mm: 6-pdr; 76.2mm: 17-pdr.
AD GUNS: 40mm: 10.

NAVY:* 9,000 incl 800 Naval Infantry.
BASES: Bassein, Mergui, Moulmein, Seikyi,
  Rangoon (Monkey Point), Sittwe.
PATROL AND COASTAL COMBATANTS: 39:
CORVETTES: 2:
  1 *Yan Taing Aung* (US PCE-827)
  1 *Yan Gui Aung* (US *Admirable* MSF).
PATROL: 37:
  COASTAL: 2 *Nawarat*
  INSHORE: 9 US PGM-401, 12 Yug Y-301, 9⟨.
  RIVERINE: 5⟨.
SUPPORT: 1 coastal tpt, 1 AGHS, 1 PC spt.

MARINES: (Naval Infantry): 800: 1 bn.

AIR FORCE: 9,000;
  26 cbt ac, no armed hel.*
COIN: 2 sqn: 12 PC-7, 4 PC-9.
TRANSPORT: 3 sqn: 5 DHC-3, 5 FH-227, 7 PC-6B.
LIAISON: 3 Cessna 180, 1 -550.
HELICOPTERS: 4 sqn: 17 Bell 205, 9 SA-316.
TRAINING: incl 10 SF-260 WB (COIN, trg), 6
  SF-260M, 9 T-37C; 10 KB-47G hel.

PARA-MILITARY: 73,000.
PEOPLE'S POLICE FORCE: 38,000;
PEOPLE'S MILITIA: 35,000.
FISHERY DEPT: ε 250: 12 patrol boats (3 *Indaw*
  (Dk *Osprey*)), 9 inshore⟨.

OPPOSITION:
Regional independence forces with loose and
  varying alliances. Only main groups listed.
BURMA COMMUNIST PARTY (BCP):
10,000 Active, 8–10,000 militia (mainly Shan State,
  South East Kachin State).
NATIONAL DEMOCRATIC FRONT (NDF):
Some 20,000: coalition of numerous ethnic gp,
  mainly in border areas incl Kachin (8,000), Shan
  and Karen (4,000) groups.

PRIVATE ARMIES (mainly narcotics linked)
Mong Tai Army (formerly Shan United Army)
  Chang Shee Fu 'Khun Sa' (narcotics warlord): 2,100.
  Kan Chit: 450. United Revolutionary Army: ε
  1,000; Kuomintang-linked. Loi Maw
  Rebels/Army: ε 3,000.

---

* Spares are short; most eqpt unserviceable.

CAMBODIA*

Population: 7,995,000

	13–17	18–22	23–32
Men:	390,000	472,000	769,000
Women:	389,000	457,000	743,000

TOTAL ARMED FORCES:
ACTIVE: some 99,300 incl provincial and
  district forces.
  Terms of service: conscription, 5 years; ages 18 to
    35. Militia serve 3 to 6 months with Regulars.

ARMY: some 42,500.
  5 Military Regions.
  6 inf div.
  3 indep inf regt.
  1 cav regt.
  4 tk bn.
  Some indep recce, arty, AD bn.
EQUIPMENT:
MBT: 80 T-54/-55, some Type 59.
LIGHT TANKS: 10 PT-76.
APC: some 150 BTR-40/-60/-152, M-113.
TOWED ARTY: some 350: 76mm: M-1942; 122mm:
  M-1938, D-30; 130mm: Type 59.
MRL: 107mm: Type-63; 132mm: BM-13-16;
  140mm: BM-14-16.
MORTARS: 82mm: M-37; 120mm: M-43; 160mm:
  M-160.
RCL: 82mm: B-10; 107mm: B-11.
AD GUNS: 14.5mm: ZPU 1/-2/-4; 37mm: M-1939;
  57mm: S-60.
SAM: SA-7.

NAVY: ε 1,000.
PATROL AND COASTAL COMBATANTS: 11:
  2 Sov *Turya* PHT with 4 × 533mm TT.
  4 Sov *Stenka* PFI, 5⟨.

AIR FORCE: ε 800.
15 cbt ac; 3 armed hel.
FIGHTER: 15 MiG-21.
ATTACK HELICOPTERS: 3 Mi-24.
TRANSPORT: 3 An-2, An-24.

HELICOPTERS: 6 Mi-8/-17.

PROVINCIAL FORCES: some 22,500.
Reports of at least 1 inf regt per province: with varying number of inf bn with lt wpn.

DISTRICT FORCES: some 32,500. Reports of
at least 1 inf bn per district: lt wpn only.

PARA-MILITARY: Some 50,000 Local Forces, org
at village level for local defence. ε 10–20 per village.

OPPOSITION:
COALITION GOVERNMENT OF DEMOCRATIC
KAMPUCHEA (CGDK):
KHMER ROUGE (National Army of Democratic Kampuchea) some 30,000 org in 20 'bde': perhaps further 15,000 spt and log.
KAMPUCHEAN PEOPLE'S NATIONAL LIBERATION ARMED FORCES (KPNLAF): some 10–12,000 org in ε 30 'bde'; ε 7 op sectors.
ARMEE NATIONALE SIHANOUKIENNE (ANS): perhaps 15–18,000 org in 7 'bde', 6 'regt', ε 5 op sectors.

EQUIPMENT: small arms, plus 12.7mm machine guns, 60mm, 82mm mor, RPG-7 RL, DK-75mm mor, RCL, SA-7 SAM reported.

FOREIGN FORCES:
VIETNAM: (Army) some 60–65,000. Complete withdrawal due September 1989.

* Data largely est. Little reliable evidence available.

FIJI

GDP	1986:	$F 1.49 bn ($US 1.32 bn)		
	1987	$F 1.46 bn ($US 1.19 bn)		
Growth	1986:	8.8%	1987:	−7.8%
Inflation	1987:	5.7%	1988:	11.8%
Debt	1986:	$US 450.0 m		
Def bdgt	1986:	$F 16.32 m ($US 14.42 m)		
	1987:	$F 16.87 m ($US 13.79 m)		
FMA	1988:	$0.05 m (US)		
$US 1 = $F	(1986):	1.132	(1987):	1.224
	(1988):	1.430		

$F = Fiji dollar

Population: 734,000

	13–17	18–22	23–32
Men:	39,900	38,100	66,400
Women:	38,300	36,900	65,700

TOTAL ARMED FORCES:
ACTIVE: 3,500.
Terms of service: voluntary.
RESERVES: some 5,000 (to age 45).

ARMY: 3,200.
4 inf bn.
1 engr coy.
EQUIPMENT:
MORTARS: 81mm: 12.
RESERVES: 2 inf bn.

NAVY: 300.
BASE: Suva.
PATROL AND COASTAL COMBATANTS: 5:
3 *Kikau* PCC (US *Redwing*), 1 with hel deck.
2 *Lautoka* PCI.
SUPPORT AND MISCELLANOUS: 2 survey⟨.

FORCES ABROAD: 1,100.
AFGHANISTAN (UNGOMAP): 4.
EGYPT (Sinai MFO): 400. 1 inf bn.
LEBANON (UNIFIL): 700; 1 inf bn.

INDIA

GDP	1987/8ε: Rs 3,292.42 bn ($253.88 bn)		
	1988/9ε: Rs 3,917.98 bn ($270.64 bn)		
Growth	1987/8ε: 2.0%	1988/9ε:	9.0%
Inflation	1987: 8.8%	1988:	10.0%
Debt	1986: $41.1 bn	1987:	$45.0 bn
Def bdgt	1988/9: Rs 130.00 bn ($8.98 bn)		
	1989/90: Rs 130.00 bn ($8.40 bn)		
Def exp	1988/9: Rs 132.00 bn ($9.12 bn)		
FMA	1988: $0.3 m (US)		
$1 = Rs	(1987/8): 12.968	(1988/9):	14.477

Rs = rupees

Population: 807,432,000

	13–17	18–22	23–32
Men:	46,162,000	41,847,000	64,480,000
Women:	43,239,000	38,123,000	59,715,000

TOTAL ARMED FORCES:
ACTIVE: 1,260,000.
Terms of service: voluntary.
RESERVES: (obligation to age 60) Army 300,000. Territorial Army (volunteers) 160,000. Air Force strength nk.

ARMY: 1,100,000.
HQ: 5 Regional Comd (= Fd Army), 10 Corps.

2 armd div (each 2/3 armed, 1 SP arty (2 SP fd, 1 med regt) bde).

1 mech div (each 3 mech (4/6 mech bn, 3 armd regt), 1 arty bde).

19 inf div (each 2–5 inf, 1 arty bde; some have armd regt).

11 mtn div (each 3–4 bde, 1 or more arty regt).

14 indep bde: 5 armd, 7 inf, 1 mtn, 1 AB/cdo.

3 indep arty bde.

6 AD bde.

4 engr bde.

These formations comprise:

53 tk regt (bn).

19 mech, 332 inf bn.

9 AB/cdo bn.

164 arty regt (bn): 1 hy, 5 MRL, 50 med (incl 11 SP), 69 fd (incl 3 SP), 39 mtn.

29 AD arty regt; perhaps 10 SAM gp (3–5 bty each).

7 sqn, 25 flt, Air Observation.

6 ATK/tpt, 4 liaison hel sqn.

EQUIPMENT:
MBT: 3,150 (ε 500 in store): some 800 T-55, 650 T-72/-M1, 1,700 *Vijayanta*.

LIGHT TANKS: 100 PT-76.

RECCE: BRDM-2.

AIFV: 700 BMP-1, some *Sarath* (BMP-2).

APC: 400 OT-62/-64, 50 BTR-60.

TOWED ARTY: some 3,860: 75mm/76mm: 900 75/24 mtn, 215 Yug M-48; 88mm: 1,000 25-pdr (retiring); 100mm: 185 M-1944; 105mm: some 800 (incl M-56 pack), some 30 IFG Mk II; 130mm: 550 M-46; 140mm: 150 5.5-in (retiring); 155mm: 50 FH-77B.

SP ARTY: 105mm: 80 *Abbot*; 130mm: 100 mod M-46

MRL: 122mm: 80 BM-21.

MORTARS: 81mm: L16A1; 82mm: M-43; 120mm: 1,000 M-43; 160mm: 200 M-43.

ATGW: SS-11-B1, *Milan*, AT-3 *Sagger*, AT-4 *Spigot*.

RCL: 106mm: 1,000+ M-40.

AD GUNS 2,750: 23mm: 140 ZU 23-2, 75 ZSU-23-4 SP; 40mm: 1,245 L40/60, 790 L40/70; 94mm: 500 3.7-in.

SAM: 26 SA-6, 620 SA-7, 20 SA-8A/-B, SA-9, 25 *Tigercat* launchers.

HELICOPTERS: 9 sqn with 180 *Chetak* (some with 4 AS-11), 4 with 100 *Cheetah*.

RESERVES:
Territorial Army: 30 inf bn.

DEPLOYMENT:
North – 1 Corps with 2 inf, 1 mtn div; 1 mtn, 1 indep inf, 1 indep arty bde. 1 Corps with 4 inf div; 2 indep armd, 1 indep inf, 2 indep arty bde.

West – 1 Corps with 1 armd, 1 mech div; 1 Corps with 2 inf div; 1 Corps with 3 inf div.

Central – 1 Corps with 1 armd, 2 inf div, plus 3 indep div (2 inf, 1 mtn).

East – 3 Corps each with 3 mtn div.

South – 1 Corps with 4 inf div.

NAVY: 47,000, incl 5,000 naval air force and 1,000 marines.
PRINCIPAL COMMANDS:
WESTERN COMD (HQ) Bombay:

BASES: Goa, Lakshadweep (Laccadive Is), Karwar (under construction).

EASTERN COMD (HQ) Visakhapatnam:

BASES: Calcutta, Port Blair (Andaman Is).

SOUTHERN COMMAND (trg); (HQ) Cochin.

NAVAL AIR: (HQ), Goa.

SUBMARINE: (HQ), Visakhapatnam.

SUBMARINES: 17:
SSGN: 1 *Chakra* (Sov *Charlie-I*) with SS-N-7 *Starbright* USGW; plus 533mm TT (presence of USGW not confirmed).

SS: 16:

6 *Sindhughosh* (Sov *Kilo*) with 533mm TT.

2 *Shishumar* (FRG T-209/1500) with 533mm TT.

8 *Kursura* (Sov *Foxtrot*) with 533mm TT.

PRINCIPAL SURFACE COMBATANTS: 28:
CARRIERS: 2:

1 *Viraat* (UK *Hermes*) (29,000t) CVV.

1 *Vikrant* (UK *Glory*) (19,800t) (in refit converting to CVV) both to operate:-
ac: 8 *Sea Harrier* attack.
hel: 8 *Sea King* ASW/ASUW (*Sea Eagle* ASM).

DESTROYERS: 5 *Rajput* (Sov *Kashin*) DDG with 2 × 2 SA-N-1 *Goa* SAM; plus 4 SS-N-2C *Styx* SSM, 5 × 533mm TT, 2 × ASW RL, 1 Ka-25 or 27 hel (ASW).

FRIGATES: 21:

3 *Godavari* FFH with 2 × *Sea King* hel, 2 × 3 ASTT; plus 4 × SS-N-2C *Styx* SSM.

6 *Nilgiri* (UK *Leander*) with 2 × 3 ASTT, 4 with 1 × 3 *Limbo* ASW mor, 1 *Chetak* hel, 2 with 1 *Sea King*, 1 × 2 ASW RL; plus 2 × 114mm guns.

1 *Talwar* (UK *Whitby*) with 1 × *Chetak* hel, 3 × *Styx* SSM.

8 *Kamorta* (Sov *Petya*) with 4 ASW RL, 3 × 533mm TT.

1 *Khukri* (ASUW) with 4 *Styx*, hel deck.

2 *Beas* (UK *Leopard*) (trg).

PATROL AND COASTAL COMBATANTS: 34:
CORVETTES: 8:

3 *Vijay Durg* (Sov *Nanuchka* II) with 4 × SS-N-2B *Styx*.

5 *Veer* (Sov *Tarantul*) with 4 × *Styx*.

MISSILE CRAFT: 13 *Vidyut* (Sov. *Osa*) with 4 × *Styx*.

PATROL, INSHORE: 13:

11 SDB Mk 2/3, 2 *Osa* PFI.

MINE WARFARE: 20:
MINELAYERS: None, but *Kamorta* FF and *Pondicherry* MSO have minelaying capability.

MINE COUNTERMEASURES: 20:

12 *Pondicherry* (Sov *Natya*) MSO.

2 *Bulsar* (UK 'Ham') MSI.

6 *Mahé* (Sov *Yevgenya*) MSI⟨.

AMPHIBIOUS: 10:

1 *Magar* LST, capacity 200 tps, 12 tk, 1 hel
.9 *Ghorpad* (Sov *Polnocny* C) LSM, capacity 140
tps, 6 tk.
Plus craft; 9 *Vasco da Gama* LCU.

SUPPORT AND MISCELLANEOUS: 18:
2 *Deepak* AO, 1 AOT, 1 *Amba* (Sov *Ugra*) sub spt,
1 tpt, 2 ocean tugs, 5 AGHS, 5 AGOR, 1 *Tir* trg.

NAVAL AIR FORCE: (5,000);
31 cbt ac, 53 armed hel.
ATTACK: 1 sqn with 8 *Sea Harrier* FRS Mk-51,
2 T-60 trg (more being delivered).
ASW: 1 ac sqn with 4 *Alizé* 1050 (land-based);
5 hel sqn with 10 *Chetak*, 5 Ka-25, 18 Ka-27, 20
Sea King Mk 42A/B.
MR: 2 sqn: 9 BN-2, 3 Il-38, 5 Tu-142M *Bear* F.
COMMUNICATIONS: 1 sqn with 6 BN-2 *Islander*,
Do-228.
SAR: 1 hel sqn with 6 *Sea King* Mk 42C.
TRAINING: 2 sqn: 6 HJT-16, 8 HPT-32 ac; 2 *Chetak*,
4 Hughes 300 hel.

MARINES: (ε 1,000);
1 regt (2nd forming).

AIR FORCE: 110,000;
836 cbt ac, 12 armed hel. 5 Air Comd.
BOMBERS: 1 lt bbr sqn with 10 *Canberra*.
FGA: 28 sqn:
4 with 60 MiG-23BN/UM;
7 with 105 MiG-21MF/U;
1 with 15 MiG-21PFMA;
5 with 70 *Jaguar* IS;
5 with 72 MiG-27;
5 with 80 *Ajeet*;
1 with 20 *Marut*.
FIGHTER: 22 sqn:
3 with 49 MiG-29UB;
3 with 52 *Mirage* 2000 (incl 45 -H, 7 -TH);
4 with 65 MiG-23MF/UM;
12 with 200 MiG-21/FL/bis/U.
Air Defence Ground Environment System.
MARITIME ATTACK: 8 *Jaguar* with *Sea Eagle*.
ATTACK HELICOPTERS: 12 Mi-25.
RECCE: 3 sqn:
1 with 8 *Canberra* PR-57;
1 with 6 MiG-25R, 2 MiG-25U;
1 with 4 HS-748.
MR/SURVEY: 2 *Gulfstream IV* SRA, 2 *Learjet* 29.
TRANSPORT:
AIRCRAFT: 12 sqn:
6 with 108 An-32 *Sutlej*;
2 with 30 An-12B;
1 with 10 DHC-3;
1 with 10 DHC-4;
1 with 16 BAe-748;
1 with 12 Il-76 *Gajraj*;

HELICOPTERS: 11 sqn with 80 Mi-8, 50 Mi-17, 10
Mi-26 (hy tpt).
VIP: 1 HQ sqn with 2 Boeing 737, 7 BAe-748.
LIAISON: flt and det: 16 BAe-748, C-47.
TRAINING: 24 BAe-748, 20 *Canberra* T-4/-13/-67,
120 HJT-16, 57 *Kiran* II, 20 HPT-32, 60 HT-2,
20 *Hunter* T-66, 5 *Jaguar* IB, 44 TS-11 ac; 20
Chetak hel.
AAM: AA-2 *Atoll*, AA-7 *Apex*, R-550 *Magic*, Matra
Super 530D.
ASM: AM-39 *Exocet*, AS-7 *Kerry*, AS-11B (ATGW),
AS-30, *Sea Eagle*.
SAM: 30 bn: 280 *Divina* V75SM/VK (SA-2), SA-3.

FORCES ABROAD:
MALDIVES: some 150.
NAMIBIA (UNTAG): 21 observers/HQ staff.
SRI LANKA: some 47,000; Army: 45,000: 4 inf div
HQ. Plus naval, air and Central Reserve Police Force.

PARA-MILITARY:
NATIONAL SECURITY GUARDS: 5,000:
anti-terrorism contingency deployment force.
Comprises elm of the Armed Forces, CRPF,
Border Guard.
CENTRAL RESERVE POLICE FORCE (CRPF):
90,000; Reserves: 250,000; 100 bn, internal
security duties and army first-line reserves.
BORDER SECURITY FORCE: 90,000; some 100 bn
(to add 44 bn by 1991), small arms, some lt arty,
tpt/liaison air spt.
ASSAM RIFLES: 40,000.
LADAKH SCOUTS: 5,000.
INDO-TIBETAN BORDER POLICE: 14,000.
SPECIAL FRONTIER FORCE: 8,000.
CENTRAL INDUSTRIAL SECURITY FORCE: 70,000.
DEFENCE SECURITY FORCE: 30,000.
RAILWAY PROTECTION FORCES: 70,000.
PROVINCIAL ARMED CONSTABULARY: 250,000.

COAST GUARD: 2,500;
FRIGATES: 1 *Kuthar* (UK Type 14).
PATROL CRAFT: 31:
6 *Vikram* PCO, 2 *Tara Bai* PCI, 8 *Rajhans* PFI, 7
Jija Bai PCI, 8⟨.
AVIATION: 3 air sqn with 11 Do-228, 2 Fokker F-27,
5 BN-2 *Islander* ac, 4 *Chetak* hel.

INDONESIA

GDP	1987/8: Rp 113,059.13 bn ($68.10 bn)	
	1988/9ε: Rp 126,739.28 bn ($74.27 bn)	
Growth	1987/8: 3.6%	1988/9: 4.1%
Inflation	1987: 9.3%	1988: 8.0%
Debt	1987: $43.2 bn	1988: $47.3 bn
Def exp	1986/7: Rp 2,318.0 bn ($1.64 bn)	

Def bdgt 1987/8: Rp 2,188.0 bn ($1.35 bn)
FMA   1988: $2.8 m (US)
$1 = Rp   (1986/7): 1,410.60 (1987/8): 1,660.25
          (1988/9): 1,706.52
Rp = rupiahs

Population: 176,379,000

	13–17	18–22	23–32
Men:	10,636,000	9,407,000	15,413,000
Women:	10,247,000	9,224,000	15,529,000

TOTAL ARMED FORCES:
ACTIVE: 285,000.

Terms of service: 2 years selective conscription authorized.

RESERVES: 800,000: Army (planned): cadre units; numbers, strengths unknown, obligation to age 45 for officers.

ARMY: 215,000.
Strategic Reserve (KOSTRAD).
　2 inf div HQ, 1 more forming.
　1 armd cav bde (–).
　3 inf bde (9 bn).
　3 AB bde (8 bn).
　2 fd arty regt (6 bn).
　1 AD arty regt (2 bn).
　2 engr bn
10 Military Area Comd (KODAM)
(Provincial (KOREM) and District (KORIM) comd)
　63 inf bn.
　8 cav bn.
　4 AB bn.
　8 fd arty bn.
　9 AD bn (6 med, 3 lt).
　6 engr bn.
　1 composite avn sqn, 1 hel sqn.
SF (KOPASSUS): 4 SF gp.

EQUIPMENT:
LIGHT TANKS: some 100 AMX-13, 41 PT-76.
RECCE: 56 *Saladin*, 58 *Ferret*.
APC: 200 AMX-VCI, 56 *Saracen*, 60 V-150 *Commando*, 80 BTR-40, 24 BTR-152.
TOWED ARTY: 76mm: M48; 105mm: 170 M-101.
SP ARTY: 105mm: 50 FV Mk 61.
MORTARS: 81mm: 500; 120mm: M-43.
RCL: 90mm: 480 M-67; 106mm: M-40.
AD GUNS 20mm: 20; 40mm: 90 M-1; 57mm: 200 S-60.
SAM: RBS-70, *Rapier*.
AVIATION:
　AIRCRAFT: 1 BN-2 *Islander*, 2C-47, 4 NC-212, 2 Cessna 185, 2 -207, 2 -310, 2 *Commander* 680, 2 O-1.
　HELICOPTERS: 16 Bell 205, 13 Bo-105, 28 NB-412, 20 Hughes 300C, 8 Soloy-Bell 47G (trg).
MARINE: LST: 1; **LCU:** 20 300t; 14 tpt.

NAVY: 43,000, incl 1,000 naval air and 12,000 marines.
PRINCIPAL COMMANDS:
WESTERN FLEET (HQ) Jakarta/Tanjung Priok:
BASES: Jakarta, Tanjung Pinang (Riau Is.), Sabang (Sumatra).
EASTERN FLEET (HQ Surabaya/Ujung); **BASES:** Surabaya, Manado (Celebes), Ambon (Moluccas).
MILITARY SEA COMMUNICATIONS COMMAND: (KOLINLAMIL): Controls some amph and tpt ships used for inter-island comms.
SUBMARINES: 2 *Cakra* (FRG T-209/1300) with 533mm TT (FRG HWT).
FRIGATES: 15
　4 *Ahmad Yani* (Nl *Van Spejk*) with 1 *Wasp* hel (ASW) (Mk 44 LWT), 2 ×3 ASTT; plus 2 with 2 × 4 *Harpoon* SSM.
　3 *Fatahillah* with 2 × 3 ASTT, 1 × 2 ASW mor, 1 with *Wasp* hel; plus 2 × 2 MM-38 *Exocet*, 1 × 120mm gun.
　3 *M.K. Tiyahahu* (UK *Ashanti*) with 1 *Wasp* hel, 1 × 3 *Limbo* ASW mor; plus 2 × 114mm guns.
　4 *Samadikun* (US *Claud Jones*) with 2 × 3 ASTT, (possibly 2 in store).
　1 *Hajar Dewantara* (trg) with 2 × 533mm TT, 1 ASW mor; plus 2 × 2 MM-38 *Exocet*.
PATROL AND COASTAL COMBATANTS: 35:
MISSILE CRAFT: 4 *Mandau* PFM with 4 × MM-38 *Exocet* SSM.
TORPEDO CRAFT: 1 *Singa* (FRG Lürssen 57m) with 2 × 533mm TT.
PATROL: 30:
　COASTAL: 8:
　1 *Hiu* (US PC 461).
　7 *Andou* (FRG Lürssen 57m) PFC.
　INSHORE: 22:
　3 Yug *Kraljevica*, 8 *Siliman* (Aus *Attack*) PCI.
　5 *Bima Samudera* (US Boeing Jetfoil) PHI, 6⟨.
MINE WARFARE: 2:
　2 *Pulau Rengat* (mod Nl *Alkmaar*) MCC.
AMPHIBIOUS: 15:
　8 *Teluk Langsa* (US LST-512) LST, capacity 200 tps, 16 tk.
　6 *Teluk Semangka* LST, capacity about 200 tps, 12 tk, 4 with 3 hels.
　1 *Teluk Amboina* LST, capacity about 200 tps, 16 tk.
Plus about 64 craft; 4 LCU, some 40 LCM, 20 LCVP.
(Note: 3 LST assigned to Mil Sea Comms Comd.)
SUPPORT AND MISCELLANEOUS: 20:
　1 *Sorong* AOR, 2 cmd/spt, 1 repair, 6 tpt (Mil. Sea Comms Comd), 2 ocean tugs, 8 survey/research.

NAVAL AIR: (ε 1,000); 18 cbt ac, 12 armed hel.
ASW: 3 NAS-332B, 9 *Wasp* HAS-1 hel.
MR: 12 N-22 *Searchmaster* B, 6 *Searchmaster* L.
OTHER:

AIRCRAFT: incl 6 C-47, 3 *Commander*, 6 NC-212;
HELICOPTERS: 1 NAS-332F, 6 NBo-105, 2 SA-313.

MARINES: (12,000);
2 inf regt (each 6 bn);
1 cbt spt regt (arty, AD)
EQUIPMENT:
LIGHT TANKS: 30 PT-76.
AIFV: 40 AMX-10 PAC-90.
APC: 57 incl 25 AMX-10P, BTR-50P.
TOWED ARTY: 122mm: 40 M-38.
MRL: 140mm: BM-14.
AD GUNS: 40mm, 57mm.

AIR FORCE: 24,000;
73 cbt ac, no armed hel.
2 Air Operations Areas:
FGA: 2 sqn with 32 A-4 (28 -E, 4 TA-4H).
FIGHTER: 1 sqn with 14 F-5 (10 -E, 4 -F).
COIN: 1 sqn with 12 OV-10F. (See also Trg)
MR: 1 sqn with 3 Boeing 737-200, 2 C-130H-MP,
4 HU-16.
TANKER: 2 KC-130B.
TRANSPORT: 4 sqn:
2 with 20 C-130 (9 -B, 3 -H, 8 -H-30);
2 with 1 Boeing 707, 7 C-47, 5 Cessna 207,
5 -401, 2 -402, 7 F-27-400M, 1 F-28-1000, 10
NC-212, 1 *Skyvan* (survey).
HELICOPTERS: 3 sqn:
1 with 12 UH-34T (updated to S-58T standard);
2 with 2 Bell 204B, 12 Hughes 500, 7 NAS-332,
12 NBo-105, 13 NSA-330, 3 SE-3160.
TRAINING: 4 sqn with 40 AS-202, 2 Cessna 172, 15
Hawk T-53 (COIN/trg), 23 T-34C, 10 T-41D.
AIRFIELD DEFENCE: 5 bn.

PARA-MILITARY:
DEPARTMENT OF DEFENCE AND SECURITY:
some 115,000: incl *Perintis* ('special police' riot
squads) and Police 'Mobile bde' org in coy:
12,000; 3 *Commander*, 1 Beech 18, 7 lt ac; 7
Bo-105, 3 Bell 206 hel.
MILITIA: 300,000 a year get 3 weeks' basic trg.
CUSTOMS: About 70 PFI⟨, armed.
HANSIP: village guards in E. Timor.
WANRA: local forces under comd of Regional
Military Commands (KOREM).
KAMRA: local police auxiliary.
MARITIME SECURITY AGENCY: 4 PFI, 6 PCI.
POLICE: About 25 PCI (armed)
SEA COMMUNICATIONS (Transport Ministry):
9 SAR craft (inshore).

OPPOSITION:

FRETILIN (Revolutionary Front for an Independent
East Timor): some 300-400 incl spt; small arms.
FREE PAPUA MOVEMENT (OPM): perhaps
500–600 (100 armed).

JAPAN

GDP	1987/8: ¥ 366,614 bn ($2,606.63 bn)	
	1988/9ε: ¥ 381,530 bn ($2,974.60 bn)	
Growth	1987/8: 5.2%	1988/9: 5.1%
Inflation	1987: 0.1%	1988: 0.7%
Debt	1987: $136.0 bn	1988: $155.0 bn
Def bdgt	1988/9: ¥ 3,700.30 bn ($28.85 bn)	
	1989/90: ¥ 3,920.00 bn ($30.09 bn)	
$1 = ¥	(1987/8): 138.35 (1988): 128.96	
	(1989): 130.26	
¥ = yen		

Population: 123,637,000

	13–17	18–22	23–32
Men:	5,147,000	4,600,000	8,114,000
Women:	4,895,000	4,380,000	7,910,000

TOTAL ARMED FORCES:
ACTIVE: 247,000.
Terms of service: voluntary.
RESERVES: Army 46,000; Navy 1,100; Air 800.

ARMY: (Ground Self-Defense Force): 156,000.
5 Army HQ (Regional Commands).
1 armd div.
12 inf div (5 at 7,000, 7 at 9,000 men each).
2 composite bde.
1 AB bde.
1 arty bde; 4 arty gp.
2 AD bde; 8 AD gp.
3 trg bde.
1 hel bde: 24 hel sqn.
2 ATK hel pl, 1 more forming.
EQUIPMENT:
MBT: 1,200: some 430 Type-61 (retiring), some 770
Type-74 (increasing).
RECCE: some 100 Type-82, 20 Type-87.
APC: 430 Type-60, 210 Type-73.
TOWED ARTY: 510: 105mm: 290 M-101;
155mm: some 40 (incl M-1, M-2), 140 FH-70;
203mm: 40 M-115.
SP ARTY: 290: 105mm: 20 Type-74; 155mm: 200
Type-75; 203mm: 70 M-110A2.
MRL: 130mm: some 70 Type-75 SP.
MORTARS: 81mm: 820 (some SP); 107mm: 560
(some SP).
SSM: 50 Type-30.
ATGW: 220 Type-64, some 100 Type-79, some 20
Type-87.

RL: 89mm: 3.5-in M-20.
RCL: 2,710: 75mm; 84mm: *Carl Gustav*; 106mm (incl Type 60 SP).
AD GUNS: 35mm: 70 twin; 37mm SP; 40mm SP.
SAM: 180 *Stinger*, some 40 Type 81 *Tan*, 200 *Improved HAWK*.
AVIATION:
  AIRCRAFT: 22: 20 LR-1, 2 TL-1.
  HELICOPTERS:
    ATTACK: 40 AH-1S;
    TRANSPORT: 3 AS-332L (VIP), 10 CH-47, 50 KV-107, 160 OH-6D/J, 130 UH-1B/H; 20 TH-55 (trg).

NAVY: (Maritime Self-Defense Force): 44,000 (including 12,000 MSDF air).

BASES: Yokosuka, Kure, Sasebo, Maizuru, Ominato.
Fleet: Surface Units org into 4 escort flotillas, of about 8 DD/FF each; based at Yokosuka (2), Sasebo and Maizuru. Submarines org into 2 flotillas based at Kure and Yokosuka. Remainder assigned to 10 regional/district units..

SUBMARINES: 15:
TACTICAL SUBMARINES: 14:
  10 *Yuushio* with 533mm TT, (US Mk 37, GRX-2 HWT), 6 with *Harpoon* USGW.
  4 *Uzushio* with 533mm TT (Mk 37 HWT).
OTHER ROLES: 1 *Uzushio* (trials)

PRINCIPAL SURFACE COMBATANTS: 63:
DESTROYERS: 6 DDG:
  2 *Hatakaze* with 1 × SM1-MR *Standard* SAM; plus 2 × 4 *Harpoon* SSM, 1 × 8 *ASROC* SUGW (Mk 46 LWT) 2 × 3 ASTT, 2 × 127mm guns.
  3 *Tachikaze* with 1 × SM1-MR; plus 1 × 8 *ASROC*, 2 × 3 ASTT, 8 × *Harpoon*, 2 × 127mm guns.
  1 *Amatzukaze* with 1 × SM1-MR; plus 1 × 8 *ASROC*, 2 × 3 ASTT.
FRIGATES: 57 (incl 8 misc roles):
FFH: 20:
  2 *Shirane* with 3 × HSS-2B *Sea King* ASW hel, 1 × 8 *ASROC*, 2 × 3 ASTT; plus 2 × 127mm guns.
  2 *Haruna* with 3 × *Sea King* hel, 1 × 8 *ASROC*, 2 × 3 ASTT; plus 2 × 127mm guns.
  4 *Asagiri* with 1 *Sea King* hel, 1 × 8 *ASROC*, 2 × 3 ASTT; plus 2 × 4 *Harpoon* SSM.
  12 *Hatsuyuki* with 1 *Sea King*, 1 × 8 *ASROC*, 2 × 3 ASTT; plus 2 × 4 *Harpoon* SSM.
FF: 37:
  4 *Takatsuki* with 1 × 8 *ASROC*, 2 × 3 ASTT, 1 × 4 ASW RL; plus 2 with 2 × 4 *Harpoon* SSM, 1 × 127mm gun; 2 with 2 × 127mm guns.
  6 *Yamagumo* with 1 × 8 *ASROC*, 2 × 3 ASTT, 1 × 4 ASW RL.
  3 *Minegumo* with 1 × 8 *ASROC*, 2 × 3 ASTT, 1 × 4 ASW RL.
  2 *Yubari* with 2 × 3 ASTT, 1 × 4 ASW RL; plus 2 × 4 *Harpoon* SSM
  1 *Ishikari* with 2 × 3 ASTT, 1 × 4 ASW RL; plus 2 × 4 *Harpoon* SSM.

11 *Chikugo* with 1 × 8 *ASROC*, 2 × 3 ASTT.
4 *Isuzu* (2 trg) with 2 × 3 ASTT, 1 × 4 ASW RL; plus 4 × 533mm TT.
1 *Akizuki* (trg) with 2 × 3 ASTT, 1 × 4 ASW RL.
2 *Murasame* (1 SS spt, 1 trials) with 2 × 3 ASTT; plus 3 × 127mm guns.
2 *Ayanami* (trg) with 2 × 3 ASTT; plus 4 × 533mm TT.
1 *Katori* (trg) with 2 × 3 ASTT, 1 × ASW RL.

PATROL AND COASTAL COMBATANTS: 14:
TORPEDO CRAFT: 5 *Juichi-go* PFT with 4 × 533mm TT.
PATROL: 9 *Jukyu-go* PCI⟨.

MINE WARFARE: 47:
MINELAYERS: 1:
  1 *Souya* (460 mines) plus hel deck, 2 × 3 ASTT, also MCM spt/comd.
MINE COUNTERMEASURES: 46:
  1 *Hayase* MCM cmd with hel deck, 2 × 3 ASTT, plus minelaying capacity (116 mines).
  21 *Hatsushima*, 11 *Takami* MCC.
  6 *Nana-go* MSI⟨.
  6 Coastal diver spt ships (ex MSC).
  1 *Utone* coastal MCM spt.

AMPHIBIOUS: 6:
  3 *Miura* LST, capacity 200 tps, 10 tk.
  3 *Atsumi* LST, capacity 130 tps, 5 tk.
  Plus craft; 3 LCT, 15 LCM, 22 LCVP.

SUPPORT AND MISCELLANEOUS: 12:
  1 *Towada* AOE, 1 *Sagami* AOE, 1 AS, 3 trg spt, 5 survey/experimental, 1 icebreaker.

MSDF AIR ARM: 12,000;
  80 cbt ac (plus 10 in store), 60 armed hel.
  7 Air Groups.
MR: 8 sqn:
  5 (1 trg) with 40 P-3C (plus 10 in store);
  3 with 30 P-2J;
ASW: 6 hel sqn (1 trg) with 60 HSS-2A/B, plus 45 in store.
MCM: 1 hel sqn with 5 KV-107A, 2 S-80 (more being delivered).
EW: 1 sqn with 2 EP-2J.
TRANSPORT: 1 sqn with 4 YS-11M.
TEST: 1 sqn with 3 P-3C, 3 UP-2J, 2 U-36A ac; 2 SH-60, 2 HSS-2B hel.
SAR: 1 sqn (7 flt) with 10 US-1/1A.
  3 rescue sqn with 10 S-61 hel.
TRAINING: 9 sqn with 30 KM-2, 10 P-3C, 22 *Queen Air* 65, 20 TC-90/UC-90, 10 YS-11T ac; 10 HSS-2A/B, 10 OH-6D/J hel.

AIR FORCE: (Air Self Defense Force): 46,000;
  362 cbt ac (plus 58 in store), no armed hel.
  6 cbt air wings; 1 cbt air unit; 1 recce gp; 1 AEW unit.
FGA: 3 sqn with 70 F-1.
FIGHTER: 9 sqn:
  6 with 120 F-15J/DJ;

3 with 72 F-4EJ (to be upgraded); 58 more in store.

RECCE: 1 sqn with 10 RF-4EJ. 5 more in store.
AEW: 1 sqn with 10 E-2C.
EW: 1 flt with 1 C-1, 4 YS-11.
AGGRESSOR TRAINING: 1 sqn with 10 T-2, 2 T-33.
TRANSPORT: 5 sqn:
   3 with 30 C-1, 10 C-130H, 10 YS-11;
   2 heavy-lift hel sqn with 6 CH-47J.
SAR: 1 wing (10 det) with 30 MU-2 ac; 30 KV-107 hel.
CALIBRATION: 1 wing with 2 MU-2J, 3 T-33A, 1 YS-11.
TRAINING: 5 wings: 10 sqn: 40 T-1A/B, 75 T-2, 40
   T-3, 20 T-4, 60 T-33A (to be replaced by T-4).
LIAISON: 11 *Queen Air* 65.
TEST: 1 wing with C-1, 3 F-4EJ, F-15J, 2 F-104J, 4
   MU-2J, T-1, 4 T-2, 2 T-3, 5 T-33A.
AAM: *Sparrow*, *Sidewinder*.

AIR DEFENCE:
   Aircraft control and warning: 4 wings; 30 radar sites.
   SAM: 6 AD msl gp (18 sqn) with 180 *Nike*-J
      (*Patriot* replacing).
   1 Air Base Defence gp with 20mm *Vulcan* AA
      guns, Type 81 *Tan*, *Stinger* SAM.

PARA-MILITARY:

MARITIME SAFETY AGENCY: (Coast Guard) 12,000:
PATROL VESSELS: Some 336:
   OFFSHORE: 83, incl 2 *Mizuho* with 2, 7 *Soya* with
      1 Bell 212 hel.
   COASTAL: 10:
   INSHORE: 243: 3 PFI, 16 PCI, some 224⟨.
MISCELLANEOUS: 90 service, 81 tender/trg vessels;
AIRCRAFT: 5 NAMC YS-11A, 2 Short *Skyvan*, 16
   King Air, 1 Cessna U-206G.
HELICOPTERS: 32 Bell 212, 4 Bell 206, 2 Hughes 369.

FOREIGN FORCES:

US: 50,500. Army (2,000): 1 Corps HQ; Navy
(8,300) bases at Yokosuka (HQ 7th Fleet) and
Sasebo; Marines (23,700): 1 MEF in Okinawa; Air
(16,500): 1 Air HQ, 1 air div some 120 cbt ac.

KOREA: DEMOCRATIC PEOPLE'S REPUBLIC (NORTH)

GDP	1986ε: won 41.54 bn ($44.09 bn)
	1987ε: won 42.90 bn ($45.54 bn)
Growth	1987: 3.3% 1988: 8.0%
Inflation	1986: 2.0% 1987: 2.0%
Debt	1986ε: $4.6 bn
Def bdgt	1988: won 3.89 bn ($4.07 bn)
	1989: won 4.06 bn ($4.17 bn)

$1 = won (1986/7): 0.948 (1988): 0.9557

Population: 22,230,000

	13–17	*18–22*	*23–32*
Men:	1,216,000	1,104,000	1,835,000
Women:	1,180,000	1,077,000	1,896,000

TOTAL ARMED FORCES:
ACTIVE: 1,040,000.
   Terms of service: Army 5–8 years; Navy 5–10
      years; Air Force 3–4 years.
RESERVES: Army 500,000, Navy 40,000.
   Mob claimed in 12 hours; up to 5,000,000 have
   some Reserve/Militia commitment. See
   Para-Military.

ARMY: 930,000.
15 Corps (1 armd, 4 mech, 1 inf, 8 all-arms, 1 arty)
   31 inf/mot inf div.
   15 armd bde.
   20 mot inf bde.
   4 indep inf bde.
1 Special Purpose corps: 80,000: 25 bde incl 3 cdo,
   4 recce, 1 river crossing regt, 3 amph, 3 AB bn, 22
   lt inf bn. 'Bureau of Reconnaissance SF'.
Arty Corps:
   Army tps: 2 hy arty, 2 mor regt; 6 SSM bn.
   Corps tps: 4 bde incl 122mm, 152mm SP, MRL.
   AD arty: 2 div; 7 regt.
RESERVE: 26 inf div.
EQUIPMENT:
MBT: some 3,200: 200 T-34, 1,600 T-54/-55, 1,200
   T-62, 175 Type-59.
LIGHT TANKS: 300 Type-63, 50 Type-62, M-1985.
RECCE: 140 BA-64.
AIFV: 200 BMP-1/BMP-2.
APC: 1,600 BTR-40/-50/-60/-152, Ch Type-531, N.
   Korean Type M-1973.
TOWED ARTY: 1,900: 76mm: M-1942; 85mm:
   D-44/SD-44; 100mm: M-1944; 122mm:
   M-1931/-37, D-74, Type-54, Type-60, D-30;
   130mm: M-46, Ch Type-59; 152mm: M-1937
   (ML-20), M-1943, M-1938, D-20.
SP ARTY: Some 2,800: 122mm: M-1981, M-1977,
   M-1985; 130mm: M-1975; 152mm: M-1974;
   180mm: M-1978.
MRL: 2,500: 107mm: Type-63; 122mm: BM-21,
   BM-11 (30 tubes); 130mm: Ch Type-63; 200mm:
   BMD-20; 240mm: BM-24.
MORTARS: 82mm: 11,000 M-37 ; 120mm: M-43.
SSM: 54 *FROG*-3/-5/-7; (some 15 *Scud* B-type
   rumoured).
ATGW: AT-1 *Snapper*, AT-3 *Sagger*.
RCL: 75mm: Type-52; 82mm: 1,500 B-10; 107mm:
   1,000 B-11.
ATK GUNS: 37mm: M-1939; 57mm: M-1943; 85mm:
   D-48 towed; 800 SU-76 and SU-100 SP.
AD GUNS: 8,000: 14.5mm: ZPU-2/-4 SP; 23mm:
   ZU-23; 37mm: Ch Type-55, M-1939; 57mm:
   ZSU-57-2 SP, S-60, Ch Type-59; 85mm: KS-12;
   100mm: KS-19. N. Korean SP AA, type unknown.

SAM: HN-5A (SA-7 type).

NAVY: 40,000.
BASES: East Coast: Wonsan (HQ), Chi-aho, Songjin Toejo.
West Coast: Nampo (HQ), Haeju, Pipaqo, Sagwon-ri. 2 Fleet HQ.
SUBMARINES: 23:
19 Ch Type-031/Sov *Romeo* with 533mm TT
4 *Sov Whiskey* with 533mm and 406mm TT.
FRIGATES: 2 *Najin* with 2 × 5 ASW RL, 1 with 3 × 533mm TT; plus 2 × 100mm guns. 1 possibly with 1 × 2 SS-N-2 *Styx* SSM.
PATROL AND COASTAL COMBATANTS: 363:
CORVETTES: 4 *Sariwan* with 1 × 100mm gun.
MISSILE CRAFT: 29:
8 *Soju*, 5 Sov *Osa* PFM with 4 × SS-N-2 *Styx*
6 *Sohung*, 10 Sov *Komar* PFM⟨ with 2 × SS-N-2.
TORPEDO CRAFT: 173:
3 Sov *Shershen* with 4 × 533mm TT.
Some 170⟨ with 2 × 533mm TT.
PATROL: 157:
COASTAL: 6 *Hainan* PFC with 4 × ASW RL.
INSHORE: some 151:
18 SO-1, 10 *Taechong*, 8 *Shanghai* II, 3 *Chodo*, 2 K-48, some 110⟨.
MINE WARFARE: About 40 MSI⟨.
AMPHIBIOUS: craft only; 14 LCM, 12 LCU, about 100 LCI⟨.
SUPPORT AND MISCELLANEOUS: 2 ocean tugs.
COAST DEFENCE: SSM: 2 regt: *Samlet* in 6 sites;
GUNS: 122mm: M-1931/-37; 130mm: SM-4-1; 152mm: M-1937.

AIR FORCE: 70,000;
650 cbt ac, 115 armed hel.
BOMBERS: 3 lt regt with 80 H-5.
FGA: 8 regt:
3 with 100 J-5;
3 with 100 J-6;
1 with 40 Q-5;
1 with 20 Su-7, 10 Su-25.
FIGHTER: 10 regt:
2 with 60 J-6;
1 with 40 J-7;
4 with 120 MiG-21;
2 with 46 MiG-23;
1 with 24 MiG-29.
ATTACK HELICOPTERS: 60 Hughes 500, 50 Mi-24.
ASW HELICOPTERS: 5 Mi-14.
TRANSPORT:
AIRCRAFT: 10 An-24, 5 Il-14, 5 Il-18, 4 Il-62M, 2 Tu-134, 4 Tu-154, 250 Y-5.
HELICOPTERS: 1 Hughes 300C, 20 -500D, 6 -500E, 40 Z-5, 70 Mi-8/-17.
TRAINING: incl 90 CJ-5, 30 CJ-6, H-5, 16 L-39, 50 MiG-15UTI, MiG-19U, 10 MiG-21U.

AAM: AA-2 *Atoll*, AA-7 *Apex*.
SAM: 4 bde (12 bn, 40 bty) with 72 SA-2 in 45 sites, 2 regt with ε 32 SA-3, 2 regt with ε 72 SA-5.

FORCES ABROAD: Advisers in 10 African
countries incl Madagascar (100), Mozambique (10).

PARA-MILITARY:
SECURITY TROOPS (Ministry of Public Security): 115,000 incl Border guards.
WORKER/PEASANT RED GUARD (WPRM): some 3 m up to age 50. Org on a provincial/town/village basis. Comd structure is bde - bn - coy - pl. Small arms with some mor and AD guns (but many units unarmed).

KOREA: REPUBLIC OF (SOUTH)

GDP	1987: won 99,790.0 bn ($121.31 bn)	
	1988ε: won 116,754.0 bn ($159.62 bn)	
Growth	1987: 11.1%	1988: 11.0%
Inflation	1987: 3.0%	1988: 7.1%
Debt	1987: $35.6 bn	1988: $32.0 bn
Def bdgt	1987: won 5,730.0 bn ($6.97 bn)	
	1988: won 6,224.7 bn ($8.51 bn)	
FMA	1988: $1.5 m (US)	
$1 = won	(1987): 822.57	(1988): 731.47

Population: 43,050,000

	13–17	18–22	23–32
Men:	2,308,000	2,260,000	4,247,000
Women:	2,169,000	2,125,000	4,067,000

TOTAL ARMED FORCES:
ACTIVE: 650,000.
Terms of service: all Services, 30–36 months.
RESERVES: 4,500,000; being re-organized.

ARMY: 550,000.
HQ: 3 Army, 7 Corps.
2 mech inf div (each 3 bde: 3 mech inf, 3 mot, 3 tk, 1 recce bn; 1 fd arty bde).
19 inf div (each 3 inf regt, 1 recce, 1 tk, 1 engr bn; 1 arty regt (4 bn)).
1 indep inf bde.
7 SF bde.
2 SSM bn with *Honest John.*
2 AD arty bde.
2 SAM bde: 3 *HAWK* bn (24 sites), 2 *Nike Hercules* bn (10 sites).
1 avn bde.
RESERVES: 1 Army HQ, 23 inf div.
EQUIPMENT:
MBT: 1,560: 200+ Type 88, 350 M-47,

950 M-48A5, 60 M-60.
AIFV: some 200 (KIFV).
APC: some 1,550 incl 450 M-113, 400 Fiat
6614/KM-900/-901.
TOWED ARTY: some 4,000: 105mm: M-101, KH-178;
155mm: M-53, M-114, KH-179; 203mm: M-115.
SP ARTY: 155mm: 100 M-109A2; 175mm: M-107;
203mm: M-110
MRL: 140 *Kooryong* (36 × 130mm).
MORTARS: 5,300: 81mm: KM-29; 107mm: M-30.
SSM: 12 *Honest John*.
ATGW: *TOW*.
RCL: 57mm, 75mm, 90mm: M67; 106mm: M40A2.
ATK GUNS: 76mm: 8 M-18; 90mm: 50 M-36 SP.
AD GUNS: 600: 20mm: incl 60 *Vulcan*; 35mm: 20
GDF-003; 40mm: 80 L60/70, M-1.
SAM: 100 *Javelin*, some *Redeye*, 130 *Stinger*, 110
HAWK, 200 *Nike Hercules*.
AVIATION:
  AIRCRAFT: 10 Cessna O-1A.
  HELICOPTERS:
    ATTACK: 48 AH-1S, 50 Hughes 500 MD.
    UTILITY: 144 Hughes 500, 5 KH-4, 34 UH-1B,
    120 UH-1H.

NAVY: 60,000 (19,000 conscripts) incl 25,000
marines.
BASES: Chinhae (HQ), Cheju, Inchon, Mokpo,
Mukho, Pukpyong, Pohang, Pusan.
3 Fleet Commands.
SUBMARINES: 3 KSS-1 *Tolgorae* SSI (175 tonnes)
with 2 × 406mm TT.
PRINCIPAL SURFACE COMBATANTS: 28:
DESTROYERS: 11:
  7 *Chung Buk* (US *Gearing*) with 2 or 3 × 2
  127mm guns; plus 2 × 3 ASTT; 5 with 2 × 4
  Harpoon SSM, 1 *Alouette* III hel (OTHT), 2 with
  1 × 8 *ASROC*.
  2 *Dae Gu* (US *Sumner*) with 3 × 2 127mm guns;
  plus 2 × 3 ASTT.
  2 *Chung Mu* (US *Fletcher*) with 5 × 127mm guns
  plus 2 × 3 ASTT.
FRIGATES: 17:
  5 *Ulsan* with 2 × 3 ASTT (Mk 46 LWT); plus 2 × 4
  Harpoon SSM.
  12 *Donghae* with 2 × 3 ASTT; plus 2 × 1 MM-38
  Exocet (weapons fit not confirmed).
PATROL AND COASTAL COMBATANTS: 79:
MISSILE CRAFT: 11:
  8 *Pae Ku*-52, 3 with 4 *Standard* (boxed) SSM, 5
  with 2 × 2 *Harpoon* SSM.
  1 *Pae Ku*-51 (US *Asheville*), with 2 × *Standard* SSM.
  2 *Kilurki-71* with 2 × MM-38 *Exocet* SSM.
PATROL, INSHORE: 68:
  32 *Kilurki-11* ('Sea Dolphin') 33m PFI.
  36 *Chebi-51* ('Sea Hawk') 26m PFI⟨.
MINE WARFARE: 9:
  1 'Swallow' (mod It *Lerici*) MHC.

8 *Kun San* (US MSC-268/289) MSC.
AMPHIBIOUS: 15:
  8 *Un Bong* (US LST-511) LST, capacity 200 tps,
  16 tk.
  7 *Ko Mun* (US LSM-1) LSM, capacity 50 tps, 4 tk.
Plus about 37 craft; 6 LCT, 10 LCM, 1 LCU about
  20 LCVP.
SUPPORT AND MISCELLANEOUS: 9:
  3 spt tankers, 2 ocean tugs, about 4 survey (civil
  manned, Ministry of Transport funded).

NAVAL AIR:
  25 cbt ac; 35 armed hel.
ASW: 2 sqn:
  1 ac with 25 S-2 (9 -A, 16 -E);
  1 hel with 25 Hughes 500MD (ASW);
  10 flt with 10 SA-316 hel (ASW),
    2 Bell 206 (liaison).

MARINES: (25,000).
  2 div, 1 bde.
  Spt units.
EQUIPMENT:
MBT: 40 M-47.
APC: 60 LVTP-7.
TOWED ARTY: 105mm, 155mm.
SSM: *Harpoon* (truck-mounted).

AIR FORCE: 40,000;
  447 cbt ac, no armed hel. 7 cbt, 2 tpt wings.
FGA: 18 sqn:
  2 with 48 F-16 (36 -C, 12 -D),
  16 with 204 F-5 (44 -A, 160 -E).
FIGHTER: 4 sqn with 68 F-4 (34 -D, 34 -E).
COIN: 1 sqn with 23 A-37B.
RECCE: 1 sqn with 10 RF-5A.
SAR: 1 hel sqn with 15 Bell UH-1B, 2 UH-1N.
TRANSPORT: 2 wings, 5 sqn:
  10 C-54, 14 C-123J/K, 3 *Commander*, 2 HS-748
  (VIP), 8 C-130H.
TRAINING: incl 20 T-28D, 33 T-33A, 34 Cessna
  (14 T-37C, 20 T-41D), 35 F-5B, 51 F-5F.
AAM: *Sidewinder*, *Sparrow*.

PARA-MILITARY:
CIVILIAN DEFENCE CORPS (to age 50): 3,500,000.
COAST GUARD: (ε 3,500)
PATROL CRAFT, OFFSHORE: 14
  8 *Ma-San-Ho* (HDP-1000)
  6 *Sea Dragon/Whale* (HDP-600)
INSHORE: 32
  12 *Sea Wolf/Shark*
  20⟨, plus numerous boats.
HELICOPTERS: 9 Hughes 500D.

FOREIGN FORCES:

US: 43,200. Army (31,600): 1 army HQ, 1 inf div, 1 SSM bty with *Lance*. Air Force (11,600): 1 div: 2 wings: 84 cbt ac.

LAOS

GDP	1985ε: kip 21.2 bn ($605.71 m)		
Growth	1985ε: 7.0%		
Inflation	1985ε: 20–30%		
$1 = kip	(1985): 35.00		

Population: 4,468,000

	13–17	18–22	23–32
Men:	264,000	227,000	218,000
Women:	274,000	238,000	229,000

TOTAL ARMED FORCES:

ACTIVE: 55,500.
Terms of service: conscription, 18 months minimum.

ARMY: 52,500.

4 Military Regions
5 inf div.
7 indep inf regt.
1 engr regt.
2 construction regt, indep construction bn.
5 arty, 9 AD arty bn.
65 indep inf coy.
1 lt ac liaison flt.

EQUIPMENT:

MBT: 30 T-34/-55.
LIGHT TANKS: 25 PT-76.
APC: 70 BTR-40/-60/-152.
TOWED ARTY: 105mm: 25 M-101; 122mm: 40 M-1938 and D-30; 130mm: 10 M-46.
MORTARS: 82mm; 120mm: M-43.
RCL: 57mm: M-18/A1; 75mm: M-20; 107mm: B-11.
AD GUNS: 23mm: ZSU-23-4 SP; 37mm: M-1939; 57mm: S-60.
SAM: SA-3, SA-7.

NAVY: (ε 650).

PATROL CRAFT, river: some 40⟨.

AIR FORCE: 2,000;

34 cbt ac; no armed hel.
FGA: 1 regt with some 30 MiG-21.
TRANSPORT: 1 sqn with 6 An-2, 5 An-24, 2 An-26, 2 Yak-40.
HELICOPTERS: 1 sqn with 2 Mi-6, 10 Mi-8.
TRAINING: 4 MiG-21U.
AAM: AA-2 *Atoll*.

PARA-MILITARY:

MILITIA SELF-DEFENCE FORCES: village 'homeguard' org for local defence.

OPPOSITION:

Numerous factions/groups. Total armed strength ε 2,000. Largest group United Lao National Liberation Front (ULNLF).

FOREIGN FORCES:

VIETNAM: 10–15,000: mostly economic construction tps. Withdrawal continues.

MALAYSIA

GDP	1987: $M 80.61 bn ($US 31.99 bn)	
	1988ε: $M 88.67 bn ($US 33.86 bn)	
Growth	1987: 4.7%	1988: 7.4%
Inflation	1987: 1.1%	1988: 2.0%
Debt	1987: $US 20.1 bn	1988: $US 18.1 bn
Def bdgt*	1988: $M 4.22 bn ($US 1.612 bn)	
	1989: $M 3.57 bn ($US 1.29 bn)	
FMA	1988: $0.95 m (US)	
$US1 = $M	(1987): 2.5196 (1988): 2.6188	
	(1989): 2.7528	

$M = ringgit

Population: 17,234,000

	13–17	18–22	23–32
Men:	894,000	847,000	1,556,000
Women:	861,000	818,000	1,519,000

TOTAL ARMED FORCES:

ACTIVE: 114,500.
Terms of service: voluntary.
RESERVES: 46,600; Army 45,000; Navy 1,000; Air 600.

ARMY: 105,000 (reducing to 97,000).

1 corps, 4 div HQ.
1 area security comd (COIN).
9 inf bde, consisting of 36 inf bn (1 APC, 1 para), 4 armd, 5 fd arty, 2 AD arty, 5 engr regt.
1 SF regt (3 bn).
RESERVES: 1 div HQ; 1 bde HQ; 12 inf regt (to reform into 3 bde); 4 highway sy bn.

EQUIPMENT:

LIGHT TANKS: 26 *Scorpion* (90mm).
RECCE: 162 SIBMAS, 140 AML-60/-90, 92 *Ferret* (modernized).
APC: 134 V-100/-150 *Commando*, 25 *Stormer*, 460 *Condor*.

TOWED ARTY: 105mm: 150 Model 56 pack, 56
M-102A1.
MORTARS: 81mm: L16.
ATGW: SS-11.
RL: 89mm: M-20.
RCL: 84mm: *Carl Gustav:* 106mm: 150; 120mm: 5.
AD GUNS: 12.7mm: 70; 40mm: 36: 24 40/70, 12 L-70.
ASSAULT CRAFT: 165 Damen.

NAVY: 12,500.

Two Regional Commands: plus Fleet.
Area 1: Malayan Peninsula (west of 109°E).
Area 2: Borneo Area (east of 109°E).
BASES: Area 1: Lumut (HQ), Tanjong Gelang,
Kuantan, Woodlands (Singapore); trg base.
Area 2: Labuan (HQ), Sungei Antu (Sarawak).
FRIGATES: 4:
2 *Kasturi* (FS-1500) with 2 × 2 ASW mor, deck for
Wasp hel; plus 2 × 2 MM-38 *Exocet* SSM, 1 ×
100mm gun.
1 *Hang Tuah* (UK *Mermaid*) with 1 × 3 *Limbo*
ASW mor, hel deck for *Wasp*; plus 1 × 2
102mm gun.
1 *Rahmat* with 1 × 3 ASW mor, 1 × 114mm gun
hel deck.
PATROL AND COASTAL COMBATANTS: 37:
MISSILE CRAFT: 8
4 *Handalan* (Sw *Spica*) with 4 MM-38 *Exocet* SSM.
4 *Perdana* (Fr *Combattante*-II) with 2 *Exocet* SSM.
PATROL: 29:
OFFSHORE: 2 *Musytari* with 1 × 100mm gun,
hel deck.
INSHORE: 27:
6 *Jerong* PFI, 3 *Kedah*, 4 *Sabah*, 14 *Kris* PCI.
MINE WARFARE: 5:
4 *Mahamiru* (mod It *Lerici*) MCO.
1 diving tender (inshore).
AMPHIBIOUS: 2:
2 *Sri Banggi* (US LST-511) LST, capacity 200 tps,
16 tk, (but usually employed as tenders to
patrol craft).
Plus 33 craft: 5 LCM, 13 LCU, 15 LCP.
SUPPORT AND MISCELLANEOUS: 3:
2 logistic/fuel spt, 1 survey.

NAVAL AIR:

No cbt ac, 6 armed hel.
HELICOPTERS: 6 *Wasp* HAS-1.

AIR FORCE: 12,000;

67 cbt ac, no armed hel, 4 Comd.
FGA: 2 sqn: with 36 A-4 (30 A-4PTM, 6 TA-4);
FIGHTER: 1 sqn with 14 F-5E.
RECCE: 1 recce/OCU sqn with 2 RF-5E, 2 F-5F.
MR: 1 sqn with 3 C-130HMP.
TRANSPORT:
AIRCRAFT: 4 sqn:

1 with 6 C-130H;
2 with 13 DHC-4;
1 with 2 HS-125 (VIP), 1 F-28 (Royal flt), 2
HU-16 *Albatross* (1 tpt, 1 VIP), 11 Cessna
402B ac; 1 NAS-332 hel.
HELICOPTERS: 4 sqn with 32 S-61A, 24 *Alouette*
III (liaison).
TRAINING: 4 trg units:
AIRCRAFT: 10 MB-339, 44 PC-7 (4 wpn trg), 11
Bulldog;
HELICOPTERS: 4 S-61, 7 *Alouette* III, 7 Bell 47.
AAM: *Sidewinder*.
AIRFIELD DEFENCE TROOPS: 1 sqn.

FORCES ABROAD:
IRAN/IRAQ (UNIIMOG): 15
NAMIBIA (UNTAG): 889: 1 inf bn, HQ staff.

PARA-MILITARY:
POLICE FIELD FORCE: 18,000; 4 bde HQ: 21 bn
(incl 2 Aboriginal); *Shorland* armd cars, 140
AT-105, SB-301 APC.
MARINE POLICE: 51 patrol, inshore:
15 *Long Hitan* (38m) PFI
9 *Sangitan* (29m) PFI
27 PCI⟨.
POLICE AIR WING: 4 Cessna 206, 7 PC-6 ac.
AUXILIARY POLICE FIELD FORCE: (Area Security
Units), 3,500 men in 89 units.
BORDER SCOUTS (in Sabah, Sarawak): 1,200.
PEOPLE'S VOLUNTEER CORPS (RELA): 180,000.

OPPOSITION:
COMMUNIST PARTY OF MALAYA (CPM): some
850 op in Thai/Malaysia border region.
NORTH KALIMANTAN COMMUNIST PARTY
(NKCP) – Sarawak East Malaysia: some 40.

FOREIGN FORCES:
AUSTRALIA: Army: 1 inf coy. Air Force: det with
P-3C ac.

---

* Excl internal sy bdgt and also $2.8 bn for defence in
5-year plan 1986–90.

MONGOLIA

GDP	1986ε: t 7.42 bn ($2.21 bn)
	1987ε: t 7.71 bn ($2.30 bn)
Growth	1987ε: 3.5% 1988ε: 4.3%
Def exp	1987: t 837.0 m ($249.44 m)
Def bdgt	1988ε: t 900.0 m ($268.38 m)
$1 = t	(1986/7/8): 3.3555
t = tugrik	

Population: 2,070,000

	13–17	18–22	23–32
Men:	119,000	105,000	158,000
Women:	116,000	108,000	157,000

TOTAL ARMED FORCES:
ACTIVE: 21,500 (perhaps 17,000 conscripts).
Terms of service: Conscription: males 18–28 years; 2 years.
RESERVES: Army 200,000.

ARMY: 21,000 (perhaps 17,000 conscripts).
4 MRD (to be reduced).
EQUIPMENT:
MBT: 650 T-54/-55/-62.
RECCE: 135 BRDM-2.
AIFV: 420 BMP-1.
APC: 450 BTR-40/-60/-152.
TOWED ARTY: 650: 122mm: M-1938/D-30; 130mm: M-46; 152mm: ML-20.
MRL: 120+: 122mm: BM-21; 132mm: BM-13-16; 140mm: BM-14-16, BM-14-17.
MORTARS: 82mm, 120mm, 160mm.
ATGW: AT-3 *Sagger* (incl BRDM-2 SP).
ATK GUNS: 100mm: T-12.
AD GUNS: 100: 14.5mm: ZPU-4; 37mm: M-1939; 57mm: S-60.
SAM: 300 SA-7.

AIR FORCE: 500; Soviet technicians;
30 cbt ac; 10 armed hel.
FIGHTER: 1 regt with 30 MiG-21 (incl trg).
ATTACK HELICOPTERS: 10 Mi-24.
TRANSPORT: at least 2 sqn:
20 An-2, 19 An-24, 1 An-26, 1 An-32.
HELICOPTERS: 1 sqn with 4 Mi-8, 10 Mi-4.
TRAINING: 2 MiG-15U, 3 PZL-104, Yak-11, Yak-18.

PARA-MILITARY:
MILITIA (Ministry of Public Security):
10,000: internal security troops, frontier guards; BTR-60/-152 APC.

FOREIGN FORCES:
USSR: ε 55,000
Army: 1 army HQ, 2 TD, 2 MRD. To be reduced to 1 MRD by end 1990.

NEPAL

GDP	1986/7: NR 58.50 bn ($2.71 bn)
	1987/8: NR 68.15 bn ($3.09 bn)
Growth	1986/7: 2.4% 1987/8: 0.5%

Inflation	1987: 10.8% 1988ε: 16.5%
Debt	1987: $877.0 m 1988: $910.0 m
Def bdgt	1987/8: NR 817.0 m ($37.04 m)
	1988/9: NR 936.60 m ($37.37 m)
FMA	1988: $0.1 m (US)
$1 = NR	(1986/7): 21.596 (1987/8): 22.055
	(1988/9): 25.061

NR = Nepalese rupees

Population: 18,651,000

	13–17	18–22	23–32
Men:	1,013,000	851,000	1,325,000
Women:	926,000	776,000	1,320,000

TOTAL ARMED FORCES:
ACTIVE: 35,000 (to be 40,000).
Terms of service: voluntary.
RESERVES: none.

ARMY:
1 Royal Guard bde: incl 1 cav sqn, 1 garrison bn.
7 inf bde: incl AB bn.
1 arty regt, 1 engr bn, 1 armd recce sqn.
EQUIPMENT:
RECCE: 25 *Ferret*.
TOWED ARTY: 75mm: 6 pack; 94mm: 5 3.7-in mtn; 105mm: 6 pack.
MORTARS: 81mm; 120mm: 18.
AD GUNS: 14.5mm: 30 Ch; 40mm: 2 L/60.

AIR FORCE:
No cbt ac, or armed hel.
TRANSPORT:
AIRCRAFT: 1 HS-748, 2 *Skyvan*.
HELICOPTERS: 1 AS-332, 1 Bell 206L, 2 *Chetak*, 2 SA-330.

FORCES ABROAD:
LEBANON (UNIFIL): 1 inf bn (850).

PARA-MILITARY:
POLICE FORCE: 28,000.

NEW ZEALAND

GDP	1987/8: $NZ 59.26 bn ($US 36.79 bn)
	1988/9: $NZ 62.81 bn ($US 40.53 bn)
Growth	1987/8: 1.3% 1988/9: −0.3%
Inflation	1987: 15.7% 1988: 6.4%
Debt	1987: $US 22.5 bn 1988: $US 20.5 bn
Def bdgt	1987/8: $NZ 1.30 bn ($US 807.94 m)
	1988/9: $NZ 1.39 bn ($US 897.06 m)
$US 1 = $NZ	(1987/8): 1.6109 (1988/9): 1.5497

$NZ = New Zealand dollars

Population: 3,347,000

	13–17	18–22	23–32
Men:	153,000	149,000	278,000
Women:	148,000	144,000	282,000

TOTAL ARMED FORCES:
ACTIVE: 12,400.

Terms of service: voluntary.

RESERVES: 9,700. *Regular* 2,900: Army 1,300, Navy 800, Air 800. *Territorial* 6,800: Army 6,100, Navy 500, Air 200.

ARMY: 5,700.
2 inf bn.
1 armd recce sqn.
1 fd arty bty.
1 SAS sqn.
1 ranger coy (to form)
RESERVES: Territorial Army: 6 inf bn, 5 fd, 1 med arty bty, 3 armd sqn (1 recce, 1 APC, 1 ATK).
EQUIPMENT:
LIGHT TANKS: 26 *Scorpion.*
APC: 78 M-113.
TOWED ARTY: 105mm: 20 M-101A1, 24 L10A1 (pack), 24 Hamel.
MORTARS: 81mm: 72.
RL: *LAW.*
RCL: 84mm: 23 *Carl Gustav*; 106mm: 13 M-40.

NAVY: 2,500.
BASE: Auckland (Fleet HQ).
FRIGATES: 4 *Waikato* (UK *Leander*) with 1 *Wasp* hel, 3 with 2 × 3 ASTT and 2 × 114mm guns, 1 with *Ikara* SUGW.
PATROL AND COASTAL COMBATANTS: 6:
2 *Pukaki* PCI.
4 *Moa* PCI (reserve trg).
SUPPORT AND MISCELLANEOUS: 4:
1 *Endeavour* AO, 1 AGHS, 1 AGOR, 1 diving spt.
IN STORE: 2 *Pukaki* PCI.

NAVAL AIR:
No cbt ac, 7 armed hel.
HELICOPTERS: 7 *Wasp* (see Air Force).

AIR FORCE: 4,200; 43 cbt ac, no armed hel.
OPERATIONAL GROUP:
FGA: 2 sqn with 17 A-4 (8 -G, 9 -K), 5 TA-4 (2 -G, 3 -K).
MR: 1 sqn with 6 P-3K *Orion.*
LIGHT ATTACK/TRG: 1 wpn trg sqn with 15 BAC-167.
ASW: 7 *Wasp* HAS-1 (Navy-assigned).
TRANSPORT: 3 sqn:
AIRCRAFT: 2 sqn: 1 with 5 C-130H;

1 with 8 *Andover*, 2 Boeing 727.
HELICOPTERS: 1 with 12 Bell UH-1H.
COMMUNICATIONS: 1 flight with 3 Cessna 421C.
SUPPORT GROUP:
TRAINING: 1 wing with 4 *Airtourer*, 15 CT-4, 3 F-27 ac; 3 Bell 47 hel.
AAM: AIM-9G *Sidewinder.*
ASM: AGM-65 *Maverick.*

FORCES ABROAD:
EGYPT (Sinai MFO): 25.
IRAN/IRAQ (UNIIMOG): 28.
SINGAPORE: 20: spt unit.

PAKISTAN

GDP	1986/7:	Rs 608.15 bn ($35.43 bn)	
	1987/8:	Rs 685.87 bn ($39.07 bn)	
Growth	1986/7:	5.4%	1987/8: 5.3%
Inflation	1987:	4.7%	1988: 12.0%
Debt	1987:	$15.9 bn	1988: $16.4 bn
Def exp	1987/8:	Rs 45.30 bn ($2.58 bn)	
	1988/9:	Rs 49.74 bn ($2.63 bn)	
FMA	1988:	$230.92 m (US)	
$1 = Rs	(1986/7): 17.165	(1987/8): 17.555	
	(1988/9): 18.882		

Rs = rupees

Population: 106,886,000*

	13–17	18–22	23–32
Men:	6,814,000	5,709,000	7,414,000
Women:	6,191,000	4,747,000	6,625,000

TOTAL ARMED FORCES:
ACTIVE: 520,000.

Terms of Service: voluntary.

RESERVES: 513,000; Army 500,000: obligation to ages 45 (men) or 50 (officers); active liability for 8 years after service. Navy 5,000. Air 8,000.

ARMY: 480,000.
7 Corps HQ.
2 armd div.
14 inf div.
5 indep armd bde.
4 indep inf bde.
8 arty bde/bde equivalents.
3 AD arty bde.
6 armd recce regt.
1 special services group (3 bn).
Avn: 1 ac, 4 hel sqn; indep observation flt.
EQUIPMENT:
MBT: 1,750: 500 M-47/-48 (incl A5), 51 T-54/-55, some 1,200 Ch Type-59.

LIGHT TANKS: Ch Type-63.
APC: 800 M-113, Ch Type-531 reported.
TOWED ARTY: 100mm: Ch Type-59; 105mm: 200 M-101 50 M-56 pack; 122mm: 100 Ch Type-54-1; 130mm: Ch Type- 59-1, M46; 140mm: 5.5in; 155mm: M-59, 60 M-114, 100 M-198.
SP ARTY: 105mm: 12 M-7; 155mm: 95 M-109A2; 203mm: 40 M-110A2.
MRL: 122mm: BM-21.
MORTARS: 81mm, 107mm, 120mm.
SSM: *Haft*-I possibly in service.
ATGW: *Cobra*, 224 *TOW* (incl 24 on M-901 SP), Ch *Red Arrow* reported.
RL: 89mm: M-20 3.5-in.
RCL: 75mm: Type-52; 106mm: M-40A.
AD GUNS: 14.5mm; 35mm; 37mm: Ch Type-55/-65; 40mm: M1; 57mm: S-60, Ch Type-59.
SAM: 100 *Stinger*, 144 RBS-70, *Anza* reported.

AVIATION:
AIRCRAFT:
  LIAISON: 1 Cessna 421, 2 *Commander* 690, 80 *Mashshaq*, 3 *Queen Air*, 1 U-8F.
  OBSERVATION: 35 O-1E, 50 *Mashshaq*.
  HELICOPTERS:
    ATTACK: 20 AH-1S (TOW).
    TRANSPORT: 7 Bell 205, 10 -206B, 16 Mi-8, 6 SA/IAR-315B, 23 SA/IAR-316, 35 SA-330, 5 UH-1H.

NAVY: 15,000 (incl Naval Air).
BASE: Karachi (Fleet HQ).
SUBMARINES: 6:
  2 *Hashmat* (Fr *Agosta*) with 533mm TT (F-17 HWT), *Harpoon* USGW.
  4 *Hangor* (Fr *Daphné*) with 533mm TT (L-5 HWT). Plus 3 SX-404 SSI SF insertion craft.
PRINCIPAL SURFACE COMBATANTS: 17.
DESTROYERS: 7:
  1 *Babur* (UK *Devonshire*) DDH with 4 × *Sea King* hel (ASW/ASUW), plus 2 × 2 114mm guns.
  6 *Alamgir* (US *Gearing*) (ASW) with 1 × 8 ASROC; plus 2 × 2 127mm guns, 2 with 3 × 2 *Harpoon* SSM.
FRIGATES: 10:
FFG: 4 *Khyber* (US *Brooke*) with SA-316B hel, 1 × 8 ASROC 2 × 3 ASTT, plus 1 × SM1-MR SAM, 1 × 127mm gun (on 5-yr lease).
FF: 6:
  2 *Shamsher* (UK *Leander*) with *Alouette* hel, 1 × 3 ASW mor, plus 2 × 114mm guns.
  4 *Badr* (US *Garcia*) with *Alouette* hel, 1 × 8 ASROC, 2 × 3 ASTT, plus 2 × 127mm guns.
PATROL AND COASTAL COMBATANTS: 29:
MISSILE CRAFT: 8:
  4 Ch *Huangfeng* with 4 × *Hai Ying* 2 SSM.
  4 Ch *Hegu⟨* with 2 × *HY-2*.
TORPEDO CRAFT: 4 Ch *Huchuan* PHT with 2 × 533mm TT.

PATROL: 17:
  COASTAL: 4 *Baluchistan* (Ch *Hainan*) PFC with 4 × ASW RL.
  INSHORE: 13:
  12 *Quetta* (Ch *Shanghai*) PFI (4 with Maritime Safety Agency), 1 *Rajshahi* PCI.
MINE WARFARE: 3 *Mahmood* (US-MSC 268) MSC.
SUPPORT AND MISCELLANEOUS: 4:
  1 *Nasr* (Ch *Fuqing*), 1 *Dacca* AO, 1 survey, 1 ocean tug.

NAVAL AIR:
  4 cbt ac, 10 armed hel.
ASW/MR: 1 sqn with 4 *Atlantic* (operated by Air Force; AM-39 ASM).
ASW/SAR: 2 hel sqn: 1 with 6 Westland *Sea King* Mk 45 (ASW, with AM-39), 4 SA-316B (ASW)
COMMUNICATIONS: 1 Fokker F-27 ac (Air Force).
ASM: AM-39 *Exocet*.

AIR FORCE: 25,000; 451 cbt ac, no armed hel.
FGA: 14 sqn:
  1 with 18 *Mirage* (15 IIIEP (some with AM-39 ASM), 3 IIIDP (trg));
  4 with 58 *Mirage* 5 (54 -5PA/PA2, 4 -5DPA/DPA2);
  9 with 135 Q-5.
FIGHTER: 12 sqn:
  9 with 150 J-6/JJ-6;
  2 with 40 F-16 (28 -A, 12 -B).
  1 with 20 J-7.
RECCE: 1 sqn with 12 *Mirage* IIIRP, 1 RT-33A.
TRANSPORT: 2 sqn:
  1 with 12 C-130 (5 -B, 7 -E), 1 L-100;
  1 with 3 *Falcon* 20, 2 F-27-200 (1 with Navy), 2 Beech (1 *Travel Air*, 1 *Baron*).
SAR: 1 hel sqn with 2 HH-43B, 4 SA-316.
TRANSPORT HELICOPTERS: 1 sqn with 4 SA-321.
TRAINING: 12 CJ-6, 30 JJ-5, 50 *Mashshaq*, 6 MiG-15UTI, 10 T-33A, 53 T-37B/C.
AD: 7 SAM bty:
  6 each with 6 *Crotale*;
  1 with 6 CSA-1 (SA-2).
AAM: AIM-7 *Sparrow*, AIM-9 *Sidewinder*, R-530, R-550 *Magic*.
ASM: AM-39 *Exocet*.

PARA-MILITARY:
NATIONAL GUARD: 75,000; incl Mujahid Force; Janbaz Force; National Cadet Corps; Women Guards.
FRONTIER CORPS: 65,000, 45 UR-416 APC.
PAKISTAN RANGERS: 15,000;
NORTHERN LIGHT INFANTRY: 7,000 some 6 bn;
COAST GUARD: 2,000.

---

* Excl Afghan refugees.

PAPUA NEW GUINEA

GDP 1986: K 2.47 bn ($2.55 bn)
1987: K 2.76 bn ($3.04 bn)
Growth 1986: 3.0% 1987: 2.9%
Inflation 1987: 3.3% 1988: 5.5%
Debt 1986: $2.3 bn 1987: $2.4 bn
Def bdgt 1987ε: K 40.0 m ($44.05 m)
1988ε: K 42.7 m ($49.27 m)
FMA 1988: $0.05 m (US)
$1 = K (1986): 0.9713 (1987): 0.9081
(1988): 0.8667

K = kina

Population: 2,580,000

	13–17	18–22	23–32
Men:	221,000	200,000	292,000
Women:	204,000	179,000	249,000

TOTAL ARMED FORCES:
ACTIVE: 3,200.
Terms of service: voluntary.

ARMY: 2,900.
2 inf regt (bn).
1 engr bn (1 more to form).

NAVY: 200.
BASES: Port Moresby (HQ), Lombrum.
PATROL AND COASTAL COMBATANTS: 5:
4 *Tarangau* (Aus Pacific Forum 32m) PCI
1 *Aitape* (Aus *Attack*) PCI
AMPHIBIOUS: craft only: 2 *Salamaua* (Aus *Balikpapan*) LCT.

AIR FORCE: 100. 3 cbt ac, no armed hel.
MR: 3 N-22B *Searchmaster* B.
TRANSPORT: 5 C-47, 1 N-22B *Missionmaster*.

PARA-MILITARY:
BORDER PATROL POLICE: 4,600.

FOREIGN FORCES:
AUSTRALIA: 100; trg unit, 1 engr unit, 30 advisers.

PHILIPPINES

GDP 1987: P 705.47 bn ($34.30 bn)
1988: P 821.84 bn ($38.96 bn)
Growth 1987: 5.9% 1988: 6.7%
Inflation 1987: 3.8% 1988: 8.7%
Debt 1987: $29.0 bn 1988: $30.0 bn
Def exp 1988ε: P 18.09 bn ($857.55 m)

Def bdgt 1989ε: P 27.34 bn ($1.28 bn)
FMA 1988ε: $127.6 m (US)
$1 = P (1987): 20.568 (1988): 21.095
(1989): 21.339

P = pesos

Population: 58,382,000

	13–17	18–22	23–32
Men:	3,239,000	3,062,000	5,278,000
Women:	3,336,000	3,055,000	5,548,000

TOTAL ARMED FORCES:
ACTIVE: 112,000.
Terms of service: voluntary.
RESERVES: 108,000. Army 80,000, (some 75,000 more have commitments); Navy 12,000; Air 16,000 (to age 49).

ARMY: 68,000.
6 Area Unified Comd (joint service).
8 inf div (7 with 3, 1 with 2 bde).
1 lt armd bde ('regt').
1 scout ranger regt (5 bn).
3 engr bde; 1 construction bn.
8 arty bn.
1 special services bde.
1 Presidential Security Group.
EQUIPMENT:
LIGHT TANKS: 41 *Scorpion*.
AIFV: 85 YPR-765 PRI.
APC: 100 M-113, 20 *Chaimite*, 165 V-150.
TOWED ARTY: 105mm: 230 M-101, M-102, M-26 and M-56; 155mm: 12 M-114 and M-68.
MORTARS: 81mm: M-29; 107mm: 40 M-30.
RCL: 75mm: M-20; 90mm: M-67; 106mm: M-40 A1.

NAVY: 28,000 (incl 10,000 Marines, 2,000 Coast Guard). 6 Naval Districts.
BASES: Sangley Point/Cavite, Zamboanga.
FRIGATES: 3:
1 *Rajah Lakandula* (US *Savage*) with 2 × 3 ASTT.
2 *Datu Siratuna* (US *Cannon*).
PATROL AND COASTAL COMBATANTS: 51:
PATROL OFFSHORE: 8:
2 *Rizal* (US *Auk*)
5 *Miguel Malvar* (US PCE-827)
1 *Magat Salamat* (US-MSF).
COASTAL: 4:
2 *Oriental* (US PC-461) PCC.
2 *Camarines Sur* (US LSSL-1) PCC.
INSHORE: 39:
4 *Kagitingan*, 5 *Basilan* (US PGM-39/71) PCI, about 30⟨.
AMPHIBIOUS: 18:
14 *Agusan del Sur* (US LST-511) LST, capacity 16 tk, 10 with accommodation for 200 tps.

4 *Isabella* (US LSM-1) LSM, capacity 50 tps, 4 tk.
Plus some 70 craft; 1 LCT, 60 LCM, 3 LCU,
   some 6 LCVP.

SUPPORT AND MISCELLANEOUS: 8:
2 AOT (small) 3 repair ships, 2 yachts/SAR craft,
   1 tpt.
(Note: The serviceability and operational capability
   of most forces listed is in considerable doubt.)

NAVAL AVIATION: 5 cbt ac, no armed hel.
MR/SAR: 5 BN-2A *Defender*, 1 *Islander*, 12 Bo-105 hel.

MARINES: (10,000):
4 bde (10 bn).
EQUIPMENT:
APC: 30 LVTP-5, 55 LVTP-7.
ARTY: towed: 105mm: 150 M-101.
MORTARS: 4.2-in. (107mm): M-30.

COAST GUARD: (2,000).
EQUIPMENT: Some 65 patrol craft incl 3 large SAR, 2
   lt ac.

AIR FORCE: 16,000;
45 cbt ac, some 71 armed hel.
FIGHTER: 2 sqn with 18 F-5 (14 -A, 4 -B).
COIN:
AIRCRAFT: 1 sqn with 18 T-28D.
   HELICOPTERS: 1 wing with 55 Bell UH-1H/M, 16
      AUH-76 (S-76 gunship conversion).
MR: 2 F-27M.
SAR: 4 HU-16 ac, 10 Bo-105C hel.
PRESIDENTIAL AIRCRAFT WING:
   AIRCRAFT: 1 F-27, 1 F-28.
   HELICOPTERS: 1 Bell 212, 2 S-70A, 2 SA-330.
TRANSPORT: 7 sqn:
   AIRCRAFT:
      1 with 3 C-130H, 3 L-100-20;
      2 with 3 C-47, 8 F-27;
      2 with 10 BN-2 *Islander*, 9 N-22B *Missionmaster*.
   HELICOPTERS: 2 sqn with 15 Bell 205, 17 UH-1H.
LIAISON: 6 Cessna 180, 2 -210, 1 -310, 5 DHC-2,
   15 U-17A/B.
TRAINING: 3 sqn:
   1 with 6 T-33, 3 RT-33.
   1 with 20 T-41D;
   1 with 14 SF-260MP, 9 -WP.
AAM: AIM-9 *Sidewinder*.

PARA-MILITARY:

PHILIPPINE CONSTABULARY (Department of
   National Defence): ε 38,000; 14 Regional Comd,
   234 provincial coy; by law part of armed forces.
**CITIZEN ARMED FORCE GEOGRAPHICAL UNITS
   (CAFGU):** Militia replaces Civil Home Defence

Force: 45,000, 56 bn. Part-time units which can
be called up for extended periods.

OPPOSITION:
NEW PEOPLE'S ARMY (NPA; Communist): 25,500
   (perhaps 16,000 armed).
BANGSA MORO ARMY (armed wing of Moro
   National Liberation Front (MNLF), muslim): ε
   15,000.
MORO ISLAMIC LIBERATION FRONT (breakaway
   from MNLF; muslim): 2,900.
MORO ISLAMIC REFORMIST GROUP (breakaway
   from MNLF): 900.

FOREIGN FORCES:
US: 17,300: Army: 600. Air: 9,200, 1 air div, 48 cbt
   ac. Navy: 5,500, base at Subic Bay.
   Marines: 2,000, 1 MEU sometimes deployed.

SINGAPORE

GDP	1987: S 41.90 bn ($20.20 bn)		
	1988ε: S 48.51 bn ($24.36 bn)		
Growth	1987: 8.8%	1988ε: 13.0%	
Inflation	1987: 0.5%	1988: 1.5%	
Debt	1986: $4.0 bn	1987: $3.4 bn	
Def bdgt	1988/9: S 2.62 bn ($1.32 bn)		
	1989/90: S 2.92 bn ($1.50 bn)		
FMA	1988: $0.05 m (US)		
$1 = S	(1987): 2.1060	(1988): 2.0124
	(1988/9): 1.9818	(1989): 1.9406

S = $ Singapore

Population: 2,658,000

	13–17	18–22	23–32
Men:	114,000	122,000	296,000
Women:	106,000	116,000	279,000

TOTAL ARMED FORCES:
ACTIVE: 55,500 (34,800 conscripts).
Terms of service: conscription; 24–30 months.
RESERVES: Army 170,000; annual trg to age 40
   for men, 50 for officers. Navy ε 4,500. Air Force ε
   7,500. People's Defence Force: ε 30,000.

ARMY: 45,000 (30,000 conscripts).
1 inf div:
   2 inf bde (each 3 inf bn).
   1 air mobile bde (3 inf bn).
   1 recce, 1 arty, 1 mor, 1 AD arty, 1 engr bn.
1 armd bde (1 tk, 2 APC bn).
1 cdo bn.
1 arty, 1 SP mor bn.

1 target acquisition bn.
1 engr bn.

RESERVES:
2 div, 1 armd, 6 inf bde HQ; 18 inf, 1 cdo, 10
arty, 2 AD arty, 3 engr bn.
People's Defence Force: some 30,000; org in 2
comd, 7 bde gp, ε 21 bn.

EQUIPMENT:
LIGHT TANKS: ε 350 AMX-13.
APC: 720 M-113, 30 V-100, 250 V-150/-200
Commando.
TOWED ARTY: 155mm: 38 Soltam M-71,
16 M-114A1 (may be in store), M-68 (may be in
store), 24 FH88.
MORTARS: 81mm (some SP); 120mm: 50 (some SP
in M-113); 160mm: 12 Tampella.
ATGW: 30 *Milan*.
RL: 89mm: M-20 3.5 in..
RCL: 84mm: *Carl Gustav*; 106mm: 90 M-40A1 (in
store).
AD GUNS: 20mm: 30; 35mm: 34 GDF-002; 40mm:
16 L/70.
SAM: RBS-70 (some SP in V-200).

NAVY: 4,500 (1,800 conscripts).
BASE: Pulau Brani (Singapore).
PATROL AND COASTAL COMBATANTS: 27:
CORVETTES: 1 *Victory* (FRG Lürssen 62m) with 8 ×
Harpoon SSM, 2 × 3 ASTT.
MISSILE CRAFT: 6 *Sea Wolf* (FRG Lürssen-45)
PFM with 5 *Gabriel*-II SSM (2 with 2 × 2
Harpoon, 2 × *Gabriel*).
PATROL, INSHORE: 20:
6 *Independence/Sovereignty* (33m).
1 *Endeavour* (trg), 1 *Panglima* (UK *Ford*) (trg);
12⟨.
MINE WARFARE: 2:
2 *Jupiter* (US *Bluebird*) MSC.
AMPHIBIOUS: 5.
5 *Endurance* (US LST-511) LST, capacity 200 tps,
16 tk.
Plus craft: 8 LCM.

AIR FORCE: 6,000 (3,000 conscripts);
188 cbt ac, some armed hel.
FGA: 4 sqn:
3 with 67 A-4S/SI, 13 TA-4S/SI.
1 with 24 *Hunter* F-74, 4 T-75.
(4 F-16A, 4 -B due to be operational in 1990.)
FIGHTER: 2 sqn with 33 F-5E, 9 F-5F.
RECCE: 4 *Hunter* FR-74.
AEW: 1 sqn with 4 E-2C.
TRANSPORT:
AIRCRAFT: 2 sqn:
1 with 4 C-130B (tkr/tpt), 6 C-130H.
1 with 6 *Skyvan* 3M (tpt/SAR).
HELICOPTERS: 3 sqn:

1 with 6 AS-350, 18 UH-1B;
1 with 4 AB-205, 5 Bell 205, 16 UH-1H
(some armed);
1 with 22 AS-332M (incl 3 SAR).
TRAINING: 3 sqn:
2 with 30 SIAI S-211;
1 with 26 SF-260 (14 -MS, 12 -WS).
AD: 4 bn: 3 SAM, 1 arty:
1 with 28 *Bloodhound* 2;
1 with 10 *Rapier* (with *Blindfire*);
1 with 6 *Improved HAWK*.
1 with 35mm Oerlikon (towed) guns.
AIRFIELD DEFENCE: 1 field defence sqn (reservists).
AAM: AIM-9 J/P *Sidewinder*.

FORCES ABROAD:
BRUNEI: (500); trg school, incl hel det (with 5 UH-1).
TAIWAN: trg camp.

PARA-MILITARY:
POLICE/MARINE POLICE: 11,600; incl some 750
Gurkhas, 10 PCI⟨ plus boats.
CIVIL DEFENCE FORCE: ε 100,000 (incl regulars,
conscripts, volunteers, ε 34,000 former army
reservists). 1 construction bde (2,500).

FOREIGN FORCES:
NEW ZEALAND: 20: spt unit.

SRI LANKA

GDP	1987:	Rs 196.72 bn ($6.68 bn)	
	1988ε:	Rs 231.35 bn ($7.27 bn)	
Growth	1987:	1.5%	1988: 3.6%
Inflation	1987:	7.7%	1988: 14.0%
Debt	1987:	$4.5 bn	1988: $4.9 bn
Def exp	1987ε:	Rs 11.40 bn ($387.16 m)*	
Def bdgt	1988ε:	Rs 18.00 bn ($583.29 m)	
FMA	1988:	$0.16 m (US)	
$1 = Rs	(1987):	29.445	(1988): 30.807
Rs = rupees			

Population: 16,733,000

	13–17	18–22	23–32
Men:	921,000	869,000	1,483,000
Women:	882,000	845,000	1,485,000

TOTAL ARMED FORCES: some 47,000 incl
recalled reservists.
ACTIVE: 22,000.
Terms of service: voluntary.
RESERVES: some 25,000; obligation: 7 years
post-Regular service.

ARMY: 40,000, incl recalled reservists (being re-org).
2 div HQ.
5 'Task Forces' (inf bde: with 5 regular, 6 reserve bn).
2 recce regt (bn) (1 reserve).
2 fd arty (incl 1 reserve), 1 AD arty regt.
1 fd engr, 1 engr plant regt.
EQUIPMENT:
RECCE: 18 *Saladin*, 15 *Ferret*, 12 Daimler *Dingo*.
APC: 10 BTR-152, 144 other (incl *Buffel*, *Saracen*).
TOWED ARTY: 76mm: 16 Yug M-48;
  85mm: 30 Ch Type-56; 88mm: 25 pdr.
  105mm; 122mm; both reported.
MORTARS: 107mm: 12 4.2-in.; 120mm: reported.
RCL: 82mm: M-60; 106mm: M-40.
AD GUNS: 40mm: 24 L-60; 94mm: 24 3.7-in.

NAVY: 5,500.
BASES: Trincomalee (HQ), Karainagar, Colombo,
  Tangalla, Kalpitiya.
PATROL AND COASTAL COMBATANTS: 36:
PATROL, COASTAL: 2 *Jayesagara* PCC.
PATROL, INSHORE: 34:
  6 *Sooraya* (Ch *Shanghai* II) PFI⟨.
  12 Is *Dvora* PFI⟨.
  16 PCI⟨.
AMPHIBIOUS: craft only; 2 LCM
SUPPORT AND MISCELLANEOUS: 3:
  3 *Abheetha*, spt/cmd.

AIR FORCE: 3,700 incl active Reservists;
  9 cbt ac, 15 armed hel.
COIN: 9 SF-260TP.
ATTACK HELICOPTERS: 11 Bell 212, 4 -412.
MR: 1 sqn with 3 Cessna 337, 3 *Dove*, 1 *Heron* ac; 2
  SA-365 hel.
TRANSPORT: 1 sqn with 2 BAe 748, 1 Cessna 421C,
  1 *Super King Air*, 10 Ch Y-12.
HELICOPTERS: 12 Bell 206.
TRAINING: incl 6 Cessna 150/152, 5 *Chipmunk*.
RESERVES: Air Force Regt, 3 sqn; Airfield
  Construction Regt, 1 sqn.

PARA-MILITARY:
POLICE FORCE: 23,500 (increase to 28,000
  planned) incl Special Task Force: 2,000-man
  anti-guerrilla unit.
NATIONAL AUXILIARY VOLUNTEER FORCE:
  5,000 (to be 10,000).
HOME GUARD: 18,000 (to be disbanded).

OPPOSITION:
LIBERATION TIGERS OF TAMIL EELAM (LTTE):
  Leader: Velupillai Pirabakaran: ε 2,000.
**EELAM PEOPLE'S REVOLUTIONARY
  LIBERATION FRONT** (EPRLF): ε 1,000: Indian
  backed Tamil group.

JANATHA VIMUKTHI PERAMUNA (JVP): People's
  Liberation Front: ε 1,200: Maoist.

FOREIGN FORCES:
INDIA: (IPKF) some 47,000. Army: 45,000, 4 inf
  div. Plus naval and air force elm. Central Reserve
  Police Force: 1,500.

---

* Incl extra allocation of Rs 2.5 bn to meet internal
security expenditure.

TAIWAN

GNP	1987:	$NT 2,791.5 bn ($US 80.42 bn)		
	1988ε:	$NT 2,820.8 bn ($US 98.79 bn)		
Growth	1987:	11.0%	1988:	11.2%
Inflation	1987:	0.7%	1988:	1.0%
Debt	1987:	$US 2.5 bn	1988:	$US 1.9 bn
Def bdgt	1988/9:	$NT 191.40 bn ($US 6.70 bn)		
	1989/90:	$NT 212.70 bn ($US 7.64 bn)		
$1 = $NT	(1987):	34.71	(1988):	28.55
	(1988/9):	29.572	(1989):	27.839

$NT = New Taiwan dollars

Population: 20,971,000

	13–17	18–22	23–32
Men:	919,000	970,000	1,958,000
Women:	867,000	916,000	1,878,000

TOTAL ARMED FORCES:
ACTIVE: 405,500.
Terms of service: 2 years.
RESERVES: 1,657,500. Army: 1,500,000 have
  some Reserve obligation to age 30. Navy 32,500,
  Marines 35,000, Air 90,000.

ARMY: 270,000.
  3 Army, 6 Corps, 1 SF HQ.
  12 hy inf div,
  96 lt inf div,
  2 mech inf div,
  1 AB bde.
  4 tk gp,
  22 fd arty bn,
  5 SAM bn: 2 with *Nike Hercules*, 3 with *HAWK*.
  6 avn sqn.
RESERVES: 9 inf div.
EQUIPMENT:
MBT: 309 M-48A5.
LIGHT TANKS: 275 M-24 (90mm gun), 675
  M-41/Type 64.
RECCE: M-8.
AIFV: 225 M-113 with 20/30mm cannon.
APC: 40 M-2 half-track, 650 M-113, 300 V-150
  Commando.

TOWED ARTY: 105mm: 650 M-101 (T-64);
155mm: M-44, 90 M-59, 250 M-114 (T-65);
203mm: 70 M-115.
SP ARTY: 105mm: 100 M-108; 155mm: 45 T-69,
110 M-109A1; 203mm: 60 M-110.
MRL: 117mm: KF VI; 126mm: KF III/IV towed and SP.
MORTARS: 81mm: M-29 (some SP); 107mm.
SSM: *Hsiung Feng* (*Gabriel*-type) coastal defence.
ATGW: *Kun Wu* (TOW-type), TOW (some SP).
RCL: 90mm: M-67; 106mm: 500 M-40/Type 51.
ATK GUNS: 76mm: 150 M-18 SP.
AD GUNS: 35mm; 40mm: 400 (incl M-42 SP, Bofors).
SAM: 36 *Nike Hercules*, 54 *HAWK*, some *Chaparral*;
Tien Kung (*Sky Bow*)-1/-2.
AVIATION:
 AIRCRAFT: 20 O-1.
 HELICOPTERS: 118 UH-1H.

DEPLOYMENT:
QUEMOY: 55,000,
MATSU: 18,000.

NAVY: 35,500.
3 Naval Districts.
BASES: Tsoying (HQ), Makung (Pescadores), Keelung.
SUBMARINES: 4:
2 *Hai Lung* (Nl mod *Zwaardvis*) with 533mm TT.
2 *Hai Shih* (US *Guppy* II) with 533mm TT.
PRINCIPAL SURFACE COMBATANTS: 36:
DESTROYERS: 26:
14 *Chao Yang* (US *Gearing*) (ASW); 13 with 1
Hughes MD-500 hel, 8 with 1 × 8 *ASROC*, all
with 2 × 3 ASTT; plus 1 or 2 × 2 127mm guns,
5 or 3 *Hsiung Feng-II* (HF-2) (Is *Gabriel*) SSM.
8 *Po Yang* (US *Sumner*) with 2 or 3 × 2 127mm
guns; plus 2 × 3 ASTT; 3 with 3 or 4 *HF-2* SSM.
4 *Kun Yang* (US *Fletcher*) with 3 or 4 127mm
guns; plus 2 × 3 ASTT with 5 *HF-2* SSM.
FRIGATES: 10:
9 *Tien Shan* (US *Lawrence/Crosley*), 8 with 2 × 3
ASTT; plus 2 × 127mm guns.
1 *Tai Yuan* (US *Rudderow*) with 2 × 3 ASTT; plus
2 × 127mm guns.
PATROL AND COASTAL COMBATANTS: 67:
MISSILE CRAFT: 52:
2 *Lung Chiang* PFM with 2 × HF-2 SSM
50 *Hai Ou* (mod Is *Dvora*)⟨ with 2 × HF-2 SSM
PATROL, OFFSHORE: 3 *Ping Jin* (US *Auk* MSF) with
3 × ASTT.
INSHORE: About 12 PCI⟨.
MINE WARFARE: 8:
8 *Yung Chou* (US *Adjutant*) MSC.
AMPHIBIOUS: 27
1 *Kao Hsiung* (US LST 511) amph comd.
1 *Cheng Hai* (US *Cabildo*) LSD, capacity about 18
tk, 200+ tps.
21 *Chung Hai* (US LST-511) LST, capacity 16 tk,
200 tps.

4 *Mei Lo* (US LSM-1) LSM, capacity about 4 tk.
Plus about 280 craft; 20 LCU, some 260 LCM.
SUPPORT AND MISCELLANEOUS: 13:
4 spt tankers, 2 repair/salvage, 6 tugs, 1
survey/research.

NAVAL AIR: 32 cbt ac; 12 armed hel.
MR: 1 sqn with 32 S-2 (25 -E, 7 -F).
HELICOPTERS: 1 sqn with 12 Hughes 500MD ASW
Defender.

MARINES: 30,000.
2 div, spt elm.
EQUIPMENT:
APC: LVT-4/-5.
TOWED ARTY: 105mm, 155mm.
RCL: 106mm.

AIR FORCE: 70,000;
469 cbt ac, no armed hel. 5 cbt wings.
FGA/FIGHTER: 14 sqn with 25 F-5A, 8 -B, 220 -E, 55
-F, 128 F-104, 33 TF-104G, 50 F-104G.
RECCE: 1 sqn with 3 RF-104G.
SAR: 1 sqn with 5 HU-16B ac, 12 S-70, 12 UH-1H hel.
TRANSPORT: 8 sqn:
 AIRCRAFT: 2 with 24 Douglas (20 C-47, 2 C-54, 1
 C-118B, 1 DC-6B);
 3 with 45 Fairchild (35 C-119G, 10 C-123B/K);
 1 with 12 C-130H.
 1 with 12 Beech 1900.
 1 VIP with 5 Boeing (1 720B, 4 727-100).
 HELICOPTERS: 5 CH-34, 1 S-62A (VIP), 14 S-70.
TRAINING: incl 60 AT-3, PL-1B, T-28A, 30 T-33A,
42 T-34C, 40 T-Ch-1 ac; 10 Bell 47G, 6 Hughes
500 hel.
AAM: AIM-4D *Falcon*, AIM-7F *Sparrow*, AIM-9J/P
Sidewinder, *Shafrir*.
ASM: AGM-12 *Bullpup*, AGM-65A *Maverick*.

PARA-MILITARY:
SECURITY GROUPS (Ministry of Defence): 25,000:
incl National Police Administration. Bureau of
Investigation. Military Police HQ.
CUSTOMS SERVICE (Ministry of Finance):
4 PCO, 5 PCC, 5 PCI; most armed.

FOREIGN FORCES:
SINGAPORE: trg camp.

THAILAND

GDP	1987:	b 1,223.20 bn ($47.55 bn)	
	1988ε:	b 1,404.23 bn ($55.52 bn)	
Growth	1987:	8.8%	1988: 11.0%

Inflation	1987:	2.6%	1988:	3.8%
Debt	1987:	$19.0 bn	1988:	$19.8 bn

Def bdgt   1987/8ε: b 44.77 bn ($1.74 bn)
           1988/9ε: b 46.30 bn ($1.83 bn)
FMA   1988ε: $24.2 m (US)
$1 = b   (1987):   25.723   (1988):   25.294
           (1989):   25.447

b = baht

Population: 54,628,000

	13–17	18–22	23–32
Men:	3,102,000	3,109,000	4,879,000
Women:	2,991,000	2,998,000	4,764,000

TOTAL ARMED FORCES:
ACTIVE: 283,000.
Terms of service: 2 years.
RESERVES: 500,000.

ARMY: 190,000 (80,000 conscripts).
4 Regional Army HQ, 2 Corps HQ.
2 cav (lt armd) div (2 cav, 1 arty regt).
1 mech inf div.
6 inf div (incl Royal Guard, 5 with 1 tk bn)
   (2 to be mech, 1 to be lt).
2 SF div.
1 arty div, 1 AD arty div (6 AD arty bn).
19 engr bn.
1 indep cav regt.
8 indep inf bn.
4 recce coy.
Armd air cav regt with 3 airmobile coy.
Some hel flt.
RESERVES: 4 inf div HQ.
EQUIPMENT:
MBT: 60+ Ch Type-69, 64 M-48A5.
LIGHT TANKS: 134 *Scorpion*, 200 M-41 (most in
   store), 20 M-24 (in store), some 9 *Stingray*.
RECCE: 32 *Shorland* Mk 3.
APC: 340 M-113, M-3A1/M-16 half-track, 150
   V-150 *Commando*, 20 *Saracen*, ε 300 Ch Type-85
   (YW-531H), 105 Ch Type-63.
TOWED ARTY: some 374. 105mm: 200 M-101/-101
   mod, 12 M-102, some M-618A2 (local
   manufacture); 130mm: 18 Ch Type-59; 155mm:
   50 M-114, 62 M-198, 32 M-71.
MRL: 130mm: Ch Type-82 reported.
MORTARS: 81mm, 107mm.
ATGW: *TOW*, 300 *Dragon*.
RL: M-72 *LAW*.
RCL: 57mm: M-18; 75mm: M-20; 106mm: 150 M-40.
AD GUNS: 20mm: 40 M-163 *Vulcan*, 24 M-167
   Vulcan; 37mm: some 30 Type-74; 40mm: 80
   M-1/M-42 SP; 104 L/70; 57mm: 24.
SAM: *Redeye*, some *Aspide*.
AVIATION:

TRANSPORT: 1 Beech 99, 4 C-47, 10 Cessna 208, 1
   Queen Air, 1 Short 330, 1 *Super King Air*.
LIAISON: 62 O-1A, 17 -E, 6 T-41A, 13 U-17A.
HELICOPTERS: 10 Bell 206, 15 -212, 6 -214, 3
   OH-58A.
TRAINING: 36 Hughes 300C, 12 OH-13, 14 TH-55.

NAVY: 50,000 (some conscripts) incl naval air
and marines.
BASES: Bangkok, (HQ) Sattahip, Songkla, Phan
   Nga, Nakhon Phanom (HQ Mekong River
   Operating Unit).
FRIGATES: 5:
   1 *Makut Rajakumarn* with 2 × 3 ASTT (*Sting Ray*
      LWT); plus 2 × 114mm guns.
   2 *Tapi* (US PF-103) with 2 × 3 ASTT (Mk 46 LWT).
   2 *Tachin* (US *Tacoma*)(trg) with 2 × 3 ASTT.
PATROL AND COASTAL COMBATANTS: 52:
CORVETTES: 2:
   2 *Ratanakosin* with 2 × 3 ASTT (*Sting Ray* LWT);
      plus 2 × 4 *Harpoon* SSM.
MISSILE CRAFT: 6:
   3 *Ratcharit* (It Breda 50m) with 4 × MM-38
      Exocet SSM.
   3 *Prabparapak* (FRG Lürssen 45m) with 5 *Gabriel*
      SSM.
PATROL: 44:
   COASTAL: 14:
      3 *Chon Buri* PFC, 6 *Sattahip*, 5 *Sarasin* (US
         PC-461) PCC.
   INSHORE: 30:
      10 T-11 (US PGM-71), about 20 PCI⟨.
MINE WARFARE: 7:
   2 *Bang Rachan* (FRG Lürssen T-48) MCC.
   4 *Ladya* (US '*Bluebird*' MSC) MSC.
   1 *Thalang* MCM spt.
AMPHIBIOUS: 10:
   2 *Sichang* (Fr PS-700) LST, capacity 14 tk, 300 tps.
   5 *Angthong* (US LST-511) LST, capacity 16 tk,
      200 tps (1 trg).
   3 *Kut* (US LSM-1) LSM, capacity about 4 tk.
   Plus 39 craft; 10 LCU, 29 LCM.
SUPPORT AND MISCELLANEOUS: 5:
   1 small tanker, 2 survey, 2 trg.

NAVAL AIR: (900); 27 cbt ac; 8 armed hel.
MR/ASW: 1 sqn with 3 F-27MPA, 5 N-24A
   Searchmaster L, 9 S-2F.
MR/SAR: 1 sqn with 2 CL-215.
MR/ATTACK: 10 Cessna T-337.
SAR: 1 hel sqn with 4 Bell 212, 5 -214, 4 UH-1H.
ASM: AGM-84 *Harpoon* (for F-27MPA).

MARINES: (20,000).
6 inf regt, 1 arty regt (3 fd, 1 AA bn);
   1 amph assault bn; recce bn.
EQUIPMENT:

APC: 33 LVTP-7.
TOWED ARTY: 155mm: 18 GC-45.
ATGW: *TOW, Dragon.*

AIR FORCE: 43,000; 145 cbt ac, no armed hel.
FGA: 1 sqn with 9 F-5A, 4 -B.
6 F-16A, 4 -B delivered; 8 more due by 1991.
FIGHTER: 2 sqn with 33 F-5E, 3 -F.
COIN: 6 sqn:
2 with 26 OV-10C;
2 with 26 AU-23A;
1 with 15 A-37B;
1 with 14 N-22B *Missionmaster.*
ELINT: 1 sqn with 3 IAI-201.
RECCE: 3 RF-5A, 3RT-33A.
SURVEY: 1 Commander 690, 2 *King Air* 90, 3 *Learjet* 35A, 2 *Merlin* IVA.
TRANSPORT: 3 sqn:
1 with 3 C-130H, 3 C-130H-30, 3 DC-8-62F.
1 with 12 C-123 (4 -B, 8-K), 6 BAe-748.
1 with 10 C-47.
  VIP: Royal flight: 2 Boeing 737-200, 1 *Merlin* IV, 1 *King Air* 200 ac; 2 Bell 412 hel.
TRAINING: 24 CT-4, 16 *Fantrainer* V-600, 12 SF-260 MS, 18 -MT, 53 T-33A, 13 T-37B, 6 -C, 11 T-41.
LIAISON: 3 *Commander*, 2 *King Air* E90, 30 O-1, 3 U-10B.
HELICOPTERS: 2 sqn:
1 with 18 S-58T.
1 with 22 UH-1H.
AAM: AIM-9B/J *Sidewinder.*
AD: 4 bn; *Blowpipe* SAM. 1 AA arty bty: 2 *Skyguard* radar, each with 4 fire units of 2 × 30mm Mauser guns.

PARA-MILITARY:
THAHAN PHRAN ('Hunter Soldiers'): 18,500 volunteer irregular force; 27 regt of some 200 coy.
NATIONAL SECURITY VOLUNTEER CORPS: 43,000.
MARINE POLICE: 1,700; 2 PFC, 1 PFI, some 30 PCI⟨
POLICE AVIATION: 500; 1 C-47 (tpt), 5 Short (3 *Skyvan*, 1 *Sherpa*, 1 330-UTT), 4 PC-6, 3 AU-23, 3 DHC-4, 1 Do-28, 2 Cessna 310, 1 *Airtourer*, 1 CT-4 ac; 44 Bell (3 212, 14 206, 27 205A), 1 S-62, 6 HH-12, 5 KH-4 hel.
BORDER PATROL POLICE: 28,000.
PROVINCIAL POLICE: ε 50,000 incl Special Action Force (ε 500).

OPPOSITION:
COMMUNIST PARTY OF MALAYA (CPM): some 850.
COMMUNIST PARTY OF THAILAND (CPT): ε 200.
THAI PEOPLE'S REVOLUTIONARY MOVEMENT (TPRM); also known as *Pak* (or *Phak*) *Mai* (New Party) New Communist Party/*Sayam Mai* (New Siam): 1,500 claimed; active guerrillas

ε 100. Vietnam/Laos-backed Communists.
ISLAMIC: Patani United Liberation Organization; Barisan Revolusi Nasional (BRN) (National Revolution Party): together ε 400.

VIETNAM

GDP	1986ε: $US 12.2–20.4 bn	
	1987ε: $US 12.6–20.8 bn	
Growth	1986ε: 3.4%	1987ε: 2.1%
Inflation	1986ε: 700%	1987ε: over 1,000%
Debt*	1987ε: $8.0 bn	1988ε: $9.0 bn
Def bdgt†	n.k.	

Population: 64,042,000

	13–17	18–22	23–32
Men:	3,633,000	3,685,000	5,916,000
Women:	3,484,000	3,483,000	5,801,000

TOTAL ARMED FORCES:
ACTIVE: 1,249,000 (often referred to as 'Main Force').
Terms of service: 3 years, specialists 4 years, some ethnic minorities 2 years.
RESERVES 'Strategic Rear Force' some 2,500,000 manpower potential see also Para-Military Forces.

ARMY: 1,100,000.
14 Corps HQ.
65 inf div (2 trg, perhaps 28 cadre).‡
10 armd bde.
15 indep inf regt.
Special Operations Force incl AB bde, demolition engr (org in regt of 5 bn).
some 10 fd arty bde.
8 engr div.
10–16 economic construction div; 20 indep engr bde.§
EQUIPMENT://
MBT: 1,600 T-34/-54/-55, 350 Ch Type-59.
LIGHT TANKS: PT-76, Ch Type-62/63.
RECCE: 80 BRDM-1/-2.
AIFV: 120 BMP.
APC: 1,500 BTR-40/-50/-60/-152, Ch Type-63, Ch Type-531, M-113.
TOWED ARTY: 100mm: incl M-1944, T-12; 105mm: M-101/-102; 122mm: incl M-1938, D-30, 130mm: 200 M-1946; 152mm: 250 D-20; 155mm: M-114.
SP ARTY: 155mm: 90 mod M-114.
ASSAULT GUNS: 100mm: SU-100; 105mm: ISU-122.
MRL: 107mm: Type 63; 122mm: BM-21; 140mm: BM-14-16.
MORTARS: 81mm, 82mm, 120mm, 160mm.
ATGW: AT-3 *Sagger.*

RCL: 57mm: Ch Type-36; 75mm: Ch Type-52, Ch Type-57; 82mm: B-10; 88mm: Ch Type-51; 90mm; 107mm: B-11.

AD GUNS: 8,000: 14.5mm; 23mm: incl ZSU-23-4 SP; 30mm; 37mm; 57mm; 85mm; 100mm.

SAM: SA-7.

NAVY: 37,000 (incl 27,000 Naval Infantry).
Four Naval Zones.

BASES: Vietnam: Cam Ranh Bay, Da Nang, Haiphong, Hanoi, Ha Tou, Ho Chi Minh City.
  Abroad: Kampuchea: (Fifth Naval Zone): Kompong Som, Ream.

FRIGATES: 7:
  1 *Phan Ngu Lao* (US *Barnegat*) (ASUW), with 2 × SS-N-2 *Styx* SSM, 1 × 127mm gun.
  5 Sov *Petya* II with 4 × ASW RL, 3 × 533mm TT.
  1 *Tran Khanh Du* (US *Savage*) with 2 × 3 ASTT.

PATROL AND COASTAL COMBATANTS: 62:
MISSILE CRAFT: 8 Sov *Osa* with 4 × SS-N-2 SSM.

TORPEDO CRAFT: 21:
  5 Sov *Turya* PHT with 4 × 533mm TT.
  16 Sov *Shershen* PFT with 4 × 533mm TT.

PATROL: 33:
  OFFSHORE: 2 US *Admirable* MSF
  INSHORE: 31:
    6 Sov So-1, 10 US PGM-59/71, 15⟨.

MINE WARFARE: 5:
  2 *Yurka* MSC, 1 *Sonya* MSC, 2 *Yevgenya* MHI⟨.

AMPHIBIOUS: 7:
  3 US LST-511 LST, capacity 200 tps, 16 tk.
  3 Sov *Polnocny* LSM, capacity 180 tps, 6 tk.
  1 US LSM-1 LSM, capacity about 50 tps, 4 tk.
  Plus about 24 craft; 12 LCM, 12 LCU

(Note: Information on serviceability, indeed continued existence, of naval units listed is extremely scarce.)

NAVAL INFANTRY: (27,000) (amph, cdo).

AIR FORCE: 12,000;
  394 cbt ac, 47 armed hel (plus many in store).//
  4 Air Div.

FGA: 5 regt:
  2 with 70 Ch J-5;
  1 with 36 MiG-23BN;
  1 with 30 Su-7B;
  1 with 40 Su-20.

FIGHTER: 6 regt with 206 MiG-21bis/PF.

ATTACK HELICOPTERS: 30 Mi-24.

MR: 12 Be-12.

ASW HEL: 17 Ka-25.

SURVEY: 2 An-30.

TRANSPORT: 3 regt: some 135 ac incl 12 An-2, 9 An-24, 50 An-26, 2 Boeing 707, 6 Il-14, 2 Il-18, 20 Li-2, 8 Tu-134, 11 Yak-40.

HELICOPTERS: 1 div (3 regt) with 200 hel incl 30 Mi-4, 20 Mi-6, 36 Mi-8.

TRAINING: 3 regt with 53 ac incl L-29, L-39, MiG-15UTI, MiG-21U, Yak-11, Yak-18.

AAM: AA-2 *Atoll*.

AIR DEFENCE FORCE: 100,000.
14 AD div:
  SAM: some 66 sites with SA-2/-3;
  4 AD arty bde: 37mm, 57mm, 85mm, 100mm, 130mm; plus People's Regional Force: ε 1,000 units.
  6 radar bde: 100 sites.

FORCES ABROAD:
CAMBODIA: 60–65,000, withdrawal continues.
LAOS: 10–15,000.

PARA-MILITARY:
PEOPLE'S REGIONAL FORCE: 500,000. Org at and op within provincial level, some div but mainly regt and coy. Although full-time also engage in economic production. Acts as reserve for Main Force

LOCAL FORCES: Some 2,500,000. Incl People's Self Defence Force (urban units), People's Militia (northern rural units), Armed Youth Assault Force (southern rural units), Centralized Militia (mainly Montagnards in Chinese border region). Comprise: static and mobile cbt units, log spt and village protection pl. Some arty, mor and AD guns. Acts as reserve for People's Regional Force.

'TACTICAL REAR FORCE': Some 500,000 manpower potential mainly ex full-time servicemen. Acts as reserve for Local Forces.

OPPOSITION: ε 25,000 incl:
UNITED FRONT FOR THE LIBERATION OF THE OPPRESSED RACES (FULRO) ε 2,500; montagnards; Cambodian border.
NATIONAL SALVATION MOVEMENT.
ARMY OF THE REPUBLIC OF VIETNAM (remnants; *Hoa Hao*).

---

* Incl some $2.3 bn owed to CMEA.
†Extensive Sov mil aid makes est of def bdgt impossible. Sov economic and mil aid est at over $1.0 bn per annum for 1986 and 1987.
‡ Inf div strengths vary from 5,000 to 12,500.
§ Men beyond normal mil age; unit strength about 4,000 each, fully armed, with mil and economic role.
// Much US, some Soviet eqpt probably inoperable.

Caribbean and Latin America

General

Debt, drugs and the traumas of transition to democratic rule continued to underlie the principal threats to security and domestic order in Latin America. While regional and domestic peace processes were pursued throughout the year, the levels of guerrilla insurgency remained unacceptably high in many countries.

Progress towards resolution of the war in **Nicaragua** continued with the five Central American governments (Nicaragua, El Salvador, Honduras, Costa Rica and Guatemala) agreeing in February 1989 to a plan to demobilize the Contras (now largely neutralized for lack of US military aid) in return for assurances by the Sandinista government that fair national elections would take place by February 1990. The following month the five states approved a plan to create a UN Peacekeeping Force to ensure that guerrillas would not launch cross-border raids, but by mid-July 1989 UN officials still considered that the establishment of such a force was a distant prospect.

Outside of Nicaragua, the most serious threats to domestic order in Central America were in **El Salvador**. President Alfredo Cristiani, who came to power with the landslide victory of his far right ARENA party in the March 1989 elections, announced in his inaugural address on 1 June his desire for a 'permanent dialogue' with leftist guerrillas of the Farabundo Martí Front for National Liberation (FMLN). The insurgency and counter-attacks have continued, with neither side accepting the other's peace proposals.

In South America, both **Peru** and **Colombia** remained beset by violence. Throughout the year in Peru the Sendero Luminoso ('Shining Path') guerrilla group demonstrated their capacity to cut essential supplies of both food and electricity to the capital, Lima, just as the group extended their sphere of influence from Ayacucho in the south to Cajamarca in the north. In Colombia violence became more widespread despite a number of government peace programmes. President Virgilio Barco was able to meet some members of the M19 movement in April, but the activities of other guerrilla groups not willing to join peace talks have served to further disrupt Colombia's economy, thus adding to the problems of internal order caused by the still powerful drug barons.

There were some signs of encouragement internationally when President Menem of **Argentina**, who before his election appeared to take a belligerent stand on the Falkland Islands, offered, after his assumption of power, to hold 'a civilized dialogue' with the UK, in which both sides would reserve their respective positions on sovereignty. In this context, Menem held out the possibility of announcing a formal end to hostilities. At the other end of the continent, however, the US dispute with President Noriega intensified; following attacks on US personnel in **Panama** the US was obliged to send reinforcements to the Canal Zone.

Military Developments

There have been virtually no developments of note in the ground forces of the region in the last 12 months; however, a few new naval units have been brought into service. Some new aircraft have also been delivered, but changes to Air Force listings principally reflect new information and reassessment. The more significant developments are listed below.

The **Chilean** Navy has taken delivery of two *Sa'ar* missile craft transferred from the Israeli Navy, and the Air Force, having cancelled an order for F-5 FGA aircraft, was unable to obtain Israeli *Kfir* FGA as the US-made engine may not be resold to Chile. The Argentine Navy has added a fourth FRG-designed *MEKO 140* frigate built locally. The US Congress has authorized the sale of spare parts to Argentina; this will allow the repair and refurbishment of M-113 APC and UH-1 helicopters. Development of the *Condor* II 800-km range SSM continues, reportedly in conjunction with Egypt.

Brazil has commissioned the first of four locally built *Inhauma*-class frigates which are armed with torpedoes and *Exocet* SSM and embark a *Lynx* helicopter. The naval *Lynx*, shown as utility helicopters last year, are now known to be armed with Mark 46 torpedoes. The

Navy, which has a long-term project to develop a nuclear-powered submarine, commissioned a small nuclear reactor as a test-bed. However, the Brazilian programme for conventional submarine construction is going very slowly and no SSN can be in service before the year 2000. The Air Force's *Mirage* III have been up-dated with new electronics and a further six aircraft have been brought into service. The Brazilian Army has procured a further 80 locally manufactured M-41 light tanks. Development of the 300-km range Avibras SS-300 SSM continues. A reappraisal of **Cuban** Army organization shows that there are nine rather than three mechanized infantry divisions

Defence Spending

The last five years have witnessed the progressive transfer of political power from military juntas to more democratically elected governments. While one of the main aims of such governments has been to reduce the influence and role of their armed forces and the usually high level of defence expenditure, this has not been possible in every case. Overall, the worsening economic predicament of many of the countries of the region presents governments with a dilemma. Defence spending must be cut if the essential reduction in public sector expenditure is to be achieved. However, internal security capabilities must be maintained and, in many cases, the military need to be compensated not only for reduced budgets but also for their loss of influence and political power.

In **Argentina** after years of profligate allocations under military rule, defence expenditure was roughly halved in 1986. Since then the military have complained continuously of their reduced budgets (which led to declining privileges, living standards and their public esteem), as well as to vilification for their abuse of human rights. After a series of small-scale rebellions, resolved by secret deals, the government made concessions in all these areas: the armed forces received four salary increases in the second half of 1988, and there was some resurgence of military influence in both internal and external affairs. In addition to a defence budget allocation estimated at between $US1–2 bn for the current fiscal year, a $US4 bn modernization programme for the armed forces was announced in January 1989 by the Alfonsín regime. There must be serious doubts, however, as to the capacity of the economy to bear such costs, particularly at a time when the new government is attempting to introduce a stringent economic regime.

In **Brazil** the continuing influence of the armed forces has been reflected in the modernization plan for the 1990s. Defence allocations have continued to grow, though recent high inflation and a faltering economy seem to have slowed down the programme. The Brazilian military have been helped by a powerful arms-production industry, until recently a vibrant exporter able to compete in world markets.

Colombia faces two serious internal threats, from the Coordinadora Nacional Guerrillera movements and from the well-organized and often well-armed drug war-lords. It is not surprising therefore that defence allocations are officially said to have increased by 37.8% in real terms between 1988 and 1989. In **Nicaragua** the complete failure of the economy has coincided with the collapse of the Contra campaign thus allowing the Sandinista regime to reduce military spending.

ARGENTINA

GDP	1986:	A 74.31 bn ($78.80 bn)
	1987ε:	A 174.63 bn ($81.44 bn)
Growth	1986: 5.5%	1987: 2.0%
Inflation	1987: 131.6%	1988: 342.7%
Debt	1987: $54.0 bn	1988: $59.0 bn
Def exp	1987ε:	A 2.63 bn ($1.22 bn)
	1988ε:	A 13.97 bn ($1.60 bn)

FMA	1988: $0.13m (US)		
$1 = A	(1986): 0.9430	(1987):	2.1443
	(1988): 8.7526	(1989):	38.3281

A = Australes

Population: 32,296,000

	13–17	18–22	23–32
Men	1,408,000	1,240,000	2,317,000
Women	1,368,000	1,207,000	2,263,000

TOTAL ARMED FORCES:
ACTIVE: 95,000 (ε 39,000 conscripts).
Terms of Service: Army, Air Force 1 year, Navy
14 months; some conscripts may serve less.
RESERVES: 377,000: Army 250,000 (National
Guard 200,000; Territorial Guard 50,000); Navy
77,000; Air 50,000.

ARMY: 55,000 (ε 30,000 conscripts).
HQ: 4 army corps, 5 Military Regions.
(Many units cadre status only.)
2 armd bde (each 2 armd cav, 1 tk regt, 1 arty bn).
2 mech inf bde (each 3 regt of 1 bn, plus armd
cav sqn, arty bn, engr coy).
2 mtn inf bde (each 3 inf, 1 arty bn, 1 engr coy,
1 recce det).
1 jungle bde (4 lt inf, 1 arty (how) bn).
1 mixed inf bde (1 inf, 1 jungle, 1 mtn regt).
Army Tps:
Presidential Guard: 1 mech inf regt, 1 mech
cav bn (ceremonial).
1 AB bde (3 AB regt, 1 arty gp, 1 trg regt).
1 indep mech inf bde (3 regt).
1 AD arty, 2 engr, 1 avn bn.
1 SF coy.
Corps Tps;
each corps 1 arty, 1 AD arty, 1 engr bn.

EQUIPMENT:
MBT: 235: 10 M-4 *Sherman*, 225 *TAM* (125 in store).
LIGHT TANKS: 60 AMX-13.
RECCE: 50 AML-90.
AIFV: 380: 180 AMX-VCI, some 200 *TAM* VCTP.
APC: 415: 140 M-3 half-track, 200 M-113,
70 MOWAG *Grenadier* (mod *Roland*), 5 BDX.
TOWED ARTY: 278: 105mm: 100 incl M-101 and
M-56; 155mm: 60 M-114, 68 CITEFA Models
77/-81, 50 M-59.
SP ARTY: 155mm: 24 Mk F3.
MRL: 105mm: SALM-Pampera; 127mm: SAPBA-1.
MORTARS: 81mm: 200; 120mm: 120 (some SP in
VCTM AIFV).
ATGW: SS-11/-12, *Cobra (Mamba)*, *Mathogo*.
RL: 89mm: M-65.
RCL: 75mm: M-20; 90mm: M-67; 105mm: M-968;
ATK GUNS: 105mm: 140 *Kuerassier* SP.
AD GUNS: 20mm: Rh 202 twin HSS-669;
30mm: HS-83/4; 35mm: K-63;
40mm: L/60, L/70; 90mm: some M-117.
SAM: *Tigercat*, *Blowpipe*, *Roland*, SAM-7.
AVIATION:
AIRCRAFT: 9 Cessna (2 -182, 5 -207, 2 *Citation*), 2
Commander (1 -560, 1 -680), 2 DHC-6-300, 1
King Air, 3 *Merlin* IIIA, 1 *Merlin* IV, 1 *Sabreliner*.
HELICOPTERS: 6 A-109, ε 15 AS-332B (24
ordered, being delivered), 5 SA-315, 1 SA-330,
7 UH- 1H, 4 UH-12E.

NAVY: 25,000 incl naval air force and marines
(incl 4,000 conscripts).
3 Naval Areas: Centre; from River Plate to
42° 45′ S: South; from 42° 45′ S to Cape Horn;
and Antarctica.
BASES: Buenos Aires, Puerto Belgrano (HQ
Centre), Mar del Plata (submarine base), Ushuaia
(HQ South), Puerto Deseado.
SUBMARINES: 4:
2 *Santa Cruz* (FRG TR-1700) with 533mm TT
(SST-4 HWT).
2 *Salta* (FRG T-209/1200) with 533mm TT
(SST-4 HWT) (1 in major refit).
PRINCIPAL SURFACE COMBATANTS: 14:
CARRIER: 1 *Veinticinco de Mayo* CVS (UK *Colossus*):
(in major refit) capacity 18 ac and hel, complement:
ac: 4 *Super Etendard*, 3 S-2;
hel: 4 S-61D.
DESTROYERS: 6:
2 *Hercules* (UK Type 42) with 1 × 2 *Sea Dart*
SAM; plus 1 *Alouette* III hel (ASW), 2 × 3
ASTT, 4 × MM-38 *Exocet* SSM, 1 × 114mm gun.
4 *Almirante Brown* (FRG *MEKO-360*) ASW with
2 × SA-316 hel, 2 × 3 ASTT; plus 8 × MM-40
Exocet SSM, 1 × 127mm gun.
FRIGATES: 7:
4 *Espora* (FRG *MEKO-140*) with 2 × 3 ASTT, hel.
deck; plus 8 × MM-40 *Exocet*.
3 *Drummond* (Fr A-69) with 2 × 3 ASTT; plus 4 ×
MM-38 *Exocet*, 1 × 100mm gun.
PATROL AND COASTAL COMBATANTS: 13:
TORPEDO CRAFT: 2 *Intrepida* (FRG Lürssen-45) PFT
with 2 × 533mm TT (SST-4 HWT)
PATROL CRAFT: 11:
OFFSHORE: 6:
1 *Teniente Olivien* (ex-US Oilfield tug).
2 *Irigoyen* (US *Cherokee* AT).
2 *King* (trg) with 3 × 105mm guns.
1 *Somellera* (US *Sotoyomo* AT).
INSHORE; 5 PCI⟨.
MINE WARFARE: 6:
4 *Neuquen* (UK 'Ton') MSC.
2 *Chaco* (UK 'Ton') MHC.
AMPHIBIOUS: 1 *Cabo San Antonio* LST (hel deck),
capacity 600 tps, 18 tk.
Plus 14 craft; 6 LCM, 8 LCVP.
SUPPORT AND MISCELLANEOUS: 9:
3 tpt, 1 ocean tug, 1 icebreaker, 2 trg, 2
survey/research.
COAST DEFENCE: some 10 arty bty: 87mm: 12
M-1898; 155mm: 16 M-3.

NAVAL AIR FORCE: 2,000;
47 cbt ac, 15 armed hel.
ATTACK: 1 sqn with 5 A-4Q, 14 *Super Etendard*.
MR/ASW: 2 sqn: 1 with 6 S-2E; 1 with 4 L-188E.

HELICOPTERS: 2 sqn: 1 ASW/TPT with 4 S-61D (ASW) and 3 tpt hel (1 S-61D, 2 ASH-3D); 1 spt with 4 SA-319B (with SS-11), 4 SA-316B.
TRANSPORT: 1 sqn with 3 F-28-3000, 3 L-188, 4 *Queen Air 80*, 7 *Super King Air*, 3 US-2A.
SURVEY: 1 *Queen Air* B-80 (photo), 4 PC-6B (Antarctic flt).
TRAINING: 2 sqn:
  11 EMB-326 *Xavante*, 6 MB-326GB, 5 MB-339A, 11 T-34C.
ASM: *Exocet* AM-39E/H, ASM-2 *Martin Pescador* (*Kingfisher*), SS-11, AS-12, AGM-12 *Bullpup*.

MARINES: 5,000.
  Fleet Forces: 2: each 2 bn, 1 amph recce gp, 1 fd arty bn, 1 hy mor, 1 ATK, 1 engr coy.
  Amph spt force: 1 marine inf bn.
  1 AD arty regt.
  1 indep inf bn.
  6 indep inf (security) coy.
EQUIPMENT:
RECCE: 12 Panhard ERC-90 *Lynx*.
APC: 15 LVT-3/-4, 19 LVTP-7, 15 LARC-5, 6 MOWAG *Roland*, 24 Panhard VCR/TT.
TOWED ARTY: 105mm: 40 M-56.
MORTARS: 81mm; 120mm.
ATGW: 20 *Bantam*, *Cobra* (*Mamba*).
RCL: 75mm, 90mm, 105mm: M-1968.
AD GUNS: 20mm, 30mm, 35mm: K-63.
SAM: 7 *Tigercat*, *Blowpipe*.

AIR FORCE: 15,000 (5,000 conscripts);
  200 cbt ac, 20 armed hel (more could be armed).
  10 air bde;
  10 AD arty bty;
  SF (AB) coy.
Air Operations Command (10 bde):
BOMBERS: 1 sqn with 5 *Canberra* B-62, 2 T-64.
FGA/FIGHTER: 4 sqn:
  2 (1 OCU) with 21 *Mirage* IIIC (18 -CJ, 3 -BJ), 13 *Mirage* IIIE (11 -EA, 2 -DA);
  2 with 9 *Mirage* 5P, 23 *Dagger* (*Nesher* ; 20 -A, 3 -B).
FGA: 3 sqn with 26 A-4P.
COIN: 3 sqn:
  2 ac with 67 IA-58A, 24 MS-760;
  1 hel with 12 Hughes 500M (armed), 8 UH-1 (armed: 3 -D, 5 -H), 7 Bell 212, 4 SA-315.
MR: 1 Boeing 707.
SURVEY: 3 *Learjet* 35A.
TANKER: 2 KC-130H.
TRANSPORT: 5 sqn with:
  AIRCRAFT: 3 Boeing 707, 4 C-47, 2 C-130E, 4 C-130H, 6 DHC-6, 12 F-27, 7 F-28, 3 IA-50, 2 *Merlin* IVA. Antarctic spt unit with 1 DHC-6, 1 LC-47.
  HELICOPTERS: 2 CH-47C, 2 S-58T, 2 S-61 (1 -R, 1 -NR).

CALIBRATION: 1 sqn with 2 Boeing 707, 1 IA-50, 2 *Learjet* 35.
LIAISON: 1 sqn with 1 *Sabreliner*, 35 Cessna 182, 1 Cessna 320, 14 *Commander*, 3 PA-28, 3 PA-34.
AIR TRAINING COMMAND:
  29 EMB-312, 18 IA-63, 10 MS-760, 45 T-34C ac. 4 Hughes 500 D hel.
AAM: AIM-9B *Sidewinder*, R-530, R-550, *Shafrir*.
ASM: ASM-2 Martín *Pescador*.

FORCES ABROAD:
ANGOLA (UNAVM): observers.
IRAN/IRAQ (UNIIMOG): observers.

PARA-MILITARY:
GENDARMERIE (Ministry of Defence): 18,000.
EQUIPMENT: *Shorland* recce, 40 M-113; ac: 3 Piper, 2 Cessna, 4PC-6; hel: 1 Hughes 500D, 3 SA-315, 6 Bo-105.
PREFECTURA NAVAL (Coast guard): (9,000);
EQUIPMENT: 6 PCO, 4 PCI, 19⟨; 3 Short *Skyvan* 3M-200 ac; 2 AS-332, 1 SA-330, 6 Hughes 500M hel.

THE BAHAMAS

GDP	1986: $B 2.08 bn ($US 2.08 bn)	
	1987ε: $B 2.27 bn ($US 2.27 bn)	
Growth	1986ε: 3.5%	1987ε: 5.0%
Inflation	1987: 6.0%	1988: 4.2%
Debt	1986: $US 249.1 m	1987: $US 264.0 m
Sy bdgt*	1988: $B 77.70 m ($US 77.70 m)	
FMA	1988: $0.03 m (US)	
$US1 = $B (1986/7/8/9): 1.0		
$B = Bahamian dollars		

Population: 248,100

	13–17	18–22	23–32
Men	12,400	13,200	21,700
Women	12,600	12,000	21,400

TOTAL SECURITY FORCES
ACTIVE: 2,750: Police (2,000); Defence Force (750).
Terms of Service: voluntary.

NAVY (750).
(ROYAL BAHAMIAN DEFENCE FORCE)
BASE: Coral Harbour, New Providence Island.
PATROL AND COASTAL COMBATANTS: 11:
  INSHORE: 3 *Yellow Elder* PFI, 1 *Marlin*, 7 PCI⟨.
AIRCRAFT: 3 *Commander* 500.

---

* Incl Police allocation.

BELIZE

GDP   1986: $BZ 431.30 m ($US 215.65 m)
          1987ε: $BZ 462.78 m ($US 231.39 m)
Growth   1987: 5.0%   1988: 7.6%
Inflation 1986: 1.0%   1987: 2.3%
Debt   1987: $US 119.0 m 1988: $US 120.8 m
Def bdgt 1988ε: $BZ 17.92 m ($US 8.96 m)
          1989ε: $BZ 19.88 m ($US 9.94 m)
FMA*   1988: $0.1 m (US)
$US1 =$BZ (1986/7/8/9): 2.0
$BZ = $ Belize

Population: 182,900

	13–17	18–22	23–32
Men	11,200	9,800	14,300
Women	11,000	9,600	13,600

TOTAL ARMED FORCES:
ACTIVE: 700.
Terms of Service: voluntary.
RESERVES (militia): ε 350.

ARMY: 650.
1 inf bn (4 Active, 3 Reserve coy).
EQUIPMENT:
MORTARS: 81mm: 6.

MARITIME WING: 50.
PATROL BOATS: 2 *Dangriga* PCI⟨.

AIR WING: 15.
1 cbt ac, no armed hel.
MR/TRANSPORT: 2 BN-2B *Defender* (1 armed), 1
Do-27A.

FOREIGN FORCES:
UNITED KINGDOM: 1,500. Army: some 1,250; 1 inf
bn + spt elm (incl *Rapier*). RAF: 300; 1 FGA flt.

---

*Plus UK military assistance, value n.k.

BOLIVIA

GDP   1987ε: B 12.33 bn ($6.00 bn)
          1988ε: B 14.65 bn ($6.23 bn)
Growth   1987: 2.2%   1988: 2.8%
Inflation 1987: 14.6%   1988: 16.0%
Debt   1987: $5.0 bn   1988: $4.8 bn
Def bdgt 1987: B 375.22 m ($182.60 m)
          1988: B 204.01 m ($86.80 m)
FMA   1988: $5.4 m (US)
$1 = B   (1987): 2.0549   (1988): 2.3502
          (1989): 2.5100

B = Bolivianos

Population: 6,987,000

	13–17	18–22	23–32
Men	384,000	329,000	517,000
Women	386,000	332,000	530,000

TOTAL ARMED FORCES:
ACTIVE: 28,000 (some 19,000 conscripts).
Terms of Service: 12 months, selective.

ARMY: 20,000 (some 15,000 conscripts).
HQ: 6 Military Regions.
Army HQ direct control:
  2 armd bn.
  1 mech cav regt.
  1 Presidential Guard inf regt.
10 'div'; org, composition varies; comprise:
  8 cav gp (5 horsed, 2 mot, 1 aslt); 1 mot inf
  regt with 2 bn. 22 inf bn (incl 5 inf aslt bn); 1
  arty 'regt' (bn) 5 arty gp (coy); 1 AB 'regt' (bn).
  6 engr bn.
EQUIPMENT:
LIGHT TANKS: 36 Steyr SK 105.
RECCE: 24 EE-9 *Cascavel*.
APC: 113: 50 M-113, 15 V-100 *Commando*,
  24 MOWAG *Roland*, 24 EE-11 *Urutu*.
TOWED ARTY: 22: 75mm: 6 M-116 pack,
  ε 10 Bofors M-1935; 105mm: 6 M-101.
MORTARS: 81mm: 200 M-29; 107mm: M-30.
RCL: 90mm; 106mm: M-40A1.
AVIATION: 4 Cessna 206, 1 *King Air* B90, 1 *Super
King Air* 200 (VIP).

NAVY: 4,000 (incl 1,000 naval inf and marines)
(perhaps 1,800 conscripts).
5 Naval Districts; covering Lake Titicaca and the
rivers; each 1 Flotilla.
BASES: Riberalta (HQ), Tiquina (HQ), Puerto
Busch, Puerto Guayaramerín (HQ), Puerto
Villaroel, Trinidad (HQ), Puerto Suárez (HQ).
RIVER PATROL CRAFT: some 10 ⟨.
SUPPORT: 1 *Libertador Bolivar* ocean tpt (uses
Arg/Uruguay ports)

NAVAL AVIATION:
AIRCRAFT: 1 Cessna 402.
MARINES: 1 bn (coy+ in each District).
NAVAL INF: 1 bn plus 5 coy.

AIR FORCE: 4,000;
69 cbt ac, 10 armed hel.
FIGHTER: 1 sqn with 14 AT-33N,
  4 F-86F (ftr/trg).

COIN: 4 AT-6G, 12 PC-7.
SPECIAL OPS: 1 sqn with 10 Hughes 500M.
SAR: 1 hel sqn with 4 HB-315B, 1 SA-315B.
TRANSPORT: 4 sqn:
  1 VIP tpt with 1 L-188 *Electra*, 1 *Sabreliner*, 3
    Super King Air, 3 Cessna (1 402, 1 404, 1 421).
  2 tpt with 2 C-130, 7 C-47, 4 IAI 201, 6 F27-400.
  1 photo-survey with 2 *Learjet* 35A, 1 Cessna 402.
LIAISON:
  AIRCRAFT: 21 Cessna, (1 -152, 2 -185, 14 -206, 1
    -210, 2 -402, 1 -404).
  HELICOPTERS: 6 UH-1H.
TRAINING: 3 Cessna 152, 23 PC-7, 6 SF-260 CB, 18
  T-23, 12 T-33A, 3 T-41D.
1 air-base defence regt (Oerlikon twin 20mm, some
  truck-mounted guns).

PARA-MILITARY:
NATIONAL POLICE: some 15,000.
NARCOTICS POLICE: some 6,000.

BRAZIL

GDP	1987:	N Cz$ 12.79 bn ($325.99 bn)
	1988ε:	N Cz$ 87.22 bn ($332.41 bn)
Growth	1987: 2.9%	1988ε: 0.1%
Inflation	1987: 229.7%	1988: 682.7%
Debt	1987: $116.0 bn	1988: $121.0 bn
Def exp	1987ε: N Cz$ 66.05 m ($1.68 bn)
	1988ε: N Cz$ 317.25 m ($1.41 bn)
FMA	1988: $0.13 m (US)

$1 = N Cz$(1987): 0.3923   (1988): 0.2624
          (1989): 1.0000
N Cz$ = New Cruzados*

Population: 146,323,000

	13–17	18–22	23–32
Men	7,474,000	6,992,000	12,668,000
Women	7,452,000	6,941,000	12,627,000

TOTAL ARMED FORCES:
ACTIVE: 324,000 (145,200 conscripts).
  Terms of Service: 12 months (can be extended by
  6 months).
RESERVES: Trained first-line 1,115,000; 400,000
  subject to immediate recall. Second-line (limited
  trg) 225,000.

ARMY: 223,000 (to be 296,000); (143,000 conscripts).
  HQ: 7 Military Comd, 12 Military Region;
  8 div (3 with Region HQ).
  1 armd cav bde (2 mech, 1 armd, 1 arty bn).
  3 armd inf bde (each 2 inf, 1 armd, 1 arty bn).
  4 mech cav bde, (each 3 inf, 1 arty bn).

12 motor inf bde (26 bn).
2 'jungle' bde (7 bn).
1 frontier bde (6 bn).
1 AB bde (3 AB, 1 SF bn).
2 coast and AD arty bde.
3 cav guard regt.
28 arty gp (4 SP, 6 med, 18 fd).
2 engr gp each 4 bn; 10 bn (incl 2 railway) (to be
  increased to 34 bn).
Avn: forming, to comprise 14 units, perhaps 250 hel.
EQUIPMENT:
LIGHT TANKS: some 630, some 140 M-3, some 80
  X-1A, 30 X-1A2 (M-3 mod); 380 M-41C.
RECCE: 160 EE-9 *Cascavel*, 30 M-8.
APC: 770: 150 EE-11 *Urutu*, 20 M-59, ε 600 M-113.
TOWED ARTY: 570: 105mm: 420 M-101/-102, Model
  56 pack; 155mm: 150 M-114.
SP ARTY: 105mm: 6 M-7/-108.
COAST ARTY: some 240 57mm, 75mm, 120mm,
  150mm, 152mm, 305mm.
MRL: 108mm: SS-06; 180mm: SS-40;
  300mm: SS-60 incl SP.
MORTARS: 81mm; 107mm: 120mm.
ATGW: 300 *Cobra*.
RL: 60mm.
RCL: 57mm: 240 M-18A1; 75mm: 20; 105mm;
  106mm: M-40A1.
AD GUNS: 12.7mm: M-55 quad; 35mm: 30; 40mm:
  60; 57mm: some 180.
SAM: 4 *Roland* II, BOFI AD system (40mm L/70
  gun with RBS-70 SAM) reported.
AVIATION: Helicopter wing forming. 36 SA-365 and
  16 HB-350 to be delivered, commencing 1989.

NAVY: 50,300 (2,200 conscripts) incl naval air
  and marines.
  6 Oceanic Naval Districts plus 1 Riverine; 1 Comd.
BASES: OCEAN: Rio de Janeiro (HQ I Naval
  District), Salvador (HQ II District), Natal (HQ III
  District), Belém (HQ IV District), Rio Grande
  (do sul) (HQ V District) Ladario (HQ VI District).
RIVERINE: Manaus, Corumba.
SUBMARINES: 7:
  1 *Tupi* (FRG T-209/1400) with 533mm TT (UK
    Tigerfish HWT).
  3 *Humaita* (UK *Oberon*) with 533mm TT
    (*Tigerfish* HWT).
  3 *Goias/Bahia* (US *Guppy* III/II) with 533mm TT.
PRINCIPAL SURFACE COMBATANTS: 17:
CARRIER: 1 *Minas Gerais* (UK *Colossus*) CVS (ASW),
  capacity 20 ac: typically 7–8 S-2E ASW ac, 8
  ASH-3H hel.
DESTROYERS: 9:
  2 *Marcilio Dias* (US *Gearing*) ASW with 1 *Wasp*
    hel (Mk 46 LWT), 1 × 8 *ASROC*, 2 × 3 ASTT;
    plus 2 × 2 127mm guns.
  5 *Mato Grosso* (US *Sumner*) ASW, 4 with 1 *Wasp*
    hel, all with 2 × 3 ASTT; plus 3 × 2 127mm guns.

2 *Piaui* (US *Fletcher*) with 5 × 127mm guns; plus 2 × 3 ASTT, 2 with 5 × 533mm TT.

FRIGATES: 7:
4 *Niteroi* ASW; with 1 *Lynx* hel, 2 × 3 ASTT, *Ikara* SUGW, 1 × 2 ASW mor; plus 2 × MM-38 *Exocet* SSM, 1 × 114mm gun.
2 *Niteroi* GP; weapons as ASW, except 4 × MM-38 *Exocet*, 2 × 114mm guns, no *Ikara*.
1 *Inhauma*, with 1 *Lynx* hel, 2 × 3 ASTT, plus 4 × MM-40 *Exocet*, 1 × 114mm gun.

PATROL AND COASTAL COMBATANTS: 24:
9 *Imperial Marinheiro* PCO.
6 *Piratini* (US PGM) PCI, 3 *Aspirante Nascimento* PCI (trg).
6 Riverine patrol.

MINE WARFARE: 6:
6 *Aratu* (FRG *Schütze*) MSI.

AMPHIBIOUS: 2:
1 *Duque de Caxais* (US *de Soto County*), capacity 600 tps, 18 tk.
1 *D'Avila* (US LST-511), capacity 200 tps, 16 tk.
Plus 36 craft; 3 LCU, 3 LCM, 30 LCVP.

SUPPORT AND MISCELLANEOUS 17:
1 *Marajo* AOR, 1 repair ship, 4 tpt, 5 survey/oceanography, 1 mod *Niteroi* FF (trg), 5 ocean tugs.

NAVAL AIR FORCE: (700);
36 armed hel.
ASW: 1 hel sqn with 10 ASH-3H.
ATTACK: 1 sqn with 8 *Lynx* HAS 21, 1 with 8 AS-350 (armed), 7 *Wasp* HAS-1, 3 HB-315.
UTILITY: 1 sqn with 3 AS-332.
TRAINING: 1 hel sqn with 10 TH-57.

MARINES: (15,000).
Fleet Force:
1 amph div (1 comd, 3 inf, 1 special ops bn), 1 arty bn (2 fd, 1 AD bty).
Reinforcement Comd:
5 bn incl 1 engr.
Internal Security Force:
6 regional, 1 special ops gp.
EQUIPMENT:
RECCE: 6 EE-9 Mk IV *Cascavel*.
APC: 16 M-113, 6 EE-11 *Urutu*, 12 LVTP-7A1.
TOWED ARTY: 105mm: 8 M-102; 155mm: 8 M-114.
MRL: 108mm: SS-06.
RL: 89mm: 3.5-in. M-20.
RCL: 106mm: M-40.
AD GUNS: 40mm: 8 M-1 towed.

AIR FORCE: 50,700;
287 cbt ac, 8 armed hel.
AD COMMAND: 1 Gp (20 cbt ac):
FIGHTER: 2 sqn with 15 F-103E (*Mirage* IIIEBR), 5 F-103D (*Mirage* IIIDBR). Ac being modernized.

TACTICAL COMMAND: 10 Gp (116 cbt ac).
FGA: 3 sqn with 26 F-5E, 4 F-5B.
AMX being delivered, from 1989.
COIN: 3 sqn with 48 AT-26.
COIN/TRG: 30 EMB-312.
RECCE: 2 sqn with 8 RC-95, 12 RT-26, 3 *Learjet* 35.
LIAISON/OBSERVATION: 6 sqn:
1 ac with 8 T-27; 5 hel with 5 SA-330, 30 UH-1H, 3 OH-13.
All sqn have some EMB-810 for liaison.
MARITIME COMMAND: 4 Gp (22 cbt ac).
ASW (afloat): 1 sqn with 12 S-2E.
MR/SAR: 4 sqn with:
   AIRCRAFT: 14 EMB-110B, 10 EMB-111;
   HELICOPTERS: 8 UH-1D armed.
TRANSPORT COMMAND: 6 Gp (6 sqn), 7 regional indep sqn:
HEAVY 2 sqn:
1 with 14 C-130; (9 -E, 5 -H);
1 with 2 KC-130H, 4 KC-137 tkr/tpt.
MED/LT: 2 sqn:
1 with 12 C-91;
1 with 23 C-95A/B.
TACTICAL: 1 sqn with 20 C-115.
VIP: 1 sqn with 1 VC-91, 10 VC/VU-93, 2 VC-96, 5 VC-97, 5 VU-9, ac; 3 VH-4 hel.
REGIONAL: 7 sqn with 7 C-115, 85 C-95A/B, 6 EC-9 (VU-9).
HELICOPTERS: 10 AS-332, 6 SA-330, 38 UH-1 (8 -D, 30 -H).
LIAISON: 50 C-42, 30 L-42.
TRAINING COMMAND:
AIRCRAFT: 79 T-27 *Tucano*, 50 AT-26, 70 EMB-110.
HELICOPTERS: 25 OH-13, 4 OH-6A.
CALIBRATION: 1 unit with 2 C-95, 1 EC-93, 4 EC-95, 1 U-93.
AAM: AIM-9 *Sidewinder*, R-530, MAA-1 *Piranha*.

FORCES ABROAD:
ANGOLA (UNAVM): Observers.

===

PARA-MILITARY:
PUBLIC SECURITY FORCES (R): some 243,000 in state military police org (State Militias) under Army control and considered an Army Reserve.

---

* A new currency unit was introduced in January 1989 at a rate of 1 New Cruzado = 1,000 cruzados and was at parity to the $US when introduced.

CHILE

GDP	1987:	pC 4,159.76 bn ($18.95 bn)
	1988ε:	pC 5,411.03 bn ($22.08 bn)
Growth	1987:	5.4%	1988ε: 7.4%

Inflation 1987: 19.8% 1988: 14.7%
Debt 1987: $19.2 bn 1988: $17.8 bn
Def exp 1988: pC 164.25 bn ($670.27 m)
Def bdgt* 1989: pC 159.80 bn ($640.12 m)
FMA 1988: $0.05m (US)
$1 = pC (1987): 219.54 (1988): 245.05
(1989): 249.64

pC = pesos Chilenos

Population: 12,862,000

	13–17	18–22	23–32
Men	626,000	631,000	1,157,000
Women	610,000	618,000	1,145,000

TOTAL ARMED FORCES:
ACTIVE: 101,000 (33,000 conscripts).
Terms of Service: 2 years all services.
RESERVES: 100,000 active; all able-bodied males have a Reserve obligation to age 45.

ARMY: 57,000 (30,000 conscripts).
6 div:
1 with 3 mot inf, 1 armd cav, 1 arty, 1 engr regt;
1 with 2 mot inf, 5 mtn, 1 armd cav, 1 arty, 1 engr regt;
1 with 2 inf, 3 mtn, 2 armd cav, 1 arty, 1 engr regt;
1 with 1 inf, 2 mtn, 2 armd cav, 1 arty, 1 engr regt;
1 with 2 inf, 2 armd cav, 1 arty, 1 engr regt, 1 cdo bn.
1 with 2 inf, 1 mtn, 2 armd cav, 1 arty, 1 engr regt.
1 bde with 1 mtn, 1 inf, 1 arty regt, 1 recce sqn.
Army tps: 1 avn, 1 engr regt.
EQUIPMENT:
MBT: 171: 150 M-4A3/M-51, 21 AMX-30.
LIGHT TANKS: 157: 50 M-24, 60 M-41, 47 AMX-13.
RECCE: 30 EE-9 *Cascavel.*
AIFV: 20 *Piranha* with 90mm gun.
APC: 330: 100 M-113, 200 Cardoen/MOWAG *Piranha*, 30 EE-11 *Urutu.*
TOWED ARTY: 108: 105mm: 72 M-101, 36 Model 56;
SP ARTY: 155mm: 12 Mk F3.
MORTARS: 81mm: M-1; 120mm (incl 50 SP).
ATGW: *Milan/Mamba.*
RL: 89mm: 3.5-in. M-20.
RCL: 57mm: M-18; 106mm: M-40A1.
SAM: *Blowpipe.*
AIRCRAFT:
TRANSPORT: 6 C-212, 4 PA-31.
TRAINING: 16 Cessna R-172.
HELICOPTERS: 2 AB-206, 2 AS-332, 11 SA-315, 11 SA-330.

NAVY: 29,000 (3,000 conscripts), incl naval air, marines and Coast Guard.
DEPLOYMENT AND BASES:

3 main commands: Fleet (includes CC, DD and FF), Submarine Flotilla, Transport. Remaining forces allocated to 3 Naval Zones:
1st Naval Zone (north of 35°S approx).
Valparaiso (HQ), Iquique.
2nd Naval Zone (35°S – 43°S approx).
Talcahuano, (HQ), Puerto Montt.
3rd Naval Zone (43°S to C. Horn), Punta Arenas, (HQ), Puerto Williams.
SUBMARINES: 4:
2 *O'Brien* (UK *Oberon*) with 533mm TT (FRG HWT).
2 *Thompson* (FRG T-209/1300) with 533mm TT (HWT).
PRINCIPAL SURFACE COMBATANTS: 11:
CRUISER: 1 *O'Higgins* (US *Brooklyn*) with 5 × 3 152mm guns, 4 × 2 127mm guns, 1 Bell hel.
DESTROYERS: 8:
3 *Capitan Prat* (UK *Norfolk*) DDG with 1 × 2 *Seaslug-2* SAM, 4 × MM-38 *Exocet* SSM, 1 × 2 114mm guns, 1 SA-319 hel.
1 *Blanco Encalada* (UK *Norfolk*) DDH with 4 × MM-38, 1 × 2 114 mm guns, up to 4 med hel.
2 *Almirante Riveros* (ASUW) with 4 × MM-38 *Exocet* SSM, 4 × 102mm guns; plus 2 × 3 ASTT (Mk 44 LWT), 2 × 3 ASW mor.
2 *Ministro Zenteno* (US *Sumner*) (ASW) with 1 × SA-319 hel, 2 × 3 ASTT, 3 × 2 127mm guns.
FRIGATES: 2 *Condell* (mod UK *Leander*) with 1 SA-319 hel, 2 × 3 ASTT; plus 2 × MM-38 *Exocet*, 1 × 2 114mm guns.
PATROL AND COASTAL COMBATANTS: 11:
MISSILE CRAFT: 4:
2 *Casma* (Is *Reshef*) PFM with 4 *Gabriel* SSM.
2 *Iquique* (Is *Sa'ar*) PFM with 4 *Gabriel* SSM.
TORPEDO CRAFT: 4 *Guacolda* (FRG, Lürssen 36m) with 4 × 533mm TT.
PATROL: 3:
2 PCO (ex US tugs).
1 PCC (ex-US PC-1638).
AMPHIBIOUS: 3:
3 *Maipo* (Fr *BATRAL*) LSM, capacity 140 tps, 7 tk.
Plus craft; 2 LCT.
SUPPORT AND MISCELLANEOUS: 6:
1 *Almirante Jorge Montt* (UK 'Tide') AO, 1 *Araucano* AO, 1 submarine spt, 2 tpt, 1 survey.

NAVAL AIR FORCE: (500);
6 cbt ac, no armed hel.
4 sqn. Bases at Viña del Mar (2nd Naval Zone), Puerto Williams (3rd Naval Zone).
MR: 1 sqn with 6 EMB-111N, 3 *Falcon* 200.
LIAISON: 1 sqn with 3 C-212A, 3 EMB-110N, 2 IAI-1124, 1 PA-31.
HELICOPTERS: 1 sqn with 8 SA-319, 3 SH-57.
TRAINING: 1 sqn with 10 Pilatus PC-7.

MARINES: (5,200).

4 gp: each 1 inf bn (+), 1 cdo coy, 1 fd arty, 1 AD arty bty.
1 amph bn.

EQUIPMENT:
APC: MOWAG *Roland*, 30 LVTP-5.
TOWED ARTY: 105mm: 16; 155mm: 35 M-114.
COAST GUNS: 155mm: 16 GPFM-3.
MORTARS: 60mm: 50; 81mm: 50.
SAM: *Blowpipe*.

COAST GUARD: (1,600)
PATROL CRAFT: 13:
2 PCC (Buoy Tenders), 11 PCI⟨.
HELICOPTER: 1 Bell 206B.

AIR FORCE: 15,000;
112 cbt ac, no armed hel.
5 Air Bde: 4 wings.
FGA: 2 sqn:
1 with 38 *Hunter* (20 F-71, 11 FGA-9, 4 FR-71, 3 T-72);
1 with 16 F-5 (13 -E, 3 -F; serviceability low).
COIN: 2 sqn with 27 A-37B (C-101 *Halcón (A-36)* to replace, ε 16 delivered).
FIGHTER/RECCE: 1 sqn with 15 *Mirage* 50 (8 -FCH, 6 -CH, 1 -DCH trg).
RECCE: 2 photo units with 2 *Canberra* PR-9, 1 *King Air* A-100, 2 *Learjet* 35 -A.
TRANSPORT: 1 sqn with:
  AIRCRAFT: 3 Boeing (1 727, 2 707), 2 C-130H, 3 Beech 99 (ELINT, tpt, trg), 16 DHC-6 (5 -100, 11 -300).
  HELICOPTER: 2 SA-315B.
LIAISON HELICOPTERS: 6 Bo-105CB, 4 UH-1H.
TRAINING: 1 wing, 3 flying schools:
  AIRCRAFT: 16 PA-28, 60 T-35A/B, 16 T-36, 30 T-37B/C, 8 T-41D.
  HELICOPTERS: 6 UH-1H.
AAM: AIM-9B *Sidewinder, Shafrir*.
ASM: AS-11/-12.
AD: 1 regt (5 gp) with:
  GUNS: 20mm: S-639/-665, GAI-CO1 twin; 35mm: 36, K-63 twin;
  SAM: *Blowpipe*, 12 *Cactus (Crotale)*.

PARA-MILITARY:
CARABINEROS: 27,000.
HELICOPTERS: 2 Bell 206, 10 Bo-105.

OPPOSITION:
FRENTE PATRIOTICO MANUEL RODRIGUEZ (FPMR): ε 1,000; leftist.
MOVEMENT OF THE REVOLUTIONARY LEFT: some 500.

---

* Excl 9.5% of proceeds from copper exports paid to the Armed Forces est at over $200 m in 1988. Incl Paramilitary Police budget.

COLOMBIA

GDP	1987:	pC 8,779.40 bn ($36.19 bn)	
	1988ε:	pC 11,544.91 bn ($38.59 bn)	
Growth	1987:	5.5%	1988ε: 3.5%
Inflation	1987:	23.3%	1988ε: 28.1%
Debt	1987:	$15.4 bn	1988: $16.5 bn
Def bdgt*	1988:	pC 71.96 bn ($240.51 m)	
	1989:	pC 132.49 bn ($374.13 m)	
FMA	1988:	$7.0 m (US)	
$1 = pC	(1987):	242.61	(1988): 299.20
	(1989)	354.12	

pC = pesos Colombianos

Population: 30,685,000

	13–17	18–22	23–32
Men	1,639,000	1,582,000	2,592,000
Women	1,587,000	1,673,000	2,826,000

TOTAL ARMED FORCES:
ACTIVE: 130,400 (some 40,400 conscripts).
  Terms of Service: 1–2 years, varies (all services).
RESERVES: 116,900: Army 100,000; Navy 15,000; Air 1,900.

ARMY: 111,400 (38,000 conscripts).
4 div HQ.
14 inf bde (Regional):
  8 with 3 inf, 1 arty bn, 1 engr gp, 1 mech or horsed cav gp;
  6 with 2 inf bn only.
Army Tps:
  1 trg bde.
  1 Presidential Guard bn (mech).
  1 mech gp.
  1 AB, 1 cdo, 1 ranger, 1 AD arty bn.
EQUIPMENT:
LIGHT TANKS: 12 M-3A1.
RECCE: 20 M-8, 120 EE-9 *Cascavel*;
APC: 171: 50 M-113, 76 EE-11 *Urutu*, 45 M-3A2 half-track.
TOWED ARTY: 105mm: 50 M-101;
MORTARS: 81mm: 125 M-1; 107mm: 148 M-2; 120mm: 120 Brandt.
ATGW: *TOW*.
RCL: 75mm: M-20; 106mm: M-40A1.
AD GUNS: 37mm: 30; 40mm: 30 M-1A1.

NAVY: 12,000 (incl 6,000 marines) (some 500 conscripts).
BASES: OCEAN: Cartagena, Buenaventura.

RIVER: Puerto Leguízamo, Puerto Orocué, Puerto Carreño, Leticia.
SUBMARINES: 2:
2 *Pijao* (FRG T-209/1200) with 533mm TT (FRG HWT).
Plus 2 *Intrepido* (It SK-506) SSI (SF delivery).
FRIGATES: 4 *Almirante Padilla* with 1 × Bo-105 hel (ASW), 2 × 3 ASTT; plus 8 × MM-40 *Exocet* SSM.
PATROL AND COASTAL COMBATANTS: 15:
PATROL:
INSHORE: 2 *Quito Sueno* (US *Asheville*) PFI.
RIVER: 3 *Arauca*, 10 ⟨.
SUPPORT AND MISCELLANEOUS: 5:
2 tpt, 2 research. 1 trg.

MARINES: (6,000); 5 bn, 2 bn naval police.
No hy eqpt (to get EE-9 *Cascavel* recce, EE-11 *Urutu* APC).

NAVAL AIR:
HELICOPTERS: 4 Bo-105.

AIR FORCE: 7,000 (some 1,900 conscripts); 54 cbt ac, 46 armed hel.
COMBAT AIR COMMAND 1:
FGA: 2 sqn:
1 with 16 *Mirage* 5 (12 -COA, 2 -COD trg, 2 -COR recce);
1 with 6 *Kfir* (4 -C2, 2 -TC2).
COMBAT AIR COMMAND 2:
COIN: 1 sqn with 1 AC-47, 10 AT-33A.
COMBAT AIR COMMAND 3:
COIN: 21 A/OA-37B ac; 24 UH-1 (6 -B, 18 -H) hel.
TACTICAL AIR SUPPORT COMMAND:
COIN: 1 sqn with 12 Hughes 500M, 10 Hughes 500D hel.
RECCE: 1 sqn with:
AIRCRAFT: 3 RT-33A;
HELICOPTERS: 7 Hughes 300C, 6 Hughes 500MG *Scout*.
MILITARY AIR TRANSPORT COMMAND:
AIRCRAFT: 1 sqn with 1 BAe 748, 1 Boeing 707, 8 C-47, 4 C-54, 1 C-130E, 2 C-130H-30, 2 Cessna 310, 1 Cessna 340, 4 Cessna 404, 1 *Commander* 560A, 4 DC-6, 10 DHC-2, 2 F-28, 2 IAI-201, 2 PA-31, 1 PA-32, 1 PA-34, 1 PA-44, 6 PC-6B, 4 *Queen Air*.
HELICOPTERS: 10 Bell 206, 3 Bell 212, 2 Bell 412, 8 UH-60.
TRAINING COMMAND:
AIRCRAFT: 20 T-34A/B, 30 T-41D.
HELICOPTERS: 2 Hughes 500E, 8 OH-13, 6 TH-55.
AAM: R-530.

FORCES ABROAD:
EGYPT (Sinai MFO): 500.

PARA-MILITARY:
NATIONAL POLICE FORCE: 80,000; 15 ac, 17 hel. (On order: Bell hel: 2 212, 2 412.)
COAST GUARD: 1,500
PATROL CRAFT: 3 inshore boats.

OPPOSITION:
COORDINADORA SIMON BOLIVAR GUERRILLERA (CGSB): loose coalition of guerrilla gp incl: Revolutionary Armed Forces of Colombia (FARC): some 5,000 active, pro-Soviet; People's Liberation Army (EPL): 800; Ejército de Liberación Nacional (ELN): ε 2,000, pro-Cuban; Movement of April 19 (M19): ε 400.

* Excl some $30 m extra for 1988 for procurement.

COSTA RICA

GDP	1987:	C 285.28 bn ($4.54 bn)	
	1988:	C 356.50 bn ($4.70 bn)	
Growth	1987:	4.8%	1988: 4.2%
Inflation	1987:	16.8%	1988: 20.8%
Debt	1987:	$3.9 bn	1988: $4.2 bn
Sy bdgt*	1988:	C 2.48 bn ($32.77 m)	
	1989:	C 2.67 bn ($33.36 m)	
FMA	1988:	$0.23 m (US)	
$1 = C	(1987):	62.776	(1988): 75.805
	(1989):	80.143	

C = colones

Population: 2,831,000

	13–17	*18–22*	*23–32*
Men	137,000	142,000	260,000
Women	132,000	138,000	251,000

TOTAL SECURITY FORCES
(Para-Military):
ACTIVE: 7,700.

CIVIL GUARD: 4,500.
2 Border Sy Comd (North, South)
Presidential Guard: 1 bn, 7 coy.
EQUIPMENT:
RL: 90mm.
MARINE: Inshore Patrol Craft: 5:
1 *Isla del Coco* (US Swift 32m) PFI. 4 PFI⟨.
AIRCRAFT: 2 Cessna 206, 3 O-2 (surveillance), 1 PA-23, 1 PA-32, 1 PA-34.
HELICOPTERS: 1 FH-1100 (VIP), 2 Hughes 500E.

RURAL GUARD: (Ministry of Government and Police): 3,200; small arms only.

* No armed forces. Figures are for Sy and Police.

CUBA

GSP*	1987ε: pC 26.50 bn ($33.81 bn)
	1988ε: pC 27.03 bn ($35.42 bn)
Growth	1987ε: nil 1988ε: 2.4%
Debt†	1987: $5.5 bn 1988: $6.4 bn
Def bdgt‡	1987ε: pC 1.30 bn ($1.66 bn)
	1988ε: pC 1.70 bn ($2.24 bn)
$1 = pC	(1987): 0.7839 (1988): 0.7584
	(1989): 0.7642

pC = pesos Cubanos

Population: 10,479,000

	13–17	18–22	23–32
Men	552,000	596,000	936,000
Women	530,000	570,000	932,000

TOTAL ARMED FORCES:
ACTIVE: 180,500 incl ε 15,000 Ready Reserves, (79,500 conscripts).
Terms of service: 3 years.
RESERVES: 130,000. Army: 110,000 Ready Reserves (serve 45 days per year) to fill out Active and Reserve units; Navy: 8,000; Air: 12,000. See also Para-Military.

ARMY: 145,000 (incl ε 15,000 Ready Reservists).
(ε 60,000 conscripts)
HQ: 4 Regional Command; 3 Army, 1 Isle of Youth.
4 corps.
3 armd div (1 Cat A, 2 Cat C).
9 mech inf div, (3 mech inf, 1 armd, 1 arty, 1 AD arty regt) (Cat B).
13 inf div (3 inf, 1 arty, 1 AD arty regt) (5 Cat B, 8 Cat C).
8 indep inf regt (Cat B/C).
AD: AD arty regt and SAM bde (Cat varies: SAM ε Cat A, AD arty B or C).
SF (ε 2,500): 2 bn (Cat A).
1 AB aslt bde (Cat A).
Forces combat readiness system is similar to that of the USSR: Cat A div fully manned by active tps; Cat B: partial manning augmented by reservists on mob; Cat C: Active cadre, full manning by reservists on mob. Time required to complete manning unknown. Possible Cat status listed above.
EQUIPMENT:
MBT: 1,100: 800 T-54/-55 (some 150 in store or static coast defence), 300 T-62.
LIGHT TANKS: 60 PT-76.
RECCE: 100 BRDM-1/-2.
AIFV: 50 BMP.
APC: 500 BTR-40/-60/-152.
TOWED ARTY: 76mm: M-1942; 122mm: M-1931/37 (A-19), D-74; 130mm: M-46; 152mm: M-1937 (ML-20), D-20, D-1.
MRL: 122mm: BM-21; 140mm: BM-14; 240mm: BM-24.
MORTARS: 82mm: M-41/-43; 120mm: M-38/-43.
STATIC DEFENCE ARTY: some 15 JS-2 (122mm) hy tk, T-34 (85mm), SU-100 (100mm) SP guns reported; all in fixed emplacements.
SSM: 65 *FROG*-4/-7.
ATGW: AT-1 *Snapper*, AT-3 *Sagger*.
ATK GUNS: 85mm: D-44; 100mm: SU-100 SP.
AD GUNS: 1,600 incl 23mm: ZU-23, ZSU-23-4 SP; 30mm: M-53 (twin)/BTR-60P SP; 37mm: M-1939; 57mm: S-60 towed, ZSU-57-2 SP; 85mm: KS-12; 100mm: KS-19.
SAM: 12 SA-6, SA-7/-9/-13/-14.

NAVY: 13,500 (8,500 conscripts).
3 Naval Districts, 4 Operational Flotillas, (SS, PFM, PFT and ASW).
BASES: Cienfuegos, Cabanas, Havana, Mariel, Punta Movida, Nicaro.
SUBMARINES: 3 Sov *Foxtrot* with 533 and 406mm TT.
FRIGATES: 3 *Mariel* (Sov *Koni*) with 2 × ASW RL.
PATROL AND COASTAL COMBATANTS: 58:
MISSILE CRAFT: 18:
18 Sov *Osa-I/-II* with 4 × SS-N-2 *Styx* SSM.
PATROL: 40 inshore:
9 Sov *Turya* PHI, 3 *Stenka*, 4 SO-1 PFI, 24 PCI⟨.
MINE WARFARE: 14:
4 Sov *Sonya* MSC
10 Sov *Yevgenya* MSI.
AMPHIBIOUS: 2 Sov *Polnocny* LSM, capacity 6 tk, 200 tps.
SUPPORT AND MISCELLANEOUS 4:
1 AO, 1 AGI, 1 ocean tug, 1 trg.

NAVAL INFANTRY: 550+.
1 amph aslt bn.

COASTAL DEFENCE:
ARTY: 122mm: M-1931/37; 152mm: M-1937; 130mm: M-46.
SSM: 2 SS-C-3 systems.

AIR FORCE: 22,000+, incl AD (11,000 conscripts); 206 cbt ac, 41 armed hel.
FGA: 5 sqn:
3 with 36 MiG-23BN;
2 with 24 MiG-17F.
FIGHTER: 8 sqn:
2 with 30 MiG-21F;
2 with 30 MiG-21PFM;
2 with 20 MiG-21PFMA;
1 with 17 MiG-21bis;
1 with 15 MiG-23 *Flogger* E.
ATTACK HELICOPTERS: 16 Mi-17, 20 Mi-25.

ASW: 5 Mi-14 hel.
TRANSPORT: 4 sqn: 30 An-2, 3 An-24, 22 An-26, 2 An-32, 20 Il-14, 4 Yak-40, 2 Il-76 (Air Force ac in civilian markings).
HELICOPTERS: 2 Mi-2, 30 Mi-4, 36 Mi-8.
TRAINING: 15 MiG-15, 15 MiG-15UTI, 10 MiG-21U, 4 MiG-23U, 20 Z-326.
AAM: AA-1 *Alkali*, AA-2 *Atoll*, AA-8 *Aphid*.
AD: 200+ SAM launchers: SA-2, SA-3, SA-6, SA-9, S-13.
Civil Airline: 10 Il-62, 7 Tu-154 used as troop tpt.

FORCES ABROAD:

ANGOLA: 40,000 (cbt units (incl 1 div, several regt) and advisers, plus some 8,000 civilian advisers). To be progressively withdrawn by 1 July 1991.
CONGO: 500,
ETHIOPIA: 2,800,
MOZAMBIQUE: 600,
S. YEMEN: 500,
NICARAGUA: some 1,200 military/security advisers; 2,000–3,000 civilians.

PARA-MILITARY:

YOUTH LABOUR ARMY: 100,000:
CIVIL DEFENCE FORCE: 50,000:
TERRITORIAL MILITIA (R): 1,300,000.
STATE SECURITY (Ministry of Interior): 15,000.
FRONTIER GUARDS (Ministry of Interior): 4,000, 4 Inshore Patrol Craft⟨.

FOREIGN FORCES:

US: 435: 1 reinforced marine coy at Guantanamo Bay.
USSR: 7,700: 1 motor rifle bde (2,800); SIGINT personnel (2,100); mil advisers (2,800).

---

* Gross Social Product: excludes the so-called 'non-productive' service sectors of the economy, such as education and housing which are included in GDP.
† Excl debt to socialist countries. Cumulative debt to CMEA ε $35–40 bn. In 1987 Castro unsuccessfully called on the USSR to forgo some $8 bn of its debt.
‡ Level of military assistance unknown. In 1986 and 1987 the level of economic assistance from the USSR dropped dramatically to $4–5 bn.

DOMINICAN REPUBLIC

GDP	1987:	$RD 21.75 bn ($US 5.66 bn)	
	1988:	$RD 31.41 bn ($US 5.12 bn)	
Growth	1987:	8.1%	1988ε: 1.0%
Inflation	1987:	16.0%	1988ε: 35.0%
Debt	1987:	$US 3.7 bn	1988: $US 3.9 bn
Def bdgt	1986:	$RD 199.50 m ($US 68.69 m)	
	1987:	$RD 294.51 m ($US 76.60 m)	

FMA 1988: $0.70 m (US)
$US 1 = $RD (1987): 3.8448 (1988): 6.1396 (1989): 6.4935
$RD = pesos República Dominicana

Population: 6,864,000

	13–17	18–22	23–32
Men	448,000	388,000	498,000
Women	443,000	387,000	550,000

TOTAL ARMED FORCES:
ACTIVE: 20,800.
Terms of service: voluntary.

ARMY: 13,000.
5 Defence Zones.
4 inf bde (with 17 bn).
1 armd, 1 Presidential Guard, 1 arty, 1 engr bn.
EQUIPMENT:
LIGHT TANKS: 2 AMX-13 (75mm), 12 M-41A1 (76mm).
RECCE: 20 AML.
APC: 8 V-150 *Commando*, 20 M-16 half-track.
TOWED ARTY: 105mm: 22 M-101.
MORTARS: 81mm: M-1; 120mm: 24 ECIA.
RCL: 106mm.

NAVY: 4,000, incl naval inf.
BASES: Santo Domingo (HQ), Las Calderas.
PATROL AND COASTAL COMBATANTS: 12:
OFFSHORE: 1 *Mella* (Cdn *River*) (comd/trg)
INSHORE: 11: 1 *Betelgeuse* (US PGM-71), 10⟨.
AMPHIBIOUS: craft only;
1 LCU.
SUPPORT AND MISCELLANEOUS: 5:
3 ex US ocean tugs (possibly used as PCO)
2 AOT (small – 1,400 tonnes).

AIR FORCE: 3,800;
12 cbt ac, no armed hel.
COIN: 1 sqn with 8 A-37B.
TRANSPORT: 1 sqn with 3 C-47, 1 *Commander* 680, 1 MU-2, 1 Rallye *Commodore*.
LIAISON: 1 Cessna 210, 5 O-2A, 2 PA-31, 3 *Queen Air* 80.
HELICOPTERS: 8 Bell 205, 1 Hughes 500D, 2 SA-318C, 1 SA-365 (VIP).
TRAINING: 2 AT-6, 2 T-28D, 6 T-34B, 3 T-41D.
AB: 1 AB sqn.
AD: 1 bn with 4 20mm guns.

PARA-MILITARY:
NATIONAL POLICE: 15,000 incl 'special ops unit': 1,000.

ECUADOR

GDP	1987:	ES 1,808.38 bn ($10.61 bn)	
	1988:	ES 2,998.29 bn ($9.94 bn)	
Growth	1987:	−5.2%	1988ε: 6.5%
Inflation	1987:	29.5%	1988: 58.3%
Debt	1987:	$9.9 bn	1988: $11.4 bn
Def bdgt	1986ε:	ES 20.40 bn ($166.15 m)	
	1987ε:	ES 32.05 bn ($188.00 m)	
FMA	1988:	$4.65 m (US)	
$1 = ES	(1986):	122.78	(1987): 170.46
	(1988):	301.61	(1989): 450.00
ES = Ecuadorean sucres			

Population: 10,372,000

	13–17	18–22	23–32
Men	587,000	523,000	816,000
Women	572,000	511,000	800,000

TOTAL ARMED FORCES:
ACTIVE: 42,000.
Terms of service: conscription 1 year, selective.
RESERVES: 100,000; ages 18–55.

ARMY: 35,000.
4 Military zones.
1 armd bde
5 inf bde (14 bn)
2 jungle bde
Army tps:
   1 SF (AB) bde (2 gp).
   1 Presidential Guard sqn.
   1 AD arty gp.
   1 avn gp.
   3 engr bn
EQUIPMENT:
LIGHT TANKS: 45 M-3, 104 AMX-13.
RECCE: 35 AML-60/-90, 10 EE-9 *Cascavel*.
APC: 20 M-113, 60 AMX-VCI, 20 EE-11 *Urutu*.
TOWED ARTY: 105mm: Model 56 pack, 50 M-101;
  155mm: 10 M-198.
SP ARTY: 155mm: 10 Mk F3.
MORTARS: 500: 81mm: M-29; 107mm: 4.2-in M-30;
  160mm: 12.
RCL: 400: 90mm: M-67; 106mm: M-40A1.
AD GUNS: 20mm: 20 M-1935; 35mm: 30 GDF-002
  twin; 40mm: 30 M-1A1
SAM: 150 *Blowpipe*.
AVIATION:
  AIRCRAFT:
    SURVEY: 1 Cessna 206, 2 *Queen Air*, 1 *Learjet* 24D.
    LIAISON: 1 Cessna 172, 1 Cessna 182, 2 Cessna
      185, 1 DHC-5, 4 IAI-201, 3 PC-6.
  HELICOPTERS:
    SURVEY: 1 SA-315B, 1 SA-316B.
    TRANSPORT/LIAISON: 10 AS-332, 5 SA-315B, 5
      SA-330, 14 SA-342.

NAVY: 4,000, incl some 1,000 marines.
BASES: Guayaquil, Jaramijo, Galápagos Islands.
SUBMARINES: 2 *Shyri* (FRG T-209/1300) with
  533mm TT (FRG SUT HWT).
PRINCIPAL SURFACE COMBATANTS: 2:
DESTROYER: 1 *Presidente Eloy Alfaro* (US *Gearing*)
  ASW with 2 × 3 ASTT, hel deck; plus 2 × 2
  127mm gun.
FRIGATE: 1 *Moran Valverde* (US *Lawrence*) with hel
  deck; plus 1 × 127mm gun.
PATROL AND COASTAL COMBATANTS: 18:
CORVETTES: 6 *Esmeraldas* with 2 × 3 ASTT, hel
  deck; plus 6 × MM-40 *Exocet* SSM.
MISSILE CRAFT: 6:
  3 *Quito* (FRG Lürssen-45) with 4 × MM-38 *Exocet*.
  3 *Manta* (FRG Lürssen-36) with 4 × *Gabriel* II SSM.
PATROL: 6 inshore⟨.
AMPHIBIOUS: 2:
  1 *Hualcopo* (US LST- 511) LST, capacity 200 tps,
    16 tk.
  1 *Tarqui* (US LSM-1) LSM, capacity 50 tps, 4 tk.
SUPPORT AND MISCELLANEOUS: 5:
  1 survey, 1 water carrier, 2 tugs, 1 trg.

NAVAL AVIATION:
AIRCRAFT: 1 Cessna 320, 3 Cessna 337, 1 *Citation* I,
  3 T-34C.
HELICOPTERS: 1 *Alouette* III.
(Note: DD, FF and corvettes have hel deck but no
  hangar or maint facilities.)

MARINES: (1,000): 3 bn: 2 on garrison duties, 1
cdo (no hy weapons/veh).

AIR FORCE: 3,000; 82 cbt ac, no armed hel.
OPERATIONS COMMAND: 1 wing, 5 sqn:
FGA: 2 sqn:
  1 with 10 *Jaguar* S, 2 -B;
  1 with 10 *Kfir* C-2, 1 TC-2.
FIGHTER: 1 sqn with 15 *Mirage* F-1JE, 1 F-1JB.
COIN: 1 sqn with 7 A-37B.
COIN/TRAINING: 1 sqn with 12 *Strikemaster* Mk 89.
MILITARY AIR TRANSPORT GROUP:
2 civil/military airlines:
TAME: 4 Boeing 727, 2 BAe-748, 1 C-130H, 2
  DC-6B, 2 DHC-5, 3 DHC-6, 1 L-188.
ECUATORIANA: 8 Boeing (3 -720, 5 -707), 1 DC-10-30.
LIAISON/SAR hel flt: 2 AS-332, 1 Bell 212, 6
  SA-316B, 1 SA-330, 2 UH-1B, 24 UH-1H.
TRAINING: incl 24 AT-33, 20 T-34C, 6 T-41.
AAM: R-550 *Magic*, Super 530, Shafrir.
1 AB sqn.
(In store: 3 *Canberra* B-6 bbr.)

PARA-MILITARY:
COAST GUARD 200: 6 PCI⟨.

EL SALVADOR

GDP	1987:	C 23.31 bn ($4.66 bn)	
	1988ε:	C 23.69 bn ($4.74 bn)	
Growth	1987:	2.8%	1988ε: 3.0%
Inflation	1987:	24.9%	1988ε: 28.0%
Debt	1987:	$1.9 bn	1988: 1.9 bn
Def bdgt	1986:	C 800.0 m ($160.00 m)	
def exp	1987:	C 1.041 bn ($208.18 m)	
FMA	1988:	$86.4 m (US)	
$1 = C	(1987/8/9):	5.0	
C = colones			

Population: 5,923,000

	13–17	18–22	23–32
Men	330,000	270,000	328,000
Women	323,000	265,000	369,000

TOTAL ARMED FORCES:

ACTIVE: 56,000 (incl 12,500 civil defence force).
Terms of service: selective conscription, 2 years: all services.
RESERVES: ex-soldiers registered.

ARMY: 40,000 (some conscripts).
6 Military Zones (14 Departments).
6 inf bde (32 inf bn).
1 arty bde (4 bn).
1 mech cav regt (2 bn).
1 engr bn.
5 rapid action bn (1,100–1,400 men).
1 AB bn (under Air Force comd).
1 AD arty bn (under Air Force comd).
EQUIPMENT:
LIGHT TANKS: 5 M-3A1 (in store).
RECCE: 12 AML-90.
APC: 66 M-37B1 (mod), 20 M-113, 10 UR-416.
TOWED ARTY: 105mm: 54 M-102.
MORTARS: 81mm: 300 M-29;
120mm: 60 UB-M52.
RL: *LAW.*
RCL: 90mm: 400 M-67.
AD GUNS: 20mm: 24 Yug M-55, 4 SP.

NAVY: 1,300.
BASE: Acajutla.
PATROL AND COASTAL COMBATANTS: 6:
PATROL INSHORE: 3 GC-6 Camcraft, 3 PCI⟨ plus boats.
AMPHIBIOUS: Craft only, 3 LCM.

AIR FORCE: 2,200 (incl AD);
32 cbt ac, 19 armed hel.
FIGHTER: 1 sqn with 8 *Ouragan* (grounded).
COIN:

AIRCRAFT: 1 sqn with 9 A-37B, 5 AC-47, 12 O-2A.
HELICOPTERS: 1 sqn with 7 Hughes (armed: 3 -500, 4 -500M), 12 UH-1M (armed), 43 UH-1H (tpt).
TRANSPORT: 1 gp: 6 C-47, 1 C-123K, 1 DC-6B, 4 IAI-201, 9 *Rallye.*
LIAISON: 6 Cessna 180, 1 Cessna 182, 1 Cessna 185 ac, 3 SA-315, 1 SA-316 hel.
TRAINING: 6 CM-170 (COIN/trg), 6 T-41.

PARA-MILITARY:
NATIONAL GUARD: 4,200.
NATIONAL POLICE: 6,000.
TREASURY POLICE: 2,400.
DEFENCA CIVIL (territorial civil defence force): 12,500 armed.

OPPOSITION:
FARABUNDO MARTI NATIONAL LIBERATION FRONT (FMLN): 6–7,000 combatants, coalition of 5 groups: People's Revolutionary Army (ERP). Popular Liberation Forces (FPL). Armed Forces of National Resistance (FARN or RN). Revolutionary Party of Central American Workers (PRTC). Armed Forces of Liberation (FAL).

GUATEMALA

GDP	1987:	q 17.38 bn ($6.95 bn)	
	1988ε:	q 20.68 bn ($7.90 bn)	
Growth	1987:	2.0%	1988ε: 2.0%
Inflation	1987:	12.3%	1988: 17.0%
Debt	1987:	$2.7 bn	1988: $2.8 bn
Def bdgt	1986:	q 245.20 m ($130.77 m)	
	1987:	q 265.80 m ($106.32 m)	
FMA	1988:	$9.4 m (US)	
$1 = q	(1986):1.8750	(1987): 2.5000	
	(1988):2.6196	(1989): 2.7050	
q = quetzales			

Population: 8,789,000

	13–17	18–22	23–32
Men	513,000	428,000	639,000
Women	496,000	415,000	626,000

TOTAL ARMED FORCES:*
ACTIVE: 42,200.
Terms of service: Conscription; selective, 30 months.
RESERVES: Army 35,000 (trained), Navy (some), Air 200.

ARMY: 40,000.*
HQ: 22 Military Zones.
4 inf bde (each 3 inf bn, 1 recce sqn, 1 arty gp).
Strategic Reserve bde (2 bn).

1 armd coy.
25 indep inf bn.
2 AB bn.
2 AD arty.
1 engr bn.

EQUIPMENT:
LIGHT TANKS: 10 M-41A3.
RECCE: 10 M-8, 10 RBY-1;
(cbt status uncertain)
APC: 10 M-113, 7 V-100 *Commando*, 18 *Armadillo*.
TOWED ARTY: 75mm: 10 M-116; 105mm: 4 M-101,
8 M-102, 48 M-56.
MORTARS: 81mm: M-1; 107mm: 12 M-30; 120mm:
12 ECIA.
RL: 89mm: 3.5-in. M-20.
RCL: 106mm.
AD GUNS: 20mm: GAI-DO1;

NAVY: 1,200 incl 700 marines (6 coy)*
BASES: Santo Tomás de Castillas (Atlantic),
Puerto Quetzal, Puerto San José (Pacific).
PATROL CRAFT, INSHORE 9:
1 *Kukulkan* (US *Broadsword* 32m) PFI, 8⟨.
AMPHIBIOUS: craft only; 1 LCM⟨.

AIR FORCE: 1,000* 17 cbt ac, 10 armed hel.
Serviceability of ac is perhaps less than 50%.
COIN: 1 sqn with 8 Cessna A-37B, 6 PC-7.
ATTACK HELICOPTERS: 4 Bell 212, 6 Bell 412.
TRANSPORT: 1 sqn with 9 C-47, 3 F-27, 7 IAI-201, 1
Super King Air (VIP).
LIAISON: 1 sqn with 4 *Cessna* 170, 8 Cessna 172, 3
Cessna 180, 1 Cessna 182, 1 Cessna 185, 3
Cessna 206.
HELICOPTERS: 1 sqn with 5 Bell 206, 7 UH-1D/-H,
3 S-76.
TRAINING: 3 CM-170 (wpn trg), 4 PC-7, 2 T-33.
TACTICAL SECURITY GROUP:
3 coy; 4 M-3A1 *White* scout cars.

PARA-MILITARY:
NATIONAL POLICE: 10,700.
TREASURY POLICE: 2,100.
TERRITORIAL MILITIA (R) (CVDC): ε 600,000,
some 15,000 lightly armed.

OPPOSITION:
**UNIDAD REVOLUCIONARIA NACIONAL
GUATEMALTECA** (URNG): some 1,000–1,500;
coalition of 4 groups: Ejército Guerrillero de los
Pobres (EGP). Partido Guatemalteco del Trabajo
(PGT). Fuerzas Armadas Rebeldes (FAR).
Organización del Pueblo en Armas (ORPA).

* National Armed Forces are combined; the Army
provides log spt to the Navy and Air Force.

GUYANA

GDP	1986:	$G 2.22 bn ($US 519.38 m)	
	1987:	$G 3.36 bn ($US 344.10 m)	
Growth	1986:	−2.3%	1987: −0.6%
Inflation	1987:	28.7%	1988ε: 36.0%
Debt	1987:	$1.7 bn	1988: $1.8 bn
Def bdgt	1986:	$G 277.71 m ($US 65.00 m)	
FMA	1988:	$0.05 m (US)	

$US 1 = $G   (1986): 4.2724   (1987): 9.7558
(1988): 10.00

$G = $ Guyanese

Population: 1,018,000

	13–17	18–22	23–32
Men	53,000	53,000	85,000
Women	53,000	52,000	89,000

TOTAL ARMED FORCES: (Combined
Guyana Defence Force):
ACTIVE: 5,450.
Terms of service: voluntary.
RESERVES: some 2,000 People's Militia.
(see Para-Military).

ARMY: 5,000.
2 inf, 1 guard, 1 SF, 1 spt wpn, 1 engr bn.
EQUIPMENT:
RECCE: 4 *Shorland*.
TOWED ARTY: 130mm: 6 M-46.
MORTARS: 81mm: 12 L16A1;
82mm: 18 M-43;
120mm: 18 M-43.
SAM: SA-7.

NAVY: 150;
BASES: Georgetown, New Amsterdam.
PATROL CRAFT: 6:
1 *Peccari* (UK Vosper 31m) PCI, 5 PFI⟨.
AMPHIBIOUS: craft only; 1 LCU.

AIR FORCE: 300;
No cbt ac, no armed hel.
TRANSPORT:
AIRCRAFT: 6 BN-2A, 2 *Skyvan* 2, 1 *Super King
Air* B-200 (VIP).
HELICOPTERS: 2 Bell 206, 1 Bell 212, 1 Bell 412,
1 Mi-8.

PARA-MILITARY:
GUYANA PEOPLE'S MILITIA (GPM): some 2,000.
GUYANA NATIONAL SERVICE (GNS): 1,500.

HAITI

GDP	1986: G 11.22 bn ($2.24 bn)	
	1987: G 9.75 bn ($1.95 bn)	
Growth	1986: 0.6%	1987: −0.6%
Inflation	1986: 3.3%	1987: −11.4%
Debt*	1987: $741.0 m	1988: $800.0 m
FMA	1987: $1.6 m	1988: $1.8 m (US)
$1 = G	(1986/7/8/9): 5.0	
G = gourdes		

Population: 5,507,000

	13–17	18–22	23–32
Men	303,000	270,000	410,000
Women	296,000	271,000	483,000

TOTAL ARMED FORCES:
ACTIVE: 7,400.
Terms of service: voluntary.

ARMY: 7,000
(has police/gendarmerie,
fire-fighting, immigration,
etc, roles).
Presidential Guard (6 inf, 1 airport security coy;
armd and arty elm).
9 military departments (27 coy).
EQUIPMENT:†
LIGHT TANKS: 6 M-5A1.
APC: 5 M-2, 6 V-150 *Commando*.
TOWED ARTY: 75mm: 4; 105mm: 6.
MORTARS: 60mm: 36 M-2; 81mm: M-1.
ATK GUNS: 37mm: 10 M-3; 57mm: 10 M-1.
RCL: 57mm: M-18; 106mm: M-40 A1.
AD GUNS: 20mm: 6 TCM-20, 4 other; 40mm: 6;
57mm: 4.

NAVY: 250 (Coast guard).
BASE: Port au Prince
PATROL CRAFT: 3: PCI⟨.

AIR FORCE: 150;
7 cbt ac, no armed hel.
COIN: 7 O-2.
COIN/TRAINING: 4 S-211 (for disposal).
TRANSPORT: 1 *Baron*, 1 BN-2, 1 C-46, 3 C-47, 1
Cessna 402, 3 DHC-2, 1 DHC-6.
HELICOPTERS: 1 Hughes 300 (liaison).
TRAINING: 3 Cessna 150, 1 Cessna 172, 1 *Bonanza*,
4 SF-260TP, 1 *Twin-Bonanza*.

* Public debt only.
† Most eqpt is inoperable.

HONDURAS

GDP	1987: L 8.02 bn ($4.01 bn)	
	1988ε: L 8.81 bn ($4.40 bn)	
Growth	1987: 4.9%	1988: 4.0%
Inflation	1987: 2.4%	1988: 4.6%
Debt	1987: $3.1 bn	1988: $3.2 bn
Def bdgt*	1987: L 135.00 m ($67.50 m)	
	1988: L 150.00 m ($75.00 m)	
FMA	1987: $60.0 m	1988: $41.0 m (US)
$1 = L	(1987/8/9) 2.0	
L = lempiras		

Population: 4,914,000

	13–17	18–22	23–32
Men	285,000	239,000	351,000
Women	284,000	237,000	347,000

TOTAL ARMED FORCES:
ACTIVE: 19,200; (13,200 conscripts).
Terms of service: conscription, 24 months.
RESERVES: 50,000.

ARMY: 15,400 (11,000 conscripts).
10 Military Zones:
4 inf bde (11 inf, 3 arty bn; 1 armd cav regt).
1 arty bde (regt).
1 indep armd cav regt.
2 indep inf, 1 SF, 1 engr, 1 AD arty bn.
EQUIPMENT:
LIGHT TANKS: 12 *Scorpion*, 3 *Scimitar*.
RECCE: 72 *Saladin*, 10 RBY Mk 1.
TOWED ARTY: 105mm: 24 M-101/-102; 155mm: 4
M-198.
MORTARS: 400 60mm, 81mm; 120mm: 60; 160mm:
30 *Soltam*.
RL: 84mm: 120 *Carl Gustav*.
RCL: 57mm: M-18; 106mm: 80 M-40A1.
AD GUNS: 80: 20mm: incl M-55.

NAVY: 1,200 incl 600 marines (900 conscripts).
BASES: Puerto Cortés, Amapala.
PATROL CRAFT: 11:
INSHORE: 11:
3 *Guaymuras* (US Swiftships 31m) PFI, 2 *Copan*
(US Lantana 32m) PFI⟨, 6 other PCI⟨.
AMPHIBIOUS: craft only; 1 *Punta Caxinas* LCT.

AIR FORCE: some 2,100 (800 conscripts);
49 cbt ac, no armed hel.
FGA: 2 sqn:
1 with 13 A-37B;
1 with 12 F-5 (10 -E, 2 -F).
FIGHTER: 1 sqn with 8 *Super Mystère* B2 (to be replaced).

TRANSPORT: 9 C-47, 1 C-123, 2 C-130A, 4
Commander, 2 DHC-5, 1 L-188, 2 IAI-201, 1
IAI-1123, 1 IAI-1124 ac; 1 S-76 hel (VIP).
LIAISON: 1 sqn with 1 *Baron*, 3 Cessna 172, 2
Cessna 180, 2 Cessna 185, 1 PA-24, 1 PA-31.
HELICOPTERS: 1 Bell 47, 10 Bell 412, 4 Hughes
500, 5TH-55, 8 UH-1B, 11 UH-1H.
TRAINING: 2 T-33, 4 C-101BB, 12 EMB-312, 5 T-41A.

PARA-MILITARY:

PUBLIC SECURITY FORCES (FUSEP) (national
police): 4,500.

FOREIGN FORCES:

US: Army: 1,500.

* Excl internal security costs.

JAMAICA

GDP	1987:	$J 15.72 bn ($US 2.86 bn)		
	1988ε:	$J 17.47 bn ($US 3.18 bn)		
Growth	1987:	5.2%	1988:	0.6%
Inflation	1987:	6.7%	1988:	8.2%
Debt	1987:	$US 4.0 bn	1988:	$US 4.5 bn
Def bdgt	1986/7:	$J 113.00 m ($US 20.62 m)		
	1987/8:	$J 137.60 m ($US 25.06 m)		
FMA	1987:	$3.3 m 1988: $3.8 m (US)		

$US 1 = $J (1986/7): 5.4794 (1987/8): 5.4899
(1988):   5.4886
$J = $ Jamaican

Population: 2,463,000

	13–17	18–22	23–32
Men	146,000	150,000	244,000
Women	141,000	148,000	243,000

TOTAL ARMED FORCES (all services form
combined Jamaica Defence Force):
ACTIVE: some 2,800.
Terms of service: voluntary.
RESERVES: some 870: Army 800; Coast guard:
50; Airwing: 20.

ARMY: 2,500.
2 inf bn.
1 spt bn.
APC: 20 V-150 *Commando*.
MORTARS: 81mm: 12 L16A1.
RESERVES: 800: 1 inf bn.

COAST GUARD: 200.

BASE: Port Royal
PATROL CRAFT: 5 Inshore:
1 *Fort Charles* PFI (US 34m), 4 PFI⟨.

AIR WING: 150;
No cbt ac, no armed hel.
AIRCRAFT: 2 BN-2, 1 Cessna 210, 1 Cessna 337, 1
King Air.
HELICOPTERS: 4 Bell 205, 4 Bell 206, 3 Bell 212.

MEXICO

GDP	1987:	pM 192,935.00 bn ($139.99 bn)	
	1988ε:	pM 405,163.00 bn ($178.24 bn)	
Growth	1987:	1.0%	1988ε: –1.0%
Inflation	1987:	134.4%	1988: 114.2%
Debt	1987:	$102.4 bn	1988: $103.0 bn
Def exp	1988:	pM 1,469.4 bn ($646.45 m)	
Def bdgt	1989:	pM 1,576.9 bn ($670.06 m)	
FMA	1987:	$0.2 m 1988: $0.23 m (US)	

$1 = pM (1987):   1,378.20 (1988):   2,273.10
(1989):   2,353.40

pM = pesos Mexicanos

Population: 84,272,000

	13–17	18–22	23–32
Men	5,360,000	4,578,000	6,929,000
Women	5,182,000	4,446,000	6,816,000

TOTAL ARMED FORCES: 261,500.
ACTIVE: 141,500 (60,000 conscripts).
Terms of service: voluntary; 1 yr conscription
by lottery.
RESERVES: 300,000.

ARMY: 105,500 regular (incl ε 60,000 conscripts).
36 Zonal Garrisons: incl 24 mot cav, 3 arty
regt, 70 inf bn.
1 mech inf bde (Presidential Guard) (3 bn).
2 inf bde (each 3 inf bn, 1 armd recce sqn,
1 arty bn).
1 AB bde (2 bn, 1 trg bn) (forms part of Air Force).
3 armd regt.
AD, engr and spt units.
EQUIPMENT:
LIGHT TANKS: 45 M-3/M-5.
RECCE: 15 M-8, 15 MAC-1, 80 Panhard ERC-90F
Lynx, 40 Panhard M-11 VBL, 39 DN-3/-5 *Caballo*.
APC: 40 HWK-11, 30 M-3 halftrack.
TOWED ARTY: 75mm: 18 M-116 pack; 105mm: 70
M-2A1, M-3.
SP ARTY: 75mm: 5 M-8.
MORTARS: 1,500 50mm, 60mm, 81mm; 120mm: 60.
ATGW: *Milan* (incl 8 Panhard M-11 VBL).

RCL: 106mm: M-40A1.
ATK GUNS: 37mm: 30 M-3.
AD GUNS: 40 12.7mm.

NAVY: 28,000, incl naval air force and marines.
2 Areas: Gulf; 5 Zones (6 Subordinate Sectors).
Pacific: 11 Zones (5 Sectors).
BASES: Gulf: Vera Cruz (HQ), Tampico,
Chetumal, Ciudad del Carmen, Yukalpetén.
Pacific: Acapulco (HQ), Ensenada, La Paz, Puerto
Cortés, Guaymas, Mazatlán, Manzanillo,
Salina Cruz, Puerto Madero, Lázaro Cárdenas,
Puerto Vallarta.
DESTROYERS: 3:
2 *Quetzalcoatl* (US *Gearing*) ASW with 1 × 8
ASROC, 2 × 3 ASTT; plus 2 × 2 127mm guns,
hel deck.
1 *Cuitlahoac* (US *Fletcher*) with 5 × 533mm TT,
5 × 127mm guns.
PATROL AND COASTAL COMBATANTS: 94:
PATROL, OFFSHORE: 44:
1 *Uxmal* (imp *Uribe*) with Bo-105 hel.
6 *Cadete Virgilio Uribe* (Sp '*Halcon*') with
Bo-105 hel.
1 *Comodoro Manuel Azueta* (US *Edsall*) (trg).
4 *Zacatecas* (US *Lawrence/Crosley*) with 1 ×
127mm gun.
1 *Durango* (trg) with 1 × 102mm gun.
18 *Leandro Valle* (US *Auk* MSF).
1 *Guanajuato* with 1 × 102mm gun.
12 D-01 (US *Admirable* MSF).
PATROL, INSHORE: 30:
30 *Quintana Roo* (UK *Azteca*) PCI.
PATROL, RIVER: 20⟨.
SUPPORT AND MISCELLANEOUS: 13:
1 PCI spt, 2 log spt, 6 ocean tugs, 4 survey.
COASTAL DEFENCE:
GUNS: 75mm: M-1902/-1906, 120mm: L/27
(probably de-activated).

NAVAL AIR FORCE: (500);
11 cbt ac, no armed hel.
MR: 1 sqn with 10 C-212, 11 HU-16 *Albatross* (SAR).
TRANSPORT: 1 C-212, 3 Cessna 310, 1 DHC-5, 1
DHC-6, 4 FH-227, 1 *King Air* 90, 1 *Learjet* 24.
LIAISON: 3 Cessna 150, 2 Cessna 180, 2 Cessna
337, 2 Cessna 402.
HELICOPTERS: 3 Bell 47, 12 Bo-105 (8 afloat), 4
SA-319B.

MARINES: (8,000).
1 bde (2 bn).
1 Presidential Guard bn.
15 gp.
32 security coy.

AIR FORCE: 8,000 (incl 2,000 AB bde);
113 cbt ac, 23 armed hel.
FIGHTER: 1 sqn with 9 F-5E, 2 F-5F.
COIN: 9 sqn:
6 with 70 PC-7;
1 with 12 AT-33;
1 with 10 IAI-201;
1 hel with 5 Bell 205, 5 Bell 206, 5 Bell 212, 8
SA-316.
RECCE: 1 photo sqn with 10 *Commander* 500S.
TRANSPORT: 5 sqn with 1 C-46, 12 C-47, 4 C-54, 2
C-118, 9 C-130A, 6 *Commander* (5 -500, 1 -680),
3 DC-7B, 2 DHC-5, 1 *Gulfstream* II, 3 *Skyvan*.
PRESIDENTIAL TRANSPORT:
  AIRCRAFT: 7 Boeing 727, 2 Boeing 737, 1
  Electra, 1 FH-227, 1 *Jetstar*, 1 *Metro*, 1
  Merlin, 6 T-39.
  HELICOPTERS: 1 A-109, 2 AS-332, 4 Bell 206, 1
  Bell 212, 2 SA-330.
LIAISON: 1 Cessna 310, 2 *King Air* (1 -90, 1 -200),
1 PA-23, 2 PA-32, 1 *Queen Air* 80.
TRAINING: 41 *Bonanza*, 20 CAP-10B, 20
Musketeer, 10 PC-7.

PARA-MILITARY:
RURAL DEFENCE MILITIA (R): 120,000.

NICARAGUA

GDP	1986:	$C 435.74 m ($US 6.50 bn)	
	1987:	$C 2,389.50 m ($US 3.41 bn)	
Growth	1987:	1.7%	
Inflation	1987:	911.9%	1988: 10,087.5%
Debt	1987ε:	$US 7.5 bn	1988ε: $US 8.4 bn
Def exp	1987ε:	$C 132.00 m ($US 1.89 bn)	
Def bdgt*	1988ε:	$C 128.00 m ($US 1.42 bn)	
$US 1 = $C	(1986): 0.0670	(1987): 0.0700	
	(1988): 90.00	(1989): 4,609.40	

$C = córdobas†

Population: 3,704,000

	13–17	*18–22*	*23–32*
Men	229,000	197,000	250,000
Women	226,000	190,000	275,000

TOTAL ARMED FORCES:
ACTIVE: 80,000 incl active duty reserves and
militia (ε 30,000 conscripts).
Terms of service: conscription, males 17–26,
2 years' service plus commitment to age 45.
RESERVES: All males 18–40 required to
register. Army/militia 134,000 (32,000 active
duty); Navy 2,500; Air none.

ARMY: 73,500: 41,500 Active (30,000 conscripts), 32,000 recalled Reserves and militia.
7 Military Regions.
2 armd bde, each 2 tk, 2 mech inf bn.
2 mot inf bde, each 3 motor inf, 1 tk bn.
2 frontier bde.
1 arty bde (4 gp: 1 MRL, 3 152mm how).
8 regional arty gp.
20 inf bn.
4 engr bn.
RESERVES: Army: 76,000 (active duty 18,000); 27 bde (125 bn).
Militia: 58,000 (active duty 14,000); 10 bde (43 bn), 62 indep bn, 49 territorial coy.
EQUIPMENT:
MBT: some 130 T-54/-55.
LIGHT TANKS: 22 PT-76.
RECCE: 72 BRDM-2.
APC: 24 BTR-60, 90 BTR-152.
TOWED ARTY: 122mm: 36 D-30; 152mm: 60 D-20.
MRL: 122mm: 36 BM-21.
MORTARS: 82mm: 625; 120mm: 42.
ATGW: AT-3 *Sagger* (12 on BRDM-2).
ATK GUNS: 57mm: 345 ZIS-2; 76mm: 84 Z1S-3; 100mm: 24 M-1944 (BS-3).
SAM: 500+ SA-7/-14/-16.

NAVY: 3,500 (some conscripts).
PATROL AND COASTAL COMBATANTS: 18:
PATROL, INSHORE: 18:
8 Sov *Zhuk* PFI, 6 North Korea *Sin Hung* PFI⟨, 4 PCI⟨.
MINE COUNTERMEASURES: 8:
4 Sov *Yevgenya*, 4 K-8 MSI⟨.

AIR FORCE: 3,000;
16 cbt ac, 10 armed hel.
COIN: 1 sqn with 6 Cessna 337, 6 L-39Z, 4 SF-260 WL.
ATTACK HELICOPTERS: 10 Mi-25.
TRANSPORT: 1 sqn with 6 An-26, 2 C-212.
HELICOPTERS: 1 sqn with 35 Mi-8/-17.
LIAISON: ac: 8 An-2, 1 *Twin Bonanza*, 2 *Commander*; plus 7 Cessna 180, 3 Cessna 185, 3 DHC-3 (serviceability doubtful).
hel: 4 Mi-2, 2 SA-316; plus 1 OH-6A (serviceability doubtful).
TRAINING: 17 L-39C.
ASM: AT-2 *Swatter* ATGW.
AD GUNS: 700+ reported: 14.5mm: ZPU-1/-2/-4; 23mm: ZU-23; 37mm: M-1939; 57mm: S-60; 100mm: KS-19.

PARA-MILITARY:
MINISTRY OF INTERIOR TROOPS (*Tropas Pablo Ubeda*): some 2,000. 1 SF bde.

OPPOSITION:
NICARAGUAN RESISTANCE ARMY (NRN):
Main contra military gp, up to 12,000 active fighters, US-backed, mainly in north, some based in Honduras. Separate wings in south and on Atlantic coast.
SOUTHERN OPPOSITION BLOC (BOS):
MISURASATA (Miskito, Sumo, Rama and Sandinista Unity) up to 3,000 not all active.

FOREIGN FORCES:
CUBA: some 1,200 mil/sy advisers.
USSR: some 100 advisers.

* Highest est of economic aid and FMA from COMECON put at $600 m and $500 m respectively in 1987.
† A currency adjustment was introduced in 1989 at a rate of 1 New córdoba = 1,000 córdobas. All data is expressed in the new currency.

PANAMA

GDP	1987: B 5.32 bn ($5.32 bn)	
	1988ε: B 4.79 bn ($4.79 bn)	
Growth	1987: 2.4%	1988ε: −10.0%
Inflation	1987: 1.0%	1988: 0.3%
Debt	1987: $4.9 bn	1988: $5.2 bn
Def bdgt	1986: B 96.50 m ($96.50 m)	
	1987: B 104.60 m ($104.60 m)	
FMA	1987: $6.4 m (US) 1988: nil	
$1 = B	(1986/7/8/9): 1.00	
B = balboas		

Population: 2,353,000

	13–17	*18–22*	*23–32*
Men	135,000	124,000	201,000
Women	130,000	121,000	194,000

TOTAL ARMED FORCES:
ACTIVE: 4,400.
Terms of service: voluntary (conscription authorized).

ARMY: 3,500.
2 bn, 8 inf, 1 SF, 2 public order, 1 engr coy, 1 cav tp.
EQUIPMENT:
RECCE: 29: 16 V-150, 13 V-300 *Commando*.
MORTARS: 60mm, 81mm, 160mm.
RL: 89mm: 3.5-in M-20.

NAVY: 400.
BASES: Balboa (HQ), Colón.
PATROL CRAFT:
INSHORE: 6:
2 *Panquiaco* (UK Vosper 31.5m), 4⟨.
AMPHIBIOUS: craft only; 4 LCM.
SUPPORT AND MISCELLANEOUS: 1 tpt (ex US LSM).

AIR FORCE: 500.
4 cbt ac, no armed hel.
MR: 4 C-212 (armed).
TRANSPORT: 2 BN-2A, 1 CN-235, 1 *Commander*, 2 DHC-6, 1 Learjet 35, 1 U-21F.
LIAISON: 1 *Bonanza*, 1 Cessna U206, 2 PA-31, 1 PA-32, 3 U-17.
HELICOPTERS: 1 AS-332 (SAR/VIP), 6 Bell 205, 6 UH-1H, 4 UH-1N.
TRAINING: 10 T-35, 1 T-41.

FORCES ABROAD:
NAMIBIA (UNTAG): 19 observers.

PARA-MILITARY:
POLICE AND NATIONAL GUARD: 11,000.

FOREIGN FORCES:
US: some 10,700. Army: 6,800; 1 inf bde and spt elm. Navy: 500. Marines: 600. Air Force; 2,800; 1 air div. Plus temporary reinforcements.

PARAGUAY

GDP	1987:	Pg 2,493.60 bn ($4.53 bn)	
	1988ε:	Pg 2,616.08 bn ($4.76 bn)	
Growth	1987:	4.3%	1988ε: 5.0%
Inflation	1987:	21.9%	1988: 24.5%
Debt	1987:	$2.3 bn	1988: $2.5 bn
Def bdgt	1987:	Pg 38.78 bn ($70.50 m)	
	1988ε:	Pg 46.37 bn ($84.32 m)	
FMA	1987:	$0.1 m 1988: $0.13m (US)	
$1 = Pg	(1987/8/9):	550.0	
Pg = guaraníes			

Population: 4,124,000

	13–17	18–22	23–32
Men	198,000	182,000	293,000
Women	190,000	177,000	293,000

TOTAL ARMED FORCES:
ACTIVE: 16,000 (9,800 conscripts).
Terms of service: 18 months; Navy 2 years.

RESERVES: some 45,000.

ARMY: 12,500 (8,600 conscripts).
HQ: 3 corps.
1 with 1 cav div (2 horsed cav, 1 armd cav, 1 mech cav regt), 2 inf div (2 inf regt, 4 frontier bn).
1 with 2 inf div (1 inf regt, 3 frontier bn), 2 cav div.
1 with 3 inf div (3 inf regt).
1 indep inf div.
1 AB bn (part of Air Force).
Cbt spt comd incl 4 arty, 6 engr bn.
EQUIPMENT:
MBT: 3 M-4A3.
LIGHT TANKS: 18 M-3A1.
RECCE: 12 M-8, M-3 half track, 20 EE-9 *Cascavel.*
APC: 10 EE-11 *Urutu.*
TOWED ARTY: 75mm: 25 Model 1927/1934; 105mm: 48 M-101; 152mm: 6 Mk V 6-in (anti-ship).
MORTARS: 81mm; 107mm: 4.2-in.
RCL: 75mm: M-20.
AD GUNS: 20mm: 10; 40mm: 10 M-1A1.
AVIATION: 3 UH-1B, 2 UH-12 hel.

NAVY: 2,500 (1,000 conscripts) (incl Marines, Harbour and River Guard).
BASES: Asunción (Puerto Sajonia), Bahía Negra, Puerto Presidente Stroessner.
PATROL AND RIVERINE COMBATANTS: 6:
COASTAL: 5
1 *Paraguay* with 4 × 120mm guns.
3 *Nanawa* (Arg *Bouchard* MSO)
1 *Itaipu* (riverine).
INSHORE: 1 *Cabral* (built 1908).
SUPPORT AND MISCELLANEOUS: 3:
2 tpt, 1 *Boqueron* spt (ex-US LSM with hel deck, carries UH 12 hel).

MARINES: 500 (200 conscripts).
1 marine bn.
1 cdo bn.

NAVAL AIR FORCE: (50).
2 cbt ac, no armed hel.
COIN: 2 AT-6G.
TRANSPORT: 1 C-47.
HELICOPTERS: 2 HB-350, 1 Bell 47G.

AIR FORCE: 1,000 (700 conscripts);
23 cbt ac, no armed hel.
COMPOSITE SQN: .
COIN: 6 AT-6, 9 EMB-326.

LIAISON: 3 Cessna 185, 6 -206, 1 -337, 1 -402.
HELICOPTER: 1 Bell 47G.
TRANSPORT: 1 sqn with 7 C-47, 1 C-131, 4 C-212, 3 DC-6B, 1 PBY-5A.
TRAINING: 6 EMB-312, 8 T-23, 5 T-25, 7 T-41.

PARA-MILITARY:
SPECIAL POLICE SERVICE: 8,000.

PERU

GDP	1987: I 567.74 bn ($33.72 bn)
	1988ε:I 3,963.50 bn ($30.76 bn)
Growth	1987: 7.0% 1988ε:−8.0%
Inflation	1987: 86.0% 1988ε:1,722.3%
Debt	1987: $15.4 bn 1988: $16.3 bn
Def exp	1988ε:I 90.50 bn ($702.50 m)
Def bdgt	1989ε:I 790.00 bn ($658.30 m)
FMA	1987: $0.7 m (US) 1988: $2.02 m (US)
$1 = I	(1987): 16.836 (1988): 128.832
	(1989): 1,200.00
I = inti	

Population: 21,564,000

	13–17	18–22	23–32
Men	1,203,000	1,077,000	1,733,000
Women	1,166,000	1,046,000	1,689,000

TOTAL ARMED FORCES:
ACTIVE: 120,000 (79,000 conscripts).
Terms of service: 2 years, selective.
RESERVES: 188,000 (Army only).

ARMY: 80,000 (60,000 conscripts).
5 Military Regions:
Army Troops:
   1 AB 'div' (bde: 3 cdo, 1 para bn, 1 arty gp).
   1 Presidential Escort regt.
   1 AD arty gp.
Regional Troops:
   2 armd div (bde, each 2 tk, 1 armd inf bn, 1 arty gp, 1 engr bn).
   1 armd gp (3 indep armd cav, 1 fd arty, 1 AD arty, 1 engr bn).
   1 cav div (3 mech regt, 1 arty gp).
   8 inf div (bde, each 3 inf bn, 1 arty gp).
   1 jungle div.
   1 SF gp.
   2 med arty gp; 2 fd arty gp.
   2 AD arty gp.
   1 indep inf bn.
   1 indep engr bn.
   3 hel sqn.

EQUIPMENT:
MBT: 350 T-54/-55 (cbt status uncertain).
LIGHT TANKS: 110 AMX-13.
RECCE: 60 M-8/-20, 20 Fiat 6616, 15 BRDM-2.
APC: 300 M-113, 225 UR-416.
TOWED ARTY: 105mm: 50 Model 56 pack, 130 M-101; 122mm: 30 D-30; 130mm: 30 M-46; 155mm: 36 M-114.
SP ARTY: 155mm: 12 M-109A2, 12 Mk F3.
MRL: 122mm: 14 BM-21.
MORTARS: 81mm: incl some SP; 107mm: incl some SP; 120mm: 300 Brandt, ECIA.
RCL: 105mm; 106mm: M40A1.
AD GUNS: 23mm: 35 ZSU-23-4 SP; 40mm: 40 towed.
SAM: 12 SA-3, SA-7.
AVIATION:
   AIRCRAFT: 1 Cessna 182, 2 -U206, 1 -337, 1 *Queen Air* 65, 3 U-10, 3 U-17.
   HELICOPTERS: 2 Bell 47G, 2 Mi-6, 34 Mi-8, 6 SA-315, 1 SA-318.

NAVY: 25,000 (12,000 conscripts) incl naval air, marines.
3 Naval Force Areas: Pacific, Lake Titicaca, Amazon River.
BASES: ocean: Callao, San Lorenzo Island, Paita, Talara. **lake:** Puno. **river:** Iquitos, Puerto Maldonado.
SUBMARINES: 11:
   6 *Casma* (FRG T-209/1200) with 533mm TT (It A184 HWT).
   1 *Pedrera* (US *Guppy* I) with 533mm TT (Mk 37 HWT).
   4 *Abtao* (US *Mackerel*) with 533mm TT.
PRINCIPAL SURFACE COMBATANTS: 14:
CRUISERS: 2:
   1 *Almirante Grau* CC (Nl *De Ruyter*) with 4 × 2 152mm guns, 8 Otomat SSM.
   1 *Aguirre* CCH (Nl *De 7 Provincien*) with 4 × SH-3D *Sea King* hel (ASW/ASUW) (Mk 46 LWT/AM-39 *Exocet*), 4 × 152mm guns.
DESTROYERS: 8:
   2 *Palacios* (UK *Daring*) with 4 × 2 MM-38 *Exocet*, 3 × 2 114mm guns, hel deck.
   6 *Bolognesi* (Nl *Friesland*) with 4 × 120mm guns, 2 × 4 ASW RL.
FRIGATES: 4 *Carvajal* (mod It *Lupo*) with 1 AB-212 hel (ASW/OTHT), 2 × 3 ASTT; plus 8 *Otomat* SSM, 2 × 20 105mm MRL, 1 × 127mm gun.
PATROL AND COASTAL COMBATANTS: 6:
MISSILE CRAFT: 6 *Velarde* PFM (Fr PR-72 64m) with 4 × MM-38 *Exocet*.
AMPHIBIOUS: 4 *Paita* (US *Terrebonne Parish*) LST, capacity 300 tps, 16 tk.
SUPPORT AND MISCELLANEOUS: 9:
   2 AO, 3 AOT, 2 tpt, 1 survey, 1 ocean tug.
RIVER AND LAKE FLOTILLAS: 10:
   4 gunboats, 6 patrol⟨.

Subscriptions to IISS Publications

From 1 January 1990 the following subscriptions are available:

Combined Subscription
>This will bring you each year:
>>1 copy of *The Military Balance*, 1 copy of *Strategic Survey*,
>>about 12 Adelphi Papers, 6 issues of *Survival*

>(For the Hardback Combined Subscription, *Survival* and Adelphi Papers will
>remain in flexi-cover)

Yearly and two-yearly subscriptions for individual publications

SUBSCRIPTION CARD (prices from 1 January 1990)

Please enter me a **Combined** Subscription for:
- ☐ 1990 (1 yr) at £118.50/$175.00 (Flexicover)
- ☐ 1990/91 (2 yrs) at £225.00/$333.00 (Flexicover)
- ☐ 1990 (1 yr) at £152.00/$225.00 (Hardback)
- ☐ 1990/91 (2 yrs) at £289.00/$428.00 (Hardcover)

Please enter me a **Military Balance** Subscription for:
- ☐ 1990 (1 yr) at £26.95/$40.00 (Personal/Flexicover)
- ☐ 1990 (1 yr) at £56.95/$84.00 (Institutional/Hardback)
- ☐ 1990/91 (2 yrs) at £108.00/$160.00 (Institutional/Hardback)

Please enter me a **Strategic Survey** Subscription for:
- ☐ 1990 (1 yr) at £13.00/$20.00 (Personal/Flexicover)
- ☐ 1990 (1 yr) at £31.00/$46.00 (Institutional/Hardback)
- ☐ 1990/91 (2 yrs) at £58.95/$87.00 (Institutional/Hardback)

Please enter me a **Survival** Subscription for:
- ☐ 1990 (1 yr) at £21.00/$30.00
- ☐ 1990/91 (2 yrs) at £39.95/$59.00

Please enter me an **Adelphi Papers** Subscription for:
- ☐ 1990 (1 yr) at £66.95/$99.00
- ☐ 1990/91 (2 yrs) at £126.00/$187.00

Please tick the appropriate boxes above and also fill in your name, address and payment details on the other side of this card.

For non-subscription orders for *The Military Balance 1989–90* and *Strategic Survey 1989–90*, please fill in the Order Form overleaf.

ORDER FORM:

Please send . . . . copies of *The Military Balance 1989–1990*

☐ at £38.00/$70.00 (Hardback) (ISBN 0 08 040352 2)
☐ or £19.00/$35.00 (Flexi) (ISBN 0 08 037569 3)

Please send . . . . copies of *Strategic Survey 1989–1990*

☐ at £34.50/$49.95 (Hardback) (ISBN 0 08 040368 9)
☐ or £15.00/$21.95 (Flexi) (ISBN 0 08 040369 7)

PAYMENT:

☐ Payment enclosed £/$ . . . . ☐ Bill me

Payment Method:

☐ Cheque   ☐ Postal Order   ☐ International Money Order

(Please make cheques, etc., payable to *Brassey's Defence Publishers* and send with this card, in an envelope, to the appropriate address below.)

Credit Cards   ☐ Access   ☐ Mastercard   ☐ Visa   ☐ Amex   ☐ Diners

Card No. ☐☐☐☐☐☐☐☐☐☐☐☐☐☐☐☐

Expiry date _____

Signature (*obligatory for credit card orders*): . . . .

PLEASE
PRINT
NAME AND
ADDRESS
CLEARLY

Name _____

Address _____

City _____   Country _____

Please fold and return this card, in an envelope, to the appropriate address:

(residents of North America):

Brassey's (US)
Maxwell House
Fairview Park
Elmsford, NY 10523
USA

(residents of ALL other countries):

Brassey's (UK)
Headington Hill Hall
Oxford
OX3 0BW
UK

(9/4)

NAVAL AIR FORCE:
8 cbt ac, 12 armed hel.
ASW/MR: 4 sqn with:
AIRCRAFT: 4 S-2E, 4 S-2G, 3 *Super King Air* B 200T.
HELICOPTERS: 6 SH-3D, 6 AB-212 ASW.
TRANSPORT: 5 C-47, 4 *Super King Air* B 200CT (tpt, recce).
LIAISON: 4 Bell 206B, 6 UH-1D hel.
TRAINING: 5 T-34C, Cessna 150.
ASM: 40 *Exocet* AM-39 (on SH-3 hel).

MARINES: (2,500).
1 Marine bde (2 bn, 1 recce, 1 cdo coy).
EQUIPMENT:
RECCE: V-100.
APC: 40 V-200 *Chaimite*, 20 BMR-600.
RCL: 106mm.
RL: 84mm.
MORTARS: ε 18 120mm.
AD GUNS: twin 20mm SP.

COAST DEFENCE: 3 bty with 18 155mm how (may have been deactivated).

AIR FORCE: 15,000 (7,000 conscripts);
119 cbt ac, 24 armed hel.
BOMBERS:
1 Gp (2 sqn) with 21 *Canberra* (3 B-72, 4 B(I)-8, 4 B-56, 8 B(I)-58, 2 T-54).
FGA: 2 Gp: 6 sqn:
3 with 41 Su-22 (incl 4 Su-22U);
3 with 29 Cessna A-37B.
FIGHTER: 3 sqn:
1 with 12 *Mirage* 2000 (10 -P, 2 -DP);
2 with 16 *Mirage* 5 (14 -5P, 2 -5DP).
ATTACK HELICOPTERS: 1 hel sqn with ε 24 Mi-24 (probably Army-assigned).
RECCE: 1 photo-survey unit with 4 *Learjet* (2 36A, 2 25B).
TANKER: 1 Boeing 707-323C.
TRANSPORT: 3 Gp (7 sqn):
AIRCRAFT: 15 An-32, 4 C-130A, 6 C-130D, 5 L-100-20, 2 DC-8-62F, 13 DHC-5, 8 DHC-6, 1 FH-227, 9 PC-6.
PRESIDENTIAL FLT: 1 F-28, 1 *Falcon 20* ac.
HELICOPTERS: 3 sqn with 8 Bell 206, 11 -212, 5 -214, 3 -412, 10 Bo-105C, 5 Mi-6, 6 Mi-8, 5 SA-316.
LIAISON: 2 Beech 99, 3 Cessna 185, 1 -320, 15 *Queen Air* 80, 3 *King Air* 90, 1 PA-31T.
LIAISON HELICOPTERS: 9 UH-1D.
TRAINING: 2 Cessna 150, 20 EMB-312, 13 MB-339A, 14 T-37B/C, 35 T-41A/-D.
TRAINING HELICOPTERS: 12 Bell 47G.
ASM: AS-30.

FORCES ABROAD:
IRAN/IRAQ (UNIIMOG): observers.
NAMIBIA (UNTAG): 20 observers.

PARA-MILITARY:
NATIONAL POLICE: 70,000 (amalgamation of Guardia Civil, Republican Guard and Policia Investigacionara Peruana); MOWAG *Roland* APC.
COAST GUARD: 600; 6 Coastal Patrol Craft, 5 inshore, some 10 riverine⟨.
RONDAS CAMPESINAS (self-defence force or People's Militia): no details.

OPPOSITION:
SENDERO LUMINOSO (Shining Path): some 4–5,000; rural gp maoist.
MOVIMIENTO REVOLUCIONARIO TUPAC AMARU (MRTA): 500; mainly urban gp.

SURINAME

GDP 1986: gld 1.75 bn ($981.01 m)
Inflation 1987: 54.0% 1988: 7.0%
Debt 1986: $871.0 m
Def bdgt 1988: gld 64.26 m ($36.00 m)
1989: gld 69.62 m ($39.00 m)
FMA 1988: $0.03 m (US)
$1 = gld (1986/7/8/9): 1.7850
gld = guilders

Population: 390,600

	13–17	*18–22*	*23–32*
Men	24,500	24,900	40,500
Women	24,000	24,600	40,800

TOTAL ARMED FORCES:
(all services form part of the Army):
ACTIVE: 3,000.
Terms of service: voluntary.

ARMY: 2,700.
1 inf bn (4 inf coy).
1 Military Police 'bde' (bn).
EQUIPMENT:
RECCE: 6 EE-9 *Cascavel*.
APC: 9 YP-408, 15 EE-11 *Urutu*.
MORTARS: 81mm: 6.
RCL: 57mm.

NAVY: 250.
BASE: Paramaribo.
PATROL CRAFT: 6 inshore:

3 S-401 (Nl 32m), 3⟨.

AIR FORCE: ε 100;
5 cbt ac, no armed hel.
COIN: 3 BN-2 *Defender*, 2 PC-7.
LIAISON: 1 Cessna U206.
HELICOPTERS: 1 Bell 205, 2 SA-316.

PARA-MILITARY:
NATIONAL MILITIA: 900.

OPPOSITION:
SURINAMESE LIBERATION ARMY or 'Jungle
Commando': 200–300; small arms only.

TRINIDAD & TOBAGO

GDP	1986: $TT 17.24 bn ($US 4.79 bn)
	1987ε: $TT 18.05 bn ($US 5.01 bn)
Growth	1987: –6.1%
Inflation	1987: 10.8% 1988: 7.7%
Debt	1987: $US 1.4 bn 1988: $US 1.7 bn
FMA	1988: $0.04 (US)
$US 1 = $TT	(1986/7): 3.60 (1988): 3.84

$TT = $ Trinidad & Tobago

Population: 1,254,000

	13–17	*18–22*	*23–32*
Men	65,000	66,000	119,000
Women	62,000	66,000	119,000

TOTAL ARMED FORCES:
(all services are part of the Army):
ACTIVE: 2,650.
Terms of service: voluntary.

ARMY: 2,000.
1 inf bn.
1 reserve bn (3 coy).
1 spt bn.
EQUIPMENT:
MORTARS: 60mm: ε 40; 81mm: 6 L16A1.
RL: 82mm: 13 B-300.

COAST GUARD: 600.
BASE: Staubles Bay.
PATROL CRAFT: Inshore: 10:
2 *Barracuda* PFI (Sw *Karlskrona* 40m).
2 *Chaguaramas* PCI (UK Vosper 31.5m), 6⟨.

AIR WING: 50.

AIRCRAFT: 1 Cessna 401.

PARA-MILITARY:
POLICE: 4,000.
MARINE WING: 2 PFI⟨, boats.
MINISTRY OF NATIONAL SECURITY; 1 SA-341,
2 S-76 (SAR) hel.

URUGUAY

GDP	1987: pU 1,700.56 bn ($7.50 bn)	
	1988ε: pU 2,797.42 bn ($7.78 bn)	
Growth	1987: 4.9%	1988ε: 2.3%
Inflation	1987: 63.5%	1988: 62.2%
Debt	1987: $5.9 bn	1988: $6.1 bn
Def bdgt	1986: pU 22.83 bn ($US 150.19 m)	
FMA	1987: $0.1 m (US) 1988: $0.13 m (US)	
$1 = pU	(1986): 151.99 (1987): 226.67	
	(1988): 359.44 (1989): 498.53	

pU = pesos Uruguayos

Population: 3,013,000

	13–17	*18–22*	*23–32*
Men	136,000	125,000	242,000
Women	131,000	120,000	235,000

TOTAL ARMED FORCES:
ACTIVE: 24,400.
Terms of service: voluntary; 1–2 years, extendable.

ARMY: 17,200.
4 Military Regions.
1 indep inf bde.
1 engr bde.
15 inf bn.
10 cav bn (4 horsed, 3 mech, 2 mot, 1 armd).
6 arty bn.
6 engr bn.
EQUIPMENT:
LIGHT TANKS, 17 M-24, 28 M-3A1, 22 M-41A1.
RECCE: 20 FN-4-RM-62, 18 EE-3 *Jararaca*,
15 EE-9 *Cascavel*.
APC: 15 M-113, 50 *Condor*.
TOWED ARTY: 75mm: 12 Bofors M-1902; 105mm:
25 M-101A1; 155mm: 5 M-114A1.
MORTARS: 81mm: 40 M-1; 107mm: 5 4.2in.
ATGW: 10 *Milan*.
RCL: 57mm: 30 M-18. 106mm: 10 M-40A1.
AD GUNS: 20mm: 6 M-167 *Vulcan*;
40mm: 2 L/60.

NAVY: 4,500 incl naval air, naval infantry.
BASE: Montevideo.
FRIGATES: 2

1 *General Artigas* (Fr *Cdt. Riviere*) with 2 × 3 ASTT, 1 × 2 ASW mor, 2 × 100mm guns.
1 *18 de Julio* (US *Dealey*) with 2 × 3 ASTT.

PATROL AND COASTAL COMBATANTS: 8:
OFFSHORE: 2:
1 *Uruguay* (US *Cannon* DE) PCO.
1 *Campbell* (US *Auk* MSF) PCO.
INSHORE: 6:
3 *15 de Noviembre* PFI (Fr *Vigilante* 42m), 1 *Salto* PCI. 2 PFI⟨.
MINE WARFARE: 1 *Rio Negro* (ex US) MSC.
AMPHIBIOUS: craft only; 2 LCM, 3 LCVP.
SUPPORT AND MISCELLANEOUS: 3:
1 tanker (VLCC, civilian charter), 1 tpt, 1 trg.

NAVAL AIR FORCE: (400);
6 cbt ac, no armed hel.
ASW: 1 flt with 3 S-2A, 3 -G.
MR: 1 *Super King Air* 200T.
TRAINING: 2 T-28, 4 T-34B, 2 T-34C, 2 TC-45.
HELICOPTERS: 1 Bell 47, 1 -222, 2 SH-34.

NAVAL INFANTRY: (500); 1 bn.

AIR FORCE: 3,000;
24 cbt ac, no armed hel.
COIN: 2 sqn:
1 with 8 A-37B, 3 AT-33.
1 with 6 IA-58B;
SURVEY: 1 *Commander* 680, 1 EMB-110B1.
SAR: 1 sqn with:
AIRCRAFT: 1 C-212.
HELICOPTERS: 2 Bell 212, 2 UH-1B, 4 UH-1H.
TRANSPORT: 3 sqn with 4 C-212 (tpt/SAR), 4 EMB-110C, 2 F-27, 2 FH-227.
LIAISON: 1 Cessna 182, 1 -310, 2 PA-18, 1 PA-23, 5 *Queen Air* 80.
TRAINING: 7 AT-6A, 24 T-34A/B, 6 T-41D.

FORCES ABROAD:
EGYPT (Sinai MFO): 70.
IRAN/IRAQ (UNIIMOG): Observers

PARA-MILITARY:
METROPOLITAN GUARD: 650.
REPUBLICAN GUARD: 500.
COAST GUARD: 1,500; 6 patrol craft⟨.

VENEZUELA

GDP	1987:	Bs 719.40 bn ($49.61 bn)	
	1988:	Bs 895.40 bn ($61.75 bn)	
Growth	1987:	3.0%	1988: 4.2%
Inflation	1987:	28.2%	1988ε: 40.3%
Debt	1987:	$36.0 bn	1988: $36.5 bn

Def bdgt*	1988ε:	Bs 12.95 bn ($892.86 m)
	1989ε:	Bs 14.11 bn ($973.00 m)
FMA	1988:	$0.13 m (US)
$1 =	Bs (1987/8/9):	14.50
Bs = bolívares		

Population: 19,081,000

	13–17	18–22	23–32
Men	1,028,000	947,000	1,579,000
Women	992,000	916,000	1,537,000

TOTAL ARMED FORCES:
ACTIVE: 70,500 incl National Guard (ε 18,000 conscripts).
Terms of service: 2 years (Navy 2¹/₂ years) selective, varies by region for all services.

ARMY: 34,000 (incl conscripts).
1 cav div with:
2 mech cav bde (1 armd, 3 mech cav, 1 fd arty bn).
1 armd bde (2 armd, 1 armd inf, 1 SP ATK bn, 1 arty gp, 1 AD bn).
4 regional inf div (incl 1 'Jungle') comprising:
7 inf bde (1 armd, 11 inf, 5 jungle bn, 5 arty, 1 AD, 5 engr bn).
1 ranger bde (6 ranger bn).
1 AB regt (2 AB bn, 1 cdo unit).
Army tps:
Presidential Guard Regt (3 bn).
1 avn regt.
1 engr regt (2 construction bn).
1 Military Police regt (2 bn).
EQUIPMENT:
MBT: 81 AMX-30.
LIGHT TANKS: 35 M-18, 36 AMX-13.
RECCE: 10 AML-245, 12 M-8, 60 M-706E1.
APC: 25 AMX-VCI, 70 V-100, 50 V-150, 20 *Dragoon* (some with 90mm gun), 46 M-113.
TOWED ARTY: 105mm: 70: 40 Model 56, 30 M-101; 155mm: 20 M-114;
SP ARTY: 155mm: 10 M-109, 20 Mk F3.
MRL: 160mm: 25 LAR SP.
MORTARS: 81mm: 100; 120mm: 85 Brandt.
ATGW: SS-11, AS-11.
RCL: 106mm: M-40A1.
AD GUNS: 110: 20mm: AML S-530 twin SP; 40mm: Bofors L/70 towed, Breda towed, M-42A1 twin SP.
SAM: 4 *Roland*.
AVIATION:
AIRCRAFT: 1 BN-2, 3 Cessna 172, 3 -182, 6 -U206, 2 G-222, 1 *King Air*, 1 *Queen Air* 80, 1 *Super King Air* 200.
HELICOPTERS:
ATTACK: 6 A-109 (ATK);

TRANSPORT: 4 AS-61R, 3 Bell 205, 6 UH-1H.
LIAISON: 2 Bell 47G, 2 -206.

NAVY: 10,000 incl naval air, marines and coast guard (ε 4,000 conscripts).
5 Commands; Fleet, Marines, Naval Avn, Coastguard, Fluvial (River Forces).
5 Fleet sqn: submarine, frigate, patrol, amph, service.
BASES: Caracas (HQ), Puerto Cabello (submarine, frigate, amph and service sqn), Punto Fijo (patrol sqn). Minor bases: Puerto de Hierro, Puerto La Cruz, Güiria, El Amparo (HQ Arauca River). Ciudad Bolivar (HQ Orinoco R).
SUBMARINES: 3:
2 *Sabalo* (FRG T-209/1300) with 533mm TT. (SST-4 HWT).
1 *Picua* (US *Guppy* III) (trg) with 533mm TT.
FRIGATES: 6 *Mariscal Sucre* (It *Lupo*) with 1 AB-212 hel (ASW/OTHT), 2 × 3 ASTT (A-244S LWT); plus 8 × *Otomat* SSM, 1 × 127mm gun, 2 × 20 105mm MLR.
PATROL AND COASTAL COMBATANTS: 13:
MISSILE CRAFT: 3 *Constitución* PFM (UK Vosper 37m), with 2 × *Otomat*.
PATROL, INSHORE: 3 *Constitución* PFI (may receive *Harpoon* SSM).
RIVERINE: 7 PCI⟨.
AMPHIBIOUS: 5:
4 *Capana* LST, capacity 200 tps, 12 tk.
1 *Amazones* (US-1152) LST, capacity 200 tps, 16 tk.
Plus craft; 2 LCU (river comd).
SUPPORT AND MISCELLANEOUS: 5:
1 log spt, 2 tpt, 1 survey, 1 trg.

NAVAL AIR FORCE: (2,000);
4 cbt ac, 6 armed hel.
ASW: 1 hel sqn (afloat) with 6 AB-212ASW. (8 S-2E ac in store).
MR: 1 sqn with 4 C-212.
TRANSPORT: 1 BAe-748, 2 C-212, 1 DHC-7.
LIAISON: 3 Cessna 310, 1 -402, 1 *King Air* 90, 1 MU-2, 1 *Super King Air* 200.
HELICOPTERS: 2 Bell 47J.

MARINES: (4,000+).
4 inf bn.
1 arty bn (3 fd, 1 AD bty).
1 amph veh bn.
1 river patrol, 1 engr, 2 para/cdo unit.

EQUIPMENT:
APC: 11 LVTP-7 (to be mod to -7A1), 30 EE-11 *Urutu*, 10 *Fuchs/Transportpanzer* 1.
TOWED ARTY: 105mm: 18.
AD GUNS: 40mm: 6 M-42 twin SP.

COAST GUARD: (ε 750).
BASE: La Guaira; operates under Naval Command and Control, but organizationally separate.
PATROL COMBATANTS: 4:
PATROL, OFFSHORE: 4:
2 *Almirante Clemente* (It FF type),
2 *Larrazabal* (US ocean tugs) (plus boats).

AIR FORCE: 6,500 (some conscripts);
147 cbt ac, 26 armed hel.
BOMBER: 1 Air Group with 18 *Canberra* B-82, B(I)-82, B(I)-88, T-84
FIGHTER/FGA: 3 Air Gp:
1 with 12 F-5 (10 -A, 2 -B), 19 T-2D;
1 with 21 *Mirage* (18 IIIEV, 2 -5V, 1 -5DV);
1 with 24 F-16 (18 -A, 6 -B).
COIN: 1 Air Gp with 12 EMB-312, 14 OV-10E.
ATTACK HELICOPTERS: 1 Air Gp with 10 SA-316, 12 UH-1D, 4 UH-1H.
RECCE: 3 *Canberra* PR-83.
TRANSPORT: 5 C-47, 7 C-123, 6 C-130H, 6 G-222.
TRANSPORT HELICOPTERS: 16 Bell 206, 2 -412, 5 HB-350B, 2 UH-1N.
PRESIDENTIAL FLT:
AIRCRAFT: 1 Boeing 737, 3 *Falcon* 20, 1 *Gulfstream* II, 1 -III, 1 *Learjet* 24D.
LIAISON: 2 Cessna 180, 9 -182, 1 *Citation* I, 1 -II, 2 *Queen Air* 65, 4 *Queen Air* 80, 5 *Super King Air* 200.
TRAINING: 1 Air Gp: 18 EMB-312, 12 *Jet Provost* T-52, 23 T-34.
AAM: R-530 *Magic*, AIM-9P *Sidewinder*.

NATIONAL GUARD: *Fuerzas Armadas de Cooperación:* 20,000 (internal security, customs).
EQUIPMENT: 25 UR-416 AIFV, 15 *Shorland* APC, 120 60mm mor, 50 81mm mor, PCI
Ac: 1 *Baron*, 1 BN-2A, 1 Cessna U206, 2 -337, 1 -402C, 4 IAI-201, 1 *King Air* 90, 1 *King Air* 200C, 2 *Queen Air* 80; Hel: 4 A-109, 15 Bell 206, 2 -214ST.
PATROL CRAFT: inshore: 26⟨; boats.

---

* A $1.9-bn modernization plan for the armed forces adopted in 1988.

2

TABLES AND ANALYSES

- Defence expenditure and manpower
- Nuclear forces
- NATO and Warsaw Pact conventional forces

Defence Expenditure: NATO, Japan, Sweden

These charts are expressed in local currency, based on 1985 prices and using a 1985 deflator. The NATO definition of defence expenditure is used, except in the cases of Sweden and Japan. The figure above each column shows the percentage increase, or decrease, from the previous year. The right-hand index

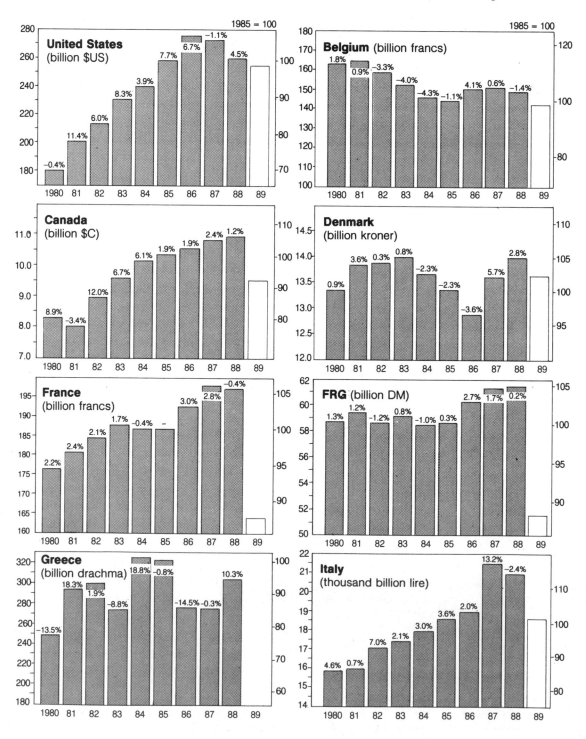

shows changes measured against a base of 100 in 1985 (the scale of this index varies for each country). The 1989 columns show defence budgets according to national defence definition and so are not directly comparable with previous years' expenditures.

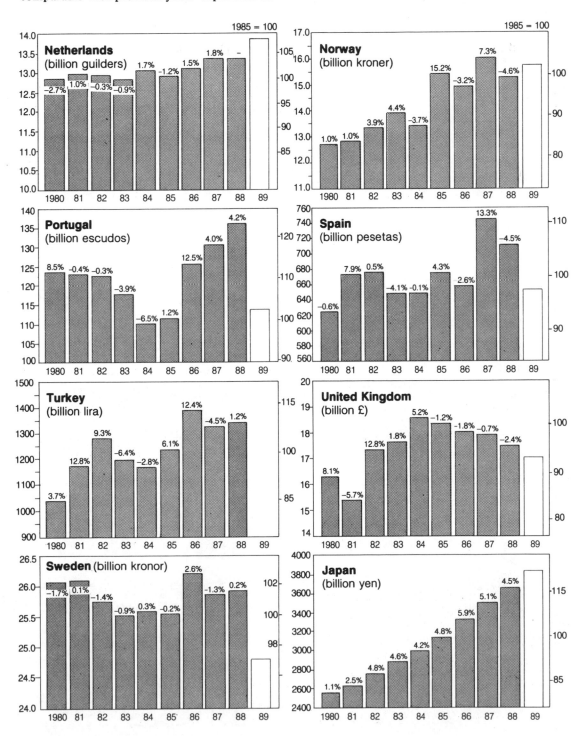

COMPARISONS OF DEFENCE EXPENDITURE AND MILITARY MANPOWER 1985–1988[a]

| Country | Defence Expenditure | | | | | | | | | | | | | | Numbers in armed forces (000) | Est. reservists[e] (000) | Para-military[f] (000) |
| | $ million[b] (1985 prices & exchange rates) | | | $ per capita (1985 prices & exchange rates) | | | % of Government spending[c] | | | % of GDP/GNP[d] | | 1988 | 1988 | 1988 |
	1985	1987	1988	1985	1987	1988	1985	1987	1988	1985	1987			
Warsaw Pact[g]														
Bulgaria	962	1,206	1,213	107	133	134	5.6	6.0	6.1	3.9	4.7	157.8	216.5	22.5
Czechoslavakia	3,698	4,195	4,182	237	267	267	7.5	9.1	7.6	4.7	4.9	197.0	280.0	11.0
GDR	6,138	7,077	7,256	365	426	437	7.8	7.6	7.4	7.5	8.0	172.0	390.0	77.5
Hungary	743	710	708	70	67	67	6.1	6.3	7.0	3.6	3.3	99.0	127.0	16.0
Poland	2,086	1,957	1,596	56	52	42	7.7	7.1	7.3	3.0	2.5	406.0	491.0	115.0
Romania	716	677	671	32	30	28	3.4	3.1	2.7	1.4	1.5	179.5	556.0	40.0
Non-Soviet WP	*14,343*	*15,822*	*15,627*	*144*	*162*	*162*						*1,211.3*	*2,060.5*	*282.0*
Soviet Union[h]	see p. 32											5,096.0	6,217.0	570.0
NATO[i]														
Belgium	2,428	2,544	2,509	245	258	254	7.6	7.3	7.1	3.0	2.9	88.3	145.0	15.9
Denmark	1,259	1,282	1,318	245	251	257	7.2	7.4	7.4	2.2	2.1	29.3	74.7	0
France	20,780	21,999	21,903	374	395	395	18.8	19.9	18.7	4.0	4.0	456.9	356.0	87.4
FRG[j]	19,922	20,820	20,870	326	341	343	22.8	22.8	22.6	3.2	3.0	488.7	850.0	21.0
Greece	2,331	1,987	2,192	225	190	218	19.1	15.2	16.9	7.0	6.2	214.0	404.0	29.0
Italy	9,733	11,234	11,178	170	196	194	5.2	5.4	5.4	2.3	2.4	386.0	769.0	219.4
Luxembourg	38	46	50	104	125	134	2.8	3.2	3.5	0.9	1.0	0.8	0	0.5
Netherlands	3,884	4,015	4,014	268	276	274	9.0	9.3	9.1	3.1	3.1	102.2	170.3	8.6
Norway	1,797	1,867	1,780	432	447	426	7.2	7.1	6.7	3.1	3.3	35.8	200.0	1.2
Portugal	654	765	797	63	73	77	9.0	8.7	8.4	3.1	3.2	73.9	190.0	42.3
Spain	3,969	4,380	4,181	100	109	107	11.0	10.5	9.5	2.4	2.4	309.5	1,030	119.7
Turkey	2,365	2,539	2,158	46	48	42	22.9	22.4	17.5	4.5	4.3	635.3	951.0	76.1
United Kingdom	23,791	23,196	22,637	424	414	402	11.3	11.2	10.9	5.2	4.7	316.7	319.8	0
NATO Europe	*92,950*	*96,672*	*95,587*	*232*	*240*	*240*						*3,137.4*	*5,459.8*	*621.1*
Canada	7,566	7,893	7,985	297	308	307	9.3	10.1	9.8	2.2	2.1	84.6	52.2	6.6
USA[h]	258,165	272,616	260,268	1,072	1,120	1,061	27.3	28.7	27.1	6.5	6.4	2,163.2	1,675.8	88.3
Total NATO	*358,681*	*377,181*	*363,840*	*293*	*303*	*299*						*5,385.2*	*7,187.8*	*716.0*
Other Europe														
Albania	108	116	116	35	37	37	11.6	11.3	11.5	4.1	4.0	42.0	155.0	12.0
Austria	892	858	811	118	114	107	3.5	3.1	2.9	1.4	1.2	54.7	242.0	0
Cyprus	87	92	n.k.	129	135	n.k.	12.3	11.2	n.k.	3.6	3.2	13.0	60.0	3.6
Finland	807	853	909	166	173	184	5.1	4.8	5.7	1.5	1.4	35.2	700.0	4.4
Ireland	320	291	247	90	82	69	4.1	3.5	2.9	1.8	1.5	13.2	16.3	0
Malta	14	17	15	36	43	39	3.5	3.8	3.4	1.4	1.5	1.2	0	0.7

Sweden[h]	3,192	3,186	3,052	381	380	364	9.1	8.9	8.8	3.3	3.0	67.0	609.0	0.5
Switzerland	1,930	1,915	1,869	295	291	282	20.9	20.1	19.7	2.1	1.9	3.5	601.5	0
Yugoslavia[k]	896	1,764	1,576	39	75	67	14.1	12.8	9.3	3.8	3.9	188.0	440.0	15.0
Middle East														
Algeria	953	957	964	44	41	41	7.7	9.2	9.6	1.7	1.9	139.0	150.0	30.0
Bahrain	151	167	171	376	389	398	5.1	5.4	5.9	3.5	5.0	3.0	0	2.2
Djibouti	32	22	19	81	57	49	22.1	n.k.	27.6	9.2	n.k.	3.0	0	1.2
Egypt	4,143	3,390	3,236	85	67	61	14.6	15.3	14.0	8.5	8.0	445.0	604.0	379.0
Iran[h]	14,223	3,605	2,736	297	70	52	36.1	12.0	n.k.	8.6	3.0	604.0	350.0	45.0
Iraq[h]	12,868	9,354	7,051	858	592	433	n.k.	n.k.	n.k.	25.9	26.8	1,000.0	650.0	4.8
Israel[h]	5,052	3,898	3,666	1,194	892	821	30.1	20.8	18.2	21.2	14.8	141.0	504.0	4.5
Jordan	523	703	631	149	185	161	29.1	27.1	23.8	12.8	16.4	82.0	35.0	4.0
Kuwait	1,796	1,277	1,371	1,051	683	703	13.7	12.3	13.3	9.1	7.2	20.0	n.k.	n.k.
Libya	n.k.	992	971	n.k.	243	226	n.k.	n.k.	36.4	n.k.	6.3	71.0	40.0	2.5
Morocco	641	640	811	29	28	34	16.4	12.1	13.7	5.4	5.0	193.0	n.k.	35.0
Oman	2,157	1,690	1,534	1,739	1,270	1,073	43.0	36.1	33.2	20.8	24.3	25.5	0	3.5
Qatar	n.k.	150	n.k.	n.k.	456	n.k.	n.k.	4.6	n.k.	n.k.	3.2	7.0	0	0
Saudi Arabia	17,693	17,467	14,444	1,527	1,375	1,103	32.0	38.1	36.0	19.6	22.7	72.0	20.0	8.5
Somalia	46	n.k.	n.k.	7	n.k.	n.k.	23.3	31.7	n.k.	4.6	n.k.	65.0	0	9.5
Sudan	207	574	n.k.	9	25	n.k.	12.6	31.7	n.k.	3.4	6.9	58.0	272.0	3.0
Syria	3,483	1,820	1,514	339	166	133	31.8	37.2	34.9	16.4	12.3	404.0	0	9.8
Tunisia	417	459	442	57	60	56	13.9	15.5	15.0	5.0	5.4	38.0	0	9.0
UAE	2,043	1,580	1,603	1,513	1,090	1,009	57.8	40.2	37.6	7.6	6.7	43.0	0	0
North Yemen	374	296	n.k.	54	40	n.k.	31.8	31.4	n.k.	8.9	8.5	36.6	40.0	5.0
Africa														
Angola[h]	1,147	n.k.	622	143	n.k.	72	37.9	n.k.	27.3	28.4	n.k.	100.0	50.0	7.0
Benin	21	n.k.	23	5	n.k.	5	16.1	n.k.	21.2	1.8	n.k.	4.3	0	2.0
Botswana	22	20	30	20	17	27	5.5	4.0	7.3	2.5	1.6	3.2	0	1.0
Burkina Faso	34	36	n.k.	5	4	n.k.	24.1	17.3	n.k.	3.3	n.k.	8.7	0	1.7
Burundi	35	30	n.k.	7	6	n.k.	20.7	17.0	n.k.	3.0	2.7	5.7	0	1.5
Cameroon	159	145	n.k.	16	13	n.k.	8.8	8.1	n.k.	1.9	2.0	7.6	0	4.0
CAR	n.k.	11	45	n.k.	4	n.k.	n.k.	10.3	n.k.	n.k.	1.7	3.8	0	2.7
Chad	37	27	n.k.	7	5	8	78.1	40.6	21.8	5.9	n.k.	17.0	0	5.7
Congo[h]	56	n.k.	n.k.	32	n.k.	n.k.	6.0	n.k.	n.k.	2.6	n.k.	8.8	12.0	1.4
Cote d'Ivoire	76	64	n.k.	8	6	n.k.	6.7	5.2	n.k.	1.1	1.1	7.1	n.k.	7.8
Ethiopia[h]	447	536	n.k.	10	12	n.k.	22.2	17.6	n.k.	9.4	8.8	315.8	0	9.0
Gabon	79	59	n.k.	69	56	n.k.	5.5	6.2	8.2	2.2	2.8	3.0	0	5.8
Ghana	63	71	91	5	5	6	7.2	6.2	n.k.	1.0	0.9	10.6	0	
Guinea Bissau	11	12	n.k.	13	14	n.k.	10.6	4.4	n.k.	n.k.	n.k.	7.2	0	2.0
Kenya	256	n.k.	n.k.	13	n.k.	n.k.	16.3	n.k.	12.7	4.3	n.k.	23.0	50.0	1.8
Liberia	28	19	24	13	8	9	9.5	8.0	n.k.	2.6	n.a.	5.8	0	2.0
Madagascar	54	45	n.k.	5	5	n.k.	11.4	4.9	n.k.	2.3	1.8	21.0	0	7.5
Malawi	21	20	n.k.	3	3	n.k.	n.k.	n.k.	n.k.	1.9	1.8	5.2	1.0	1.0

For notes see p. 211.

	Defence Expenditure											Numbers in armed forces (000)	Est. reservists[e] (000)	Para-military[f] (000)
	$ million[b] (1985 prices & exchange rates)			$ per capita (1985 prices & exchange rates)			% of Government spending[c]			% of GDP/GNP[d]				
Country	1985	1987	1988	1985	1987	1988	1985	1987	1988	1985	1987	1988	1988	1988
Mali	30	39	n.k.	4	4	n.k.	8.1	11.8	n.k.	2.7	3.1	7.3	0	4.8
Mozambique	239	567	831	19	43	61	42.2	n.k.	38.0	9.4	n.k.	36.7	0	9.5
Niger	12	13	14	2	2	2	3.3	4.5	4.8	0.8	0.8	3.3	0	4.5
Nigeria	1,251	841	954	13	8	9	10.2	4.6	5.2	1.3	0.7	94.5	0	12.0
Rwanda[h]	n.k.	29	26	n.k.	4	4	n.k.	13.3	6.2	n.k.	1.8	5.2	0	1.2
Senegal[h]	63	63	67	10	9	10	13.3	6.4	6.2	2.4	n.k.	9.7	0	n.k.
The Gambia	2	n.k.	n.k.	3	n.k.	n.k.	2.9	n.k.	n.k.	1.2	n.k.	0.6	0	0.4
Seychelles	8	10	n.k.	120	137	n.k.	8.0	8.8	n.k.	5.0	n.k.	1.3	0	0
Sierra Leone[h]	5	n.k.	n.k.	1	n.k.	n.k.	4.0	n.k.	n.k.	0.4	n.k.	3.1	0	0.8
South Africa	1,951	2,214	2,376	62	67	69	12.4	14.4	18.4	3.6	4.1	125.5	455.0	57.0
Tanzania	280	n.k.	n.k.	13	n.k.	n.k.	16.0	n.k.	n.k.	4.4	n.k.	40.0	10.0	1.5
Togo	19	n.k.	n.k.	6	n.k.	n.k.	7.0	n.k.	n.k.	2.6	n.k.	4.3	0	1.5
Uganda[h]	53	139	40	3	8	2	15.6	8.0	13.0	2.7	8.3	35.0	0	0
Zaire[h]	81	41	n.k.	3	1	n.k.	8.1	3.9	n.k.	2.7	1.6	26.0	0	25.0
Zambia	n.k.	22	n.k.	n.k.	3	n.k.	n.k.	1.8	n.k.	n.k.	0.6	16.2	0	1.2
Zimbabwe[h]	284	347	345	34	40	37	17.5	15.7	12.7	6.0	7.9	47.0	0	18.0
Asia														
Afghanistan	287	n.k.	n.k.	20	n.k.	n.k.	n.k.	n.k.	n.k.	8.7	n.k.	55.0	n.k.	107.0
Australia	4,668	4,415	4,221	296	272	254	10.2	9.5	9.3	3.0	2.7	70.5	27.6	0
Bangladesh	169	183	n.k.	2	2	n.k.	15.5	14.0	n.k.	1.2	1.2	101.5	30.0	35.0
Brunei	205	179	n.k.	856	728	n.k.	n.k.	n.k.	n.k.	6.0	n.k.	4.0	0	2.8
Burma	228	173	171	6	4	4	20.7	30.0	35.5	3.3	3.3	186.0	0	38.0
China[h]	6,357	6,137	5,283	6	6	5	10.1	8.0	7.7	2.2	1.9	3,200	0	1,830
Fiji	14	14	n.k.	20	19	n.k.	4.5	4.2	n.k.	1.2	1.2	3.5	1,200	0
India	6,263	8,551	8,247	8	11	10	18.0	21.5	27.6	3.0	3.8	1,362.0	5.0	655.0
Indonesia	2,341	1,704	n.k.	14	10	n.k.	12.5	9.6	0.0	2.8	1.9	284.0	240.0	115.0
Japan	13,151	14,641	15,298	109	120	125	5.6	6.5	6.6	1.0	1.0	245.0	800.0	12.0
North Korea	4,156	4,106	3,943	207	196	182	13.9	13.2	12.3	9.9	9.3	842.0	46.4	38.0
South Korea	4,399	5,219	6,309	107	148	147	28.7	33.8	32.5	5.1	5.7	629.0	540.0	3.5
Malaysia	1,764	1,455	1,641	113	88	99	16.1	13.4	15.3	5.6	4.6	113.0	47.6	22.7
Mongolia	233	244	257	123	121	127	13.3	13.5	13.5	11.0	10.9	24.5	200.0	15.0
Nepal	36	34	36	2	2	2	8.3	7.1	6.8	1.5	1.4	35.0	0	28.0
New Zealand	454	495	497	140	151	148	5.0	3.7	4.3	2.0	2.2	12.8	9.7	0
Pakistan	2,076	2,624	2,649	22	26	26	35.3	35.4	35.0	6.9	7.4	480.6	513.0	89.0
Papua New Guinea	34	37	37	10	11	11	4.5	4.5	4.7	1.5	1.4	3.2	0	4.6
Philippines	474	766	855	9	13	15	11.0	13.4	14.7	1.4	2.1	104.0	48.0	43.5
Singapore	1,188	1,078	1,184	464	413	455	24.7	19.9	20.7	6.7	5.6	55.5	182.0	11.6

Sri Lanka	228	361	500	14	22	31	11.4	18.3	26.6	3.8	5.8	22.0	25.0	26.0
Taiwan	4,136	4,041	3,961	208	199	192	39.8	37.6	39.6	6.6	6.3	405.5	1,657.0	25.0
Thailand	1,517	1,579	1,573	29	29	29	19.0	19.7	19.0	4.1	3.7	256.0	500.0	90.7

Latin America

Argentina	1,889	993	1,192	62	32	37	12.1	9.2	n.k.	2.9	1.5	95.0	377.0	28.0
Belize	4	11	8	22	64	49	6.4	10.0	10.0	1.8	4.9	0.7	0.3	0
Bolivia	127	198	93	20	29	13	24.9	n.k.	9.5	2.0	3.0	27.6	0	21.0
Brazil	1,731	1,318	809	13	9	6	3.1	11.2	n.k.	0.8	0.3	319.0	1,115.0	243.0
Chile[h]	1,242	816	621	102	65	49	24.8	18.4	15.5	7.8	4.5	101.0	100.0	27.0
Colombia	274	317	269	10	11	9	5.3	5.5	n.k.	0.8	0.8	86.0	117.0	94.0
Costa Rica	29	40	31	12	14	11	3.4	3.6	2.8	0.7	0.9	0	0	9.5
Cuba	1,597	1,344	1,677	157	131	162	13.0	n.k.	n.k.	0.9	0.5	180.0	130.0	19.0
Dominican Republic	51	74	n.k.	8	11	n.k.	8.1	11.1	n.k.	1.1	1.4	21.0	0	1.0
Ecuador	284	289	n.k.	30	29	n.k.	11.8	n.k.	n.k.	1.8	1.8	40.0	n.k.	0.2
El Salvador	252	253	n.k.	52	50	n.k.	23.6	36.4	n.k.	4.4	4.5	55.0	n.k.	12.6
Guatemala	197	173	n.k.	25	20	n.k.	16.6	13.0	n.k.	1.8	1.5	42	5.0	11.6
Guyana	45	n.k.	n.k.	46	n.k.	n.k.	12.2	n.k.	n.k.	9.7	n.k.	5.5	2.0	1.5
Haiti	31	n.k.	n.k.	6	n.k.	n.k.	n.k.	n.k.	n.k.	1.5	n.k.	7.6	0	
Honduras[h]	72	63	67	16	14	14	4.7	6.7	6.9	2.1	1.7	18.7	50.0	5.0
Jamaica	18	20	n.k.	8	8	n.k.	2.0	2.0	n.k.	0.9	0.9	2.5	0.7	0
Mexico	1,241	568	619	16	7	7	2.7	n.k.	1.4	0.7	0.3	138.0	300.0	n.k.
Panama	97	104	n.k.	44	46	n.k.	6.2	8.5	n.k.	2.0	2.0	7.3	0	12.3
Paraguay	60	79	76	16	20	20	14.1	21.2	18.5	1.3	1.6	16	36.0	7.5
Peru[h]	641	217	n.k.	33	10	n.k.	25.2	n.k.	n.k.	4.5	1.4	118.0	188.0	71.0
Suriname	23	n.k.	32	59	n.k.	82	5.1	n.k.	n.k.	2.4	n.k.	3.0	0	0.9
Trinidad & Tobago	73	n.k.	n.k.	62	n.k.	n.k.	2.3	n.k.	n.k.	1.0	n.k.	2.7	0	4.0
Uruguay	128	n.k.	n.k.	44	n.k.	n.k.	10.9	n.k.	n.k.	2.5	n.k.	24.0	0	2.7
Venezuela	824	n.k.	933	48	48	48	6.5	n.k.	10.2	1.3	n.k.	49.0	0	20.0

a In this edition total defence expenditures and per capita defence expenditures are given in 1985 prices and in 1985 dollars. Where possible exchange rates have been taken from the IMF, otherwise posted average annual exchange rates have been calculated. The consumer price indices have been taken from the IMF where possible, or, where necessary, constructed from known inflation rates.

b Some military expenditures include internal security expenditures; in other cases these and research costs are born by other ministries' budgets.

c Calculation based on local currency. This series is designed to show national trends only. International trends may be invalidated by differences in the scope of the government sector and in budgetary definitions. Where possible, total government outlays (including development or capital expenditure) have been used.

d Based on local currency. See country entries. For most countries, GDP figures are used. For WP countries, GNP figures are derived from NMP. In some cases commercial bank estimates

have been used.

e Normally, only men within 5 years of their active service period are included, unless a country entry specifies a different parameter. Home Guard manpower has not been included.

f Part-time and reserve para-military forces are not included.

g The difficulty in calculating suitable exchange rates makes conversion to dollars and international comparison imprecise and unreliable. It is important to refer to individual country entries and to the local-currency figures for defence expenditures and the size of the economy.

h See country entry.

i Defence expenditures are based on NATO definition.

j Excl aid to West Berlin (DM 16.3 bn in 1987, DM 16.7 bn in 1988).

k Central government spending is the total of Federal Government budget, plus state and regional government budgets. Gross Material Product is used instead of GDP.

The Strategic Nuclear Balance

A. Current US Strategic Forces under SALT and START Counting Rules

Counting rules		SALT/START	SALT		START	
		Launchers deployed	Warheads/ launcher[a]	Total warheads	Warheads/ launcher[b]	Total warheads
ICBM	*Minuteman* II	450	1	450	1	450
	Minuteman III	500	3	1,500	3	1,500
	MX	50	10	500	10	500
Sub-total (ICBM)		1,000		2,450		2,450
SLBM	*Poseidon* C-3	224	14	3,136	10	2,240
	Trident C-4	384	8	3,072	8	3,072
Sub-total (SLBM)		608		6,208		5,312
Bombers	B-1B[c]	97	12	1,164	1	97	(97)
	B-52G/H (non-ALCM)	69	12	828	1	69	(69)
	B-52G (ALCM)	98	20	1,960	10 (12)	980	(1,176)
	B-52H (ALCM)	96	20	1,920	10 (20)	960	(1,920)
Sub-total (bombers)		360		5,872		2,106	(3,262)
TOTAL		**1,968**		**14,530**		**9,868**	(11,024)

B. Current Soviet Strategic Forces under SALT and START Counting Rules

Counting rules		SALT/START	SALT		START	
		Launchers deployed	Warheads/ launcher[a]	Total warheads	Warheads/ launcher[b]	Total warheads
ICBM	SS-11	400	1	400	1	400
	SS-13	60	1	60	1	60
	SS-17	138	4	552	4	552
	SS-18	308	10	3,080	10	3,080
	SS-19	350	6	2,100	6	2,100
	SS-24	30	10	300	10	300
	SS-25	165	1	165	1	165
Sub-total (ICBM)		1,451		6,657		6,657
SLBM	SS-N-6	240	1	240	1	240
	SS-N-8	286	1	286	1	286
	SS-N-17	12	1	12	1	12
	SS-N-18	224	7	1,568	7	1,568
	SS-N-20	100	9	900	10	1,000
	SS-N-23	80	10	800	4	320
Sub-total (SLBM)		942		3,806		3,426
Bombers	*Bear* (ALCM)	75	20	1,500	10 (8)	750	(600)
	Bear (non-ALCM)	100	2	200	1	100	(100)
	Blackjack[c]	20	12	240	1	20	(20)
Sub-total (bombers)		195		1,940		870	(720)
TOTAL		**2,588**		**12,403**		**10,953**	(10,803)

[a] The figures in this column are derived primarily from SALT II Treaty, Article IV, Paragraph 10, First Agreed Statement and Common Understanding.

For Soviet missiles deployed since the signing of the Treaty, warheads are assigned as follows: SS-24, ten; SS-25, one; SS-N-20, nine; SS-N-23, ten.

The number of gravity bombs and SRAM was not limited in SALT, so the IISS best estimate is used.

The number of ALCM assigned to each heavy bomber is 20 (SALT II Treaty, Article IV, Paragraph 14, Second Agreed Statement).

[b] In this column the figures for ballistic missile warheads are taken from the December 1987 Washington Communique. ALCM numbers reflect the latest US negotiating position of attributing 10 ALCM to each ALCM-carrier. The Soviet position is to attribute to each the maximum number of ALCM with which it could be equipped, but recent figures have not been publicly released. The numbers in parentheses are IISS estimates of maximum loading capability for each bomber type.

US–USSR Strategic Nuclear Developments

Changing the Counting Rules

The arms-control counting rules for strategic nuclear weapons remain in transition. Tables A and B reflect current inventories as described by both SALT and START counting rules. The essay in *The Military Balance 1988–1989* (pp. 230–32) discusses each approach. The change from SALT to START affects the numbers of accountable warheads, rather than launchers, and is especially pronounced in three areas: SLBM (*Poseidon* C-3, *Trident* D-5, SS-N-20, SS-N-23), gravity bombs and ALCM. START counting rules reduce the accountable warhead totals for the current inventories of both sides; most significantly for the United States. Adopting these rules would artificially magnify the cuts of a START agreement.

The START Negotiations

Negotiations resumed in June 1989, after a pause during which the Bush Administration conducted a review of the US position. The review emphasized the need to stress crisis stability and ICBM survivability in START, rather than reductions for their own sake. Modifications in the current US negotiating position were considered, including: banning MIRV-equipped mobile ICBM but permitting single-warhead mobiles; raising the ceiling on strategic nuclear delivery vehicles above the agreed limit of 1,600; banning all SS-18s; and reverting to SALT counting rules for ballistic missile warheads. None of these changes was adopted by the United States before the June session, although they may re-emerge as the negotiations progress. Instead, President Bush chose to pre-empt a difficult Senate ratification debate by proposing that appropriate verification measures should be tested before final agreement on a treaty. The Soviet Union has agreed to this proposal in principle, although it has increased the number of items to be verified.

In the negotiations themselves, difficulties lie ahead over the basic principles of at least four major issues: linkage between an ABM Treaty non-withdrawal period and START; SLCM limits and SLCM verification; the US proposal to ban all mobile ICBM; and ALCM counting rules. Scope for progress is apparent on only the last two, with the introduction of new ideas for mobile ICBM verification and signs that the Joint Chiefs of Staff favour modifying the US position on ALCM counting rules.

Consequences of Ongoing Modernization

Both super-powers are continuing to replace ageing nuclear systems with modern weapons that could create problems for both strategic stability and the START negotiations. In the 1990s, both super-powers could deploy highly accurate SLBM with hard-target kill capability. Silo-based ICBM and bomber forces on both sides would become more vulnerable to a short-warning attack, and the deployment of mobile missiles would become more important for strategic security. Only the Soviet Union has deployed mobile ICBM (SS-24, SS-25) at this stage, and the number of warheads on these missiles has more than doubled in the past year (from 200 to 465); Soviet opposition to a ban on mobile ICBM could stiffen as a result. In April the Bush Administration announced its intention to seek Congressional support for two mobile missiles (MX in rail garrison mode and *Midgetman*), but approval remains far from certain. Without a viable US mobile ICBM, Congressional consent for a START treaty appears unlikely.

Meanwhile, the United States continues to convert penetrating bombers to ALCM carriers, with 36 B-52H being retrofitted during the past year. Adopting the ALCM counting rules proposed by the USSR would require the US to cut about 1,100 more ALCM from the force structure than would adoption of US counting rules; the new ALCM deployments might thus harden the US position on ALCM counting rules.

Finally, the emergence of *Brilliant Pebbles* SDI technology may hold out some prospect of the earlier deployment of a lower-cost and more survivable SDI system. This could further complicate the already difficult negotiations on the ABM Treaty non-withdrawal period.

Outlook

Given existing negotiating problems, the prospect for new US positions that could modify the previously agreed START framework, the impact of force modernization programmes, and the higher priority now being given to conventional force reductions in Europe, it is quite conceivable that it may take several more years of negotiations to complete a START Treaty.

---

c Although the B-1B is capable of carrying 8 ALCM internally and 12 externally, the US Air Force plans initially to deploy the B-1B as a penetrator. Similarly, the Soviet *Blackjack* is capable of carrying up to 12 ALCM internally (and perhaps more externally), but it will probably be equipped as a penetrator at first. With limited information available on *Blackjack's* gravity bomb load and ALCM configuration, this year's figures treat the B-1B and *Blackjack* on an equivalent basis.

NATO/WARSAW PACT NUCLEAR DELIVERY MEANS
(Other than US/Soviet Strategic Weapons: see p. 212)

Category and type of system[a]	Countries deploying	NATO Guidelines Area[b]		Atlantic to Urals		Global	
		NATO	WP	NATO	WP	NATO	WP
LAND-BASED LAUNCHERS							
IRBM							
SSBS-S3	France	–	–	18	–	18	–
SS-20[c]	USSR	–	–	–	n.k.	–	340
GLCM							
BGM-109G[c]	US	n.k.	–	n.k.	–	98	–
SS-C-1b *Sepal*[d]	USSR	–	–	–	40	–	40
MRBM							
Pershing II[c]	US	n.k.	–	n.k.	–	109	–
SS-4[c]	USSR	–	–	–	43	–	43
SRBM							
Pershing IA[e]	FRG	72	–	72	–	72	–
Pluton	France	–	–	32	–	32	–
Lance	US	36	–	36	–	65	–
Lance	Other NATO[f]	52	–	58	–	58	–
SS-23[c]	USSR	–	–	–	n.k.	–	76
Scud B	USSR	–	150	–	510	–	630
Scud A/B	Other WP[f]	–	88	–	151	–	151
FROG/SS-21	USSR	–	104	–	713	–	930
FROG/SS-21	Other WP[f]	–	148	–	234	–	234
Artillery[g]	US	1,294	–	1,294	–	5,025	–
	Other NATO[f]	1,578	–	3,915	–	4,022	–
	USSR	–	1,776	–	4,800	–	9,200
	Other WP[f]	–	294	–	717	–	717
Aircraft[gh]	US	156	–	368	–	2,606	–
	Other NATO[f]	484	–	1,822	–	1,861	–
	USSR	–	225	–	2,004	–	3,110
	Other WP[f]	–	255	–	295	–	295

Category and type of system[a]	Countries deploying	European/Atlantic waters		Global	
		NATO	WP	NATO	WP
MARITIME LAUNCHERS					
SLBM[i]	France	96	–	96	–
	UK	64	–	64	–
	USSR	–	18	–	36
NUCLEAR-ARMED SHIPS[j]					
SLCM					
Land Attack	US	29	–	45	–
(submarine)	USSR	–	6	–	10
Land Attack (surface)	US	16	–	19	–
Anti-Ship	USSR	–	40	–	66
(submarine)					
Anti-Ship (surface)[k]	USSR	–	21	–	26
ASW (air flight)					
SUBROC	US	12	–	16	–
SS-N-15	USSR	–	23	–	35
ASROC	US	71	–	132	–
SS-N-14/SUW-N-1	USSR	–	43	–	65
Torpedoes[l]	USSR	–	337	–	536
MARITIME AIRCRAFT[m]					
Carrier-based strike	US	470	–	1,291	–
	France	64	–	64	–
	UK	46	–	46	–
Land-based bombers	USSR	–	260	–	355
Land-based ASW	US	27	–	488	–
	Other NATO[f]	150	–	150	–
	USSR	–	120	–	195

[a] For system performance details, see Table 1.
[b] Territories of Be, FRG, Lux, Nl, Cz, GDR, Po.
[c] To be eliminated under terms of INF Treaty.
[d] May no longer be nuclear-capable.
[e] US warheads to be withdrawn.
[f] For breakdowns of the relevant NATO and WP holdings, see Table 1.
[g] Aggregates of all theoretically nuclear-capable weapons.

[h] Excl long-range strategic; land-based naval bombers are listed with maritime ac.
[i] 400 US SLBM warheads also assigned to SACEUR.
[j] Numbers mounting relevant nuclear systems.
[k] Excl patrol combatants fitted with anti-ship msls as unlikely to carry nuclear warheads.
[l] Excl torpedo craft as unlikely to carry nuclear warheads.
[m] Excl all helicopters.

NUCLEAR-CAPABLE DELIVERY VEHICLES: NATO, WARSAW PACT AND CHINA

Many delivery systems are dual-capable; we show the total number in service, even though a high proportion may not be assigned a nuclear role. Maximum aircraft loadings are given, though often fewer stores may be carried. Some loadings differ from those under SALT/START counting rules.

Category and type	First year deployed	Range (km)[a]	Throw-weight (000 lb)[b]	CEP (m)[c]	Launcher total 6/89	Munition/warhead	Yield per warhead[d]	Remarks
UNITED STATES								
LAND-BASED								
Strategic								
ICBM								
LGM-30F *Minuteman* II	1966	11,300	1.6	370	450	Mk 11C; W-56	1.2 MT	
LGM-30G *Minuteman* III	1970	14,800	2.2	220	200	3 × Mk 12 MIRV; W-62	170 KT	
	1980	12,900	2.4	220	300	3 × Mk 12A MIRV; W-78	335 KT	
LGM-118 *Peacekeeper* (MX)	1986	11,000	7	100	50	10 × Mk 21 MIRV; W-87	300 or 400 KT	In mod *Minuteman* silos
Intermediate-/medium-range								
GLCM								
BGM-109G[e]	1983	2,500	–	20	98	W-84	10–50 KT(s)[d]	313 msl
MRBM								
Pershing II[e]	1983	1,800	3	40	109	W-85	5–10 KT(s)[d]	200 msl
Tactical								
SRBM								
MGM-52C *Lance*	1972	110	0.5	150–400	65	W-70 mods 0, 1, 2 / W-70 mod 3	3 values: 1–10 KT / 1 KT(−) or 1 KT(+)	
Artillery[f]								
M-110A1/A2 203mm SP	1977/9	21.3	–	170	} 1,172	M-422 shell; W-33 / M-753 rocket-assisted projectile; W-79[g]	0.5 or 10 KT / 0.5, 1 or 2.5 KT	Some enhanced radiation (ER) warheads stored in US
	1981	29	–	200–500				
M-109 155mm SP (3 mods)	1963	18/24/30	–	n.k.	2,531	M-454 shell; W-48 or	0.1 KT	
M-198 155mm towed	1979	14	–	n.k.	1,012	XM-785 shell; W-82[g]	under 2 KT	W-82 still under development, potentially ER capable
M-114 155mm towed	1940	19.3	–	n.k.	310			
SEA-BASED								
Strategic								
SLBM								
UGM-73A *Poseidon* C-3	1971	4,600	3.3	450	224	10 × Mk 3 MIRV; W-68	40 KT	Installed in 14 SSBN
UGM-93A *Trident* C-4	1980	7,400	3.0+	450	384	8 × Mk 4 MIRV; W-76	100 KT	Installed in 20 SSBN

	Year	Radius of action (km)[a]	Max speed (mach)	Weapon load (000 kg)	No.	Max ordnance load[i] / Warhead	Yield	Comments
Tactical								
SLCM								
BGM-109A *Tomahawk*[h]	1983	2,500	–	280	–	TLAM-N; W-80	200 KT	Some 258 of 758 TLAM-N warheads produced. 45 submarines, 35 surface combatants have launchers
ASW								
UUM-44A *SUBROC*	1965	50	–	–	–	W-55	1–5 KT	Some 285 warheads produced. Installed in 16 submarines. To be withdrawn by end 1989
RUR-5A *ASROC*[h]	1961	11	–	–	–	W-44	1 KT	Some 500 warheads remain. Installed in 132 surface combatants. Normal weapon load is conventional homing torpedo. To be withdrawn by end 1990
AIR								
Strategic								
Long-range bombers[h]								
B-52G	1959	4,600	0.95	29.5	98	Internal: 12 bombs (B-43/-53/-61/-83) or 8 SRAM; External: 12 ALCM		Incl 9 ac in store
					69			In conventional role but could re-role. Incl 8 ac in store
B-52H	1962	6,140	0.95	29.5	96	Internal: 12 bombs (B-43/-53/-61/-83) or 8 SRAM or 8 ALCM; External: 12 ALCM *Harpoon*		Incl 12 ac in store
B-1B	1986	4,580	1.25	61	97	Internal: 8 ALCM plus 8 SRAM; or 24 SRAM; or 24 B-61 bombs; External: 14 ALCM or 14 SRAM or 14 bombs (B-43/-61/-83)		Incl 7 ac in store
Medium-range bombers[h]								
FB-111A	1969	1,890	2.2	13.15	62	2 bombs (B-43/-61/-83) plus 4 SRAM		Incl 14 ac in store
Tactical								
Land-based[h]								
F-111D/E/F	1967	1,750	2.2/2.5	13.1	140	3 bombs (B-43/-57/-61)		
F-4D/E	1969	840	2.4	5.9	775	3 bombs (B-28RE/-43/-57/-61)		Incl 350 in store

For notes, see p. 225.

Category and type	First year deployed	Radius of action (km)[a]	Max speed (mach)	Weapon load (000 kg)	Launcher total 6/89	Max ordnance load	Remarks
F-16	1979	550/930	2+	5.4	1,385	1 bomb (B-43/-61)	Incl 367 in store
A-4E/F/M	1970	1,230	0.9	4.5	98	1 bomb (B-28/-43/-57/-61)	USMC
AV-8	1985	890	0.95	2.8	146	n.k.	USMC
Carrier-borne							
A-6E	1963	1,250	0.9	8.1	391	3 bombs (B-28/-43/-57/-61)	Incl 54 USMC, 125 in store
A-7E	1966	880	0.9	6	210	4 bombs (B-28/-43/-57/-61)	
F/A-18	1982	850	2.2	7.7	550	2 bombs (B-57/-61)	Incl 118 in store, 186 USMC 2 hours endurance at radius of action. Total endurance 5 hours
S-3A (ASW)	1974	575	0.6	n.k.	140	1 B-57 depth charge	
Maritime							
P-3 (ASW)	1961	1,140	0.66	19	488	2 B-57 depth charges	8 hours endurance at radius of action; total endurance 18 hours. Incl 115 in store

	First year deployed	Range (km)[a]	Max speed (mach)	Weapon load (000 kg)	Missile total	Munition/warhead	Yield per warhead[d]	Remarks
ALCM								
AGM-86B[h]	1982	2,400	0.66	60	ε 1,660	W-80	170–200 KT	Planned total of 1,175 warheads
ASM								
AGM-69A (SRAM)	1972	56 (low) 220 (high altitude)	3.5	ε 0.03	ε 1,100	W-69	170 KT	

BOMBS[j]

Type	Yield per warhead[d]	No. in stockpile mid-1989	Remarks	Type	Yield per warhead[d]	No. in stockpile mid-1989	Remarks
B-28	70, 350 KT, 1.1, 1.45 MT	380	Replaced by B-61, B-83 by 1990	B-61 (strategic)	100–500 KT(s) (3 yields)	900	In-flight yield selection and fusing, hard target penetration
B-43	1 MT and others	500	Hard target penetration	B-61 (tactical)	1–345 KT	2,025	Replacing B-28, B-43, B-53
B-53	9 MT	50		B-83	1–2MT	1,000	1,500 more planned, to replace B-28, -43, -53
B-57	5–20 KT	825	Depth-charge capability				

NATO (excluding US)[k]

LAND-BASED

Intermediate-range

IRBM

Category and type	First year deployed	Range (km)[a]	Throw-weight (000 lb)[b]	CEP (m)[c]	Launcher total 6/89	Munition/warhead	Yield per warhead[d]	Remarks
SSBS S-3D	1980	3,500	n.k.	n.k.	18	TN-61	1 MT	Fr
Tactical								
SRBM								
MGM-31A/B *Pershing* 1A	1971	160–720	0.8	400	72	Mk 50 mod 1; W-50	60 or 200 or 400 KT	FRG msl, US warheads. For withdrawal after INF elimination
Pluton	1974	120	n.k.	150–300	32	AN-51	15 or 25 KT	Fr
MGM-52C *Lance*	1976	110	0.5	150–400	58	W-70	3 values: 1–100 KT	Be (5), FRG (26), It (6), Nl (7), UK (14)
Artillery[f]								
M-110 203mm sp	1962	21.3	–	170	399	M-422 shell; W-33	0.5 or 10 KT	Be (11), FRG (226), Gr (24), It (18), Nl (76), Tu (16), Sp (12) UK (16)
M-115 203mm towed	1940	16.8	n.k.	n.k.	127	M-422 shell; W-33	0.5 or 10 KT	Dk[l] (12), Gr (44), It (23), Tu (48)
M-109 155mm sp	1964	18/24/30	–	–	1,859	M-454 shell; W-48	0.1 KT	Be (165), Cdn[l] (76), Dk[l] (76), FRG (586), Gr (90), It (260), Nl (222), No[l] (130), Port (6), Sp (96), Tu (42), UK (110)
M-114 155mm towed	1940	19.3	n.k.	n.k.	1,637	M-454 shell; W-48	0.1 KT	Cdn[l] (57 in store), Dk[l] (96), Gr (240), It (423), Nl (140), No[l] (155), Port (40), Sp (84), Tu (402)
SAM[h]								
MIM-14B *Nike Hercules*	1962	140	1.12	–	375	W-31	1–2 or 20+ KT	Be (36), It (96), Gr (36), No[l] (128) Sp (4), Tu (128). Only some 75 W-31 warheads remain in service
SEA-BASED								
Strategic								
SLBM								
Polaris A-3 TK	1967	4,600	1.5	900	64	3 × MRV; W-58 (*Chevaline*)	200 KT	UK. In 4 SSBN
M-20	1977	3,000	n.k.	n.k.	48	TN-60	1 MT	Fr. In 3 SSBN, incl 1 in refit
M-4	1985	6,000	n.k.	n.k.	48	6 × MIRV; TN-70/-71	150 KT	Fr. In 3 SSBN

For notes, see p. 225.

AIR[h]

Tactical
Land-based

Category and type	First year deployed	Radius of action (km)[a]	Max speed (mach)	Weapon load (000 kg)	Launcher total 6/89	Max ordnance load	Remarks
F-104G/S	1958	830	2.2	1.8	334	1 B-28/-57/-61 bombs	Gr (74), It (25), Tu (235)
F-4E/F	1967/73	840	2.4	5.9	286	1 B-61 bomb	FRG (152), Gr (34), Tu (100)
F-16	1982	930	2+	5.4	315	1 B-61 bomb	Be (86), Dk[k] (57), Nl (109), No[j] (63)
CF-18	1986	740	2.2	7.7	93	2 bombs	Cdn[l]
Mirage IIIE	1964	960	1.8	19	15	1 or 2 AN-52 bombs	Fr
Mirage IVP	1986	930	2.2	9.3	18	1 *ASMP*	Fr. Incl 2 in store
Mirage 2000N	1988	690		6.3	30	1 *ASMP*	Fr
Jaguar A	1974	850	1.4	4.75	161	1 or 2 AN-52 bombs	Fr (43), UK (118)
Tornado IDS	1981	1,390	0.95	6.8	609	n.k.	FRG (311), Italy (98), UK (200). Only UK ac certified for nuclear ops

Carrier-borne

Category and type	First year deployed	Radius of action (km)[a]	Max speed (mach)	Weapon load (000 kg)	Launcher total 6/89	Max ordnance load	Remarks
Super Etendard	1980	650	1.0	2.1	64	1 or 2 AN-52 bombs	Fr. 53 to be converted for *ASMP*
Sea Harrier	1980	460/750	0.98	2.3	46	1 (maybe 2) WE-177 bombs	UK

Maritime

Category and type	First year deployed	Radius of action (km)[a]	Max speed (mach)	Weapon load (000 kg)	Launcher total 6/89	Max ordnance load	Remarks
P-3B/C	1961	1,140	0.66	9.1	23	2 B-57 depth-charge	Nl (13), No[j] (4), Sp (6). 8 hrs endurance at radius of action. Total endurance 18 hrs
Nimrod	1969	1,000	0.85	6.1	36		UK. 8 hrs endurance at radius of action. Total endurance 12 hrs
Atlantic	1965	1,300	0.57	3.8	32		FRG (14), It (18). 8 hrs endurance at radius of action. Total endurance 18 hrs
Buccaneer	1963	1,410	0.85	7.3	59		UK

Category and type	First year deployed	Range (km)[a]	Max speed (mach)	Weapon load (000 kg)	Launcher total 6/89	Munition/warhead	Yield per warhead[d]	Remarks
ASM								
ASMP	1986	100–300	2	n.a.	n.a.		45 KT	Fr
Bombs								
AN-22	–	–	–	–	–		15, 300 KT	Fr
WE-177	–	–	–	–	–		10, 200, 400 KT	UK. Depth-charge capability

SOVIET UNION

LAND-BASED

Strategic
ICBM

			Range (km)[a]	Throw-weight (000 lb)[b]	CEP (m)[c]	Launcher total 6/89	Munition/ warhead	Yield per warhead[d]	Remarks
SS-11 *Sego*	mod 2	1973	13,000 }[m]	2.5	1,100	400	single RV	1 MT	
	mod 3	1975	10,600				3 × MRV	100–300 KT	
SS-13 *Savage*	mod 2	1968	9,400	1.3	1,800	60	single RV	600 KT	
SS-17 (RS-16)	mod 3	1982	10,000[m]	6.4	400	138	4 × MIRV	500 KT	
Spanker									
SS-18 (RS-20)	mod 4	1982	11,000	16.7	250	308	10 × MIRV	500 KT	
Satan	mod 5	n.k.	ε 9,000	16	250	–	10 × MIRV	750 KT	
SS-19 (RS-18)	mod 3	1982	10,000[m]	7.5	300	350	6 × MIRV	550 KT	
Stiletto									
SS-24 *Scalpel*		1987/8	10,000	ε 8	200	30+	10 × MIRV	100 KT	Rail-based. Solid fuel
SS-25 (RS-12M) *Sickle*		1985/6	10,500	ε 1.6	200	165+	single RV	550 KT	Road-mobile. Solid fuel

Intermediate-/medium-range
I/MRBM

			Range (km)	Throw-weight	CEP (m)	Launcher total 6/89	Munition/ warhead	Yield per warhead	Remarks
SS-4 (R-12) *Sandale*		1959	2,000	3	2,000	43	single RV	1 MT	
SS-20 (RSD-10)									
Sabere	mod 2	1977	5,000	n.k.	400	340	3 × MIRV	150 KT	

Tactical
SRBM

		Range (km)	Throw-weight	CEP (m)	Launcher total 6/89	Munition/ warhead	Yield per warhead	Remarks
FROG-7 (*Luna*)[h]	1965	70	n.k.	400	630	–	200 KT	
SS-21 *Scarab* (*Tochka*)[h]	1978	120	n.k.	300	300	–	100 KT	
SS-1c (R-17) *Scud B*[h]	1965	300	n.k.	900	630	–	KT range	
SS-23 (OTR-23) *Spidere*	1979/80	500	n.k.	350	76	–	100 KT	

GLCM

		Range (km)	Throw-weight	CEP (m)	Launcher total 6/89	Munition/ warhead	Yield per warhead	Remarks
SS-C-1b *Sepalh*	1962	450	n.k.	n.k.	40	–	350 KT	Coastal defence. Nuclear role doubtful

Artillery[f]

		Range (km)	Throw-weight	CEP (m)	Launcher total 6/89	Munition/ warhead	Yield per warhead	Remarks
M-1976 152mm SP towed	1978	27	–	n.k.	ε 1,000	–	2–5 KT	
2S5 152mm SP	1980	27	–	n.k.	ε 2,100	–	2–5 KT	
D-20 152mm towed	1955	17.4	–	n.k.	ε 2,000	–	2 KT	
2S3 152mm SP	1972	27	–	n.k.	ε 3,500+	–	under 5 KT	
2S7 203mm SP	1975	18+	–	ε 200	ε 200	–	2–5 KT	
2S4 240mm SP mor	1975	12.7	–	n.k.	ε 400	–	n.k.	

For notes, see p. 225.

Category and type	First year deployed	Range (km)[a]	Throw-weight (000 lb)[b]	CEP (m)[c]	Launcher total 6/89	Munition/ warhead	Yield	Remarks
SAM								
ABM-1B Galosh	1964	320	n.k.	–	100	–	3 MT	Deployed Moscow only.
SH-11 mod Galosh	1983/84	n.k.	n.k.	–		–	n.k.	
SH-08 Gazelle	–	n.k.	n.k.	–		–	n.k.	
SA-10 Grumble[h]	1981	100	n.k.	–	1,500	–	n.k.	
SA-5 Gammon[h]	1967	300	0.132	–	2,000	–	n.k.	
SEA-BASED								
Strategic								
SLBM								
SS-N-5 Sark	1964	1,400	n.k.	2,800	18	single RV	1 MT	In 6 SSB
SS-N-6 Serb	1968	2,400	1.5	1,300	240	single RV	500 KT	In 15 SSBN
mod 3	1974	3,000	1.5	1,300		2 MRV	ε 500 KT	
SS-N-8 Sawfly mod 1	1972	7,800	1.5	1,500	286	single RV	500 KT–1 MT	In 23 SSBN
mod 2	1973	9,100	n.k.	900			800 KT	
SS-N-17 Snipe	1977	3,900	2.5	1,460	12	single RV	500 KT	In 1 SSBN
SS-N-18 mod 1	1977	6,500	n.k.	1,400	224	3 MIRV	500 KT	In 14 SSBN
Stingray mod 2	1977	8,000	n.k.	900		single RV	500 KT–1 MT	
mod 3	1978	6,500	n.k.	900		5 MIRV	500 KT	
SS-N-20 Sturgeon	1981	8,300	n.k.	500	100	6 MIRV	100 KT.	In 5 SSBN
SS-N-23 Skiff	1985	8,300	n.k.	<900	80	10 MIRV	ε 100 KT	In 5 SSBN
Tactical								
SLCM								
SS-N-3a/b Shaddock[h]	1962	450	–	n.a.	346	–	350 KT	In some 32 SSGN/SSG[n], 8 CG
SS-N-7 Starbright[h]	1968	n.a.	–	n.a.	80	–	200 KT	In 10 SSGN
SS-N-9 Siren[h]	1968/9	100	–	n.a.	242	–	200 KT	In 7 SSGN, 30 corvettes, 1 msl craft
SS-N-12 Sandbox[h]	1973	550	–	n.a.	84	–	350 KT	In some 12 SSGN[n], 4 CVV, 3 CG
SS-N-19 Shipwreck[h]	1980	550	–	n.a.	180	–	500 KT	In 5 SSGN, 3 CGN
SS-N-21 Sampson	1987	3,000	–	n.k.	47+	–	n.k.	In 2 SSGN, 7 SSN (no. of launchers n.k.)
SS-N-22 Sunburn[h]	1981	400	–	n.k.	152	–	200 KT	In 10 DDG, 12 corvettes
SS-NX-24	–		–	n.k.	n.k.	–	n.k.	In trials SSGN
ASW								
SS-N-14 Silex[h]	1974	55	–	n.a.	346	ASROC type	1 to 5 KT	In 1 CGN, 17 CG, 10 DD, 32 frigates
SS-N-15 Starfish	1982	45	–	n.k.	n.k.	SUBROC type	about 5 KT	In 35 SSN
SUW-N-1 (FRAS-1)	1975	30	–	n.k.	10	ASROC type	5 KT	In 3 CVV, 2 CGH
Type 53-68 HWT	1970	14	–	–	n.k.	torpedo	20 KT	Usable from all 533mm TT
Type 65 HWT	1981	50	–	–	n.k.	torpedo	20 KT	Usable from all 650mm TT
Mines								
	n.k.	–	–	n.k.	–	–	5–20 KT	

AIR

Strategic
Long-range bombers

		Radius of action (km)[a]	Max speed (mach)	Weapon load (000 kg)	Weapon total	Max ordnance load	
Tu-95 *Bear A/B*	} 1956	5,690	0.9	11.3	175	2–3 bombs	Some 40 ac
Bear B/G	}					1–2 AS-3/4 ALCM	Some 60 ac
Bear H						up to 8 AS-15 ALCM	Some 75 ac
Tu-160 *Blackjack*	1988	7,300	2.3	16.3	20	n.k.	
Medium-range bombers							
Tu-16 *Badger*	1955	2,180	0.91	9	276	1–2 AS-5/-6 ALCM, 1 bomb	140 Strategic Aviation, 135 Navy
Tu-22 *Blinder*	1962	1,500	1.4	10	160	1 AS-4 ALCM, 1 bomb	120 Strategic Aviation, 40 Navy
Tu-26 *Backfire*	1974	4,430	1.92	12	355	1–2 AS-4 ALCM, 2 bombs	175 Strategic Aviation, 180 Navy
Tactical[b]							
Land-based							
MiG-21 *Fishbed* L	1970	480	2.1	1.5	180	2 bombs	
MiG-27 *Flogger* D/J	1971	390/600	1.7	4.5	855	2 bombs	
Su-17 *Fitter* D/H/K	1974	430/680	2.1	4	810	2 bombs	480 under TVD control
Su-24 *Fencer*	1974	320/1,130	2.3	8	830	2 bombs	
Maritime ASW							
Tu-142 *Bear* F	1972	1,510	0.83	10	60	2 bombs	8 hrs endurance at radius of action.
Il-38 *May*	1970	1,700	0.64	7	45	ε 2 bombs	8 hrs endurance at radius of action. Total endurance 15 hrs
Be-12 *Mail*	1965	600	0.5	10	90	2 bombs	8 hrs endurance at radius of action. Total endurance 12 hrs

		Range (km)[a]	Max speed (mach)	Weapon load (000 kg)	Weapon total	Yield[d]	
ALCM							
AS-3 *Kangaroo*	1961	500	2	n.k.	n.k.	800 KT–1 MT	
AS-4 *Kitchen*	1962	300	3.3	n.k.	n.k.	1 MT	
AS-6 *Kingfish*	1977	300	3	n.k.	n.k.	350 KT–1 MT	
AS-15 *Kent*	1984	1,600	0.6	n.k.	n.k.	250 KT	
Bombs	n.k.	–	–	–	n.k.	Strategic: 5, 20, 50 MT; Tactical: 250, 350 KT	
Depth-charges	n.k.	–	–	–	n.k.	–	Known to exist; no details available

For notes, see p. 225.

WARSAW PACT (excluding USSR)[o]

LAND-BASED

Category and type	First year deployed	Range (km)[a]	Throw-weight (000 lb)[b]	CEP (m)[c]	Launcher total 6/89	Munition/ warhead	Yield per warhead[d]	Remarks
Tactical								
SRBM[h]								
Scud B	1965	300	n.k.	900	157	–	KT range	Bu (36), Cz (36), GDR (28), Hu (9), Pol (30), Ro (18)
FROG-3/-5/-7	1957/65	70	n.k.	400	212	–	200+ KT	Bu (36), Cz (30), GDR (44), Hu (18), Po (52), Ro (32)
SS-21 *Scarab*	1986	120	n.k.	300	16	–	100 KT	Cz (8), GDR (8)
Artillery[f]								
M-55/D-20 152mm towed	1955	17.4	–	n.k.	565	–	2 KT	Bu (ε 20), GDR (180), Hu (315), Ro (ε 50)
2S3 152 mm SP	1980	27	–	n.k.	128	–	under 5 KT	Bu (ε 20), GDR (90), Hu (18)
2S7 203mm SP	1975	18+	–	ε 200	12	–	2–5 KT	Cz (12)
2S4 240mm SP mor	1975	12.7	–	n.k.	12	–	n.k.	Cz (12)

AIR

Category and type	First year deployed	Radius of action (km)[a]	Max speed (mach)	Weapon load (000 kg)	Launcher total 6/89	Max ordnance load	Remarks
Tactical[h]							
Land-based strike							
Su-7 *Fitter A*	1959	210/320	1.6	2.5	30	2 bombs	Pol (30)
Su-20 *Fitter C*	1974	430/680	1.6	4	50	2 bombs	Pol (50)
MiG-23BN *Flogger H*	1975/6	390/600	1.2	4.4	105	2 bombs	Bu (40), Cz (40), GDR (25)
Su-22 *Fitter K*	1986	430/680	1.6	4	110	2 bombs	GDR (35), Pol (75)

CHINA	First year deployed	Range (km)ᵃ	Throw-weight (000 lb)ᵇ	CEP (m)ᶜ	Launcher total 6/89	Munition/ warhead	Yield per warheadᵈ	Remarks
LAND-BASED								
Strategic								
ICBM								
CSS-4 (DF-5)	1981	15,000	4.4	n.k.	2	single RV	5 MT	
CSS-3 (DF-4)	1978/9	7,000	4.4	n.k.	6	single RV	3 MT	
IRBM								
CSS-2 (DF-3)	1970	2,700	4.4	n.k.	60	single RV	2 MT	
SEA-BASED								
Strategic								
SLBM								
CSS-N-3 (JL-1)	1983/4	2,200– 3,000	n.k.	n.k.	12	–	ε 2 MT	Installed in 1 SSBN

AIR	First year deployed	Radius of action (km)ᵃ	Max speed (mach)	Weapon load (000 kg)	Launcher total 6/89	Maximum ordnance load	Yield per warheadᵈ	Remarks
Strategicʰ								
Medium-range bombers								
H-6	1968/9	2,180	0.91	9	up to 120	ε 2 bombs	n.k.	

Chinese *tactical* nuclear weapons have been reported, but no details are available.

SOURCES: include Cochrane, Arkin and Hoenig, *Nuclear Weapons Databook*, vol. I (Cambridge, MA: Ballinger 1984); Cochrane, Arkin, Norris and Hoenig, *Nuclear Weapons Databook*, vol. II (Cambridge, MA: Ballinger, 1987); Hansen, *US Nuclear Weapons, The Secret History* (New York: Orion, 1988); *Bulletin of the Atomic Scientists* (various issues).

a Ranges and aircraft radii of action in km; for nautical miles, multiply by 0.54. A missile's range may be reduced by up to 25% if max payload is carried. Radii of action for ac are in normal configuration, at optimum altitude, with a standard warload, without in-flight refuelling. When two values are given the first refers to a low-low-low mission profile and the second to a high-low-high profile.

b Throw-weight is the weight of post-boost vehicle (warhead(s)), guidance systems, penetration aids and decoys). Weights are the max for the weapon system in question and are not necessarily for the range cited.

c CEP (circular error probable) = the radius of a circle around a target within which there is a 50% probability that a weapon aimed at that target will fall.

d Yields vary greatly; figures given are estimated maxima. KT range = under 1 MT; MT range = over 1 MT. Yield, shown as 1–10 KT means that the yield is between these limits; if shown as 1–10 KT(s) it means that yields between these limits can be selected. Yields shown as 1 or 10 KT mean that either yield can be selected.

e Weapons to be eliminated under the terms of the INF Treaty.

f Numbers cited are totals of theoretically nuclear-capable pieces. Not all will be certified for nuclear use, and in practice relatively few are likely to be in a nuclear role at any one time. All artillery pieces listed are dual-capable.

g Congressional limit of 925 on W-79 and W-82 production.

h Dual-capable. All aircraft types in this table are dual-capable.

i External loads are additional to internal loads.

j All bombs have five option fusing: freefall airburst or surface burst, parachute retarded airburst or surface burst, and retarded delayed surface burst (except B-57, which has no freefall/retarded surface burst, and B-53, which has no freefall surface burst).

k Except for French and UK national weapons, nuclear warheads held in US custody.

m No nuclear warheads held on Canadian, Danish or Norwegian territory.

n Variable range, capable of striking IRBM/INF targets.

n Some SSGN/SSG can carry either SS-N-12 *Sandbox* or SS-N-3 *Shaddock*.

o Nuclear warheads in Soviet custody.

NATO and Warsaw Pact
Conventional Forces

Introduction

The past year has seen three developments which, respectively, impact significantly on perceptions of the state of the East–West conventional balance and on its actual and impending reality. These developments are: the formal publication of data on conventional forces in Europe by both NATO and the Warsaw Pact, the announcement and inception of unilateral force reductions and some force restructuring by the Soviet Union and its East European allies, and the opening of the Vienna negotiations on conventional armed forces in Europe (CFE). This essay reviews each of these by way of introduction to the IISS aggregation of the conventional force strengths of the two sides.

Data

GENERAL

NATO's November 1988 publication of force comparison data, 'Conventional Forces in Europe: The Facts' was the first of its kind since 1984. The Warsaw Pact (WP) compilation on the 'Correlation of Forces in Europe', published at the end of January 1989, was its first ever such essay in military *glasnost* and, as such, a highly significant and very welcome breakthrough. Not surprisingly, there were significant differences between the data produced by the two sides, and between both sides' figures and those of the IISS. It is not the intention to discuss the detail of these differences here, but rather to analyse the underlying problems they illustrate.

Some of the differences merely concern the overall scope of the assessments and the categories of equipment addressed, where there were mismatches. Some doubtless reflect the fact that, quite apart from security considerations which will have inhibited both NATO and the WP, the compilers of such comparisons can only draw on the information they possess. Theoretically, this should have provided them with firm information about 'own troops', less certain intelligence estimates – and in some cases gaps in relevant information – about the other side. The IISS faces similar problems in its compilation and aggregation (and, moreover, has no 'own troops'). It would, however, be intellectually dishonest to attempt to withhold or modify the known figures of one side in order to 'compensate' for unknowns on the other, in the hope of thus creating a more

realistic picture of the balance. The IISS eschews this, although this raises problems discussed further below, principally in the context of reserve equipment stocks. It is less easy to be entirely confident that elements of creative accounting, or at least ambiguity, have not affected the official publications – indeed it is difficult to understand some of the figures adduced without suspecting such practices. To a very large degree, however, the differences clearly reflect differing counting rules and conventions. These will need to be resolved for CFE purposes; thereafter all analyses may be able to draw on a uniform data base. However, since the existing differences usefully illustrate the critical nature of counting rules, they are examined in some detail below.

First, however, three other points warrant comment, if only to explain the IISS approach. Essays in earlier issues of *The Military Balance* (notably pp. 223–5 of the 1986–1987 edition, pp. 226–31 of the 1987–1988 edition, and pp. 233–6 of the 1988–1989 edition) have made clear IISS reservations about force comparisons based on 'bean counts' except in the context of quantitative arms control, where equipment (and possibly manpower) 'beans' represent a measurable currency on which to base bargains. Our aggregates are therefore compiled with this in view. The geographical boundaries of the CFE region and the categories of equipment do not, however, always square with the form and detail in which the IISS possesses data. While the IISS is striving to acquire the necessary fine-grained information, it has remained necessary in some cases to estimate a breakdown of aggregated data (notably in the cases of the USSR and Turkey) to match the limited geographical area covered by the Atlantic-to-the-Urals (ATTU) zone. Similarly, specific total holdings of some weapon types for some countries have had to be estimated on the basis of organizational and reserve stock norms. For this reason, aggregated data in Table A will not always be readily reconcilable with the sum of the country holdings listed in the earlier part of the book. Compilers of the NATO and WP data publications have assuredly faced similar problems.

Secondly, there are undeniably important differences in status between equipment (and personnel) in active units, in units which can only be activated after mobilization and reinforcement (e.g., US POMCUS stocks, and Warsaw Pact Category C and mobilization divisions), and in maintenance and battle-attrition replacement stocks. The differences between the first two categories relate, however, only to time; they are very important in respect of the threat of surprise attack, but their relevance diminishes with warning and preparation time. The third category is critical to sustainability and very relevant in the context of some analyses which seek to adjust apparent force balances by applying differential factors for equipment serviceability. The two official publications take very different lines on this question. The NATO document lists, by country, equipment in fully or partially manned units (thereby including low-category Warsaw Pact divisions but excluding US POMCUS stocks from this count). In footnotes to its count it also aggregates NATO equipment held 'in storage' (including POMCUS) but does not quantify parallel WP 'in storage' holdings, merely stating that in all cases these are estimated to exceed NATO holdings. The WP document attempts no such discrimination, providing only total holdings per country. The IISS, for the present, similarly provides only aggregated data, but hopes progressively to be able to distinguish between the three categories. IISS aggregates also include training and operational conversion unit equipment where this is known to be combat-capable; this most notably affects combat aircraft totals. We judge that it would be manifestly absurd to disregard the ready reinforcement potential of such equipment and the trained manpower represented by associated instructors (and others filling peacetime posts which lapse on transition to war). We are, however, very conscious that our data on WP equipment reserves and training holdings is limited, and some Pact totals *may* therefore be understated. The conventional wisdom is that the WP is very slow to discard or scrap old equipment, and 'elephant's graveyard' equipment parks are known to exist.

Third, in the arms-control context, it is necessary to distinguish between indigenous and stationed forces. Both alliance documents do this to varying extents; previous IISS force comparison tables have not done so (although country entries showed them, and the insert map in *The Military Balance 1988–1989* aggregated them for key equipments). Table A now shows the relevant breakdown for all force components covered.

DETAIL

Manpower. Despite initial NATO reluctance, manpower is now an agreed part of the CFE negotiations. It is, however the least meaningful (or verifiable) measure of combat capability, and one that poses special problems. The NATO document includes aggregated active ground-force strength figures, seemingly including WP ancillaries such as railway and construction troops (who, General Yazov has recently asserted, do not undergo even basic military training). The WP document also includes active air force, air defence force, naval and civil (territorial) defence force strengths, all carefully itemized. Neither includes strengths of mobilizable reserves, highly relevant to combat ratios after build-up and to sustainability. The IISS will continue to present active and reserve ground force strengths and to exclude (but note the existence of) potentially usable ancillary ground forces. Neither NATO, WP nor IISS tables include para-military manpower, although this is often substantial, heavily armed and well-trained and could clearly fulfil wartime rear-area and line-of-communication security tasks, releasing army manpower for combat zone roles.

Divisions. Because of wide differences in strengths and armaments (see p. 5) divisions (or division equivalents, calculated on the assumption that three all-arms brigades or four regiments equate to a division) are a particularly meaningless unit of account except as an indication of the availability of potentially quasi-autonomous formations. The NATO document counts them (arguably inflating the Pact figures by including artillery divisions and brigades). The WP document does not. We have, for the present, retained them – not least as illustrating the differences between peacetime and war-mobilized potential – but stress that raw numbers of divisions are not comparable.

Tanks. Tank counts well illustrate the problems of definition despite, at least *prima facie*, being relatively simple to identify. NATO's figures take a 90mm or larger-calibre gun as the yardstick, thereby omitting T-34 tanks. The WP definition is unclear. It certainly includes light tanks and possibly some armoured reconnaissance vehicles mounting guns; it also appears, in its figures for NATO, to include tank museums, target hulks on ranges, scrapyard detritus and (e.g., in crediting Portugal with 470 tanks) a degree of imagination which might suggest that the West has overrated the capabilities of the KGB and GRU. The IISS continues to count all tanks with 85mm or larger guns.

Other Armoured Vehicles. NATO presented separate counts for what it termed armoured infantry fighting vehicles (AIFV – which at the time it defined as cannon-armed and incorporating infantry firing ports) and 'other armoured vehicles' (a miscellany of light tanks, AIFV *lacking* infantry firing ports (e.g., the UK *Warrior*), armoured personnel carriers (APC), command and support vehicles). The WP amalgamated IFV, APC and scout vehicles in a single count. The CFE negotiations currently seek to limit 'armoured troop carriers' (ATC), a combination of APC and AIFV (with a sub-limit on the latter), and NATO now accepts that the AIFV category should include cannon-armed infantry vehicles, whether or not they have firing ports. We agree this definition and list AIFV and APC numbers which, in combination, equate to the CFE ATC category.

Artillery and Mortars. Any aggregation of artillery, multiple rocket launchers (MRL) and mortars is inevitably somewhat simplistic, imputing equal value to weapons with substantially differing weight and nature of munitions (the true artillery weapon), range, rate of fire, etc. It also poses questions about weapons with actual or potential dual roles for direct-fire anti-tank (ATK) use and indirect-fire artillery bombardment. The NATO document aggregates all indirect-fire weapons with calibres of 100mm or greater. The WP takes guns and MRL of 75mm calibre and above, including weapons viewed in the West as primarily anti-tank, thereby inflating Pact figures. But it also includes mortars down to 50mm, which are extremely short-range and in some cases have no HE capability, thereby inflating NATO figures. Any counting criteria must to some extent be arbitrary. In the arms-control context large numbers of small-calibre weapons present obvious verification difficulties. The IISS judges 105mm to be a sensible minimum calibre above which to count for artillery, MRL and mortars, and the figures in Table A reflect this criterion.

ATK Weapons. Anti-tank weapons present four major difficulties. First, the question, already alluded to, of attributing guns (which may be of up to 100mm calibre) between the ATK and artillery roles. Secondly, the existence of a wide range of smaller anti-tank rocket launchers. Thirdly, the proliferation of anti-tank guided weapons (ATGW), including their fitment on some armoured fighting vehicles (AFV) in a *secondary* role, where they will on occasion have ATK utility (notably in a meeting engagement) but will not normally be available for deployment to formal integrated ATK defences. And, finally, the deployment of ATGW on helicopters, in some cases as a (near) permanent fit, in others as an optional configuration. The NATO approach has been to aggregate all ground, vehicle-borne and helicopter-mounted ATGW, ATK guns and recoilless rifles, while noting the proportion of AFV and helicopters for which this is a secondary function (some 13% in the NATO case, but 52% for the Warsaw Pact). The WP includes ATK guns in its artillery count, disregards rocket launchers, leaves helicopter-borne systems to a general 'catch-all' combat helicopter category (discussed below) and confines its 'anti-tank guided missile systems' count to vehicle-mounted weapons at regimental level and above, together with portable systems in battalions. The IISS continues to confine its figures to ground-launched ATGW and those fitted on vehicles with a *primary* ATK role.

Air Defence. Air defence (AD) weaponry comprises anti-aircraft cannon artillery (with calibres ranging from as little as 23mm to 100mm or even 130mm) and both fixed and mobile surface-to-air-missiles (SAM) with very different capabilities and (generally) far greater slant ranges. Their role varies between protection of the homeland and defence of the field army. Their contribution to offensive 'invasion capability' is important but, arguably, only secondary. The WP document ignores them. The NATO document aggregates both cannon and SAM and both homeland and field army defence weapons; the calibre criterion used for AA artillery appears to be set very low, thereby catching larger numbers of Pact weapons than may be genuinely significant in combat. In Table A, the IISS lists SAM and AD artillery separately, counting both homeland defence and field army assets in both cases but excluding shoulder-launched SAM (*Blowpipe, Stinger, Mistral*, SA-7/-14/-15) which are widely proliferating (although including pedestal-mounted variants, where these exist) and counting AD guns only of 20mm calibre and above.

Combat Helicopters. Helicopters increasingly fill a range of combat, combat-support, transport and logistic functions; some on a dedicated basis, others reconfiguring between roles. Discrimination in terms of their importance to combat capability and relevance to arms-control is therefore difficult. The NATO document aggregates armed, ATK and assault/transport helicopters (consciously double-counting with its explicit ATK weapon category). The WP counting rules add in many other helicopter functions – scout/reconnaissance, electronic warfare (EW) and even utility – and, moreover, include naval helicopters. The IISS remains of the view that in the land/air context the combat helicopter count should be confined to those equipped and roled primarily to deliver ordnance over the battlefield, and that naval helicopters are best aggregated under a discrete maritime category. (The combat helicopter definition used by NATO in its July 1989 CFE proposal broadly follows the land/air aspect of this approach.)

Combat Aircraft. Both official documents list the aircraft types they aggregate under this category, but their numbers differ considerably. Contributory factors are the WP inclusion of

NATO carrier-based aviation (which NATO excludes) and the exclusion of *Backfire* (which NATO figures include) – but these factors alone do not wholly account for the differences. Pact figures are also broken down between parent services (air forces, air defence forces and navies) and to some extent between roles (albeit some attribution of roles to NATO multi-role aircraft is, to say the least, debatable). NATO figures attempt no such breakdown, and, while the totals listed include reconnaissance and electronic warfare aircraft, they explicitly exclude stored and combat-capable training aircraft, though numbers of these are given in notes. (NATO's subsequent CFE proposal, however, revises its combat aircraft definition to comprise all permanently land-based fixed-wing or swing-wing aircraft designed or converted to deliver ordnance and any variants of such aircraft, regardless of their roles.)

The IISS continues to define combat aircraft as those normally equipped to deliver ordnance and, as stated earlier, includes relevant training, OCU and stored aircraft in the count. It accepts the relevance of naval aviation based on carriers within combat radius of European land targets, but – given that carrier-based aircraft represent, in every respect, a floating population – judges it most appropriate to list these under an explicit maritime heading. For the benefit of analysts we continue to disaggregate land combat aircraft into sub-strategic bomber, ground attack and air defence roles, in the case of multi-role aircraft discriminating on the basis of parent unit role and aircrew training.

It is, however, important to stress two points. First, although up-to-date role training is an important determinant, the boundary between fighter ground attack and air defence/fighters is extremely porous. Multi-role aircraft can to some extent switch missions, notwithstanding their parent unit's primary role. Thus too much weight should not be attached to the attribution to roles at Table A, although it usefully illustrates the apparent respective priorities of the two sides. Secondly, it would be a misconception to regard the air defence/fighter category as essentially defensive – not solely because of the scope for re-roling but because effective counter-air operations are essential to securing *air superiority*. Moreover, such operations will not solely be confined to friendly airspace. Hence if combat aircraft are to be subject to arms-control regulation, this should not be confined to ground attack aircraft alone.

Naval Forces. The NATO document, due no doubt to the exclusion of naval forces from the CFE mandate, makes no reference to them other than to include land-based naval aviation in its combat aircraft count. The WP – which has been at pains to assert that NATO's naval superiority counterbalances its own (welcome) admission of substantial ground-force advantages to the extent of providing 'rough parity' – lists submarines (omitting SSBN and SSB) and large surface ships, which it categorizes as of 1,200-tonne displacement or greater. Within the larger surface ship category, it identifies numbers in some key categories (aircraft carriers, cruise-missile-equipped vessels and amphibious ships). What is interesting and revealing here is the effect of the 1,200-tonne criterion. There is of course, no magic displacement criterion. In its own count the IISS has used a yardstick of 1,000 tonnes, which, if nothing else, is manifestly a round number. The effect of moving the goal-posts by 200 tonnes is, however, substantial. The relevant figures for the number of Warsaw Pact 'larger surface ships' in European/Atlantic waters is 246 of 1,000 tonnes or greater and 147 at 1,200 tonnes or more; the equivalent figures for NATO ships are 438 and 406 respectively. The point here is not to argue that WP counting-rules and conventions are self-serving (or noticeably more so than NATO's) but to illustrate the difference a relatively small change in an arbitrarily determined yardstick can make. Table A continues to apply the IISS 1,000-tonne criterion and to break down vessels by types. As indicated earlier, it also continues to address naval fixed- and rotary-wing aviation under this 'maritime' heading, distinguishing between roles in the same manner as for land-based combat aircraft (but with the same provisos).

Other Categories. Each of the official documents introduces one category of equipment not addressed in Table A. In the WP case this is 'tactical missile systems', which we do not consider strictly a part of conventional forces and therefore tabulate separately at pp. 214–15. NATO lists armoured vehicle launched bridges, reporting a Pact holding in active units of 2,550 against NATO's aggregate of 454. The IISS recognizes the importance of these equipments as part of an offensive or counter-offensive capability but as yet lacks sufficient data on which to base an independent aggregate figure. We have, however, no reason to doubt the NATO count.

Unilateral Reductions
Starting with President Gorbachev's UN speech of 7 December 1988, Warsaw Pact countries have announced a series of sizeable unilateral troop reductions and withdrawals to be effected by 1991, together with some substantial restructuring of remaining forces in the forward area. Subsequent announcements by officials

have elaborated on the details and the timetable, although some differing statements have left the precise number of men and equipment involved a little obscure. The reductions have already started, and the reorganization of remaining forces into a structure described by the WP as being 'clearly defensive' is reportedly under way. In the case of Soviet forces, it has been stated that this restructuring will involve the removal of one tank regiment (94 tanks) from each tank and motor rifle division, but the addition of further anti-tank, air defence and mine-laying assets. Non-Soviet Warsaw Pact forces organized on Soviet lines may be expected to follow a similar pattern.

The reductions – principally involving the withdrawal of six Soviet tank divisions (including two from the Western Group of Forces, formerly called the Group of Soviet Forces in Germany, which some reports suggest were earmarked for Operational Manoeuvre Group (OMG) roles), the removal of substantial additional numbers of tanks from remaining tank and motor rifle divisions in Central Europe, reductions in artillery, assault crossing and assault landing troops and equipment, together with some 13% (using WP figures) of forward-deployed Soviet combat aircraft – clearly address key areas of NATO concern over Warsaw Pact capabilities for short-notice attack and large-scale offensive action. Once complete, and with the announced plans for the destruction or conversion to civilian use of a significant proportion of the relevant equipment having been effected, the military picture in Europe will be substantially altered – particularly in Central Europe, where, for example, there will be approximate parity in tank numbers between NATO and the Warsaw Pact (albeit at differing levels of manning and readiness). Such a situation will make the short-warning or 'surprise attack' scenario (already highly improbable) barely plausible. Longer-warning scenarios will be less affected but the necessary preparation time for the Warsaw Pact will be increased, which should in turn enhance NATO warning and – provided warning is heeded – preparation times. And the Pact's ability to achieve and sustain desired levels of force superiority will be diminished.

Of course, little of this has yet happened, but, barring unforeseen reactions in Eastern Europe or the Soviet Union, we see no reason to doubt the sincerity of a programme which derives at least as much from pressing domestic imperatives in the East (which will not go away) as from a revised view of East–West relations (which exists, but could change). It would, nevertheless, be even more encouraging to see clear evidence, currently lacking, that Soviet weapon production rates were declining in proportion to the planned reductions. The programme has, however, impli-

cations for *The Military Balance* and for its uses. *The Military Balance* has always been a snapshot of military organizations and strengths, hoping to be accurate as at its cut-off date for information but recognizing that the picture will change over the year up to the next issue. Hitherto this has not led to serious inaccuracies; the pace of military change has generally been gradual. The picture for Warsaw Pact force levels, organization, equipment holdings and deployment now looks set to move too rapidly for *The Military Balance* figures necessarily to be able to hold good for a full twelve months. Analysts and other users may need to seek periodic updates on the state of play with unilateral changes.

Whatever the reorganizations, however, readers will need to be cautious before accepting that any measures can create forces which are unambiguously defensive in nature and structurally incapable of offensive action. This is not to belittle Eastern plans or to undervalue the significance of their announced intentions. But even reorganized Warsaw Pact divisions, with much reduced tank strengths, will remain highly potent formations, and capability for offensive action will remain, as ever, predominantly a matter of *relative* strengths and capabilities.

The Vienna CFE Negotiations

Beyond the unilateral Warsaw Pact reductions – and encouraged by them – negotiations on conventional force reductions in Europe have begun in propitious circumstances and with a rapid convergence of the negotiating objectives and positions of the two sides. While difficulties remain (not least the questions of counting rules and definitions, discussed earlier, and of verification) and while unforeseen obstructions may (and probably will) yet appear, the remaining differences appear capable of being bridged by skilful negotiation – though this may take more time than optimists currently envisage. But the essential ingredient, political will, is manifestly present on both sides.

Success in the CFE negotiations will of course, pose a new challenge to *The Military Balance*'s snapshot of the force array in Europe as reductions, redeployments and reorganization are effected. But this problem is not yet with us – and would be a small price for analysts to pay for a properly constructed bargain which satisfies the CFE mandate of establishing 'a secure and stable balance of conventional forces at lower levels' and eliminates any 'capability for launching surprise attack and for initiating large-scale offensive action'.

The state of the CFE negotiations does, however, impinge on *The Military Balance* in one respect. Our primary aim in providing aggregate totals of conventional force elements in Table A is explicitly for use in the arms-control context (and even in that connection we are, as already indicated, uneasy about any rigid categorization of aircraft). We have grave reservations about the figures being put to other uses. With this in mind, and anticipating an approach which would seek to differentiate between parts of the ATTU zone and apply appropriate sub-limits to each, we last year provided figures for three geographical divisions of Europe (the NATO Guidelines Area (NGA), comprising the territories of the FRG, the Benelux countries, the GDR, Poland and Czechoslovakia; the 'Jaruzelski' area, which adds Denmark and Hungary to the NGA; and the complete ATTU zone) as well as global totals. At this stage of the negotiations, however, the subregions remain still to be agreed, with NATO proposing three sub-divisions within the ATTU zone and the Warsaw Pact three other (different) ones. It would be impracticable – and potentially highly confusing – to attempt to lay out figures for all these potential alternatives. We have therefore repeated our practice of 1988–1989.

The Balance

Recent editions of *The Military Balance* have made clear why the IISS feels unable to offer any overall judgments on the state of the NATO/WP conventional balance. No new analytical tools or methods have emerged to alter that situation. Nor have the changes over the past year altered our long-standing view that the force relationship is such that 'general military aggression in Europe would be a high-risk option with unpredictable consequences, particularly so long as the risk of nuclear escalation exists'. Equally, for the present it remains true that, to Western eyes, Soviet conventional forces in the ATTU zone, and particularly in the forward area, exceed realistic Eastern defence needs and, by virtue of their organization and deployment, justify continued Western concern.

But the situation is already in the process of significant change. Eastern force reductions have begun and, together with reorganization plans and reported changes in doctrine and training patterns (though the latter are difficult to discern with absolute assurance), do now support Soviet claims of new thinking. Even the unilateral reductions will, once complete, virtually eliminate the surprise attack threat which has so long concerned NATO planners. Success in the CFE negotiations appears achievable on terms which would revolutionize the East–West security relationship. It is at last becoming possible to look forward to the prospect of a situation of much diminished concern as to the state of the balance, the meaning of the figures or the prospects for and potential outcome of general military aggression in Europe.

The Tables

That Utopia is, however, not yet here. Table A presents aggregated data on NATO and Warsaw Pact conventional forces and equipment, as at 1 June 1989, compiled on the basis of the counting rules and the unavoidable elements of estimation and extrapolation discussed earlier in this essay. Tables B and C seek to continue our practice of putting some flesh on the bare bones of these data by, respectively, setting out the key characteristics of the artillery weapons of both sides and of the world's principal navies. Other relevant insights are provided by the table and note on demographic trends in both East and West on pp. 238–9, and the essay on reserve forces on pp. 240–46.

Table A: Conventional Force Data: NATO and Warsaw Pact

This Table presents aggregated data for a large number of national forces, divided on the basis of their geographical deployment. Its compilation has required some extrapolation (generally from estimated Tables of Organization and Equipment (TO & E)) and estimation (generally to break out gross holdings between geographical areas on a proportionate basis) to augment the information shown in individual country entries. It therefore embodies some data in which the IISS has a lesser degree of confidence. Totals in parentheses are numbers of stationed forces (i.e. those outside national borders) in Europe.

	NATO Guidelines Area (NGA)[a]		Jaruzelski Area[b]		Atlantic to Urals		Global	
	NATO[c]	WP	NATO[c]	WP	NATO[c]	WP	NATO[c]	WP
1. LAND/AIR								
Manpower (000)								
Total active ground forces[d]	793 (353)	975 (490)	810 (353)	1,109 (555)	2,243 (359)	2,317 (555)	2,992	2,855
Total ground force reserves[e]	969	920	1,024	1,060	4,136	3,908	5,488	4,658
Divisions[f]								
Manned in peacetime[g]	$29\frac{2}{3}$ (13)	$50\frac{1}{3}$ ($28\frac{2}{3}$)	$31\frac{2}{3}$ (13)	$58\frac{1}{3}$ ($32\frac{1}{2}$)	$94\frac{2}{3}$ (13)	114 ($32\frac{1}{2}$)	$119\frac{2}{3}$	$153\frac{2}{3}$
Manned on mobilization of reserves[h]	11	18	$12\frac{2}{3}$	$19\frac{2}{3}$	42	$106\frac{2}{3}$	$58\frac{1}{3}$	$135\frac{2}{3}$
Total war mobilized	$40\frac{2}{3}$ (13)	$68\frac{1}{3}$ ($28\frac{1}{2}$)	$44\frac{1}{3}$ (13)	78 ($32\frac{1}{2}$)	$135\frac{2}{3}$ (13)	$220\frac{2}{3}$ ($32\frac{1}{2}$)	173	$289\frac{1}{3}$
Ground Force Equipment[i]								
Main battle tanks	13,100 (7,200)	19,800 (8,700)	13,300 (7,200)	22,400 (9,900)	21,900 (7,200)	58,500 (9,900)	34,400	78,200
AIFV[j]	6,000 (2,600)	11,500 (8,100)	6,000 (2,600)	13,100 (9,200)	7,000 (2,600)	24,700 (9,200)	11,500	34,400
APC	10,700 (4,100)	11,900 (2,300)	11,200 (4,100)	13,500 (2,900)	27,000 (4,100)	49,300 (2,900)	55,600	68,100
Artillery, MRL and mortars[k]	6,100 (2,600)	14,000 (6,000)	6,600 (2,600)	16,000 (6,900)	18,100 (2,600)	49,600 (6,900)	26,700	67,100
ATGW, ground-based[l]	7,300 (3,600)	3,000 (1,400)	7,500 (3,600)	3,600 (1,700)	13,200 (3,600)	11,500 (1,700)	32,000	16,300
AD guns[m]	3,500 (700)	2,500 (600)	3,500 (700)	2,700 (600)	10,300 (700)	11,300 (600)	11,200	13,800
SAM[m]	1,000 (600)	2,900 (1,200)	1,100 (600)	3,300 (1,300)	2,200 (600)	11,300 (1,300)	3,200	15,700
Armed hel[n]	615 (350)	640 (410)	615 (350)	730 (460)	1,100 (350)	1,515 (460)	3,180	2,400
Land Combat Aircraft[o]								
Bombers[p]					18	285	80	455
Ground attack[q]	1,010 (350)	1,140 (740)	1,100 (350)	1,350 (950)	3,210 (670)	2,510 (950)	4,930	3,400
Air defence/fighters[r]	340 (120)	1,230 (350)	340 (120)	1,470 (490)	1,200 (140)	4,240 (490)	2,960	5,440

	European/Atlantic waters		Global	
	NATO	WP	NATO	WP

2. MARITIME

Naval Forces

Submarines[s]	185	191	231	289
Carriers	13	2	20	4
Battleships/cruisers	26	26	50	37
Destroyers/frigates	328	183	418	252
Amphibious[t]	71	87	108	113

Naval Air[o]

Bombers	–	260	–	355
Attack	650	} 100	1,060	} 215
Air defence/fighter	310		620	
ASW fixed-wing ac	500	120	820	195
ASW hel	430	200	590	290

[a] The territories of Be, FRG, Lux, Nl, GDR, Po and Cz.

[b] NATO Guidelines Area plus territory of Dk and Hu.

[c] Fr and Sp forces are not part of NATO's integrated mil comd, but are incl in relevant totals. A proportion of Turkish forces have been excluded from the Atlantic-to-Urals count, as forces in the south-east of Turkey facing Syria, Iraq and Iran are not being counted in CFE.

[d] Ground Forces exclude para-military forces, such as border guards and sy tps, though these incl formations of up to div size, hold hy eqpt and would probably fulfil some rear area sy functions in war. Marines and Naval Inf have been incl, but tps manning AD units, when these are part of an Air Force or a separate service, are not. Where elms of forces are organized on a joint-service basis (e.g., Canadian Medical Services, French *Service de Santé*, Soviet MOD staff and units) a proportion of these have been added to ground-force totals. WP figures could also be increased by including a proportion of railroad and contruction troops, but these have not been included.

[e] Normally only men within 5 years of their active service period are incl, unless a country entry specifies a different parameter. Home Guard manpower has not been incl.

[f] Div are not a standard formation between armies; manpower and eqpt totals vary considerably (see Table on p. 5). For the purposes of this table we have counted div equivalents as being either three manoeuvre bde (normally of three bn plus some spt units) or four regt (normally groups of bn of inf or armd only).

[g] Incl all Sov and WP Category A and B div and NATO formations manned at over 50% of war establishment.

[h] Comprises only forces mob within the relevant geographical area. North American-based US and Cdn forces earmarked for reinforcement of Europe are shown under the 'Global' heading.

[i] Totals incl all known stocks of materiel whether manned by active or reserve forces, held as maint reserves, or in POMCUS. It should be noted that information on WP reserve holdings is much more limited than for NATO and the relevant figures much lower. This may be at least in part accounted for by the WP op practice of replacing spent div by follow-on echelons rather than topping them up from reserve stocks.

[j] AIFV comprise all armd wheeled or tracked inf fighting veh armed with a cannon of not less than 20mm calibre.

[k] Incl arty MRL and mor of not less than 105mm calibre; excl ATK guns.

[l] The figures shown are est aggregates of all dismounted ATGW and those veh-mounted wpn with a primary ATK role.

Totals exclude ATGW on AIFV (e.g. M-2/-3 *Bradley*, BMP, BMD) or fired by MBT main armament (e.g. T-80) and do not, therefore, represent total available ATGW for either side.

[m] SAM launchers exclude shoulder-launched wpn (e.g., *Javelin, Blowpipe, Stinger*, SA-7/-14/-16). Air Force and separate AD force SAM and AD guns are incl.

[n] Comprises all hel whose primary function is CAS or ATK.

[o] Totals incl OCU and trg ac of the same type as those in front-line sqn.

[p] Long-range strategic bombers have been excluded. Only *Mirage* IVP, FB-111A, Tu-16, Tu-26 and Tu-22 are included.

[q] Comprises all aircraft whose prime role is to attack ground targets, incl dual-capable bomber/ground attack, FGA, CAS, radar-suppression, COIN.

[r] Multi-role ac are incl as ground-attack ac unless specified in the national entry as belonging to an AD unit or having AD as their prime role.

[s] Excludes SSB, SSBN and 'other role' submarines.

[t] Only amph ships (i.e. over both 1,000 tonnes full-load displacement and 60 metres overall length) are incl.

Table B: NATO and Warsaw Pact Artillery, Multiple Rocket Launchers and Mortars: Key Characteristics

This table does not aim to compare the capabilities of individual artillery pieces but is included to allow readers to estimate, in conjunction with the entries in country sections, the scale and capability of artillery which could be brought to support the ground forces of NATO and the Warsaw Pact. However, artillery is purely the delivery means, whilst ammunition is the true weapon. Logistic support is therefore critical.

Notes:

1. CALIBRE: This is given in millimetres (mm). Only weapons with calibre of 105mm or above are included.
2. TYPE: The abbreviations used to show the type of weapon are:
   AB = airborne; HOW = howitzer; MOR = mortar; MRL = multiple rocket launcher; SP = self-propelled.
3. MOBILITY: weapons are shown as either towed or SP. The latter are either wheeled, in which case we show the number of driven wheels, or tracked. Mobility is highly important when counter-bombardment fire can be expected within 5–7 minutes.
4. PROTECTION: The abbreviations used are: AC for armoured chassis only (where the gun and, when firing, crew are not protected); T for turret-mounted gun, where protection equates more to that of an APC than a tank. Protection can also be derived from dispersion, which can be more easily achieved with the availability of automatic-data-processing-assisted fire control and autonomous navigation systems.

Calibre	Designation	Country of design	Type	Mobility	Protection	Max range
105	OTO-Melara	It	HOW	Pack (122 Kg)	–	14,600
105	Light gun	UK	GUN	Towed	–	17,200
105	M-101	US	HOW	Towed	–	14,500
105	Abbot	UK	SP GUN	Track	AC + T	17,000
105	M-108	US	SP HOW	Track	AC + T	15,000
107	M-30	US	MOR	Pack / Track	– / APC	8,000
107	M-107 (2S12)	USSR	MOR	Towed		6,300
110	LARS	FRG	SP MRL	Wh 6 × 6	–	14,000
120	MO-120-RT	Fr	MOR	Towed		13,000
120	M-43	USSR	MOR	Towed	–	5,700
120	M-84	Sp	MOR	Tow / Track	– / APC	6,725
120	Tampella	Finland	MOR	Track	–	6,000
120	2S9	USSR	AB SP HOW	Track	AC + T	10,500
122	BM-21V	USSR	AB SP MRL	Wh 4 × 4	–	15,000
122	BM-21	USSR	SP MRL	Wh 4 × 4	–	20,500
122	FIROS-30	It	SP MRL	Wh 6 × 6	–	30,000
122	RM-70	Cz	SP MRL	Wh 8 × 8	–	20,500
122	D-30	USSR	HOW	Towed	–	21,900+
122	2S1	USSR	SP HOW	Track	AC + T	21,900
130	M-51	Cz	SP MRL	Wh 6 × 6	–	8,200
140	WP-8	Pol	AB MRL	Towed	–	9,810
140	RPU-14	USSR	AB MRL	Towed	–	9,810
152	D-1	USSR	HOW	Towed	–	12,400
152	D-20	USSR	GUN / HOW	Towed	–	24,000+
152	2S5	USSR	SP GUN	Track	AC	30–35,000
152	2S3	USSR	SP GUN / HOW	Track	AC + T	30,000
152	Dana	Cz	SP HOW	Wh	–	22,000
155	FH-70	FRG / UK / It	HOW	Towed	–	31,000
155	TR	Fr	GUN	Towed	–	32,500
155	M-114 / 39	Nl	HOW	Towed	–	30,000
155	M-114	US	HOW	Towed	–	19,300
155	M-198	US	HOW	Towed	–	30,000
155	AU-F-1	Fr	SP GUN	Track	AC + T	31,500
155	Mk F-3	Fr	SP GUN	Track	AC	24,800
155	AS-90	UK	SP GUN	Track	AC + T	31,500
155	M-44	US	SP HOW	Track	AC	14,600
155	M-109G	US	SP HOW	Track	AC + T	23,500
175	M-107	US	SP GUN	Track	AC	32,800
203	M-110	US	SP HOW	Track	AC	30,000
203	2S7	USSR	SP GUN	Track	AC	35,000+
220	BM-22	USSR	SP MRL	Wh 8 × 8	–	40–45,000
230	MLRS	US	SP MRL	Track	AC crew	30,000
240	M-240	USSR	MOR	Towed	–	9,700
240	2S4	USSR	SP MOR	Track	AC	12,700+

5. MAXIMUM RANGE: This is given in metres and is the range achieved by the furthest-reaching projectile for that equipment, often an RAP. It should be noted that RAP are only used when essential, as they are far more expensive than normal HE rounds.

6. RATES OF FIRE: Two examples are given, in rounds per minute: one for sustained rates, which can be maintained for considerable periods of time, and one for maximum or burst rates, which can only be sustained for short periods at intervals. For MRL we have shown the number of tubes mounted and the time taken to reload after a complete salvo has been fired; this data is marked with an asterisk.

7. AMMUNITION NATURES: The abbreviations used are:
NUC = nuclear; HE = high-explosive; RAP = rocket-assisted projectile; FRAG = fragmentation; AP GREN = anti-personnel grenade (sub-munition); AP MINE = anti-personnel mine (sub-munition); ATK MINE = anti-tank mine (sub-munition); ERBS = extended-range bomblet shell; CW = chemical warfare agent; HEAT = high-explosive anti-tank; HESH = high-explosive squash-head; SMK = smoke; ILL = illuminating; MKR = marker; ICM = improved conventional munition.

8. AMMUNITION HOLDINGS: We give ammunition holdings purely on the SP chassis or the towing vehicle. Where dedicated ammunition vehicles are provided for each gun, the relevant holding is shown in brackets. Holdings are often reinforced by 'dumping' particularly in defence and when a high rate of expenditure can accurately be anticipated.

9. EXTRAS: Here we include relatively unique characteristics, such as permanently fitted flotation equipment (flot), amphibious capability (amph), parachute dropping capability (para), automatic and hydraulic loading systems (auto and hydraulic) and nuclear and chemical warfare protection (NBC).

Rates of fire		Amunition natures	Ammo holding	Extras	Designation
Sustained	Max/burst				
4	8	HE / RAP / AP GREN / SMK / ILL	n.k.	–	OTO Melara
3	6	HE / HESH / SMK / ILL / MKR	n.k.	–	Light gun
3	10	HE / RAP / AP GREN / SMK / ILL	n.k.	–	M-101
3	8	HE / HESH / SMK / ILL / MKR	40	flot	*Abbot*
1	3	HE / RAP / AP GREN / CW / SMK / ILL	87	–	M-108
9	18	HE / SMK / ILL	n.k.	–	M-30
n.k.	15	HE / SMK / ILL	n.k.	–	M-107 (2S12)
36*	15 min*	HE / ATK MINE / FRAG / SMK	36	–	*LARS*
10–12	10 in 30 sec	HE / RAP / ILL	n.k.	–	MO-120-RT
10	–	HE / FRAG / SMK / ILL	n.k.	–	M-43
6 per 5 min	12	HE / FRAG / SMK / ILL	n.k.	auto	M-84
15	15	HE / SMK / ILL	n.k.	–	Tampella
8–10	n.k.	HE / HEAT / SMK / ILL / INC	60	para / amph / auto	2S9
12 in 10 sec*	n.k.*	HE / CW / SMK	12	–	BM-21V
40 in 20 sec*	n.k.*	HE / CW / SMK	40	–	BM-21
40 in 20 sec*	n.k.*	HE / AP MINE / ATK MINE	40	–	FIROS 30
40 in 20 sec*	2–3 min*	HE	80	–	RM-70
7–8	n.k.	HE / RAP / CW / HEAT / SMK / ILL	n.k.	–	D-30
5	n.k.	HE / RAP / CW / HEAT / SMK / ILL	40	NBC	2S1
32*	2 min*	HE	96	–	M-51
8*	2 min*	HE / CW / SMK	8	–	WP-8
16*	4 min*	HE / CW / SMK	16	–	RPU-14
4	n.k.	HE	n.k.	–	D-1
4	5	NUC / HE / RAP / CW / HEAT / SMK / ILL	10–15	–	D-20
4–5	n.k.	NUC / HE / RAP / CW / HEAT	40	–	2S5
4–5	6	NUC / HE / RAP / HEAT / SMK / ILL	40	–	2S3
4–5	n.k.	HE / RAP / SMK / ILL	n.k.	–	*Dana*
2	3 in 15 sec	HE / SMK / ILL / ICM	68	auto	FH-70
6	3 in 18 sec	HE / RAP / SMK / ILL	48	hydraulic	TR
n.k.	4	HE / ERBS	n.k.	–	M-114/39
40 per hr	2	NUC / HE / AP GREN / CW / SMK / ILL	n.k.	–	M-114
4	n.k.	NUC / HE / RAP / AP GREN / ATK MINE / CW / SMK / ILL	n.k.	–	M-198
8	6 in 45 sec	HE / RAP / ATK MINE / SMK / ILL	42	auto / NBC	AU-F-1
1	4	HE / RAP / SMK / ILL	– (+ 25)	–	Mk F-3
2	3 in 15 sec	HE / SMK / ILL	48	auto	AS-90
n.k.	n.k.	HE / AP GREN / CW / SMK / ILL	24	–	M-44
1	3	NUC / HE / RAP / AP GREN / ATK MINE / HEAT / SMK / ILL	34 (+ 93)	–	M-109G
1 per 2 min	2	HE	2 (+ 98)	–	M-107
1 per 2 min	2	NUC-RAP / HE / RAP / AP GREN / CW	2 (+ 98)	–	M-110
1	2	NUC / HE / RAP / CW	10	–	2S7
16 in 10 sec*	15–20 min*	HE (sub-munition) / FRAG / ATK MINE / CW	16	–	BM-22
12*	n.k.*	SUB / ATK MINE (FRG) / CW	12	–	MLRS
1	n.k.	NUC / HE / CW	40	–	M-240
2	n.k.	NUC / HE / CW	n.k.	–	2S4

Table: C Major Fleet Capabilities

Notes:

1. The aim of this table is to present the vital statistics of the major Navies of the world in a form which makes it possible to gain a view, not only of their absolute capabilities but also of their shape and posture and of the fundamental strategic thinking that has gone into their constitution. Strategic Naval Forces data are omitted from all but the three manpower columns.
2. MANPOWER: We include all active-service Naval and Naval Aviation personnel and exclude Marines, Naval Infantry, Coastal Defence and other similar organizations. The totals have been amplified to give first, the percentage of personnel serving afloat (to provide a measure of teeth-to-tail ratio) and, second, the percentage of conscripts (to provide a very general measure of likely training states).
3. COMBAT TONNAGE: This column lists the aggregate tonnage of ocean-capable vessels – assessed as all tactical submarines and surface combatants above 1,000 tonnes full load/dived displacement. The entry in this column determines the country's position in the table.
4. ORGANIC AIRCRAFT: Two columns, one for fixed-wing and one for rotary-wing, list the aircraft which can be embarked in the fleet at full strength – that is, with all air-capable ships at their full normal aircraft complement. More may be embarked in an emergency, but maintenance, armament and fuel facilities will be overstretched in consequence. The numbers in parentheses indicate the number of additional aircraft of specific seagoing types held supernumary to the afloat complement.

Country	Manpower total	% afloat[a]	% conscript[b]	Combat tonnage	Subs	Carriers	Other PSC	Organic Air FW	Organic Air HEL
USA	584,000	35	none	3,208,000	98[c]	14[c]	215[c]	1,020 (400)[d]	226 (122)
USSR	437,000	32	77 (36)	2,585,000	280[c]	4[f]	260[c]	52 (52)	164 (11)
UK	57,000	37	none	336,000	27[c]	2[f]	47	16 (30)	78 (86)
China	227,000	24	13 (48)	325,000	92[c]	0	56	0	3 (3)
Japan	44,000	39	none	242,000	14	0	63	0	28 (32)
France	63,000	27	29 (12)	229,000	16[c]	2	42	62 (34)	37 (1)
India	46,000	25	none	170,000	17	2[f]	26	16 (−8)[g]	36 (19)
Taiwan	35,500	39	n.k. (24)	121,000	4	0	36	0	13 (−1)[g]
Italy	51,000	18	53 (12)	113,000	10	1[f]	29	0	54 (44)
Turkey	51,000	20	75 (18)	99,000	15	0	22	0	4 (2)
Brazil	35,300	20	6 (12)	92,000	7	1	16	8 (4)	19 (6)
Spain	30,500	28	63 (12)	84,000	8	1[f]	18	8 (15)	20 (22)
Greece	19,500	43	61 (24)	80,000	10	0	21	0	6 (8)
Peru	22,500	27	48 (24)	77,000	11	0	14	0	8 (4)
Canada	17,100	29	none	72,000	3	0	19	0	15 (20)
Netherlands	14,100	30	8 (14)	70,000	6	0	15	0	23 (−1)[g]
Pakistan	15,000	41	none	69,000	6	0	17	0	14 (−4)[g]
Chile	22,200	23	10 (24)	66,000	4	0	11	0	12 (−1)[g]
South Korea	35,000	24	32 (n.k.)	61,000	3[h]	0	28	0	7 (3)
FRG	36,000	21	28 (15)	60,000	24[h]	0	14	0	12 (7)
Argentina	20,000	23	16 (14)	60,000	4	1	13	7 (18)	14 (1)
Australia	15,700	25	none	59,000	6	0	12	0	4 (2)
North Korea	40,000	24	n.k. (n.k.)	42,000	23	0	2	0	0 (0)
Indonesia	31,000	17	none	37,000	2	0	15	0	10 (2)
Egypt	20,000	17	50 (36)	30,000	10	0	6	0	0 (0)

Footnotes

[a] Numbers serving afloat are derived by totalling the full complements of all combatant vessels – submarines, PSC, patrol and coastal, amphibious and mine warfare. Support ship complements of all types are excluded because these are often wholly or partially civilian-manned. The calculation used does not allow for Naval Aviation personnel permanently based ashore. When their numbers are substantial, the 'percentage afloat' is lower than would otherwise be the case.

[b] Figures in parentheses indicate length of conscript service in months, where appropriate.

[c] Indicates that a proportion of the units listed are nuclear-powered.

[d] Figures given do not include US Marine Corps fixed-wing aircraft. A substantial proportion of their 141 AV-8B V/STOL air-

5. AMPHIBIOUS LIFT: This is presented in terms of the military force that listed specialist amphibious shipping can deliver, in numbers of men, MBT equivalents (at 50 tonnes or 30m^2 per MBT) and transport helicopters, for which there are operating facilities. There is no correlation between the figures given and the numbers of Marines or Naval Infantry or their allocated equipment listed in the country entries.

6. AFLOAT SUPPORT RATIO: Here we provide a measure of the sustainability of the nation's surface forces in a prolonged conflict remote from their national bases. The ratio shown is that of front-line, underway-replenishment-capable support ships to the total number of Principal Surface Combatants listed. In general a figure of 0.20 or better (ie one support ship to 5 PSC) indicates a good level of sustainability; 0.10 or less, poor.

7. LAND-BASED AIRCRAFT: In this category we include all permanently land-based maritime aircraft of all roles: MR, ASW, ASUW and SAR, divided again into FW and hel. No distinction is made between naval attack aircraft (such as the FRG naval *Tornados*) and patrol aircraft (such as *Atlantique* and *Nimrod*). No distinction is made between maritime aircraft operated by the listed nation's Air Force and Navy.

8. PATROL AND COASTAL COMBATANTS: This column lists all patrol and coastal combatants under Naval command in peacetime. Numbers will usually be augmented by Coastguard and equivalent vessels and other unarmed patrol craft requisitioned from civil resources in the mobilization process.

9. MINE WARFARE FORCES: This column lists all permanent mine warfare units maintained in operational condition in peacetime. MCM vessels allocated to reserve units as training craft are included.

Amphibious lift			Afloat support ratio	Land-based air		Patrol/ coastal	Mine warfare	Country
Men	MBT	Hel		FW	Hel			
51,000	1,316^e	182^e	0.26	904^d	47	30	29	USA
17,000	752	10	0.17	866	120	410	37	USSR
2,500	112	11	0.27	71	37	44	38	UK
6,200	374	0	0.07	294	62	915	56	China
1,000	45	0	0.03	92	17	14	47	Japan
1,900	91	8	0.16	35	0	23	24	France
1,500	66	1	0.07	29	6	33	20	India
4,600	370	0	0	37	24	67	8	Taiwan
1,000	20	10	0.07	18	0	13	15	Italy
2,800	99	0	0.05	22	3	48	39	Turkey
600	18	0	0.06	24	25	24	6	Brazil
4,400	54	0	0	6	0	59	12	Spain
2,450	154	1	0	8	4	35	16	Greece
1,200	64	0	0.14	12	0	6	0	Peru
0	0	0	0.16	33	0	12	2	Canada
0	0	0	0.14	15	0	0	26	Netherlands
0	0	0	0.12	4	0	29	3	Pakistan
420	21	3	0.18	9	0	11	0	Chile
1,950	156	0	0	25	42	79	9	South Korea
0	0	0	0.29	133	22	45	56	FRG
600	18	0	0	26	0	13	6	Argentina
350	14	1	0.08	20	20	22	3	Australia
0	0	0	0	0	5	363	40	North Korea
3,000	216	10	0.07	27	0	35	2	Indonesia
300	15	0	0	1	17	43	9	Egypt

craft will normally be embarked in appropriate amphibious ships. Some of the remaining 347 combat aircraft may be allocated to USN carriers.

^{e} Excludes capacity of US Marine Corps prepositioned shipping.

^{f} Carriers indicated do not have catapults and arrester gear and are thus limited to V/STOL aircraft operations.

^{g} The negative figures in parentheses indicate more sea billets for aircraft than current holdings. In most cases procurement of additional aircraft is known to be imminent.

^{h} A proportion (in some cases all) submarines listed are of less than 1,000 tonnes dived displacement and are thus not included in aggregated tonnage.

Demographic Trends Facing NATO and the Warsaw Pact

The declining numbers of young men reaching the age for military service during the next decade foreshadows problems for the NATO countries if armed forces are to continue to be maintained at current strengths. These problems will be particularly acute for the Federal Republic of Germany. The Warsaw Pact countries do not yet face similar quantitative problems, but there are potential difficulties over the demographic make-up of Soviet forces, with the proportion of men of Russian origin falling from 56% in 1979 to under 53% in 1989.

The table opposite shows the current armed forces annual conscript intake (recruit intake requirement for countries without conscription), length of service obligations for ground force conscripts (the largest manpower component), and the demographic trends to the start of the next century. A comparison of the numbers reaching the age of 18 with those required to meet conscription targets apparently shows there is little problem, but such a comparison makes no allowance for national minimum standards for health or education, nor for the exemption of certain categories.

If full-time armed forces are to be maintained at current manpower levels, the options open to those countries facing large shortfalls in manpower are:

– *Increasing the length of conscript service.* This is obviously an unpopular option, and hence politically undesirable. It is, however, probably the most advantageous from a military point of view, since longer service allows higher training standards to be reached before men are transferred to the reserves. The FRG had already decided on this course, and from 1 June 1989 conscript service was to have been increased from 15 to 18 months; this would have maintained uniformed manpower levels (after a restructuring process which increases the proportion of reserves in active formations) while conscript recruit availability fell by 17%. However, implementation of the decision has now been postponed until 1992.

– *Increasing the number of long-service career servicemen.* Countries without conscription can only recruit the same numbers from a reduced manpower pool by increasing the attractions of service life. Countries primarily relying on conscription may ease their manpower problems if they can increase the regular component. The penalty is increased costs for salaries, pensions and 'quality of life' enhancements. Increased manpower expenditure will be difficult to reconcile with generally static or decreasing defence budgets and spiralling equipment procurement costs.

– *Lowering medical standards.* Naturally men in combat units must be fully fit, but there are many relatively undemanding tasks in the rear areas which can well be performed by the less physically able.

– *Use of mercenaries.* British armed forces embody some 9,700 personnel enlisted outside the UK, predominantly in the Brigade of Gurkhas. The French Foreign Legion is some 8,500 strong. The United States still incorporates South Korean soldiers in the units stationed in the ROK. It is, however, highly doubtful whether there is scope, or political acceptability, for wider use of non-indigenous forces by NATO nations – notwithstanding periodic suggestions that the FRG should recruit from among its (principally Turkish) *gastarbeiter*. In any event, the concept poses organizational problems – whether to integrate such mercenaries as individuals in the employing nation's own units or to raise units and/or formations exclusively manned (though not necessarily officered) by mercenaries. Either course has implications for force cohesion and effectiveness. The use of mercenaries also generally carries administrative and logistic problems.

– *Tightening the rules governing exemption.* The problem of exemptions is currently most acute for the FRG, where some 20% of those fit for conscription claim exemption each year. A significant proportion of exemptions arise on grounds of conscientious objection, a phenomenon now also generating dissent in Poland, the GDR and Hungary. Tightening the rules would have both positive and negative political implications: it can be portrayed as introducing a fairer application of the national service burden, but it will inevitably provoke strident protests from those denied exemption as a consequence. The negative political effects are likely to be the more pronounced.

– *Linking national service to further education.* In the US, a proposal is being laid before Congress under which further education grants of $20,000 would be provided in exchange for two years in the combat branches of the military at reduced rates of pay. The measure has been proposed primarily for financial reasons, but it has been estimated that some 200,000 young people might volunteer each year. The concept could be adopted by other countries and has the advantage that only those fit for higher education, and hence of good intellectual quality, would be eligible.

– *Increasing the use of women*. Most armed forces already employ volunteer servicewomen in many fields short of combat duty, and there is scope for the increased use of women here. In some countries there is growing pressure to drop all or many of the restrictions placed on the employment of women in combat units, and, for example, women now serve on naval fighting ships in Canada, the Netherlands and Norway, while Denmark has gone so far as to introduce full equality of opportunity for women throughout the armed forces. In some other countries however, extension beyond the support role

(principally medical) would not be politically sustainable. No European country currently conscripts women for military service. This would clearly be one possible solution to manpower shortfalls, but it is doubtful whether any nation would ever require conscript service-women to engage in combat.

None of the foregoing options (nor any combination of them) appears likely fully to solve the manpower problems likely to face the NATO nations during the coming decade, should negotiated arms control fail to produce substantial force reductions. The most likely course is an increased reliance on reserves, both to 'flesh out' undermanned active units and as reserve units/formations *per se*. The current status of reserves and reservists is discussed in the next essay.

Comparison of Conscript Requirement and Number of 18-year-old Men

Country	Conscript intake 1989 (000)[a]	Conscript service (months)[b]	Number of men per year reaching age 18 (000)							% change 1989–2000
			1989	1990	1992	1994	1996	1998	2000	
Bulgaria	47	24	66	64	72	72	67	64	62	−6
Czechoslovakia	59	24	112	116	131	144	142	137	122	+9
GDR	63	18	117	108	92	92	113	113	119	+2
Hungary	43	18	75	76	92	92	85	74	67	−11
Poland	115	24	271	289	307	327	325	344	352	+30
Romania	80	16	195	189	208	205	205	202	174	−11
Soviet Union	3000	24	2,092	2,109	2,173	2,330	2,330	2,330	2,474	+18
Belgium	26	12	71	69	63	61	62	63	61	−14
Canada	(7)	–	202	190	180	185	183	189	187	−7
Denmark	8	9–12	39	38	36	34	32	29	27	−30
France	238	12	452	451	410	369	376	406	401	−9
FRG	178	15	399	353	306	299	290	312	315	−21
Greece	80	21	73	73	74	76	76	77	71	−9
Italy	270	12	465	456	445	402	363	325	322	−31
Netherlands	40	14–16	122	116	99	92	89	89	91	−20
Norway	23	12	34	33	31	28	27	27	27	−20
Portugal	34	16	88	89	89	89	79	74	77	−13
Spain	206	12	337	339	340	336	318	292	259	−13
Turkey	384	18	613	613	613	627	627	542	–	−15
UK	(34)	–	452	424	372	345	336	378	369	−18
USA	(312)	–	1,971	1,810	1,664	1,653	1,768	1,799	1,870	−5

[a] For Canada, UK and US the average annual recruit intake requirement is given.

[b] Ground Forces length of service. In some countries Naval (particularly sea-going) and Air Force conscripts serve longer.

Reserve Forces and Reservists: NATO and the Warsaw Pact

Introduction

On mobilization for war, NATO and Warsaw Pact countries rely – albeit to varying degrees – on calling up reservists to bring peacetime units up to war establishment, to man reserve formations and units to complete their order of battle, and to provide a pool of battle casualty replacements. Even in peacetime, some use reservists on short periods of recall to flesh out active units to operable strength levels. This reliance on reservists is likely to increase, so far as many NATO countries are concerned for resource reasons – both demographic (see pp. 238–9) and financial (reserve units are significantly less expensive to maintain than active forces). Successful arms control is also likely to enhance the importance of reserve forces. This essay examines the factors affecting the combat efficiency of reservists and reserve units and describes the main methods employed to maintain reserve forces and individual reservists ready for war.

As a yardstick for comparison it is worth describing the system in Israel, a state which depends on reservists and reserve formations for at least 75% of its wartime strength and which has established a well-tried mobilization process, tested at the start of three wars and on innumerable 'stand-tos' in response to perceived threats and practice alarms. Israeli conscripts serve for three years (with a fourth year for officers); thereafter they are posted to a front-line reserve formation and normally serve there in the same platoon or tank crew for at least 15 years before moving to a second-line unit. Israeli women serve for two years as conscripts and then as reservists until their 24th birthday or marriage, whichever comes first. In most years each individual carries out at least four weeks reserve duty, ideally split between two weeks field training at unit or formation level and two weeks, often more, on border, internal security or guard duty. Reserve formations are equipped on the same scale and usually with identical weapons and equipment as the standing army units in which their soldiers carried out their conscript service. With this level of training and equipment Israeli reserve forces have made an indispensable contribution to Israel's battlefield success.

There are two main systems of manning reserves: one, as in the UK and US for example, relies on volunteers (often without previous military experience) to man reserve units, coupled with a reserve liability for ex-servicemen; the second, practised by most European continental countries, relies entirely on both ex-regular

servicemen and ex-conscripts to provide the required manpower. The two approaches are not, of course, mutually exclusive but can operate in parallel. Employment patterns also vary: all countries use reservists to bring active-duty units up to war strength and to provide pools of manpower to replace battle casualties. In some forces, the FRG for example, units and sub-units of reservists complete formation and unit wartime orders of battle; in others, such as the US, France and the Netherlands, there are divisions and brigades formed entirely of reservists (other than for permanent staff and training cadres); in yet others, principally the Warsaw Pact (WP) armies, a proportion of units and formations are manned in peacetime at substantially below operational levels and 'fleshed out' by reservists on mobilization.

In general, states with the smallest armed forces rely most heavily on reserve forces, which are accordingly more closely integrated with active forces and tend to carry out more training and to serve for longer periods than in other, stronger, forces. Such states normally operate a 'total defence' concept and do not distinguish between active forces and reserves, considering all men to be members of the armed forces belonging to either standing or mobilized forces. In these countries a number of military support tasks (transport, medical and logistic support) devolve onto the civil sector on mobilization.

The preponderance of reservists serve in the ground forces and in the support elements of air forces (including ground and air defence) and shore establishments of navies. Few NATO or WP reservists fly or sail; such reservists as do will be discussed separately.

Combat Capability

The combat capability of reserves depends on three elements: the individual competence of reservists, the standard of collective training of units or formations, and the availability and effectiveness of the weapons with which they are equipped. Their utility is, of course, also dependent on the existence of a sound (and preferably adequately practised) system for their timely mobilization, shake-down training where necessary, movement to the operational area and integration into the active forces.

The combat capability of *individual* reservists depends on two factors: the length of their full-time military service and the frequency, length and effectiveness of training whilst a reservist. It is true to say that, in general, volunteer reservists (without previous military experience) require, and usually undertake, far more training than ex-servicemen with a reservist liability. So far as the latter are concerned, a British Army study concludes that, for ex-servicemen with at least three full years full-time service, loss of skills necessitates refresher training within at most three years of discharge and at regular intervals thereafter. Ex-conscript servicemen with lesser periods of full-time service would almost certainly require longer and more frequent periods of continuation training. So far as volunteers without former full-time service are concerned, with the possible exception of specialist professions such as the medical services, lack of military experience coupled with problems of continuity and turnover require training to be repeated frequently to achieve a unit norm. It has been assessed that, for example, a reserve company commander aged 34, who joined at the age of 20 and served dutifully since, could only have gained the equivalent of something under two years full-time experience at all levels of commands. Table 1 shows the length of conscript service and reservist liability of NATO countries.

The combat capability of a reserve *unit or formation* depends on the capability of the individual reservists in the unit, the amount of collective training carried out and the extent to which the unit or formation embodies an active force cadre (particularly of leaders – both officers and NCOs – and key specialists). While volunteer reserve units generally carry out both unit and formation collective training at regular, if infrequent, intervals, units composed entirely of reservists, or of a combination of conscripts and reservists (in the Warsaw Pact style), tend to train far less frequently, normally only at formation level, and then only when that formation is mobilized to take part in higher-level training (when the training value for individuals is normally very limited). In these circumstances reservists may typically be recalled for training only once in a three- to five-year period; on mobilization such units will need several weeks intensive training before they can be considered combat-ready. It must also be questionable whether conscripts who serve in undermanned units/formations ever receive the same training experience as their contemporaries in fully manned units.

The quality and modernity of *equipment* is the final element in judging the combat capability of reserve units. More often than not, reserve unit equipment is a generation behind that of active units and is therefore unlikely to be of the same type as that on which most recently demobilized reservists have been trained. Reserve forces equipped with different weapons systems from active forces will be less compatible with them, particularly in respect of communications and logistics. Some forces attempt to equip their reserves on the same scale as their active forces, and, while this may be achieved in respect of major weapons such as tanks, artillery, APC, etc., these units often lack key ancillary items of equipment, such as manpack radio, night-vision aids, etc. In this respect it has been estimated that completion of the equipment of the US Army National Guard alone would cost $8.6 bn for provision of items which would still be outstanding at end 1992, taking into account equipment currently on order. If this is the case, the situation must be considerably worse in forces financially less well catered for.

Table 1: NATO Conscripts Full-time and Reserve Liability

Country	Full-time service (months)	Reserve liability to age[a]	Training liability and pattern
Be	10 or 12	45 (54)	Total 66 days spread over 8 (or 15) years
Dk	9–12	51	Not more than 70 days in first 20 years
Fr	15	45 (60)	No fixed period and only during 5 years after active service
FRG	15	45 (60)	14 days every 4 years (12 days alternate years from 1989)
Gr	21–25	50	Up to 30 days every 3 years
It	12	45	No fixed period
Nl	14–17	35 (45)	Up to 60 days in any 3 years, but max 6 call-out periods overall
No	12–15	44 (55)	4 × 3-week periods in Field Army units to age 35
Port	16–24	45	3 weeks per year for 8 years
Sp	12	34	No training
Tu	18	41	15 days in each 5 years

Annual training liability for volunteer reservists: UK, 36 days per year; US, 60 days per year.

[a] Figures in parentheses are requirements for officers.

NATO Ground Forces Reserves

A number of schemes have been developed for the efficient employment of reservists in war, and these are described in general terms below. Some countries employ more than one of these schemes. Luxembourg has neither conscription nor reserve forces and so is not considered further, nor is Iceland, which has no military forces.

The Voluntary System

The United States, United Kingdom and Canada, which do not have conscription, all maintain volunteer reserve forces (in addition to a reserve liability for regular servicemen).

THE UNITED STATES.   In the US there are two forms of reserve force: the all-volunteer National Guard (Army and Air Force only) and the Reserves. In peacetime the National Guard has a dual loyalty both to its parent state, by which it can be called out to cope with emergencies or civil disturbances, and to the Federal Government, which is responsible for its wartime role, equipment and training. The Reserves are subordinate to the Department of Defense alone and so are, to some extent, more readily available to support the active forces in situations less than war (aerial refuelling for the Libyan air raid, transport operations to Grenada, Marine evacuation from Beirut are recent examples), and their training overseas cannot be inhibited by individual States' policies. The Reserves comprise both volunteers and former active-duty servicemen (all who join the US forces must complete a total of six years with either active forces or Ready Reserves).

The organization of the reserve forces, whether National Guard or Reserves of all services, follows the same pattern. There are three major categories: the Ready Reserve, the Standby Reserve and the Retired Reserve:

The Ready Reserve has two categories, the Selected Reserve and the Individual Reserve.
- The Selected Reserve provides all organized reserve formations and units and the majority of trained individuals to augment and reinforce the active forces in emergency. Selected Reserve personnel are required to carry out 48 days of drills spread over the year, plus a two-week period of training.
- Individual Ready Reserve personnel have the same recall liability but a reduced, or no, training commitment.

Ready Reserve units also include Active Guard and Reserve members who have agreed to join for full-time duty for the purpose of administering and training their units, as well as Military Technicians, who are civilian Federal employees who maintain and administer the units of which they are also Guard or Reserve members. The President can, without a prior declaration of war, order not more than 200,000 of the Ready Reserve to active duty, in the first instance for 90 days. The Ready Reserve (for all services) numbers some 1,655,900, compared with Active Component strength of 2,124,900. The Army and Marine Corps together field 21 Active divisions, as against 11 National Guard and Reserve divisions.

The Standby Reserve is a pool of trained individuals (former active-force servicemen who did not complete 20 years service and former Reserve members) who could be mobilized if necessary. It has no training commitment and can only be ordered to active duty in time of war or emergency declared by Congress.

The Retired Reserve comprises all active force retirees (with 20 years service in any service) and also Reserve officers who receive retired pay. It constitutes a source of trained individuals who would normally be used to augment support and training facilities. They may be ordered to active duty at any time in the interest of national defence.

Training and readiness are two high-priority requirements of all reserve forces. In respect of training the US scores well; training commitments are adhered to, and time devoted to training often well exceeds the minimum required. Individual training is taken seriously and, for those without active duty experience, includes a 12-week full-time basic training period. Officer Candidate School lasts 9 weeks, and specialists are expected to attend courses to qualify for appointments. A large number of units train overseas each year, often in the theatre to which they might be deployed. The quality of training and motivation can be judged by retention rates which, in 1987, were 83.5% for the ARNG. In the ARNG some 22 units are earmarked to deploy overseas within 24 hours, but larger formations will take longer; 4 divisions are to be ready to deploy in 30–60 days with a further 5 within 90 days.

THE UNITED KINGDOM.   The UK has a dual, volunteer and post-active-service, system for providing reserves for all three services. Reserve units are manned by volunteers, while former regular servicemen who have a reserve commitment are used to bring both active and reserve units up to war strength and to provide replacements for battle casualties.

Volunteers train regularly, the minimum annual commitment for the Territorial Army (TA) being 22 days of training drills and a two-week training camp, often held overseas. The TA provides units of all arms and services for the reinforcement of NATO and for Home Defence. The Royal Naval Reserve is mainly used to man mine counter-measure vessels, augment shore-based staffs and communications units and set up the Naval Control of Shipping Organization to manage convoys. The Royal Auxiliary Air Force and RAAF Regiment only provide units for airfield ground and air defence. A major problem is the rate of turnover, as high as 30% a year in some units, which makes unit and sub-unit training difficult; a recent report considered that the TA (and presumably its naval and air force counterparts) would not be ready for their operational tasks without a limited period of work-up training.

There are a number of different categories of ex-active-service reservist with varying call-out liabilities; the most important category is the Regular Reserve Section A, in which non-commissioned soldiers with less than six years active service serve for the balance of seven years with the reserve, and those with between six and twelve years active service for the balance of twelve years. Certain categories of reservist now report for one day a year for checking and limited familiarization training, and a scheme for reservists to carry out one week's refresher training in the third year of their reserve service has been introduced, but attendance is voluntary. All these reservists have had a minimum of three years active service and so will have been more fully trained than their continental counterparts, who carry out much shorter periods of conscription. However, they do not carry out any regular form of training, may not rejoin their original unit and are purely a large pool of individuals. In the context of a NATO war, British reserves, including the TA, can be recalled to service by administrative order – a Queen's Order – which does not require the prior approval of Parliament.

CANADA. Canada also has both volunteer and ex-active-service reserves, known as the Primary Reserve and Supplementary Reserve respectively, and organized very much on the British model. Canada plans to expand its reserve forces substantially over the next 15 years, but today primary reserve units are well below war strength and are normally composed of unit HQ, HQ elements and one sub-unit. The reserve force expansion programme will only double the number of sub-units, and Primary Reserve units will continue to rely heavily on supplementary reservists to reach war establishment and will require extensive training before becoming combat-ready. A further element of the Canadian Primary Reserve is The Canadian Rangers comprised of Inuit and others living in the North West Territories, the Yukon, Quebec province, Newfoundland and Labrador, who form a recce and observation force on the northern approaches to the country.

The Post-Conscript Service System
RESERVE FORMATIONS BASED ON TRAINING SCHOOLS. Both France and Italy have reserve formations – France has two light armoured divisions and Italy an armoured, a mechanized and a mountain brigade – mobilized from the training staffs and demonstration units of the main combat arms schools and brought up to war strength with reservists and stockpiled equipment. This option has obvious penalties in regard to the possibility of carrying on training during the transition to war and hostilities, which could have serious implications in a long war. However, in operational terms, such formations with a strong active-force element, particularly in Headquarters, will be more effective than their all-reserve counterparts. At least some WP mobilization formations, notably in the GDR, are established on a similar basis.

MIXED ACTIVE AND RESERVE FORMATIONS. This pattern is favoured by the FRG where active armoured and armoured infantry battalions in peacetime hold and maintain an additional company's-worth of equipment. These equipment-holding companies, when manned on mobilization by reservists, are regrouped to form a fourth battalion in each brigade. In the '*Heeresstruktur* 2000' restructuring plan, caused by the downward demographic trend, a number of brigades will be reorganized to consist of only two active battalions and two equipment-holding battalions (brigades with covering-force-type roles will, however, retain a higher proportion of active units). The existing training cycle is for reserve units to be mobilized for two weeks training every four to five years; after restructuring, training will be increased to 12 days every second year. Other nations utilize this course in other ways: the UK reinforces active divisions with reserve units and, in one case, forms a division from an active brigade and two reserve brigades; the US reinforces some active divisions with 'round-out' brigades from the Army Reserve and Army National Guard.

HOME/TERRITORIAL DEFENCE UNITS. Most, but not all, units earmarked for home defence are manned by reservists. Most NATO members have home defence units which can vary in capability from fully mobile brigades, sometimes with armour and artillery, down to Home Guard detachments with very localized responsibilities. In general, home defence units carry out much less (if any) training than reserve units earmarked to reinforce or support active forces. Table 2 summarizes NATO home defence forces.

RECALLING RESERVISTS TO THEIR ORIGINAL ACTIVE UNIT. A number of armies keep time-expired conscripts on the mobilization books of the units in which they carried out their conscript service. The French Army does so for four

Table 2: Summary of NATO Home Defence Units

Country	Mobile	Area	Local
Belgium	Motor Inf Regt	–	–
Denmark	Regt combat teams	Inf bn	Home Guard
France	Defence Zone Bde	Territorial regt	–
FRG	Home Defence Bde and Regt	Home Defence coy	Security pl
Greece	National Defence Bde	National Defence bn	–
Italy	–	Frontier Inf bn	Security coy
Netherlands	–	–	Home Guard
Norway	–	Independent coys	Home Guard
Portugal	–	–	–
Spain	–	–	–
Turkey	National Guard Bde	National Guard bn	–
UK	–	Home Defence TA bn	Home Service Force coy

months, the Italian for two years. This system has the great merit of ensuring that the most up-to-date reservists are recalled and that they return to units which they know and in which they are known. The Greek Army also practices this method in conjunction with a unit classification system similar to that used by the Warsaw Pact, with Class A units being 85% or more manned and considered combat-ready, and with Class B and C units at 60% and 20% manning with a commitment to be ready within 24 and 48 hours respectively. This system has been further refined by the Netherlands with 'Rechtstreeks Instromend Mobilisabel' (RIM). The RIM system is based on forming companies (tank, infantry, artillery) as new intakes of conscripts are called up and keeping them as entities, with the same men, throughout basic training which lasts four months, conscript service with active units (a further 10–12 months) and 18 months with a RIM reserve unit. Active units usually consist of two combat-ready companies, the third consisting of recruits under training; this last would be replaced in emergency by the most recent company to have completed its active service (which is described as being on 'short leave'). After four months of being ready for immediate recall that company joins a reserve battalion composed of companies released earlier from the same active unit. The system maintains sub-unit continuity for nearly three years. At the end of their RIM service, conscripts have a reserve liability to the age of 35 (officers to 45) and on mobilization would join units enrolled for home defence. It is claimed that RIM units can be ready to move within 24 hours and would need no further training. Dutch mobilization is practised annually, with battalions called out on a random basis.

TOTAL DEFENCE CONCEPT. In this concept both civil and military authorities co-operate closely, with the civil sector being responsible for aspects, such as medical support and transport, which are military responsibilities in other countries. The concept is followed by Norway and, to a lesser extent, Denmark, as well as by neutral states such as Switzerland and Sweden. In general this concept allows for a period of full-time compulsory military service much shorter than usual but a far longer and more committed period of reserve duty. But the term 'reserves' is shunned in countries following the total defence concept, those not in the active forces being referred to as mobilizable forces. 'Mobilizable' service normally concludes with duty in home guard territorial defence units. In peacetime Norwegian Armed Forces number some 34,000 regulars and conscripts, but within 72 hours mobilization would expand this force to around 320,000. The Norwegian Army maintains only one fully-manned brigade in peacetime but can field a further 13 on mobilization.

Sea-going Reserves

Few navies include reservist-crewed ships in their order of battle. In NATO only those countries with volunteer reserves maintain naval reserve forces. Canada provides its maritime reserve with half a dozen patrol craft for training; this fleet is likely to be expanded by two newly purchased offshore support ships and possibly, in the future, with new mine counter-measures (MCM) vessels. The UK also maintains inshore patrol craft for training and wartime operations crewed by the Royal Naval Reserve (RNR), but the most important element of the RNR is the MCM squadron with eleven *Waveney*-class minesweepers operated entirely by reservists. The US Naval Reserve Surface Forces comprise some 22 frigates, 18 MCMV and two amphibious ships. However, the crews of these are some 60% regular and so are capable of undertaking limited sea-going operations without mobilizing reservist crew members. After mobilization they would be more combat-capable than similar ships with all-reservist crews.

Other nations employ naval reservists to complete ships' companies and to form maritime home guards with small craft. A number of navies have plans to requisition civil shipping, principally for minesweeping, but no training is carried out in peacetime.

Flying Reserves

So far as we can establish, only the US and Canada have air force flying units manned by reservists who are regularly trained and so qualified to fly service aircraft or helicopters. Though most retired aircrew in other countries have a reserve commitment, few are able to maintain their flying currency other than in the transport field.

The Canadian Air Reserve comprises two wings and three squadrons. The wings each have two squadrons of CH-136 *Kiowa* helicopters. Two of the separate squadrons are twinned with active air force units, one in the SAR and light transport role, the other with a reconnaissance and fisheries patrol role. The remaining squadron is in the process of being re-equipped with its own DHC-8 *Dash 8* aircraft, primarily for a navigator training role. There are also eight augmentation flights (similar to US associate squadrons) with aircrew who train regularly and maintain their currency.

The United States maintains flying units in all elements of its reserves (Air Force Reserve, Air National Guard, Army Reserve, Army National Guard, Naval Reserve Aviation and Marine Corps Reserve Aviation), and units operate virtually every type of aircraft other than strategic bombers. In peacetime reserve aircrew fly alongside their active-force counterparts in numerous

Table 3: Comparison of US Active and Reserve Aviation Assets (by squadrons)

Type	Active	Reserve/ Guard
Air Force (incl AFR and ANG)		
Fighter	50	26
FGA	37	29
Recce	12	5
Transport	32	38
Tanker	35	26
SF	10	2
Army (incl AR and ARNG)[a]	40	29
Navy		
Fighter	26	4
Attack	42	7
AEW	15	2
MR	24	13
ASW incl hel	37	4
Tanker		
Marine Corps		
Fighter	12	3
FGA	13	5
Transport hel	15	3

[a] Battalions: combat avn, ATK, med tpt, recce, comd.

exercises and operations, recent examples of which include: transport sorties for the Beirut evacuation and Grenada invasion, and tanker support for the Libyan bombing raids. The US considers its aviation reserves a cost-effective force which competes on equal terms with active units in air meets and tactical competitions. Table 3 shows the relative strengths of US active and reserve aviation assets. The US Air Force also maintains 21 associate squadrons of personnel only, which are linked to active transport and tanker squadrons and, by providing additional air and ground crew, allow these squadrons to utilize their aircraft to the maximum.

The British Army maintains one helicopter squadron in the TA.

WARSAW PACT FORCES

The Warsaw Pact use of reservists is quite different from that of NATO (except for Greece). Reservists either make up the war strength of formations and units which are undermanned in peacetime or form para-military organizations which have a home-guard-type role.

The Military Balance employs the NATO system of categorization of Warsaw Pact divisions. This system follows very closely what is known of the Soviet method of classification:

- Category A: 75% to full strength, equipment complete, combat-ready. Includes units described by the USSR as units at wartime establishment and units at reduced wartime establishment;
- Category B: 50–75% strength, equipment normally complete, full manning planned to take 3 days. Units described as at peacetime establishment by the USSR; NATO and WP consider them combat-ready;
- Category C: some 20–50% strength, equipment possibly complete with older models, planned to be fully manned in 7 days and retrained in less than 60 days. Units described as at reduced peacetime establishment by the USSR;
- Mobilization divisions: these have a maximum of 5% manning and a stockpile of much older equipment. The USSR describes them as 'invisible' or shadow divisions. Will take some months to become combat-ready.

Table 4 shows the breakdown of WP divisions (tank, motor rifle and airborne) by category.

A very rough calculation shows that some 59% of the manpower required to man all of these divisions fully must be provided by reservists.

Most divisions below Category A carry out both a training exercise and a mobilization practice each year, but not all elements of the division will necessarily be mobilized on every occasion. The complete division is unlikely to train more frequently than once every three years.

Table 4: Summary of Warsaw Pact Divisions by Category

	Cat A (75%+)	Cat B (50–75%)	Cat C (20–50%)	Mob (5% max)
Soviet Union	54	53	106	3
Bulgaria	–	5 (plus 5 bdes)	3	–
Czechoslovakia	4	3	3	5
GDR	6	–	–	5
Hungary	(ground forces reorganized on a brigade basis; categorization not yet known)			
Poland	8	–	5	2
Romania	2	4	4	–

Specialist training, for example for radar operators, ATGW controllers, etc., is carried out more frequently, and each Soviet Military District has a centre for training reservists in each group of specialists: air defence, anti-tank, etc. The aim is to retrain all specialists once a year; it is not known how successful this training scheme is.

All WP and some NATO countries employ large numbers of reservists to man local defence units (which *The Military Balance* normally categorizes as para-military forces and excludes from comparative force counts). These have a home-guard-type role, are unlikely to be deployed away from their local area and are normally only lightly armed, but WP strength is considerable.

Conclusion
Accurately establishing the alliances' relative dependence on reserve forces on mobilization is difficult. In virtually all countries the legal reserve liability lasts much longer than the time during which the most recently released men are considered militarily useful, at least in a combat or technically demanding capacity without considerable re-training. The theoretical availability of manpower thus invariably exceeds the initial mobilization requirement. Nor is it possible accurately to quantify the combat capability of reservists of different countries, as training methods and the time devoted to training vary considerably, but the preceding paragraphs give a very general impression of relative worth.

It is clear that, with the exception of US reserves, reserve forces of both NATO and the WP will need some (and some may need considerable) training before they can be considered combat-ready. This applies especially to formations and units formed wholly or predominantly of reservists. Units with a substantial component of fully trained active forces can tolerate fairly substantial dilution by reservists (possibly up to 50%) without serious loss of combat efficiency, and can give their reinforcements rapid, concentrated 'on-the-job' training. The problem is more acute for NATO, as low category WP divisions are unlikely to be committed in the leading echelons. It is most acute in NATO's Central Region, where the 1st Belgian Corps relies on reserve forces for two of its six brigades and in the 1st Netherlands Corps, where one of the three divisions is comprised of reserve units. The main reserve fighting component of 1st British Corps is two brigades of the UK-based infantry division which initially has a rear-area protection role. The existing organization of West German brigades provides three active and one reserve battalions but this is to alter in most brigades to two active and two reserve under the *Heeresstruktur* 2000 plan. Any further dilution of the ratio of active/reserve front-line combat formations could have serious implications, particularly in short-warning scenarios.

Reliance on reserve forces, particularly on units forming part of front-line divisions, carries a number of risks, not the least being the question of readiness. The decision to mobilize reserve forces is a high-profile political move, and it is quite possible that, to avoid sending the wrong signals, decision-taking could be delayed, thus jeopardizing early deployment. Conversely, once mobilization has been decided upon, political and military leaders may find themselves locked into a dangerously escalatory process along August 1914 lines. Therefore, heavier reliance on reserves as a result of either demographic and economic pressures or negotiated active-unit reductions should be examined with particular care in terms of its impact on crisis stability as well as its military implications.

DESIGNATIONS OF AIRCRAFT AND HELICOPTERS LISTED
IN *THE MILITARY BALANCE*

The use of [square brackets] shows the type from which a variant was derived. 'Q-5 . . . [MiG-19]' indicates that the design of the Q-5 was based on that of the MiG-19.

(Parentheses) indicate an alternative name by which an aircraft is known – sometimes in another version. 'L-188 . . . *Electra* (P-3 *Orion*)' shows that in another version the

Lockheed Type 188 *Electra* is known as the P-3 *Orion*.

Names given in 'quotation marks' are NATO reporting names – e.g. 'Su-27 . . . *'Flanker'* '.

When no information is listed under 'Origin' or 'Maker', take the primary reference given under 'Name/designation' and look it up under 'Type'.

Type	Name/designation	Origin	Maker	Type	Name/designation	Origin	Maker
AIRCRAFT				Bronco	(OV-10)		
A-3	*Skywarrior*	US	Douglas	Buccaneer		UK	BAe
A-4	*Skyhawk*	US	MD	Bulldog		UK	BAe
A-6	*Attacker*	US	Grumman	C-1		Japan	Kawasaki
A-7	*Corsair* II	US	LTV	C-2	*Greyhound*	US	Grumman
A-10	*Thunderbolt*	US	Fairchild	C-4M	*Kudu* (AM-3)	S. Africa	Atlas
A-37	*Dragonfly*	US	Cessna	C-5	*Galaxy*	US	Lockheed
AC-130	(C-130)			C-7	DHC-7		
AC-47	(C-47)			C-9	*Nightingale* (DC-9)		
Airtourer		NZ	Victa	C-12	*Super King Air* (*Huron*)	US	Beech
AJ-37	(J-37)			C-18	[Boeing 707]		
Ajeet	(Folland *Gnat*)	India/UK	HAL	C-20	(*Gulfstream* III)		
				C-21	(*Learjet*)		
Alizé		France	Breguet	C-22	(Boeing 727)		
AlphaJet		France/FRG	Dassault/Breguet/Dornier	C-23	(*Sherpa*)	UK	Short
				C-42	(Neiva *Regente*)	Brazil	Embraer
				C-45	*Expeditor*	US	Beech
AM-3	*Bosbok* (C-4M)	Italy	Aermacchi	C-46	*Commando*	US	Curtis
An-2	*'Colt'*	USSR	Antonov	C-47	DC-3 (*Dakota*) (C-117 *Skytrain*)	US	Douglas
An-12	*'Cub'*	USSR	Antonov				
An-14	*'Clod'*	USSR	Antonov	C-54	*Skymaster* (DC-4)	US	Douglas
An-22	*'Cock'*	USSR	Antonov	C-91	HS-748		
An-24	*'Coke'*	USSR	Antonov	C-93	HS-125		
An-26	*'Curl'*	USSR	Antonov	C-95	EMB-110		
An-32	*'Cline'*	USSR	Antonov	C-101	*Aviojet*	Spain	CASA
An-124	*'Condor'* (*Ruslan*)	USSR	Antonov	C-115	DHC-5	Canada	De Havilland
				C-117	(C-47)		
Andover	[HS-748]			C-118	*Liftmaster* (DC-6)		
Atlantic	(*Atlantique*)	France	Dassault/Breguet	C-119	*Packet*	US	Fairchild
				C-123	*Provider*	US	Fairchild
AS-202	*Bravo*	Switz	FFA	C-127	(Do-27)	Spain	CASA
AT-3	*Halcón* (C-101)			C-130	*Hercules* (L-100)	US	Lockheed
AT-3		Taiwan	AIDC				
AT-6	(T-6)			C-131	Convair 440	US	Convair
AT-11		US	Beech	C-135	[Boeing 707]		
AT-26	EMB-326			C-137	[Boeing 707]		
AT-33	(T-33)			C-140	(*Jetstar*)	US	Lockheed
AU-23	*Peacemaker* [PC-6B]	US	Fairchild	C-141	*Starlifter*	US	Douglas
				C-160		France/FRG	Transall
AV-8	*Harrier* II	US/UK	MD/BAe				
Aztec	PA-23	US	Piper	C-212	*Aviocar*	Spain	CASA
B-1		US	Rockwell	C-235		Spain	CASA
BAC-111		UK	BAe	CA-25	*Winjeel*	Aus	Commonwealth
B-52	*Stratofortress*	US	Boeing				
BAC-167	*Strikemaster*	UK	BAe	Canberra	(B-57)	UK	BAe
BAe-146		UK	BAe	CAP-10		France	Mudry
BAe-748	(HS-748)			CAP-20		France	Mudry
Baron	(T-42)			CAP-230		France	Mudry
Be-6	*'Madge'*	USSR	Beriev	Caravelle	SE-210	France	Aérospatiale
Be-12	*'Mail'* (*Tchaika*)	USSR	Beriev	CC-08	DHC-4		
Beech 95	*Travel Air*	US	Beech	CC-109	(Convair 440)	US	Convair
BN-2	*Islander, Defender, Trislander*	UK	Britten-Norman	CC-115	DHC-5		
				CC-117	(*Falcon* 20)		
Boeing 707		US	Boeing	CC-129	C-47		
Boeing 727		US	Boeing	CC-132	(DHC-7)		
Boeing 737		US	Boeing	CC-137	(Boeing 707)		
Boeing 747		US	Boeing	CC-138	(DHC-6)		
Bonanza		US	Beech	CC-144	CL-600/-601	Canada	Canadair

Type	Name/ designation	Origin	Maker	Type	Name/ designation	Origin	Maker
CF-18	F/A-18			EMB-110	*Bandeirante*	Brazil	Embraer
CF-116	F-5			EMB-111	*Maritime*		
Cheetah	[*Mirage* III]	S. Africa	Atlas		*Bandeirante*	Brazil	Embraer
Cherokee	PA-28	US	Piper	EMB-120	*Brasilia*	Brazil	Embraer
Cheyenne	PA-31T	US	Piper	EMB-121	*Xingu*	Brazil	Embraer
	[*Navajo*]			EMB-312	*Tucano*	Brazil	Embraer
Chieftain	PA-31-350	US	Piper	EMB-326	*Xavante* (MB-326)	Brazil	Embraer
	[*Navajo*]			EMB-810	[*Seneca*]	Brazil	Embraer
Chipmunk	DHC-1			EP-3	(P-3 *Orion*)		
Citabria	Cessna 150	US	Cessna	*Etendard*		France	Dassault
Citation	(T-47)	US	Cessna	EV-1	(OV-1)		
CJ-5	[*Yak-18*]	China		F-1		Japan	Mitsubishi
CL-215		Canada	Canadair	F-4	*Phantom*	US	MD
CL-44		Canada	Canadair	F-5	-A: *Freedom*	US	Northrop
CL-601	*Challenger*	Canada	Canadair		*Fighter*;		
CM-170	*Magister*	France	Aérospatiale		-E: *Tiger* II		
	[*Tzugit*]			F-6	J-6		
CM-175	*Zéphir*	France	Aérospatiale	F-7	J-7		
Cochise	T-42			F-8	J-8		
Comanche	PA-24	US	Piper	F-8	*Crusader*	US	Republic
Com-	*Aero-/Turbo-*	US	Rockwell	F-14	*Tomcat*	US	Grumman
mander	*Commander*			F-15	*Eagle*	US	MD
Commod-	MS-893	France	Aérospatiale	F-16	*Fighting Falcon*	US	GD
dore				F-21	*Kfir*	Israel	IAI
Corvette	SN-601	France	Aérospatiale	F-27	*Friendship*	Neth	Fokker
CP-3	P-3 *Orion*			F-28	*Fellowship*	Neth	Fokker
CP-121	S-2			F-33	*Bonanza*	US	Beech
CP-140	*Aurora* (P-3 *Orion*)	US	Lockheed	F-35	*Draken*	Sweden	SAAB
CT-4	*Airtrainer*	NZ	Victa	F-84	*Thunderstreak*	US	Lockheed
CT-39	*Sabreliner*	US	Rockwell	F-86	*Sabre*	US	N. American
CT-114	CL-41 *Tutor*	Canada	Canadair	F-100	*Super Sabre*	US	N. American
CT-133	*Silver Star*	Canada	Canadair	F-104	*Starfighter*	US	Lockheed
	[*T-33*]			F-106	*Delta Dart*	US	Convair
CT-134	*Musketeer*			F-111		US	GD
Dagger	(*Nesher*)			F-172	(Cessna 172)	France/	Reims-
Dakota		US	Piper			US	Cessna
Dakota	(C-47)			F/A-18	*Hornet*	US	MD
DC-3	(C-47)			*Falcon*	*Mystère-Falcon*		
DC-4	(C-54)			FB-111	(F-111)		
DC-6		US	Douglas	FH-227	(F-27)	US	Fairchild-
DC-7		US	Douglas				Hiller
DC-8		US	Douglas	*Flamingo*	MBB-233	FRG	MBB
DC-9		US	MD	FT-6	JJ-6		
Deepak	(HT-32)			G-91		Italy	Aeritalia
Defender	BN-2			G-222		Italy	Aeritalia
Devon		UK	De Havilland	*Galaxy*	C-5		
DH-100	*Vampire*	UK	De Havilland	*Galeb*		Yug	SOKO
DHC-1	*Chipmunk*	Canada	DHC	*Gardian*	(*Falcon* 20)		
DHC-2	*Beaver*	Canada	DHC	*Genet*	SF-260W		
DHC-3	*Otter*	Canada	DHC	GU-25	(*Falcon* 20)		
DHC-4	*Caribou*	Canada	DHC	*Guerrier*	R-235		
DHC-5	*Buffalo*	Canada	DHC	*Gulfstream*		US	Gulfstream
DHC-6	*Twin Otter*	Canada	DHC				Aviation
DHC-7	*Dash-7* (*Ranger*,	Canada	DHC	*Gumhuria*	(Bücker 181)	Egypt	Heliopolis Ac
	CC-132)			H-5	[*Il-28*]	China	Harbin
DHC-8		Canada	DHC	H-6	[*Tu-16*]	China	Xian
Do-27	(C-127)	FRG	Dornier	*Harrier*	(AV-8)	UK	BAe
Do-28	*Skyservant*	FRG	Dornier	*Hawk*		UK	BAe
Do-128		FRG	Dornier	HC-130	(C-130)		
Do-228		FRG	Dornier	*Heron*		UK	De Havilland
Dove		UK	De Havilland	*Heron*		Aus	Riley
E-2	*Hawkeye*	US	Grumman	HF-24	*Marut*	India	HAL
E-3	*Sentry*	US	Boeing	HFB-320	*Hansajet*	FRG	Hamburger
E-4	[Boeing 747]	US	Boeing				FB
E-6	[Boeing 707]	US		HJ-5	(H-5)		
EA-3	[A-3]			HJT-16	*Kiran*	India	HAL
EA-6	[A-6]			HPT-32		India	HAL
Electra	(L-188)			HS-125	(*Dominie*)	UK	BAe
EC-130	[C-130]			HS-748	[*Andover*]	UK	BAe
EC-135	[Boeing 707]			HT-2	[DHC-1]	India	HAL

Type	Name/designation	Origin	Maker	Type	Name/designation	Origin	Maker
HT-32	*Deepak*	India	HAL	*Marut*	HF-24		
HU-16	*Albatross*	US	Grumman	*Mashshaq*	MFI-17	Pakistan/	PAC/
HU-25	(*Falcon 20*)					Sweden	SAAB
Hunter		UK	BAe	*Matador*	(AV-8B)		
HZ-5	(H-5)			MB-326		Italy	Aermacchi
IA-35	*Huanquero*	Argentina	FMA	MB-339	(*Veltro*)	Italy	Aermacchi
IA-50	*Guaraní*	Argentina	FMA	MBB-233	*Flamingo*		
IA-58	*Pucará*	Argentina	FMA	MC-130	(C-130)		
IA-63	*Pampa*	Argentina	FMA	*Mercurius*	(HS-125)		
IAI-201/-202	*Arava*	Israel	IAI	*Merlin*		US	Fairchild
IAI-1124	*Westwind, Seascan*	Israel	IAI	*Mescalero*	T-41		
IAR-28		Rom	IAR	*Metro*		US	Fairchild
IAR-93	*Orao*	Yug/Ro	SOKO/IAR	MFI-15	*Safari*	Sweden	SAAB
Il-14	'Crate'	USSR	Ilyushin	MFI-17	*Supporter*, (T-17)	Sweden	SAAB
Il-18	'Coot'	USSR	Ilyushin	MH-1521	*Broussard*	France	Max Holste
Il-20	(Il-18)			MiG-15	'Midget' trg	USSR	MiG
Il-28	'Beagle'	USSR	Ilyushin	MiG-17	'Fresco'	USSR	MiG
Il-38	'May'	USSR	Ilyushin	MiG-19	'Farmer'	USSR	MiG
Il-62	'Classic'	USSR	Ilyushin	MiG-21	'Fishbed'	USSR	MiG
Il-76	'Candid' (tpt)	USSR	Ilyushin	MiG-23	'Flogger'	USSR	MiG
	'Mainstay' (AEW)			MiG-25	'Foxbat'	USSR	MiG
	'Midas' (tkr)			MiG-27	'Flogger D'	USSR	MiG
Impala	[MB-326]	S. Africa	Atlas	MiG-29	'Fulcrum'	USSR	MiG
Islander	BN-2			MiG-31	'Foxhound'	USSR	MiG
J-2	[MiG-15]	China		*Mirage*		France	Dassault
J-5	[MiG-17F]	China	Shenyang	*Mission-master*	N-22		
J-6	[MiG-19]	China	Shenyang	*Mohawk*	OV-1		
J-7	[MiG-21]	China	Xian	MS-760	*Paris*	France	Aérospatiale
J-8	[Sov Ye-142]	China	Shenyang	MS-893	*Commodore*		
J-32	*Lansen*	Sweden	SAAB	MU-2		Japan	Mitsubishi
J-35	*Draken*	Sweden	SAAB	*Musketeer*	Beech 24	US	Beech
J-37	*Viggen*	Sweden	SAAB	Mya-4	'Bison'	USSR	Myasishchev
JA-37	(J-37)			*Mystère-Falcon*		France	Dassault
Jaguar		France/	SEPECAT				
		UK		N-22	*Floatmaster, Missionmaster*	Aus	GAF
JAS-39	*Gripen*	Sweden	SAAB	N-24	*Searchmaster* B/L	Aus	GAF
Jastreb		Yug	SOKO	N-262	*Frégate*	France	Aérospatiale
Jet Provost		UK	BAe	N-2501	*Noratlas*	France	Aérospatiale
Jetstream		UK	BAe	*Navajo*	PA-31	US	Piper
JJ-6	(J-6)			NC-212	C-212	Spain/	CASA/
JT-3	*Halcón* (C-101)	Chile	Enaer			Indon	Nurtanio
JZ-6	(J-6)			NC-235	C-235	Spain/	CASA/
KA-3	[A-3]					Indon	Nurtanio
KA-6	[A-6]			*Nesher*	[*Mirage* III]	Israel	IAI
KC-10	*Extender* [DC-10]	US	MD	NF-5	(F-5)		
KC-130	[C-130]			*Nightingale*	(DC-9)		
KC-135	[Boeing 707]			*Nimrod*		UK	BAe
KE-3	[E-3]			O-1	*Bird Dog*	US	Cessna
Kfir	(F-21)	Israel	IAI	O-2	(Cessna 337,	US	Cessna
King Air		US	Beech		Skymaster)		
Kiran	HJT-16			OA-4	(A-4)		
Kraguj		Yug	SOKO	OA-37	*Dragonfly*		
Kudu	C-4M			*Orao*	IAR-93		
L-4	(L-18)			*Ouragan*		France	Dassault
L-18	*Cub*	US	Piper	OV-1	*Mohawk*	US	Rockwell
L-19	O-1			OV-10	*Bronco*	US	Rockwell
L-21	*Super Cub*	US	Piper	P-2J	[SP-2]	Japan	Kawasaki
L-29	*Delfin*	Czech	Aero	P-3		Switz	Pilatus
L-39	*Albatros*	Czech	Aero	P-3	*Orion*	US	Lockheed
L-70	*Vinka*	Finland	Valmet	P-95	EMB-110		
L-100	C-130			P-149		Italy	Piaggio
	(civil version)			P-166	*Albatross*	Italy	Piaggio
L-188	*Electra* (P-3 Orion)	US	Lockheed	PA-18	*Super Cub*	US	Piper
L-410	*Turbolet*	Czech	LET	PA-23	*Aztec*		
L-1011	*Tristar*	US	Lockheed	PA-24	*Comanche*	US	Piper
Learjet	(C-21)	US	Gates	PA-28	*Cherokee*	US	Piper
Li-2	[DC-3]	USSR	Lisunov	PA-31	*Navajo*	US	Piper
Lightning		UK	BAe	PA-34	*Seneca*	US	Piper
LR-1	(MU-2)						
Magister	CM-170						

ABBREVIATIONS

⟨	under 100 tons
–	part of unit is detached/less than
+	unit reinforced/more than
ε	estimated
' '	unit with overstated title/ship class nickname
AA	anti-aircraft
AAM	air-to-air missile(s)
AAW	anti-air warfare
AB	airborne
ABD	airborne division (Sov)
ABM	anti-ballistic missile(s)
about	the total could be higher
ac	aircraft
ACV	air cushion vehicle/vessel
AD	air defence
adj	adjusted
AE	auxiliary(ies), ammunition carrier
AEF	auxiliary(ies) explosives and stores
AEW	airborne early warning
AF	stores ship(s) with RAS capability
AFR	Air Force Reserve (US)
AGHS	hydrographic survey vessel(s)
AGI	intelligence collection vessel(s)
AGOR	oceanographic research vessel(s)
AGOS	ocean surveillance vessel(s)
AH	hospital ship(s)
AIFV	armoured infantry fighting vehicle
AIP	air-independent propulsion
AK	cargo ship(s)
ALCM	air-launched cruise missile(s)
amph	amphibious/amphibian(s)
ANG	Air National Guard (US)
AO	tanker(s) with RAS capability
AOE	auxiliary(ies), fuel and ammunition, RAS capability
AOT	tanker(s) without RAS capability
AP	passenger ship(s)
APC	armoured personnel carrier(s)
AR	repair ship(s)
AR	Army Reserve (US)
Arg	Argentina
armd	armoured
ARNG	Army National Guard (US)
arty	artillery
AS	submarine depot-ship(s)
aslt	assault
ASM	air-to-surface missile(s)
ASTT	anti-submarine TT
ASUW	anti-surface-ship warfare
ASW	anti-submarine warfare
AT	tug(s)
ATBM	anti-tactical ballistic missile
ATGW	anti-tank guided weapon(s)

ATK	anti-tank
ATTU	Atlantic to the Urals
Aus	Australia
avn	aviation
AVT	aviation training ship
AWACS	airborne warning and control system
BA	Budget Authority
BB	battleship(s)
bbr	bomber(s)
bde	brigade(s)
bdgt	budget(s)
Be	Belgium
bn	battalion(s)/billion(s)
BSAG	battleship surface attack group
bty	battery(ies)
Bu	Bulgaria
CAS	close air support
Cat	Category
cav	cavalry
cbt	combat
CBW	chemical and biological warfare
CC	cruiser(s)
Cdn	Canada
cdo	commando
CG	SAM cruiser(s)
CGF	Central Group of Forces (Sov)
CGH	CG with helicopters
CGN	nuclear-fuelled CG
cgo	freight aircraft
Ch	China (PRC)
COIN	counter-insurgency
comb	combined/combination
comd	command
comms	communications
CONUS	Continental United States
coy	company(ies)
CV	aircraft carrier(s)
CVBG	carrier battle group
CVN	nuclear-fuelled CV
CVV	V/STOL and hel CV
CW	chemical warfare
CY	current year
Cz	Czechoslovakia
DD	destroyer(s)
DDG	destroyer(s) with area SAM
DDH	destroyer(s) with hel
def	defence
defn	definition
det	detachment(s)
div	division(s)
Dk	Denmark
ECM	electronic counter-measures
ELINT	electronic intelligence
elm	element(s)
engr	engineer(s)
EOD	explosive ordnance disposal
eqpt	equipment
ESM	electronic support measures
est	estimate(d)
EW	electronic warfare
excl	excludes/excluding
exp	expenditure

FAC	forward air control
fd	field
FF	frigate(s)
FFG	frigate(s) with area SAM
FFH	frigate(s) with helicopter
FGA	fighter(s), ground-attack
flt	flight(s)
FMA	foreign military assistance
Fr	France
FRG	Federal Republic of Germany
ftr	fighter(s) (aircraft)
FW	fixed-wing
FY	fiscal year
GA	Chinese Integrated Group Army
GDP	gross domestic product
GDR	German Democratic Republic
GLCM	ground-launched cruise missile(s)
GNP	gross national product
GP	general-purpose
gp	group(s)
Gr	Greece
GW	guided weapon(s)
hel	helicopter(s)
HWT	heavy-weight torpedo(es)
Hu	Hungary
hy	heavy
ICBM	intercontinental ballistic missile(s)
imp	improved
incl	includes/including
indep	independent
inf	infantry
INF	intermediate nuclear forces
IRBM	intermediate-range ballistic missile(s)
Is	Israel
It	Italy
kg	kilogram(s)
km	kilometre(s)
KT	kiloton(s)
LCA	landing craft, assault
LCAC	landing craft, air cushion
LCM	landing craft, mechanized
LCT	landing craft, tank
LCU	landing craft, utility
LCVP	landing craft, vehicles and personnel
LHA	landing ship(s) assault
LKA	assault cargo ship(s)
log	logistic
LPD	landing platform(s), dock
LPH	landing platform(s), helicopter
LSD	landing ship(s), dock
LSM	landing ship(s), medium
LST	landing ship(s), tank
lt	light
LWT	light-weight torpedo(es)
m	million(s)
MAC	Military Airlift Command (US)

maint	maintenance
MARV	manoeuvring re-entry vehicle(s)
MBT	main battle tank(s)
MCC/I/O	mine counter-measures vessel(s), coastal/inshore/offshore
MCMV	mine counter-measures vessel(s)
MCR	Marine Corps Reserve (US)
MD	Military District(s)
mech	mechanized
med	medium
MEF/B/U	Marine Expeditionary Force(s)/Brigade(s)/Unit(s) (US)
MFO	Multi-National Force and Observers
MHC/I/O	minehunter(s), coastal/inshore/offshore
MICV	mechanized infantry combat vehicle(s)
mil	military
MIRV	multiple independently-targetable re-entry vehicle(s)
misc	miscellaneous
Mk	mark (model number)
ML	minelayer
mob	mobilization
mod	modified/modification
mor	mortar(s)
mot	motorized
MPS	marine prepositioning squadron(s)
MR	maritime reconnaissance/motor rifle
MRBM	medium-range ballistic missile(s)
MRD	motor rifle division (WP)
MRL	multiple rocket launcher(s)
MRV	multiple re-entry vehicle(s)
MSC/I/O	minesweeper(s), coastal/inshore/offshore
msl	missile(s)
MT	megaton(s)
mtn	mountain
n.a.	not applicable
NBC	nuclear, biological and chemical
NCO	non-commissioned officer
NGA	NATO Guidelines Area
NGF	Northern Group of Forces (Sov)
n.k.	not known
Nl	Netherlands
NMP	net material product
No	Norway
NR	Naval Reserve (US)
nuc	nuclear
OCU	operational conversion unit(s)
off	official
op/ops	operational/operations

org	organized/organization
OTH	over-the-horizon
OTHR	over-the-horizon radar
OTHT	over-the-horizon targeting
para	parachute
pax	passenger(s)/passenger transport aircraft
PCC/I/O	patrol craft, coastal/inshore/offshore
pdr	pounder
PFC/I/O	fast patrol craft, coastal/inshore/offshore
PFM	fast patrol craft, SSM
PFT	fast patrol craft, torpedo
PHM/T	hydrofoil(s), SSM/torpedo
pl	platoon(s)
Pol	Poland
POMCUS	prepositioning of matériel configured to unit sets
Port	Portugal
PSC	principle surface combatants
RAS	replenishment at sea
RCL	recoilless launcher(s)
recce	reconnaissance
regt	regiment(s)
RL	rocket launcher(s)
Ro	Romania
ro-ro	roll-on, roll-off
RPV	remotely piloted vehicle(s)
RV	re-entry vehicle(s)
SAC	Strategic Air Command (US)
SALT	Strategic Arms Limitation Treaty
SAM	surface-to-air missile(s)
SAR	search and rescue
SDI	Strategic Defense Initiative
SES	surface-effect ship(s)
SF	Special Forces
SGF	Southern Group of Forces (Sov)
SIGINT	signals intelligence
sigs	signals
SLBM	submarine-launched ballistic missile(s)
SLCM	sea-launched cruise missile(s)
SLEP	service life extension programme
some	up to
Sov	Soviet
Sp	Spain
SP	self-propelled
spt	support
sqn	squadron(s)
SRAM	short-range attack missile(s)
SRBM	short-range ballistic missile(s)
SS(C/I)	submarine(s) (coastal/inshore)
SSB	ballistic-missile submarine(s)

SSBN	nuclear-fuelled SSB
SSGN	SSN with dedicated non-ballistic missile launchers
SSM	surface-to-surface missile(s)
SSN	nuclear-fuelled submarine(s)
START	Startegic Arms Reduction Talks
STOL	short take-off and landing
STOVL	short take-off, vertical landing
SUGW	surface-to-underwater GW
Sw	Sweden
sy	security
TA	Territorial Army (UK)
tac	tactical
TAC	Tactical Air Command (US)
TD	tank division (WP)
tk	tank(s)
tkr	tanker(s)
tps	troop(s)
tpt	transport(s)
trg	training
TT	torpedo tube(s)
Tu	Turkey
UK	United Kingdom
UN	United Nations
UNAVM	UN Angolan Verification Mission
UNDOF	UN Disengagement Observation Force
UNFICYP	UN Force in Cyprus
UNGOMAP	UN Good Offices Mission in Afghanistan and Pakistan
UNIFIL	UN Interim Force in Lebanon
UNIIMOG	UN Iran/Iraq Military Observer Group
UNTAG	UN Transition Assistance Group (Namibia)
UNTSO	UN Truce Supervisory Organization
URG	underway replenishment group(s)
USGW	underwater-to-surface GW
US	United States of America
USMC	US Marine Corps
UUGW	underwater-to-underwater GW
veh	vehicle(s)
VIP	very important person(s)
VLS	vertical launch system(s)
V(/S)TOL	vertical(/short) take-off and landing
WGF	Western Group of Forces (Sov)
WP	Warsaw Pact
wpn	weapon
Yug	Yugoslavia

Type	Name/designation	Origin	Maker
PA-44	*Seminole*	US	Piper
PBY-5	*Catalina*	US	Consolidated
PC-6	*Porter*	Switz	Pilatus
PC-6A/B	*Turbo Porter*	Switz	Pilatus
PC-7	*Turbo Trainer*	Switz	Pilatus
PC-9		Switz	Pilatus
PD-808		Italy	Piaggio
Pembroke		UK	BAe
Pillán	T-35		
PL-1	*Chien Shou*	Taiwan	AIDC
Porter	PC-6		
PZL-104	*Wilga*	Poland	PZL
PZL-130	*Orlik*	Poland	PZL
Q-5	'Fantan' [MiG-19]	China	Nanchang
QU-22	*Bonanza*		
Queen Air	(U-8)		
R-160		France	Socata
R-235	*Guerrier*	France	Socata
RC-21	(C-21)		
RC-47	(C-47)		
RC-95	(EMB-110)		
RC-135	[Boeing 707]		
RF-4	(F-4)		
RF-5	(F-5)		
RF-35	(F-35)		
RF-84	(F-84)		
RF-104	(F-104)		
RF-172	(Cessna 172)	France	Reims-Cessna
RT-26	(EMB-326)		
RT-33	(T-33)		
RU-21	(*King Air*)		
RV-1	(OV-1)		
S-2	*Tracker*	US	Grumman
S-3	*Viking*	US	Lockheed
S-208		Italy	SIAI
S-211		Italy	SIAI
Safari	MFI-15		
Safir	SAAB-91 (SK-50)	Sweden	SAAB
SC-7	*Skyvan*	UK	Short
SE-210	*Caravelle*		
Sea Harrier	(*Harrier*)		
Seascan	IAI-1124		
Searchmaster B/L	N-24		
SF-37	(J-37)		
Seneca	PA-34 (EMB-810)	US	Piper
SF-260	(SF-260W *Warrior*)	Italy	SIAI
SH-37	(J-37)		
Shackleton		UK	BAe
Sherpa	C-23		
Short 330		UK	Short
Sierra 200	(*Musketeer*)		
SK-37	(J-37)		
SK-50	(*Safir*)		
SK-60	(SAAB-105)	Sweden	SAAB
SK-61	(*Bulldog*)		
Skyvan		UK	Short
SM-1019		Italy	SIAI
SN-601	*Corvette*		
SNJ	T-6 (Navy)		
SP-2H	*Neptune*	US	Lockheed
SR-71	*Blackbird*	US	Lockheed
Su-7	'Fitter A'	USSR	Sukhoi
Su-15	'Flagon'	USSR	Sukhoi
Su-17/-20/-22	'Fitter'	USSR	Sukhoi
Su-24	'Fencer'	USSR	Sukhoi
Su-25	'Frogfoot'	USSR	Sukhoi
Su-27	'Flanker'	USSR	Sukhoi

Type	Name/designation	Origin	Maker
Summit Sentry	(O-2)		
Super Etendard		France	Dassault
Super Galeb	[*Galeb*]		
Super Mystère		France	Dassault
T-1		Japan	Fuji
T-2	*Buckeye*	US	Rockwell
T-2		Japan	Mitsubishi
T-3		Japan	Fuji
T-6	*Harvard*	US	N. American
T-17	(*Supporter*, MFI-17)	Sweden	SAAB
T-23	*Uirapurú*	Brazil	Aerotec
T-25	Neiva *Universal*	Brazil	Embraer
T-26	EMB-326		
T-27	*Tucano*	Brazil	Embraer
T-28	*Trojan*	US	N. American
T-33	*Shooting Star*	US	Lockheed
T-34	*Mentor*	US	Beech
T-35	*Pillán* [PA-28]	Chile	Enaer
T-36	(C-101)		
T-37	(A-37)		
T-38	*Talon*	US	Northrop
T-39	(*Sabreliner*)	US	Rockwell
T-41	*Mescalero* (Cessna 172)	US	Cessna
T-42	*Cochise* (*Baron*)	US	Beech
T-43	(Boeing 737)		
T-44	(*King Air*)		
T-47	(*Citation*)		
TB-20	*Trinidad*	France	Aérospatiale
TB-30	*Epsilon*	France	Aérospatiale
TC-45	(C-45, trg)		
T-CH-1		Taiwan	AIDC
Texan	T-6		
TL-1	(KM-2)	Japan	Fuji
Tornado		UK/FRG/Italy	Panavia
TR-1		US	Lockheed
Travel Air	Beech 95		
Trident		UK	BAe
Trislander	BN-2		
Tristar	L-1011		
TS-8	*Bies*	Poland	PZL
TS-11	*Iskra*	Poland	PZL
Tu-16	'Badger'	USSR	Tupolev
Tu-22	'Blinder'	USSR	Tupolev
Tu-26	'Backfire'	USSR	Tupolev
Tu-28	'Fiddler'	USSR	Tupolev
Tu-95	'Bear'	USSR	Tupolev
Tu-134	'Crusty'	USSR	Tupolev
Tu-126	'Moss'	USSR	Tupolev
Tu-142	'Bear F'	USSR	Tupolev
Tu-154	'Careless'	USSR	Tupolev
Turbo Porter	PC-6A/B		
Twin Otter	DHC-6		
Tzugit	[CM-170]	Israel	IAI
U-2		US	Lockheed
U-3	(Cessna 310)	US	Cessna
U-7	(L-18)		
U-8	(*Twin Bonanza/Queen Air*)	US	Beech
U-9	(EMB-121)		
U-10	*Super Courier*	US	Helio
U-17	(Cessna 180, 185)	US	Cessna
U-21	(*King Air*)		
U-36	(*Learjet*)		